Special Ed **Using**

Corel® WordPerfect® 9

que®

Quite a few commercial Web sites are devoted to publishing job listings and maintaining huge electronic résumé databases. Some of these sites have résumé-building programs to help get you started. The following list of Web sites gives you a place to start looking:

www.americasemployers.com

www.apnjobs.com

www.careeravenue.com

www.careerpath.com

www.careershop.com

www.computerjobs.com

www.headhunter.com

www.jobs.com

www.jobbankusa.com

www.jobexchange.com

www.monster.com

www.net-temps.com

You probably use a search engine or two to locate information on the Internet. What you might not realize is that the most popular search engines also maintain job listings on their sites. The listings are usually organized into regions or states. Some of these sites have links to other Web sites that might prove helpful during your job search. Figure 8 shows the Yahoo! employment page.

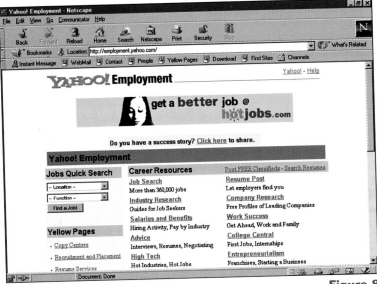

Figure 8

Special Edition
Using
Corel® WordPerfect® 9

Laura Acklen

Read Gilgen

que®

A Division of Macmillan Computer Publishing, USA
201 W. 103rd Street
Indianapolis, Indiana 46290

CONTENTS AT A GLANCE

SPECIAL EDITION USING COREL® WORDPERFECT® 9

International Standard Book Number: 0-7897-1620-8

Library of Congress Catalog Card Number: 97-81316

Printed in the United States of America

First Printing: June 1999

01   00   99   4   3   2   1

TRADEMARKS

Executive Editor
John Pierce

Acquisitions Editors
Jill Byus
Jamie Milazzo

Development Editor
Susan Hobbs

Managing Editor
Thomas F. Hayes

Project Editors
Lori A. Lyons
Linda Seifert

Copy Editor
Kitty Jarrett

Indexer
Larry Sweazy

Proofreader
Jeanne Clark

Technical Editors
Jim Gray
Darralyn McCall
Kent Easley

Layout Technician
Eric S. Miller

Cover Designers
Dan Armstrong
Ruth Lewis

Book Designers
Lousia Klucznik
Ruth Lewis

CONTENTS

III Organizing Information

ABOUT THE AUTHORS

Laura Acklen obtained her BBA at Southwest Texas State University in 1985, completing a senior DBMS project with one of the first dual-floppy 8086 IBM PCs and pfs:WRITE software. After learning WordPerfect 4.2 in early 1988, she developed custom courseware and trained law offices that were converting from Wang systems to PC-based Local Area Networks. In 1990, she began teaching classes for the international training company, Productivity Point International (PPI), and progressed into courseware development for their corporate headquarters. Her student and instructor manuals were distributed internationally for use in all PPI training centers.

In 1993, Laura wrote her first book for Que, with Michael Miller, called *Oops! What To Do When Things Go Wrong with WordPerfect*. Her second book, *WordPerfect 6.0 SureSteps*, was written that same year. Since that time, she has authored or co-authored six other books for Que, including *Que's First Look at Windows 95* and three editions of the *Special Edition Using WordPerfect* books (for versions 6, 6.1, and 7).

Laura has also written extensively for Que Education and Training, completing nine student manuals and three instructor manuals designed for both corporate and academic training centers.

Laura was a contributing editor for the *WordPerfect for Windows Magazine* for almost four years. She wrote the monthly "Basics" column for the first year before switching over to the "Troubleshooting" column, which also appeared in every issue.

When she isn't chained to her computer, Laura enjoys scuba diving, cooking, reading, and chasing small children around the backyard. She lives in Austin, Texas with her husband, Jeff, and their three children. Laura has big plans to have her Web site up and running this summer, so stop by www.wpwriter.com.

Read Gilgen completed his BA at Brigham Young University, and his MA and PhD in Latin American Literature and Linguistics at the University of California, Irvine. He taught Spanish at the University of North Carolina, Chapel Hill, and at the University of Wisconsin before becoming director of UW's L&S Learning Support Services (the language labs) in 1981.

His professional interests include instructional technology in higher education, especially in foreign language education. He is currently president of the International Association for Language Learning Technology.

He has taught and written extensively on DOS, Windows, and WordPerfect since the early 1980s. He is author of Que's *WordPerfect for Windows Hot Tips* and contributing author to several Que books, including the Special Editions of *Using WordPerfect Suite 8* and *Using Microsoft Office 97 Professional*.

DEDICATIONS

From Laura:

To my children, Ben, Lindsey, and Sarah, who tolerated fewer trips to the park, the absence of homemade cookies, and my total preoccupation with this project.

From Read:

To my wife, Sue, a talented woman in her own right, for her unending and loving support.

ACKNOWLEDGMENTS

Read and I would like to thank everyone who helped bring this book to fruition. Jill Byus, our first acquisitions editor, was such a pleasure to work with that we actually enjoyed the process of negotiating contracts and submission dates. Her successor, Jamie Milazzo, has our undying gratitude for taking charge and keeping the book on schedule, despite all the little surprises that inevitably come up during a lengthy project.

Our development editor, Susan Hobbs, did an excellent job coordinating the efforts of the editing team and two increasing tired and slightly cranky authors. After Jamie was lured away to Florida, Suz took over as our point of contact, which meant she responded to many, many email messages, followed up on countless details, and kept the work flow moving. Her good humor and flexibility allowed us to preserve our individual writing styles while keeping the coverage consistent. Suz got extra brownie points for working late nights and weekends right along with us.

We would also like to thank Lori Lyons, Linda Seifert, Jeanne Clark, and Eric Miller for their thoughtful attention to detail in the final push.

From Laura:

I simply could not ask for a more understanding and supportive family. They suppress their giggles and try not to roll their eyes when I promise that this project won't be as time-consuming as the last one. First and foremost, I want to thank my husband, Jeff, for doing more than his share of the chores and for entertaining the children on the weekends so I could hide in my office and work. Thanks to my mother, Jennie, and my sister, Heather, for their constant support and encouragement. My in-laws have been wonderful in offering to take a child or two off our hands for a weekend. Last, but certainly not least, I want to extend my warmest thanks to Read. I couldn't have asked for a better writing partner.

From Read:

No acknowledgment would be complete without thanking those closest to you who support you when you've gone into hiding to write. My wife, Sue, watched far too many movies by herself over the last few months. I probably should also acknowledge my kids who made taking on this project necessary. Finally, I also owe a heartfelt and sincere thank you to Laura for inviting me to collaborate on this project, and for having the patience and determination to see it through.

TELL US WHAT YOU THINK!

As the reader of this book, *you* are our most important critic and commentator. We value your opinion and want to know what we're doing right, what we could do better, what areas you'd like to see us publish in, and any other words of wisdom you're willing to pass our way.

As the Executive Editor for the General Desktop Applications team at Macmillan Computer Publishing, I welcome your comments. You can fax, email, or write me directly to let me know what you did or didn't like about this book—as well as what we can do to make our books stronger.

Please note that I cannot help you with technical problems related to the topic of this book, and that due to the high volume of mail I receive, I might not be able to reply to every message.

When you write, please be sure to include this book's title and author as well as your name and phone or fax number. I will carefully review your comments and share them with the authors and editors who worked on the book.

Fax: 317-581-4666

Email: office_que@mcp.com

Mail: Executive Editor
         General Desktop Applications
         Macmillan Computer Publishing
         201 West 103rd Street
         Indianapolis, IN 46290 USA

INTRODUCTION

If you've picked up this book, it means you've either purchased Corel WordPerfect Office 2000, or you're seriously thinking about it. Good for you! WordPerfect is *without a doubt*, the most powerful, customizable, and easy-to-use program that you can get your hands on. Period. WordPerfect lets you work the way *you* want to work, not the way programmers *want* you to work.

File compatibility with Microsoft Word and other applications has been enhanced to the point where document migration is virtually seamless, so it no longer matters what your clients and associates are using. What *does* matter is that you have a choice. Get WordPerfect and go to work!

Don't let the size of the book intimidate you. We won't bore you with minute details of every little feature. Nope—this book is crammed full of tips, tricks, and practical examples that you won't find anywhere else. We explain what a feature is, but more importantly, we tell you *why* you want to use it. What's in it for you? How can it save you time? What features can be used together to achieve a higher level of productivity? All this and more, just waiting for you to start turning the pages.

WHO SHOULD BUY THIS BOOK

If you've used a word processor before, and you want to learn how to take advantage of all that WordPerfect has to offer, this book is for you. We made a few assumptions about our audience when we developed the outline for this book. We decided that most of you already know the basics of creating and formatting documents, even if you've done the work in another application. Many of you have used a previous version of WordPerfect, so your interest lies not only in the new features, but also in how you might use the familiar features more effectively.

NEW FEATURES AND ENHANCEMENTS IN WORDPERFECT 9

This latest version of WordPerfect includes some very exciting new features and some welcome improvements that speed up navigation and formatting. WordPerfect Office 2000 supports more cross-platform, open-standard formats than any other word processor on the market. Here are some highlights:

- Corel's RealTime Preview shows you what a formatting change will look like, before you make it. For example, as you highlight fonts in the Font drop-down list, the document text is reformatted in that font, on-the-fly. RealTime Preview works for fonts, font sizes, zoom, justification, lines, borders, shading, and color, just to name a few.

- Install-As-You-Go saves disk space by not installing extra components that you might not use. If you try to use something that hasn't been installed yet, you'll get a message to that effect and, if you like, the Setup program takes care of installing that component for you.

- Corel's Scrapbook gives you quick access to your clip art images by organizing them into folders by category. You can search for and preview images, sounds, and movies, and then drag and drop those objects into your documents. With the Scrapbook, you can organize a vast collection of items by creating your own categories and then adding items from your hard drive, CD-ROM, or network drive. Upgraders will be thrilled to find that they can import items from Corel WordPerfect versions 7 and 8 clip art storage.

- New navigational tools like the AutoScroll feature let you use a regular mouse to scroll through a document as if you had a wheel mouse. A new Browse button lets you move through a document by page, heading, table, box, footnote, endnote, edit position, or comment. The Back and Forward buttons move you to and from your previous editing position (similar to the way your Internet browser buttons work).

- In response to an overwhelming number of user requests, the Print Preview feature is now fully editable, so you don't have to switch back to the regular view to make changes to the document. Print Preview is fully compatible with Corel RealTime Preview, so you can experiment with formatting options without actually applying them to the document.

- Collating multiple pages while printing has been enhanced. You can now print on both sides of the page regardless of what kind of printer you have. You can enlarge or reduce a document to fit any paper size, without reformatting the page. Also, you can now print a page of thumbnail pages—as many as 8 rows and 8 columns—enabling you to print up to 64 thumbnail pages on a single piece of paper.

- With the addition of Adobe® Acrobat® Reader, you can view, navigate, and print PDF files. A much-anticipated feature is the ability to save your own documents as PDF files so that they can't be edited by the recipient.

- Although WordPerfect's file format hasn't changed since version 6, other applications' file formats change like the weather. WordPerfect Office 2000 comes with updated conversion drivers to make the transfer of documents between WordPerfect and

Microsoft Word cleaner than ever. You can even set the default file save format to Microsoft Word (.doc) so that the user doesn't have to intervene at all.

- If you can't beat 'em, join 'em. Corel has incorporated Microsoft Word 97 menus and toolbars that you can display in place of the WordPerfect default menus and toolbar. There is even a Microsoft Word Help item on the Help menu that takes you to a page with links to notes for converting files between the two programs, and a side-by-side comparison of their features.

- All of you "road warriors" out there will appreciate the Embedded Fonts feature. Now, you can save your fonts with a document so that no matter where you are, or whose machine you are using, you'll get the appearance you expect when you view and print your documents.

- Improved accessibility features make it easier than ever to integrate third-party accessibility tools with WordPerfect. The support of High-Contrast mode, large font mode, and keyboard equivalents for virtually every feature ensures an equal opportunity for everyone to enjoy the power of WordPerfect.

- Documents destined for the Internet or an intranet can be published directly to Trellix, a Web page tool that helps you organize long documents into segments that are easily navigated. Trellix allows Webmasters to delegate content ownership to specific users. Thankfully, you don't need specialized knowledge of HTML or graphic design to create and maintain content for online use.

- WordPerfect 9 has writing tools for more than 15 languages so that you can spell check, hyphenate, look up synonyms, and check grammar in any one language or a combination of languages. The Euro symbol has been included in Corel fonts to help meet the needs of multinational users.

- You'll be able to work with SGML and XML documents in the familiar WYSIWYG environment. WordPerfect's XML authoring tool incorporates the Document Type Definition (DTD), layout information, and mapping files into one template. It's important to note that Microsoft Word doesn't include the DTD information in XML documents, so other users can't truly make use of that file.

- Unparalleled support for open standards and programming interfaces—such as PDF, VBA, HTML, ODBC, Java™, SGML, XML and OLAP—make it easier than ever to work with users from all over the world. Support for ODMA standards make WordPerfect compatible with document management applications, such as iManage™, PC DOCS, SoftSolutions®, and WORLDOX®.

- Support for Microsoft Visual Basic for Applications (VBA) is included, so now you have a very powerful alternative to the PerfectScript macro language. WordPerfect is the only mainstream word processor to offer two powerful programming languages that can be used separately or in combination.

- With In-Place Editing, you can edit an object without switching to a different window. If you click the object, buttons and list boxes temporarily change to work specifically with that object.

- The In-Place Activation feature allows for seamless integration with third-party applications. When you double-click the OLE object, the originating application is launched from inside WordPerfect.

- Miscellaneous goodies: You can use Make It Fit on a block of text, there are over 100 new shapes, the chart module has been enhanced with new chart types, and you can skew table cells.

HOW THIS BOOK IS ORGANIZED

Special Edition Using Corel WordPerfect 9 is designed for users who have some experience using a word processor and want to learn how to use WordPerfect's more advanced features. The book is divided into sections to help you focus on the areas that you are particularly interested in. The first section is a good place to start because some fundamental concepts are covered, but beyond that, you are free to jump around and read about what interests you.

PART I: LEARNING THE BASICS

Chapters 1 through 6 cover the fundamentals of using WordPerfect to create, edit, save, and print documents. A short basic formatting chapter covers the features that you need to use right away, such as changing fonts, applying bold, italic, and underline, and adjusting the margins. The file management chapter is in this first section because managing files is such an integral part of what you do every day. After all, what good is all your hard work if you can't find the file? In the other chapters, you learn how to use the writing tools and how to print, fax, and email your documents. If you're tempted to skip this part because you've already used a word processor, don't. It's loaded with tips and practical advice on how to use the basic features to be more productive.

PART II: FORMATTING DOCUMENTS

Chapters 7, 8, and 9 focus on formatting documents. Chapter 7 sticks to formatting lines and paragraphs, so you learn how to align and indent text, set tabs, keep text together, and add line numbers and borders. Chapter 8 tackles formatting page elements: page numbers, paper size, headers and footers, subdividing the page, columns, borders, and Make It Fit. Chapter 9 explains how to create and implement styles for consistency and speedier formatting. Bet you didn't know that if you modify a style, the text that is formatted with that style is automatically updated, every bit, all at once.

PART III: ORGANIZING INFORMATION

Chapters 10 and 11 cover organizing information into tables, lists, and outlines. You learn everything you need to know about creating and formatting tables. Bulleted and numbered lists are used in all types of documents to present (sequential and nonsequential) pieces of information in an easy-to-read list. Obviously, the Outline feature can be used to create outlines that show the structure of a document or an idea. The outline styles can also be used to create numbered sections of text where the numbers are automatically updated as you rearrange the text.

Part IV: Working with Graphics

In this section, Chapters 12, 13, and 14 teach you how to incorporate graphic images and effects in your documents. You learn how to insert clip art and other types of images, such as GIF files that you download from the Internet. You learn how to create custom graphic lines and borders and how to insert the new shapes. Chapter 13 shows you how to customize graphics and Chapter 14 focuses on the Draw and TextArt features. In Chapter 14, you also learn how to customize WordPerfect graphics and bitmap graphics in Presentations.

Part V: Integrating Information from Other Sources

Chapters 15 and 16 show you how to use information from other applications. You learn how to use the Windows Clipboard to copy information between applications. We show you how to use OLE to create a link so that the information is automatically updated in the document any time it's been modified in the originating program. You learn how to import documents, spreadsheets, and databases from other applications. The conversion drivers have been improved dramatically so that the transport between WordPerfect and Microsoft Word is virtually seamless. Chapter 16 focuses on creating data charts and organizational charts.

Part VI: Publishing Documents

This section has some very weighty chapters in it. Chapter 17 covers the document collaboration features, such as document comments, reviewing and comparing documents, and using the Corel Versions feature to maintain a record of the revisions to a document. Chapter 18 talks about the features geared toward long documents, such as bookmarks, footnotes, endnotes, cross references, and the Master Document feature. Chapter 19 covers the creation of tables of contents, tables of authorities, and indexes. Chapter 20 presents information on creating interactive and multimedia documents with hypertext links, links to Web pages, and embedded video and sounds. Chapter 21 covers WordPerfect's Web publishing features and is packed with practical advice on how to get your documents published on the Internet or your company intranet.

Part VII: Automating Everyday Tasks

This last section discusses ways that you can use WordPerfect's automation tools to speed up repetitive tasks. Chapter 22 covers templates, from using the project templates that come with WordPerfect to creating your own templates (both from existing documents and from scratch). You learn how to insert prompts that guide the user through the template and how to link fields in a template to the Address Book fields. Chapter 23 covers the Merge feature. A brief overview of a typical mail merge is given, but the focus is on using other sources for names and addresses and creating documents other than form letters during a merge. A section on the

Address Book is included here. Chapter 24 shows you how to use the PerfectExpert panel to create and edit documents without searching through the menus for an elusive command. The bulk of this chapter focuses on macros—running macros that others have developed (including the shipping macros), and creating your own macros with the Macro Recorder. The steps to assign macros to toolbars, keystrokes, and menus are included, as well as information about using macros from previous versions and whether or not you need to install VBA support.

CONVENTIONS USED IN THIS BOOK

Que, as well as all of Macmillan Computer Publishing's various imprints, has more than 10 years experience creating the most popular and effective computer reference books available. From trainers to programmers, Que's authors have invaluable experience using—and most importantly—*explaining* computer and software concepts. From basic to advanced topics, Que's publishing experience, and its authors' expertise and communication skills, combine to create a highly readable and easily navigable book.

Tip #1001 from
Laura and Read

Liberally sprinkled throughout the text, tips are places where Read and I share insights that we've gained after using, teaching, and writing about WordPerfect for the past 10 years.

Note

Notes contain extra information or alternative techniques for performing tasks that we feel will enhance your use and/or understanding of the current topic.

Caution

If we want to warn you about a potential problem, you'll see that information in a caution note. Believe me, after years in a classroom, we know all about the pitfalls!

 This element is designed to call your attention to areas where you are likely to get into trouble. When you see a Troubleshooting note, you can skip to the Troubleshooting at the end of the chapter to learn how to solve (or avoid) a problem.

Sidebars
Sidebars are used when we want to pass on supplemental information that isn't necessarily "required reading." Sidebars have clear, descriptive titles so you'll know right away why we want you to read it.

CROSS REFERENCES

Cross references are used whenever possible to direct you to other sections of the book that give complementary or supportive information. If you want to learn how to use WordPerfect features together, pay close attention to the cross references.

BUTTONS

Whenever a button is referred to in an explanatory paragraph or step-by-step procedure, the button will appear in the left margin, next to the paragraph or step that mentions it. This visual reminder helps you quickly locate the button on the toolbar so that you can remember it for future use.

KEYBOARD SHORTCUTS

Whenever a combination of keys can be pressed to execute a command, they'll appear paired by a plus sign, as in Ctrl+Home (to move to the top of a document) or Ctrl+P (to open the Print dialog box). When using a keyboard shortcut, press the first key, and while that key is depressed, tap the second key, and then release the first key.

UNDERLINED HOT KEYS

If you're like most people, you probably spend more time with your hands on the keyboard than on the mouse. Why would you want to take your hands off the keyboard and use the mouse to open a menu when you can do it from the keyboard? There are keystrokes that can be used to select menu commands and options in dialog boxes. You'll find the under-lined letters as they appear onscreen underlined in the text. For example, File, Print tells you that pressing Alt+F to open the File menu, followed by P will open the Print dialog box. After you're in the Print dialog box, Alt+E tells WordPerfect that you want to print the Current Page.

TYPEFACES

Throughout this book, a variety of typefaces are used, each designed to draw your attention to specific text:

Typeface	Description
Monospace	Screen messages, text you type, and Internet addresses appear in this special typeface.
Italic	New terminology and emphasized text will appear in italic.

END-OF-CHAPTER EXAMPLES

Every chapter ends with a Troubleshooting section, where you'll find answers to frequently encountered problems. We've addressed more than just the simplest problems and solutions here—we cover the pitfalls you're likely to encounter when you push WordPerfect to the limit.

The Project element is designed to complement the information presented in the chapter. In some chapters, you'll see "before and after" shots that illustrate how features can be used to enhance a document. In others, there will be a practical and real-world example of how you can implement the features covered in the chapter. And in one or two chapters, we've shown you how to prepare information for use with a particular feature.

LEARNING THE BASICS

CHAPTER **1**

GETTING COMFORTABLE WITH WORDPERFECT

In this chapter

Creating documents isn't just typing letters and memos anymore. You can run a small business by using all the features in Corel WordPerfect. From typical correspondence to complex mail merges to tables with spreadsheet formulas to desktop publishing to document collaboration to Web publishing, WordPerfect has the tools you need to accomplish any task.

The challenge becomes uncovering the features and shortcuts that you need. That's where this book comes in. Written by two WordPerfect professionals who've been involved with the program since the early days of the DOS versions, we show you the best ways to harness the power of WordPerfect. Along the way, we share tips, tricks, and shortcuts that we've gained from years of using the program, and from teaching the program to others.

This chapter covers the basics of creating and saving documents, so if you've used WordPerfect before, you might think you can just skip it. Don't. You'll find lots of useful information and some great shortcuts that you can use every day.

STARTING WORDPERFECT

 The quickest way to start WordPerfect is to have a *shortcut* on the desktop. Double-click it, and away you go! If you don't have the shortcut, using the Start menu is easy—it just takes a few more mouse clicks:

1. Click the Start button.
2. Highlight Programs.
3. Highlight WordPerfect Office 2000 to open the submenu (see Figure 1.1).
4. Click WordPerfect 9.

You're now ready to start working in WordPerfect.

Figure 1.1
You can start WordPerfect 9 from the Start menu with a click, two slides, and a click.

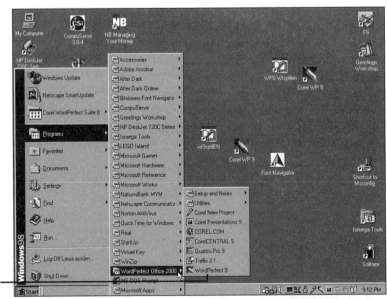

Click here to start WordPerfect.

⚠ *If you can't find the WordPerfect Office 2000 folder on your Programs menu, see "Having Trouble Starting WordPerfect" in the Troubleshooting section at the end of this chapter.*

TOURING THE WORDPERFECT SCREEN

All Windows 95/98 applications look essentially the same. They all have title bars, menus, toolbars, and control buttons. This gives you a distinct advantage because using one Windows application prepares you to learn another.

Tip #1 from
Laura and Read

In WordPerfect 9, as in WordPerfect 8, you can click anywhere in a document and move the insertion point to that place. No more pressing Enter or Tab until the insertion point is where you want it. Just click and start typing.

When you start WordPerfect, a blank document appears (see Figure 1.2), so you can start typing immediately. The insertion point shows you where the text will appear. The shadow cursor shows you where the insertion point will be if you click the mouse button.

Figure 1.2
The WordPerfect screen includes elements that you have seen in other Windows applications.

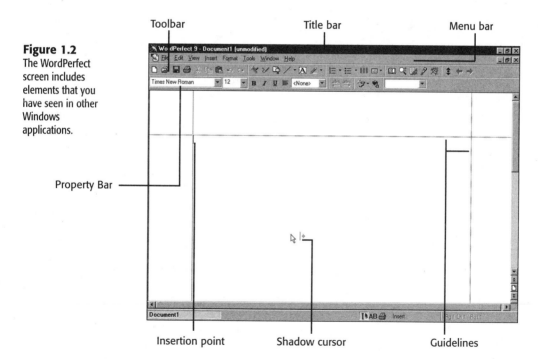

Toolbar   Title bar   Menu bar

Property Bar

Insertion point   Shadow cursor   Guidelines

Tip #2 from
Laura and Read

The Shadow Cursor On/Off button on the application bar shows whether the shadow cursor is turned on (the button appears pressed in). Click the button to turn the shadow cursor on and off.

The gray lines you see onscreen are called *guidelines*. They help you see the text area of your page by marking the top, bottom, left, and right margins. Clicking and dragging the guidelines is a quick way to change the margins.

Turn Off the Guidelines
If you find the guidelines distracting, you can turn them off by opening the View menu and selecting Guidelines. In the Guidelines dialog box, remove the check mark next to Margins, and then click OK.

→ To learn more about changing the margins with guidelines, **see** "Changing Margins with Guidelines," **p. 67**

SAVING TIME WITH TOOLBARS

The Property Bar is like a shape-shifter from a science fiction story; it changes depending on the task at hand (refer to Figure 1.1). You start out with the text Property Bar, but as soon as you create a table, it switches to the table Property Bar. When you create an outline, you get the outline Property Bar, and so on. It's handy because the buttons you need magically appear, and you get your work done twice as fast because you aren't hunting around in the menus for a command.

Note

The new "shape-shifting" Property Bar replaces QuickSpots, which were used in WordPerfect 7 to give you quick access to formatting commands for certain objects, such as paragraphs and tables.

Displaying QuickTips
If you point to a button on any of the toolbars and pause, a QuickTip appears that describes the function of that button.

The toolbar is different from the Property Bar—it doesn't change unless you tell it to. The one you see in Figure 1.2 is called the WordPerfect 9 toolbar and has buttons for general editing tasks. There are 20 other toolbars to choose from, including WordPerfect 7, WordPerfect 8, and Microsoft Word 97 toolbars. Other toolbars contain buttons for working with tables, graphics, outlines, fonts, macros, and so on.

To begin working with toolbars, follow these steps:

1. Right-click the toolbar to open the Toolbar QuickMenu (see Figure 1.3). Notice that the WordPerfect 9 toolbar already has a check mark next to it. A check mark next to the name means that the toolbar is already on. To see a complete list of available toolbars, choose <u>M</u>ore.

PART

I

CH

1

QuickMenus

Windows 95 introduced the concept of right-clicking on an object to display a pop-up menu of context-sensitive commands. These menus are called *QuickMenus* in WordPerfect. There's one for just about everything you do. Start right-clicking on things and discover how much time these menus can save you.

Figure 1.3
You can right-click the toolbar to open the QuickMenu, where you can switch to another toolbar or turn the toolbar(s) off.

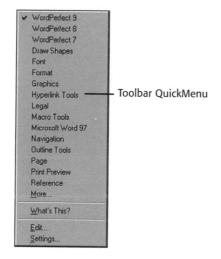

Toolbar QuickMenu

2. Click the toolbar you want to turn on (clicking an *unchecked* toolbar name turns it on; clicking a *checked* toolbar name turns it off).

Clearing a QuickMenu

You might change your mind and decide not to use a QuickMenu. Just click in the document window and the QuickMenu disappears.

 If you can't find the toolbar or the Property Bar, see "The Missing Property Bar and Toolbar" in the Troubleshooting section at the end of this chapter.

 If the QuickTips aren't showing up, see "QuickTips Don't Appear" in the Troubleshooting section at the end of this chapter.

CREATING DOCUMENTS

With WordPerfect, you can start typing as soon as the program is loaded. A blank document, with all the standard settings in place, stands ready for you. Table 1.1 lists some of WordPerfect's default settings. Others are discussed in later chapters.

Tip #3 from
Laura and Read

Templates are documents with formatting and *form text* already in place. All you have to do is fill in the blanks and print (or email, or fax). There are templates for fax cover sheets, invoices, balance sheets, proposals, purchase orders, calendars, labels, and more.

→ To learn about creating documents with templates, **see** Chapter 22, "Building Documents with Templates," **p. 613**

What Does *Default* Mean?

When you first use a program, there are settings already in place for you. These are called *default* settings. As you read through this book, you'll see this term often when a new feature is introduced. For example, in the section on changing margins, it's explained that the default margins are one inch on each side.

You can set up your own default settings, which define how you want your documents formatted in most cases. This way, you make only minor adjustments, which saves you loads of time in the long run.

TABLE 1.1 WORDPERFECT'S DEFAULT SETTINGS

Element	Default Setting
Margins	1 inch at the top, bottom, left, and right
Line spacing	Single-spaced
Font	Times New Roman 12 point
Tabs	Every 1/2 inch
Paper size	8 1/2 inches×11 inches
Automatic backup	Every 10 minutes

→ To learn more about defaults, **see** "Editing Styles," **p. 238**
→ To learn how to change the margins, **see** "Changing Margins with Guidelines," **p. 67**
→ To learn how to change line spacing, **see** "Adjusting the Spacing Between Lines and Paragraphs," **p. 178**
→ To learn how to change the font, **see** "Choosing the Right Font," **p. 58**
→ To learn how to change tab settings, **see** "Setting Tabs," **p. 173**
→ To learn how to change the paper size, **see** "Choosing Different Paper Sizes," **p. 204**
→ To learn how to change the automatic backup interval, **see** "Saving Documents," **p. 20**

TYPING TEXT

One of the coolest features in WordPerfect is the capability to click anywhere in a document, and then start typing. No pressing Enter, or Tab, or any of that—just click and type!

PART
I
CH
1

Note If you're working in one document and you want to create a new one, click the New button on the toolbar.

To create a WordPerfect document, do the following:

1. Click anywhere in the document area. The insertion point moves to the new place.
2. Begin typing text.

As you type along, you may notice that occasionally strange things happen automatically. For example, if you forget to capitalize the first word in a sentence, WordPerfect corrects it for you. When you type ordinal numbers, WordPerfect changes the two letters to superscript text so that the number has the proper format (such as 1st, 2nd, 3rd). This is the Format-As-You-Go feature working for you. Format-As-You-Go corrects common mistakes as you type.

→ To learn how to customize the Format-As-You-Go feature, **see** "Customizing Format-As-You-Go," **p. 136**

ERASING TEXT

We all make mistakes when we're typing—especially when we're thinking faster than our fingers can move! The problem is that if you stop and correct every little mistake, you lose your train of thought. A better idea is to correct only those mistakes that you notice right away, and then go back later and fix the rest.

There are three ways to erase text:

- If you make a mistake and you notice it right away, press the Backspace key to backspace over and erase the mistake.
- Click to the left of the word(s) you want to delete and press the Delete key repeatedly until the text has been erased.
- Select the text, then press Delete.

 If you've been a little heavy-handed with the Delete key and you've accidentally deleted too much text, see "Heavy-Handed Deletions" in the Troubleshooting section at the end of this chapter.

INSERTING TODAY'S DATE

You might be surprised at how many times a day you type out the date. With just one keystroke, you can insert today's date anywhere in a document.

1. Click in the document where you want the date to appear.
2. Press Ctrl+D.

WordPerfect gets the date and time from the Windows Date/Time Properties dialog box, so if the date or time you insert is wrong, you need to reset the clock. Double-click the time on your taskbar to open the Date/Time Properties dialog box, where you can make the needed changes.

You can also insert the time. Choose Insert, Date/Time to open the Date/Time dialog box (see Figure 1.4). Select the 12-hour format or the 24-hour format (scroll down the list), and then click Insert.

Figure 1.4
You can choose a format for the date and time in the Date/Time dialog box.

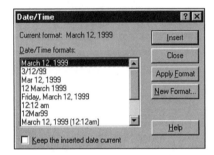

Tip #4 from
Laura and Read

You can use automatic dates in documents that you use over and over again. This date is automatically updated every time you open or print the document. Consider using it in fax cover sheets, memos, press releases, invoices, receipts, and so on. To insert this type of date, press Ctrl+Shift+D. Or select Keep the Inserted Date Current in the Date/Time dialog box.

WORDPERFECT'S AUTOMATIC PROOFREADING FEATURES

As you type, you may notice that red dashes appear under some words. The Spell-As-You-Go feature has marked these words as possible misspellings. Spell-As-You-Go is one of the two automatic proofreading features in WordPerfect—the other is Grammar-As-You-Go, which checks for grammatical errors. The theory behind these two features is that it's faster to correct these errors while you are typing than to go back and fix them later.

 Have you incorrectly spelled a word, but don't see the red dashes under it? See "Spell-As-You-Go Gone" in the Troubleshooting section at the end of this chapter.

Note

If Grammar-As-You-Go is activated instead of Spell-As-You-Go, you may see blue dashes in the text as well.

Note

Spell-As-You-Go was introduced in WordPerfect 7; Grammar-As-You-Go was introduced in WordPerfect 8. So if you've been using WordPerfect 6.1, you've got two new toys to play with!

To correct a word with Spell-As-You-Go, follow these steps:

1. Right-clicking an underlined word displays a list of suggested replacement words that you can choose from (see Figure 1.5).

Figure 1.5
You can right-click an underlined word to choose from a list of suggested replacement words.

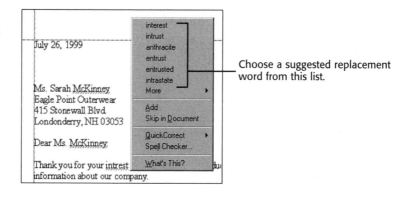

Choose a suggested replacement word from this list.

2. Click the correctly spelled word in the list. That's it—you just corrected the misspelled word. Selecting a word from this list automatically replaces the underlined word with the word you chose.

If you find these proofing marks distracting, you can disable the Spell-As-You-Go and Grammar-As-You-Go features by following these steps:

1. Choose the Tools menu and select Proofread from the submenu. Notice that Spell-As-You-Go has a bullet next to it—this means it's turned on (see Figure 1.6). You can switch to using Grammar-As-You-Go, but both options cannot be selected at the same time. However, because Grammar-As-You-Go includes Spell-As-You-Go, choosing Grammar-As-You-Go turns them both on.

Figure 1.6
The bullet next to Spell-As-You-Go means it is on. Choosing Grammar-As-You-Go activates both Grammar-As-You-Go and Spell-As-You-Go.

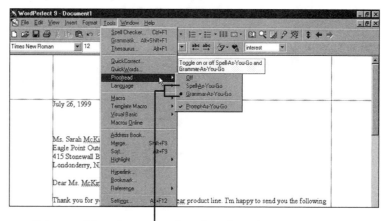

Only one of these features can be selected at a time.

2. Choose <u>O</u>ff. Choosing <u>O</u>ff turns off both Spell-<u>A</u>s-You-Go and <u>G</u>rammar-As-You-Go.

Bullets and Checks

Have you ever noticed that in menus, some items have a check mark next to them and others have a bullet? Besides showing you which item is currently selected, is there any other difference? Yes! Bullets are there to tell you that only one of the options in that group can be selected at one time. Check marks tell you that more than one option in that group can be selected at one time.

SAVING DOCUMENTS

Electronic filing has virtually replaced paper filing, so even if you don't expect to work with a document again, it's a good idea to save it so you have a record of it.

Follow these steps to save a document:

 1. Click the Save button.

- If you've already named this document, it will seem like nothing has happened. Because the document has already been named, WordPerfect saves the changes without any intervention from you. But you'll see (unmodified) after the filename in the title bar—that's how you know a document has been saved.

- If you haven't named the document yet, the Save File dialog box appears (see Figure 1.7). This is where you type a name and location for the file.

Figure 1.7
You use the Save File dialog box to save your files, giving each a name and a location.

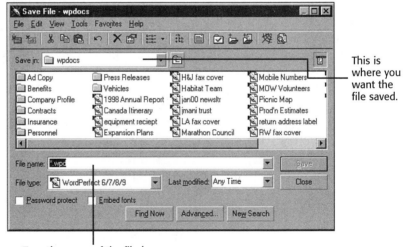

This is where you want the file saved.

Type the name of the file here.

2. Type a filename and press Enter (or click the <u>S</u>ave button).

- Filenames can contain letters, numbers, and spaces. Some symbols can be used, but not others, so to avoid problems, stick with dashes (-) and underscores (_).

- You can include the name of the drive and the *folder* where you want the document to be saved when you type the filename. For example, typing c:\reports\FY1998 saves the document FY1998 to drive C: in the reports folder.

- When you type a filename without selecting a location, the document is saved in the default folder, which is the folder that WordPerfect is currently pointing to.

→ To learn more about how to change to a different folder, **see** "Finding and Opening Documents," **p. 36**

Naming Files in Windows 95/98

If you're new to Windows 95/98, you may not realize that you have the freedom of using up to 255 characters (including spaces) in your filenames. The idea of using filename extensions (the three letters after the period) has gone by the wayside because you can give such a complete description of the file in the name itself. WordPerfect assigns an extension of .wpd to all documents. In most file-oriented dialog boxes, you'll notice that the extensions don't even show up.

Tip #5 from
Laura and Read

WordPerfect has a Timed Document Backup feature that automatically makes a backup copy of your document while you work. It's already turned on and set to make a backup every 10 minutes. You can adjust the interval and take a look at where your backup files are created in the Files Settings dialog box. Choose Tools, Settings, Files. If necessary, click the Document tab. You can adjust the Timed Document Backup interval by typing a new value in the Timed Document Backup Every text box or by clicking the spinner arrows next to the text box.

Hands Off the Original

If you want to preserve the original document, use Save As to save the file under a different name. Do this right away, so you don't accidentally replace the original with your revised version.

CREATING AN ENVELOPE

Despite the capability to fax and email documents in WordPerfect, some of us still mail them out the old-fashioned way—in an envelope. To make creating an envelope as easy as possible for you, WordPerfect pulls in the mailing address for you so you don't have to retype it. How? The program looks for three to six short lines of text (each one ends with a hard return) followed by a blank line. If two address blocks are in a letter, such as a return address followed by a mailing address, WordPerfect grabs the second address.

To create an envelope, follow these steps:

1. Open the Format menu and choose Envelope from the drop-down list. WordPerfect creates an envelope at the end of the document. The margin guidelines show you the dimensions of the mailing and return address blocks. The Property Bar contains

buttons for adding the return address, mailing address, and a bar code, and for changing the envelope size and position (see Figure 1.8).

Caution	If the margin guidelines aren't turned on, it's hard to see where you're supposed to type the return and mailing addresses. To turn on the margin guidelines, choose View, Guidelines to open the Guidelines dialog box. Place a check mark next to Margins, and then click OK.

2. If you want to include a return address, you have a couple options:

- Click in the return address area and type the information.
- Click the Return Address button on the Property Bar and choose an address from the pop-up list. Choose Address Book from the pop-up list if you want to select an address from any of the available address books (they vary depending on your email capabilities).

Envelope buttons on Property Bar

Figure 1.8
WordPerfect finds the mailing address and inserts it in the envelope so that you don't have to type it twice.

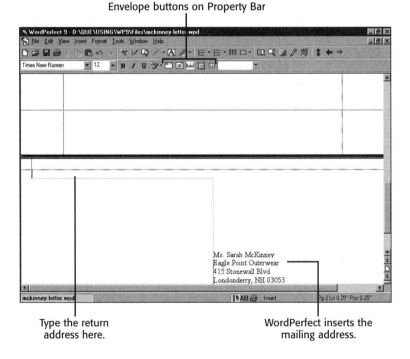

Type the return address here.

WordPerfect inserts the mailing address.

3. If necessary, you can do the following:

- Use another mailing address—You can either manually replace the mailing address or click the Mailing Address button and choose a mailing address from one of the available address books.

- Insert a bar code—Click the Bar Code button, and then type the recipient's zip code and choose a position for the bar code.

- Adjust the address positions—Click the Envelope Positions button, and then adjust the placement of the return and mailing addresses.

- Choose a different envelope size—Click the Envelope Size button, and then choose a size from the pop-up list.

Note

In previous versions of WordPerfect, the Format, Envelope command took you to the Envelope dialog box, where you typed the return address and set all the envelope options. In WordPerfect 9, the envelope is created at the end of the document and you type the return address on the envelope itself. The buttons on the Property Bar give you access to most of the options you formerly found in the Envelope dialog box.

PREVIEWING AND PRINTING DOCUMENTS

Unless you plan to email or fax a document, you'll need to print it. However, before you print a document, you should preview it. Often, the way a document appears onscreen can be quite different from the way it appears when printed.

SWITCHING TO PRINT PREVIEW

The Print Preview feature shows you exactly what your document will look like when you print it. Use it often. You'll save time, paper, printer resources, and let's not forget frustration.

Earlier versions of WordPerfect included a Print Preview feature, but you couldn't make any changes while in it. This time around, you can freely edit the text, reposition graphics, and so on.

To use the Print Preview feature, follow these steps:

1. Open the File menu and choose Print Preview. The current page is displayed (see Figure 1.9). Using buttons on the Print Preview toolbar, you can switch to a Two Page view, or you can use the Zoom feature (covered next) to adjust the size of the page.

2. When you are finished, click the Print Preview button to switch back to the document window.

Click here to switch to
Two Page view.

Click here to adjust the
zoom setting.

Print Preview toolbar

Figure 1.9
Print Preview displays
a fully editable
representation of
how the document
will look when
printed.

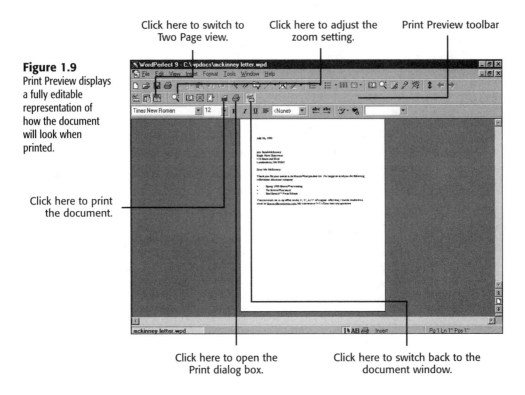

Click here to print
the document.

Click here to open the
Print dialog box.

Click here to switch back to the
document window.

ADJUSTING THE ZOOM SETTING

No matter where you choose to edit your document—in the document window or in Print
Preview—you can adjust the zoom setting to control the size of the document onscreen.
Don't be shy about it—changing the zoom setting does *not* affect the size of the printed
document. Adjust the zoom by following these steps:

1. Click the Zoom button on either the Standard toolbar or the Print Preview toolbar. A
   pop-up list of zoom settings appears (see Figure 1.10).

Zoom Ratios
The ratio is the size of the document onscreen compared to its size when printed. A zoom setting of 50%
displays the document at half the printed size, a setting of 100% displays the document at the printed size, a
setting of 200% displays the document at twice the printed size, and so on.

---

2. Select a zoom setting.

This is the current setting.

Figure 1.10
Clicking the Zoom button opens a pop-up menu of standard choices. Hover over any setting for a RealTime Preview.

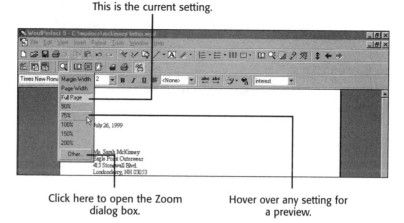

Click here to open the Zoom dialog box.

Hover over any setting for a preview.

Tip #6 from
Laura and Read

Is a zoom setting of 100% too big and 75% too small? Don't worry—you're not bound by the standard settings on the pop-up menu. Either choose Other from the pop-up menu or open the View menu and choose Zoom. This opens the Zoom dialog box, where you can type in your own zoom setting.

Tip #7 from
Laura and Read

Sometimes it takes a little experimenting to find the right zoom setting for the task. Fortunately, RealTime Preview shows you a preview of each setting before you choose it. After you click the Zoom button, point to and hover over any of the zoom settings. WordPerfect immediately redisplays the document with the new setting.

New in WordPerfect 9—RealTime Preview
One of the improvements that you'll notice right away is RealTime Preview. How many times have you changed a format only to discover that it wasn't exactly what you wanted? You might reselect three or four times before finding just the right one. No more—now you can preview a formatting change before you ever apply it to the text! RealTime Preview works on borders, columns, color fills, fonts, font attributes, frames, justification, outlines, and zoom. In many cases, the change is reflected in the text in the document window. In other situations, the preview text in the dialog box is a portion of text from your document.

PRINTING DOCUMENTS

After you've previewed your document and checked it for accuracy, you're ready to print. If you're printing an envelope, have the envelope ready. (Most printers accept envelopes through a manual feed tray.) Follow these steps to print an envelope:

1. Press Ctrl+P, or open the File menu and select Print to open the Print dialog box.

2. Press Enter to send the document to the printer. You can do this type of quick print only if you want to print the whole document and you don't need to select another printer.

Tip #8 from
Laura and Read

The Print Preview toolbar has a Print Document button that sends the document to the printer, bypassing the Print dialog box.

→ To learn how to set print options, **see** "Using Print Options," **p. 149**
→ To learn how to fax a document, **see** "Faxing Documents," **p. 161**
→ To learn how to email a document, **see** "Sending Documents via Email," **p. 163**

CLOSING DOCUMENTS

When you've finished working on a document, you clear it off your screen by closing the document window. If you haven't saved it yet, you get the chance to do that now. Follow these steps to close a document:

1. Click the Close button on the menu bar.

   If you haven't made any changes since the last time you saved, WordPerfect closes the document. If you *have* made some changes, you'll be prompted to save the document (see Figure 1.11).

Document Close button

Figure 1.11
When you click the Close button, WordPerfect prompts you to save your changes before clearing the document off the screen.

Click Yes to save your changes.

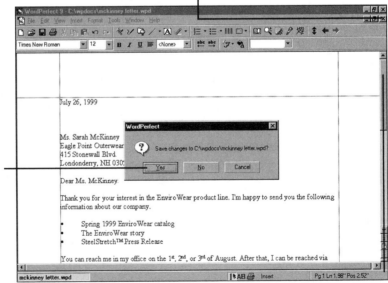

2. Click <u>Y</u>es if you want to save your work; click <u>N</u>o if you want to close the document without saving.

   If you click <u>Y</u>es and you haven't yet given this document a name, the Save File dialog box appears (refer to Figure 1.7). This is where you can type a name and location for the file. Otherwise, WordPerfect saves and closes the document.

3. Type the filename and press Enter.

GETTING HELP

Corel WordPerfect 9 offers an unprecedented level of support to help you become productive as quickly as possible. With all the different ways to automate your tasks and so many places to go for help, it's almost like having someone sitting right next to you, telling you which keys to press.

Even if you don't know *exactly* what you're looking for, you can still find help when you need it. Here are the places where you can get help while you're working:

- Find out what a button stands for by pointing to it with the mouse and pausing. A QuickTip appears and gives you either the name or a brief description of the button. You can use this on all types of screen elements, not just toolbar buttons.

- Get descriptions of menu items by pointing to the item and pausing. A QuickTip appears with a description.

- Press Shift+F1 to change the mouse pointer into a What's This pointer. Then click on a screen element for a description.

- In dialog boxes, click the What's This button, and then click the dialog box option you want help on. A QuickTip appears with a description for that option (see Figure 1.12). For more help, click the <u>H</u>elp button in the lower-right corner. This opens a Help window with the help topic for that dialog box or feature.

Figure 1.12
If a dialog box has a question mark next to the Close button, you can click the question mark, and then click a dialog box component to display a QuickTip on that component.

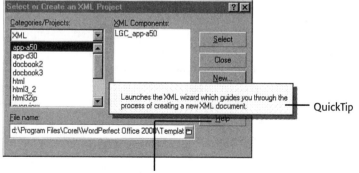

Click here to display the help topic.

- When you know what you want to do, and you don't want to poke around the help screens until you find it, you can use the PerfectExpert. You type a question in your own words and get a list of possible solutions. Choose the Help menu, and then select Ask the PerfectExpert. (You'll learn more on this a little later in the chapter.)

- You can learn a lot about a program by looking around in Help, so don't overlook the Help system. The Contents section is task oriented, so you're likely to discover features as they relate to a specific project, such as adding images to your documents or using Internet tools. Choose the Help menu, choose Help Topics, and then click the Contents tab. Double-click the book icons to open more topics. Next to each help page is a question mark icon (see Figure 1.13). You can double-click these icons to display help topics.

Figure 1.13
The Contents tab of the Help Topics dialog box organizes help topics using a book-and-chapter model.

Double-click this icon to display a help topic.

Double-click the book icon to open more topics.

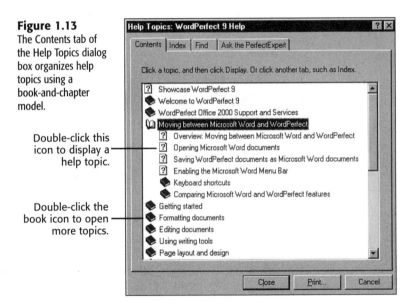

- The Help Index is great when you want to search for a subject and get a list of help topics to choose from. Choose the Help menu, choose Help Topics, and then click the Index tab. Type a keyword (or just the first few letters) to jump down through the index (see Figure 1.14). Double-click an index entry to display the help topic, or in some cases, a list of possible help topics to choose from.

- If you have an Internet connection, you can go up to Corel's Web site for help. Choose Help, Corel on the Web, Technical Support. WordPerfect launches your Internet browser and takes you to its Technical Support page (see Figure 1.15). You'll find links to its technical support documents, tips and tricks, file downloads (updates, patches, and utilities), and its newsgroups.

- The real muscle in Corel's online support arm is the searchable knowledge base. In WordPerfect, choose Help, Help Topics, and then click the Corel Knowledge Base tab. Type your question in the text box, and then click Search. In your Internet browser, go to http://kb.corel.com. Either way, you can search through thousands of technical information documents (TID) furnished by Corel's Technical Support Department. You'll find solutions for the problems you're encountering, along with helpful tips, shortcuts, and detailed explanations of how features work.

Figure 1.14
The Index tab of the Help Topics dialog box organizes help topics alphabetically in an index.

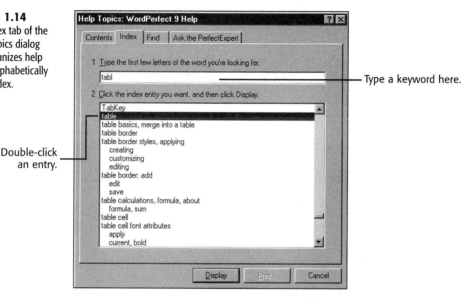

Type a keyword here.

Double-click an entry.

Figure 1.15
Corel's Technical Support Web page has links to technical support documents, tips and tricks, and updates.

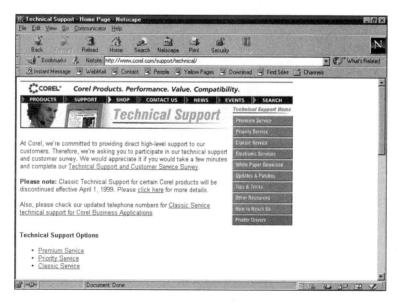

- For those making the transition from Microsoft Word, there is a special help section just for you. Choose the <u>H</u>elp menu, and then select <u>M</u>icrosoft Word Help.

■ For the ultimate in point-and-click productivity, choose <u>H</u>elp, Perfect<u>E</u>xpert. The PerfectExpert panel opens on the left side of the screen, with buttons to help you design virtually every aspect of a document (see Figure 1.16). Rather than searching for the right command in the menus, you can click buttons from the well-organized lists.

→ For more information on using the PerfectExpert panel, **see** "Using the PerfectExpert," **p. 686**

Figure 1.16
The PerfectExpert panel has frequently used features organized so that you don't have to search for items in the menus. All you have to do is click a button and choose from a list.

Click here to start a new document.

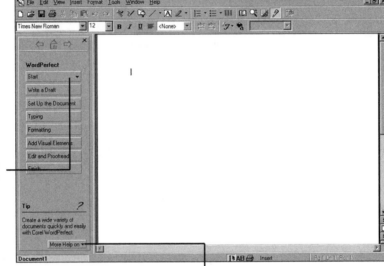

Click here to get help.

ASKING FOR HELP IN YOUR OWN WORDS

What could be better than asking a question in your own words and getting a list of places where you can go to find the answer? Even when you don't know the name of a feature, if you know what you're trying to do, the PerfectExpert can help.

Let's say you need to create a Web page. Search the PerfectExpert for creating a Web page, and you'll get access to help topics on the process of designing and publishing a Web page.

To ask the PerfectExpert, do the following:

1. Open the <u>H</u>elp menu and choose Ask the <u>P</u>erfectExpert.
2. Type your question and press Enter. WordPerfect searches through the help topics projects to compile a list of possible solutions (see Figure 1.17).

Figure 1.17
With the PerfectExpert, you can ask questions in your own words.

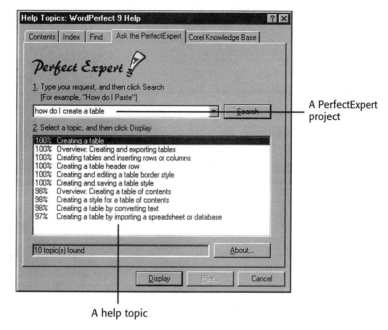

A PerfectExpert project

A help topic

3. To display a help topic, double-click the topic.

EXITING WORDPERFECT

The quickest way to exit WordPerfect is to click the application Close button. You'll see two Close buttons in the upper-right corner. Don't let this confuse you—the top one is the application Close button; the bottom one is the document Close button.

When you closed your document, you clicked the bottom Close button. Now, click the top Close button to close the application window and exit WordPerfect.

Tip #9 from
Laura and Read

Would you like to be able to pick up *right* where you left off when you start WordPerfect again? Let's say you're working on three documents, and you want to be able to save your place in one of the documents. The next time you start WordPerfect, you want those same three documents open and your insertion point where you left it. No problem—choose the Tools menu and select Settings, and then Environment to open the Environment Settings dialog box. Click the Interface tab. In the Save Workspace section, select Always (to save automatically each time you exit) or Prompt on Exit (to selectively save the workspace). Click OK and then Close to return to the document.

Exit WordPerfect by doing the following:

1. Click the application Close button. Before closing the program, WordPerfect prompts you to save your changes (in every open document window).

2. If necessary, give filenames to any documents that you have not yet saved and named.

TROUBLESHOOTING

HAVING TROUBLE STARTING WORDPERFECT

I'm trying to start WordPerfect, but I can't find WordPerfect Office 2000 on my Programs menu.

The program hasn't been installed on your system yet. Insert the Corel CD in the CD-ROM drive. The Setup program should start automatically. If it doesn't, choose Start, Run. Type the drive letter for the CD-ROM drive, followed by a colon (:), and then type setup.exe. (You can also click the Browse button to locate the CD-ROM drive if you can't remember the drive letter.) Press Enter to start the Setup program.

THE MISSING PROPERTY BAR AND TOOLBAR

I don't see the Property Bar or the toolbar on my screen.

It's possible that another user has placed these bars somewhere else on the screen. Look on the left and right sides of the document window. Also, look at the bottom of the screen, just above the status bar. The Property Bar and toolbar might also be positioned as a "floating palette" anywhere in the document window. To move them back, point to a blank section (or the title bar of the palette) and wait for a four-pronged arrow to appear. Click and drag the bar back up to the top of the screen. When the gray guidelines appear as a long rectangle, release the mouse button.

If you don't see the bars at all, they've probably been turned off. Choose View, Toolbars. Place a check mark in the box next to Property Bar and WordPerfect 9.

QUICKTIPS DON'T APPEAR

When I point to a toolbar button, a QuickTip doesn't appear.

Perhaps another user turned off QuickTips. Choose Tools, Settings to open the Settings dialog box. Click the Environment icon, and then click the Interface tab. Place a check mark in the QuickTips check box, click OK, and then click Close.

HEAVY-HANDED DELETIONS

I got in a big hurry and deleted way too much text. How can I get it back?

You mean, you don't remember exactly what you just deleted so you can just type it back in really fast? Well, no one else does either. Press Ctrl+Z or click the Undo button to reverse the last action taken on the document. If this doesn't work, you've done something else after you deleted the text. Press Ctrl+Z or click the Undo button until the text comes back.

If you click Undo too many times, you can click Redo to undo the last Undo. Say that three times fast!

SPELL-AS-YOU-GO GONE

I don't see any dashes under any words onscreen, even if I type a misspelled word.

The Spell-As-You-Go feature has been turned off. Choose Tools, Proofread, Spell-As-You-Go to turn it back on.

PROJECT

In the "Saving Documents" section, I talked about the Timed Document Backup feature and how it's turned on and set to make backups of your documents every 10 minutes. In the event of a system crash, the most you stand to lose is 10 minutes of work (or less, if you decrease the backup interval). You're probably wondering how you can get to this backup file if your system locks up.

If you fail to exit WordPerfect properly, the next time you start the program, you'll see a message box, telling you that you have a backup file available (see Figure 1.19). You have to choose one of the three options before you can get into the program.

Figure 1.19
In the Timed Backup message box, you can open, rename, or delete the backup file.

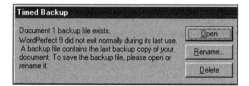

I strongly suggest that you open the backup file so you can see what's in it before you even considering deleting it. When you delete the backup file, it's gone; you can't restore it from the Recycle Bin.

Backup files are named wp{wp}.bk#, where the # stands for the number of the document. If you have four documents open, you'll have four different backup files: wp{wp}.bk1, wp{wp}.bk2, wp{wp}.bk3, and wp{wp}.bk4. Bear in mind that only the active document is backed up when the backup interval comes up, so if you're in document number 3, that document is backed up. If you're in another document when the interval comes up again, that document is backed up. Maybe some day they can engineer a Timed Document Backup feature that backs up all the open documents during the backup interval, but it hasn't happened yet.

Choose Open to open the backup file so that you can take a look. I usually open the named document so that I can do a visual comparison to see which is the most recent version. You can even do a Document Compare to compare the two so you can see the differences. With the backup copy open, choose File, Document, Compare. Type the name of the named document or browse for it. Choose Compare Only to start the comparison.

When you've figured out which copy is the most recent, you can save it. If the backup file has changes that the named document doesn't, close the named document, and then save the backup document with that name to overwrite the older file. If the named document has the most recent information, then you can close the backup document without saving it.

If you want to take a look at the backup file, but not right now, rename it so you can get back to it later. Choose Rename to open the Rename File dialog box (see Figure 1.20). The original filename is shown. Type the new filename in the New Name text box, and then click OK. The named backup file is saved in the current folder unless you type a different drive and folder name when you name the file. I suggest saving the named backup file to the Backup folder so you know where to find it.

Figure 1.20
You can rename a Timed Document Backup file so that you can go back and look at it later.

The current filename is displayed here.

Type the new name here.

Now, if for some strange reason, you don't get the Timed Backup dialog box, you can go look for the backup files and open them manually. They are stored in the folder that's specified in the Files Settings dialog box. Choose Tools, Settings, and then click Files. If necessary, click the Document tab. The name of the backup folder is shown in the Backup Folder text box. Open the Open File dialog box and move to that folder. The backup files all follow the same naming convention—wp{wp}.bk#. If you aren't sure which one you need, choose View, Details to see the date and time the file was last saved.

It's a good idea to do some periodic housekeeping in the Backup folder. Delete the files that you don't need anymore and move the files that you want to keep.

CHAPTER 2

OPENING AND EDITING DOCUMENTS

In this chapter

FINDING AND OPENING DOCUMENTS

Although much of what you work on in WordPerfect is new, original material, most of the time you will find yourself modifying and correcting existing documents. That, after all, is the real value and power of the word processing program: It saves you time and energy as you perfect your work.

WordPerfect's Open File dialog box is the easiest way to locate and to open existing files. It's WordPerfect's friendlier equivalent to Windows 95/98 Explorer. Simply choose File, Open (or press Ctrl+O or F4), and WordPerfect displays the dialog box shown in Figure 2.1.

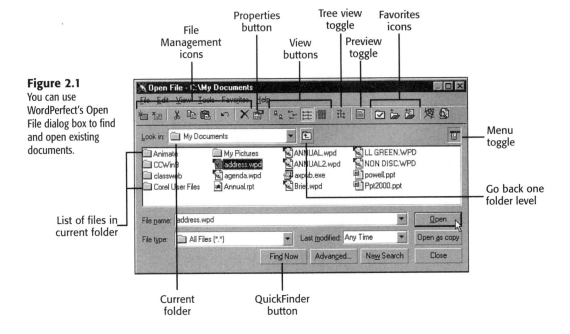

Figure 2.1
You can use WordPerfect's Open File dialog box to find and open existing documents.

Tip #10 from
Laura and Read

WordPerfect's *QuickOpen* feature remembers the last nine documents you worked on and lists these at the bottom of the File menu. Simply click File, and then click the name of the document you want to open. That's it! WordPerfect opens the document, and you're ready to begin editing.

WordPerfect automatically opens the default, or currently selected, folder—for example, c:\My Documents. To open a file in this folder, scroll through the list, click the file you want to open, and click Open. You can also double-click the file to select and open it at the same time.

UNDERSTANDING THE OPEN FILE DIALOG BOX

You'll probably be surprised at how useful WordPerfect's file management system (the Open File dialog box) can be. You'll find yourself here often as you find, open, delete, rename, or copy files. After a quick overview, you'll be able to use this tool much more effectively.

The View buttons determine how WordPerfect displays filenames in the file list. You can choose from the following View button options (refer to Figure 2.1):

- Large Icon shows each file with a large icon. This isn't terribly useful unless you like large pictures!

- Small Icon shows the list of files with small icons, arranged alphabetically by row from left to right.

- List is the default view, and files are shown with small icons, arranged alphabetically by column from top to bottom.

- Details is perhaps the most useful view (see Figure 2.2). Files are listed with small icons, arranged alphabetically from top to bottom. However, you also see the date and time the file was last modified, and its relative size.

PART

I

CH

2

Figure 2.2
The Details view of the Open File dialog box offers the most information about files, and also enables you to sort your files.

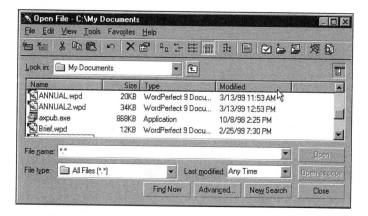

Tip #11 from
Laura and Read

The column heading buttons in the Details view can do much more than look pretty. Click the Modified button, for example, and WordPerfect arranges the list of files in chronological order of when the files were last modified. Click it again to sort in reverse chronological order. Click the Name button, and you get an alphabetical listing. This procedure also works in other Windows applications where the files are listed with column headings.

If you really want to make the WordPerfect Open File dialog box look like the Windows Explorer, click the Toggle Tree View On/Off button (see Figure 2.3).

Tip #12 from
Laura and Read

Don't forget that you can size the Open File dialog box window just as you do most Windows windows. A larger Open File dialog box is particularly useful if you choose the Details view.

Figure 2.3
If you toggle the Tree View on, the Open File dialog box looks and works very much like the Windows Explorer.

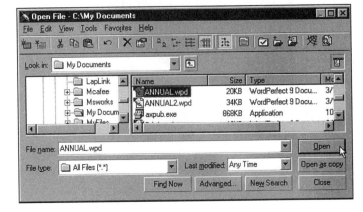

PREVIEWING FILES

If you want to preview a file before opening it, click the Preview toggle button (see Figure 2.4).

Figure 2.4
The Preview view shows you a thumbnail sketch of a page of your document.

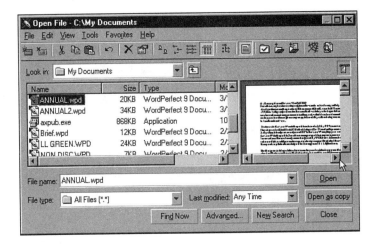

Unfortunately, what you actually see in the Preview window is so small that it's not terribly useful as you try to determine the contents of the file. However, you can remedy this by creating a larger Preview window. Follow these steps:

1. Right-click the Preview window to display a menu of choices.

2. Choose <u>U</u>se Separate Window. WordPerfect displays a separate Previewer window (see Figure 2.5). Alternatively, you can choose <u>V</u>iew, <u>P</u>review, <u>U</u>se Separate Window to display the separate Previewer window.

Figure 2.5
The Preview window can be detached from the Open File dialog box and sized larger to make the document more readable.

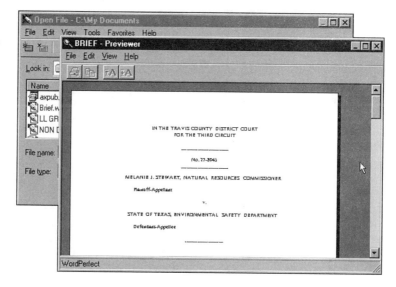

3. Size the Previewer window so that it's large enough to display the document in a readable format.

4. Close the Previewer window to return to the Open File dialog box.

The next time you click the Preview toggle button, WordPerfect displays the document preview in this separate window. To cancel the separate preview window, right-click the Previewer window and uncheck <u>U</u>se Separate Window.

Note

When you size the Previewer window, WordPerfect remembers that size the next time you click the Preview toggle button in the Open File dialog box. However, if you maximize the Previewer window, the next time you access it WordPerfect once again displays the smaller-sized window.

Another method for previewing files is to use the QuickView program that comes with Windows 98. While in the Open File dialog box, right-click the file you want to view and choose <u>Q</u>uickView from the menu that appears. If the option doesn't appear, that means the program has not been installed or that you are trying to view a file not supported by QuickView. Make sure the program is installed by accessing the Control Panel, and then choosing Add/Remove Programs, Windows Setup, Accessories, QuickView.

CHANGING TO ANOTHER FOLDER

What happens when you don't see the file you want in the current folder? Assuming that you did save the file, the most likely reason you don't see it is that you saved it in a different folder.

To navigate to another folder, first look in the list of files for other folders that might contain the file. Double-click a folder to open it and to see its contents.

If you don't find the file there, you may have to return to the next level up. Just click (once) the Go Back One Folder Level button (refer to Figure 2.1) and then decide whether to try another folder or to go back another folder level.

When you finally find the file you want, open it.

Caution	If you change folders, the last opened folder becomes the default folder. The next time you access the Open File dialog box, you get a listing of files in that folder. This can be confusing if you're not mindful of which folder you are in.

Tip #13 from *Laura and Read*	If you want to always open the same default folder, choose Edit, Change Default Folder (make sure it does *not* have a check beside it). Now, regardless of how often you browse for files in other folders, you'll always return to the default folder when you access the Open File dialog box.

 If you still have trouble making the proper default folder come up when you access the Open File dialog box, see "Setting the Default Folder" in the Troubleshooting section at the end of this chapter.

USING QUICKFINDER TO LOCATE DOCUMENTS

Sometimes you simply can't remember the name of the document you're looking for. Often, however, you remember a word or phrase that you know is contained in the document itself. WordPerfect's *QuickFinder* feature enables you to search for and find documents based on their contents.

Access the Open File dialog box, and in the File Name text box, type the word you want to find. Then click Find Now. Do *not* click Open and do *not* press Enter. WordPerfect searches all the documents in the current folder and its subfolders, and returns the results in the QuickFinder Results dialog box. Select the file you want, and click Open.

Tip #14 from	If you know the name of the file you're looking for, but just can't seem to find it, don't for-get that you can use the Windows Find feature. Click the Start button, choose Find, Files or Folders, and then search for your file by name.
Laura and Read	

OPENING A COPY OF A DOCUMENT

Sometimes you want to edit a copy of a document, but you want to leave the original intact. Follow these steps:

1. Access the Open File dialog box (by selecting File, Open).
2. Find and select the file you want to work on.
3. Click the Open as Copy button (not the Open button). WordPerfect opens a copy of the file, which you can edit.
4. When you finish making changes, choose File, Save. WordPerfect forces you to provide a new filename.
5. Choose Save, and you now have a modified copy of the original, and the original is still intact.

CONVERTING DOCUMENTS ON OPEN

Believe it or not, not everyone uses Corel WordPerfect! Even if they do, they don't always use the most recent version. Fortunately, WordPerfect's built-in file conversion feature enables you to open nearly every kind of word processing document.

Tip #15 from	If you have a ton of old WordPerfect files, there is no need to worry about losing them when you switch to WordPerfect 9. Just leave them alone until you need them, and then open them in WordPerfect 9 just as you open any other document. WordPerfect converts the older WordPerfect formats to the new WordPerfect 9 format. When you save the con-verted file, choose the WordPerfect 6/7/8/9 format.
Laura and Read	

When you save a converted document, WordPerfect asks if you want to save it in the latest WordPerfect format (WordPerfect 6/7/8/9) or in the original format from which it was con-verted. If you're returning the document to someone who isn't using WordPerfect, simply select the original format and choose OK.

MOVING AROUND IN A DOCUMENT

When you have found a document to edit, you need to know the most efficient ways of get-ting around so you can quickly make changes to the document. Before you can make a change, you must reposition the insertion point (that is, the cursor) at the point where you want to make the change.

As in other parts of the Windows environment, you can move the insertion point by using either the mouse or the keyboard.

Mouse or Keyboard?

It's easy to get into a rut of using primarily the mouse or the keyboard. It's a good idea to become familiar with both methods of moving around your document so that as the need arises, you can use the most appropriate method. For example, if your hands are already on the keyboard, it might make more sense to use the keyboard to move the insertion point instead of having to move your hand to the mouse to move the insertion point.

USING THE MOUSE TO MOVE AROUND

You move the insertion point with the mouse in the following ways:

- Point and click—Position the mouse pointer at the location in the text where you want to place the insertion point. (The mouse pointer will be either an arrow or an I-beam, depending on the Shadow Cursor options you have chosen.)

→ To learn more about the Shadow Cursor and how to enable or disable it, **see** "Touring the WordPerfect Screen," **p. 13**

- Scrollbar—As in any Windows application, you can scroll bit by bit simply by clicking the up and down arrows at either end of the vertical scrollbar. You can scroll more quickly by clicking and dragging the scroll box found between the two arrows. When you use the scroll box, WordPerfect displays a QuickTip that indicates the page number you see on the screen.

- Browse buttons—These buttons are located at the bottom of the vertical scrollbar (see Figure 2.6). By default, you browse by page. Click the up arrow to go to the previous page, and click the down arrow to go to the next page. To toggle among other methods of browsing, click the Browse By button, located between the up and down arrows. You can browse by page, table, box, footnote, endnote, heading, edit (cursor) position, or comment.

- The Autoscroll feature—You can click the *Autoscroll* icon on the toolbar to activate automatic scrolling. The mouse pointer automatically positions itself in the middle of the screen, and displays a dot with up and down arrows (see Figure 2.7). As you move the mouse pointer up, the pointer changes to a dot with an upward arrow, and the text scrolls toward the top of the document. Pull the mouse downward to scroll toward the bottom of the document. The closer the mouse pointer is to the center of the screen, the slower the text scrolls. Click the mouse to reposition the insertion point, and at the same time turn off Autoscroll.

Tip #16 from
Laura and Read

Using the Autoscroll feature, you can read your document as you scroll. Simply move the mouse pointer a short distance downward, away from the center of the screen to scroll slowly and thus read the text before it disappears from the screen.

Figure 2.6
You can browse your document by page, table, box, and so on by using the Browse buttons on the vertical scrollbar.

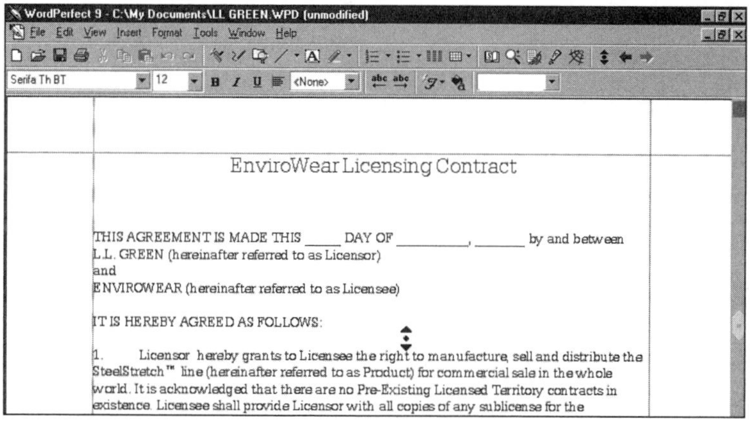

Previous (page, or whatever option you have selected)

Scroll box

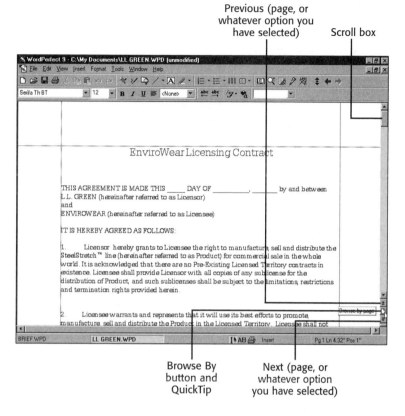

Browse By button and QuickTip

Next (page, or whatever option you have selected)

Figure 2.7
Autoscroll makes it easy to scroll through your document by moving your mouse pointer up or down on the screen.

USING THE KEYBOARD TO MOVE AROUND

Sometimes moving the insertion point with the mouse can be imprecise, and even tedious. Moving it by using the keyboard can be quicker and more accurate.

Tip #17 from *Laura and Read*	Don't worry if the list of possible keystrokes seems overwhelming. Actually there are relatively few *different* procedures, each with two or more directions (up or down, for example). Try one or two, and add to your repertoire until you can move around your documents like greased lightning.

Table 2.1 shows keyboard shortcuts for repositioning the insertion point. These keystrokes are standard in all Windows applications, except as noted (with an asterisk).

TABLE 2.1   WORDPERFECT'S KEYBOARD SHORTCUTS

Keystroke(s)	Insertion Point Moves
Right-arrow	One character to the right
Left-arrow	One character to the left
Down-arrow	One line down
Up-arrow	One line up
Ctrl+right-arrow	One word to the right
Ctrl+left-arrow	One word to the left
Ctrl+down-arrow	One paragraph down
Ctrl+up-arrow	One paragraph up
Home	To beginning of current line
End	To end of current line
Page Down	To bottom of current screen
Page Up	To top of current screen
Alt+Page Down*	To top of next physical page
Alt+Page Up*	To top of previous physical page
Ctrl+End	To end of document
Ctrl+Home	To beginning of document

This keystroke is not standard in other Windows programs.

WORKING WITH SELECTED TEXT

Can you imagine having to format your text or delete whole paragraphs one character at a time? Fortunately, you can select a chunk of text and delete it or apply formatting to it.

SELECTING TEXT

Although typically you use the mouse or the keyboard to select text, you can also use the Edit menu to select the text. Choose Edit, Select to discover these choices:

- Sentence—WordPerfect selects the sentence in which the insertion point is found.
- Paragraph—WordPerfect selects the entire paragraph, including the extra blank space between paragraphs.
- Page—WordPerfect selects the entire current page.
- All—WordPerfect selects the entire document.

PART

I

CH

2

None of these options are terribly common, however. Instead, you'll probably end up using the mouse or the keyboard to select text. Let's look first at selecting text using the keyboard. This procedure is simple once you've mastered the cursor control keystrokes in Table 2.1. To select a portion of text, position the insertion point at the beginning of the area you want to select, hold down the Shift key, and use any cursor movement to move to the end of the selection.

For example, to select text a word at a time, hold down the Shift key while pressing Ctrl+right-arrow. To select everything from the cursor to the end of the document, hold down the Shift key and press Ctrl+End.

Note

Selecting text using the Shift key along with cursor movement keys or along with repositioning the insertion point with the mouse is standard in all Windows applications.

Selecting text with the mouse is also easy, although a bit of dexterity and practice may be necessary before you become really good at it.

Table 2.2 shows several methods of using the mouse to select text. Again, these methods are standard in all Windows applications, except as noted (with an asterisk).

TABLE 2.2   SELECTING TEXT IN WORDPERFECT BY USING THE MOUSE

Mouse Action	What It Selects
Drag across text	One whole word at a time
Alt+drag across text	One character at a time
Double-click	Entire word
Triple-click*	Entire sentence
Quadruple-click*	Entire paragraph
Single-click in left margin*	Entire sentence
Double-click in left margin	Entire paragraph

This mouse action is not standard in other Windows programs.

The methods listed in Table 2.2 are used only for selecting text. The mouse is used differently to select graphics objects or cells of a table.

→ To learn more about selecting graphics objects, **see** Chapter 12, "Adding Graphics to Your Documents," **p. 317**

→ To learn more about selecting tables and table cells, **see** Chapter 10, "Organizing Information with Tables," **p. 251**

Finally, with text selected, you can further refine your selection by choosing Edit, Select and selecting one of the following options:

- Tabular Column—If your text is arranged in tabular columns and you want to select the column, select your text from the beginning of the tabular column to the end of the tabular column. WordPerfect selects all text, including other columns, but choosing this option changes the selection to include only the desired tabular column.

- Rectangle—If you want to select a specific rectangle of text, first select from the beginning of the rectangle to the end of the rectangle. WordPerfect selects all text. Choosing this option changes the selection to include only the rectangle of text.

- Select Table—With the cursor positioned inside a table, this option selects the entire table.

Although you probably won't use these options frequently, they can be useful when you have to edit and reformat text that was poorly formatted to begin with.

Deleting Text

You already know how to delete text by using the Backspace key (erasing to the left of the insertion point) or the Delete key (erasing to the right of the insertion point). However, you can also quickly delete a selected block of text. After selecting the text you want to delete, you can use one of these methods:

- Press Delete.
- Press Backspace.
- Right-click the selection and choose Delete from the *QuickMenu (page 15)*.

Moving and Copying Text

So you've got some text selected. Besides deleting it, what else can you do with it? The "bread and butter" of word processing consists of moving text from one place to another. When you move the text, but leave a copy in the original location, you are *copying and pasting* text. If you move it and delete the original location, you are *cutting and pasting* text.

WordPerfect likes to try to please everyone, so there are several different ways to cut and paste selected text. The basic procedure is this:

1. Select the text you want to move.

2. Copy (or cut) the selected text.

3. Reposition the insertion point at the target location.

4. Paste the text you copied (or cut).

You can paste copied text as many times as you like, until you copy or cut something new.

Note	The Windows Clipboard is an area of your computer's memory that stores information that you cut or copy. If you cut or copy another selection, this selection replaces whatever was in your Clipboard. If you turn off your computer, you lose entirely whatever is in the Clipboard.

The various methods for copying, cutting, and pasting are listed in Table 2.3. Use the method that helps you work the fastest. For example, if your hands are already on the keyboard, try using the keyboard methods. Otherwise, you might want to use the mouse.

TABLE 2.3   METHODS FOR MOVING TEXT

Action	Method
Copy	Choose Edit, Copy Click the Copy toolbar icon Right-click the selection and choose Copy Press Ctrl+C Press Ctrl+Insert
Cut	Choose Edit, Cut Click the Cut toolbar icon Right-click the selection and choose Cut Press Ctrl+X Press Shift+Delete
Paste	Choose Edit, Paste Click the Paste toolbar icon Right-click and choose Paste Press Shift+Insert

Tip #18 from
Laura and Read

Typically when you cut or copy material, it replaces anything you previously cut or copied to the Windows Clipboard. You can also cut or copy a series of selections, and append them to the Windows Clipboard. Select the text, and choose Edit, Append. You then paste at once from the Clipboard everything you appended.

Tip #19 from
Laura and Read

A fast and easy-to-remember sequence for cutting and pasting involves using the Shift key: Shift+cursor to select the text, Shift+Delete to cut the text, and then Shift+Insert to paste the text. If you learn these keystrokes, you can save incredible amounts of time as you cut and paste.

 If what you paste isn't what you thought you copied, see "Pasting Things Correctly" in the Troubleshooting section at the end of this chapter.

WordPerfect also enables you to use the mouse to drag selected text from one location and drop it in another. This drag-and-drop feature can be useful in many situations. To *drag and drop* text, follow these steps:

1. Use the mouse or the keyboard to select the text you want to move.

2. Position the mouse pointer on the highlighted text. The pointer changes to an arrow.

3. Click and hold down the left mouse button.

4. Drag the mouse to the target location. The mouse pointer changes to an arrow, along with a small rectangular box (see Figure 2.8). An insertion point also appears, showing you exactly where the text will be copied when you release the mouse button.

Figure 2.8
You can use the mouse to quickly drag and drop text.

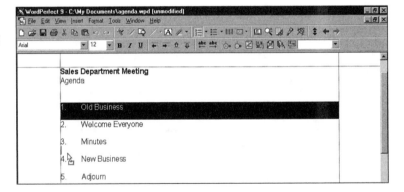

5. Release the mouse button. WordPerfect continues to highlight the text. If you didn't quite hit your target, you can drag again, or you can choose Undo and start over again.

6. When you have the selection where you want it, click the selection to deselect it.

Tip #20 from
Laura and Read

In addition to moving text, you can also copy selected text by holding down the Ctrl key while dragging and dropping the text.

Oops (Using Undo)

When your finger slips and you type the wrong letter, it's no big deal. Backspace quickly zaps the letter and you're back on track. But when you make a change to a large amount of text, reconstructing the original can be tedious and time-consuming. Fortunately, WordPerfect gives you the capability to undo your actions quickly and easily.

You can use any of the following methods to undo an action:

- Choose Edit, Undo.
- Click the Undo icon on the toolbar.
- Press Ctrl+Z.

Even better, WordPerfect remembers up to the last 10 things you did, and enables you to undo them sequentially in reverse order.

If you get carried away and undo too many steps, you can also redo those steps by clicking the Redo icon on the toolbar or choosing Edit, Redo.

> **Caution**
>
> Both Undo and Redo operate sequentially. If you need to undo or redo a step or two, do so immediately. Otherwise, you may not be able to back up or move forward without undoing correct steps or redoing incorrect steps.

By default, WordPerfect does not save Undo information with your document—but you can save it if you want. If you want to save Undo information, choose Edit, Undo/Redo History, Options and check Save Undo/Redo Items with Document. Then, if you or someone else opens the document later, you can still undo the last 10 steps performed on the document. Note, however, that if you are deleting or moving large quantities of text or graphics, and you save the Undo information, the size of your saved file can increase dramatically.

What Happened to Undelete
Nearly since its inception, WordPerfect has included an Undelete feature. Long-time WordPerfect users looking for Undelete will find that the feature no longer is available. Instead, use Undo when you delete text accidentally, and use standard cut and paste to move text.

Working with Reveal Codes

The capability to look behind the scenes and to see how specific codes control the flow of a WordPerfect document is called *Reveal Codes* (see Figure 2.9). For many, this is the single most important distinguishing feature between WordPerfect and other word processing programs. Some people love using the feature, and others don't. But even the critics have to admit that Reveal Codes does give you detailed control over your document.

Figure 2.9
The Reveal Codes
screen enables you to
view what's controlling
the format of your
document.

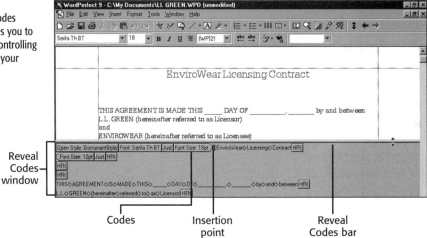

You can use any of the following methods to turn on Reveal Codes:

- Choose View, Reveal Codes.
- Press Alt+F3.
- Right-click the editing screen and choose Reveal Codes from the QuickMenu.
- Drag the Reveal Codes bar located at the bottom of the vertical scrollbar (refer to Figure 2.9).

Control codes appear in the Reveal Codes screen as buttons mixed in with the text. The insertion point is shown as a small red box. You can reposition the insertion point by clicking the mouse in the Reveal Codes window, in addition to using the usual mouse and keyboard methods.

Deleting with Reveal Codes On
When Reveal Codes is off, Delete and Backspace remove text but don't necessarily delete formatting codes. In Reveal Codes, WordPerfect assumes that you see the codes, and that you intend to delete them when you use Delete or Backspace. If you accidentally delete a formatting code, just use Undo to restore it.

Generally, when you make a change in your WordPerfect document, you do so at the insertion point. Sometimes you make changes that you don't even see but that cause problems with the document's formatting. Using Reveal Codes enables you to find errant codes and delete them. Simply position the insertion point before or after the code and press Delete or Backspace as appropriate.

WordPerfect's AutoCode Placement feature also places certain codes at more appropriate locations. For example, codes that clearly affect paragraphs, such as margin or tab settings, are placed at the beginning of the paragraph in which the insertion point is resting. Codes that pertain to pages, such as page numbering or headers, are placed at the beginning of the current page.

You can also use the mouse in the Reveal Codes screen to delete or edit codes:

- You can delete codes by clicking and dragging them up, out of the Reveal Codes screen (see Figure 2.10).

PART

I

CH

2

Figure 2.10
You can use the mouse to drag codes out of the Reveal Codes screen to delete them.

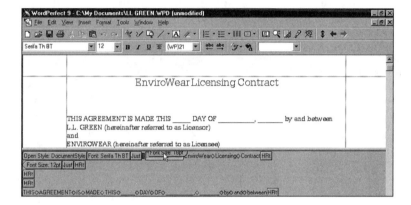

- You can edit many format settings by double-clicking their codes in the Reveal Codes screen. This brings up the appropriate dialog box, which enables you to make changes in the code setting.

Some WordPerfect aficionados prefer to work all the time with the Reveal Codes screen on. However, it's also quite easy to toggle Reveal Codes back off again. Simply press Alt+F3, choose <u>V</u>iew, Reveal <u>C</u>odes, right-click the Reveal Codes window and choose Hide Reveal Codes, or drag the Reveal Codes separator bar all the way to the bottom of the screen.

 Having trouble seeing a Reveal Codes window? See "Sizing the Reveal Codes Window" in the Troubleshooting section at the end of this chapter.

EDITING MORE THAN ONE DOCUMENT

If your desk looks anything like mine, you realize that we rarely work on just one thing at a time. While we're correcting the annual report, someone calls and asks for the action list from last week's board meeting.

Fortunately, WordPerfect makes it easy for us to work this way by giving us up to nine separate document windows.

To open a document in another WordPerfect window, simply access the Open File dialog box and open the document. If you want to open more than one file at a time, simply access the Open File dialog box, and then while holding down the Ctrl key, click each file you intend to open and click Open. However, don't forget that WordPerfect cannot open more than nine documents at once.

To open a new window with a blank document, click the Create a Blank Document icon on the toolbar. You can also choose File, New or press Ctrl+N.

When you have more than one document open, you have to remember what documents you have open and learn to jump quickly from one document to another. WordPerfect's title bar displays the name of the currently active document window, and the application bar displays the titles of all open documents (see Figure 2.11).

Figure 2.11
Tabs on the application bar display each open WordPerfect document. Clicking a document enables you to switch to that document.

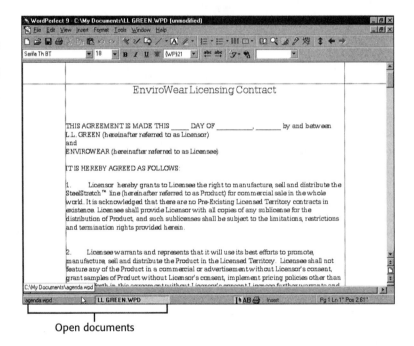

Open documents

You can switch from one document to another by using any of the following methods:

- On the application bar, click the name of the document you want to work on, and WordPerfect opens that window for you.
- Choose Window and then click the document you want.
- Press Ctrl+F6 repeatedly until WordPerfect displays the document you want to work on.

Tip #21 from	Remember that you can copy and paste from one document to another. Simply cut or copy while viewing one document, and then switch to another document and paste.
Laura and Read	

→ To learn more details about moving information from one WordPerfect document to another, **see** Chapter 15, "Importing Data and Working with Other Programs," **p. 403**

TROUBLESHOOTING

PASTING THINGS CORRECTLY

Sometimes when I paste I get something other than what I wanted to copy.

The Windows Clipboard remembers the last thing you copied or cut. When you paste something you previously copied or cut, this is because you didn't cut or copy correctly. Simply undo what you pasted, and then go back and cut or copy the selection again.

SETTING THE DEFAULT FOLDER

When I open the Open File dialog box, I can't seem to make the default folder what I want it to be.

Even if you turn off Change Default Folder, WordPerfect still remembers the last folder you were in. Access the Open File dialog box, toggle the menu on if necessary, and then choose Edit, Change Default Folder (make sure there is a check mark beside this menu item.) Next, browse to the folder you want to become the default folder, and choose Close. Access the Open File dialog box again and choose Edit, Change Default Folder to turn off this feature, and then click Close. Now, each time you open the Open File dialog box, you'll find yourself in the correct default folder. Note that after you exit WordPerfect, the Open File dialog box opens to the default folder (for example, c:\My Documents) specified in your settings.

SIZING THE REVEAL CODES WINDOW

Even if I choose View, Reveal Codes, I still don't see a Reveal Codes window.

If you dragged the Reveal Codes bar to size the Reveal Codes window, you may have sized it so small that you don't realize the window is still open. When you turn on Reveal Codes, if you see a solid gray bar at the bottom of the document window, then you must drag this bar up to make a larger Reveal Codes window. You can also drag the bar completely to the bottom of the screen to turn off the Reveal Codes window.

PROJECT

Selecting text and moving it by using cut and paste is the heart and soul of word processing. All programs let you cut and paste standard selections of text, but WordPerfect enables you to select nonstandard selections.

Suppose, for example, that someone has sent you a file that contains text arranged in columns. However, the text is formatted using spaces or tabs instead of using the column feature. Arranging the text into one long sequential column is a snap using WordPerfect. Follow these steps:

1. Begin by selecting the second column, from the beginning of the column to the end of the column. WordPerfect selects all text between the beginning and ending points (see Figure 2.12).

Figure 2.12
If you try to select a column of text, WordPerfect first selects all text.

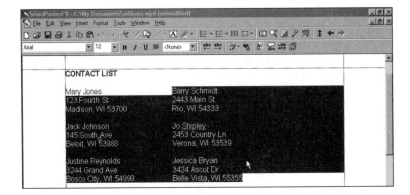

2. Choose Edit, Select, Rectangle to select only the material in a rectangle defined by the beginning and the end of the selection (see Figure 2.13).

Figure 2.13
WordPerfect can refine a selection to select only a rectangle.

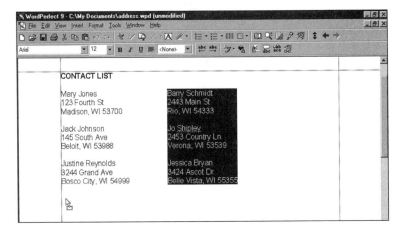

3. Use the cut feature to remove only the rectangle.

4. Position the cursor after the first column, and paste the rectangle. You now have a single, sequential column of text (see Figure 2.14)

Figure 2.14
Cutting and pasting a rectangular selection allows you to move columns of text.

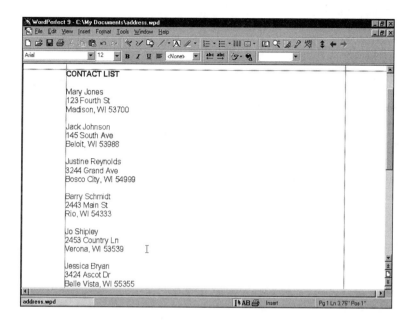

Before formatting the new single column (for example, into newspaper-style columns), you may have to remove extra spaces or tabs following the lines from the original first column.

CHAPTER **3**

BASIC FORMATTING

In this chapter

CHOOSING THE RIGHT FONT

You've tirelessly researched the facts and figures. You've chewed your nails down to the quick trying to think of *just the right* words. You're almost done, when your co-worker stops by and expresses concern that your document won't get the attention it deserves if it isn't easy to read. "Wonderful," you think. You've got three seconds to finish this document and *now* you have to worry about making it easy to read!

What can you do? Choose attractive fonts to generate interest in your subject. Make the titles and headings larger than the body text so that they really stand out. It only takes a few minutes, and the results are well worth your effort.

Caution

As you format your document, remember to always, always, always position the insertion point first. As a general rule, your changes take effect at the insertion point, which may or may not be where you want them. If you forget and get some unexpected results, you've got a safety net: You can click the Undo button to reverse the last action (or continue clicking to reverse the last several actions).

Corel WordPerfect Fonts

Corel offers more than 1,000 fonts—enough to satisfy even the most discriminating fontmeisters. Of these, 24 are the character set fonts, which contain the symbols and foreign language alphabets. Another 56 fonts are installed during a typical installation. The rest can be installed separately, using either the Corel Setup Wizard or the Fonts folder. In the Fonts folder, choose <u>F</u>ile, <u>I</u>nstall New Font.

 If you received an error message during setup saying that you had too many fonts selected, see "Too Many Fonts" in the Troubleshooting section at the end of this chapter.

SELECTING FONTS AND FONT SIZES

The quickest way to choose a different font is to click the Font Face drop-down arrow on the Property Bar. A drop-down list of fonts appears, and a large preview window pops up at the top of the document (see Figure 3.1). As you point to a font in the list, the sample text in the preview window morphs into that font. Thanks to RealTime Preview, the text in the document does the same thing. You don't have to play guessing games, trying to figure out how a font will look from a tiny piece of sample text—you can see how a whole page of text will look. When you find the font that you want, click it.

Tip #22 from
Laura and Read

WordPerfect keeps a list of the 10 most recently used fonts at the top of the Font Face drop-down list.

PART

I

CH

3

Note

The sample text you see in the preview window varies, depending on where the insertion point is. If the insertion point is at the top of the document, a small snippet of text from the beginning of the document is shown. If the insertion point is in a word, that word is used. If the insertion point is in blank space, four letters (A, B, X, Y) are used. Finally, if you've selected text, a short section of that text appears.

Caution

When you're changing the font (or font size) for existing text, such as a title or heading, select it first. Otherwise, the new font (or size) takes effect at the insertion point and stays in effect for the rest of the document (unless, of course, you change the font—or size—again later).

Figure 3.1
As you hover over fonts in the drop-down list, the sample text in the Preview window and the text in the document morphs into that font.

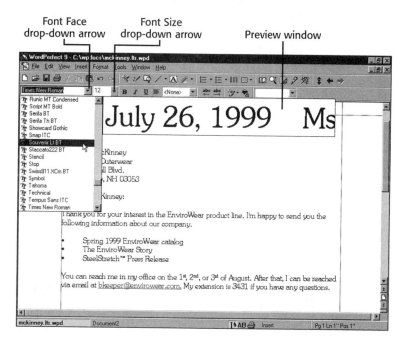

Font Face drop-down arrow   Font Size drop-down arrow   Preview window

Choosing a different font size works essentially the same way as choosing a different font. Click the Font Size drop-down arrow on the Property Bar to open a drop-down list of sizes. If you click the scroll arrows, you'll see that the list has sizes ranging from 6 points to 72 points. A preview window with sample text opens next to the list. As you move the mouse down through the list, the sample text and the document text expand and contract to show the new size.

Tip #23 from
Laura and Read

If you want to use a font size that isn't in the list, click the Font Size box (to select the current size), and then type the size you want.

When you've decided which font you want to use for the body text, set that as the default font for the document. Likewise, if you select a font that you want to use for most, if not all, your documents, set that as the default for all new documents. Choose Format, Font to open the Font Properties dialog box. Make your selections, and then choose Settings. Choose Set as Default for This Document or Set Face and Point Size as Default for All Documents.

Tip #24 from *Laura and Read*	One of the new features in WordPerfect 9 is that you can embed fonts in a document so that they go where the document goes. Choose Embed Fonts in the Save File dialog box. WordPerfect compresses the fonts and saves them with the file.

Tip #25 from *Laura and Read*	Ever wish you had a "font catalog" that you could flip through? Call me old-fashioned, but I'll take a printout over an onscreen sample *any day*. WordPerfect includes a nifty macro that prints out a sample of the fonts on your system. Choose Tools, Macro, Play, and then double-click the Allfonts icon.

→ To find a list of all the macros that ship with WordPerfect, along with the steps to create your own macros, **see** Chapter 24, "Experts and Macros," **p. 685**

SELECTING RECENTLY USED FONTS BY USING QUICKFONTS

Let's say you're formatting a lengthy report. You're finished experimenting, so you know which fonts you want to use for your headings and key terms. Even with the Font Face and Font Size drop-down lists, reselecting the same fonts and sizes over and over is tedious. It's QuickFonts to the rescue! The last 10 fonts (with sizes and effects) you selected are kept in the QuickFonts list for fast access. Click the QuickFonts button on the Property Bar (see Figure 3.2), and then click the font you want to reuse. Sorry—no RealTime Preview here.

QuickFonts button

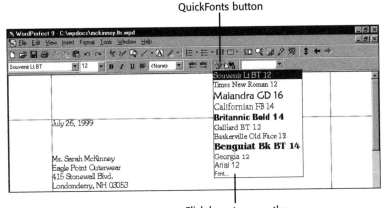

Figure 3.2
Click the QuickFonts button to select from the 10 most recently used fonts.

Click here to open the Font Properties dialog box.

MANAGING FONTS WITH BITSTREAM'S FONT NAVIGATOR

With so many fonts included with WordPerfect and thousands more available on the Internet, it's a full-time job to keep track of them all. Bitstream saw this coming and developed a font manager program called Font Navigator. It's bundled with Corel WordPerfect Office 2000, so you've already got it.

To start Font Navigator, choose Start, Programs, WordPerfect Office 2000, Utilities, Font Navigator 3.0.1. If this is the first time you've ever run Font Navigator, you'll get the Font Navigator Wizard, which helps you locate the fonts on your system. Follow the prompts and let the wizard search your system for fonts.

The Font Navigator window is divided into four panes: one for the fonts files that are found on your system, one for the installed fonts, one for font groups, and one that displays a font sample (see Figure 3.3).

Figure 3.3
You can use Bitstream's Font Navigator to help organize your fonts into manageable groups.

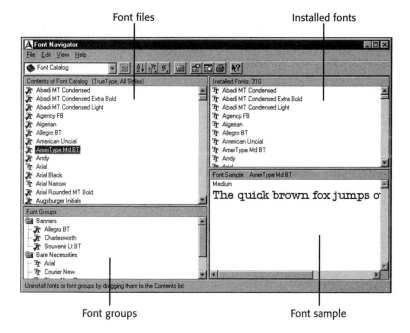

Font files   Installed fonts

Font groups   Font sample

The advantage of the multipane window is that you can click and drag fonts from one list to another. For example, to install fonts, you click and drag them from the Font Catalog list to the Installed Fonts list. They can be uninstalled by clicking and dragging them from the Installed Fonts list back to the Font Catalog.

With Font Navigator, you can do the following:

- Locate available fonts—You can search for fonts on a local or network drive, a floppy disk, a removable drive, a CD-ROM, or only in certain folders on a disk or drive. Choose File, Find Fonts. When Font Navigator is finished, a list of available fonts is displayed in the Font Catalog list.

- View font samples—Select a font in any of the three lists—Font Catalog, Installed Fonts, or Font Groups—to display a sample in the Font Sample pane (refer to Figure 3.3). You can see a more detailed font sample as well: Select a font, and then click the Explore Font button to view a sample of each font variation in eight different sizes.

> **Note**
> The Font Catalog displays the family name for a font (for example, Goudy Old Style), rather than listing all of the different variations (for example, Goudy Old Style Regular, Goudy Old Style Bold, Goudy Old Style Italic).

- Print font samples—To print a sample, select one or more fonts, and then click the Print Font Sample button or choose <u>F</u>ile, <u>P</u>rint Samples.

- Install fonts—You can click and drag a font from the Font Catalog list to the Installed Fonts list. To install multiple fonts, click the first font, and then hold down the Ctrl key as you click the other fonts. Click and drag the selected fonts to the Installed Fonts list.

> **Note**
> When you install fonts in Font Navigator, the fonts are *not* copied to the Fonts folder. The fonts don't have to be in the Fonts folder for you to use them, so Font Navigator doesn't copy these files unnecessarily.

- View properties for a font—You can select a font in one of the lists, and then click the View Properties button. You'll see the name of the file and where it's located, as well as a complete character chart.

- Create font groups—You can click the Create New Font Group button or choose <u>F</u>ile, <u>N</u>ew Font Group. A new font group folder appears in the Font Groups list, with an editing border around it. Type a name, and then press Enter. To view a list of fonts in a font group, double-click the font group name.

- Install font groups—You can select one or more font groups, and then click and drag them to the Installed Fonts list.

- Arrange fonts in the Font Catalog—Fonts can be arranged by format and by style. You can click the View Fonts by Format button and then choose a file format from the list. Or you can click the View Fonts by Style button and select a style from the list. Figure 3.4 shows the Serif fonts in the Font Catalog.

- Customize the view—You can control which fonts are displayed (for example, by style, format, or vendor) in the Font Catalog list. Choose <u>V</u>iew, Customize <u>V</u>iew to display the Customize View dialog box. Click the drop-down list arrows and choose the fonts you want displayed in the list.

- Browse through fonts in a specific folder or on a CD—You can view fonts and print samples without adding the fonts to the Font Catalog. Click the drop-down list arrow at the top of the dialog box to switch to a different folder or drive. The fonts on that folder or drive are displayed in the list, so you can view and print samples as well as install selected fonts—all without actually adding them to the Font Catalog.

Figure 3.4
Viewing fonts by style narrows down the list of fonts to only those in a particular style.

Click here to display all fonts.   Only serif fonts are displayed.

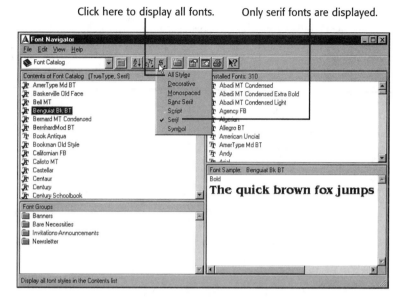

You can explore fonts on your hard drive, floppy disks, removable drives, CD-ROMs, or network drives.

■ Associate a font group with an application or a document—You can associate a font group with an application or a document so that when you activate the font group, the fonts are installed, the application is started, and the document is opened—without running the Font Navigator. Right-click a font group, and then choose Properties. In the Font Group Properties dialog box (see Figure 3.5), click Browse to look for the application file or the document that you want to associate with this font group. Select Auto Install Font Group if you want to install these fonts without confirmation.

Figure 3.5
You can create an association to an application or a document in the Font Group Properties dialog box.

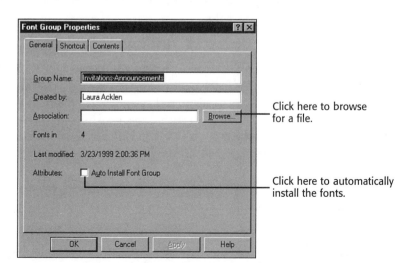

Click here to browse for a file.

Click here to automatically install the fonts.

- Create a shortcut for a font group—If you routinely install the same font groups over and over, consider creating a shortcut to each font group. Shortcuts can reside on the desktop, in the Start menu, or in the Programs folder. Right-click a font group, and then choose Properties. In the Font Group Properties dialog box, click the Shortcut tab. Select Create a Shortcut for This Group. Select a location for the shortcut, and then choose the type of confirmation you want before the fonts are installed. Choose Apply, and then click OK. If you've associated an application or a document with a font group, selecting the font group shortcut installs the fonts, loads the application, and opens the document.

Tip #26 from
Laura and Read

It's a good idea to create a font group that contains the basic fonts that you need when you're working in Windows. A font group makes it easier to locate and restore the essential fonts after you've installed fonts for a specific project.

EMPHASIZING IMPORTANT TEXT

When you speak, you use inflection for emphasis. To get an important point across, you might raise your voice and pronounce each word slowly and clearly. This gets the audience's attention and it gives them a point of reference.

You can do the same thing with your printed document. Judicious use of bold, italic, underline, and other effects can guide readers through the text and draw attention to important points (but not so much that readers lose their train of thought).

Using a Light Touch

Don't get carried away with all the different fonts and font effects that you can choose from! A light touch is all you need. Too many fonts, too many effects, or too much color will frustrate the reader.

Try to keep things simple: Don't use more than three or four fonts on a page, don't apply bold *and* italics *and* underline (all at once), don't apply color to long passages of text, don't use a bunch of different font sizes, and choose a font that suits the subject matter.

USING BOLD, ITALIC, AND UNDERLINE

Before there were gazillions of fonts to play with, the only way you could vary the look of the text was with bold, italic, and underline. These old standbys still have their place. Case in point—the designers for the *Special Edition Using* books decided to use italic to point out important terms and to emphasize words, and underline to show hotkeys. Titles and headings are bold so they really stand out. All these things make it easier for you to understand the information being presented.

To apply bold, italic, or underline, select the text, and then click the Bold, Italic, or Underline button (or any combination of the three).

⚠ *If you can't figure out why your bold, italics, and underline disappeared after you changed the font, see "Disappearing Act" in the Troubleshooting section at the end of this chapter.*

ADDING COLOR

I can't remember the last time I printed a document for someone to read. Like many others, I use email most of the time. I just attach the file to an email message. The recipient pulls it up in his or her word processing program and they read it onscreen.

This method of reviewing documents (plus my new color printer) gave me the excuse I needed to start adding color to my documents. I began using it to draw attention to titles and headings, and progressed to using it for key terms, statistics, quotes, references, headers and footers, and so on.

I'm not too ashamed to admit that I really get a kick out of it. It's fun! I also like to think that if the finished product gets your attention, you're more likely to *read* it, rather than *skim* it.

Collaborating in Color

By the time you read this chapter, no fewer than six people have reviewed and edited the text. Proofreaders, tech editors, development editors, and production staff have all added their two cents. We would all go crazy if we didn't have a good method for keeping everyone's comments separate. Our solution? We let everyone use a different color (hopefully one that's easy to read).

To add color to your text, follow these steps:

1. If you've already typed some text to which you want to add color, select the text you want to add color to. Otherwise, position the insertion point where you want to start typing the colored text.

Caution

When you finish typing the colored text, you'll have to switch the color back to black. For this reason, it's easier to type the text, select it, and then choose the color.

 2. Click the Font Color button on the Property Bar (see Figure 3.6).

3. Click one of the color boxes to choose one of the standard colors.

Tip #27 from
Laura and Read

If you use the same colors over and over, you'll love this! WordPerfect places the last seven colors you've selected on the top row of the palette. I really appreciate this with the custom colors because I don't have to reselect them each time.

Font Color button

Figure 3.6
Clicking the Font
Color button on the
Property Bar is the
fastest way to open
the color palette. This
palette is also avail-
able in the Font
Properties dialog box.

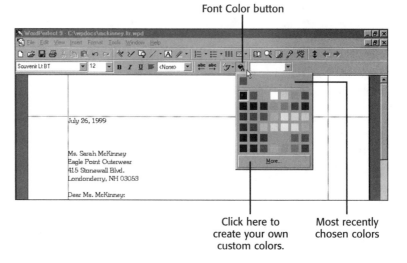

Click here to
create your own
custom colors.

Most recently
chosen colors

Tip #28 from
Laura and Read

So 42 colors isn't enough for you? When you've got to have just the right shade of
blue/green (and you've got a few minutes to play), choose More from the color palette to
open the Select Color dialog box. Click anywhere on the color wheel to move the little
selection box and display the color you've created in the New Color section. You can make
minor adjustments by tweaking the numbers in the Color Values section.

→ To learn how to use the highlighter to accentuate sections of text, **see** "Using the Highlight Tool," **p. 480**

USING OTHER FONT EFFECTS

Bold, italic, underline, and color all have buttons on the Property Bar, so they are the easiest
font effects to add. The other effects, also called *attributes*, are found in the Font Properties
dialog box. First, position the insertion point where you want the effects to start (or select
some existing text). Choose Format, Font or press F9 to open the Font Properties dialog
box (see Figure 3.7).

The font attributes are listed in the Appearance section. As you select attributes, the sample
text in the lower-left corner shows you how the attributes will look when applied to the text.
The RealTime Preview feature pops up again here—WordPerfect pulls in a short section of
text from your document and uses it as the sample text. (If you're working in a blank document, the sample text is the name of the currently selected font.) Click OK when you're
done choosing effects.

Tip #29 from
Laura and Read

If you use font attributes a lot, consider adding buttons for them to the toolbar. Or create a
new Fonts toolbar and add *all* your favorite buttons to it. Choose Tools, Settings, Customize.
To add a button to an existing toolbar, select the toolbar, and then choose Edit. Open the
Feature Categories drop-down list and choose Format. Select the feature in the list, and
then choose Add Button. To create a new toolbar, choose Create, type a name for the toolbar, and then click OK. Add buttons as previously described.

Figure 3.7
You can use the Font Properties dialog box if you need to set multiple font options or if you want to preview your changes first.

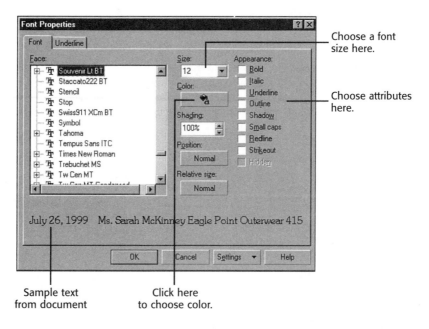

Choose a font size here.

Choose attributes here.

Sample text from document

Click here to choose color.

Tip #30 from
Laura and Read

You can use the Font Properties dialog box anytime you need to set more than a couple font options at once. For example, if you need to choose a different font and size, and apply bold and italics, it's faster to do it all at once in the Font Properties dialog box than to choose each one separately from the Property Bar.

 If you're selecting options in the Appearance section of the Font Properties dialog box and the sample text isn't changing to reflect your changes, see "Disappearing Act" in the Troubleshooting section at the end of this chapter.

CHANGING MARGINS WITH GUIDELINES

Believe it or not, you can make your document easier to read by adjusting the margins. A wider margin creates more white space around the text and limits the number of words on a line. The shorter the line, the less likely the readers are to lose their place.

On the other hand, if you're trying to keep the number of pages down, you might want to make the margins smaller so you can fit more on a page. For example, if you plan to use headers and footers, you might want to cut the top and bottom margins down to 1/2 inch. By default, the margins are set to 1 inch on all sides (see Table 1.1 on page 16).

To adjust the margins, position the mouse pointer over a guideline and wait until the pointer changes into a double-arrow. Click and drag the guideline. As you click and drag, you'll see a dotted guideline and a bubble. The dotted guideline shows you where the new margin will be, and the bubble tells you what the new margin will be (in inches) when you release the mouse button (see Figure 3.8).

If you accidentally drag a margin guideline and end up with wacky margins, see "Bad Dragging" in the Troubleshooting section at the end of this chapter.

Click-and-Drag Phobia
If you're not a big fan of clicking and dragging, or if you just want to be more precise, you can make your changes in the Margins dialog box. Choose Format, Margins, and then either type the measurements in the text boxes or click the spinner arrows to bump the value up or down—in this case, 0.1 inch at a time.

The dotted guideline marks the new margin.

New margin setting

The original guideline marks the original margin.

Figure 3.8
Clicking and dragging guidelines is the fastest way to adjust the margins. The dotted guideline and bubble show you what the new margins will be when you release the mouse button.

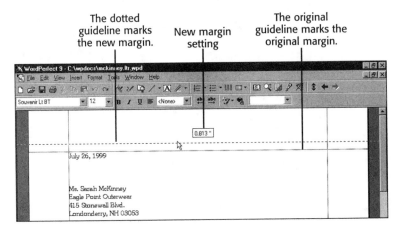

Caution

Many printers (such as inkjet and laser printers) aren't capable of printing to the edge of the paper. This area is called the *unprintable zone*. The size of this zone varies from printer to printer, so the information is kept in the printer's setup. All this means is that that if you try to set a margin within the unprintable zone, WordPerfect automatically adjusts it to the printer's minimum margin setting.

JUSTIFYING TEXT

Justification controls how text flows between the left and right margins. The most obvious example of this is centering text on a line. WordPerfect does the math, and you get the same amount of space on the left and right sides. No matter what you do to the left and right margins, that text stays centered.

The default setting in WordPerfect is left justification, which creates a smooth left margin and a ragged right margin. The result is an open, informal appearance that is accessible and easy to read. For that reason, this book has been formatted with left justification.

There are four other justification options that you might be interested in, especially if you work with columns, newsletters, and formal documents (see Figure 3.9).

Figure 3.9
This sample document illustrates the different justification settings.

Justification button

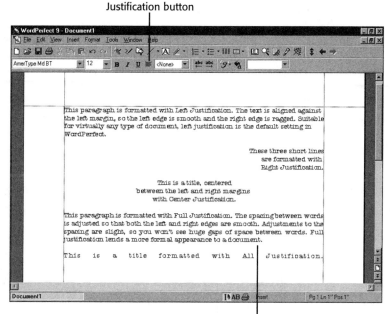

The last line isn't justified.

WordPerfect offers the following justification options:

- Left—Text is aligned against the left margin so the left margin is smooth and the right is ragged. It's suitable for almost every type of document, especially those with long passages of text. To apply left justification, choose Format, Justification, Left, or press Ctrl+L.

- Right—Text is aligned against the right margin so the right side is smooth and the left is ragged. The unique placement draws attention, but because it's hard to read, you might not want to use it on more than three or four lines. To apply right justification, choose Format, Justification, Right, or press Ctrl+R.

- Center—Text is centered between the left and right margins. It's common practice to center titles and headings to differentiate them from the rest of the text. To apply center justification, choose Format, Justification, Center, or press Ctrl+E.

- Full—Text is aligned against the left and right margins, so both edges are smooth. How? WordPerfect makes slight adjustments to the spacing between words so that each line extends from the left to the right margin. Full justification gives documents a more formal and organized appearance. To apply full justification, choose Format, Justification, Full, or press Ctrl+J.

- All—This type of justification stretches lines of text between the left and right margins, regardless of their length. Whereas full justification adjusts the spacing between words, all justification adjusts the spacing between letters as well. This setting is used for letterhead, informal titles and headings, and special effects. To apply all justification, choose Format, Justification, All.

PART

I

CH

3

Before you choose which type of justification you want to use in your document, decide where you want the justification to take effect, and then move the insertion point there. This may be at the top of the document, the top of a column, or the beginning of a paragraph. If you want to apply justification to a section of text, such as a multiline title, select the text first.

 Instead of using the menus, you can click the Justification button on the Property Bar, and then choose the justification setting from the pop-up list. This method offers an advantage over the others in that you get a RealTime Preview of each justification setting when you hover over it.

Caution	With justification set to full, the last line in a paragraph won't be justified if it doesn't extend to the right margin (or pretty close to it). Refer to Figure 3.9 for an example of how this looks.

Tip #31 from *Laura and Read*	Have you noticed that articles in the newspaper are formatted into columns with smooth left and right margins? When the column edges are well-defined, side-by-side columns don't look cluttered or disorganized. You can achieve the same result by setting justification to full. This can be done before or after you type the text into columns.

→ To learn how to define columns, **see** "Setting Up Columns," **p. 215**

USING QUICKBULLETS

I use lists in all sorts of documents. They're easier to follow than long, drawn-out explanations, so readers really appreciate them. WordPerfect's QuickBullets feature makes it easy for you to create a bulleted list on-the-fly. Simply type a symbol, and then press Tab—WordPerfect converts the symbol to a bullet. Table 3.1 lists the QuickBullet symbols.

Inserting QuickBullets is easy when you use the following steps:

1. Type one of the QuickBullets symbols, and then press Tab. As soon as you press Tab, WordPerfect converts the symbol to a bullet.

Note	If you type more than one line of text next to the bullet, you'll notice that the text automatically wraps under the text, not under the bullet. WordPerfect actually converts the tab to an indent so the list has the proper format.

2. Type the text, and then press Enter. Notice that you automatically get another bullet when you press Enter (see Figure 3.10).

3. When you are finished with the list, press Enter, and then backspace to delete the bullet.

Figure 3.10
You can use the QuickBullets feature to create bulleted lists with just one or two keystrokes.

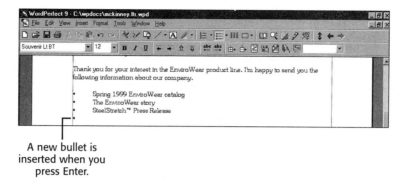

A new bullet is
inserted when you
press Enter.

Note

If for some reason you don't like the QuickBullets feature, you can easily turn it off. Choose the Tools menu and select QuickCorrect, Format-As-You-Go. Deselect (that is, remove the check mark from) the QuickBullets option.

PART

I

CH

3

Table 3.1 lists the six bullet symbols you can create with symbols on the keyboard. You can also refer to the help topic on this for a quick reminder.

TABLE 3.1   QUICKBULLETS SYMBOLS

Press This	To Get This
+ then Tab	★
^ then Tab	◆
o or * then Tab	•
O then Tab	●
> then Tab	▶
- then Tab	—

→ To learn how to indent text, **see** "Indenting Text," **p. 176**

→ To learn how to insert bullets by using the Bullets and Numbers dialog box, **see** "Working with Bulleted and Numbered Lists," **p. 290**

INSERTING SPECIAL CHARACTERS

Special characters, or symbols, are one of the many areas where WordPerfect distinguishes itself from the competition. WordPerfect has more than 1,500 special characters, including entire foreign language alphabets, that you can insert anywhere in your document.

It's the Font That Counts
Not all special characters are available in every font. Depending on the font you have selected, you may see empty boxes instead of special characters, which means that those characters aren't available. On the other hand, certain fonts, such as Wingdings, are composed entirely of special characters.

To insert special characters, follow these steps:

1. Click in the document where you want the special character to appear.
2. Press Ctrl+W to open the Symbols dialog box (see Figure 3.11). You might need to scroll down to see the symbol you want.

Figure 3.11
Through the Symbols dialog box, you can insert more than 1,500 special characters.

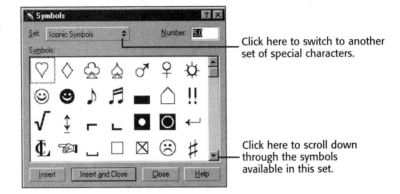

Click here to switch to another set of special characters.

Click here to scroll down through the symbols available in this set.

3. If you don't see the character you need, click the Set button, and then select a different character set from the list.
4. Select the symbol, and then choose Insert and Close. You can also double-click a symbol in the list to insert it and close the Symbols dialog box. When you need to insert more than one symbol, choose Insert instead. This leaves the dialog box open so you can choose another symbol.

Tip #32 from
Laura and Read

I don't like leaving the Symbols dialog box open because it always seems to be in the way—like when other passengers monopolize the armrests on a plane. At least you can shove a dialog box out of the way! Just click and drag the title bar to move it to a more friendly spot on the screen.

Tip #33 from
Laura and Read

If you insert the same symbols over and over, you'll appreciate this shortcut. The next time you select a symbol, look for the two numbers in the Number text box. Then, when you need to insert that character again, press Ctrl+W, type the two numbers (separated by a space or a comma), and then press Enter. For example, to insert the heart symbol shown in Figure 3.11, press Ctrl+W, and then type 5,0.

The QuickCorrect feature is designed to automatically correct common spelling errors and typos while you type. There are five symbols that you can insert with QuickCorrect (see Table 3.2).

TABLE 3.2 CREATING SYMBOLS WITH QUICKCORRECT	
To Get This	**Type This**
Copyright symbol	(c
Registered trademark symbol	(r
$^1/_2$	1/2
en dash	-- or n-
en dash	--- or m-

If you don't want QuickCorrect making these automatic replacements, you can take these symbols out of the list. Choose Tools, QuickCorrect. Select the symbol you want to remove, and then choose Delete Entry.

TROUBLESHOOTING

TOO MANY FONTS

During a custom installation, I got the error message "Too Many Fonts Selected" after I marked the fonts I wanted to install. The installation continued, but now I'm not sure which fonts were installed.

All the fonts you marked were copied to your hard drive, but not all of them were registered. There is a limit to the number of fonts that can be registered in the Windows Registry. When you exceed this limit, all sorts of problems can crop up—from fonts not displaying correctly to buttons showing symbols instead of text. I've seen conflicting reports on what the actual limitation is, but Corel recommends that you keep a maximum of 300 fonts registered at one time. This number includes any fonts that you already had on your system (such as Windows 95/98 fonts and fonts installed with other applications). Corel suggests that you run a typical installation so that the character set fonts and default fonts are safely installed before you attempt to install additional fonts.

To see the fonts that are currently registered on your system, open the Fonts folder (choose Start, Settings, Control Panel, Fonts). To make room for the Corel fonts, select and delete the fonts that you don't use. Then choose File, Install New Font to add fonts that were copied to the hard drive but not registered during setup.

BAD DRAGGING

I accidentally grabbed a margin guideline with the mouse and before I knew what was happening, half my page had new margins. How do I fix this?

It's really faster to undo the change than to try to drag the guideline back to its original position. Either click the Undo button or choose Edit, Undo.

DISAPPEARING ACT

After spending 15 minutes selecting text and applying italics, I decided to change the font. Now all the text I italicized is back to normal. How do I restore the italics I originally had?

Sometimes changing the font causes your bold, italics, underline, or other font effects to disappear. Why? Because the new font doesn't support those effects. This doesn't happen very often—it happens mostly with the more decorative fonts—but when it does, it's disconcerting. You can either switch to another font and see if it supports them, or you can just forget about the effects.

PROJECT

It's easy to get overwhelmed by all the formatting choices you have with WordPerfect. You can spice up a plain vanilla document with interesting fonts and font effects. You may even find yourself getting carried away with all the colors you can use.

Unfortunately, there are few hard-and-fast rules for formatting documents. Other than the unspecific rule of thumb "try to avoid too many fonts on a page," you'll be hard pressed to find a good set of guidelines.

Because, as they say, "a picture is worth a thousand words," here are two examples for you. Figure 3.12 illustrates a newsletter where some common mistakes were made:

- There are too many font changes on the page.
- The font for the date in the masthead is difficult to read and it leaves too much white space at the end of the line.
- Bold, italic, and underline are not applied well.
- The two title fonts are dissimilar.
- A sans serif font is used for the body text, and a serif font is used for the headings.
- This list is difficult to read both because the first line is indented and because of the font used.
- The margins of the newsletter text leave too much white space on either side.

Figure 3.13 shows the same newsletter with some small, vital corrections:

- The same font is used for both titles and the newsletter text.
- The masthead font is easy to read and blends well with the title text.
- A wider font was chosen so the title stretches completely across the line.
- A serif font is used for both the body text and the headings.
- The margins for the body text line up with the newsletter masthead.
- Bold and italic are applied to the headings for subtle emphasis.

This font is
difficult to read.

Serif font

These two fonts
don't have much
in common.

Too much white
space on either side

Figure 3.12
This newsletter illus-
trates common mis-
takes that are made
when applying fonts,
font effects, and mar-
gin formatting.

Sans serif font

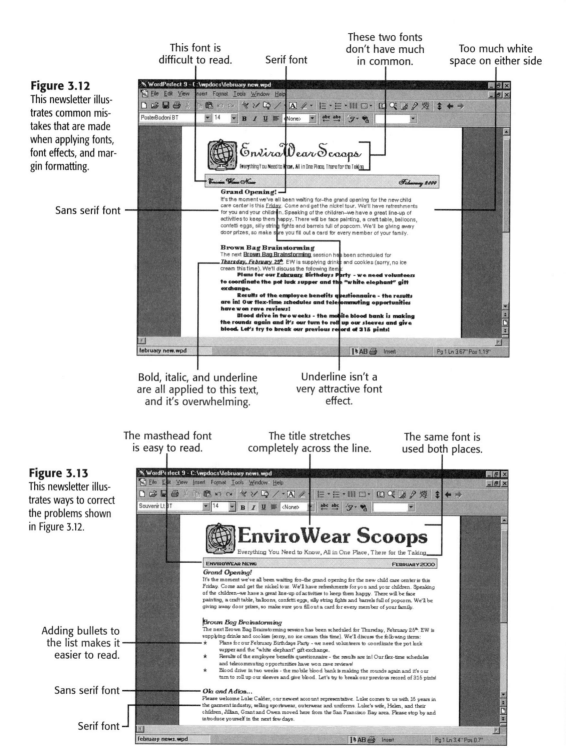

Bold, italic, and underline
are all applied to this text,
and it's overwhelming.

Underline isn't a
very attractive font
effect.

The masthead font
is easy to read.

The title stretches
completely across the line.

The same font is
used both places.

Figure 3.13
This newsletter illus-
trates ways to correct
the problems shown
in Figure 3.12.

Adding bullets to
the list makes it
easier to read.

Sans serif font

Serif font

CHAPTER 4

MANAGING FILES AND FOLDERS

In this chapter

ORGANIZING FILES AND FOLDERS

One of the most valuable skills you can learn is how to properly organize your files. Our increasing dependence on electronic copies of files has made it a matter of survival—you *must* be able to quickly locate important information.

Creating an electronic filing system is very similar to creating a system with manila folders, hanging folders, and filing cabinets. You decide how you want to group files together (such as by client, project, department, or case number), and then you create a folder for those files. Existing files can be copied into the folder and new files can be saved there.

Every bit of this can be done within WordPerfect, so you don't even have to start My Computer or Explorer to get the job done. In every situation where you need to choose a file, you can do it in a file management dialog box. The figures in this chapter show the Open File dialog box, but no matter which file management dialog box you're in (it could be Save File, Insert File, Insert Image, Play Macro, or any other), you have the same capabilities.

SELECTING FILES TO WORK WITH

You probably already know how to select a file—you just click it. And you may know how to select a group of files with the Ctrl and Shift keys. What you may *not* know is that you can rearrange the list to make it easier to group files together.

Here are two methods for selecting multiple files:

- To select a group of files that are one right after the other, click the first file, hold down the Shift key, and then click the last file. Everything between the first click and the second click is selected (see Figure 4.1).

Figure 4.1
By using the Shift key, you can select a list of files in just two clicks.

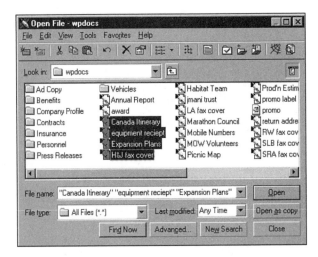

- To select a group of files that are scattered throughout the list, click the first file, hold down the Ctrl key, and then click the other files, one at a time. While you're selecting, you can scroll up or down through the list, but you can't switch to another folder. If you accidentally select the wrong file, click it again to deselect it.

Tip #34 from
Laura and Read

If you accidentally select the wrong files, you don't have to start over. Just hold down the Ctrl key and click the offending files.

 If you're having a hard time selecting multiple files, see "Can't Select Multiple Files" in the Troubleshooting section at the end of this chapter.

The following are methods for grouping files together:

- To group files with similar names, type all or part of the name in the File Name text box. For example, to display only files that begin with etheridge, type etheridge*, and then press Enter. The resulting list of files contains only files that begin with etheridge (regardless of what follows etheridge in the filename). The asterisk is a *wildcard*, like a one-eyed jack in poker: You can use it to represent one or more characters in a filename.

- To arrange files differently, choose View, Arrange Icons. Choose By Name to arrange files in alphabetical order. Choose By Type to arrange files by type (such as documents, presentations, and spreadsheets). Choose By Size to arrange files from smallest to largest. Choose Date to arrange files from the most recently edited to the least recently edited. To return to the default arrangement, choose Name.

 - To view additional file details, choose View, Details or click the drop-down arrow next to the Views button and then click Details (see Figure 4.2). In the Details view, you can click a column heading to sort the list by that item. Click the column heading once to sort in ascending order; click again to sort in descending order.

PART
I

CH
4

Tip #35 from
Laura and Read

There are four view options: large icons, small icons, details, and list. Clicking the Views button switches you automatically to the next view. Keep clicking, and you'll cycle through all four view options.

- To view a particular type of file, click the File Type drop-down list arrow and select a file type from the list. Choose All Files (*.*) to reset the file list.

- To view files that were modified within a specific time frame, click the Last Modified drop-down list arrow and select a time frame from the list.

Caution

Any changes you make in the Details view are "sticky," which means they remain in effect even after you switch to another view. For example, if you sort the files by date, and then switch back to List view, the files remain grouped together by date, even though you can't see the file dates in the list.

Figure 4.2
Grouping files makes it easy to sort by a specific criterion.

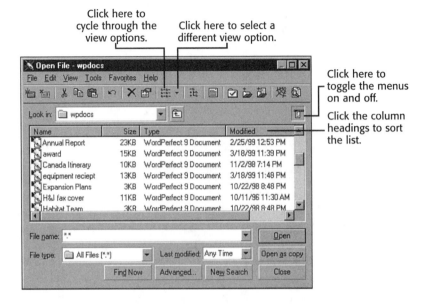

Click here to cycle through the view options.

Click here to select a different view option.

Click here to toggle the menus on and off.

Click the column headings to sort the list.

Tip #36 from
Laura and Read

After you've grouped your files together, you can print a list for future reference (or just because you want to be able to put a check mark next to each one when you're finished with it). Choose File, Print File List, select the options you want in the Print File List dialog box, and then click OK. If you've selected files and you want to print a list of only those files, make sure you select the Print List of Selected Entries option in the Listing Options section.

ADDING ITEMS TO THE FAVORITES FOLDER

When I first started surfing the Net, it didn't take long before I wanted to create a list of my favorite sites so I didn't have to remember, and type in, the exact addresses. You can do the same thing with folders—you can create a list of your frequently used folders so you don't have to navigate through the labyrinth of drives and folders every time you want to grab a file.

Windows 95/98 has a special place to put your favorite stuff—it's called the Favorites folder. It's a Windows feature, so it's not specific to WordPerfect. This is important because you're likely to see items in the Favorites folder that have been added in other applications (such as your Internet browser).

You can add items to the Favorites folder from any file management dialog box. Here are the steps for adding folders, drives, and files:

- To add a drive, open it in the list, and then choose Favorites, Add, Add Favorite Folder. A shortcut to the drive is added to the Favorites folder.

- To add a folder, open it in the file list. Choose Favorites, Add, Add Favorite Folder. A shortcut to the folder is added to the Favorites folder.

Caution

In the previous two items, the steps won't work if you *select* the drive or folder, rather than open it. Just make sure you read the items in the <u>A</u>dd menu carefully before you select one.

- To add a file, select it in the list, and then choose Favo<u>r</u>ites, <u>A</u>dd, Add Favorite <u>I</u>tem. A shortcut to the file is added to the Favorites folder.

After you've added a bunch of items to the Favorites folder and you're ready to use them, click the Go To/From Favorites button on the toolbar, or choose Favo<u>r</u>ites, <u>G</u>o To/From Favorites. The file list displays the contents of the Favorites folder (see Figure 4.3).

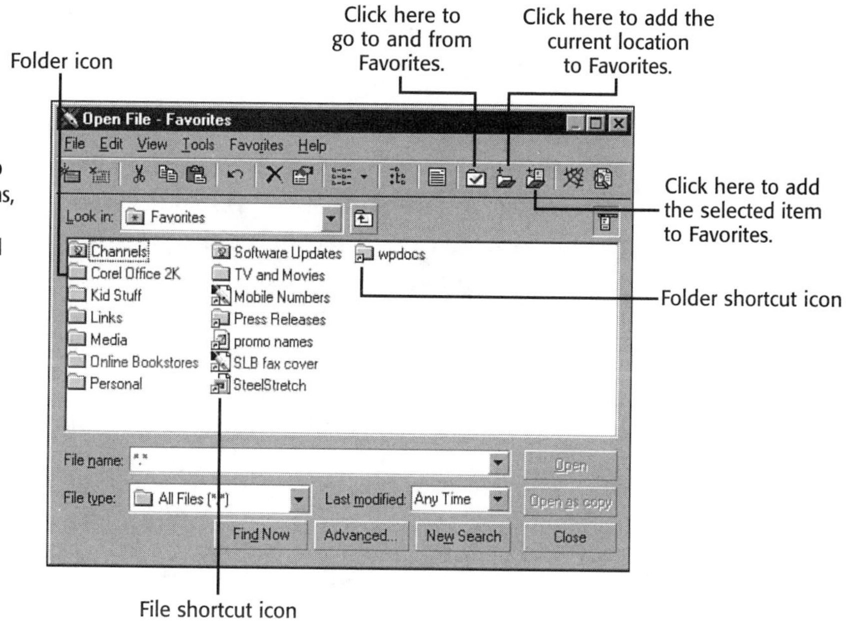

Figure 4.3
The Favorites folder contains shortcuts to frequently used items, such as drives, folders, and files, as well as items that have been added in other Windows applications.

Folder icon

Click here to go to and from Favorites.

Click here to add the current location to Favorites.

Click here to add the selected item to Favorites.

Folder shortcut icon

File shortcut icon

PART

I

CH

4

There are three types of icons: folders, shortcuts to folders, and shortcuts to files. You double-click a folder shortcut to switch to that folder and double-click a file shortcut to open that file. If Windows doesn't know which application to use to open the file, it prompts you to pick one (this shouldn't be a problem with WordPerfect documents).

If you can't get one of your shortcuts to work, see "My Shortcut Stopped Working" in the Troubleshooting section at the end of this chapter.

After a while, you'll have quite a collection of shortcuts in the Favorites folder, and finding the one you want will take a little longer. At that point, you should create some folders for related shortcuts. You may already be familiar with this concept if you've been keeping URLs for your favorite Web sites organized into folders in your Web browser's Favorites or bookmarks list. I've got a folder for financial pages, one for kid stuff, one for Corel information, and so on.

You can create folders and move shortcuts by using the same techniques that are described in the next section, so read on for more information.

MANAGING FILES AND FOLDERS

Now that you can select and group files together, you're ready to roll up your sleeves and get some things done. Most of the commands you'll need are on the File menu. If you've toggled the menu bar off, you can still get to the commands with a QuickMenu. To open a QuickMenu, right-click a file or folder (see Figure 4.4).

> **Note**
>
> Depending on what you have selected, the options on a QuickMenu (and the File menu) change. For example, the file QuickMenu has Quick View and Print; the folder QuickMenu has Sharing and Explore.

Figure 4.4
The file QuickMenu has all the commands you need to effectively manage your files from within WordPerfect.

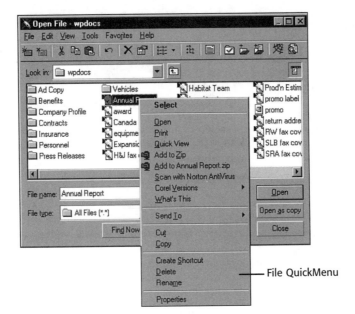

MOVING FILES AND FOLDERS

Occasionally, a file (or folder) gets saved to the wrong folder and you need to move it. You don't want to copy it because then you'll have two copies of the same file (or folder). To move a file (or folder), follow these steps:

1. Right-click the file (or folder) and choose Cut. Or you can select it and then click the Cut button.

2. Switch to the folder where you want to store the file (or folder).

3. Right-click anywhere in the file list, and then choose Paste; or just click the Paste button.

| Tip #37 from | There is a command on the File menu—Move to Folder—that you can use to move files and |
| *Laura and Read* | folders (a file must be selected for this item to appear). Rather than switch to the destination folder, you can choose it from the Select Destination Folder for Move dialog box. This way you don't have to navigate back to the original folder after you've pasted the file (or folder). While we're on the subject, there is a Copy to Folder command that you can use as well—it works the same way as the Move to Folder command. |

⚠ *If you can't find a file that you just moved, see "Misplaced Files" in the Troubleshooting section at the end of this chapter.*

COPYING FILES AND FOLDERS

Network administrators implement security measures so that your co-workers can't get into your folders and accidentally delete or modify your files. If you want to share your files, you can usually copy them to someone else's folder or to a shared area on the network. Because you do the copying, you maintain control over who has access to your files.

→ To learn more about sharing documents, **see** Chapter 17, "Collaborating on Documents," **p. 475**

To copy a file (or folder), follow these steps:

1. Right-click the file (or folder) and then choose Copy. Or you can select the file (or folder) and then click the Copy button.

2. Switch to the folder where you want to store the file (or folder).

3. Right-click anywhere in the file list, and then choose Paste; or click the Paste button.

PART

I

CH

4

| Tip #38 from | The best way to ensure the integrity and accuracy of your documents is to keep a copy of |
| *Laura and Read* | every file you share. If a person using one of your documents makes any changes, either accidentally or on purpose, you're protected because you still have a clean copy. |

| Tip #39 from | As usual, you can use the Cut, Copy, and Paste buttons on the toolbar rather than select |
| *Laura and Read* | from the menus. |

| **Caution** | If you select a second file, a group of files, or a folder, and choose Cut or Copy before you |
| | paste, you'll lose the information for that item. You have to go back to the folder where the original items were located and cut or copy the file(s) again. |

RENAMING FILES AND FOLDERS

When you create a folder or save a file, you try to give it a descriptive name. Later, however, that name may no longer seem appropriate. To rename a file or folder, select it and then choose File, Rename. You can also right-click the file or folder, and then choose Rename.

An editing box appears around the file (or folder) name, and the name is selected (see Figure 4.5). Type the new name and then press Enter.

Figure 4.5
You can always change a file or folder name later.

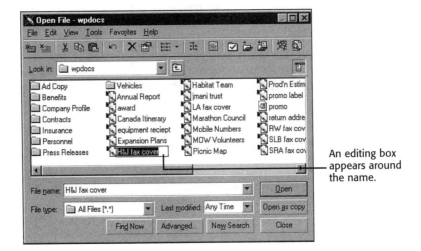

An editing box appears around the name.

There is one other method for renaming files and folders that doesn't require selecting from a menu. Click the filename or folder name (not the icon), pause, and then click the name again. The editing box should appear. Type the new name and press Enter.

If you're clicking a file twice and you can't get the editing box to appear, see "Can't Click Twice to Rename" in the Troubleshooting section at the end of the chapter.

Caution
You can't rename a file that is currently open, either in your application or in someone else's (if you're working on a networked computer).

DELETING FILES AND FOLDERS

Periodic housekeeping is an important part of managing your files. One method for keeping your drives uncluttered is to archive folders and files that you no longer use. You might decide to move these onto floppy disks, zip disks, or tape backup. The important thing is that you aren't getting rid of them permanently—if the need arises, you can always use the archive copy.

 If you decide that you'll never, ever, ever need a file or folder again, you can delete it off the drive. Select the file(s) or folder(s) in the list and either press the Delete key or click the Delete button. Alternatively, you can right-click the file or folder and then choose <u>D</u>elete from the QuickMenu. If necessary, choose Yes to confirm the deletion.

Caution
Be extremely careful about removing folders. Deleting a folder removes all the subfolders and files within that folder.

When you delete files and folders from a local drive, Windows 95/98 moves them to the Recycle Bin (see Figure 4.6). (Files deleted from a floppy disk or removable drive aren't moved to the Recycle Bin.) The good news is that you can get an accidentally deleted file or folder back. To restore a file or folder, open the Recycle Bin, select the file(s) or folder(s) you didn't really mean to throw away, and choose File, Restore.

The bad news about the Recycle Bin is that when you delete a file or folder and it goes to the Recycle Bin, you haven't actually freed up any disk space. To physically remove deleted files and folders, open the Recycle Bin and choose File, Empty Recycle Bin. Just make sure you look them over carefully, because once you empty the Recycle Bin, they are gone for good!

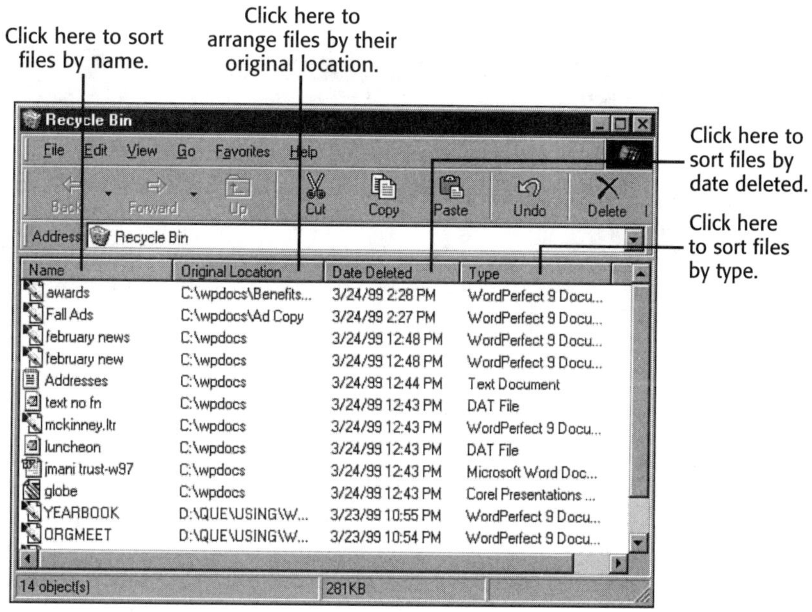

Figure 4.6
The Recycle Bin is the ultimate safety net. If you accidentally delete files or folders, you can restore them to their original locations from the Recycle Bin.

Click here to sort files by name.

Click here to arrange files by their original location.

Click here to sort files by date deleted.

Click here to sort files by type.

PART

I

CH

4

COPYING FILES TO A FLOPPY DISK

Electronic mail has revolutionized our ability to share files with one another. Unfortunately, not everyone has an email address, so sometimes you share files the old-fashioned way: You have to copy the files to a disk and send the disk to the person who needs the file or folder. To copy a file to a floppy disk, select it and then choose File, Send To (or right-click it and choose Send To). Click 3½ Floppy in the list.

| Tip #40 from
Laura and Read | I don't need to give you a speech about how important it is to back up your files. Sooner or later, you'll find out for yourself. What I can tell you is this: Copy important files to a floppy disk at the end of the day—you'll sleep better at night. You can use the Send To command on the QuickMenu to copy files (and folders, if necessary) to a floppy disk. |

SENDING FILES VIA EMAIL

If you have email capabilities, you can send a file directly from a file management dialog box. The Mail command in a file management dialog box works the same way as the Mail command in the document window. The difference is that in a file management dialog box, you can only send the file as an attachment; you can't send the file as a message, and you can't send selected text.

To send a file, right-click it, and then choose Send To, Mail Recipient (or select the file and choose File, Send To, Mail Recipient). If the Choose Profile dialog box appears, select a profile from the drop-down list. WordPerfect switches you to your mail program, and attaches the document to an email message (see Figure 4.7). You can type your message text, and then address and send the message as you normally would.

Figure 4.7
If your mail program supports MAPI or CMC standards, you can send files as attachments to email messages from within a file management dialog box.

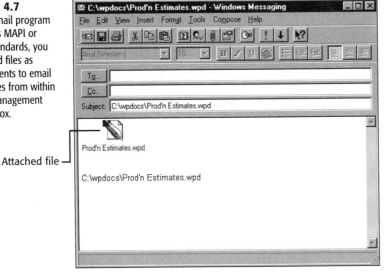

Attached file

Tip #41 from
Laura and Read

Downloading large files can really be a pain. Be nice and zip up your files with a file compression utility. One of the most popular is WinZip, a shareware program that you can download from http://www.winzip.com. After you install it, you'll see an option on the QuickMenu to add the file(s) or folder(s) to a zip file. Another good reason to zip up files? Some Internet service providers (ISPs) can't handle more than one file at a time. If you want to send multiple files to someone on AOL, for example, you can either create a message for each file or you can zip them up into one file.

→ To learn more about sending files, **see** "Sending Documents via Email," **p. 163**

CONNECTING TO NETWORK DRIVES

 If you're connected to a network, you can map to a network drive from within a file management dialog box. Choose Tools, Map Network Drive, or if your menus are turned off, click the Map Network Drive button. In the Map Network Drive dialog box (see Figure 4.8), select a drive from the Drive list box, and then type the path in the Path text box. (Don't forget to start the path name with \\.)

Figure 4.8
You can use the Map Network Drive dialog box to map a drive letter to any drive on the network that you have rights to.

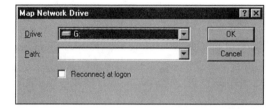

 When you're ready to disconnect from this drive, choose Tools, Disconnect Network Drive, or click the Disconnect Network Drive button. Select the drive, and then click OK.

Caution

If the drive doesn't map to the path you've typed, you may not have rights to that area of the network. Consult your network administrator.

CREATING SHORTCUTS ON THE DESKTOP

My Programs menu became so full that I needed another monitor just to see it all. That's when I decided to create some shortcuts to the programs that I use often. Now all I have to do is double-click the shortcut icon to start the application.

There is a shared folder on my network where anyone can copy files for others to use. I open that folder a dozen times a day to retrieve all sorts of files. I can't access it from within an application because I don't always know what type of file I'll be getting—it could be a spreadsheet, a document, or a presentation. So I created a shortcut to that folder on my desktop. Now all I have to do is open the folder and double-click the file. If all goes well, the originating application loads and opens the file for me.

To create a shortcut to a folder, select the folder, and then choose File, Send To, Desktop as Shortcut. (You can also right-click the file and choose Send To, Desktop as Shortcut.)

Now let's turn to those files that you open over and over during the day: lists of mobile phone numbers, account numbers for shipping services, timesheets, project tracking tables—any file that you use often. Normally, you would load an application and then open the file. With a shortcut to the file on the desktop, all you have to do is double-click the shortcut icon to load the application and open the file.

To create a shortcut to a file, select the file, and then choose File, Send To, Desktop as Shortcut. (You can also right-click the file and choose Send To, Desktop as Shortcut.)

When you double-click a file in Explorer or My Computer, Windows loads the application that is associated with that file and then opens the file. The same thing happens when you double-click a shortcut to a file on the desktop. This may seem like magic, but it really boils down to how file extensions are associated with applications in the Registry. For various reasons, Windows may not know which application to load for a particular file. If this happens, you are prompted to select an application from a list.

When WordPerfect creates shortcuts on the desktop, it uses the name of the file or folder for the shortcut. You can assign a more descriptive name by using the same technique you use for renaming files (discussed in the "Renaming Files and Folders" section).

 If one of your shortcuts has mysteriously stopped working, see "My Shortcut Stopped Working" in the Troubleshooting section at the end of this chapter.

VIEWING AND OPENING INTERNET PAGES

You can view Web pages on the Internet, or your company's intranet, from within a file management dialog box. When you find the page you want, you can open it directly into WordPerfect. You must have an Internet browser, such as Netscape Navigator or Microsoft Internet Explorer, already installed on your system for this to work.

To view Internet pages, type the name of the Internet (or intranet) page you want to view in the File Name text box, and then press Enter. If you've viewed this page before, the page loads automatically. Otherwise, an Internet connection is initiated and the page is displayed in the list box. The toolbar has some new browser buttons that you can use (see Figure 4.9)

Figure 4.9
You can view and open Internet (and intranet) pages from within WordPerfect's file management dialog boxes.

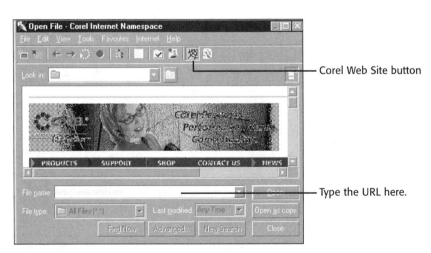

— Corel Web Site button

— Type the URL here.

 You can use the Back, Forward, Refresh, and Stop buttons to navigate through the site. If you find a page that you want to open in WordPerfect, click Open.

When you're ready to return to the default file management dialog box, click the Corel Web Site button.

Tip #42 from
Laura and Read

If you haven't already maximized the dialog box, you'll definitely want to do it here so you can view the Web page without scrolling back and forth. You can also click and drag a border to resize the dialog box. How? Point to a border and pause–the pointer changes to a double-headed arrow. Click and drag the border; the guideline shows you how large the box will be when you release the mouse button.

PROTECTING SENSITIVE FILES

With the advent of flexible work hours and job-sharing, you may have to share your computer with a co-worker. Or, if your assistant has rights to your folders on the network, you may need to protect your sensitive files.

There are two levels of security in WordPerfect: read-only and password-protected. If you specify a file as read-only, someone else can open the file, but he or she can't save it back under the original name. In other words, the person can't save any changes to the file. The drawback to this approach is that a savvy user could modify the properties for a file and remove the read-only attribute. Follow these steps to specify a file as read-only:

1. In a file management dialog box, select the file.

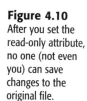 2. Click the Properties button, or right-click the file and choose Properties. The Properties dialog box for that file appears (see Figure 4.10).

3. Place a check mark next to Read-only in the Attributes section of the Properties dialog box.

4. Click Apply, and then click OK.

PART

I

CH

4

Figure 4.10
After you set the read-only attribute, no one (not even you) can save changes to the original file.

Click here to set the read-only attribute.

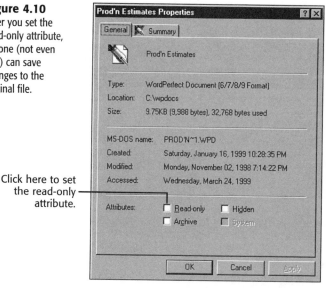

The next time you (or anyone else) try to open this file, you'll get a message reminding you that this file is set to read-only (see Figure 4.11). If you attempt to save the file by clicking the Save button (or by using the File, Save command), the Save As dialog box opens, and you are forced to type a new filename before you can save the file.

Figure 4.11
WordPerfect reminds you with this message that a file has been set to read-only and you'll have to save your changes to a different filename.

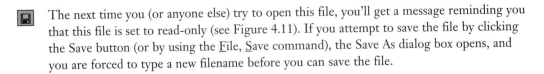

The second level of security is setting a password for a file. The advantage of this approach is that when you save a file with a password, no one can open it unless he or she knows the password. The disadvantage is that if you forget the password, you can't get to the file. At least that's the way it's supposed to work. There are programs that can crack WordPerfect passwords. Admittedly, some people use these programs to get into documents that they shouldn't see, but realistically speaking, these programs are invaluable to system administrators when employees forget their passwords.

If you can safely assume that the people you are trying to keep away from your sensitive files don't know about those programs, you can use password protection with confidence. Otherwise, save those files on a floppy disk and lock them up! Follow these steps to password protect a file:

1. With the file open in the document window, choose File, Save As to open the Save As dialog box (see Figure 4.12).

Figure 4.12
After you save a document with a password, you must know the password to open the file from then on.

Click here to set a password.

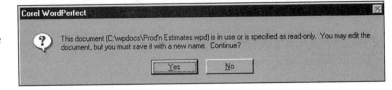

2. If necessary, type a name for the file in the File <u>N</u>ame text box.

3. Place a check mark in the <u>P</u>assword Protect check box.

4. Click <u>S</u>ave. The Password Protection dialog box opens (see Figure 4.13).

Figure 4.13
If you'll be sharing this file with someone who has WordPerfect 6.x, make sure you choose Original Password Protection in the Password Protection dialog box.

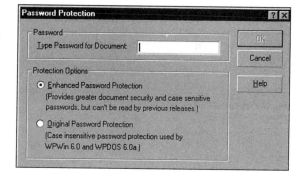

5. Type the password in the <u>T</u>ype Password for Document text box.

6. Choose the type of password protection you want to use, and then click OK.

7. Retype the password, and then click OK to save the file.

Note

If you opt for Enhanced Password Protection, the password is case sensitive. In other words, you must type the password in the same case that you used when you assigned it. Original Password Protection is not case sensitive, so if you think you'll have trouble remembering the case, choose this option instead.

Caution

I spent about an hour searching the Internet for programs that can crack WordPerfect passwords. I found several Web sites offering password-cracking programs and services, so consider yourself warned. WordPerfect's passwords are not 100% guaranteed to prevent prying eyes.

SAVING WORDPERFECT FILES IN A DIFFERENT FORMAT

Unfortunately, not everyone uses WordPerfect. And even if they do, there are quite a few different versions floating around. How can you be sure that the file you create today can be opened by someone else? You can start by saving it to the correct format for that person's application.

If someone opens your WordPerfect 9 file in a previous version of WordPerfect, document features (in the form of codes) that are not supported in that version won't work (they are converted to Unknown codes). But the codes are preserved so that when you open the document again, everything is in place.

When you save a file to another application's format, you lose the elements that aren't supported in that application. Thankfully, WordPerfect conversion drivers do an excellent job of translating WordPerfect features into comparable features in other applications. To save a file in a different format, follow these steps:

1. With the file open in the document window, choose File, Save As. The Save As dialog box appears.

2. Click the File Type drop-down list arrow. A list of available save formats appears (see Figure 4.14).

Figure 4.14
When you save a file, you can choose a different file format from the File Type drop-down list.

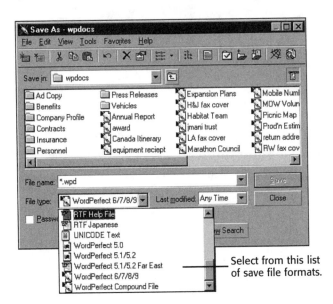

Select from this list of save file formats.

3. Scroll through the list and choose a format.

4. If necessary, type a name (and location) for the document in the File Name text box, and then click Save.

Tip #43 from
Laura and Read

When saving files to another format, it might be helpful to include an abbreviation of the name of that format in the filename, so that you don't confuse that file with the one in Word-Perfect format. For example, a file in Word 97 format might be called `jmani trust-w97`.

Importing and Exporting Files

WordPerfect really shines when it comes to importing and exporting files. You can convert files from more than 50 different file formats to WordPerfect and you can export WordPerfect documents to more than 75 file formats. What does this mean? It essentially means that it doesn't matter what applications your clients and associates are using—you can open their files in WordPerfect and then save them back to their native format. Search for the help topic *file formats*, and then double-click Import or Export underneath File Formats to display the Import and Export File Formats for WordPerfect 9 help topic.

Using Document Summaries

One of the lesser-known, but incredibly powerful, file management features is the document summary. Some people don't even know it exists, but those of us who thrive on full-text search and retrieval techniques we can't live without it. Document summary information can be viewed from the file management dialog boxes, so you can learn a lot about a file without opening it first.

Document summaries go hand-in-hand with QuickFinder because you can narrow down a search from the entire document to the document summary. This not only speeds up the process, it also enables you to search for information that isn't included in the document text, such as an author's name, a client's account number, and so on. The next section discusses searching for files with WordPerfect's QuickFinder.

Filling Out a Document Summary

Before you start thinking that you don't have time to fill out a document summary, think of all the time you'll save later, when you need to locate and organize related files. There's no rush—a document summary can be completed whenever you want, as long as you have the document open.

To fill out or edit a document summary, with the document open, choose File, Properties. The Properties dialog box appears (see Figure 4.15). Some of this information may already be filled in for you, such as the creation date, the author, and the typist. WordPerfect grabs the author/typist name from the User Information section of the Environment Settings (which you get to by choosing Tools, Settings, Environment).

PART
I

CH
4

Figure 4.15
The Properties dialog box has tabs for the document summary and the document information.

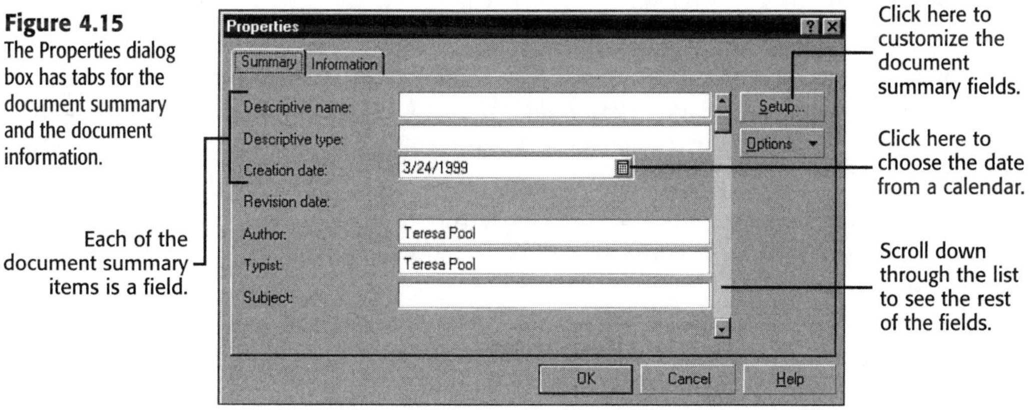

Each of the document summary items is a field.

Click here to customize the document summary fields.

Click here to choose the date from a calendar.

Scroll down through the list to see the rest of the fields.

To type information in a field, click in the field. You can also press Tab to move to the next field or Shift+Tab to move back to the previous field. When you're finished, click OK. Make sure you save the document so that the summary information you just typed is saved.

CUSTOMIZING DOCUMENT SUMMARY FIELDS

Document summaries can be customized so that they contain only the fields you will use. In a networked environment, a standard document summary can be designed and implemented. Users can quickly locate files by narrowing down the search to only those fields in the standard document summary.

To customize document summary fields, choose File, Properties, Setup. The Document Summary Setup dialog box appears (see Figure 4.16). The left side contains a list of all the document summary fields you can choose from. The right side shows the fields that are currently displayed.

The fields that you can choose from   The fields that are currently displayed

Figure 4.16
You can choose from more than 50 fields to create a document summary that captures the information that's important to you.

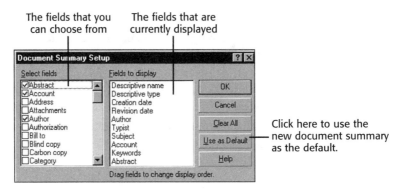

Click here to use the new document summary as the default.

You can customize the document summary by using the following techniques:

- If you want to remove a field from the Fields to Display list, deselect the field in the Select Fields list. Either click the check box or click the field name to remove the check mark.

- If you want to start from scratch, choose Clear All to remove all the fields from the Fields to Display list.

- Click and drag the fields in the Fields to Display list to arrange them in the proper order (such as the most important fields at the top). This way, you're sure to fill in the important fields because you'll see them first.

- If you want to use the new document summary as the default, click Use as Default, and then click Yes to confirm that you want to save the new configuration as the default. Otherwise, your changes are reflected in the document summary for this document only.

- If you change your mind and you want to return to the default document summary, choose Cancel to close the Document Summary Setup dialog box without saving your changes.

SETTING DOCUMENT SUMMARY OPTIONS

Now that you've invested the time to get everything set up the way you want it, bear with me for a few more minutes, while I show you a few more ways to use the document summary information.

In the Properties dialog box (refer to Figure 4.15), click Options to display a pop-up list with the following options:

- Print Summary—Choose this option if you want to print the document summary information for future reference. You can also choose Document Summary in the Print dialog box.

- Delete Summary from Document—Choose this option if you want to delete all the information in the document summary. You can then enter updated information without going to the trouble of erasing the old information first. Keep in mind that if you've customized the document summary, you'll lose those changes. When you delete the summary, WordPerfect replaces it with a blank, default document summary.

- Extract Information from Document—Choose this option to have WordPerfect pull the first 800–850 characters from your document and place them in the Abstract field (you may have to scroll down the list to see this field). The Extract command also pulls text from the document for the Subject field. The default subject search text is *Re:* so if the Extract command finds this text in your document, it grabs the information next to *Re:* and puts it in the Subject field. In Chapter 5, "Using the Writing Tools," you'll learn how to change the default subject search text that Extract looks for.

- Save Summary as New Document—Choose this option if you want to save the summary information to a file.

PART

I

CH

4

CUSTOMIZING DOCUMENT SUMMARY SETTINGS

WordPerfect has always differentiated itself from other applications by giving you full rein to customize its features. Buried in a dizzying array of customization options is the capability to customize how you use document summaries. The most important one for me is turning on the prompt that reminds me to fill in the document summary when I save a document for the first time.

Choose Tools, Settings, Summary to open the Document Summary Settings dialog box (see Figure 4.17). From here you can do the following:

- Change the default subject search text that the Extract command uses to fill in the Subject field.

- Type a default descriptive type to be used in the Descriptive Type field for all document summaries.

- Turn on a prompt that reminds you to fill in the document summary when you save (or exit) a new document.

- Convert a descriptive filename to a long filename when you open the document.

- Insert the filename in the Descriptive Name field when you save the document.

Figure 4.17
You can choose the Create Summary on Save/Exit option if you have trouble remembering to fill in document summaries.

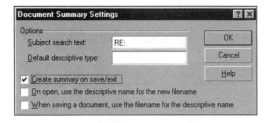

Tip #45 from
Laura and Read

You don't have to change the default subject search text if you use *Re:* in your documents instead of *RE:*. The Extract command finds *Re:*, *re:*, and *RE:*.

Converting Descriptive Filenames

Windows 95 introduced long filenames of up to 255 characters, which freed us from the DOS 8-character filename, 3-character extension limitation we were accustomed to. Some of us got around this limitation by creating descriptive filenames in document summaries and setting our file management dialog boxes up so that these filenames displayed as well. If a document created in a previous version of WordPerfect has been saved with a descriptive filename, you can use that name as the new long filename. Furthermore, a macro that ships with WordPerfect Office 2000, called longname.wcm, converts the names of selected documents from the DOS filenames to long filenames.

→ For more information on playing macros, **see** "Playing Macros," **p. 689**

FINDING MISSING FILES BY USING QUICKFINDER

Most new computers ship with 8–16GB of hard disk space. The number of files you can store on a drive of that size is astounding—it's like trying to get your mind around how much a trillion dollars is. Believe me, you don't want to search through every folder on an 8GB drive "by hand" for a file, and that's assuming you can remember the name of the file you're looking for. No, when it comes to finding files, QuickFinder is the tool you want to reach for.

QuickFinder allows you to search for files based on the filename, content, date modified, or type. You can build a search that's as simple as looking for every file that contains the word *recycle*. Or you can create a complex search designed to display a very narrow selection of documents (which is often the case when searching through legal, scientific, and medical documentation).

For example, with QuickFinder, you can search for all the files on drive C that contain any form of the word *recycle* and the phrase *#3 plastic* on the same page—but not *#5 plastic* and *glass* in the same paragraph—that were modified within the past week, with *021753-4* in the Client field of the document summary.

You don't have to be in WordPerfect (or any other application) to use QuickFinder. Choose Start, Find, Using QuickFinder. If you don't see this option on the Find menu, choose Start, Programs, WordPerfect Office 2000, Utilities, Corel QuickFinder 9 Searcher.

PERFORMING A BASIC SEARCH

I call it a "basic search" but actually you can do quite a bit with the options you have available in the file management dialog boxes. (The next section discusses how to use the options in the Advanced Find dialog box.)

If you've used previous versions of WordPerfect, the new interface is a little disconcerting. Rest assured that the functionality is still here—it's just been reorganized a bit. Before, you had to click the QuickFinder tab or button to switch to another dialog box, where you set the criteria for a search. Now, some of this functionality is incorporated into the file management dialog boxes so you can get to it right away.

For example, in previous versions of WordPerfect, in the QuickFinder dialog box, there was a text box where you could type in a filename (all or part of it), and a separate text box where you could type text that you wanted to search for. In WordPerfect 9, the functions of these two text boxes have been combined into one: Now you can type filenames and content in the File Name text box of any file management dialog box (see Figure 4.18).

Figure 4.18
In WordPerfect 9, you can perform a basic search without switching to another dialog box. Some of the QuickFinder tools have been added to file management dialog boxes.

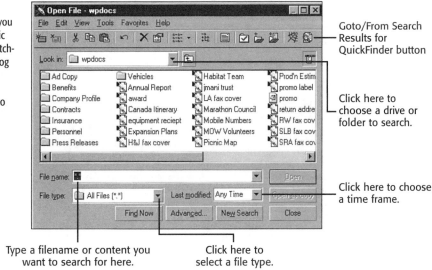

Goto/From Search Results for QuickFinder button

Click here to choose a drive or folder to search.

Click here to choose a time frame.

Type a filename or content you want to search for here.

Click here to select a file type.

The following are the options for creating a basic search in a file management dialog box:

- Choose the drive or folder that you want to search in the Look In text box.
- Type all or part of a filename in the File Name text box. If you don't know the entire name, use the asterisk wildcard to replace one or more characters. For example, type

gateway* to locate Gateway Development, Gateway Board, Gateways Center, Gateways PUD, and so on.

■ Type the content you want to search for in the File Name text box. This might be a word, part of a phrase, or a combination of both. If you can't remember the exact text, use the asterisk wildcard to replace one or more characters. For example, type lymph* to locate lymph glands, lymphoma, lymphocyte, lymphatic, lymphangial, and so on.

■ Select a file type from the File Type text box. The default is to search every file, so if you know you're looking for a WordPerfect document, choose WP Documents from the list. It almost goes without saying, but this really cuts down on the time it takes to find a file.

■ Select a time frame from the Last Modified list box. For example, if you want to locate the documents that you've modified in the past month, choose Last Month from the list.

Each of these options can be filled in separately or in combination. When you're finished, click Find Now. When the search is complete, the QuickFinder Search Results folder is displayed, with a list of files (and their locations) that matched the criteria (see Figure 4.19).

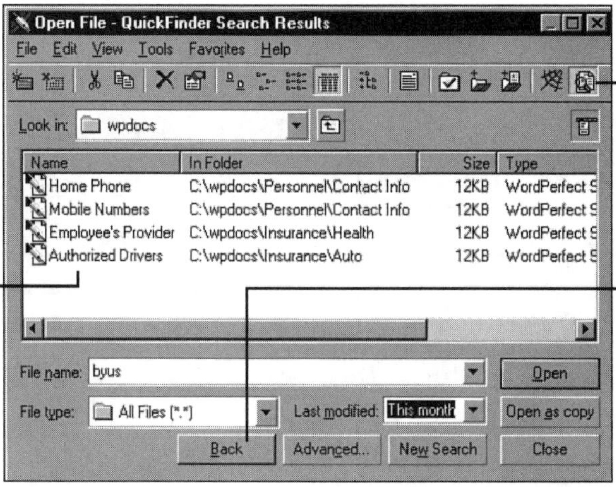

Figure 4.19
When QuickFinder completes a search, the results are placed in the QuickFinder Search Results folder.

List of files that matched the search criteria

Click one of these buttons to switch back to the regular file management dialog box.

If you want to open a file, double-click it. To open a group of files, select them and then click Open. Otherwise, use the same techniques you learned earlier in this chapter to manage the files.

When you're ready to return to the "regular" file management dialog box, click the Goto/ From Search Results for QuickFinder button or the Back button. Use the Goto/From Search Results for QuickFinder button to toggle back and forth between the two file lists.

Tip #47 from
Laura and Read

Did your search return too many files? Then continue to narrow down the list of files by searching through the QuickFinder Search Results folder.

PERFORMING AN ADVANCED SEARCH

If you're ready to take your searches one step further, you're ready for Advanced Find. From the Advanced Find dialog box, you can search through document summary fields (didn't I tell you this would come up again?) and you can refine your contents searches by using operators. WordPerfect old-timers, this is where you'll find the options you're used to seeing when you click the QuickFinder tab of a file management dialog box.

After you've entered the criteria you want in the file management box, choose Advanced to open the Advanced Find dialog box (see Figure 4.20). From here, you can build on those criteria by adding operators and limitations on where QuickFinder can search.

Criteria entered into the file
management dialog box

Click here to add
document summary fields.

Figure 4.20
In the Advanced Find
dialog box, you can
search through docu-
ment summary fields
and add operators to
your content search.

Double-click here
to create a new
property.

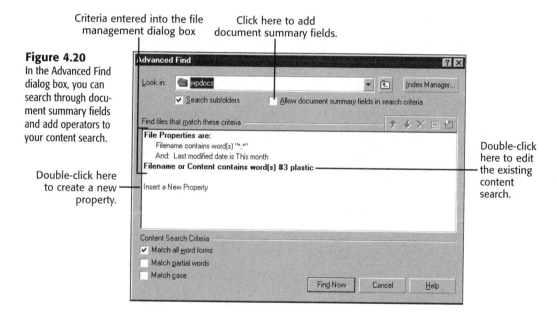

Double-click
here to edit
the existing
content
search.

PART

I

CH

4

The following are ways you can create a more complex search:

- Double-click the filename or content search criteria to edit the existing criteria in the Find Files That Match These Criteria list box.

- Double-click the Insert a New Property item in the Find Files That Match These Criteria list box to create a new search criterion.

- Choose the And or Or operator from the first drop-down list (see Figure 4.21).

- Click the second drop-down list arrow and choose where you want QuickFinder to search (such as Content, File name, Both). This is where the document summary fields appear if you have selected Allow Document Summary Fields in Search Criteria (see Figure 4.22).

Figure 4.21
The first drop-down list contains the And and Or operators so that you can create word combinations in a content search.

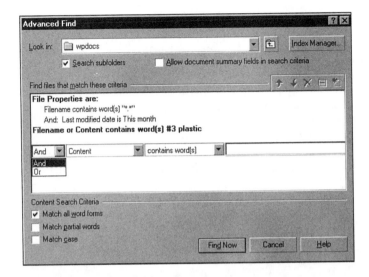

Figure 4.22
Click the second drop-down list arrow to specify a filename or content search. You can also choose from a list of document summary fields if you choose Allow Document Summary Fields in Search Criteria.

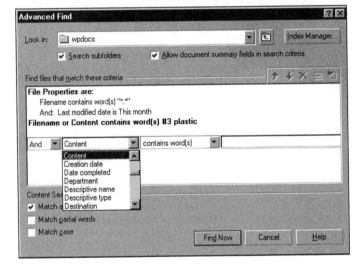

- Click the third drop-down list arrow and select the proximity criteria you want to use for the content search (see Figure 4.23). Type the content in the text box on the right.

In the Content Search Criteria section of the Advanced Find dialog box, you can select from the following options:

- Choose Match All Word Forms if you want QuickFinder to look for all the different forms of a word. For example, if you search for *recycle*, QuickFinder finds the words *recycle*, *recycled*, *recycles*, and *recycling*.

- Choose Match Partial Words if you want QuickFinder to search for the content text even if it's in the middle of another word. For example, searching for *sulfur* locates the following: *sulfuric*, *sulfurous*, *sulfuryl*, and *sulfurate*.

Figure 4.23
Click the third drop-down list arrow to choose the proximity limitation you want to impose on the content search.

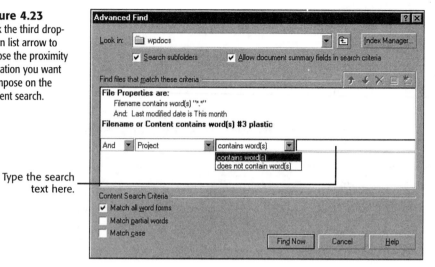

Type the search text here.

- Choose Match <u>C</u>ase if you want QuickFinder to look for the content by using the exact case that you've typed in. For example, you may want QuickFinder to locate the word *Water*, but only if it's capitalized.

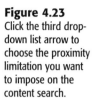

Tip #48 from
Laura and Read

The Advanced Find options are sticky, which means they stay in effect until you close the File Management dialog box. To clear the Advanced Find options, click Ne<u>w</u> Search in the File Management dialog box.

QuickFinder Versus Document Management Programs
As you can see, QuickFinder is capable of performing complex searches that put it one step below dedicated full-text search and retrieval programs. The true beauty of QuickFinder lies in the fact that because it is built in to WordPerfect, you don't have to learn another program. Besides that, *you* name your files; you don't have a program name your files for you with cryptic filenames that no one but the program can decipher.

Are you getting frustrated because you're searching for a file that you know *is in a folder and you* know *it contains the text you're searching for, but QuickFinder won't find it? See "QuickFinder Doesn't Find the File" in the Troubleshooting section at the end of this chapter.*

CREATING A FAST SEARCH

There is one more important aspect of QuickFinder that you should know about. It's called the QuickFinder Manager, and you use it to create files that contain a list of every word in a series of documents. Rather than search through the text of every file, QuickFinder searches through the fast search file.

The most obvious advantage is the significant decrease in the amount of time it takes to locate files. A less obvious advantage is that you can combine text from documents in different folders and drives and search it all at once (rather than perform a series of QuickFinder searches on each folder or drive).

You create fast searches in the QuickFinder Manager (see Figure 4.24). You can click Index Manager in the Advanced Find dialog box or you can choose Start, Programs, WordPerfect Office 2000, Utilities, QuickFinder 9 Manager.

Figure 4.24
In the QuickFinder Manager, you can create two types of fast search files, each geared toward saving you time as you search for information in your files.

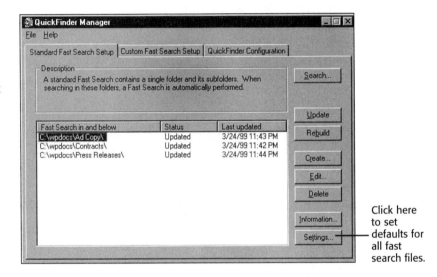

Click here to set defaults for all fast search files.

CREATING A STANDARD FAST SEARCH

There are two types of fast searches: standard and custom. A standard fast search searches through only one folder (and all its subfolders); a custom fast search can search through multiple folders (with or without their subfolders). The following steps show you how to create a standard fast search:

1. If necessary, click the Standard Fast Search Setup tab in the QuickFinder Manager dialog box.
2. Click Create. The QuickFinder Standard Fast Search dialog box appears (see Figure 4.25).

Figure 4.25
A standard fast search can only search through one folder, so it's pretty straightforward to set up.

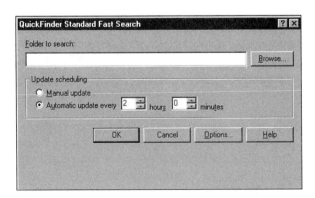

3. Type the path for the folder you want to search or click the <u>B</u>rowse button to look for the folder.

4. Select one of the update options:

- If you choose <u>M</u>anual Update, you have to remember to update the file when you add, remove, or edit files in the folder.

- If you choose A<u>u</u>tomatic Update, QuickFinder updates the fast search at the specified interval (as long as your computer is on and Windows is running).

5. Click the <u>O</u>ptions button to open the QuickFinder Fast Search Options dialog box (see Figure 4.26), where you can finish configuring the fast search. The options that you choose here override the settings you made in the QuickFinder Settings dialog box (click the Se<u>t</u>tings button in the QuickFinder dialog box shown in Figure 4.24).

Figure 4.26
You can fine-tune a fast search with options in the QuickFinder Fast Search Options dialog box.

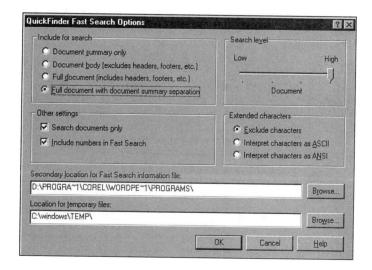

6. Click OK twice to return to the QuickFinder Manager dialog box, where the new fast search appears in the list. When the status is Updated, the fast search file has been created and is ready for use.

Tip #49 from
Laura and Read

If you don't want to include the subfolders of a folder in a standard fast search, create a custom fast search instead. A custom fast search can be created to search through a folder with or without the subfolders.

Note

By default, QuickFinder creates the fast search file in the folder that you selected for the standard fast search.

CREATING A CUSTOM FAST SEARCH

A custom fast search is more flexible than a standard fast search because you're free to build a list of folders to search in one pass; you don't have to conduct a separate QuickFinder search for each folder. You can select folders from different drives (including network drives), and you can exclude certain subfolders when necessary. Follow these steps to create a custom fast search:

1. Click the Custom Fast Search Setup tab in the QuickFinder Manager dialog box.

2. Click Create. The QuickFinder Custom Fast Search dialog box appears (see Figure 4.27).

Figure 4.27
With a custom fast search, you can build a list of multiple folders to search through. The folders can all reside on the same drive, or they can be scattered across multiple drives.

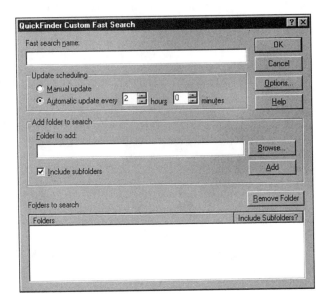

3. Type a name for the fast search in the Fast Search Name text box.

4. Select one of the update options:

   - If you choose Manual Update, you have to remember to update the file when you add, remove, or edit files in the folder.

   - If you choose Automatic Update, QuickFinder updates the fast search at the specified interval (as long as your computer is on and Windows is running).

5. Type a folder name in the Folder to Add text box or click the Browse button to look for the folder.

> **Note**
> Unless your system has gobs of memory and tons of free disk space, resist the urge to create a fast search for your entire hard drive. Instead, create fast searches for folders that have a common thread (such as projects, clients, customers, suppliers, and distributors).

6. Select or deselect the Include Subfolders option to either include or exclude the subfolders for the folder you specified in step 5.

7. Click Add to insert this folder in the Folders to Search list box.

Tip #50 from
Laura and Read

If you accidentally add the wrong folder to the list, or if you forget to select/deselect the Include Subfolders option, you can remove a folder from the list. Select the folder, and then click the Remove Folder button.

8. Repeat steps 5–7 to include all the folders that you want in the fast search.
9. Choose Options to open the QuickFinder Fast Search Options dialog box (refer to Figure 4.26), where you can finish configuring the fast search. The options you choose here override the settings you made in the QuickFinder Settings dialog box (click the Settings button in the QuickFinder dialog box shown in Figure 4.24).
10. Click OK twice to return to the QuickFinder Manager dialog box, where the new fast search appears in the list. When the status reads Updated, the fast search file has been created and is ready for use.

Note

The fast search file for a custom fast search is created in `\program files\corel\ wordperfect office 2000\programs`.

Caution

Take care not to accidentally delete a fast search information file (with the `.idx` extension). The name of the file is cryptic and can easily be mistaken for a misplaced temporary file.

Tip #51 from
Laura and Read

On some networks, it's up to the network administrator to create fast search files for the network drives. These can be distributed across the network and imported into the individual user's custom fast search list. In a file management dialog box, right-click the `.idx` file and choose Add to Custom Search List. (Occasionally, when you import an `.idx` file, it comes in without a name. You can still see it in the list, with Imported in the Status column.) Select it and choose Edit to type a fast search name. Use the same steps if a co-worker has created a large fast search file and you want to use it.

Selecting a Fast Search in QuickFinder

Now that you've got a nice, neat list of fast search files, you're probably wondering how to tell QuickFinder which fast search to use. The answer is by selecting them from a custom indexes list in the Advanced Find dialog box.

The first step is to add your fast searches to the list. To do this, you have to locate the search file so that you can select it and add it to the list. You can do this in one of two ways: You can look in the Properties dialog box for each fast search, or you can search for all the fast search files at once.

To look at the properties for a fast search, select it in the QuickFinder Manager dialog box (refer to Figure 4.24), and then click Information. The QuickFinder Fast Search

Information dialog box appears (see Figure 4.28). The path for the index file is shown in the dialog box. Jot this down—this is where you need to go to find the file. Go back to the Open File dialog box and navigate to that folder. The index filename starts with ~QF. Right-click the file, and then choose Add to Custom Search List.

Figure 4.28
The path for the fast search file is shown in the QuickFinder Fast Search Information dialog box.

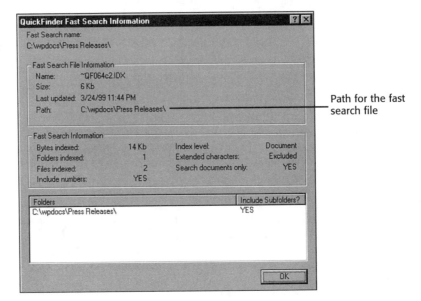

Path for the fast search file

You can also search for all the index files at once and then selectively add them to the Custom Indexes list. In the Open File dialog box, select a drive from the Look In drop-down list. Type ~qf in the File Name text box, and then choose Find Now. When the search results appear, right-click the files you want to add and choose Add to Custom Search List.

Now you have the files in the list. To search in a fast search, click the Look In drop-down list arrow in the Advanced Find dialog box. Scroll up to the top of the list. You should see Custom Indexes at the very top. Click the plus sign to open the list (see Figure 4.29). Select the fast search that you want to use, and then fill out the rest of the search criteria.

Note

You won't be able to choose a QuickFinder fast search from the Look In drop-down list in the Open File dialog box (or any other file management dialog box for that matter). You must be in the Advanced Find dialog box to get to that option.

⚠️ *Does QuickFinder find some, but not all of the files you are searching for? See "QuickFinder Doesn't Find All the Files" in the Troubleshooting section that follows.*

A fast search in the Custom Indexes list

Figure 4.29
You can choose a fast search in the <u>L</u>ook In drop-down list of the Advanced Find dialog box.

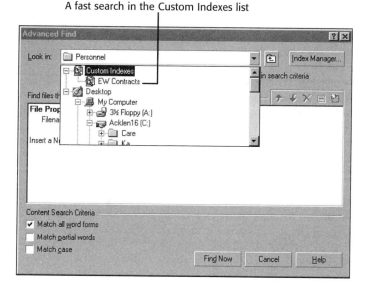

TROUBLESHOOTING

CAN'T SELECT MULTIPLE FILES

I can't seem to select more than one file from my file list. When I try to select the second file, the first is deselected.

Selecting multiple files can be tricky. You have to remember to hold down the Ctrl key when you select the second and subsequent files. If the files are one after the other, you can select them all at once: Click the first one, hold down the Shift key, and then click the last one.

MISPLACED FILES

I just moved (or copied) a file to another folder, but now I can't find it.

Maybe you are looking for the wrong filename. Or you could be looking in the wrong folder. Either way, the fastest way to find the file is to use QuickFinder to search for it. You can either search for the filename, or if you are unsure about the filename, you can search for text in the file. See the section "Finding Missing Files by Using QuickFinder" in this chapter for more information.

CAN'T CLICK TWICE TO RENAME

I'm trying to click twice to rename a file, and I can't get the editing box to appear.

This method for renaming files and folders is faster than choosing Rena<u>m</u>e from a menu, but it's a little trickier. You have to be sure to click the name, not the icon. If you click the icon, WordPerfect selects the file, not just the name. Also, make sure you pause a moment between the first and second clicks.

MY SHORTCUT STOPPED WORKING

I can't get one of the shortcuts in the Favorites folder to work. When I double-click the shortcut icon, nothing happens.

If the file (or folder) has been deleted, moved, or renamed, the shortcut won't be able to find it. Try to locate the file (or folder) by browsing through the other folders on your system, or try to find the file by searching for a piece of text in the file (with QuickFinder). When you find the file, delete the old shortcut, and then create a new shortcut for the file.

QUICKFINDER DOESN'T FIND THE FILE

I'm trying to search for a file by using text that is in the file. QuickFinder doesn't find the file. I know it is in the folder somewhere. What am I doing wrong?

First, make sure you're searching the correct drive or folder. Second, try using the Match All Word Forms option to search for alternate forms of a word or the Match Partial Words option to find the word even if its embedded inside another word. Third, broaden the search by removing some of the criteria. Remember that if one criterion doesn't match, QuickFinder won't find the file.

QUICKFINDER DOESN'T FIND ALL THE FILES

I'm searching for all the files that contain watershed ordinance. *QuickFinder finds some of the files, but not all of them. Am I doing something wrong?*

Probably not. It sounds like a damaged entry in the Windows Registry. This type of error also comes up when running QuickFinder on a network drive. It could also be a corrupt `.idx` file on the hard drive.

Let's start with the Registry. There is a utility that removes all WordPerfect entries and keys from the Registry. After you clear out all the WordPerfect information, you can reregister WordPerfect to correct the damaged entries.

First, exit all your applications. Then choose Start, Run, and type `c:\program files\corel\wordperfect office 2000\programs\pfreg.exe` (if necessary, substitute the correct drive letter for `c`). In the PerfectFit Component Registration dialog box, choose Unregister, and then click Register.

If this doesn't work, try rebuilding the files. First, delete all the `.idx` files from your hard drive. Make sure you search all the drives where you may have created fast searches. Remember that by default, a standard fast search creates the file in the folder you specified for that fast search.

Open QuickFinder from the Start, Find menu to search for all the fast search files on your system (type ~qf in the File Name text box). Select all the files, and then press Delete. Don't worry—this doesn't delete the fast search information! Now, open QuickFinder Manager and rebuild all the fast search files (both standard and custom) by selecting them and clicking the Rebuild button. If you forget, and you try to update the fast search, you get an error because the file for that fast search doesn't exist.

PROJECT

Daily backups are incredibly important, but like many other things in life, if it isn't fast and easy to do, it doesn't get done. Lots of backup programs claim to automate the entire backup process, but you still have to remember to load the program and start the backup. By using the Open File dialog box, you can search for all the files that you worked on throughout the day and copy them to a floppy disk.

Start by opening the Open File dialog box. Choose a drive (or folder) from the Look In drop-down list. Open the Last Modified drop-down list and choose Today. If you are interested in only the WordPerfect documents you modified, open the File Type drop-down list and choose WP Documents (*.wpd), otherwise, leave the filter set to All Files (*.*). Choose Find Now to start the search.

When the search results appear, select the files you want to back up. You probably don't want to back up all the files, especially if you searched for All Files. You'll see plenty of temporary files and other system files that are created or modified every day. You can ignore them and concentrate on the documents, spreadsheets, address books, databases, presentations, calendars, and so on.

When you are finished selecting the files, choose File, Send To, 3½ Floppy Disk.

CHAPTER 5

USING THE WRITING TOOLS

In this chapter

SPELL CHECKING A DOCUMENT

Writing thoughtful and original material is enough of a challenge, without having to worry about misspelled words! If you leave misspellings, the reader can be distracted. And, like it or not, some readers question the intelligence level of the author…and your credibility rating drops a notch.

Who would have thought something as simple as a few misspelled words could undermine all your hard work? Save yourself (or your boss) the potential embarrassment by running Spell Checker on every document, no matter how short, before you send it off.

In Chapter 1, "Getting Comfortable with WordPerfect," you learned how to use the Spell-As-You-Go feature to catch misspelled words (and other potential errors) as you type. If you've turned off Spell-As-You-Go, or if you want to check through the entire document all at once, you have to run Spell Checker from the Tools menu.

→ To learn more about using Spell-As-You-Go and Grammar-As-You-Go, **see** "WordPerfect's Automatic Proofreading Features," **p. 18**

Tip #52 from	Call me paranoid, but I've gotten in the habit of saving my documents before starting any of the writing tools. This way, if I make some changes that I decide I don't want to keep, I can always revert to my saved copy. Also, in rare cases, the writing tools can cause your system to freeze, so you'll want to be able to get back to your saved document after you restart.
Laura and Read	

Here's how to start Spell Checker and correct mistakes in your document:

1. Choose Tools, Spell Checker or click the Spell Checker button. The writing tools dialog box with tabs for Spell Checker, Grammatik, and the Thesaurus appears (see Figure 5.1). Spell Checker immediately begins checking the document for misspelled words, duplicate words, and irregular capitalization. A potential error is highlighted, and suggested replacement word(s) appear in the Replacements list box.

2. Choose from the following options to correct the misspelled word, add the word to the dictionary, or skip the word:

   - To correct a misspelled word manually, click in the document window, correct the problem, and then choose Resume to continue spell checking.

   - To replace a misspelled word with the correctly spelled word, select the correctly spelled word in the Replacements list box, and then choose Replace. In the case of duplicate words and irregular capitalization, you can select the single word, or the word with correct capitalization, in the Replacements list box (before choosing Replace).

   - If this is a frequently misspelled word, select the correct spelling in the Replacements list box, and then choose AutoReplace to add the combination to the QuickCorrect list. (See "Adding and Removing QuickCorrect Entries" later in this chapter for more information.)

Figure 5.1
Spell Checker, Grammatik, and the Thesaurus are all integrated into the same dialog box. Click the appropriate tab to switch to another writing tool.

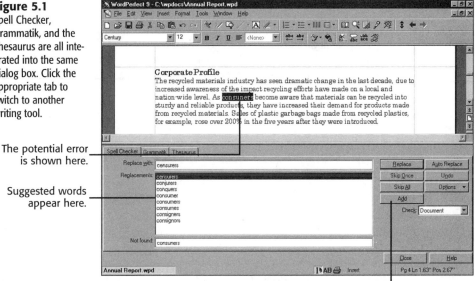

The potential error is shown here.

Suggested words appear here.

Click here to add the word to the active user word list.

Tip #53 from
Laura and Read

If the correct spelling doesn't appear in the Replacements list, edit the word manually in the Replace With box, and then choose Replace.

- To skip the word here but have Spell Checker stop if it finds it again, click Skip Once.
- To skip the word here and for the rest of the document, click Skip All.
- To add this word to the active user word list, click Add.

Caution

If you accidentally add a misspelled word to the user word list, see the section "Editing User Word Lists" later in this chapter for information on removing entries.

- If you accidentally replace the misspelled word with the wrong replacement word, click Undo.

Tip #54 from
Laura and Read

The Spell Checker/Grammatik/Thesaurus combo dialog box is a strange beast. It is an integrated dialog box that's anchored to the bottom half of the screen. It doesn't have to stay that way, though, because you can click and drag it wherever you want. Point to the gray area next to the Thesaurus tab. The pointer changes to a four-headed arrow. Click and drag the dialog box up into the document window. But be careful—don't go too far, or you'll anchor it to the top half of the screen. Whenever you see the gray rectangular outline, you

PART

I

CH

5

continues

continued

can drop it. Now it looks like the other dialog boxes—it has a blue title bar and a Close button. To put it back, point to the title bar and wait for the four-headed arrow, and then drag the dialog box down to the bottom of the screen. When you get close to the bottom, the rectangular guideline changes to one that stretches horizontally across the screen. When you see the horizontal guideline, release the mouse button to anchor it at the bottom of the screen.

By default, Spell Checker checks the entire document. If you don't want to check the whole document, you can select just a portion. To specify which portion of the document you want checked, click the Check drop-down list arrow and select an option.

 If you are tired of skipping over your name, company name, company address, and so forth, see "My Name Is Not Misspelled" in the Troubleshooting section at the end of this chapter.

 If you are frustrated because after adding a bunch of words in Spell Checker, it still stops on those words in another document, see "My Words Aren't Being Added" in the Troubleshooting section at the end of this chapter.

Tip #55 from *Laura and Read*	You can create more user word lists for specific types of documents. The active, or currently selected, word list is the one that Spell Checker adds words to when you choose Add. To create a new user word list, choose Options, User Word Lists, Add List. Type a name for the file, and then choose Open. The new user word list appears in the list, with an × in the box, indicating that it's active for this document. Choose Set Default if you want this user word list to be active in new documents.

Document Word List

Choosing Skip All adds the word to the document word list, which is saved with the document and doesn't affect other documents. The strength of this feature becomes clear when you work with long documents that are full of technical terminology. It only takes a few mouse clicks, and after you've built the list, Spell Checker runs a lot faster because it isn't stopping on those terms anymore.

CUSTOMIZING SPELL CHECKER

By default, Spell Checker starts checking the document immediately and looks for misspellings, duplicate words, and irregular capitalization. Phonetically spelled words are included in the Replacements text box to give you more suggested replacement words to choose from. You can alter these default settings by selectively turning on and off the options that you want to use.

In the Spell Checker dialog box, choose Options to open the pop-up list of options (see Figure 5.2). A check mark next to an option means that it's already turned on. You can choose from the following options:

■ Deselect Auto Start if you don't want Spell Checker to start checking the document immediately. You have to click Start in the Spell Checker dialog box to start the spell check.

- Select Beep on Misspelled if you want Spell Checker to beep every time it stops on a word. This is helpful if you want to turn to something else while Spell Checker is running and you want to be notified if Spell Checker stops.

- After you've completed a spell check of the document, the next time you run Spell Checker on the document, it checks only the parts of the document that have been edited or added. If you want to force Spell Checker to recheck the entire document, choose Recheck All Text.

- If you want Spell Checker to check words that contain both letters and numbers, select Check Words with Numbers.

- Deselect Check Duplicate Words if you don't want Spell Checker to stop when it finds duplicate words (that is, two identical words next to each other).

- Deselect Check Irregular Capitalization if you don't want Spell Checker to flag words with irregular capitalization (for example, McKinney, PowerPC, or NationsBank).

- Select Prompt Before Auto Replacement if you want WordPerfect to prompt you before replacing a word that you've added to the user word list with Auto Replace.

- Deselect Show Phonetic Suggestions if you don't want Spell Checker to show you suggestions that are phonetically similar to (that is, they sound like) the word that Spell Checker has stopped on.

Figure 5.2
You click Options to customize how the Spell Checker operates and to work with the word lists.

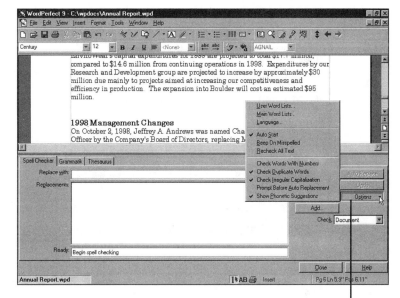

Click here to open the pop-up menu.

PART

I

CH

5

Tip #56 from
Laura and Read

The settings you make on the Options list stay in place until you change them again.

EDITING USER WORD LISTS

As the capabilities of the Spell Checker program grew, the dictionary files of earlier versions outgrew the term *dictionary* and became *word lists*. Every new document is created with a document word list and the default user word list. You can add entries to the word lists whenever Spell Checker stops on a word. Choosing Add adds the word to the user word list; choosing Skip All adds the word to the document word list.

If you accidentally add a misspelled word to a word list, you have to edit the list to remove the entry (otherwise, Spell Checker thinks that misspelled word is okay). You can edit both document word lists and the user word lists to add or remove entries.

In the Spell Checker dialog box, choose Options, User Word Lists. The User Word Lists dialog box appears (see Figure 5.3). Select the word list that you want to edit. From here you can do the following:

- If you want to remove an entry, select it in the list box and choose Delete Entry.

- If you want to add an entry, type the word/phrase you want to add in the Word/Phrase text box, and then choose Add Entry.

- If you want to add an entry with a replacement word, type the word/phrase in the Word/Phrase text box, type the replacement word/phrase in the Replace With text box, and then click Add Entry.

- To add multiple replacement words (which will be displayed in the Replacements list box as suggested replacement words), type the word/phrase in the Word/Phrase text box, type the replacement word/phrase in the Replace With text box, and then choose Add Entry. Type that *same* word/phrase in the Word/Phrase text box, type *another* replacement word/phrase in the Replace With text box, and then click Add Entry. Repeat for all the replacement words that you want associated with this word/phrase.

- If you want to edit an entry, select the entry in the list box. Edit the word or phrase in the Replace With text box and then click Replace Entry.

Figure 5.3
In the User Word Lists dialog box, you can select additional user word lists to use. You can also edit the word lists to add, remove, and replace entries.

This is the default user word list.

Click here to set the selected user word list as the default.

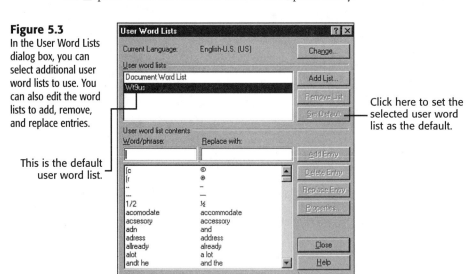

If the word list you want to edit doesn't appear in the list, click Add List to browse for .uwl files. When you find the one you need, select it, and then choose Open.

 If you just realized that you've added a bunch of incorrect entries in the user word list file, see "I Trashed the User Word List" in the Troubleshooting section at the end of this chapter.

USING OTHER DICTIONARIES

When you spell check a document, Spell Checker scans two types of word lists: the user word lists and the main word lists. It scans the user word list first, and if it doesn't find the word, it scans the main word list. If it still doesn't find the word, Spell Checker stops checking the document and flags the word as a possible error.

That's the macro view. The micro view is that you can link up to 10 user word list files and up to 10 main word list files together to check your documents. I know, I know, it sounds like overkill—but I've been known to link together a few main word lists when I wanted to use several language word list files together. (Each language comes with its own main word list file.) This is how you add specialized third-party dictionaries, such as medical and legal dictionaries, so they can be integrated into Spell Checker.

I've known serious keyboard pounders to create a library of word lists for different types of documents, particularly those of a technical nature. No matter how many word lists you use, Spell Checker checks all the user word lists before moving to the main word lists.

To add main word lists, choose Options, Main Word Lists, Add List (see Figure 5.4). Select a file from the folder, and then choose Open.

Figure 5.4
When additional language modules are installed, the main word list files are saved in the 9.0 subfolder of the Writing Tools folder.

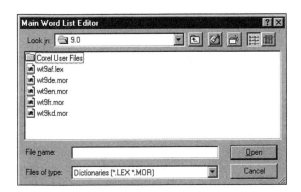

Tip #57 from
Laura and Read

If you don't see the language file that you need, run Corel's Setup program and install additional language modules. The name of the file is wp9xx.mor, where xx is the language code.

To add user word lists, choose Options, User Word Lists, Add List. Select a file from the list (or browse the system to locate other word lists), and then click Open. When a user word list file is in the list, you can select and deselect it to make it active or inactive as needed (see Figure 5.5).

Figure 5.5
You can use up to 10 user word lists together to check your documents, including the default user word list (WT9US).

This word list is inactive.

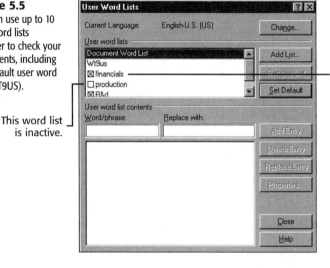

This word list is active.

Tip #58 from
Laura and Read

Spell Checker looks through these files in the order in which they appear in the list, so add the word lists that contain the most relevant words at the top.

Tip #59 from
Laura and Read

If you've been using an earlier release of WordPerfect, you can use the supplementary dictionary files or user word files that you created. In the Spell Checker (or Grammatik), choose Options, User Word Lists, Add List. Open `wt80xx.uwl` for version 8, `wt61xx.uwl` for version 7, or `wtspelus.sup` for version 6.1.

RUNNING SPELL UTILITY

WordPerfect 9 ships with the Spell Utility program, which you can use to convert word lists and dictionaries from previous versions of WordPerfect. You can also view the contents of a main word list, add and remove words, merge a word list with another word list, and create new main word lists. Spell Utility is a program called `wt9sptlen.exe`, and it's stored in the `\program files\corel\shared\writing tools\9.0` folder. Locate the file in Explorer or My Computer, and then double-click it to start it. The Spell Utility dialog box appears (see Figure 5.6).

Figure 5.6
Spell Utility is a separate program that you run outside of WordPerfect.

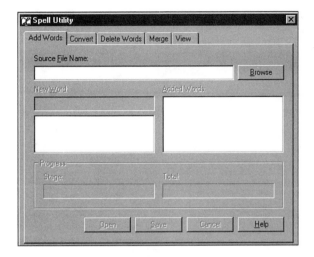

If you can't find the `wt9sptlen.exe` file on your system (or on the network), you can copy it directly from the CD. Insert the Corel WordPerfect Office 2000 CD in the drive, and then use Explorer or My Computer to look in the `\corel\shared\writing tools\9.0` folder. Right-click the file and choose Copy. Now, switch to the `\program files\corel\shared\writing tools\9.0` folder on your system. Right-click in the file list and choose Paste.

Using the Spell Utility, you can

- Add words to a main word list—Click the Add Words tab, and then click the Browse button to select the main word list file (`\program files\corel\shared\writing tools\9.0\wt9en.mor` is the default main word list file). Choose Open to open the file and activate the rest of the dialog box. Type the word you want to add in the New Word text box, and press Enter. Continue adding words until you've built your list. Choose Save to add the words in the Added Words list.

- Convert dictionaries and word lists—Click the Convert tab. Click the Conversion Type drop-down list arrow and choose an item from the list (see Figure 5.7). Choose Browse to select the source file. Specify a name for the word list you are creating in the Destination File Name text box. Choose Convert.

Tip #60 from
Laura and Read

If you don't see the item you need on the Conversion Type drop-down list, you might have to do a two-step conversion. Try converting the file to a WordPerfect 9 Document, and then convert the WordPerfect 9 Document to a WordPerfect 9 Dictionary.

PART

I

CH

5

Figure 5.7
Using the Convert
feature, you can con-
vert dictionaries and
word lists from previ-
ous versions of
WordPerfect into
WordPerfect 9 word
lists.

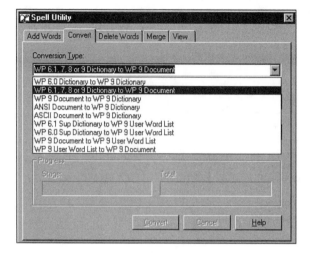

- Create a new main word list—Create a list of words in a WordPerfect document, an ANSI text file, or an ASCII text file. In Spell Utility, click the Convert tab. Select the appropriate conversion type, and then browse for the source file. Type a name for the file you are creating in the Destination File Name text box (make sure you use an .lex extension). Choose Convert.

- Delete words that you've added to a main word list—Click the Delete Words tab. Choose Browse to select the main word list file (\program files\corel\shared\writing tools\9.0\wt9en.mor is the default main word list file), and then choose Open. A list of words that you've added appears in the User Words list box. Select a word, and then choose Delete. Choose Save when you're done.

- Merge two main word lists together into one list—Click the Merge tab. Click the Merge Type drop-down list arrow and choose an item from the list. Browse for the source file. Specify a name for the file that you want to contain both lists in the Target File Name text box. Choose Add Words in Source to Target, and then choose Merge. If you decide later that you want to remove the merged words, follow these same steps, except choose Delete Words in Source from Target.

- View words in a main word list—Click the View tab. Click the Browse button to select a main word list file (\program files\corel\shared\writing tools\9.0\wt9en.mor is the default main word list file). Choose Open to open the file and activate the rest of the dialog box. Type the word (or a partial word) that you want to look up in the Word text box. The search results appear in the Results list box. For a more complete list, choose Look Up.

CHECKING THE GRAMMAR IN A DOCUMENT

Grammatik is a built-in grammar checker that proofs your documents for correct grammar, style, punctuation, and word usage, and thus catches many of the errors that pass by Spell

Checker. Interestingly, Spell Checker is integrated into Grammatik, so you only need to run Grammatik in order to run both.

Grammatik follows a strict set of grammatical rules when checking a document for problems. Many good writers, however, often bend these rules to make a point. Don't feel compelled to fix every problem or accept every solution if it changes the meaning of your words. Follow these steps to run Grammatik:

1. Choose Tools, Grammatik. If you already have the writing tools dialog box open, click the Grammatik tab. Grammatik immediately starts checking the document and, like Spell Checker, stops and highlights a potential error (see Figure 5.8).

Figure 5.8
Grammatik has many of the same options as Spell Checker to correct a potential problem or move past it.

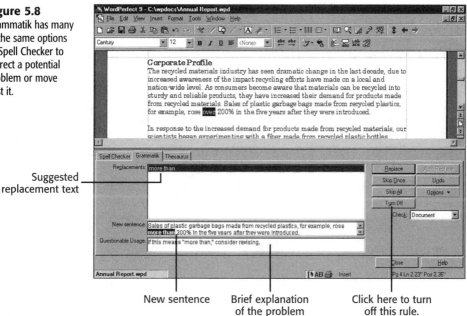

Suggested replacement text

New sentence   Brief explanation   Click here to turn
                of the problem   off this rule.

PART

I

CH

5

2. Choose from the following options to correct the error, skip the error, or turn off the rule:

- To correct a writing error manually, click in the document window, correct the problem, and then click Resume to continue the grammar check.

- To replace a writing error, select one of the suggestions in the Replacements list box, and then click Replace. If no suggestions are listed, you have to manually correct the text.

- To skip the writing error here but have Grammatik stop if it finds the error again, click Skip Once.

- To skip the writing error here and for the rest of the document, click Skip All.

- The rules by which Grammatik checks your document are organized into *rule classes*. To disable a particular rule class, choose Turn Off. This change is temporary; it affects only the current Grammatik session.

- If you correct a problem, and then change your mind, choose Undo to reverse the last action taken by Grammatik.

By default, Grammatik checks the entire document. If you want to check only a portion of the document, click the Check drop-down list arrow and select an option.

Note Because Spell Checker is integrated into Grammatik, when you run Grammatik, you also correct errors that are flagged by Spell Checker.

 If you want Grammatik to stop flagging a certain error, see "My Sentences Are Not Too Long" in the Troubleshooting section at the end of this chapter.

SELECTING A DIFFERENT CHECKING STYLE

Different types of documents must conform to particular grammatical rules and require varying levels of formality. To accommodate these differences, Grammatik offers 11 predefined checking styles, and you can create your own. By default, Grammatik uses the Quick Check style to check your documents. You can select another style, change the threshold settings, and choose a formality level. In the Grammatik dialog box, choose Options, Checking Styles to display the Checking Styles dialog box (see Figure 5.9).

Figure 5.9
You can select a checking style to match the type of document you are checking.

To choose a checking style, select it in the list, and then click Select. A checking style remains in effect until you choose another one.

To edit a checking style, select it in the list, and then click Edit. The Edit Checking Styles dialog box appears (see Figure 5.10).

 If you're having trouble getting your changes to a checking style to stick, see "My Edits to a Checking Style Aren't Getting Saved" in the Troubleshooting section at the end of this chapter.

Figure 5.10
You can modify any of the predefined checking styles to enable or disable rule classes, modify the threshold settings, or choose a different formality level.

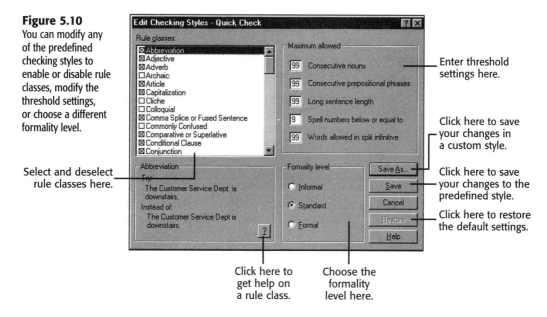

Enter threshold settings here.

Click here to save your changes in a custom style.

Select and deselect rule classes here.

Click here to save your changes to the predefined style.

Click here to restore the default settings.

Click here to get help on a rule class.

Choose the formality level here.

CUSTOMIZING GRAMMATIK

By default, when you run Grammatik, it starts checking the document immediately, prompts you before an automatic replacement, and suggests spelling replacement words. You can alter these default settings by selectively turning on and off the options that you want to use.

In the Grammatik dialog box, click the Options button to open the pop-up list of options (see Figure 5.11). A check mark next to an option means that it's already turned on. Choose from the following options:

- Choose Checking Styles to open the Checking Styles dialog box, where you can select another style (see the section "Selecting a Different Checking Style" earlier in this chapter).

- Choose Turn On Rules to display a list of the rules that you have turned off during this session. You can select a rule from this list to turn it back on.

- Choose Save Rules to save the rules that you turned off during this session as a new checking style.

- Choose User Word Lists to select, add, and edit user word lists. See the section "Editing User Word Lists" earlier in this chapter for more information.

- Choose Language to open the Language dialog box, where you can select a different language for this session. See the section "Switching to a Different Language" later in this chapter for more information.

- Choose Analysis to generate statistics and readability reports (see "Generating Readability Reports" later in this chapter).

- Deselect Auto Start if you don't want Grammatik to start checking the document immediately. You have to click Start in the Grammatik dialog box to start the grammar check.

PART

I

CH

5

- Deselect Prompt Before <u>A</u>uto Replacement if you don't want WordPerfect to prompt you before replacing a word that you've added to the user word list with A<u>u</u>to Replace.

- Deselect Suggest Spelling <u>R</u>eplacements if you still want Grammatik to flag spelling errors, but you don't want to see suggested replacement words in the Re<u>p</u>lacements list box.

- Select <u>C</u>heck Headers, Footers, Footnotes if you want to include these elements in the grammar check. Use this option if you've discovered an error in the document and there is a chance that you may have duplicated the error in a header, footer, or footnote.

Figure 5.11
You can click the Options button to customize how Grammatik operates, to edit checking styles, and to gener-ate statistical reports.

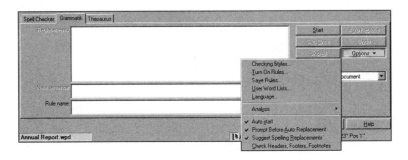

The settings you make on the O<u>p</u>tions list stay in place until you change them again.

GENERATING READABILITY REPORTS

Grammatik can compile three different statistical reports on your document: a readability report, basic counts, and a flagged list. You can also display a parse tree and a parts of speech diagram. To generate these reports, choose Options, Anal<u>y</u>sis. Choose from the following options:

- <u>P</u>arse Tree—This diagram identifies the clauses in the sentence where the insertion point lies.

- <u>P</u>arts of Speech—This diagram identifies each word as a noun, a pronoun, an adjective, a verb, an adverb, or another part of speech. This diagram dissects the sentence where the insertion point lies.

- <u>B</u>asic Counts—This is a count of words, sentences, and paragraphs, along with the average number of syllables per word, words per sentence, and sentences per paragraph (see Figure 5.12).

- <u>F</u>lagged—This report displays a list of errors and the number of times they were flagged during this session.

- <u>R</u>eadability—This report compares your document to one of three comparison documents (or a document of your choosing) to give you an idea of the skill required to comprehend the document content (see Figure 5.13).

Figure 5.12
The Basic Counts report is similar to the Information sheet in the Properties dialog box, but it is more precise.

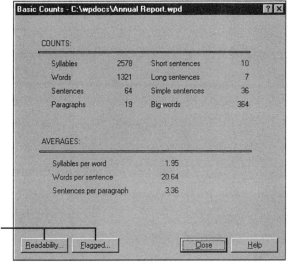

Click here to display a different report.

Figure 5.13
The Readability report gives you an idea of how easy or difficult it is to understand the document.

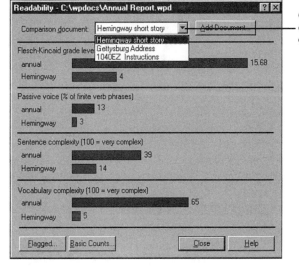

Click here to choose a different comparison document.

LOOKING UP WORDS IN THESAURUS

A thesaurus helps you find the right words to express your thoughts. Some thoughts and ideas are more complex than others, and most ideas can be expressed in a number of ways. Using the right words enables you to convey exactly the message you want to get across to the reader.

WordPerfect's Thesaurus looks up synonyms (that is, words with similar meanings) for a selected word. You can start the Thesaurus from a blank screen, but if you click on a word first, Thesaurus looks up that word. Choose Tools, Thesaurus, or, if you already have the writing tools dialog box open, click the Thesaurus tab. Thesaurus looks up the word and, by default, displays a list of synonyms (see Figure 5.14).

Figure 5.14
Thesaurus helps you refine your writing by showing you different words to use.

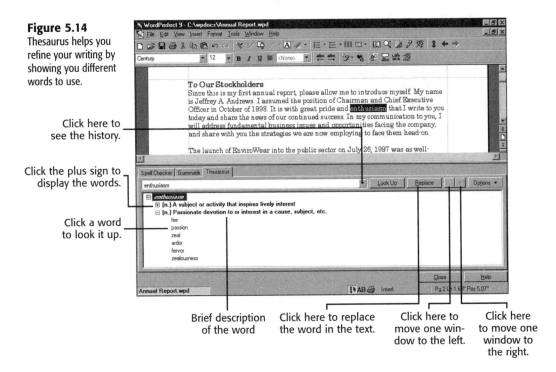

Click here to see the history.

Click the plus sign to display the words.

Click a word to look it up.

Brief description of the word

Click here to replace the word in the text.

Click here to move one window to the left.

Click here to move one window to the right.

If the insertion point is within a word, Thesaurus looks up synonyms for that word and displays them in the first window. Otherwise, you need to type the word you want to look up in the text box and then click Look Up.

Each word has its own window in the writing tools dialog box. When you fill up more than three windows, new ones are created. You can click the scroll arrows to move one window to the left or right.

To look up a word in one of the windows, click it. To replace the word in the document with the word from Thesaurus, double-click the word. If you change your mind, you can click Edit, Undo.

Thesaurus maintains a history list of all the words you look up during this session so that you can quickly get back to a word that you noticed earlier. Click the drop-down list arrow next to the Look Up button to select from a list of words.

As with the other writing tools, Thesaurus is set up to start looking up words immediately, and to create a list of synonyms for a word. You can turn off Auto Look Up and choose the types of words Thesaurus looks up. In the Thesaurus dialog box, click the Options button to open the pop-up list of options (see Figure 5.15). You can choose from the following options:

- Deselect Auto Look Up if you don't want Thesaurus to look up words right when you start it.

- Select Auto Close if you want Thesaurus to close after you choose a word for the document.

- Select Spelling Assist if you want Thesaurus to give spelling suggestions for misspelled words.

- Select Language to select a different language (which has its own Thesaurus data file).

- Select Set Data File to set the data file for a language.

- Select Synonyms to look up words with the same or similar meaning. For example, if you look up *pretty*, Thesaurus finds *handsome*, *attractive*, *ravishing*, and so on.

Figure 5.15
You can click the Options button to choose the type of words Thesaurus looks up, to choose a different language, or to activate Spelling Assist.

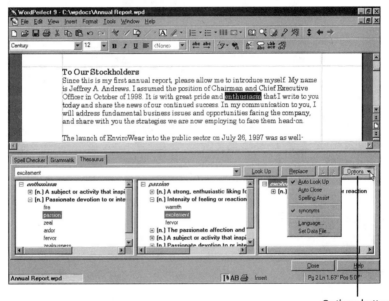

Options button

Caution

Make sure you don't accidentally deselect Synonyms in the Options menu. If you do, Thesaurus looks up the different meanings of the word and displays a brief description for each one, but it doesn't look up any words.

- Select Antonyms to look up words with an opposite meaning. For example, if you look up *ugly*, Thesaurus finds *attractive* and *pretty*.

- Select Related Words to look up words that have a similar meaning. For example, if you look up *old*, Thesaurus finds words such as *senior* and *original*.

- Select Related Information to produce a list of words associated to the genus of a word. For example, if you look up *tree*, Thesaurus finds *plants*, *leaves*, *roots*, and so on.

- Select Hypernyms to display the superordinate of a word. For example, the hypernym of *peach* is *fruit*.

- Select Hyponyms to display the subordinate of a word. For example, a hyponym of *fruit* is *peach*.

- Select Cross References to look up information from other documents.

- Select Phrases to look up different meanings of a word. For example, if you look up *time*, Thesaurus suggests phrases such as *it's about time* and *time to go now*.

Tip #61 from
Laura and Read

Not every lookup option is supported in every language. For example, the English version of WordPerfect supports only synonyms. There is a table in Help that tells you which Thesaurus options each language supports. Choose Help, Help Topics, and then click the Contents tab. Double-click Editing Documents, double-click Using Writing Tools, double-click Using Thesaurus, double-click Customizing Look Up Options, and double-click Overview: Languages and Support Look Up Options. You can print this out if you want to make it easier to read. In the Help window, choose File, Print Topic.

SWITCHING TO A DIFFERENT LANGUAGE

Writing in different languages is more than being able to enter, display, and print non-English characters. You also need to be able to correct spelling, check grammar, and look up terms in Thesaurus, in addition to using the proper date conventions and currency symbols. WordPerfect supports multiple languages in three ways:

- You can purchase WordPerfect in a different language so that the menus, prompts, messages, dictionaries, and Thesaurus are all in that language.

- You can mark sections of a document as being in one of the more than 30 languages supported by WordPerfect. Additional language modules can be installed that support Spell Checker, Grammatik, Thesaurus, Document Properties, and Hyphenation.

- A Language Resource File (LRS file), which comes with the program and each language module, contains the information for formatting numbers and footnote-continued messages, among other things. You can edit this file to customize these options.

If you want to mark only a section of text, select it first. Otherwise, click in the text where you want to switch to a different language (and thus use different writing tools to check the text). Choose Tools, Language, Settings. The Language dialog box appears, with a list of available language modules (see Figure 5.16). Scroll through the list and double-click the language you want.

Tip #62 from
Laura and Read

You can add or remove a language while running Spell Checker or Grammatik. Choose Options, Language. Click the Add button to add a language. To remove a language, select it in the Language list box, and then click the Remove button. You can also click the Change button in the User Word Lists dialog box to switch to a different language.

Figure 5.16
You can disable the writing tools for sections of text that need to be checked in a different language.

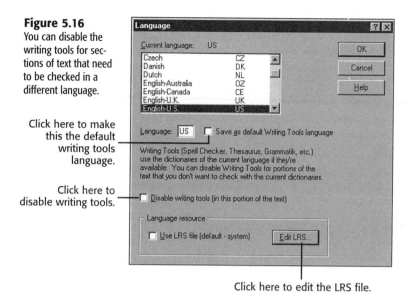

Click here to make this the default writing tools language.

Click here to disable writing tools.

Click here to edit the LRS file.

Tip #63 from
Laura and Read

Help has a list of the languages and the writing tools they support. Choose Help, Help Topics. If necessary, click the Contents tab. Double-click Editing Documents, double-click Using Writing Tools, double-click Choosing a Language, and double-click Overview: Writing Tools Supported Languages. You can print this out if you want to make it easier to read. In the Help window, choose File, Print Topic, OK.

SEARCHING FOR TEXT BY USING FIND AND REPLACE

PART
I

CH
5

The Find and Replace feature enables you to quickly locate text or codes and replace them if desired. I like to use Find to find the section of text that I need to work on. (Obviously this isn't necessary for short documents, but for long ones, believe me, WordPerfect can search faster than you can read!)

Here's an example of how you might use the Replace feature with Find: Let's say you accidentally misspelled an important client's name. You can search for all occurrences and replace them with the correct spelling. The same thing goes for codes. If you decide you want to search for a particular font and replace it with another one, you can do it with Find and Replace. To search for (and replace) text, follow these steps:

1. Choose Edit, Find and Replace to open the Find and Replace dialog box (see Figure 5.17).

2. Type the text you want to search for (this might be a complete or partial word, phrase, or number) in the Find text box.

3. Type the replacement text (this should be exact) in the Replace With text box.

4. Click Find Next to start the search.

Tip #64 from
Laura and Read

You can search for a symbol and replace it with another symbol. Click in the Find text box and press Ctrl+W. Select the symbol from any of the character sets, and then click Insert and Close. Click in the Replace With text box and press Ctrl+W. Select the symbol from any of the character sets, and then click Insert and Close. Choose Find Next. When WordPerfect stops, choose Replace All to do a global replacement.

Tip #65 from
Laura and Read

If you want to delete all or some instances of the search text, leave <Nothing> in the Replace With text box (or leave it blank). As you go through the search, you can selectively replace (or not replace) the search text with nothing, deleting it from the document.

Figure 5.17
You can do complex searches by choosing from the menus in the Find and Replace dialog box.

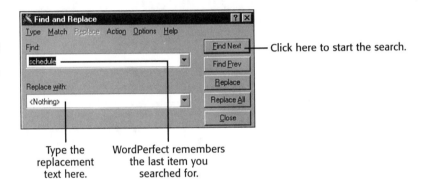

Click here to start the search.

Type the replacement text here.

WordPerfect remembers the last item you searched for.

When WordPerfect locates the search text, you have the following options:

- Click Find Next to continue the search.
- Click Find Prev to move back to the previous instance.
- Click Replace to replace the search text with the replacement text.
- Click Replace All to replace all the rest of the occurrences without further confirmation from you.
- Click Close if you're just using Find to locate your place in a document and you want to get to work.

SEARCHING FOR CODES

You can extend a search into the document codes to either locate a particular code so that you can edit or delete it, or to replace the code with another one. For example, if you're cleaning up a converted document, you might want to strip all the extraneous codes out. Or you might want to search for a symbol and replace it with another symbol. Here's how to search for a code:

1. Choose Edit, Find and Replace.
2. Choose Match, Codes from the menu in the Find and Replace dialog box. This opens the Codes dialog box (see Figure 5.18).

Figure 5.18
Using Find and Replace, you can search for any code in the Codes dialog box.

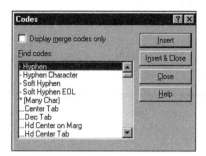

3. When you find the code you want to find, click it and then click Insert & Close.

4. Click Find Next. When WordPerfect stops, close the Find and Replace dialog box, and then turn on Reveal Codes. The insertion point is right after the code.

5. To delete the code, press Backspace. Otherwise, double-click the code to edit it.

Tip #66 from
Laura and Read

If you often work with converted documents, Find and Replace can be your best friend. After you identify the codes you want to get rid of, you can search for the codes and delete them. Some documents are so poorly formatted that it's quicker to clean out the codes and start over. Although that might take numerous find and replace operations, it's still faster than manually deleting each code.

To find and replace a code, follow these steps:

1. Complete steps 1–3 above.

2. Click in the Replace With text box.

3. Choose Replace, Codes. The same Codes dialog box shown in Figure 5.18 opens. This time, only the codes that can *replace* the code you are searching for are available. All the others are grayed out. For example, you can't replace a Center Tab code with a Date Format code.

4. When you find the code you want, click it and then click Insert & Close.

5. Click Find Next. When WordPerfect stops, choose Replace to replace this code and move on to the next one; choose Replace All to replace the rest of the codes without further confirmation.

To find and replace codes with specific settings, follow these steps:

1. Choose Edit, Find and Replace.

2. Choose Type, Specific Codes to open the Specific Codes dialog box (see Figure 5.19).

3. Select a code from the list and then click OK. Based on your selection, a modified Find and Replace dialog box appears, with options for you to select the setting that you are searching for. Figure 5.20 shows the dialog box you get after choosing the Font code.

PART

I

CH

5

Figure 5.19
To search for a code with a specific setting, select the code from the Specific Codes dialog box. This produces a modified Find and Replace dialog box, where you can choose the setting.

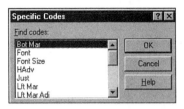

Figure 5.20
When you select Font from the Specific Codes dialog box, you get the Find and Replace Font dialog box.

4. Use the Find and Replace Font dialog box options to specify exactly what you want to find (and replace). For example, you could search for Century Bold and replace it with Humanist Bold, or you could search for all the 14-point text and replace it with 16-point text.

5. Click Find Next to start the search.

Tip #67 from *Laura and Read*	In the modified Find and Replace dialog box that you get when you're searching for specific code settings, put a check mark in the Replace with Nothing check box if you want to replace the code with nothing, thus deleting it from the document.

Tip #68 from *Laura and Read*	You might not have thought of this yet, but you can combine text and codes in the Find text box to look for text that is followed (or preceded) by a certain code.

RUNNING CASE-SENSITIVE SEARCHES

For times when you want to search for a word, but only if it's capitalized, you can narrow down a search by making it case-sensitive. You can actually make a case-sensitive replacement, too.

For example, if you want to find the word *Water*, but not *water*, type Water in the Find text box, and then choose Match, Case. The text Case Sensitive appears underneath the Find text box. Click Find Next.

Here's another example: Let's say you want to replace all instances of *water quality ordinance* with *Water Quality Ordinance*. However, you don't want to replace *WATER QUALITY ORDINANCE* with *Water Quality Ordinance*. First, enter the exact phrases, with the correct capitalizations, in each of the text boxes. Then click in the F̲ind text box and choose M̲atch, C̲ase. Click in the Replace W̲ith text box and choose R̲eplace, C̲ase. The text Case Sensitive now appears under both text boxes (see Figure 5.21). Click F̲ind Next.

Figure 5.21
When you perform a case-sensitive find and replace, you have to set the Case option for both text boxes.

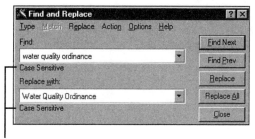

Verify that Case Sensitive appears under both text boxes.

OTHER FIND AND REPLACE OPTIONS

I could probably write an entire chapter on all the different types of searches you can do by using Find and Replace. Case-sensitive searches and codes searches are the most frequently used of the options available, so they get the most coverage. Some other options might prove helpful:

- Choose T̲ype, W̲ord Forms to find all forms of the word you are searching for. For example, if you search for the word *litigate*, you'll locate *litigating*, *litigation*, and *litigated*, as well as *litigate*.

- Choose M̲atch, W̲hole Word to find the word only if it appears by itself, and not as a part of a larger word.

- Choose M̲atch, F̲ont to open the Match Font dialog box (see Figure 5.22), where you can select a font, font size, and font attributes. WordPerfect finds the search text only if it's been formatted with the font, size, and attributes that you select. (If you click in the Replace W̲ith text box and choose R̲eplace, F̲ont, you get the Replace Font dialog box, which is identical to the Match Font dialog box.)

PART
I

CH
5

Caution

The W̲ord Forms option won't work if you have more than one word or if you have codes in the F̲ind text box.

Click here to choose a font.

Figure 5.22
You can use the
Match Font dialog box
options if you want
to locate text in the
selected font, font
size, and attributes.

Click here to
choose a font size.

Select one or
more attributes.

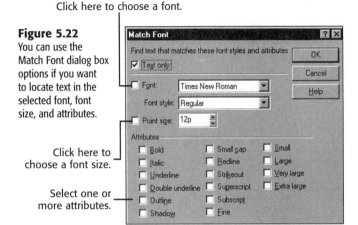

UNLEASHING THE POWER OF QUICKCORRECT

QuickCorrect automatically corrects common mistakes while you type. QuickCorrect cleans up extra spaces between words, fixes capitalization errors, corrects common spelling mistakes and typos, inserts special symbols, and replaces regular straight quotation marks with typeset-quality curly quotation marks. It also helps you create graphic lines, bulleted lists (recall the discussion of QuickBullets in Chapter 3, "Basic Formatting"), ordinal numbers, and hyperlinks to Internet (or intranet) addresses or to files on your network or local hard drive. QuickCorrect is a robust feature with a lot of tools that do some of the work for you.

Choose Tools, QuickCorrect to open the QuickCorrect dialog box (see Figure 5.23). There are tabs for all the different features that fall under the QuickCorrect umbrella. The QuickWords feature is discussed in the section "Setting Up QuickWords," later in this chapter.

Figure 5.23
In the QuickCorrect
dialog box, you can
add, remove, and edit
the QuickCorrect
entries. You can also
turn off QuickCorrect
so that it doesn't
correct words while
you type.

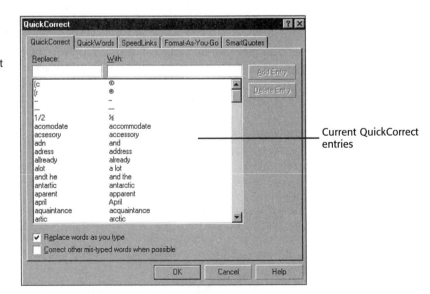

Current QuickCorrect
entries

ADDING AND REMOVING QUICKCORRECT ENTRIES

QuickCorrect includes an extensive list of frequently misspelled words and typos as well as some symbols you can insert by using just a few keystrokes. After you add your own common typos and their corrections to the QuickCorrect list, you'll spend less time proofing your documents with the writing tools.

To add words or phrases to QuickCorrect, type the word or phrase in the Replace text box. Type the replacement word or phrase in the With text box (see Figure 5.24). Click Add Entry.

Figure 5.24
You can add your frequent misspellings and typos to the QuickCorrect list and let WordPerfect fix your mistakes for you as you type.

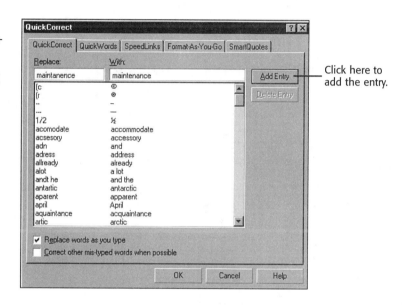

Click here to add the entry.

If you don't like QuickCorrect, you can turn it off completely. Choose Tools, Quick-Correct, and deselect Replace Words as You Type (that is, remove the check mark). A better solution might be to remove the entries that you don't like so that you can continue to take advantage of those that are helpful. To remove an entry, select it in the list, and then click Delete Entry, Yes.

PART
I
CH
5

Tip #69 from
Laura and Read

Think of ways you can use QuickCorrect to insert long or hard-to-type words when you type a few characters. For example, you could add an entry to replace *wp2k* with *Corel WordPerfect Office 2000* or *adm* with *antidisestablishmentarianism*. (My Dad used that word to teach me how to spell by sounding out words.)

Transferring QuickCorrect Entries from Previous Versions
If you've been using WordPerfect 7 or 8, you can use the QuickCorrect entries that you created in those versions. You just need to add the user word list file to the list of user word lists. Choose Tools, Spell Checker, Options, User Word Lists, Add List. Open wt80us.uwl for version 8 or wt61us.uwl for version 7.

INSERTING SPEEDLINKS

The SpeedLinks feature creates a hyperlink whenever you type the beginning of an Internet address, such as www, ftp, http, or mailto. This also works for email addresses such as *yourname*@compuserve.com. You can then give that hyperlink a friendlier name. For example, when you type the URL http://kb.corel.com, SpeedLinks creates the hyperlink to the Web page.

Choose Tools, QuickCorrect, and then click the SpeedLinks tab (see Figure 5.25). Type the friendlier name that you want to use to activate the hyperlink in the Link Word text box (the @ symbol is inserted automatically). Type the location to link it to in the Location to Link To text box. If necessary, click the Files icon to browse your system (or the network) and select a drive, folder, or file.

Figure 5.25
Using SpeedLinks, you can create a link word that automatically creates a hyperlink to a Web page, email address, document, folder, or drive.

All link words begin with an @.

Click here to deselect automatic hyperlinks.

Click here to browse your system or network.

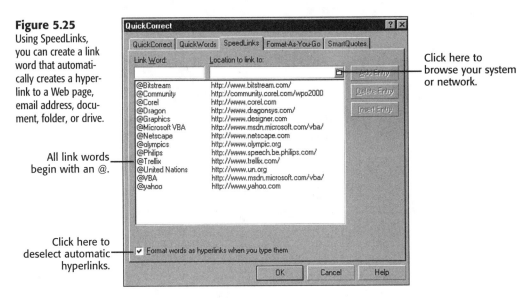

To insert a SpeedLinks entry in a document, type the @ symbol followed by the link word. When you press the spacebar or Enter, WordPerfect creates the hyperlink.

Tip #70 from
Laura and Read

If you often work with hyperlinks, there is a toolbar that you can turn on. Right-click the toolbar and then click Hyperlink Tools. This toolbar has buttons to help you create and edit hyperlinks, move from the next to the previous hyperlink, activate and deactivate hyperlinks, create bookmarks, and edit the hyperlink style. When you're ready to turn it off, right-click a toolbar, and then click Hyperlink Tools again.

CUSTOMIZING FORMAT-AS-YOU-GO

The Format-As-You-Go feature helps keep your sentence structure accurate by cleaning up extra spaces between words and sentences. I can't get enough of the automatic capitalization at the beginning of a new sentence—I don't have to press that Shift key nearly as often. Format-As-You-Go also fixes most of your capitalization mistakes: If there are two capital letters at the beginning of a word, the second letter is changed to lowercase.

You can choose Tools, QuickCorrect to open the QuickCorrect dialog box, and then click the Format-As-You-Go tab. By default, all the options in the Sentence Corrections section are selected, and End of Sentence Corrections is set to None (see Figure 5.26).

Figure 5.26
The Format-As-You-Go feature has six different tools to help you quickly create bulleted lists, graphic lines, ordinal numbers, en dashes, and em dashes.

Remove the check mark to disable the feature.

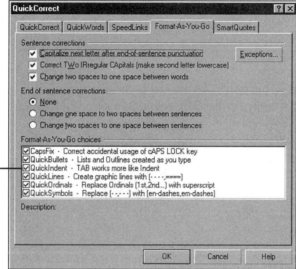

All the following Format-As-You-Go tools are selected by default, but you can deselect the ones you don't want to use. The tool remains deselected until you select it again.

- CapsFix—Fixes problems with capitalization when Caps Lock is on by mistake and you hold down the Shift key to capitalize the first letter (such as tHIS). CapsFix works only if Caps Lock is on.

- QuickBullets—Helps you quickly create bulleted lists.

→ For more information on using the QuickBullets feature to create bulleted lists, **see** "Using QuickBullets," **p. 70**

- QuickIndent—Pressing Tab at the beginning of the first and second lines of a paragraph creates a left indent for that paragraph.

- QuickLines—Typing four dashes and then pressing Enter creates a single horizontal line from the left to the right margin; typing four equal signs and then pressing Enter creates a double horizontal line from the left to the right margin.

- QuickOrdinals—Typing ordinal text after a number converts the ordinal text to superscript when you press the spacebar.

- QuickSymbols—Typing two hyphens followed by a space inserts an en dash; typing three hyphens followed by a space inserts an em dash.

PART
I

CH
5

TURNING ON SMARTQUOTES

The mild-mannered feature SmartQuotes converts the regular straight quotation marks to typeset-quality curly quotation marks as you type. It doesn't sound like a big deal, but for materials that should have a more polished appearance, this is one of those small details that can really help. To turn off SmartQuotes or select different quotation characters:

1. Choose Tools, QuickCorrect, and then click the SmartQuotes tab to display the SmartQuotes options (see Figure 5.27).

2. Deselect the option that you don't want to use.

3. To change the quotation character, click the Open and Close drop-down list arrows and select another character.

Figure 5.27
The SmartQuotes feature replaces straight quotation marks with curly quotation marks for a more polished, professional appearance.

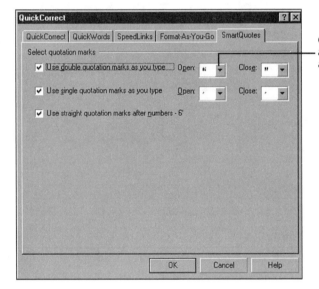

Click a drop-down arrow to choose another character.

Tip #71 from
Laura and Read

You can insert one of the symbols from the Symbols dialog box in place of a quotation character. Select one of the quotation characters, and then press Delete. Press Ctrl+W to open the Symbols dialog box. Select a symbol, and then click Insert and Close.

SETTING UP QUICKWORDS

QuickWords simplify the process of typing frequently used words and phrases. You assign an abbreviation to a word or phrase, use the abbreviation when typing the document, and then expand the abbreviation. QuickWords aren't limited to words or phrases—you can assign QuickWords to text that contains formatting codes, such as font attributes and graphics that you would use for logos.

If you're upgrading from WordPerfect 6.1 or 7, you'll see that the Abbreviations feature is now called QuickWords.

You can assign entire paragraphs to a QuickWords entry, and then use them to quickly build documents that consist of form paragraphs (such as wills, leases, contracts, and so on). Here's how to create a QuickWords entry:

1. Select the text or graphic you want to assign to QuickWords. If you want to insert a graphic or logo with a QuickWords entry, turn on Reveal Codes and position the red cursor to the left of the box code, and press Shift+right arrow to select the box code.

2. Choose <u>T</u>ools, QuickW<u>o</u>rds to display the QuickWords tab of the QuickCorrect dialog box (see Figure 5.28).

Figure 5.28
With QuickWords, you can assign an abbreviation to text or graphics, and then simply type the abbreviation to insert them into a document.

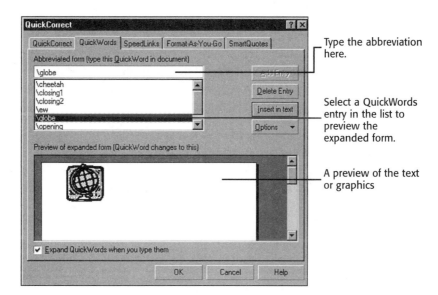

Type the abbreviation here.

Select a QuickWords entry in the list to preview the expanded form.

A preview of the text or graphics

PART

I

CH

5

3. Type the abbreviation you want to use in the Abbreviated Form (Type This Quick-Word in Document) text box. The abbreviation can be a few letters or a one- or two-word phrase.

Note

Try using words that won't normally come up in your documents for QuickWords. For example, you could use *compadd* to expand your company address, *clogo* for the company logo (not just *logo*), or *sigblock* for your signature block.

Caution

If you're creating a QuickWords entry for a graphic image, make sure Expand as Text with Formatting is selected on the Options menu. Otherwise, the graphic won't appear in the document.

4. Click Add Entry.

Tip #72 from
Laura and Read

The QuickWords feature has been touted as an accessible alternative to creating macros for inserting frequently used sections of text or graphics. It's faster, more flexible, and it's easier to edit a QuickWords entry than it is to edit a macro.

➔ For more information on creating and running macros, **see** Chapter 24, "Experts and Macros," **p. 685**

It's easy to update a QuickWords entry when the form text changes (in the case of form paragraphs) or if you want to insert a different graphic image with a certain QuickWords entry. To replace a QuickWords entry, follow these steps:

1. Select the text or graphic.

2. Choose Tools, QuickWords.

3. Select from the list the QuickWords entry that you want to assign to the selected text or graphic.

4. Click the Options button and choose Replace Entry.

5. Click Yes in the confirmation message box.

You can also rename a QuickWords entry when necessary. On the QuickWords tab of the QuickCorrect dialog box, select the QuickWords entry, and then click Options, Rename Entry. Type the new name, and then click OK.

Every now and then, it's a good idea to go through the QuickWords entries and remove the ones you aren't using anymore. To delete a QuickWords entry, choose Tools, QuickWords. Select the QuickWords entry you want to delete, and then click Delete Entry.

Finally, you can turn off QuickWords if you don't want to expand the QuickWords as you type. In the QuickWords dialog box, deselect Expand QuickWords When You Type Them.

Tip #73 from
Laura and Read

To expand all the QuickWords at once, choose Tools, Macro, Play, and then double-click expndall. See Chapter 24, "Experts and Macros," for more information on the macros that ship with WordPerfect Office 2000.

TROUBLESHOOTING

MY NAME IS *NOT* MISSPELLED

Spell Checker (and Grammatik) stop on my name, company name, company address, and all sorts of other words that are correctly spelled. How can I tell Spell Checker and Grammatik that the word is spelled correctly so that it won't stop on it again?

In either Spell Checker or Grammatik, you can add correctly spelled words to the user word list so they won't stop on the word again (unless, of course, the word is misspelled). The next time that Spell Checker or Grammatik stops on the word, click Add to add it to the selected user word list. Also, make sure you are adding it to the user word list, not the document word list. Choose Options, User Word Lists, and make sure that WT9US is selected.

I TRASHED THE USER WORD LIST

I wasn't paying attention and I added a bunch of words to the user word list that I should have added to another user word list file. Is there some way I can revert to the default user word list file without manually removing all the entries?

You can restore the default contents by deleting the file and letting WordPerfect re-create it the next time you start the program. Delete the file wt9xx.uwl (where xx stands for the language code) in the \program files\corel\shared\writing tools\9.0\corel user files folder in Windows 95/98 and the d:\winnt\profiles\<user name>\personal\corel user files in Windows NT.

This solution also works if you open the QuickCorrect dialog box and the QuickCorrect list is empty.

MY WORDS AREN'T BEING ADDED

I just finished spell checking a document, and I see that I added a bunch of words to the word list. Now when I check another document, Spell Checker still stops on those words. What's the deal?

The words that you added during a spell check were inserted in the document word list, which is available only to this document, not the user word list, which is available to other documents. You need to set the user word list as the default word list. In the Spell Checker dialog box, choose Options, User Word Lists, select wt9xx.uwl in the list, and then click Set Default.

MY EDITS TO A CHECKING STYLE AREN'T GETTING SAVED

I made some changes to one of the checking styles, but I can't seem to save the edits.

Any of the 11 predefined checking styles can be modified, but you must be sure to choose Save or Save As before you exit the Edit Checking Styles dialog box. If you choose Save, the changes are saved to the selected checking style. If you choose Save As, you can specify another name for the checking style. A modified checking style is shown with an asterisk (*) next to it in the Checking Styles dialog box.

MY SENTENCES ARE NOT TOO LONG

Grammatik is constantly flagging long sentences in my documents. Is there any way I can change this?

Each checking style has its own threshold settings in the Maximum Allowed section of the Edit Checking Styles dialog box. You can increase the number of words in the Long Sentence Length text box to change the threshold setting for long sentences. You can set up to a maximum of 99 words.

PROJECT

Rather than leave it up to individual employees of your company to add frequently used words to their user word list, you can create a standard user word list and distribute it throughout the company. You can even take things a step further—instead of just adding the company name, company address, names of clients, and technical terms, you can take advantage of the capability to create a custom list of replacement terms when a certain word is encountered. For example, if the word *chairman* is found, suggested replacement words such as *chairperson* or *chair* could be given.

A server installation must be performed first, and then a workstation installation. From this workstation, start WordPerfect and open the user word list by choosing Tools, Spell Checker, Options, User Word Lists. Select wt90us in the list, and then add entries for your company name and address, clients, key personnel in the company, technical terms, and so on. Leave the Replace With text box blank, so the word is added as a <skip> word.

To add QuickCorrect replacements, type both the word and the replacement. If you add more than one replacement word for the same word, the suggested replacements appear on the Spell-As-You-Go list when a user right-clicks the underlined word. Also, an entry with more than one replacement is not automatically corrected while you type.

When you are finished, use Windows Find File to locate this customized user word list file. Search the Windows folder and its subfolders. Make a copy of the file and name it wt90us.sav. Replace the wt90us.sav file on the server with the customized wt90us.sav file.

Before you do the rest of the workstation installations, make sure there isn't a user word list file already on the system (from a previous installation). If there is already a wt90us.uwl file on the workstation, WordPerfect won't copy the customized wt90us.sav file (which is renamed wt90us.uwl on the workstation).

CHAPTER **6**

PRINTING, FAXING, AND EMAILING

In this chapter

The Basics of Printing

Despite predictions of the "paperless office," the end result of most WordPerfect documents is still printed pages. This way of thinking and working might be changing as we move toward publishing documents to the World Wide Web, or as we share documents via email. But the printer continues to be an important part of the office, and printing is one of the essential tasks for any user of WordPerfect.

Selecting a Printer

WordPerfect is a *WYSIWYG (what you see is what you get)* program. However, to truly see onscreen what your document will look like, WordPerfect has to know what printer you are planning to use so it can display the proper fonts and print attributes. To select a printer, follow these steps:

1. Choose File, Print to display the Print dialog box (see Figure 6.1). The options you see on the Print tab of this dialog box may vary, depending on your printer's features.

Figure 6.1
WordPerfect's Print dialog box is the heart and soul of all printing options.

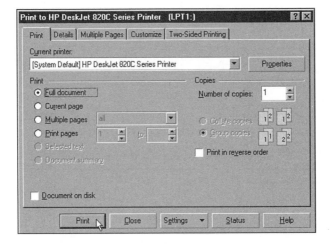

2. In the Current Printer list box, WordPerfect displays the currently selected printer. If the printer name displayed is the printer you will be using, you can click Close to return to your document, or you can proceed to print your document.

3. If the printer is not correct, click the drop-down list that displays the default Windows printer along with any other printers or fax drivers that have been installed in Windows.

4. Select the printer to which you want to print.

5. Click Close to return to your document.

Tip #74 from
Laura and Read

You can quickly check which printer is selected by moving the mouse pointer to the printer icon on the application bar. A QuickTip appears that displays the name of the currently selected printer. If this is not the printer you want, click the printer icon to go to the Print dialog box, where you can change the selected printer.

With the proper printer selected, you can create or format your document with confidence, knowing that what you see on the screen will match what your printer can print.

Select Printer Before Formatting a Document
If you don't have the proper printer selected, you can still change the printer before printing. However, some formatting probably will change, including some printer fonts, line spacing, and so on. If you know the printer you'll use, it's best to choose it before spending too much time on your document.

PREVIEWING PRINTED OUTPUT

If you are working in Page view (which you get to by choosing View, Page), WordPerfect shows you on the screen exactly what you will see on the printed page. However, even if you're working in Draft view, WordPerfect also enables you to preview your printed output quickly and easily.

To preview your document before printing, choose File, Print Preview. Print Preview zooms the document to a full-page view, thus enabling you to see the whole page while at the same time allowing you to edit the document (see Figure 6.2). The Print Preview toolbar also appears, helping you to perform tasks that typically precede printing. These include the following:

- Ruler—Click this icon to display a ruler above the document to help verify page layout measurements.

- View Page—This default Print Preview view displays a full page of the document. Although the text is probably too small to read, you can edit or modify the page layout while in Print Preview.

- Two Page View—This option shows two pages, side-by-side.

- Zoom—If you want to see the document close up, you can zoom in by using this option.

- Spell Checker—One of the last things you do before printing is check the document's spelling. This icon makes it easy to access Spell Checker.

- Make It Fit—If after previewing your document you decide that you need to squeeze your document into fewer pages, use this icon to access the Make It Fit feature.

- Page Setup—If you decide to change the paper size or orientation, access the Page Setup dialog box by clicking this icon.

- Print Document—This option sends the document directly to the printer, bypassing the Print dialog box.

PART

I

CH

6

■ Print—If you want to make changes in the number of copies or what pages to print, access the Print dialog box by clicking this icon.

 ■ Print Preview—Click this icon to turn off Print Preview.

Print Preview toolbar

Figure 6.2
You can use Print
Preview to preview
the document layout
before printing.

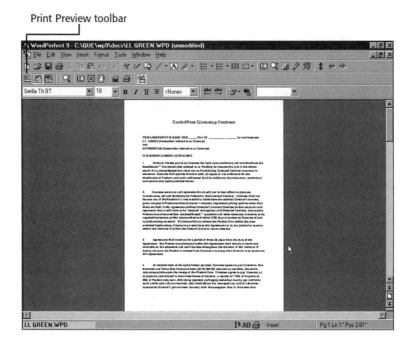

 If you are satisfied with what you see in Print Preview, and if you want to print a single copy of the entire document, you can send the document directly to the printer by clicking the Print Document icon. Otherwise, click the Print icon to proceed to the Print dialog box (refer to Figure 6.1).

Tip #75 from
Laura and Read

If you want to bypass the Print dialog box, simply press Ctrl+Shift+P. Unless you have made changes previously in the Print dialog box, this prints a single copy of the entire document.

PRINTING MULTIPLE COPIES

One of the most commonly used printing options is to specify the number of copies of the document you want to print. To change the number of copies, simply change the number in the Number of Copies text box.

If you to print more than one copy, you can choose to Collate copies, or to Group copies (the default). The illustrations in the Print dialog box (shown in Figure 6.3) show the effect of selecting these options.

Figure 6.3
The Print dialog box enables you to choose many options for printing your document, including number of copies, collating options, and even printing only selected text.

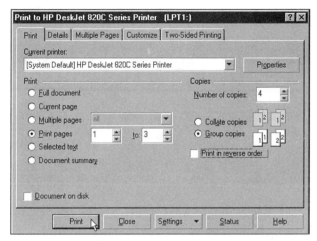

PRINTING SPECIFIC DOCUMENT PAGES

Although you typically print a full document (WordPerfect's default), you can also print selected pages of the document. The options on the Print tab of the Print dialog box include

- Current Page—This option prints only the page on which the cursor currently resides. This is the quickest way to print a single page in a large document.

- Multiple Pages—Using this option you can choose specific nonsequential pages. For example, if you need to print pages 1 through 4, and page 15, you type 1-4, 15 in the text box.

> **Note**
> If you click the Multiple Pages tab of the Print dialog box, you see a number of examples and explanations as to how you can print multiple pages or labels, secondary pages, chapters, and volumes. However, under the Print tab you can indicate only page numbers.

> **Caution**
> The numbers you enter in the Multiple Pages text box must be in numeric order; otherwise, all the pages may not print. For example, if you specify 12-15, 4, only pages 12–15 print. To print these specific pages, you must enter 4, 12-15.

- Print Pages—This option enables you to specify a range of pages. Simply specify the beginning page in the first text box, and the ending page in the second text box. If you don't indicate an ending page, WordPerfect prints to the end of the document.

- Selected Text—If you have selected text before accessing the Print dialog box, this option prints only the selected text.

PART

I

CH

6

Note

When you choose to print selected text, the output appears on the printed page in the same location in which it would have appeared had you printed the surrounding text. For example, if you select the last paragraph on the page, the paragraph prints by itself at the bottom of the page.

- Document Summary—This option prints only the document summary but none of the body of the document.

 If you try to print and nothing happens, see "When Nothing Happens" in the Troubleshooting section at the end of this chapter.

CONTROLLING PRINT JOBS

Both WordPerfect and Windows enable you to check the status of any current print jobs and to control multiple print jobs. To control a print job from within WordPerfect, follow these steps:

1. Access the Print dialog box by choosing File, Print (refer to Figure 6.3).

2. Click the Status button. WordPerfect displays the Print Status and History dialog box (see Figure 6.4), which in turn displays information about the various print jobs waiting to be printed, along with a list of recently completed print jobs.

Note

If you don't see any print jobs in the Print Status and History dialog box, choose Display, and uncheck Hide Completed Jobs.

Figure 6.4
WordPerfect's Print
Status and History
dialog box provides
information about
current as well as
recent print jobs, and
enables you to pause
or cancel print jobs in
progress.

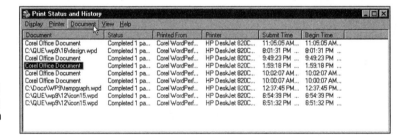

3. Locate and select the print job you want to control.

4. Choose Document, Pause Printing if you want to temporarily pause printing.

5. Choose Document, Cancel Printing to stop the print job, even if it's in progress.

6. Choose Document, Remove to delete a print job from the list.

7. Close the Print Status and History dialog box to return to the Print dialog box.

WordPerfect's Print Status and History dialog box works the same as the Windows Printer dialog boxes, but the Windows dialog box is a bit easier to access. When you begin printing, Windows displays a printer icon on the Windows taskbar (see Figure 6.5). Double-click the icon to display the Printer dialog box (see Figure 6.6). You then can select a print job and pause or cancel it.

Figure 6.5
The Windows printer icon on the Windows taskbar appears only when a print job is in progress.

Figure 6.6
The Windows Printer dialog box is similar to the WordPerfect Print Status and History dialog box, but is easier to access, thus enabling you to more quickly cancel a print job.

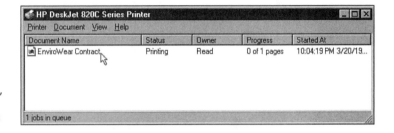

Note

You can pause or cancel the printing of all documents on a printer that is attached to your computer. If you are using a network printer, you may see other print jobs listed that are not yours. However, you can pause or cancel only your own documents.

Caution

If you are connected to a network, you may have access to several different printers that are also connected to the network. Be careful, however, to select only those printers where you really want to print. Otherwise, you may end up sending a print job to a printer in a far-flung area of the company or, worse, to someone who shouldn't see your printed output.

PART

I

CH

6

USING PRINT OPTIONS

You now know about some of the most common printing tasks and procedures you are likely to encounter. WordPerfect also offers a wide array of options for printing nearly any kind of document.

PRINT AND DETAIL OPTIONS

On the Print tab of the Print dialog box (refer to Figure 6.1), you can use the following options:

- Print in Reverse Order—Depending on how your printer stacks pages as they're completed, you may want to print the pages in reverse order so that they are stacked in the proper order.

- Document on Disk—You need not open a file before you print it. Instead, simply select this option, and in the text box that appears, enter the name of the document you want to print. WordPerfect then prints the file directly from your disk to the printer.

On the Details tab of the Print dialog box (see Figure 6.7), you can modify settings related to the current printer and change the color and resolution settings:

- In the Current Printer section, you can add a printer, modify a printer setup, specify how the paper feed works, choose a default initial font for the currently selected printer, or specify whether this is a fax printer (see the section "Faxing Documents" later in this chapter.)

- By default, your print job goes to the printer device specified in the printer setup—for example, to a local printer or to a network printer. However, you can also send the output to a file if you choose Print to File and provide a filename. You should use this option if you want to copy a print image directly to a printer—for example, a PostScript file to a PostScript printer.

- The Resolution options apply only if your printer allows them. Some printers do not permit changes in resolution (*dots per inch*, or *dpi*), whereas others print at the highest resolution possible, regardless of the setting.

- Color printing is more often affected by the printer setup than by the WordPerfect setting. If you're having a problem printing in black and white only, try deselecting Print in Color and see if that works. If the document still prints in color, you have to change your printer's setup properties (on the Print tab) in order to print in only black and white. If you have a laser printer that prints only in black and white, the color options are not available.

- You can choose Print Text Only if you don't want to print your graphic images (for example, in a draft). WordPerfect still preserves the formatting of the text, leaving blank spaces where the graphics would normally print.

- You can also select Print Text as Graphics, if for some reason your printer doesn't print text properly. For example, some laser printers don't print white text on a black background (such as in a table heading). Choosing this option overcomes that limitation.

 If your graphics don't look good, see "Better Graphics Printing" in the Troubleshooting section at the end of this chapter.

Figure 6.7
The Details tab of the Print dialog box enables you to control output options, such as color, graphics, and paper feed.

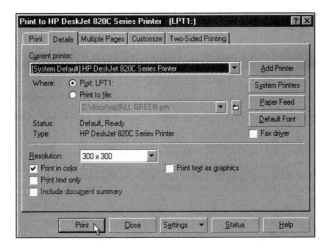

ENLARGING AND REDUCING PRINT OUTPUT

Life would be simple if all we ever had to do was print our documents to standard *portrait* orientation (8 1/2 inches wide by 11 inches tall) or standard *landscape* orientation (11 inches wide by 8 1/2 inches tall). Fortunately, WordPerfect recognizes that we sometimes need to print both larger and smaller versions of documents.

One common printing need is for posters that display more than one page. For example, if you are making a presentation and want the audience to be able to read a printed page, you could create a poster that consists of up to six pages wide and six pages tall.

To create a poster, first create the page in WordPerfect as you normally would. Then follow these steps:

1. Access the Print dialog box.
2. Click the Customize tab. WordPerfect displays options for enlarging and reducing your printed output (see Figure 6.8, which shows the P̲oster option already selected).
3. Choose P̲oster.
4. Click the drop-down menu by the P̲oster text box to display several options, including 2×2, 3×3, 4×4, 5×5, and 6×6.
5. Select the size you want, and WordPerfect displays a sample of how the page will be printed.

PART

I

CH

6

> **Note**
>
> WordPerfect does not display a preview of your document, but only a preview of the page layout. Also, the resulting printed pages are complete pages expanded or squeezed to fit the page layout you select.

Figure 6.8
You can use the Customize tab of the Print dialog box to print posters or thumbnails of your document, or to scale your document pages to different paper shapes and sizes.

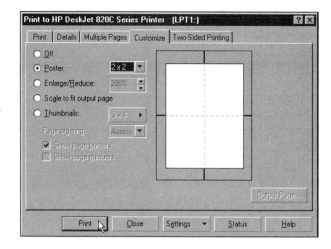

6. Click Print to print the document. After WordPerfect prints the pages, you must trim and paste the pages together to complete the poster.

You can also specify the exact size of the printed document. For example, if you want to create quarter-page printouts, choose the Enlarge/Reduce option, and then specify the percentage (for example, 50%). Again, the preview box displays the size of the output (see Figure 6.9).

Figure 6.9
The preview box shows how your reduced or enlarged pages will appear when printed.

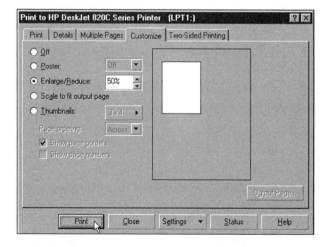

Note

Remember that 50% is half the height and *also* half the width. You probably need to experiment with size settings until you get a feel for what works best.

If you want to use a smaller (or larger) paper size, but you still want the equivalent of your 8 1/2-inch by 11-inch page on the target paper size, follow these steps:

1. While in the Customize tab of the Print dialog box, select Scale to Fit Output Page.
2. Click the Output Page button to display the Page Setup dialog box (see Figure 6.10).

Figure 6.10
You can use the Page Setup dialog box to select the paper size you'll be using for your custom print output.

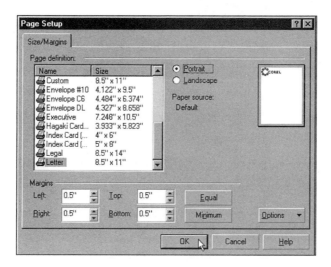

3. Choose the target paper size from the Page Definition list, and click OK.
4. Click Print, and WordPerfect formats the document to fit the target paper size.

A *thumbnail* is a small, but complete, view of a page, which gives the reader an idea of what the full-size page contains. Several thumbnails can be included on one full printed page. If you want a thumbnail summary of your document pages, choose the Thumbnails option. You then can choose the following options:

- You can determine how many thumbnails you want per page—up to eight across and eight down.
- You can select the order of the thumbnail pages—either across or down.
- You can show borders around each thumbnail, to help set them off and make them appear more like printed pages.
- You can also choose to display a page number beneath each thumbnail that corresponds to the normal printed page.
- You can select the size and shape of the output page (for example, a landscape page).

After you determine the options you want, click Print to print the page of thumbnails. Figure 6.11 shows a printed example.

PART
I

CH
6

Figure 6.11
To create a summary of your document, you can print several thumbnail pages on one page.

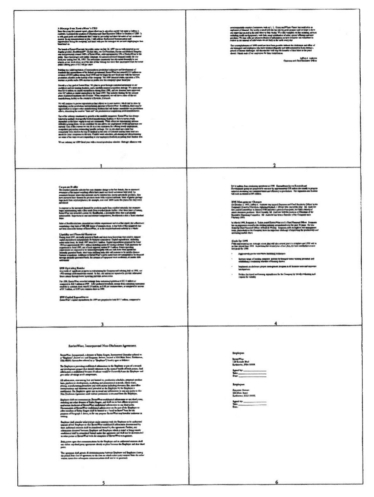

PRINTING ENVELOPES

Certain documents, such as envelopes, labels, or booklets, must be printed to nonstandard forms. When you set up the page size for these types of documents, WordPerfect automatically knows how to format the output to fit those particular page sizes.

Suppose, for example, you want to print an envelope. Figure 6.12 shows a typical envelope, ready to print.

→ For details on how to create and address an envelope, **see** Chapter 1, "Getting Comfortable with WordPerfect," **p. 11**

To verify that the page is set up properly, choose File, Page Setup. WordPerfect displays the Page Setup dialog box, shown in Figure 6.13. Note that WordPerfect has selected the Envelope page definition and expects to find it in the paper tray.

Figure 6.12
After you set up your envelope, WordPerfect knows how to print it perfectly on an envelope that's the size you select.

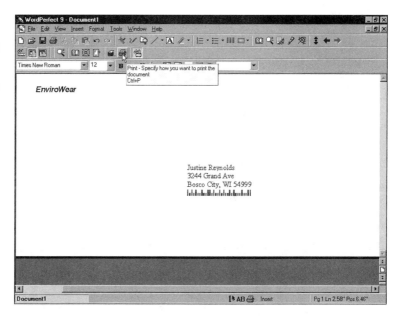

Figure 6.13
You can use the Page Setup dialog box to change the envelope (or other page) size before printing.

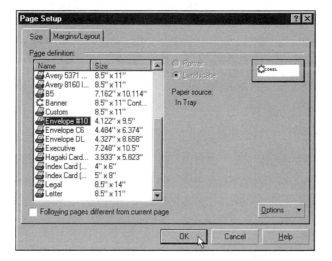

Printer Selection Determines Page Definition

WordPerfect chooses a page definition and source based on your currently selected printer. For example, if you are using a laser printer with an envelope bin, WordPerfect automatically selects that source. However, if you don't have an envelope bin, WordPerfect looks for an envelope in the manual feed tray of the laser printer.

When you print, WordPerfect automatically selects the proper form and prints the correct size to match that form. Depending on your printer, WordPerfect typically waits for you to insert the proper form if it isn't a standard 8 1/2-inch by 11-inch sheet of paper.

PRINTING LABELS

Labels are another different-sized form, but generally labels come on a standard 8 1/2-inch by 11-inch sheet, or for a dot-matrix printer, on a continuous roll.

Before you print your labels, make sure you set up the label form correctly by choosing Format, Labels. WordPerfect displays the Labels dialog box (see Figure 6.14). You then can choose from the entire list of label definitions, or just from the Laser-printed, or Tractor-fed labels. The preview box displays the label definition you choose.

Figure 6.14
WordPerfect prints pages of labels, as shown in the preview box of the Labels dialog box.

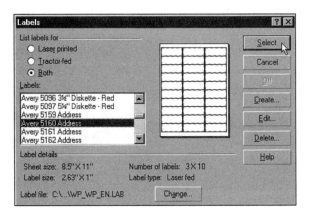

 If the label definition is correct, you simply access the Print dialog box and choose Print. If you're printing to a laser printer, WordPerfect prints an entire page of labels (for example, 30 labels on a 3-column by 10-row page of labels).

WordPerfect defines each label as a separate page. Thus, if you specify that you want to print pages 1–15, only the first 15 labels print, leaving blank the last 15 labels on a 30-label page.

Tip #76 from
Laura and Read

If you're using an inkjet printer, you can reuse a partially used sheet of labels by making sure that the first label you want to print corresponds to the first available label on the sheet. For example, to begin with label 16, access the Print dialog box, and choose Print Pages, beginning at 16.

Caution

You might be tempted to send a partially used sheet of labels through your laser printer again to print on the unused labels. However, the heat process from printing the sheet the first time can loosen unused labels, causing them to come off in the printer the second time around. Cleaning stuck labels from inside a laser printer is both time-consuming and costly.

PRINTING BOOKLETS

You can divide pages to print in a booklet style (with pages folded in half). Typically you use landscape orientation so that each half page ends up 8 1/2 inches tall by 5 1/2 inches wide. Then, using WordPerfect's booklet feature, you can print the pages so that they are numbered and ordered automatically.

Note

Booklets are like labels in that more than one page is printed on each sheet of paper. However, you can only print booklets that contain two booklet pages per sheet of paper.

To set up booklet printing, follow these steps:

1. Choose File, Page Setup to access the Page Setup dialog box (see Figure 6.15, shown with Landscape selected.)

Figure 6.15
You choose Landscape in the Page Setup dialog box when setting up a typical booklet page.

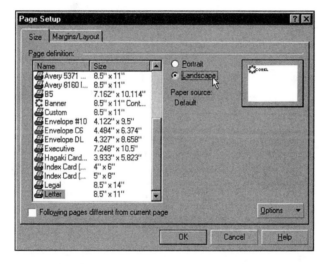

2. Choose the target paper size, typically Letter size (8 1/2 inches by 11 inches).
3. Choose the paper orientation, typically Landscape.
4. Click the Margins/Layout tab (see Figure 6.16)
5. Set your margins as desired. 1-inch margins in booklets are too large, so choose something smaller, such as 1/2 inch.
6. Click the Divide Page button and choose 2×1 (commonly used with landscape pages), or 1×2 (often used with portrait pages). Note how the pages look in the preview box and make any adjustments you want.
7. Choose OK to return to your document.
8. Choose File, Print Preview to make sure the pages are laid out the way you want them.

PART

I

CH

6

Figure 6.16
When setting up a booklet, reduce the margins and use Divide Page to specify what type of booklet you want.

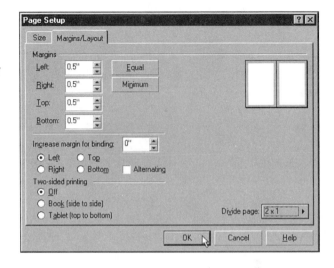

Now you can print your pages and also make sure they appear in the proper order so you don't have to cut and paste to prepare them for the printer.

To illustrate, normally if you print a four-page booklet, WordPerfect prints page 1 on the left side of the first sheet and page 2 on the right side of the first sheet (see Figure 6.17).

Figure 6.17
Normally WordPerfect prints divided pages sequentially, which is proper for some folded brochures, but which doesn't work for folded booklets.

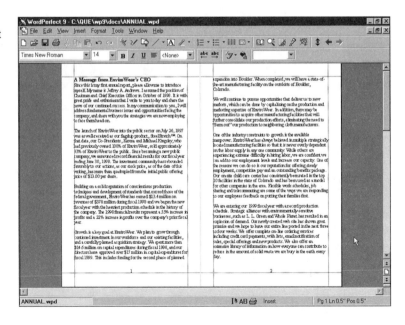

Instead, you want page 4 on the left side of the first sheet, and page 1 on the right side (see Figure 6.18). On the back side, you want page 2 on the left side and page 3 on the right side.

Figure 6.18
WordPerfect's booklet printing option organizes divided pages properly so that they appear in proper sequence for a folded booklet.

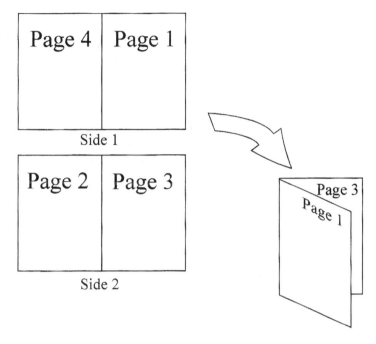

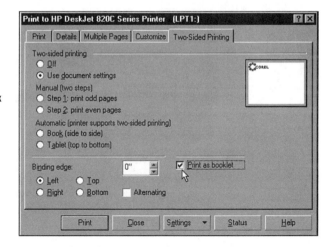 To print booklet pages in the proper order, first access the Print dialog box. Then click the Two-Sided Printing tab (see Figure 6.19), and select the Print as Booklet check box. WordPerfect automatically arranges all the pages correctly and begins to print all of one side of each sheet of paper. WordPerfect then prompts you to reinsert the pages to print the second side of the paper.

Figure 6.19
The Two-Sided Printing tab of the Print dialog box enables you to print booklets as well as carry out other duplex printing procedures.

PART

I

CH

6

Tip #77 from	If you plan to take the printed output to a printer or duplicating service, you do not need to
Laura and Read	reinsert the pages. Simply click OK when prompted to reinsert a page, and WordPerfect prints the second sides on new sheets of paper. It's easier for the printer to duplicate single-sided sheets than sheets that have been printed on both sides.

Tip #78 from	The first time you print double-sided booklets, you might have to experiment with your
Laura and Read	printer so that the reinserted sheets print properly. Start with a short (for example, four-page) test booklet to try it out before printing a longer booklet.

USING CUSTOM PRINT SETTINGS

Sometimes you use a customized printing procedure over and over again. WordPerfect lets you save customized settings so that you can recall them quickly when needed.

Suppose, for example, you have a standard report that requires you to print four copies of the last page to send to potential investors. Follow these steps to save and use a custom print setup:

1. From the Print dialog box, make the various setup changes you need to print exactly what you want (for example, change the Number of Copies, use Multiple Pages to select the exact pages you want, and choose Group Copies to group the output.)

2. Without printing yet, click Settings and choose Named Settings. WordPerfect displays the Named Settings dialog box (see Figure 6.20).

Figure 6.20
You can use the Named Settings dialog box to save customized print settings for future use.

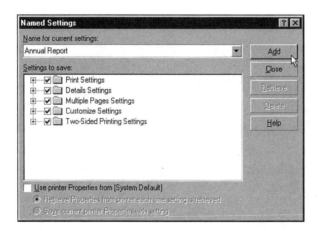

3. Change the Name for Current Settings (for example, Annual Report).

4. You can ignore the Settings to Save list because you have already made the changes you want.

5. Uncheck the <u>U</u>se Printer Properties from [System Default] box at the lower-left corner of the dialog box.

6. Click the A<u>d</u>d button, which automatically replaces the Replace button when you change the setting name.

7. Click <u>C</u>lose.

Tip #79 from
Laura and Read

To change the default print settings for every time you print, modify the options in the Print dialog box, click S<u>e</u>ttings, choose <u>A</u>pplication Default, and then choose Repl<u>a</u>ce. If you later decide you want the original print settings, simply click S<u>e</u>ttings, choose <u>A</u>pplication Default, and then choose R<u>e</u>store.

Now whenever you want to print using your named setting, simply access the Print dialog box and click the S<u>e</u>ttings button. At the bottom of the button are listed any named settings you created. Click the one you want (for example, Annual Report), and WordPerfect modifies the Print dialog box setup. Click Print to print using the new settings.

Tip #80 from
Laura and Read

When you make changes to the Print dialog box setup, WordPerfect remembers those settings for that document until you close the document. If you want to quickly restore the default print settings without closing the document, access the Print dialog box, click S<u>e</u>ttings, choose <u>A</u>pplication Default, and then choose R<u>e</u>trieve.

FAXING DOCUMENTS

Printing to paper through a local or network printer is only one method of getting your document out to the world. WordPerfect can also fax your document directly from within WordPerfect to anywhere in the world, quickly and painlessly. However, first the following conditions must be met:

- A fax board must be installed in your computer (or connected to your network). Most modems come with faxing capabilities built in, so if you have a modem, you probably already have the hardware needed to fax. Check your modem manual for more information.

- A Windows-based fax program must be installed on your computer. When fax software is installed, a fax printer appears in your list of available printers. You can check this by clicking the Windows Start button and choosing <u>S</u>ettings, <u>P</u>rinters (see Figure 6.21), or by accessing the WordPerfect Print dialog box and clicking the drop-down list under C<u>u</u>rrent Printer. Many modems also ship with fax software. Check your modem documentation for more information.

- The person to whom you send the fax must have a fax machine or a computer-based fax program and a fax/modem to receive the fax.

Figure 6.21
If you have a fax printer installed in your Windows system, that printer appears along with other printers in the Windows Printers dialog box.

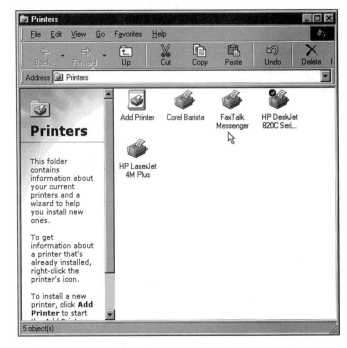

Assuming that the listed conditions are met and the hardware and software are properly set up, follow these steps to fax a document from WordPerfect:

1. With the document that you want to fax in the active window, choose File, Print, or press F5.

2. Choose the fax printer from the drop-down list under Current Printer.

3. Make other changes to the print setup as desired (for example, which pages to print).

4. Click Fax to fax the document. WordPerfect then prepares the document for faxing and hands it off to your fax software for faxing.

Tip #81 from
Laura and Read

You can also quickly access the Fax (Print) screen by choosing File, Send To, Fax. WordPerfect automatically chooses the fax printer and displays the Fax (Print) screen.

---

5. Your fax software should display a dialog box that enables you to designate where to send the fax. If the dialog box doesn't appear, click the fax software icon on the Windows taskbar or press Alt+Tab to toggle to the fax software.

6. Fill in the destination information in the fax program's dialog box, and then send the fax. Figure 6.22 shows a typical setup screen for the Fax Talk Messenger fax program.

After the document is scheduled for sending, you can use the fax program's software to monitor the fax status, check the fax logs, or even cancel the fax if it hasn't yet been sent.

Figure 6.22
Fax software "prints" your document to your fax/modem and sends it to the fax/phone you specify. Your Fax dialog box may be different than shown, but it should include most of the same information.

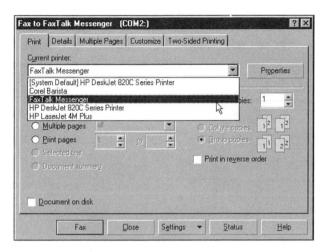

If the recipient of your fax complains about page breaks appearing in the wrong places, see "Fax Has Bad Page Breaks" in the Troubleshooting section at the end of the chapter.

SENDING DOCUMENTS VIA EMAIL

If you use an email program, you can send all or part of your document in the message body, or send the entire document as an attachment to a message.

To determine whether your mail program has been installed and is integrated with WordPerfect, choose File, Send To. Supported mail programs are listed on the menu, as is a Mail option (see Figure 6.23).

If you want to send the entire file as an email attachment, simply choose Send To GroupWise Recipient (or whatever email program you're using). Windows switches you to your mail program, which then adds the document as an attachment and enables you to send a message with the attachment (see Figure 6.24).

If your email program does not appear on the WordPerfect File, Send To menu, you still have these options:

- You can enable your mail program so that WordPerfect recognizes it. You can do this on the Windows Control Panel. Find the Mail icon, open it, and follow the procedures listed there for adding a mail program.

- You can save your document, and then open your mail program separately and add the document as an attachment.

- You can copy text from a WordPerfect document and paste it in the body of the mail message. Using this method removes most, if not all, of WordPerfect's formatting. However, it also enables you to copy just part of your document into the message.

PART
I
CH
6

Figure 6.23
If your mail program is installed and recognized by WordPerfect, it appears on the File, Send To menu.

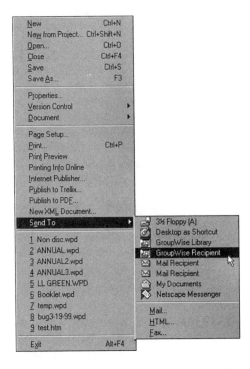

Figure 6.24
If you send your document as an attachment, the receiver can then download the attachment and open it in WordPerfect to preserve all of the document's formatting.

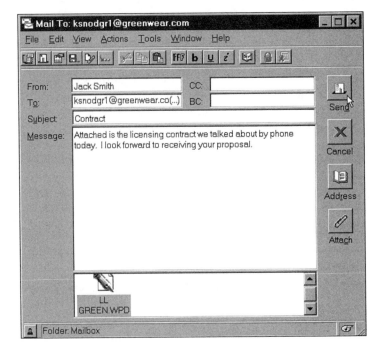

Tip #82 from
Laura and Read

Don't forget that you can also copy text from WordPerfect and paste it into your mail message, even if your mail program isn't integrated with WordPerfect.

TROUBLESHOOTING

WHEN NOTHING HAPPENS

I chose Print from the Print dialog box, but nothing happened. What am I doing wrong?

First, make sure your printer is on and online. Usually, if a printer is not available or is offline, you get an error message telling you so. Next, make sure you have selected the proper printer. If you're connected to a network, selecting the wrong printer may send your document to someone else's printer.

BETTER GRAPHICS PRINTING

When I print a document with graphics, the graphic images don't look good even though I'm using a laser printer.

The problem may be that you haven't selected the best print resolution. Make sure you choose <u>P</u>rint, click the Details tab, and set <u>R</u>esolution to its highest setting (for example, 600×600). Text usually isn't affected by a lower resolution setting.

FAX HAS BAD PAGE BREAKS

I sent a fax from WordPerfect, but the person I sent it to says page breaks are in the wrong places.

Whenever you change printers, small formatting changes often take place, primarily because the fonts and their horizontal and vertical spacing are slightly different for each printer. Before printing, or in this case faxing, go back through your document and check the layout. When you've verified that it's okay, go ahead and send the document to the fax (printer).

PROJECT

Printing is a pretty mundane task…except when it comes to preparing booklets. Suppose you have a 13-page policy handbook that you want to prepare in a 5 1/2-inch-wide by 8 1/2-inch-high format. You get the whole thing ready, and it looks great in Print Preview, but when you print it and fold it, the pages are all in the wrong places!

WordPerfect makes it easy to set up and print booklet-type pages in the correct order. If you've ever had to cut and paste pages (with scissors and glue!) to arrange them in the right order, you'll appreciate this huge time-saving feature.

To create and print a booklet, follow these easy steps:

1. Prepare the content of the booklet as you normally do and save it (as you should at every step in these procedures).

2. Choose Format, Page, Page Setup to display the Page Setup dialog box.

3. On the Size tab, choose Landscape, using the Letter (8 1/2 inches by 11 inches) Page Definition.

4. On the Margins/Layout tab, set all margins equally to .5 inch, and choose 2×1 from the Divide Page palette. Figure 6.25 shows the Margins/Layout tab with these options.

Figure 6.25
You can use the Margins/Layout tab of the Page Setup dialog box to set options for dividing landscape pages with narrow margins in preparation for booklet printing.

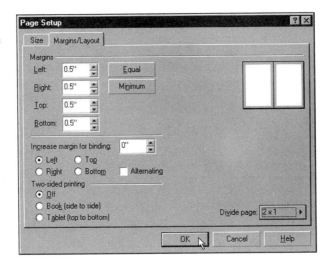

5. Click OK to return to the document. WordPerfect displays half pages, side by side, on the landscape page.

6. Add title pages, headers, footers, page numbering, and other elements that make your document look like a handbook (see Figure 6.26).

7. Consider whether there should be blank pages. For example, the first page might be a title page, but the inside cover would be blank, followed by the inside title page or table of contents. Insert blank pages (by pressing Ctrl+Enter or selecting Insert, New Page) at the appropriate locations.

8. Use the two-page view of Print Preview to verify that the pages are laid out correctly (see Figure 6.27).

9. Choose File, Print and click the Two-Sided Printing tab. Choose Print as Booklet and click Print.

10. WordPerfect assumes that you want to print on both sides of the paper. If this is the case, insert the pages again when prompted by WordPerfect and click OK. Otherwise, just click OK at each prompt and print the second side on a separate sheet of paper.

Figure 6.26
Format each half page as you would a full-size page, including headers, footers, page numbering, and so on.

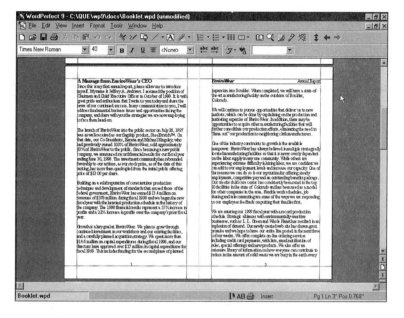

Figure 6.27
The two-page view of Print Preview helps you see how your booklet pages are laid out.

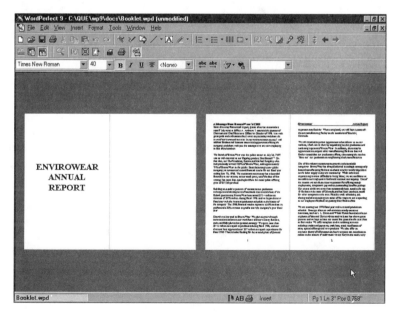

WordPerfect calculates the number of pages and organizes them so that each appears in the proper place when the pages are folded. No muss, no fuss!

PART

II

FORMATTING DOCUMENTS

CHAPTER 7

FORMATTING LINES AND PARAGRAPHS

In this chapter

CENTERED AND FLUSH RIGHT TEXT

One of the most common formatting tasks is centering a line. Flush right is a little less common, but it still has an important place, especially in legal documents. In Chapter 3, "Basic Formatting," you learned how to use *justification (page 68)* to make lines of text centered and flush right. In this chapter, you'll learn how to use the Center and Flush Right features to make lines of text centered and flush right.

What's the difference, you ask? When you change the justification to Center, every line you create from then on is centered, until you change the justification to something else. This is fine for title pages, where you have multiple lines that you want centered, but it's not the most efficient option for single lines. In this situation, the Center feature is the best choice.

- To center a line of text, press Shift+F7, and then type the text. If you've already typed the text, click at the beginning of the line, and then press Shift+F7.

- To make a line of text *flush right*, or align it against the right margin, press Alt+F7, and then type the text. If you've already typed the text, click at the beginning of the line, and then press Alt+F7.

If you've accidentally pressed Shift+F7 or Alt+F7 in the middle of a line, see "My Title Is Split in Half" in the Troubleshooting section at the end of the chapter.

You can also find Center and Flush Right commands in the menus. Choose Format, Line (see Figure 7.1). Note the keyboard shortcuts listed next to the commands.

Figure 7.1
The Line menu has commands to make lines of text centered and flush right.

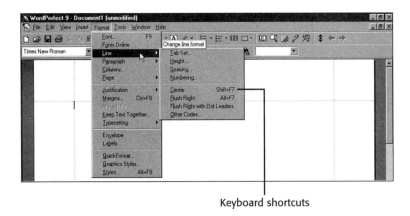

Keyboard shortcuts

Tip #83 from
Laura and Read

Here's something you can't do with justification—you can have centered text and flush right text on the same line. How? Press Shift+F7, type the centered text, press Alt+F7, and type the flush right text.

If you press Shift+F7 twice, you'll get *dot leaders* (periods with spaces between them) leading to the text. Likewise, if you press Alt+F7 twice, you'll get dot leaders across the line to the text. Change your mind? Press Shift+F7 or Alt+F7 again to remove the dot leaders.

SETTING TABS

Tabs—you either love 'em or you never use 'em. Although they were once the only way to create columns, tabs have fallen out of favor now that we have the Tables feature.

Still, tabs have their place, and in some cases, they are easier to set up than a table. For example, if you want to create three columns, one of which is a dollar amount, it's probably faster to turn on the ruler and set two regular tabs and one decimal-align tab than it is to create a table, format the dollar amount column to decimal alignment, and remove the table lines.

There are four types of tabs:

- Left Align—Text flows from the right side of the tab stop. This is the "normal" tab.
- Center—Text is centered over the tab stop.
- Right Align—Text flows from the left side of the tab stop.
- Decimal Align—The numbers are aligned on their decimal points, which rest on the tab stop. You can change the alignment character to something other than a period (decimal point).

Note

You can add dot leaders to each of the four tab types. Dot leaders are useful when the space between columns is wide because they help the reader's eye travel across the gap. They are especially useful when preparing a table of contents.

If you don't already have the ruler displayed, turn it on by choosing View, Ruler. The default tab settings (every 1/2 inch) are shown with triangles (see Figure 7.2). The gray area identifies the margin area; the white area is the text area.

Figure 7.2
Using the Ruler, you can set all types of tabs with just a few mouse clicks.

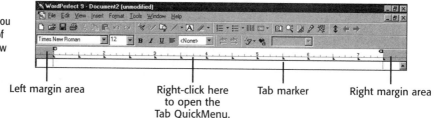

Left margin area   Right-click here to open the Tab QuickMenu.   Tab marker   Right margin area

In most cases, you want to clear the default tabs so that you can create specific tabs. Right-click in the tab area of the ruler (refer to Figure 7.2) or right-click any tab marker to open the *Tab QuickMenu* (see Figure 7.3). Choose Clear <u>A</u>ll Tabs to delete the default tabs.

Figure 7.3
Using the Tab QuickMenu, you can clear the default tabs, set specific types of tabs, and then return to the default settings.

Margin icon

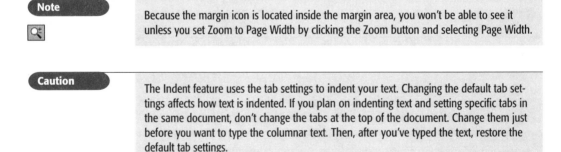

Tab QuickMenu

Setting new tabs is easy—just click on the ruler where you want the tab stop (this inserts the default tab, which is a left-aligned tab). To remove a tab, drag it off the ruler. When you set a tab (or modify the default tab settings in any way), a margin icon appears in the left margin area (refer to Figure 7.3). Click the margin icon to display a tab bar, which shows the tab settings for the current paragraph. Click anywhere in the document to clear the tab bar.

Note

Because the margin icon is located inside the margin area, you won't be able to see it unless you set Zoom to Page Width by clicking the Zoom button and selecting Page Width.

Caution

The Indent feature uses the tab settings to indent your text. Changing the default tab settings affects how text is indented. If you plan on indenting text and setting specific tabs in the same document, don't change the tabs at the top of the document. Change them just before you want to type the columnar text. Then, after you've typed the text, restore the default tab settings.

To move a tab, click and drag the tab marker (on the ruler or on the tab bar). When you do, a bubble appears, telling you where the tab will fall when you release the mouse button, and a *guideline (page 14)* appears in the text so that you can see the effect on existing text (see Figure 7.4). The mouse pointer changes, too, whenever you point to a tab marker—it changes to a *move pointer* (that is, a pointer with a box and a box guideline).

To change the tab type, right-click the tab and choose a tab type from the QuickMenu. Then click on the ruler to set the tab. After you've changed the tab type, it stays selected until you select another tab type. So if you change the tab type to Decimal, every time you click on the ruler, you'll set a decimal tab.

This bubble identifies the tab's position on the page.

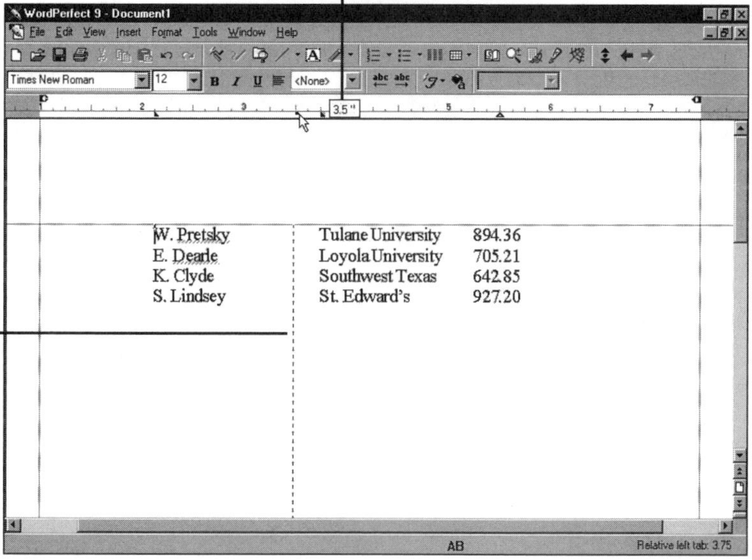

Figure 7.4
If you've already typed the text, you can still move the tabs around. The guideline helps you see where the text will be as you click and drag the tab.

Tab guideline —

When you're working with tabs, it's extremely important to position the insertion point first. Be sure that you're creating new tab settings exactly where you want them, so they don't reformat the wrong text. Furthermore, when you edit your tab settings to adjust the spacing between columns, be sure you click at the beginning of the text. Otherwise, some of the text is formatted with the original tab settings and the rest of the text is formatted with the new tab settings. It's not a pretty sight, believe me. Remember your old friend Undo?

After you've typed the text, you can go back and edit the tab settings. You can click and drag them on the ruler (or the tab bar) to adjust the spacing between columns. You can even switch to a different tab type if necessary. Just be sure you click at the top of the text that you've formatted with tabs before you start making changes.

When you're ready to return to default tab settings (so you can use regular tabs and indent later on in the document), right-click in the document where you want to make the change and choose Default Tab Settings.

It wouldn't be fair not to mention the Tab Set dialog box (see Figure 7.5). Everything you can do from the ruler and more is available in this dialog box. Right-click the ruler, and then choose Tab Set (refer to Figure 7.3). Or choose Format, Line, Tab Set to display the Tab Set dialog box.

PART

II

CH

7

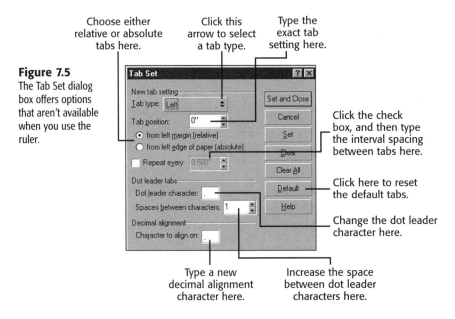

Choose either relative or absolute tabs here.

Click this arrow to select a tab type.

Type the exact tab setting here.

Figure 7.5
The Tab Set dialog box offers options that aren't available when you use the ruler.

Click the check box, and then type the interval spacing between tabs here.

Click here to reset the default tabs.

Change the dot leader character here.

Type a new decimal alignment character here.

Increase the space between dot leader characters here.

⚠ *If you press Tab, only to have WordPerfect indent the whole paragraph, see "Pressing Tab Indents the Paragraph" in the Troubleshooting section at the end of this chapter.*

INDENTING TEXT

Indentation is often used for quotations, to emphasize text, or to place a paragraph in a subordinate position beneath another paragraph. When you create a bulleted or numbered list, WordPerfect inserts an Indent command after the bullet or number so that the text you type isn't aligned under the bullet or number, but rather under the first line of text.

→ For more information on creating outlines and bulleted/numbered lists, **see** Chapter 11, "Organizing Information with Lists and Outlines," **p. 289**

There are four ways to indent text:

- Indent moves every line on the left within a paragraph to the next tab setting. By default, this moves the text over 1/2 inch every time you choose Indent.

- Double Indent moves every line in a paragraph in from the left and right sides, to the next tab setting. By default, this indents the text by 1/2 inch on the left and 1/2 inch on the right.

- Hanging Indent leaves the first line at the left margin—all the other lines are indented (on the left side) by 1/2 inch. Hanging Indent has the opposite effect of Indent.

Caution

Here's the annoying thing about the Hanging Indent option. If you've cleared all the tabs, the hanging indent begins the first line at the left *edge* of the paper, which may or may not work, depending on your printer. You'll need two tabs: one where the first line should begin and one where the subsequent lines should begin. For example, you might set a tab at 1/2 inch and one at 1 inch for a hanging indent that formats the first line 1/2 inch into the left margin and the subsequent lines at the left margin.

■ Back Tab is like Margin Release on a typewriter (uh oh, I just dated myself). It temporarily releases the left margin so the first line of a paragraph starts in the left margin area; the other lines align at the left margin.

To indent a new paragraph, press F7, and then type the text. Press Shift+Ctrl+F7 for a double indent and Ctrl+F7 for a hanging indent. As usual, if you've already typed the text, click in the paragraph before applying an indent style.

You can choose Indent, Double Indent, and Hanging Indent, as well as Back Tab, from the Paragraph menu (see Figure 7.6). Choose Format, Paragraph to open the Paragraph menu.

Figure 7.6
One of the Indent commands on the Paragraph menu, Back Tab, doesn't have a shortcut key assigned to it.

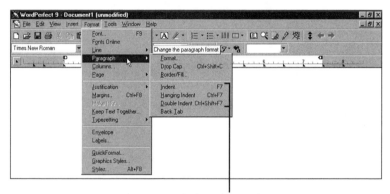

Indent shortcut keys

Tip #85 from
Laura and Read

WordPerfect can display symbols for spaces, hard returns, tabs, indent, center, and flush right, as well as a few others. If you don't want to see these symbols, choose View, Show ¶, or press Ctrl+Shift+F3.

Tip #86 from
Laura and Read

Because the QuickIndent feature is turned on by default, you can quickly indent paragraphs with the Tab key. When you press Tab at the beginning of the first and second lines, QuickIndent converts those tabs into an indent. You can also quickly create a hanging indent by pressing Tab at the beginning of any line *except* the first line in a paragraph. If you find this behavior annoying, you can turn off QuickIndent by choosing Tools, QuickCorrect. Click the Format-As-You-Go tab, and then remove the check mark next to QuickIndent in the list of Format-As-You-Go choices.

→ For more information on enabling and disabling the QuickIndent feature, **see** "Customizing Format-As-You-Go," **p. 136**

PART
II

CH
7

If you want the first line of every paragraph to be indented automatically (rather than pressing Tab each time), use the First Line Indent option. Choose Format, Paragraph, Format to open the Paragraph Format dialog box (see Figure 7.7). Type the amount that you want the first line indented in the First Line Indent text box. (A tab indents the first line by 1/2 inch.)

Click OK. All new paragraphs from this point on will have the first line indented. Set the value back to 0 (zero) inches for no indent.

Figure 7.7
Type the value for the first-line indent in increments of inches. For example, 1/4 inch would be .25".

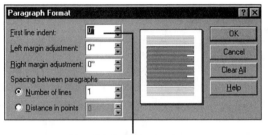

Type the indent value here.

⚠ *Are you having a hard time sorting paragraphs that have been indented with tabs, indents, or hanging indents? See "Sorting Indented Paragraphs" in the Troubleshooting section at the end of this chapter.*

ADJUSTING THE SPACING BETWEEN LINES AND PARAGRAPHS

As you may recall from Chapter 1, "Getting Comfortable with WordPerfect," the default line spacing setting is single-spacing. Some types of documents, such as grants and formal reports, require a certain line-spacing setting. If I'm planning on printing out a document for someone else to review, I'll change to double- or triple-spacing, so that person has room to write comments. After I've incorporated that person's changes, I'll switch the document back to single-spacing.

To change line spacing, click where you want the change to take effect (or select the text you want to change). Choose Format, Line, Spacing to open the Line Spacing dialog box (see Figure 7.8). Either type a value or click the spinner arrows to increase or decrease the value in the Spacing text box.

Figure 7.8
You can specify the number of lines that you want between each line by typing the value or clicking the spinner arrows. Type 1 for single-spacing, 1.5 for one-and-a-half spacing, 2 for double-spacing, and so on.

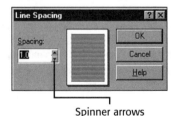

Spinner arrows

The new line-spacing setting takes effect at the beginning of the paragraph where the insertion point is resting, and it remains in effect through the rest of the document, or until you change the line spacing again. For example, in a double-spaced document, it's common to switch to single-spacing for lists or quotations.

Note
> The actual amount of space between lines depends on the current font and font size. WordPerfect automatically adjusts the line height to accommodate the tallest character, so if you switch to a line-spacing setting of 1.5 lines, you'll get space equal to one-and-a-half times the height of a line.

The accepted standard is to leave a blank line between paragraphs, so you just press Enter twice after you type a paragraph, right? That's not a problem—until you decide to change the line spacing to double. Now you've got the space of two lines between each paragraph. Furthermore, these extra lines leave space at the top of a page.

Rather than insert extra blank lines, you can adjust the spacing between paragraphs. This way, you always get the same amount of space between each paragraph (no matter what you do to the line spacing), and you don't have extra blank lines floating around.

To change the paragraph spacing, click where you want the change to take effect. Choose Format, Paragraph, Format to open the Paragraph Format dialog box (refer to Figure 7.7). In the Spacing Between Paragraphs section, you can enter the number of lines or the number of points that you want between each paragraph. Either type the value or click the spinner arrows to increase or decrease the value.

Note
> You may be familiar with the term *points* as it relates to font sizes. An inch is 72 points. You probably won't ever use points as a unit of measure, but, just in case you want to, it's there.

KEEPING TEXT TOGETHER

As you type along, you never have to worry about running out of room—WordPerfect creates a new page for you as soon as you reach the bottom of the current page. It's so transparent that you don't even stop to think about it—until you preview the document and realize that you've got headings at the bottom of one page and the corresponding paragraph at the top of the next page. Some other examples of page-formatting problems are a page break in the middle of a list of numbered paragraphs or a figure separated from the explanatory text.

You can prevent these situations by marking the text that should stay together when a page break is encountered. You can use three features to do this: Widow/Orphan Protection, Block Protect, and Conditional End of Page. Choose Format, Keep Text Together to display the Keep Text Together dialog box (see Figure 7.9).

PART
II

CH
7

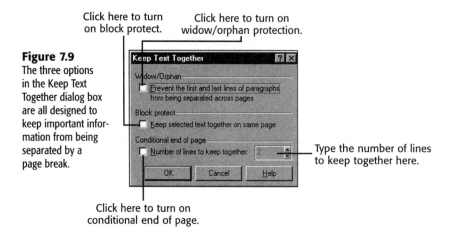

Click here to turn on block protect.

Click here to turn on widow/orphan protection.

Figure 7.9
The three options in the Keep Text Together dialog box are all designed to keep important information from being separated by a page break.

Type the number of lines to keep together here.

Click here to turn on conditional end of page.

ENABLING WIDOW/ORPHAN PROTECTION

Widow/orphan protection is designed to protect against single lines of a paragraph getting left behind at the bottom of a page or getting pushed to the top of the next page. This improves the document's appearance and makes it easier to read.

The first line of a paragraph that gets left behind at the bottom of a page is called an *orphan*. A *widow* is the last line of a paragraph that gets pushed to the top of a page.

Position the insertion point where you want widow/orphan protection to start (usually at the top of the document). In the Keep Text Together dialog box, select Prevent the First and Last Lines of Paragraphs from Being Separated Across Pages.

USING BLOCK PROTECT

You use the block protect feature when you want to keep a section of text together on the same page. As you edit the document, and the block moves near a page break, WordPerfect decides whether the block will fit on the current page. If it doesn't fit, the entire block gets moved to the top of the next page. Block protect works well for keeping figures or tables and explanatory text together. You can also use it to protect numbered paragraphs and other lists.

To turn on block protect, select the text (and figures or tables) that you want to keep together. In the Keep Text Together dialog box, choose Keep Selected Text Together on Same Page.

Caution

Block-protecting large sections of text can result in big chunks of white space in the middle of a document.

SETTING A CONDITIONAL END OF PAGE

The Conditional End of Page feature keeps a certain number of lines together when a page break is encountered. You might use Conditional End of Page at the beginning of a heading so you can specify how many lines of the following paragraph you want to keep with the heading.

To turn on Conditional End of Page, position the insertion point at the beginning of the heading. In the Keep Text Together dialog box, choose <u>N</u>umber of Lines to Keep Together. In the text box type the number of lines that you want to keep together. Count the heading line as one of the lines, and if there is a blank line between the heading and the paragraph, count that, too.

 If you're having trouble getting conditional end of page to work for you, see "Conditional End of Page Isn't Working Right" in the Troubleshooting section at the end of this chapter.

INSERTING LINE NUMBERS

Line numbers are used in many documents, such as legal documents, to give an easy point of reference. For example, you can tell your client to look for a change that was made on "page 13, line 5." Line numbers can also make it easier to proofread and revise many different types of documents.

To turn on line numbering, click in the line (or paragraph) where you want the line numbers to start. Choose Fo<u>r</u>mat, <u>L</u>ine, <u>N</u>umbering to open the Line Numbering dialog box (see Figure 7.10). Choose Turn Line Numbering <u>O</u>n.

Click here to turn
on line numbering.

Figure 7.10
In the Line
Numbering dialog
box, you can turn on
line numbers, select a
line number style,
and specify the posi-
tion and font for
the numbers.

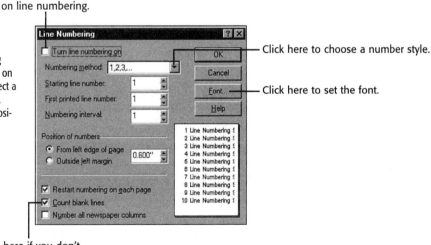

Click here to choose a number style.

Click here to set the font.

Click here if you don't
want to count blank lines.

After you've turned on line numbers, choose from the following options:

- Click the Numbering <u>M</u>ethod drop-down list arrow and choose a style for the numbers.
- Specify the starting line number, the first printed line number, and the numbering interval. (Regardless of the style that you use for the line numbers, you still set these line number options numerically.)

■ Change the location of the line numbers by setting the distance between the line numbers and the left edge of the page or the distance between the line numbers and the left margin.

As you make changes to the line numbering options, the sample document is updated to reflect the changes.

■ Deselect Restart Numbering on <u>E</u>ach Page if you want the lines numbered consecutively through the end of the document.

■ Deselect <u>C</u>ount Blank Lines if you don't want to skip blank lines in the line number count.

■ Select N<u>u</u>mber All Newspaper Columns if you want to use line numbers in newspaper columns.

■ Click <u>F</u>ont to open the Line Numbering Font dialog box (see Figure 7.11). Select the font and the font size. If desired, select a color, shading, or appearance *attribute (page 66)* to visually separate the numbers from the body text.

Figure 7.11
You can select the font, font size, color, shading, and text attributes that you want to assign to the line numbers in the Line Numbering Font dialog box.

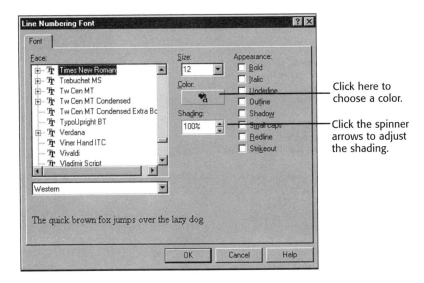

WordPerfect has a *macro (page 688)* that sets up a blank legal pleading paper, with line numbers and a vertical double line that separates the line numbers from the document text (see Figure 7.12). To run the macro, choose <u>T</u>ools, <u>M</u>acro, <u>P</u>lay, and then double-click pleading.wcm. You can also click the Pleading button on the Legal toolbar to run this macro.

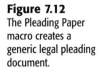

Figure 7.12
The Pleading Paper macro creates a generic legal pleading document.

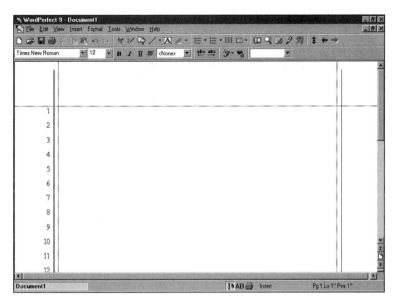

ADDING BORDERS, DROP SHADOWS, AND FILLS

Strictly speaking, a paragraph is any amount of text followed by a hard return, so a date on a line by itself is treated as a paragraph. You can create a box around any paragraph or paragraphs by using the Border feature. A well-chosen border creates a frame around the paragraph, emphasizing it and setting it apart from the rest of the text. You can create a drop shadow behind the box, and you can add a background (fill) to the area inside the border.

Choosing Borders Elsewhere

You can add borders around a page, a column, or a graphics box. The dialog boxes are virtually identical to the Paragraph Border/Fill dialog box, so rather than repeat this discussion in those respective sections, I'll refer you to this section for information on choosing the border, the drop shadow, and the fill.

ADDING BORDERS

There are 32 different predefined borders to choose from. Because you can edit these borders to change the color and the line style, there are endless possibilities.

Follow these steps to add a border around a paragraph or selected paragraphs:

1. Click in the paragraph, or select the paragraphs, around which you want to create a border.

2. Choose Format, Paragraph, Border/Fill. The Paragraph Border/Fill dialog box opens (see Figure 7.13).

PART

II

CH

7

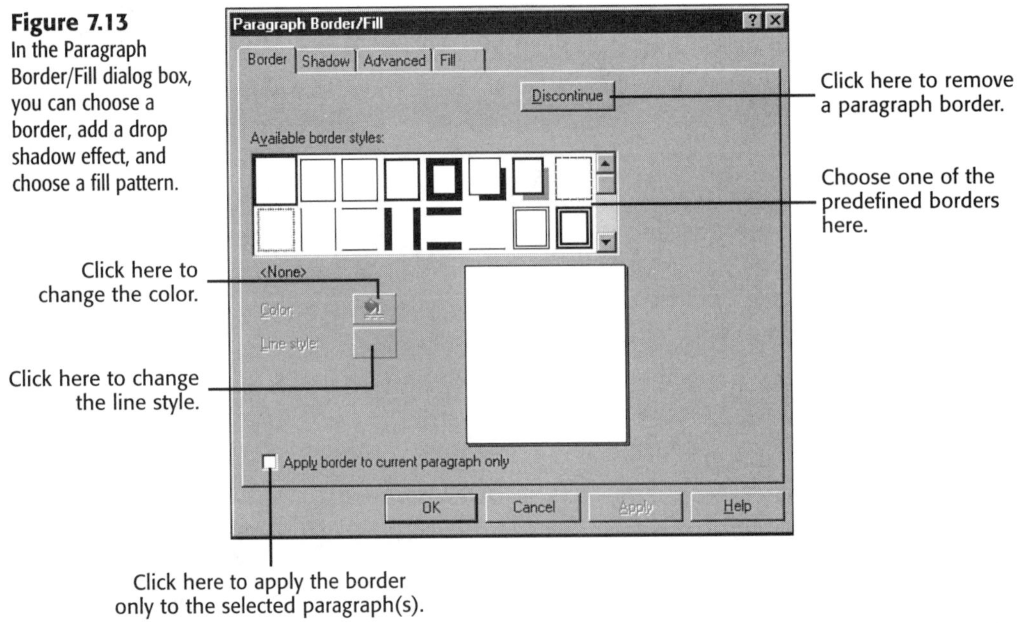

Figure 7.13
In the Paragraph Border/Fill dialog box, you can choose a border, add a drop shadow effect, and choose a fill pattern.

Click here to remove a paragraph border.

Choose one of the predefined borders here.

Click here to change the color.

Click here to change the line style.

Click here to apply the border only to the selected paragraph(s).

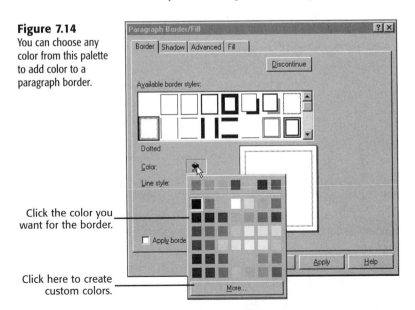

3. Click a border in the A̲vailable Border Styles list box. Scroll down through the list to see all the predefined borders. After you've chosen a border, you have the following options:

- To change the color of the border, click the C̲olor button and then click a color on the palette (see Figure 7.14).
- To change the line style used in the border, click the L̲ine Style button and then click a line style from the palette (see Figure 7.15).

Figure 7.14
You can choose any color from this palette to add color to a paragraph border.

Click the color you want for the border.

Click here to create custom colors.

Figure 7.15
You can choose a line style from this palette for the paragraph border.

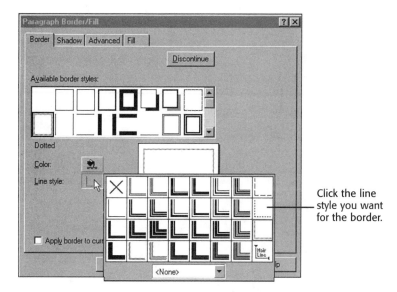

Click the line style you want for the border.

4. Select Apply Border to Current Paragraph Only if you only want the border applied to the current paragraph or selected paragraphs. Otherwise, the border starts with the current paragraph(s) and stops at the end of the document.

To remove a paragraph border, click in the paragraph, choose Format, Paragraph, Border/Fill to open the Paragraph Border/Fill dialog box, and click the Discontinue button.

Tip #87 from
Laura and Read

If you want to add graphic borders from other programs to the list of available border styles in the Border/Fill dialog box, you must convert the file to WPG format. Open the file in Presentations, and then save it in the `\Program Files\Corel\Wordperfect Office 2000\graphics\borders` folder in WPG format.

Tip #88 from
Laura and Read

I found help topics that talk about the ability to round corners on both paragraph and page borders. Unfortunately, the two commands to round paragraph borders aren't present in the Advanced tab of the Paragraph Border/Fill dialog box. Don't give up hope yet—I have a feeling this eventually will be implemented, so look for it in the next service release. When it does appear, refer to the steps included in the "Adding Borders Around Pages" section of Chapter 8, "Formatting the Page," for more information on rounding corners.

ADDING DROP SHADOWS

A *drop shadow* gives your borders a distinctive look by adding depth behind the frame. You might want to use a drop shadow border for special announcements, advertisements, or important sections of a form. A drop shadow also looks great when applied to a page border for letterhead, a title page, or flyer.

PART

II

CH

7

Follow these steps to create a drop shadow:

1. Choose Format, Paragraph, Border/Fill, and then click the Shadow tab. There are 25 different drop shadow effects (see Figure 7.16). Click one of the effects to have it applied to the sample document.

Figure 7.16
You can select one of the shadow effects in the Shadow tab of the Paragraph Border/Fill dialog box.

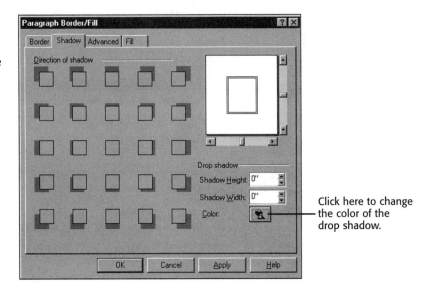

Click here to change the color of the drop shadow.

 Note

If you've been using WordPerfect 7 or 8, you're accustomed to working with only one drop shadow effect in the Advanced tab of the Border/Fill dialog box. In WordPerfect 9, there are 25 different drop shadow effects. A separate Shadow tab was created so all the effects could have their own area.

If you're trying to choose a drop shadow and nothing happens, see "I Can't Choose a Drop Shadow" in the Troubleshooting section of this chapter.

2. (Optional) Enter a value for the height and width of the shadow.

3. (Optional) Click the Color button and select a color for the drop shadow.

4. Choose Apply to apply the drop shadow and leave the Paragraph Border/Fill dialog box open; choose OK to apply the drop shadow and close the dialog box.

CHOOSING FILL PATTERNS

Borders and fill are independent of each other, so you can apply a fill pattern to a paragraph (or selected paragraphs) without choosing a border first. Although the most common use of fill is to add shading, you can have some fun combining patterns with foreground and background colors.

Here's how to add a fill pattern:

1. Click in the paragraph, or select the paragraphs to which you want to add the fill pattern.

2. Choose Fo_rmat, P_aragraph, B_order/Fill, and then click the Fill tab. There are 32 different predefined fill patterns to choose from.

3. Click a fill pattern to apply it to the sample document. The name of that fill pattern appears under the A_vailable Fill Styles list box (see Figure 7.17).

Figure 7.17
After you've selected a fill pattern, you can add color to it by selecting another foreground and/or background color.

Name of the ———— selected fill

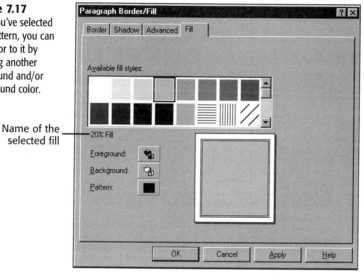

4. After you've selected a fill pattern, you can
   - Click the F_oreground button and choose a color for the foreground.
   - Click the B_ackground button and choose a color for the background.
   - Click the P_attern button and choose another fill pattern.

Choose A_pply to apply the fill pattern to the paragraph(s) and leave the Paragraph Border/Fill dialog box open; choose OK to apply the fill pattern and close the dialog box.

Caution

Try to avoid using a gray fill pattern with more than a 30% shading, or your black text will be too hard to read.

INSERTING DROP CAPS

A *drop cap* is the first letter in a paragraph, enlarged and positioned so that the top of the letter lines up with the top of the first sentence. The rest of the letter drops down into the text, hence the term "drop cap." Drop caps are used to draw the reader's eye to a specific point in the page, such as to a pull quote or to the beginning of a chapter or section.

PART

II

CH

7

To add a drop cap at the beginning of a paragraph, click in the paragraph, and then choose Format, Paragraph, Drop Cap or press Ctrl+Shift+C. WordPerfect grabs the first character, enlarges it, and wraps the rest of the paragraph around it (see Figure 7.18).

Figure 7.18
You can use a drop cap to decorate the beginning of a page, chapter, or column.

Drop cap

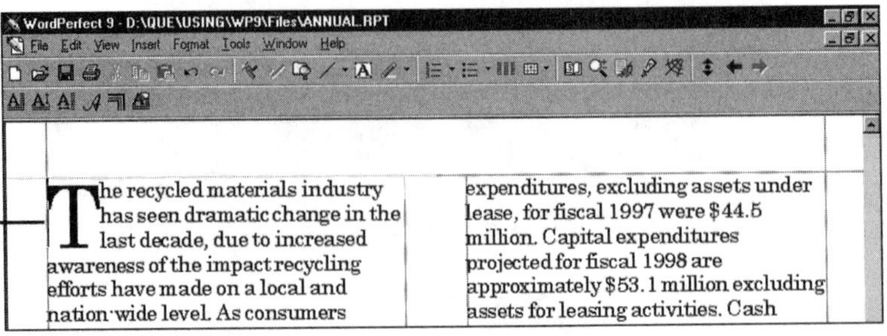

You can click in front of the drop cap to use the tools on the Property Bar to edit a drop cap:

 ■ Click the Drop Cap Style button to choose a different drop cap style from the palette.

 ■ Click the Drop Cap Size button to choose how tall you want the drop cap to be (in lines). The default is 3 lines high.

 ■ Click the Drop Cap Position button to place the drop cap in the text or in the margin.

 ■ Click Drop Cap Font button to choose a font, color, shading, or font attribute for the drop cap.

 ■ Click the Drop Cap Border/Fill button to choose a border, drop shadow, or fill pattern.

 ■ Click the Drop Cap Options button to choose how many letters you want in the drop cap. You can choose to have the first word made into a drop cap. You can also choose to adjust for diacriticals and descenders.

> **Note**
> To switch from the Drop Cap Property Bar to the regular Property Bar, click in the body text.

TROUBLESHOOTING

MY TITLE IS SPLIT IN HALF

I accidentally pressed Shift+F7 in the middle of a title and now the title is split in half. How can I fix this?

If you accidentally press Shift+F7 or Alt+F7 in the middle of a line, strange things can happen! If the line is short, it just splits the text up, but in a paragraph, it can cause the letters to get all crunched up together. If you notice this problem right away, press Backspace to delete the Center or Flush Right code. Next, press Home to move to the beginning of the line so you can try again. If you notice this problem minutes later, turn on Reveal Codes (Alt+F3), click at the beginning of that line, and start looking for the code. When you find it, click and drag it out of the Reveal Codes window to delete it.

PRESSING TAB INDENTS THE PARAGRAPH

When I press Tab, the whole paragraph is indented. I want to indent just the first line, not the entire paragraph.

To indent only the first line of a paragraph, press Tab at the beginning of the first line. If you *then* press Tab at the beginning of *any other line* in the paragraph, QuickIndent converts the tab to an indent, which indents the whole paragraph.

Pressing Tab at the beginning of any line in a paragraph except the first line creates a hanging indent. In this case, only the first line of the paragraph is lined up against the left margin, and the remaining lines are indented to the next tab stop (1/2 inch).

To turn off the QuickIndent feature, choose Tools, QuickCorrect. Click the Format-As-You-Go tab, and then deselect QuickIndent.

SORTING INDENTED PARAGRAPHS

After painstakingly creating a list of contributors for a fundraising campaign, I can't get the list to sort correctly. I indented each entry so it would be formatted underneath some other text. What am I doing wrong?

You aren't doing anything wrong—tab and indent codes act as field delimiters in a sort. In other words, they count as fields, moving the first field (the first word) over to the second or third field. In the case of a hanging indent, there are two codes inserted—left indent and back tab—so the first word in the line is actually the third field. The same thing happens if you have flush right, center, and margin release codes at the beginning of a line.

The best thing to do is turn on Reveal Codes and figure out how many codes you have at the beginning of each line. Then adjust the field number in your sort to skip past the codes.

CONDITIONAL END OF PAGE ISN'T WORKING RIGHT

I've used Conditional End of Page to keep the first three lines of a paragraph with a heading, but it isn't working. Only the first line stays with the heading. What am I doing wrong?

First, be sure you click at the beginning of the heading line before you insert the Conditional End of Page code. Second, when you specify how many lines to keep together, be sure that you count the heading as a line. Furthermore, if there is a blank line between the heading and the paragraph, you have to count that, too. So if you have a heading, a blank line, and then the paragraph, and you want to keep three lines of the paragraph together with the heading, you need to keep five lines together.

I CAN'T CHOOSE A DROP SHADOW

I'm in the Shadow tab in the Paragraph Border/Fill dialog box, but whenever I click a drop shadow effect, nothing happens. The sample document doesn't show me the drop shadow effect and nothing is inserted in my document when I click OK.

You probably forgot to choose a border style first. If you don't choose a border in the Available Border Styles list box, the options in the Shadow tab won't have any effect because they manipulate the borders. The Fill tab still works, without a border selected, because you can add fill to a paragraph without adding a border.

PROJECT

It's amazing what a difference a few minor changes can make! Take the company newsletter in Figure 7.19, for example. It looks okay, but a few things could be done to improve the appearance. Figure 7.20 shows the same newsletter after a few improvements have been made. The information that you need to make these changes is included in this chapter, so I won't duplicate the steps here.

Figure 7.19
Although this newsletter looks pretty good as it is, improvements can be made.

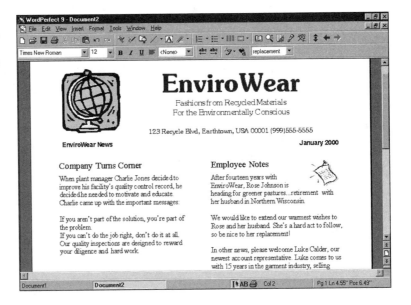

A paragraph border has been added around the last line in the masthead to separate the masthead from the text of the newsletter. A gray fill was added to shade the text and enhance the border's appearance. A drop cap was added at the top of each column. The messages mentioned in the first column were indented on both sides to identify them as quotations. Finally—and this is a change that you won't notice by looking at the document—the graphic image in the second column has been attached to the Employee Notes paragraph with block protect so that the graphic stays with the paragraph.

Figure 7.20
With a little formatting and tweaking, the newsletter looks much more attractive.

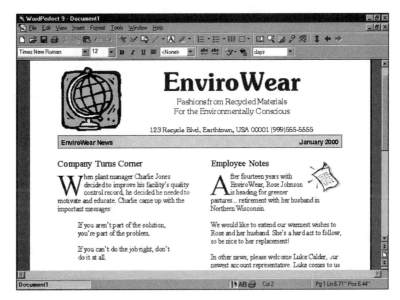

CHAPTER **8**

FORMATTING THE PAGE

In this chapter

CHANGING MARGINS

In Chapter 1, "Getting Comfortable with WordPerfect," you learned how to change the margins by using the guidelines. If you find it awkward to click and drag the guidelines, you can always use the dialog box, where you can type in the margin settings directly.

To change the margins in a dialog box, choose Format, Margins. You can also choose File, Page Setup, and then click the Margins/Layout tab. Figure 8.1 shows the Page Setup dialog box. Type the margin settings in the text boxes, or click the spinner arrows to increment/decrement the values.

Figure 8.1
The Margins/Layout tab of the Page Setup dialog box has options for setting and adjusting the margins.

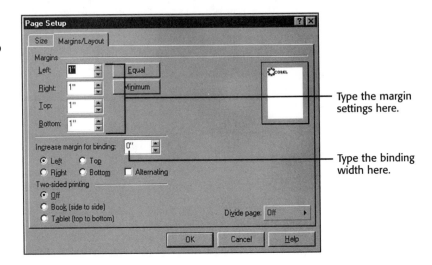

Type the margin settings here.

Type the binding width here.

If you want to set equal margins on all sides, type the margin setting in one of the four text boxes, and then click the Equal button. Click the Minimum button to set the margins according to the minimum margin requirements for the currently selected printer.

Tip #89 from
Laura and Read

If you type a fraction (such as 1/4, 1/3, 2/3) in the text box, WordPerfect converts it to the decimal equivalent.

 If you've been trying unsuccessfully to adjust the top and bottom margins to center text on a page, see "Can't Find the Right Margins to Center the Page" in the Troubleshooting section at the end of this chapter.

 If you notice that margins are changing in the middle of a document and you can't find any margin codes to delete, see "I've Got Gremlins Formatting My Document" in the Troubleshooting section at the end of this chapter.

Setting the Binding Width

If you need to shift the margins to accommodate binding, you can set a binding width that functions independently of the margin settings. Type the amount of margin space that the binding will require, and then choose Left, Right, Top, or Bottom, depending on where the binding will be placed. To set up alternating pages, place a check mark in the Alternating check box. The sample document in the dialog box shows what the bound pages will look like with the settings you have made. To set the binding for double-sided documents, choose Book or Tablet in the Two-sided printing section, and then choose to increase the binding width on the inside margin or the outside margin (these two options don't appear if Off is chosen).

Tip #90 from
Laura and Read

WordPerfect's default margins of 1 inch on all sides may be fine for most folks, but if you prefer to use different margins in your documents, you can alter the settings in the default template. This way, you don't have to set new margins every time you create a new document.

→ To change the settings in the default template, **see** "Editing the Default Template," **p. 619**

Tip #91 from
Laura and Read

Headers, footers, footnotes, endnotes, and watermarks use the margin settings in the DocumentStyle, not the margin settings that you insert in the document. If you have these elements in your document, be sure you change the margins in the DocumentStyle. To edit the DocumentStyle, choose View, Reveal Codes to turn on Reveal Codes. Double-click the DocumentStyle code, and then choose Format, Margins from the Styles Editor dialog box to open the Page Setup dialog box, where you can set the margins.

INSERTING PAGE BREAKS

No doubt you've noticed that WordPerfect automatically creates a new page for you whenever you fill up the current one. It's transparent, so you don't even have to think about it. For times when you want to start a new page and you haven't reached the bottom of the current page, you need to insert a *page break*, which is also known as a *hard page*. *Soft page breaks* are inserted by WordPerfect as you type; *hard page breaks* are those that you insert.

To insert a hard page, press Ctrl+Enter. In Draft view mode, a page break displays as a horizontal double line. In Page view mode, you see a space between the two pages (see Figure 8.2).

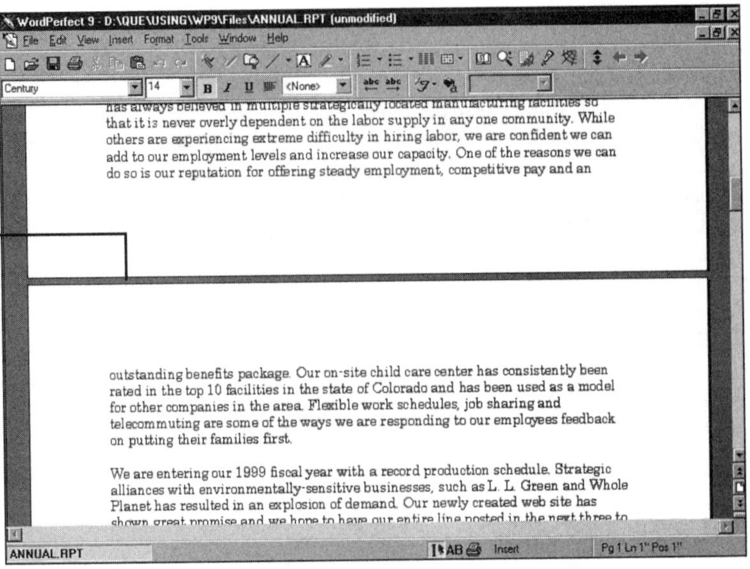

Figure 8.2
In Page view mode, the physical page is displayed, so you can see the space between pages.

Page break

When you insert a page break, a hard page code [HPg] is inserted in the document. To remove a page break, delete the [HPg] code. You can also click at the end of the paragraph, just before a page break, and press Delete. In a style-heavy document, you might inadvertently delete a style code with this method, in which case you need to reapply the style.

In a long document, you might decide to precede a major section with a hard page break so that each section begins on a new page. If, during heavy revisions, these hard pages get moved around to the wrong places, you can use Find and Replace to quickly strip out all the hard page codes, or only the ones that you don't need anymore.

→ To get a refresher on how to search for a code and delete it from the document, **see** "Searching for Codes," **p. 130**

Tip #92 from	If the red cursor is to the left of a code, press Delete; if the red cursor is to the right of a
Laura and Read	code, press Backspace. You can also click and drag a code out of the Reveal Codes window to delete it.

When you're printing on both sides of the paper, you'll want to start new chapters or sections on the right side of facing pages. The simplest way to do this is to use the Force Page feature. First, click in the paragraph where you want to force a new page.

Choose Format, Page, Force Page to open the Force Page dialog box (see Figure 8.3). Choose Current Page Odd to force a new odd-numbered page. (Pick this if you want to start new chapters and sections on the right side.) Choose Current Page Even to force a new even-numbered page. Choose Start New Page to create a new page at the beginning of the current paragraph.

Figure 8.3
As with hard page breaks, if further editing moves the new page to an undesirable location, you can turn on Reveal Codes and delete the [Force] code.

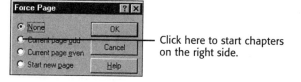

Click here to start chapters on the right side.

ADDING PAGE NUMBERS

Numbering pages in WordPerfect can be as simple as printing a page number at the bottom of every page or as complex as numbering chapters individually and choosing different page numbering styles for various sections of a document.

INSERTING PAGE NUMBERS AT THE TOP OR BOTTOM OF THE PAGE

You can choose from 10 preset page number positions that place the page number at the top or bottom of the page. If you're printing on both sides of the paper, you might want to place the page numbers at alternating top or bottom corners.

To insert a page number, click on the page where you want the numbering to start. Choose Format, Page, Numbering to display the Select Page Numbering Format dialog box. Click the Position drop-down list arrow to open the list of positions that you can choose from (see Figure 8.4). Select a page number position from the list.

Choose a page number position here.

Figure 8.4
The quickest way to insert a page number is to choose one of the preset page number positions and page number styles.

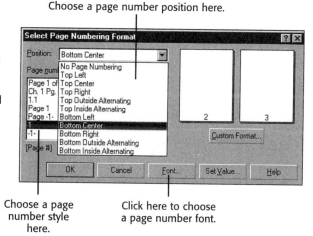

Choose a page number style here.

Click here to choose a page number font.

Page Number Placement
Page numbers are printed on the top or bottom line in the text area of the page, not in the margin space. WordPerfect inserts a blank line to separate the page number from the rest of the document text. This reduces the amount of text that would normally fit on the page by two lines. If you decrease your top or bottom margin (depending on where you put the page numbers) to approximately 2/3 inch, you can regain the lost space, and the page numbers will appear to print in the margin space.

At this point, you can click OK to insert a basic page number that starts on the current page (as page 1) and continues through the rest of the document. Figure 8.5 shows a document with simple page numbers at the bottom center of the page.

Page number

Figure 8.5
The most common page numbering scheme is to position the number at the bottom center of every page.

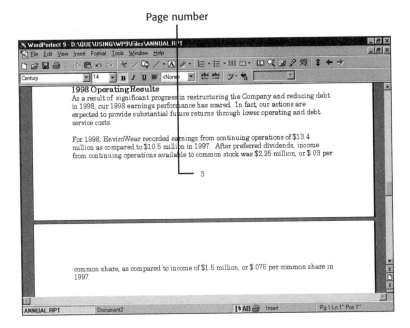

There are other page numbering options you can choose:

- You can choose a page number format from the Page Numbering Format list box. Scroll down through the list to see the letter and Roman numeral styles.

Using a "page x of y" Page Number
A "page x of y" page number tells you the number of the current page (x) and the total number of pages in the document (y). To create a "page x of y" page number, select Page 1 of 1 in the Page Numbering Format list box. Click OK.

- You can click the Font button to open the Page Numbering Font dialog box, where you can choose a font, font size, color, or attributes for the page number.

Caution

WordPerfect uses the font set in the Document Initial Font dialog box for page numbers, not the font that you may have set in the document. So either set the font that you want for the body text *and* the page number in the Document Initial Font dialog box (by choosing File, Document, Default Font) or choose a font in the Page Numbering Font dialog box that matches the one you've used in the document.

- You can choose <u>C</u>ustom Format to open the Custom Page Numbering dialog box. From here, you can create a combination page number style that can include the volume number, chapter number, or secondary page number. You can also create a customized "page x of y" page number style that tells the current page number and the total number of pages in the document. See the section "Switching to a Different Page Numbering Scheme" later in this chapter for more information.

- You can choose Set <u>V</u>alue to open the Values dialog box, where you can type the new number to use for any of the page numbering components. This is where you reset page numbering by setting the page number back to 1. See the section "Changing the Page, Chapter, or Volume Numbers" later in this chapter for more information.

Tip #93 from
Laura and Read

It's common practice to use different numbering styles for the introductory pages, the body of the document, and the closing sections. To accomplish this, select the format for the page numbers at the top of the document, again at the main body, and then again at the closing section. In addition to switching to a different number format, you should restart the page numbering. See the section "Setting Page, Chapter, and Volume Numbers" later in this chapter for more information on restarting page numbers.

SWITCHING TO A DIFFERENT PAGE NUMBERING SCHEME

To accommodate long or complex documents, WordPerfect has five types of page numbers that can be used individually or in combination with one another:

- Page and secondary page numbers that increase automatically—Journals and newsletters sometimes use the secondary page numbers in addition to the regular page numbers. One set numbers every page consecutively throughout the year, and the other numbers the pages in the individual issues.

- Chapter and volume numbers that you increase or decrease where appropriate— Chapter numbers are used for different sections in a document; volume numbers are used to number multiple documents. You can also use these with journals and newsletters to provide volume (year) and chapter (issue/month) numbers.

- A total pages number that displays the total number of pages currently in the document—You use this page number in conjunction with the regular page number to create "page x of y" page numbers.

To create a custom page numbering scheme, move the insertion point to the page where you want the page numbering to start, and then follow these steps:

1. Choose Format, Page, Numbering, Custom Format to open the Custom Page Numbering dialog box (see Figure 8.6).

Select a style here.

Figure 8.6
You can create a combination page number style that includes page numbers with chapter numbers, volume numbers, secondary numbers, and a total pages number.

Build the custom page number style here.

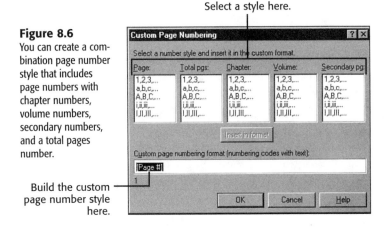

2. Click a number style in the list box of the page number type that you want to use. For example, to select volume numbering with lowercase Roman numerals, click the fourth item in the Volume list box (see Figure 8.7).

Figure 8.7
After you've selected a number type and format, you insert it as a code in the list box.

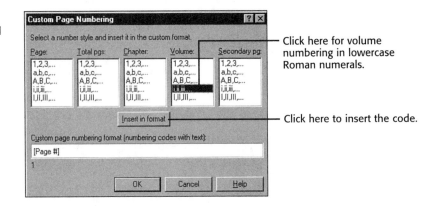

Click here for volume numbering in lowercase Roman numerals.

Click here to insert the code.

3. Click Insert in Format to insert that number style in the Custom Page Numbering Format (Numbering Codes with Text) text box.

4. If necessary, type the text that you want to appear before or after the number. For example, type Volume in front of the [Vol #] code.

5. To create a combination page number, insert the other code in the list box and type the necessary accompanying text. An example of the resulting page number appears below the text box (see Figure 8.8).

Figure 8.8
The more complex the document, the more important it is to have accurate and descriptive page numbering.

Example of the resulting page number

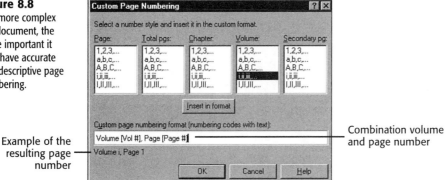

Combination volume and page number

6. When you're satisfied with the way the page number looks, click OK to return to the Select Page Numbering Format dialog box.

7. Make any necessary adjustments to the font or the placement, and then click OK to insert the page number in the document.

 If you've just made some adjustments to your custom page numbers and the changes are affecting some of the pages but not others, see "Editing a Custom Page Number" in the Troubleshooting section at the end of this chapter.

SETTING PAGE, CHAPTER, AND VOLUME NUMBERS

Documents with introductory materials often have two sets of page numbers—one for the introductory pages and another for the body text. One common type of formatting uses lowercase Roman numerals (for example, i, ii, iii) for the table of contents and other introductory material, and then Arabic numbers (for example, 1, 2, 3) for the text.

Whether or not you change the format for the page numbers, it's common practice to restart page numbering after the introductory pages. Furthermore, WordPerfect doesn't automatically increment chapter and volume numbers—you have to do that manually.

To change the page number beginning on the current page, follow these steps:

1. In the Select Page Numbering Format dialog box, click the Set Value button to open the Values dialog box (see Figure 8.9).

Figure 8.9
You can set the starting value for page numbers, chapter numbers, and volume numbers in the Values dialog box.

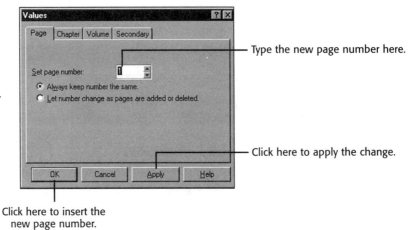

Type the new page number here.

Click here to apply the change.

Click here to insert the new page number.

2. If necessary, click the Chapter, Volume, or Secondary tab. Although the options are identical in every tab, the values on each are tied to the corresponding page number codes in your document.

3. Type the new number in the Set Page Number text box (or click the spinner arrows).

4. Choose one of the following:

- Always Keep Number the Same—Use this option when you don't want the page number to change, no matter how much editing takes place. For example, you might want the first page of the body text to be numbered as page 1, no matter how many introductory pages there are.

- Let Number Change as Pages Are Added or Deleted—Choose this option when you want the page number to be updated as you edit the document.

Tip #94 from
Laura and Read

If you want the freedom to rearrange chapters, be sure you choose Let Number Change as Pages Are Added or Deleted when you set the chapter number.

INSERTING PAGE NUMBERS ELSEWHERE IN A DOCUMENT

You're not limited to the 10 predefined page number positions. You can insert a page number anywhere in the document. For example, you might want to refer to the current page, chapter, or volume number within the text. Or you might want to insert a chapter or volume number directly into a title.

To insert a page number elsewhere in a document, follow these steps:

1. Position the insertion point where you want the page number to appear.

2. Choose Format, Page, Insert Page Number. The Insert Page Number dialog box has options for inserting primary and secondary page numbers, chapter and volume numbers, and the total pages number (see Figure 8.10).

Figure 8.10
You can use the Insert Page Number dialog box to insert a page number in a location other than the predefined page number positions.

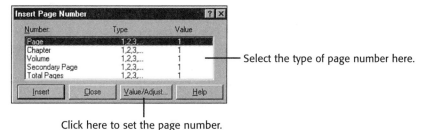

Select the type of page number here.

Click here to set the page number.

3. Click the type of number that you want to insert in the list box.

4. If necessary, click the Value/Adjust button to open the Value/Adjust Number dialog box, where you can change to a different page number method (numbers, letters, or Roman numerals) or set the page number (see Figure 8.11). Click Apply and then OK when you're done.

Figure 8.11
In the Value/Adjust Number dialog box, you can choose a different numbering method, and you can set the page, chapter, and volume numbers.

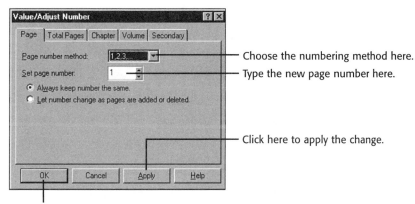

Choose the numbering method here.

Type the new page number here.

Click here to apply the change.

Click here when you're done.

5. Click Insert (in the Insert Page Number dialog box). The number is inserted at the insertion point.

6. You can continue inserting numbers. Click in the document window and reposition the insertion point, and then click in the dialog box to make it active again. Choose another number type, and then click Insert.

7. Click Close when you're finished inserting page numbers.

Tip #95 from
Laura and Read

You might think that this is the feature you should use to insert page numbers in headers and footers. You're close, but it's actually a little easier than this. When you're working with headers and footers, you can use the Page Numbering button on the Property Bar to open a drop-down list of numbering types (page, secondary, chapter, volume, total pages).

If you have page numbers cropping up for no apparent reason, see "I've Got Gremlins Formatting My Document" in the Troubleshooting section at the end of this chapter.

CHOOSING DIFFERENT PAPER SIZES

The default paper size in the U.S. version of WordPerfect is 8 1/2 inches by 11 inches (other countries have different standards for paper size). The text is formatted in *portrait* orientation, which means the paper is taller than it is wide. If all you ever do is create standard business documents, you might never have to change the paper size. However, when the time comes that you have to create an envelope, print on legal size paper, or rotate a document to landscape orientation, you do so by choosing a different paper size.

Choose Format, Page, Page Setup (or choose File, Page Setup). If necessary, click the Size tab to display the paper sizes that are available for the current printer (see Figure 8.12).

Click here to switch to landscape orientation.

Figure 8.12
You can choose a different paper size or switch to a different orientation in the Page Setup dialog box.

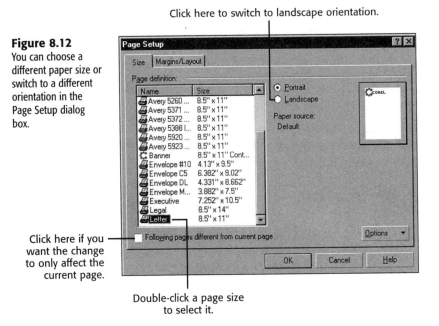

Click here if you want the change to only affect the current page.

Double-click a page size to select it.

If all you want to do is rotate your text into a *landscape* orientation (where the page is wider than it is tall), choose Landscape. Select Following Pages Different from Current Page if you want to change the paper size only for the current page. Otherwise, double-click a paper size in the Page Definition list to insert a paper size code at the top of the current page.

 If your document inexplicably prints on two different types of paper, see "I've Got Gremlins Formatting My Document" in the Troubleshooting section at the end of this chapter.

CREATING AND EDITING PAPER SIZES

Every printer has a list of paper sizes that it can handle. If you switch to a different printer, or computer, the paper size you chose may not be available. When this happens, WordPerfect makes a best guess and selects a similar paper size. If this doesn't work, you have to edit an existing paper size or create your own. If you decide to create your own custom paper sizes, you're restricted by the limitations of the printer. In other words, you aren't able to create a paper size that doesn't work with that printer.

It's faster to edit an existing paper size than to create one from scratch, so look for a size in the list that's similar to the size you want to create. Select it in the list, and then choose Options, Edit. Choose Portrait to edit the definition for the portrait orientation; choose Landscape to edit the definition for landscape orientation; choose Both to edit the definition for both orientations. The Edit Page Definition dialog box appears (see Figure 8.13). Depending on which orientation you chose to edit, some of the options in the dialog box may not be available.

Click here to select paper type. ¬   ┌ Click here to choose a size.

Figure 8.13
You can edit an existing paper size in the Edit Page Definition dialog box.

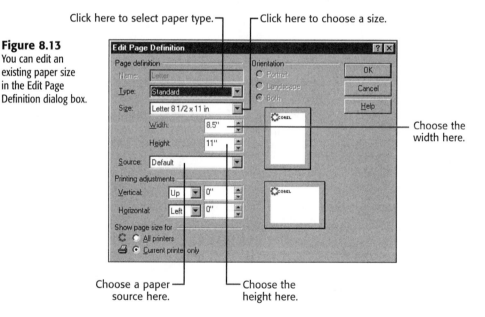

Choose the width here.

Choose a paper source here. ───   ─── Choose the height here.

To create a definition from scratch, choose Options, New to display the New Page Definition dialog box (see Figure 8.14), which is identical to the Edit Page Definition dialog box except that all the options are available. Now you can work with the following options:

- If you're creating a new definition, type a name in the Name text box.
- You can click the Type drop-down list arrow and choose a paper type from the list.
- You can click the Size drop-down list arrow and choose a paper size from the list. If you don't see the size you need, choose User Defined Size.

Figure 8.14
You can choose User Defined Size if you don't see the dimensions that you want to use in the list.

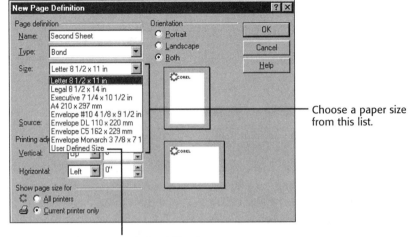

Choose a paper size from this list.

Choose User Defined Size if you want to specify the width and height.

- If you chose User Defined Size, enter the page width in the <u>W</u>idth text box and the page height in the H<u>e</u>ight text box. Or you can click the spinner arrows to increase or decrease the size.

- You can click the <u>S</u>ource drop-down list arrow and choose a source for the paper. For example, unless you have an envelope tray attached to your printer, you need to choose Envelope manual feed so you can insert the envelopes manually.

- If for some reason the text doesn't print using to the margins you have set, you can reposition the text on the page with printing adjustments. Click the <u>V</u>ertical drop-down list arrow, choose Up or Down, and then type the amount of adjustment in the text box. Or click the H<u>o</u>rizontal drop-down list arrow, choose Left or Right, and then type the amount of adjustment in the text box.

- You can choose <u>P</u>ortrait, <u>L</u>andscape, or <u>B</u>oth to set the orientation capabilities of the page definition.

Click OK when you're finished making your changes. The new paper size appears in the P<u>a</u>ge Definition list box.

Caution

Remember that the new definition you've created or the definition that you've edited isn't available if you choose another printer. When you switch to a different printer, WordPerfect makes a best-guess match to the paper sizes available on that printer. You can, however, create and edit the definitions on that printer to match the definitions on the first printer.

Tip #96 from
Laura and Read

When you're printing a long letter, usually the first page is on letterhead and the remaining pages are on plainer "second sheets." If you have two paper trays on your printer, you can put letterhead in one and second sheet in the other. I have only one tray, so I either pull the tray out and place the letterhead on top of the second sheets, or I manually feed the letterhead and let the printer pull second sheets from the paper tray. Either way, the trick is to tell the printer where to get the paper. By creating a separate page definition for the letterhead, you can specify where your letterhead paper is. Then you insert a paper size code for the letterhead on the first page and a paper size code for the second sheets on the second page.

You can delete unused paper sizes by selecting them in the list and choosing Options, Delete. Keep in mind that the next time you open a document with that paper size, it won't be available and WordPerfect will make a best-guess match from the other sizes.

If you accidentally delete the wrong paper size, you can restore it from the current printer driver. In the Page Setup dialog box, choose Options, Regenerate. Choose one of the two available options:

- All Sizes from Printer—Choose this option to restore the original page definitions from the current printer driver. Use this option carefully—if you've edited one of the paper sizes in the list, restoring the paper sizes from the printer driver wipes out your changes.

- New Sizes Only—Choose this option if you need to add new definitions that may have been created since the last time the list was generated.

Tip #97 from
Laura and Read

If you routinely use a paper size other than the default 8 1/2 inches by 11 inches, you can replace the default paper size in the default (wp9us) template.

→ For more information on creating and editing templates, **see** Chapter 22, "Building Documents with Templates," **p. 613**

SUBDIVIDING PAGES

A single, physical page can be divided into separate, logical pages. A physical page maintains the original dimensions of the paper. *Logical pages* are pieces of the physical page, but they are still considered individual pages for purposes of page numbering. For example, if you subdivide a page into six logical pages then turn on page numbering, the logical pages are numbered 1 through 6. The Labels feature utilizes the same concept to separate a sheet of paper into individual labels.

In the "Printing Booklets" section of Chapter 6, "Printing, Faxing, and Emailing," you learned how to divide the page to create a booklet. Another example of why you would want to subdivide a page is invitations. You can subdivide an 8 1/2-inch by 11-inch piece of paper into four 4 1/4-inch by 5 1/2-inch sections and place four invitations on a page.

To subdivide a page, choose Fo<u>r</u>mat, <u>M</u>argins. Click the Di<u>v</u>ide Page button to open the palette (see Figure 8.15).

Figure 8.15
Using the divide page feature, you can divide a physical piece of paper into multiple logical pages.

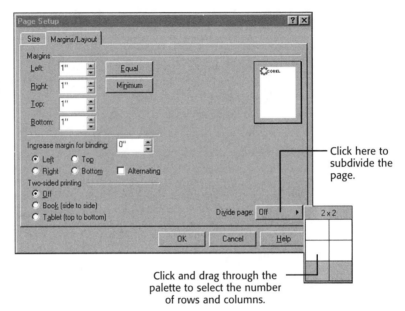

Click here to subdivide the page.

Click and drag through the palette to select the number of rows and columns.

Click and drag through the palette to choose the number of rows and columns. The sample page in the palette illustrates how the paper will be subdivided.

Before you click OK, take a look at the margin settings. WordPerfect uses the current margins for each logical page, so if you keep the default 1-inch margins, you'll have a 1-inch border around each logical page that you won't be able to use. That's a lot of wasted space. Click the Mi<u>n</u>imum button to quickly set the margins to the minimum allowed by your printer. Figure 8.16 shows the first logical page in a subdivided page. To move to the next page, press Ctrl+Enter.

Finally, when you divide the current page, it dominoes down through the rest of the document. To go back to a full-size page, choose Fo<u>r</u>mat, <u>M</u>argins. Click the Di<u>v</u>ide Page button, and then click the upper-left corner to select 1 × 1, which means one row and one column, or one page.

Logical page   Press Ctrl+Enter to move to the next logical page.

Figure 8.16
Each logical page can be formatted separately with the page formatting options.

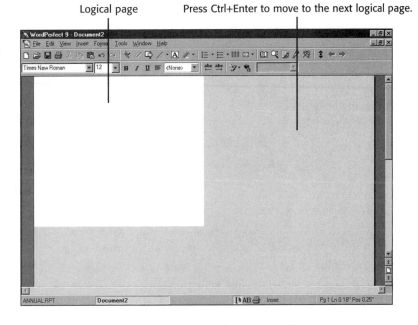

Tip #98 from
Laura and Read

You can center text on a subdivided page with the Center Page feature. Remember that each section is a logical page, so you format it just as if it were a full-size page. Click in the section (page) that you want to center, and then choose Format, Page, Center. Choose Current Page if you only want to center the current page, or choose Current and Subsequent Pages to center all the pages from this point forward.

ADDING HEADERS AND FOOTERS

Headers hold information that you want printed at the top of every page; *footers* hold information that you want printed at the bottom of every page. You can create two headers and two footers on every page, although usually one header/footer is for odd pages and the other header/footer is for even pages. Headers and footers can contain graphics, page numbers, titles, the filename, revision dates, or any other information about the document.

You create the header or footer on the page where you want it to start. For ease of editing, this is usually the top of the document. For pages where you don't want the headers and footers to print (such as title pages or the first page of a letter), you can suppress the header and footer. You can also use Delay Codes to postpone the effect of a formatting code. See the section "Suppressing and Delaying Codes" later in this chapter.

Formatting codes, such as margin changes and fonts, that you want to affect headers and footers as well as the body text, should be inserted in the DocumentStyle, rather than in the document itself. To edit the DocumentStyle, choose File, Document, Current Document Style.

To insert a header or footer, follow these steps:

1. Click Insert, Header/Footer to open the Headers/Footers dialog box (see Figure 8.17).

Figure 8.17
In the Headers/Footers dialog box, Header A is selected by default.

2. If necessary, select Header B, Footer A, or Footer B.

3. Click Create. What happens next depends on which view mode you're using. Either way, the Property Bar now has some handy buttons you can use:

    • In Page mode, the insertion point moves up to the top of the page, within the header guidelines (see Figure 8.18).

    • In Draft mode, the insertion point moves to a header/footer editing window.

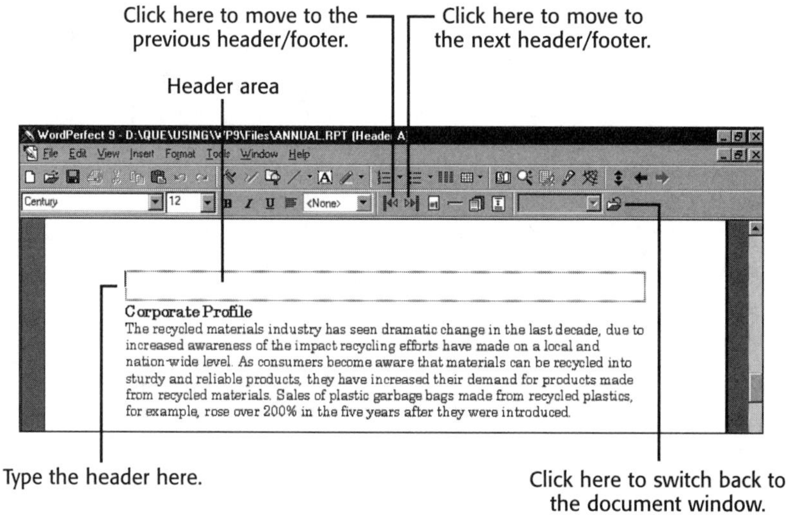

Click here to move to the previous header/footer. ———— Click here to move to the next header/footer.

Header area

Figure 8.18
In Page view mode, you create and edit the header or footer onscreen, not in a separate window, as with Draft mode. In either mode, you have some new buttons on the Property Bar.

Type the header here.

Click here to switch back to the document window.

4. Type the text of the header or footer. Using the menus, add the necessary graphics, tables, and other formatting elements. (Features that can't be used in a header or footer are grayed out on the menus.)

Tip #99 from
Laura and Read

Header and footer text in the same font size as the document text is distracting at its best, and downright ugly at its worst. If you're using a 12-point font for the body text, step down at least 2 points, preferably 4 points, for the header or footer text. If you're using a sans serif font (such as Arial) for your headings and a serif font (such as Times New Roman) for your text, you might also consider using the sans serif font for the header and footer text to further set it apart from the body text.

Caution

WordPerfect automatically inserts a blank line between the document text and the header or footer. Don't insert a blank line in the header or footer unless you want to increase the distance to two lines.

Tip #100 from
Laura and Read

In another lifetime, I installed local area networks in law offices and trained the staff in WordPerfect. One of the first standards we recommended was inserting the path and file-name (in a tiny 6- or 8-point font) in a footer that printed on every page but the first page. Anyone who read the document knew exactly where to find the file on the network. (Whether or not they had rights to the file was up to a system administrator.) To insert the filename in a header or footer, choose Insert, Other. Choose Filename or Path and Filename.

5. Click the Close button to switch back to the document window.

If you're in Page mode, you'll see the header or footer text onscreen with the rest of the document text. If you're working in Draft mode, you won't see header or footer text unless you edit the header or footer. To edit a header or footer, choose Insert, Header/Footer. Select the appropriate header or footer, and then click Edit.

Because headers and footers are printed within the text area of a page, you should probably decrease the margins to allow more space for the body text. It's more attractive to pull the header or footer into the margin space. Remember to change the margins in the DocumentStyle, or the changes won't affect the placement of the headers and footers.

 If your header or footer prints on top of the page numbers, see "Headers/Footers Versus Page Numbers" in the Troubleshooting section at the end of this chapter.

 If you have headers and footers popping up in places where they shouldn't, see "I've Got Gremlins Formatting My Document" in the Troubleshooting section at the end of this chapter.

Note

WordPerfect 7 users are used to a feature bar with the buttons for header and footer functions. In WordPerfect 9, you access these functions by using buttons on the "shape-shifter" Property Bar.

That's how you create a header or footer. The following are some of the other options you can take advantage of:

■ You can insert page numbers by clicking the Page Numbering button on the Property Bar. A drop-down list of options appears (see Figure 8.19). Select the type of page number you want to insert.

Select a page number type from the list. ──┐

Figure 8.19
Click the Page Numbering button to insert any of the five types of page numbers in a header or footer.

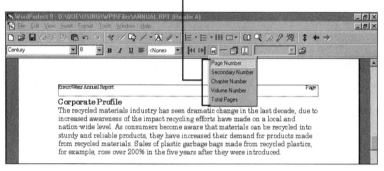

 ■ Click the Horizontal Line button to insert a graphic line in the header or footer.

Caution

Make sure the insertion point is on a blank line when you click the Horizontal Line button. Otherwise, the graphics line plops down right on top of text.

 ■ Click the Header/Footer Placement button to open the Header or Footer Placement dialog box (see Figure 8.20). The default is to print the header or footer on every page.

Figure 8.20
Specify on which pages you want the header or footer to print in the Placement dialog box.

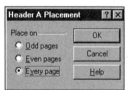

Overlapping Headers
Although I usually create one separate header for odd pages and another for even pages, occasionally I use two headers on the same page. One usually contains something standard, such as the title of the document. The other contains something that changes periodically in the document, such as chapter numbers and names. To keep the two headers from overlapping, I keep the first header's text at the left margin and the second header's text flush against the right margin. I make sure to use short titles and chapter names so that they don't run into each other in the middle of the page!

■ Click the Header/Footer Distance button, and then type the distance that you want between the header or footer and the body text in the Distance dialog box (see Figure 8.21).

Figure 8.21
You can adjust the space between the header (or footer) and the text in the Distance dialog box.

Type the measurement or click the spinner arrows.

Tip #101 from
Laura and Read

When you're working in a header or footer, the Numbering option on the Format, Page menu is gray and there is no option for Value/Adjust under Insert Page Number. So how are you supposed to adjust the page number in a header or footer? First, insert the page number in the header or footer. Switch back to the document window and choose Format, Page, Numbering. Change Position to No Page Numbering, and then click Set Value and change the page number there. Click OK twice to get back to the document.

SUPPRESSING AND DELAYING CODES

The Suppress feature prevents headers, footers, watermarks, and page numbers from printing on a particular page. It's frequently used to keep these elements from printing on the title page. You have to place a Suppress code at the top of every page on which you don't want a header, footer, page number, or watermark to print.

Click on the page where you want to suppress a header, footer, page number, or watermark, and then choose Format, Page, Suppress. The Suppress dialog box opens (see Figure 8.22). Place a check mark next to the elements that you want to suppress, or choose All to select all the elements at one time. Click OK.

Figure 8.22
In the Suppress dialog box, choose the page elements you do not want to print on the current page.

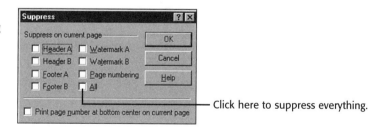

Click here to suppress everything.

The Delay Codes feature postpones the effect of formatting changes for a specified number of pages. A delay code is used in situations where you want to skip more than one page (for example, if you want to skip past the table of contents, preface, or other introductory material before printing headers, footers, or page numbers).

With Delay Codes, you can insert all your formatting at the top of the document, and then selectively apply the formatting after a certain number of pages. To go one better, you can put all the delay codes in the DocumentStyle, where they can't accidentally be deleted during editing.

To create a delay code, follow these steps:

1. Choose Format, Page, Delay Codes. The Delay Codes dialog box appears (see Figure 8.23).

Figure 8.23
Type the number of pages that you want to skip in the Delay Codes dialog box.

2. Type the number of pages in the Number of Pages to Skip Before Applying Codes text box (or click the spinner arrows to select the number). Click OK to switch to the Define Delayed Codes editing window (see Figure 8.24).

The title bar identifies the window.

Click here to create a watermark.

Click here to return to the document window.

Figure 8.24
You can postpone the action of many formatting codes by placing them in delay codes. Delay codes can be inserted in the document or in the DocumentStyle.

Click here to insert a graphic image.

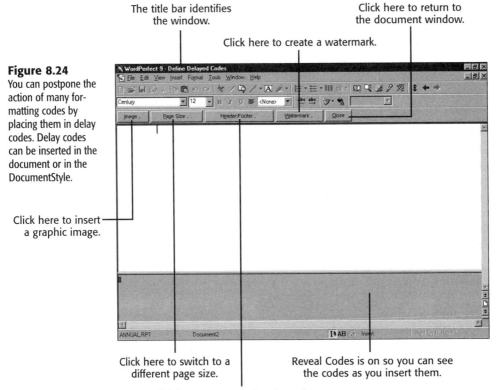

Click here to switch to a different page size.

Click here to create a header or footer.

Reveal Codes is on so you can see the codes as you insert them.

3. Use the menus or the buttons on the feature bar to insert the necessary formatting codes.

4. Click the <u>C</u>lose button to return to the document window.

No matter where you are on the page, WordPerfect automatically inserts this Delay code to the top of the page: [Delay: #]. The # represents the number of pages you want to skip. (WordPerfect calculates the number of pages to skip based on physical pages, not page numbers). If your insertion point is on page 5 and you set a Delay code to skip 3 pages, the code [Delay: 3] is inserted at the top of the page 5. On the page where the formatting takes effect, a [Delay: codes] code is inserted at the top of that page. If you move the red cursor to the left of this code, it expands to show you the codes within.

The trick to this feature is to realize that you are actually inserting formatting codes *into* a code—a delay code. If you create Header A in a delay code, you can't edit that code from the document window; you can only create another Header A. The two headers are independent of each other. The header/footer that you create in a delay code overrides the header/footer that you create in the document. To modify a formatting code in a delay code, you have to edit the delay code by turning on Reveal Codes and double-clicking the [Delay: #] code to edit the contents.

Setting Up Columns

Columns help to break up information and make it easier to read. Take a look at your daily newspaper—it's much easier to read across a short section of text than it is to read across an entire page (especially with small fonts). There are three types of columns in WordPerfect:

- Newspaper—Text flows down the first column until the bottom of the page is reached, then wraps up to the top of the next column. Newspaper columns are used in newsletters, magazine articles, and newspapers.

- Balanced Newspaper—Text flows across from column to column so that the columns stay (roughly) the same length, no matter how much text you type in. Since the text is constantly readjusting, typing in balanced columns is awkward. It's best to type the text and then turn on the columns.

- Parallel—Text flows down the first column until you push it over to the next column. Typing in parallel columns isn't bad because *you* decide when you want to move to the next column. However, editing in parallel columns is about as much fun as working on your income taxes. For this reason, most WordPerfect users turn to the Tables feature when they need side-by-side columns.

→ To learn how to create and edit tables, **see** Chapter 10, "Organizing Information with Tables," **p. 251**

DEFINING COLUMNS

Columns can be defined before or after you type text. During heavy revision, you may find it easier to work outside columns. When you're finished revising, you can turn columns on and have WordPerfect reformat the text.

To define columns, position the insertion point where you want the columns to start. You can also select a portion of text to be formatted into columns so the rest of the text isn't affected.

Tip #102 from
Laura and Read

> It's common to have a title or heading that spreads across the top of the columns, so you might want to leave a blank line or two at the top of the document, and then define the columns underneath.

The fastest way to define columns is to click the Columns button and then choose the number of columns (see Figure 8.25). It is common to define newspaper columns with the default half-inch *gutter* (that is, space between columns).

Click here to turn on columns.

Figure 8.25
You can click the Columns button to turn on columns.

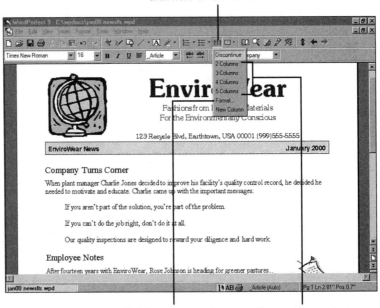

Click here to open the Columns dialog box.

Choose the number of columns here.

You can adjust the column and gutter widths by clicking and dragging the column guidelines (or the markers on the ruler). This might be all you need to know. However, if you want to define balanced columns, or if you want a little more control (and who doesn't), you can use the Columns dialog box to define the columns.

To define columns with the Columns dialog box, follow these steps:

1. Choose Format, Columns to display the Columns dialog box (see Figure 8.26).

Specify the number of columns here.

Adjust the gutter width here.

Figure 8.26
You use the Columns dialog box if you want to define balanced columns or if you want more control over the column definition.

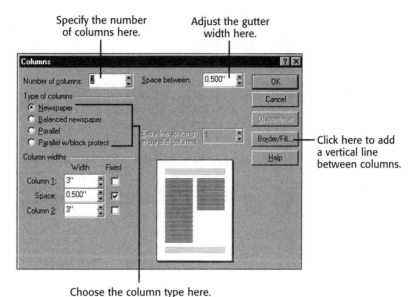

Click here to add a vertical line between columns.

Choose the column type here.

2. If you want more than two columns, type the number of columns in the Number of Columns text box.

3. If necessary, increase or decrease the gutter width in the Space Between text box.

4. Choose a column type in the Type of Columns section.

5. If necessary, adjust the individual column widths and space between the columns in the Column Widths section.

6. If you want a vertical line to appear between the columns, click the Border/Fill button. Scroll down through the Available Border Styles list box until you see the Column Between style (see Figure 8.27). Click OK.

→ If you're curious about graphic lines and how to customize the line styles, **see** Chapter 12, "Adding Graphics to Documents," **p. 317**

→ For more information on adding borders, shading, and drop shadows, **see** "Adding Borders, Drop Shadows, and Fills," **p. 183**

Figure 8.27
The Column Between border style applies a thin vertical line between each set of columns.

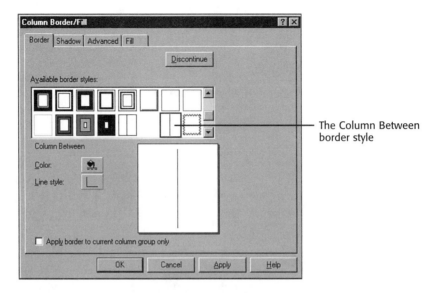

The Column Between border style

Don't worry if you don't see the vertical line between the columns on the sample document in the Columns dialog box. Because you applied the line in the Column Border/Fill dialog box, you'll see the line on the sample document there, not in the Columns dialog box.

7. Click OK to close the Column Border/Fill dialog box and turn on the columns (see Figure 8.28).

Figure 8.28
In this document, three balanced newspaper columns have been defined. The gutter space has been reduced to .3 inches.

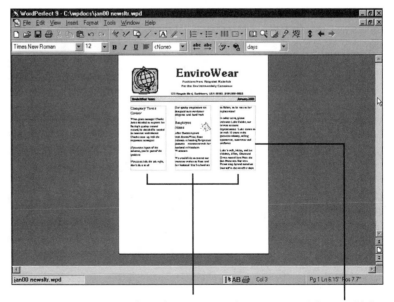

Balanced newspaper columns   Column guideline

If your balanced columns are not balanced, see "My Balanced Newspaper Columns Are Uneven" in the Troubleshooting section at the end of this chapter.

 You can turn columns on and off as often as you like. To turn off columns, click the Columns button, and choose Discontinue (or choose Format, Columns, and then click Discontinue). When you're ready to turn columns on again, either click the Columns button and choose the number of columns (to define the default newspaper columns with .5-inch gutter), or choose Format, Columns to define columns with settings other than the defaults.

TYPING AND EDITING IN COLUMNS

Typing and editing in columns can be a little tricky. You can save yourself some frustration if you finish typing and editing the text before you turn on columns. If for some reason you need to work in columns, the mouse is the quickest method for moving the insertion point—just click where you want to go. Table 8.1 lists some keyboard shortcuts you can use.

TABLE 8.1 SHORTCUTS FOR MOVING AROUND IN COLUMNS	
Press This	**To Move Here**
Alt+right arrow	One column to the right
Alt+left arrow	One column to the left
Alt+End	Last line in the column
Alt+Home	First line in the column

Tip #103 from
Laura and Read

When you're formatting text into columns, hyphenating words becomes an important issue. If you hyphenate too much, you frustrate the reader; if you don't hyphenate enough, you get gaps in the text. You can let WordPerfect decide where words should be hyphenated with the hyphenation feature (choose Tools, Language, Hyphenation, and then choose Turn Hyphenation On and click OK). If you want to decide where words are hyphenated, insert a *soft hyphen*, which remains invisible until the word moves close to the end of a line, and then it's used to hyphenate the word. Press Ctrl+Shift+hyphen to insert a soft hyphen.

USING MAKE IT FIT

Didn't your mother tell you there would be days like this? Your letter's signature block spills over to the second page...or your newsletter doesn't have quite enough text to fill the page. It happens to the best of us. Before you run screaming from the room at the prospect of spending an hour adjusting font sizes and margins, take a deep breath and let WordPerfect do the dirty work.

Make It Fit does just that—it makes text fit however many pages you specify. Now, you can't make one page of text stretch out into three pages, and you can't take three pages of text and expect to squeeze it into one page. The number of pages that you specify must be *at least* 50% of the current size.

You can use Make It Fit on selected text or on the entire document, so if you want to work on only a section of text, select it first. Choose Format, Make It Fit to open the Make It Fit dialog box (see Figure 8.29). (If you selected text, the Top Margin and Bottom Margin options are not available.)

Note

WordPerfect 9 introduces a new angle on Make It Fit: It's called Block Make It Fit. You can select a block of text and apply Make It Fit to only that text, leaving the rest of the document unaffected.

Type the desired number of pages here.

Figure 8.29
Make It Fit adjusts margins, font size, and line spacing to expand or contract text so that it fits within a specified number of pages.

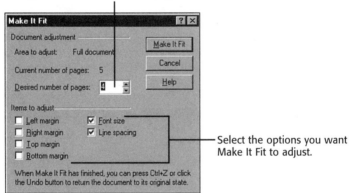

Select the options you want Make It Fit to adjust.

Take a look at the current number of pages, and then type the number of pages that you want to fill in the Desired Number of Pages text box. Select the options that you want Make It Fit to use to reformat the text, and then click Make It Fit.

Note

If you have hard page codes in the document, you get a message that warns you that these codes might affect how well the document is formatted.

ADDING BORDERS AROUND PAGES

Adding page borders is so similar to adding borders around paragraphs that I'm only going to cover the difference between the two here. Refer to "Adding Borders, Drop Shadows, and Fills" in Chapter 7, "Formatting Lines and Paragraphs," for more information.

There are 54 additional borders available for pages in the Page Border/Fill dialog box—they are called *fancy borders*. To see them, click the Border Type drop-down list arrow and choose Fancy. When you choose Fancy borders, a Change button appears in the dialog box (see

Figure 8.30). Click the Change button to open the Change Folder dialog box, where you can choose another borders folder.

Click here to switch between Line and Fancy borders.

Figure 8.30
The fancy borders are available only in the Page Border/Fill dialog box.

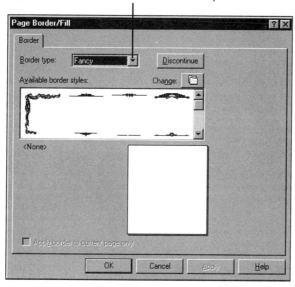

Caution

When you create a border using the line styles, WordPerfect automatically allows space between the text and the border, which is positioned on the margins. A fancy border can overwrite the text, so you may have to make some adjustments to the margins.

To apply a page border to the current page only, choose Apply Border to Current Page Only. In most cases, you apply a page border to the all pages in the document to maintain consistency. However, you can turn the border off on certain pages if you want. Click on the page where you want the border to stop, and then choose Format, Page, Border/Fill, Discontinue.

Tip #104 from
Laura and Read

The Page Border/Fill dialog box offers a list of fancy borders. You can customize these borders in presentations and then save them with the same name or a different name. The fancy borders are located in the folder specified in the File Settings dialog box. Choose Tools, Settings, Files, click the Graphic tab, and look in the Default Fancy Borders Folder text box for the location.

Tip #105 from
Laura and Read

Round-cornered borders add an interesting effect. You can change the border corners for the line borders to anything from slightly rounded to almost circular. To round off the corners on a border, choose Format, Page, Border/Fill. Click the Advanced tab, and then click Rounded Corners. To adjust the amount of roundness, type a value in the Corner Radius text box. Keep an eye on the sample document to see how the roundness looks.

TROUBLESHOOTING

CAN'T FIND THE RIGHT MARGINS TO CENTER THE PAGE

I've been trying unsuccessfully to adjust the top and bottom margins so that I can center titles on the title page. There must be an easier way!

There is—it's called Center Page, and it only takes a second to set it up. Choose Format, Page, Center. Choose Current Page to center the current page. Choose Current and Subsequent Pages to center pages from the insertion point on. Choose No Centering to stop centering pages (after you've used the Current and Subsequent Pages option).

EDITING A CUSTOM PAGE NUMBER

I decided to go back and add some text to a plain page number. After I made the change, I noticed that part of my document has the revised page number, but the rest has only the original page number. What's going on here?

When you edit a custom page number, you have to be sure you go back to the page where you created the custom page number. This might be at the top of the document or the beginning of a new section or chapter. Going back to the original page gives you the opportunity to edit the original code, rather than create another code (with your changes) later on in the document that conflicts with the original code.

MANUAL FEED IS ON ALL THE TIME

I made a few changes to one of the paper size definitions, and now whenever I print something, I have to insert every piece of paper into the manual feed tray.

You've accidentally changed the paper source to manual, so the printer thinks that you *want* to insert the paper by hand. This is a great feature when you want to manually feed in the letterhead and allow the printer to grab second sheets from the tray, but it's a real pain when it gets turned on by accident. Select the paper size in the Page Setup dialog box and choose Options, Edit, Both. Click the Source drop-down list arrow and choose Default.

HEADERS/FOOTERS VERSUS PAGE NUMBERS

I've got my page numbers positioned in the bottom center of every page, but they are printing on top of the footer text. Isn't there some way to print the footer text in one place on the line and the page number somewhere else?

As you've already surmised, page numbers, headers, and footers all use the same area of the page. Most of the time they all get along. When a conflict occurs, the page number doesn't replace the header or footer (or vice versa); they are both printed, one on top of the other.

You have two choices: You can either choose another position for the page number (such as the bottom right), or you can insert the page number as part of the footer.

I've Got Gremlins Formatting My Document

I don't know what I did to deserve this, but I'm working on a document for a friend, and all sorts of crazy things are happening. I've got headers and footers popping up in places where they don't belong, page numbers that start midway through the document, and margin changes out of nowhere. When I print, the document comes out on two different types of paper. The worst part about the whole thing is that I can't find a code to delete or edit and I've even used Find and Replace to try to locate it.

It *is* rather unsettling to see formatting changes that can't be traced back to a code. One of two things can cause this type of situation: styles and delay codes. There could be styles in the document that contain the offending formatting codes, or the formatting codes might be inside a delay code. Either way, you can't remove or edit the formatting codes until you've located the style or delay code that contains the codes. Start at the top of the document and look for a [Delay:#] code. Double-click the code to edit the contents.

A style code could be anywhere. Use Find and Replace to locate the style code, and then double-click it to edit the contents.

My Balanced Newspaper Columns Are Uneven

I've defined balanced columns and typed in text, but the columns aren't all the same length.

You've probably got some blank lines in there throwing things off. Turn on Reveal Codes and delete any extra [HRt] codes. You might also have some formatting options that conflict with columnar formatting. Click in the paragraph that isn't balanced, and then choose Format, Keep Text Together and deselect all the options.

Rounded Corners Don't Display Correctly

I've rounded the corners on a page border, but the corners still look square on the screen.

Rest assured, the rounded corner will print correctly even though they aren't displayed onscreen. In order to display rounded corners, WordPerfect would have to redraw the screen every time you type a character, which would result in a serious performance degradation.

Project

Just as you saw in Chapter 7, "Formatting Lines and Paragraphs," a few small changes can make all the difference in the world. Take pity on the annual report that you see in Figure 8.31. The information is no doubt comprehensive and exhaustively researched. The only problem is that it's dull and boring. Figure 8.32 shows the same annual report with a few improvements. The information that you need to make these changes is included in this chapter, so I won't duplicate the steps here.

A decorative page border has been added to the title page. This border was discontinued on the second page so that it only affects the first page. Headers and footers were created at the top of the first page, but they are suppressed on the title page. The header contains document identification text. The footer has a "page x of y" page number centered on the line. Finally, the top and bottom margins have been reduced to .667 to reclaim the space taken up by the header and footer.

Figure 8.31
This annual report contains everything you need to know about the company, but it doesn't look interesting to read.

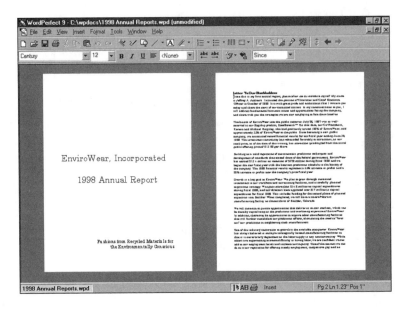

Document information in the header

Margins reduced to reclaim the space lost by the header and footer

Figure 8.32
This annual report looks more inviting and gives the impression that the person who prepared it paid close attention to details.

Fancy page border —

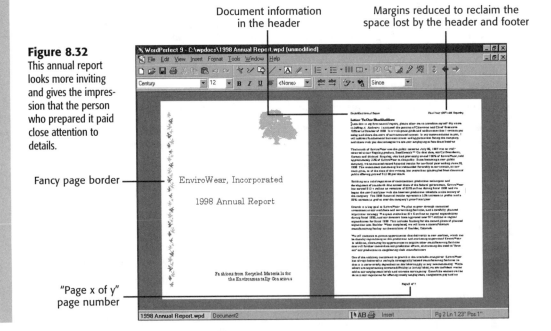

"Page x of y" page number

CHAPTER **9**

FORMATTING WITH STYLES

In this chapter

A QUICK OVERVIEW OF STYLES

You like doing things in style. But you also like to be quick about it. WordPerfect has just the answer for you: styles.

Most of us begin making our documents look good by using the "brute force" method. If the document needs to be fixed, we just add a formatting code here or there until it approximates what we're looking for. Unfortunately, if you have to create that kind of document again, you'll spend lots of time trying to duplicate the steps you took, and often you don't really end up with the same results.

Suppose, for example, you want each section heading in your document in a certain font and size, and you want them all bold and italic, with a horizontal line underneath that extends the width of the page. Instead of applying each of those elements to each heading, one by one, you can apply to each heading a style that already includes all those elements.

Styles are named collections of formatting procedures, such as fonts, margins, tabs, and so on. When you apply a style in your document, you apply one or more formatting options. Thus, everything with a particular style has the same look.

In addition, any change you make to a style automatically changes any text where you already applied that style. For example, if you decide you don't want your headings in italics, you can remove the italics format from your style, and WordPerfect removes it from each place the style was used. The other formats, such as font, size, and so on, remain intact.

Much like many of WordPerfect's features, styles can be both easy to use and complex. More often than not, you'll find yourself using styles occasionally to make your work easier and more professional looking. But when you need the full power that styles have to offer, you won't be disappointed because WordPerfect will be there to help.

STYLES VERSUS MACROS VERSUS QUICKWORDS

Just what is the difference between styles and macros? Couldn't you just create a macro to accomplish the formatting you want?

Indeed, macros are powerful and can perform many formatting tasks. However, after you run a macro, you end up with formatting codes in your document as if you placed them there yourself. *Macros (page 688)* automate the process of inserting format codes, but otherwise there is nothing in the document to distinguish the fact that you used a macro instead of formatting the text one step at a time.

Styles, on the other hand, remain in the document and format the text they are applied to. If you remove the style, you remove all the formatting it provided, not only in one location, but everywhere it appeared in the document. If you change a style, the change takes place automatically throughout the document. Thus styles offer much more flexibility and control for formatting than do macros.

QuickWords is another powerful formatting tool. But like macros, the end result is simply text and format codes as if you had created each code yourself.

➜ For information on using QuickWords, **see** Chapter 3, "Basic Formatting," **p. 57**
➜ For more information on macros, **see** Chapter 24, "Experts and Macros," **p. 685**

USING QUICKFORMAT TO CREATE STYLES ON-THE-FLY

WordPerfect's QuickFormat feature enables you to make and use styles on-the-fly. You begin by formatting text, and then copying and applying the results at other locations in the document. Consider, for example, the document shown in Figure 9.1. Suppose you want to make each header stand out by changing its font and making it both bold and italic. Follow these simple steps:

PART

II

CH

9

Figure 9.1
The use of styles makes it easy to apply consistent formatting throughout a document—for example, in section headings.

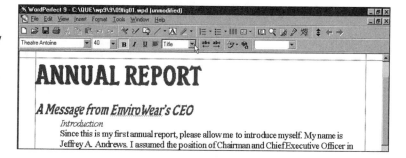

1. Begin by applying the formatting you want to the first section heading. For example, if you change the font, and add bold and italic, you get the result you see in Figure 9.1.

 2. Position the insertion point anywhere on the formatted heading, and choose Format, QuickFormat, or click QuickFormat on the toolbar. WordPerfect displays the QuickFormat dialog box (see Figure 9.2.)

Figure 9.2
The QuickFormat dialog box enables you to capture a formatting style and apply it to selected text or to heading paragraphs.

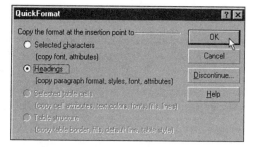

3. Because you want to produce consistent-looking headings, choose the Headings option.

4. Click OK, and WordPerfect returns you to the document, but now the mouse pointer is shaped like a paint roller with a trailing swath of paint (see Figure 9.3)

Figure 9.3
The mouse pointer changes to indicate that you will apply a heading style when you click the mouse.

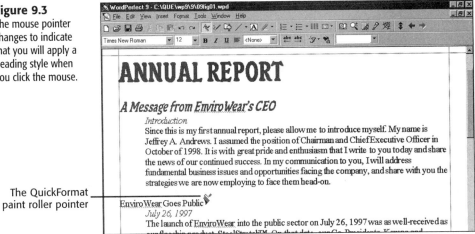

The QuickFormat paint roller pointer

5. Move to the next section heading, point the tip of the paint swath at the heading, and click. WordPerfect applies the styles from the first heading to the heading you click.

6. Continue through the document, clicking each heading to apply the QuickFormat style.

7. To turn off the QuickFormat process, choose Format, QuickFormat; or simply click the QuickFormat button on the toolbar.

Each time you create a QuickFormat style, WordPerfect adds the style to your style list and numbers it (for example, QuickFormat1, QuickFormat2, and so on). If you want to use the style again, you can follow the same procedures listed previously or you can apply the style from the style list, following these steps:

1. Position the cursor on the heading you want to format.

2. Choose Format, Styles. WordPerfect displays the Styles dialog box (see Figure 9.4).

Figure 9.4
You can use the Styles dialog box to select and apply a style to your document.

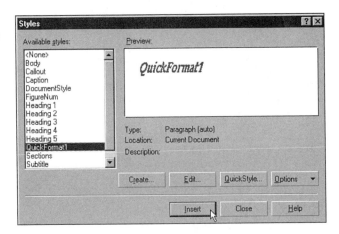

3. Click the QuickFormat style you created for the headings (for example, QuickFormat1).

4. Click Insert. WordPerfect applies the style to the heading.

Heading format styles apply to entire paragraphs. If you want to copy only fonts and attributes and apply them to selected text, the procedure is a bit different:

1. Begin by applying the formatting you want to your text. For example, you can add fancy underlining to bold, italic text, as shown in Figure 9.5.

Figure 9.5
You can use QuickFormat to pick up special formatting and apply it to selected text.

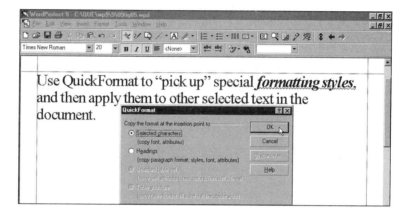

 2. Position the insertion point anywhere on the formatted text, and choose Format, QuickFormat, or click QuickFormat on the toolbar. WordPerfect displays the QuickFormat dialog box (refer to Figure 9.2).

3. Because you now want to copy fonts and attributes, choose Selected Characters.

4. Click OK, and WordPerfect returns you to the document, but now the mouse pointer is shaped like a paint roller with an I-beam.

5. Move to the text you want to format and use the mouse to select it (see Figure 9.6). When you release the mouse button, WordPerfect applies the styles from the original text to the text you just selected.

Figure 9.6
QuickFormat by characters applies formatting style to selected text instead of to whole paragraphs.

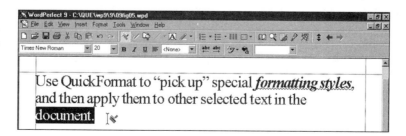

6. Continue through the document, selecting text to which you want to apply the QuickFormat style.

7. Turn off QuickFormat by choosing Fo_r_mat, _Q_uickFormat, or by clicking the QuickFormat icon on the toolbar.

> **Note**
>
> QuickFormats are saved with the current document, but are not available to other documents you create. For more information on renaming, editing, and saving styles for use in all your documents, see the section "Creating Custom Styles," later in this chapter.

UNDERSTANDING STYLES

Styles are primarily formatting tools. A style consists of various format elements that you apply collectively to all or part of a document. If all you ever need is a quick and easy way to apply basic formatting, QuickStyles will probably do the trick. But if you need to explore the full power of WordPerfect's styles, you also need to understand how and where they work.

TYPES OF STYLES

Although styles are relatively easy to create and use, you can become confused when you first encounter paragraph styles, template styles, or system styles. It helps to think about styles as different types, depending on their function or location.

First, there are three basic *types* of styles, each with its own purpose, and named according to the portion of the document they affect:

- Document (or open) styles
- Paragraph styles
- Character styles

Second, there are three *locations* for styles:

- Document styles (styles saved with a document)
- Template styles (styles saved in templates)
- System styles (WordPerfect's default styles)

Finally, there are *feature* styles that apply to specific types of text, such as the following:

- Specialized text styles, such as hyperlinks and headings.
- Outline styles for bullets, numbered paragraphs, and outlines.
- Graphics styles for graphics boxes, text boxes, equation and figure numbers, and so on.
- Footnote and endnote styles.
- Header, footer, and watermark styles.

→ For information on bullet, list, and outline styles, **see** Chapter 11, "Organizing Information with Lists and Outlines," **p. 289**

→ For information on style for graphics boxes, **see** Chapter 13, "Customizing Graphic Shapes and Images," **p. 347**

→ For details on footnote, endnote, and other specialized heading styles, **see** Chapter 18, "Working with Large and Multipart Documents," **p. 497**

Styles can be a combination of any of these categories. For example, a numbered outline style is also a paragraph style, and can be stored in the current document or in a template for use in all your documents.

DOCUMENT, PARAGRAPH, AND CHARACTER TYPES OF STYLES

Document styles are found at the beginning of the document because they establish certain features such as paper size, margins, tab stops, line spacing, and font for the entire document. These are *open* styles, as opposed to *paired* styles, because they are turned on and left open throughout the document. In earlier versions of WordPerfect the DocumentStyle style is called Document Initial Styles.

If you insert formatting codes in your document but don't get the results you expect (for example, page numbers are in the wrong font), you probably need to look at the DocumentStyle (see the section "Editing Styles" later in this chapter).

Paragraph styles, as the name indicates, affect entire paragraphs. You typically use paragraph styles for such things as headings, headlines, titles, and bibliographic entries.

A paragraph style overrides DocumentStyle settings, or other settings created by the insertion of formatting codes. To apply a paragraph style, simply place the insertion point anywhere in the paragraph, and then choose Format, Styles. WordPerfect displays the Styles dialog box (refer to Figure 9.4). Select the style you want and click Insert to apply that style. Note, in Figure 9.7, that the style affects the entire paragraph, but does not affect paragraphs before or after the style.

Figure 9.7
A paragraph style formats the entire paragraph to which it is applied, but does not change the formatting before or after the paragraph. Note the pair of style codes in Reveal Codes.

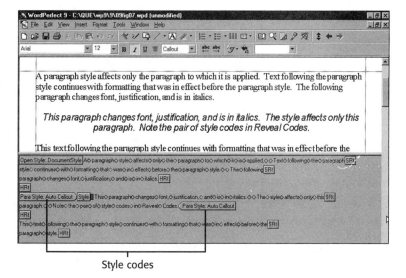

Style codes

Character styles affect sections of text, but not whole paragraphs or documents, and are usually limited to text attributes such as font, font size, bold, and italic. They also override paragraph or document styles.

Although character styles seem similar to pairs of WordPerfect attribute codes (such as bold), they are much more easily changed. For example, you can use a style called Citation to apply underlining to books you reference. If you later decide to put citations in italics instead of underlining them, you simply change the style, and WordPerfect automatically updates all citations.

Tip #106 from
Laura and Read

To apply a character style, you must first select the text you want. WordPerfect normally selects entire words at a time, but you can select the specific characters you want by holding down the Alt key while dragging the mouse. You also can select text one character at a time by holding down the Shift key while moving the cursor with the keyboard.

THE LOCATION OF STYLES

WordPerfect always stores styles you create or import in the document itself (see Figure 9.8, which illustrates the location of styles and where they can be stored). You can edit such styles, but they affect only the current document. However, if you save custom styles to a template, you can apply them to other documents as well.

Figure 9.8
WordPerfect styles that come from the WordPerfect system and from templates can be modified or created by the user within a document. Modified styles can be saved with the document or to other templates.

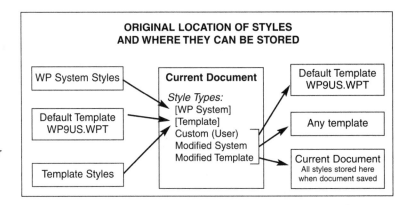

Certain default styles are part of the WordPerfect system, and as such are always available to restore settings that you may have changed. You cannot change these styles, but you can import them and then change them for the current document. Further, you can save system style changes to a template.

All WordPerfect documents are based on templates that contain styles, macros, toolbars, keyboard definitions, and so on. By default, regular documents start by using the wp9us.wpt template (*us* varies, depending on the language and country version of WordPerfect you use). Other specialized documents, such as calendars, newsletters, and fax cover sheets, are based on templates that contain their own special styles.

Thus, the current document contains styles that came from a template (either the default template or a specialized template) or from the WordPerfect system. The current document can also contain styles you create or edit.

You can save styles with the current document only, or you can save them to one of the specialized templates or to the default template for use with future documents. You cannot change the system settings because these are used to restore styles to their default settings.

The following sections describe how to use, and how to create, edit, save, and retrieve styles.

FEATURE-SPECIFIC STYLES

This chapter explores how to create and edit styles in general. These principles and procedures also apply to feature-specific styles, such as footnotes or graphics. However, you may have to approach them differently. For example, the Styles list does not include a footnote style. However, if you edit that style (by choosing Insert, Footnote/Endnote; and then in the Footnote/Endnote dialog box choosing Options, Advanced; and in the Advanced Footnote Options dialog box, editing the numbering style), WordPerfect adds the edited style to the current document's style list (see Figure 9.9).

Figure 9.9
If you modify WordPerfect system styles, the modified style appears in the list of available styles in that document. Otherwise, unless you import them, WordPerfect system styles do not appear in the list.

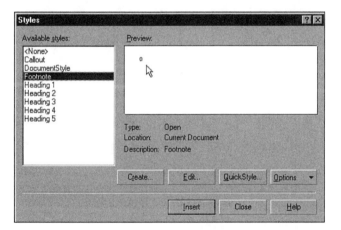

You can also import WordPerfect's system styles to the current document, and then edit a system style (such as footnotes) directly from the document's styles list (see "Editing Styles," later in this chapter). To import system styles, from the Styles dialog box, choose Options, Retrieve, and then in the Retrieve Styles From dialog box, choose System Styles, and click OK.

USING WORDPERFECT'S STYLES

Whether your document contains few or many styles, and whether these styles come from a template, from the WordPerfect system, or from your own creation, using styles is simple.

Determine exactly where you want to apply a style. You can apply styles to

- The entire document—This requires editing the DocumentStyle (see the section "Editing Styles," later in this chapter) or positioning the cursor at the beginning of the document to apply an open style.

- A paragraph—Simply position the cursor anywhere in the paragraph you want to format.

- A selection of text—Use the mouse or the keyboard to select the specific text you want to format.

To apply a style, follow these steps:

1. Click the Styles drop-down list on the Property Bar (see Figure 9.10).

Figure 9.10
The fastest way to select a style is to choose one from the Styles list on the Property Bar.

2. Click the style you want to use.

If you want a bit more control over which style you use, follow these steps instead:

1. Choose Format, Styles or press Alt+F8. WordPerfect displays the Styles dialog box (see Figure 9.11).

Figure 9.11
The Styles dialog box enables you to select, create, edit, or save styles. You can also preview the effect of a style before you insert it.

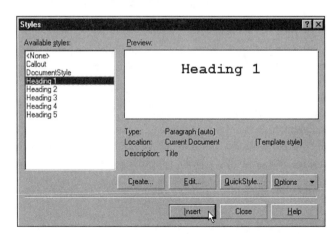

2. In the Available Styles list, click the style you want to use. WordPerfect displays an approximation of the effect of the style in the Preview box.

3. To apply the style to the document, click <u>I</u>nsert.

4. To close without applying the style, click Close, or press Esc.

Where Styles Come From

The list of styles you see varies depending on the template you start with, the styles you import, changes you make to feature styles (such as footnote numbering), and custom styles you create, including QuickFormat or QuickStyle styles.

CREATING CUSTOM STYLES

Predefined styles may be of some use to you, but you'll notice the real value of styles only after you create and use your own. Fortunately, styles are easy to create and edit.

CREATING QUICKSTYLES

One of the easiest ways to create a basic formatting style is to first format some text as you want the style to look and then use the QuickStyle feature.

To use QuickStyle, follow these steps:

1. Format the text selection or paragraph with the features you want to include in the style. For example, in Figure 9.12, the paragraph is 10-point Arial italic, and is right justified.

Figure 9.12
You can format text first, and then use QuickStyle to create a style based on the format you used.

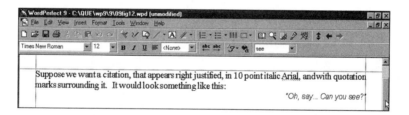

2. Position the cursor anywhere in the selection or paragraph. You need not select the text.

3. Choose Fo<u>r</u>mat, <u>S</u>tyles (or press Alt+F8) to access the Styles dialog box.

4. Click <u>Q</u>uickStyle to display the QuickStyle dialog box (see Figure 9.13).

Figure 9.13
In the QuickStyle dialog box you name the style and designate the type of style you want it to be. You can also add an optional description that helps you remember what the style is used for.

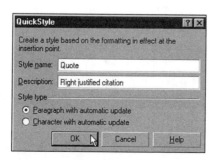

Tip #107 from
Laura and Read

You can also select the QuickStyle feature by clicking the drop-down Styles list on the Property Bar and selecting QuickStyle.

5. In the Style Name text box, type the name of the style, using 20 or fewer characters.

6. You can also type a longer description in the Description text box. This can be useful later if you want to use the style, but can't remember what it does by the name alone.

7. Choose Paragraph if you want the style to apply to entire paragraphs, or Character if you want to format only selected text.

Note

QuickStyle does not always convert formatting settings to a style. For example, if you change the margins for a single paragraph, or use a tab to indent the first line, QuickStyle does not save these formatting changes. However, QuickStyle does recognize paragraph formatting that you change using the Paragraph Format dialog box (which you reach by choosing Format, Paragraph, Format).

8. Click OK to add the style to your current document and to return to the Styles dialog box. Your new style appears in the Available Styles list (see Figure 9.14).

Figure 9.14
The Preview box in the Styles dialog box enables you to preview the effect of a selected style.

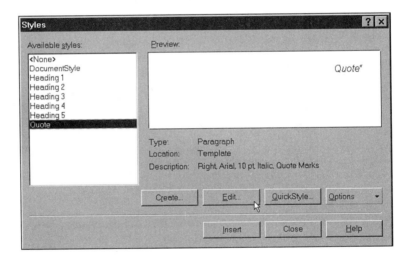

When you click a style, note that WordPerfect displays the effect of the style in the Preview box, and also displays the longer description that you provided.

CREATING STYLES

If you know what you want in your style, you can often create the style more quickly and with more control by accessing the Styles Editor dialog box and adding style information directly into the style. In addition, you can add specific text or special characters, along with formatting information.

For example, to create the Quote style, first set up the style by following these steps:

1. Open the Styles dialog box by choosing Format, Styles or by pressing Alt+F8.

2. Click Create to open the Styles Editor dialog box. Figure 9.15 shows the Styles Editor dialog box, with Show 'Off Codes' already selected and codes added to the editing screen.

Figure 9.15
The Styles Editor dialog box, shown here with both on and off codes, gives you control over the content and effect of a style.

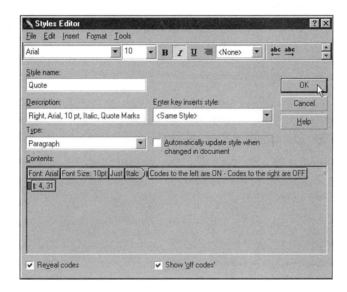

3. Provide a style name (for example, Quote).

4. Provide a description (for example, right justified, italic Arial text.)

5. By default, when you press Enter at the end of a paragraph that uses a style, the next paragraph continues using the same style. If you want to turn off the paragraph style when you press Enter, replace <Same Style> with <None> in the Enter Key Inserts Style box.

6. Because you want to apply the style to an entire paragraph, be sure Paragraph appears in the Type box.

7. If you want changes to one Quote-style paragraph to appear automatically in all other Quote-style paragraphs, check the Automatically Update Style When Changed in Document check box.

8. Do *not* click OK yet; you want to stay in this dialog box.

You're now ready to add the style's formatting codes to the Contents box. This box displays the style in a Reveal Codes format, where you can add text, special characters, and format codes. Suppose, for example, you want your Quote paragraph to add a quotation mark at the beginning of the paragraph, and another at the end, along with other formatting codes (refer to Figure 9.15). Follow these steps:

1. Choose the font style from the Font list on the Property Bar or from the Font dialog box (which you access by choosing Format, Font).

Using the Styles Editor
The menus and Property Bar in the Styles Editor are similar to those in the regular WordPerfect screen, but features that cannot be added to styles are not included in the menus. For those features that are available, you access and insert format codes with the same menu choices or keystrokes that you do in a regular WordPerfect document.

---

2. Choose the font size from the Property Bar or from the Font dialog box.
3. Choose italic from the Property Bar or from the Font dialog box.
4. Choose right justification from the Property Bar or from the menu (which you access by choosing Format, Justification, Right).
5. Type a quotation mark (").

   All the codes you see are those that begin the paragraph. WordPerfect automatically turns off these codes and reverts to the document codes at the end of the paragraph. However, you also want to close your paragraph with a quote mark. Continue with the following steps.

6. Click Show 'Off Codes'. WordPerfect displays a separator button. Codes to the left of the button are those that begin the paragraph, and those to the right of the button are those that end the paragraph.
7. Position the cursor to the right of the separator button.
8. Type another quotation mark (").

Tip #108 from
Laura and Read

If you're using WordPerfect's SmartQuotes, the Styles Editor inserts another opening quotation mark where you should have a closing quotation mark. Simply type any character, such as a space, before typing the quotation mark to get the proper closing quotation mark. Then delete the character, leaving only the closing quotation mark to close the paragraph.

---

9. Check your style settings one more time then choose OK to save your style in your current document.

EDITING STYLES

To edit a paragraph or character style, access the Styles dialog box, select the style you want to edit, and click Edit. WordPerfect displays the Styles Editor dialog box, where you can make changes just as you do when you create a new style (see the preceding section, "Creating Styles").

Tip #109 from
Laura and Read

Instead of creating new styles from scratch, you can often save time by editing an existing style that's similar to the one you want to create. Simply give the style a new name and make any changes you want.

Editing DocumentStyles follows a similar approach, but has more far-reaching impact on your document. You can access the Styles Editor and view the DocumentStyle style in three ways:

- Choose File, Document, Current Document Style.

- Choose Format, Styles, and from the Available Styles list, select DocumentStyle and click Edit.

- Access Reveal Codes (by choosing View, Reveal Codes, or pressing Alt+F3). In the Reveal Codes window, double-click the Open Style: DocumentStyle button at the beginning of the document.

PART

II

CH

9

WordPerfect displays the Styles Editor dialog box (see Figure 9.16).

Figure 9.16
You can also use the Styles Editor to edit an open, or a document, style that affects an entire document.

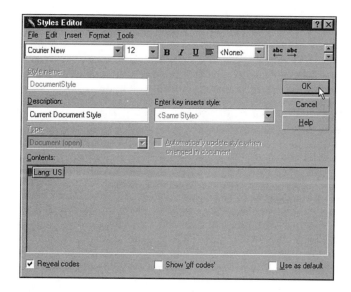

Out of the box, WordPerfect comes with certain preset styles. For example, by default documents are in portrait orientation, have 1-inch margins on all sides, are singled-spaced, and have tab stops at every 1/2 inch.

Note that none of these settings appear in the DocumentStyle. However, if you want to change the default settings, this is the place to do it.

To change the document styles for just the current document, edit the DocumentStyle style just as you do other styles. If you also want to make these changes the default for all your new documents, click Use as Default. WordPerfect then saves the Document Style information to your default template so that any new documents you create use these changed styles.

Note

Changes to the default template do *not* change the styles in documents that you have already created. Such changes apply only to new documents that you create after making the changes.

Tip #110 from
Laura and Read

One of the most common problems WordPerfect users encounter is that they insert a formatting code, but find that it doesn't format everything they expect it to. For example, if you insert a margins code at the beginning of the document, that code affects the body of the text, but headers, footers, and footnotes all retain the original default margins.

To ensure that a formatting code affects the entire document, change the settings in the DocumentStyle style.

SAVING STYLES

When you create or edit a style, that style is automatically saved in your current document. If you later open the document, the style is still there, available for your use. Unfortunately, custom styles are not automatically available to you in other documents or templates.

However, you can save your custom styles to WordPerfect's default template for use in all documents you create. You can also save a style to a custom template, one that you use only for a specific type of document (for example, a news release).

Note

When you save a style to another template, you actually copy the style from the current document to that template.

To save a style to the default WordPerfect template, follow these steps:

1. Open the document that contains the style you want to save.

2. Access the Styles dialog box by choosing Fo<u>r</u>mat, <u>S</u>tyles or by pressing Alt+F8.

3. Select the style you want to save to the default template and choose <u>O</u>ptions, <u>C</u>opy. WordPerfect displays the Styles Copy dialog box (see Figure 9.17).

Figure 9.17
To save a style, you copy the style to another document or template.

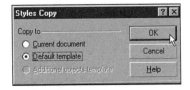

4. Choose <u>D</u>efault Template and click OK.

WordPerfect now displays the style in the Available <u>S</u>tyles list, with the notation that it's located both in the current document and also in a template as a template style.

Now, if you open a new blank document, your style appears in the style list. You can use the style as you do any other style.

The procedure for copying a style from your current document to another template is a bit more complicated, but only because there are more steps to follow:

1. Copy the style from your current document to the default template, as described in the preceding steps.

Tip #111 from
Laura and Read

If you want a custom style available to you in all your documents, including templates, you need not copy it to individual templates. By copying it to the default template, it is accessible from all your documents.

2. Choose File, New from Project or press Ctrl+Shift+N to display the PerfectExpert dialog box (see Figure 9.18).

Figure 9.18
You can use the PerfectExpert dialog box to open a template file and then import styles to be used with the template.

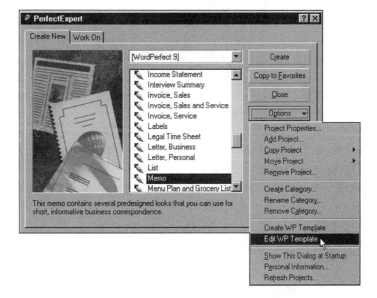

3. From the Create New tab, select the template to which you want to copy your custom style.

4. Click Options, and select Edit WP Template. WordPerfect displays the WordPerfect editing screen, along with the template you are editing, and the Template toolbar (see Figure 9.19).

5. Click the Copy/Remove Object button on the Template toolbar. WordPerfect displays the Copy/Remove Template Objects dialog box, as shown in Figure 9.20.

Figure 9.19
You can use the Template toolbar to copy styles and to save them with the current template document.

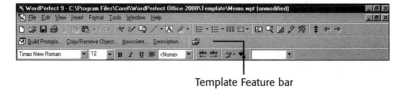

Template Feature bar

Figure 9.20
You can use the Copy/Remove Template Objects dialog box to copy styles from another document or template to the current document.

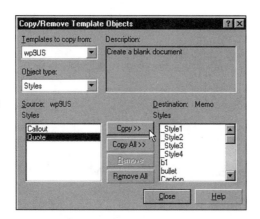

6. From the Templates to Copy From list, choose the default WordPerfect template, wp9US.wpt, if it isn't already chosen.

7. Select Styles from the Object Type drop-down list. WordPerfect displays your custom styles in the Styles list on the left side of the dialog box.

8. Click the style you want to copy, even if there's only one style listed, and click the Copy>> button to add it to the list of styles in the current template.

9. Click Close to return to the template.

 10. Click the Close button on the Template toolbar and answer Yes when asked whether you want to save changes to the template.

Now, whenever you create a new document based on your edited template, your custom style is available to you, even if the style is later removed from your default template.

→ If you need help working with WordPerfect templates, **see** "Using WordPerfect's Templates," **p. 614**

DELETING STYLES

If you create a style, it stays in the document unless you delete it. Sometimes you simply want to clean up your document and remove any unnecessary custom styles.

To remove a custom style from your current document or from the default template, follow these steps:

1. Access the Styles dialog box by choosing Format, Styles or by pressing Alt+F8.

2. Select the style you want to remove. Note the type of style it is, and whether it is a template style or in the current document only.

3. Click Options, and select Delete. WordPerfect displays the Delete Styles dialog box (see Figure 9.21), which includes all custom styles that can be deleted, whether from the current document or from the default template.

Figure 9.21
You can remove styles from the current document by using the Delete Styles dialog box.

Note

You can remove only custom styles; you cannot delete system styles. If you choose a system style, the Delete option is grayed out and you cannot delete it.

4. Select the style or styles you want to delete.

5. Choose how you want to delete the style. You can delete the style by choosing one of these options:

   • Including Formatting Codes—This removes the style and the formatting it produces.

   • Leave Formatting Codes in Document—This removes the style, but replaces it with formatting codes that become part of the text, but that you must remove or format one by one, as you do with normal text.

6. Click OK to delete the style.

USING STYLES TOGETHER

You can increase the power of styles by linking them together in the same document. For example, if you have a style that defines your company logo, you can nest that style in other styles used in newsletter headings, company letterhead, fax cover sheets, and so on. Then if you change the logo style, it automatically updates other styles in which it is embedded.

To insert one style inside another, access the Styles dialog box, select the style in which you want to embed another style, and choose Edit. Then, in the Contents box of the Style Editor, choose Format, Styles and select a style to insert, and then click Insert.

Note

Generally, styles that contain other styles should be document (open) styles because paragraph styles can be difficult to use. In any case, you cannot embed one paragraph style within another.

Styles that usually follow one another can be made to *chain*, or link, from one style to the next. For example, after you type a section heading, WordPerfect could automatically switch to the next style, such as a subtitle or a paragraph that begins with a drop cap.

To link two styles, follow these steps:

1. Access the Styles dialog box and select the first style you want to use.

2. Click Edit to display the Styles Editor dialog box.

3. In the Enter Key Inserts Style box, select the second style you want to use from the drop-down list of available styles (see Figure 9.22). Only custom styles appear; template and system styles do not.

Figure 9.22
In the Styles Editor dialog box, you can choose to chain, or link, a style to another style.

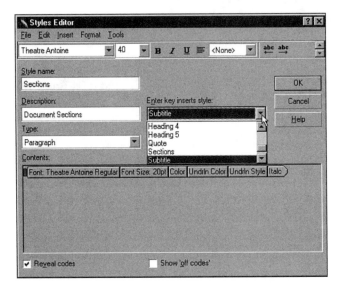

4. Click OK to return to the Styles dialog box.

5. If you want to link the second style to a third style, repeat steps 1–4. Otherwise, click OK to save the linked styles in the current document.

Note

You cannot link from document (open) styles or from system styles.

Tip #112 from
Laura and Read

Don't forget that the default for all paragraph styles is to continue with the same style when you press Enter. If you want to turn off the style when you press Enter, you can choose <None> from the Enter Key Inserts Style box.

WORKING WITH STYLES FROM OTHER FILES

If you, or someone else, creates a document that contains styles you want to use, you might have to import those styles to your current document. For example, if you want to use a style that you know exists, but that doesn't show up on the Styles list, find the file or template, and then import the style and make it part of the current document.

To import styles from one file or template into a current document that doesn't have the styles, follow these steps:

1. Open the document that does not currently have the styles you want.

2. Access the Styles dialog box, click Options, and choose Retrieve. WordPerfect displays the Retrieve Styles From dialog box (see Figure 9.23).

Figure 9.23
To import styles from the WordPerfect system or from another template, you use the Retrieve Styles From dialog box.

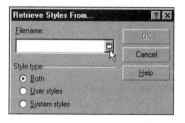

3. Use the Browse button to locate the file or template that contains the styles you want to retrieve.

4. You can choose to retrieve only user styles, only system files, or both.

5. When asked whether you want to overwrite current style, answer Yes.

WordPerfect imports the style types you requested and adds them to the styles you already have in your current document. Save your current document to save the styles with that document.

Tip #113 from
Laura and Read

If you aren't sure about the styles you imported, you should check them out *before* you save your document. Also, you can always close the document without saving, which also discards the imported styles.

Tip #114 from
Laura and Read

Another easy way to move a single style from one document to another is to open both documents and use Reveal Codes to copy the style code from the first document and paste the code into the second document.

TROUBLESHOOTING

TOO MUCH UNINTENDED QUICKSTYLE

I tried to apply a QuickStyle to a heading, but applied it to a whole paragraph instead.

This can happen when you're trying to apply formatting by using the mouse. Simply click Undo on the toolbar or press Ctrl+Z. Then try it again.

CREATING A GLOBAL STYLE

I created a style, but now it doesn't appear on the list of available styles.

When you create a style, you save it in your current document only. If you want to make the style available for all your documents, you must copy the style to the default template. Choose Format, Styles, and then select the style you want to copy. Click Options, and select Copy. Choose Default Template and click OK.

MISSING CUSTOM STYLES

I saved my custom style to the default template, but when I open my documents, that style doesn't seem to be available.

Styles saved to the default template are available only for newly created documents. You must import custom styles from your default template to the current document.

TOO MANY CHANGES

I wanted to change a bold, italic paragraph back to normal text, but when I did, other paragraphs changed also.

You tried to change a paragraph style that automatically updates when you change the text. Instead, access the Styles drop-down menu on the Property Bar and select <None>, or delete the styles codes in Reveal Codes.

PROJECT

Nearly any repetitive formatting task can be accomplished more easily and with more consistency by using styles. One simple example is a product list, such as the one shown in Figure 9.24. Each item in the list has a name, a part number, and a description. Suppose you want to set off each element with a different font, style, size, and color. You also want to make it easy to type the entries, chaining one style to the next.

Follow these steps to create three chained styles: PartName, PartNumber, and Description:

1. Create at least one set of entries for each type of text, such as Widget, 45N-5000, and "Primary pin assembly for the wombat mechanism in the Regenta product line." (Refer to Figure 9.24.)

2. Apply formatting to each element:

   - PartName—Choose a sans serif font (for example, Arial), make it 14 point, and change the color to blue.

Figure 9.24
A product list is a perfect candidate for styles because it needs repetitive yet consistent formatting of the name, part number, and description.

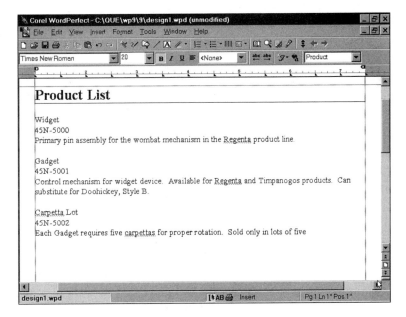

- PartNumber—Add italics.
- Description—No change to the body of the text.

3. Click the PartName heading and choose QuickFormat from the Styles list on the Property Bar.

4. Supply the name of the style to be used (for example, PartName).

5. Choose Paragraph with Automatic Update, and click OK.

6. Repeat steps 3–5 for the other two styles (PartNumber and Description).

Having created the basic style for each element, you now must modify two of the styles to add an indent code and also to chain the styles together. Follow these steps:

1. Access the Styles dialog box by choosing Format, Styles or by pressing Alt+F8.

2. Select the PartName style and click Edit.

3. Click the drop-down menu for Enter Key Inserts Style, and choose the style you want to chain to (for example, PartNumber).

4. Unless you need to make other changes, click OK.

5. Select the PartNumber style and click Edit.

6. Click the drop-down menu for Enter Key Inserts Style, and choose the Description style.

7. Position the cursor at the beginning of the codes in the Contents box and choose Format, Paragraph, Indent to insert a hard left indent code.

8. Make other changes as needed and click OK.

9. Select the Description style and click Edit.

10. Click the drop-down menu for Enter Key Inserts Style, and choose the PartName style.

Note

If you want to end the sequence after the description style, choose <None> from the Enter Key Inserts Style menu.

11. Position the cursor at the beginning of the codes in the Contents box and choose Format, Paragraph, Indent to insert a hard left indent code.

12. Make any other desired changes and click OK.

13. If you want to add these styles to your default template, choose Option, Copy, Default Template and click OK.

Finally, to use the styles, simply apply them to preexisting text or on a new line, by following these steps:

1. Choose the PartName style, type part name heading, and press Enter.

2. Type the part number and press Enter.

3. Type the description and press Enter.

4. Repeat steps 1–3 until you complete your product list.

The completed list, with styles applied appears in Figure 9.25. If you decide to change the style of any of these three elements, change the format of the text where the style is applied to change it in all locations of that style (for example, change Arial to Lucida in the PartName heading.)

Figure 9.25
The product list, with consistent styles, is more appealing, easier to read, and better organized. Making formatting changes in any paragraph result in the same changes being made to all paragraphs with the same style.

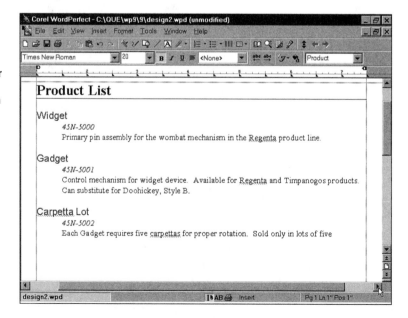

ORGANIZING INFORMATION

CHAPTER 10

ORGANIZING INFORMATION WITH TABLES

In this chapter

UNDERSTANDING TABLES

Of all WordPerfect's special features, the Table feature offers perhaps more practical uses and enables you to enhance the effectiveness and attractiveness of your documents more than any other.

A *table* consists of rows and columns of data arranged and formatted to make the data easy to read or understand. For example, consider the WordPerfect table shown in Figure 10.1.

Figure 10.1
Even simple data lists look better and are easier to read in a WordPerfect table.

Item	Part Number	Bin Number
Widget	34-222	24-A
Gadget	33-245	26-B
Doodad	33-249	13-F

The structure of a table is very much like the structure of a spreadsheet, and in fact, you can even use WordPerfect tables for spreadsheet functions. In a table, WordPerfect labels the rows with numbers (1, 2, 3...) and the columns with letters (A, B, C...). The intersection of a column and a row is a *cell*. You identify each cell according to the row and column in which it resides (A1, B3, C14, and so on). In Figure 10.1, for example, the word *Widget* is in the first column (A) and the second row (2); therefore, *Widget* is in cell A2.

→ For information on WordPerfect's table spreadsheet capabilities, **see** Chapter 15, "Importing Data and Working with Other Programs," **p. 403**

All other table features are options. For example, you can change the appearance of the lines that WordPerfect uses to separate table cells, or you can omit them altogether. You can change text justification, rotate or *skew (page 272)* text, and add text attributes. You can adjust the width and height of any column or row. You can even create formulas to calculate numeric information.

Using WordPerfect's table formatting options, you can create any kind of table—from simple lists to complex invoices, from schedules to calendars, from programs to scripts, and more (see Figure 10.2).

Designing, creating, and modifying a table is a visual and artistic venture. Don't be afraid to experiment, and don't be upset if the results are not quite what you expected. Simply try again.

Figure 10.2
With WordPerfect's Table feature, you can even create complex forms, such as invoices.

EnviroWear

**Fashions from Recycled Materials
For the Environmentally Conscious**

123 Recycle Blvd, Earthtown, USA 00001 999-555-1234
http://www.envirowear.com/

Quantity	Description	Unit Cost	Amount
2 ea	Plastic Sunglasses (#2 Plastic)	$18.99	$37.98
1 ea	Cloth rope sandal	$25.99	$25.99
			$0.00
			$0.00
Comments:		Subtotal	$63.97
Thank you for your business		Tax (5.5%)	$3.52
		TOTAL	$67.49

PART

III

CH

10

PLANNING TABLES

Before you actually create a table, you can save a great deal of time by doing some preliminary planning. First, ask yourself what you want to accomplish with your table. Do you merely want to present straightforward information more clearly, or do you want to design a more complex, heavily formatted form?

Next, determine the approximate number of rows and columns you want. You can have up to 64 columns and 32,767 rows (or 2,097,088 cells), although it's unlikely you'll ever use that many. You do not need to know the exact number of rows or columns because you can add or insert them while you work with your table. Knowing this information in advance, however—especially the number of columns—can make creating, modifying, and using your table much easier.

You can also benefit from determining and selecting the font style and size you want to use before you begin. Again, this is not critical because you can change fonts as you work with your table.

Finally, consider the number and placement of tables. You might need to place two tables of dissimilar structure one after the other, rather than try to create just one table. Also, you might need to place two tables beside each other, in which case you might want to use columns or graphics boxes.

CREATING TABLES

After you determine the number of rows and columns you want, you create WordPerfect tables using one of two easy methods: using the menus or using the toolbar.

To use the menus to create a table, follow these steps:

1. Position the insertion point in your document where you want to insert a table.

2. Choose Insert, Table or press F12. WordPerfect displays the Create Table dialog box (see Figure 10.3).

Figure 10.3
The Create Table dialog box lets you specify the number of columns and rows you want in your table.

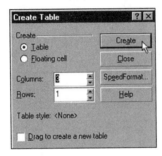

3. Type the number of columns and the number of rows you want.

4. Click Create to create the table (see Figure 10.4).

Figure 10.4
A simple table with four columns and five rows: Notice that the columns are evenly spaced and extend from margin to margin, and the Property Bar shows table-specific functions.

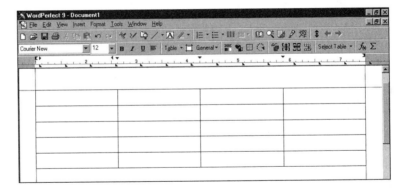

> **Note**
>
> The Drag to Create a New Table option in the Create Table dialog box enables you to create a table inside a text box. You drag the area where you want the text box, and then WordPerfect inserts the table you specify in the dialog box. After the table is created, you can work with it as described in this chapter. Choosing this option makes it the default until you deselect it.

→ For more information on creating and manipulating text boxes, **see** Chapter 12, "Adding Graphics to Documents," **p. 317**

To create the same table by using the toolbar, follow these steps:

1. Position the insertion point in your document where you want to insert a table.

2. Click the Table QuickCreate button, and hold the mouse button down to display a grid.

3. Drag the mouse down and to the right until the pop-up grid highlights the number of columns and rows you want (see Figure 10.5). If you need more columns or rows than are displayed on the grid, keep dragging the mouse; WordPerfect expands the grid until it is up to 32 columns by 45 rows. At the top of the grid, WordPerfect specifies the number of columns and rows, in that order, that you have selected.

Figure 10.5
Using the Table QuickCreate button on the toolbar, you click and drag the mouse to select the number of rows and columns you want in a table.

PART
III

CH

10

4. After you have displayed the number of columns and rows you want, release the mouse button. WordPerfect creates the table with the number of columns and rows you indicated.

Note

If you selected <u>D</u>rag to Create a New Table in the Create Table dialog box, you also have to drag to create using the QuickCreate button. To turn off this option, choose <u>I</u>nsert, <u>T</u>able and uncheck <u>D</u>rag to Create a New Table.

Tip #115 from
Laura and Read

If you decide you don't want to create a table, simply drag the mouse pointer to the top of the grid and when `No Table` appears, release the mouse button.

TOOLS FOR WORKING WITH TABLES

Although earlier versions of WordPerfect include a menu category just for tables, you'll soon discover that WordPerfect menus no longer offer help in modifying or working with tables. However, help is still available using the Property Bar and QuickMenus.

With the insertion point located inside a table, the Property Bar changes to display several table-related options. Click the T<u>a</u>ble drop-down menu to find most of the table-related options you're likely to need (see Figure 10.6). Many of the other buttons on the Property Bar repeat what you find on the menu.

Figure 10.6
Table-related menu items can be found on the Table menu of the Property Bar.

You can also quickly access a menu of options by right-clicking on a table. The Table QuickMenu is nearly identical to the one you find on the Property Bar (see Figure 10.7).

Figure 10.7
The Table QuickMenu is nearly identical to the one you find on the Property Bar.

Note

If the insertion point is located anywhere outside the table, the Property Bar does not display table-related options. Likewise, the QuickMenu does not work if you right-click outside the table area.

USING SPEEDFORMAT

By default, all the cells in a WordPerfect table are surrounded by single lines, and the table has no border. You can customize the lines and borders of a table, and WordPerfect's SpeedFormat feature makes it easy to modify the design of your table.

Tip #116 from
Laura and Read

Although you can change the design and format of a table at any time, SpeedFormat usually works best if applied *before* making other format changes. Thus, if you know what kind of look you want, use SpeedFormat immediately after creating your table.

If you create the table using the menus, you can choose the SpeedFormat feature from the Create Table dialog box (refer to Figure 10.3). If you have already created a table, you can position the cursor anywhere inside the table and choose SpeedFormat from the Table drop-down menu on the Property Bar, or from the Table QuickMenu. WordPerfect then displays the Table SpeedFormat dialog box (see Figure 10.8, which shows a style already selected).

Figure 10.8
When you select a SpeedFormat style such as Fancy Fills, you apply a predefined set of formats, lines, and fills to your table.

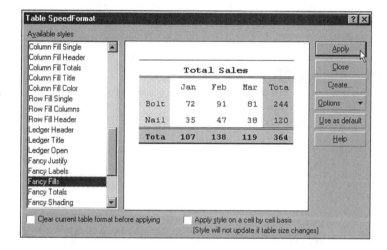

PART
III

Cʜ
10

The Available Styles list box lists several predefined table formats. When you click a style, WordPerfect displays a sample table in the preview box. For example, if you select the Fancy Fills style, WordPerfect formats your table with a centered title bar and with shading and line changes to set off the data (refer to Figure 10.8).

Tip #117 from
Laura and Read

Not all designs match the function of the table you are creating. For example, the Single Bold Title style actually changes the structure of your table. If you don't like the format you select, you can simply select other styles until you find the one that works best for your table.

CONVERTING TABULAR COLUMNS TO TABLES

You may have existing text that you want to place in a table, but you don't want to retype that text. Fortunately, WordPerfect provides a simple method for creating a table from text that is formatted in tabular columns. In fact, this capability may be the easiest yet most practical use for tables.

Suppose that you have a list of company employees that includes names, offices, and telephone numbers. The three columns of data are separated by single tabs, as follows:

Cramer, Ron	VH299	7-3456
Jansen, Lisa	VH287	7-1126
Leisses, Sue	VH297	7-6543

To convert data in tabular columns to a table, follow these steps:

1. With the mouse or keyboard, select all the text to the end of the last line of data. Don't include the final hard return, or you end up with an extra row in your table.

2. Choose Insert, Table or press F12. WordPerfect displays the Convert Table dialog box (see Figure 10.9). Alternatively, you can click the Tables QuickCreate button on the toolbar and choose Tabular Columns from the drop-down list.

Figure 10.9
The Convert Table dialog box is used for converting preexisting data to a table.

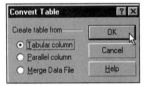

3. Choose Tabular Column (the default), and click OK. WordPerfect converts your tabular columns of data into a table (see Figure 10.10).

Figure 10.10
After converting data from tabular columns into a table, you might need to use column width and other formatting to adjust the layout of the data.

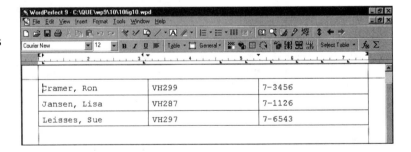

Although this procedure is easy, the key to successfully converting tabular columns to a table lies in the format of the original text. You should use tab settings for each column so that only *one* tab separates each column of data. If, for example, you use WordPerfect's default 1/2-inch tab settings and use more than one tab to separate some of the entries, WordPerfect adds extra cells in the table for the extra tabs. The result can be quite messy.

WORKING WITH TABLES

If you thought it was easy to create a table, you'll find it even easier to work with the information you place in tables.

Consider each table cell a miniature document with its own margins and formatting. As you enter text, WordPerfect wraps the words within the cell, vertically expanding the row to accommodate what you type (see Figure 10.11). You can enter and edit text in a cell just as you do in a document.

Figure 10.11
A table can contain more than one line of text in a cell. Notice that the row automatically expands vertically to accommodate the text you enter.

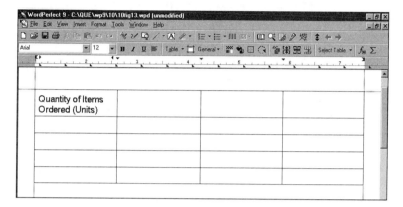

MOVING AROUND IN A TABLE

When you first create a table, WordPerfect positions the cursor at the upper-left corner of the table, in cell A1. Notice that the General Status indicator, on the application bar at the bottom of the screen, displays the name of the current table (Table A in this case) and the cell location of the cursor, Cell A1 (see Figure 10.12). When you move the cursor to a new cell, WordPerfect indicates on the status bar the location of the new cell.

Figure 10.12
When the cursor in located within a table, WordPerfect displays the current cell location on the application bar.

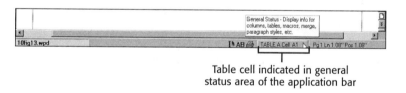

Table cell indicated in general status area of the application bar

To move the cursor one cell to the right, press the Tab key. To move the cursor one cell to the left, press Shift+Tab.

Note that if the cursor is in the last cell of a row, pressing Tab moves the cursor to first cell of the next row. Pressing Shift+Tab while the cursor is in the first cell of a row moves the cursor to the last cell of the previous row.

When you reach the last cell of the last row of your table and press Tab, WordPerfect adds a row and advances the cursor to the first cell of the next row.

→ For more information on how to insert or delete rows and columns in a table, **see** "Changing Table Size," **p. 267**

Of course you can also use the mouse or the arrow keys to move the cursor in your table (see Table 10.1). However, if you're using the keyboard, it is usually quickest and most efficient to use the Tab and Shift+Tab keys.

TABLE 10.1 MOVING THE INSERTION POINT IN A TABLE

Action	Result
Tab	Advances one cell to right
Shift+Tab	Moves one cell to the left
Arrow keys	Move any direction (must travel through text)
Home, Home	Move to left column in row
End, End	Move to right column in row
Mouse click	Click directly in the target cell

USING QUICKFILL

The idea behind WordPerfect's QuickFill feature is that WordPerfect can examine the first few entries in a series and automatically determine the pattern that is being used. WordPerfect then fills in the remaining blank cells in the series based on that pattern.

WordPerfect can automatically insert such things as numbers, days, months, and so on. To use QuickFill to automatically fill in table cells, follow these steps:

1. Type the data you want in the first three cells of a series of cells. For example, type Mon, Tue, and Wed at the top of the first three columns.

2. Select the cells you want filled, including the first three you already typed (see Figure 10.13).

Figure 10.13
You can select a sequence of cells and several blank cells, and use QuickFill to fill the missing data.

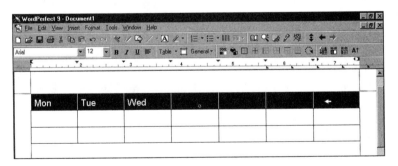

3. Choose QuickFill from the Table menu on the Property Bar or from the Table QuickMenu. WordPerfect automatically supplies the remaining information (see Figure 10.14).

Figure 10.14
QuickFill knows how to fill in the remaining cells in a series.

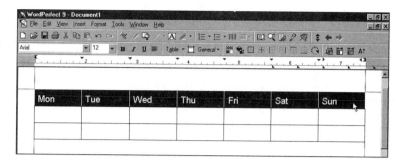

Some of the series that QuickFill can complete for you include the following:

- Numbers—For example, 1, 2, 3,... or 5, 10, 15...
- Days—For example, Monday, Tuesday, Wednesday... or Mon, Tue, Wed...
- Months—For example, Jan, Feb, Mar...

Note

If you supply information that WordPerfect cannot extrapolate, it simply repeats the cells that contain information across the remaining selected cells.

SELECTING TEXT AND CELLS

Within a single cell, you select text the same way you do in a document—by using the mouse or the keyboard.

If you cross a cell boundary while selecting, WordPerfect begins selecting entire cells. For example, if you click the mouse in the middle of the text in cell A1 and begin dragging the mouse toward cell B1, WordPerfect highlights just the text until the mouse pointer crosses over into cell B1. At that point, the entire cells (A1 and B1), are highlighted and the mouse pointer changes to an arrow (see Figure 10.15). As you continue to drag the mouse to other cells, these cells also become part of a selected block.

Tip #118 from
Laura and Read

To select only part of the text from more than one cell, without selecting an entire cell, use the Select key (F8), which enables you to precisely select the text you want.

You can use this method to select rows of cells, columns of cells, and entire tables of cells. However, to select a single cell, you position the mouse pointer within the cell you want to select and move the pointer slowly toward the left line of the cell until the pointer changes to a single arrow. This arrow indicates that you are about to select cells rather than just contents. Click once to select the cell. Click twice to select the entire row of cells. Click three times to select the entire table.

PART
III

CH
10

Figure 10.15
You can select entire cells by dragging the mouse pointer across the edge of the cell until the pointer turns into an arrow. Continue dragging the pointer across cells to select multiple cells at once.

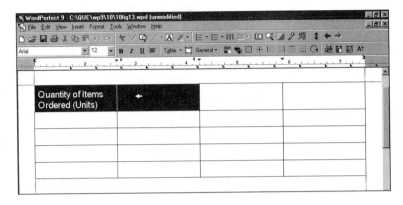

To select a column, move the pointer toward the top line of any cell in the column until the pointer turns into a single upward-pointing arrow. Click once to select the cell, twice to select the column, and three times to select the entire table.

 If you've been having trouble with selected cell text moving where you don't want it, see "But I Didn't Want That There!" in the Troubleshooting section at the end of this chapter.

Tip #119 from
Laura and Read

If you choose T<u>a</u>ble, Ro<u>w</u>/Col Indicators to display the row and column indicators at the edge of the screen, you can click the number of a row or the letter of a column to select an entire row or column.

DELETING TEXT FROM CELLS

To remove text from within a single cell, you use the Delete and Backspace keys as you do with any other text.

A quicker and easier method for deleting the contents of entire cells, especially if the cell contains a large amount of text, is to select the entire cell using the method described in the preceding section. Then press Backspace or Delete, and WordPerfect removes the entire contents of the cell.

Tip #120 from
Laura and Read

Don't forget to use Undo if you accidentally delete the contents of a cell.

You can use the same method for deleting the contents of an entire row, column, or table. However, because this can be a bit more destructive, WordPerfect displays a dialog box asking exactly what you want to delete. For example, if you select all of Row 1 and press Delete or Backspace, the Delete Structure/Contents dialog box appears, with <u>R</u>ows selected (see Figure 10.16). If you click OK, you actually remove the entire row from the table. If you choose C<u>e</u>ll Contents Only, then click OK, only the contents of that row are removed; the row itself remains.

Figure 10.16
The Delete
Structure/Contents
dialog box enables
you to delete the con-
tents of cells or entire
rows or columns.

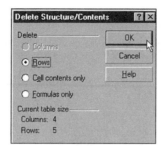

If you select and attempt to delete all the cells in the table, WordPerfect offers several options in the Delete Table dialog box (see Figure 10.17)

Figure 10.17
The Delete Table dia-
log box enables you
to delete the entire
table, remove all the
data from the table,
or convert the table
to a merge data file.

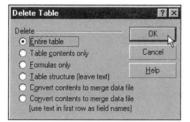

CUTTING, COPYING, AND PASTING TEXT IN TABLES

You can cut, copy, and paste text to and from table cells the same way you do in text documents.

By selecting entire cells, you can quickly and easily cut or copy all the text along with its formatting to a new location. For example, suppose that you want to copy all of Row 1 to Row 2. Select the entire row and then choose Cut or Copy, and the Cut or Copy Table dialog box appears (see Figure 10.18).

Figure 10.18
You can use the Cut
or Copy Table dialog
box to cut and paste
entire rows, columns,
or groups of cells.

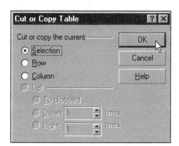

Now you can choose to move the current selection (the contents, but not the table struc-ture), the entire row (the contents and the structure), or the entire column. To cut the entire row, select Row, and then click OK. Position the cursor where you want to paste the row, and choose Paste to insert the row at the insertion point.

Tip #121 from	One of the best uses for the drag-and-drop method of cutting and pasting is when you
Laura and Read	need to move table cells, rows, and columns from one location to another. After selecting the cells you want to move, simply use the mouse to drag the selection to the new table location and release the mouse button.

DELETING, CUTTING, AND COPYING TABLES

To delete, cut, or copy an entire table, including its structure, select the table from before the table to beyond the end of the table; then delete, cut, or copy the table.

To restore a deleted table, you can use Undo (Ctrl+Z). If you cut or copied the table, you can paste it in the new location.

SAVING AND PRINTING TABLES

A table is always part of a document, even when the table is the only element in the document. The procedure for saving tables, therefore, is exactly the same as the method for saving documents.

If you want to save a table alone, or just part of your table, first select the table or the cells you want to save, and then choose File, Save As (or press F3). WordPerfect asks if you want to save the entire file or just the selected text. If you choose Selected Text and provide a filename, WordPerfect saves just the selected cells, along with their format and contents.

Also, you print tables the same way you print other kinds of text. If you print using a dot-matrix printer, you may want to turn off table lines to speed printing (dotted or dashed lines actually increase printing time). However, table lines do not significantly affect printing speed on inkjet or laser printers.

→ For more information on saving a WordPerfect document, **see** Chapter 1, "Getting Comfortable with WordPerfect," **p. 11**

→ For information on printing, **see** Chapter 6, "Printing, Faxing, and Emailing" **p. 143**

EDITING TABLE STRUCTURE

When you create a WordPerfect table, certain default settings apply:

- Evenly spaced columns and rows
- No special formatting of the contents of the cells
- Single lines that separate the cells of the table
- No special border around the table
- Full-justified tables (the tables themselves extend from margin to margin)

The real beauty of the Table feature is that you can easily make all kinds of adjustments to these default settings. When you make changes to the shape and size of table cells, columns, and rows, you are editing the layout of the table, or the table structure.

WordPerfect offers several methods for changing the layout of tables: the Property Bar (including the Table drop-down menu), the Table QuickMenu, the mouse, and the ruler bar.

→ For details on table editing tools, **see** "Tools for Working with Tables," **p. 255**

Tip #122 from
Laura and Read

Don't forget that in order to use table editing tools, you first need to position the cursor somewhere inside the table.

CHANGING COLUMN WIDTHS

Often, instead of evenly spaced columns, you need a table with columns of unequal width. To quickly change the width of a column, position the mouse pointer directly on the line separating two columns until the pointer changes into a double-headed arrow (see Figure 10.19). When you click and hold down the mouse button, WordPerfect displays a dotted guide that helps you position the new column margin. Notice that a QuickTip box also appears, displaying the exact widths of the column to the left and the column to the right. Simply drag the column divider right or left until you have the desired width.

PART

III

CH

10

Figure 10.19
You can change column widths by dragging the column divider with the mouse.

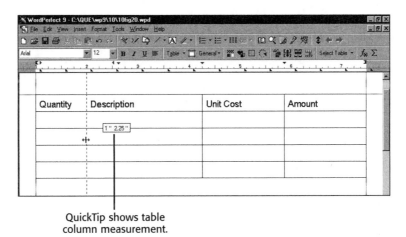

QuickTip shows table column measurement.

Tip #123 from
Laura and Read

Don't forget that Undo can be very useful as you experiment with table adjustments.

You can perform the same task by dragging the inverted triangles on the ruler bar (see Figure 10.20). Notice that the status bar also displays the exact position of the column separator line: Position: 4.25.

Figure 10.20
You can use the mouse to drag the inverted triangles on the ruler bar to size your table columns.

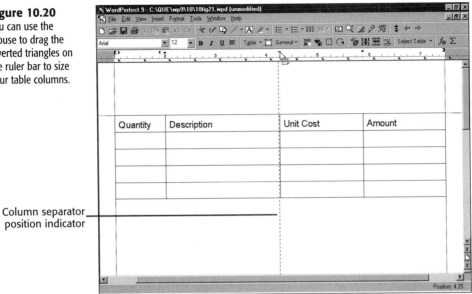

Column separator position indicator

Tip #124 from
Laura and Read

To change column widths proportionally, hold down the Shift key while moving the column separators. For example, in a four-column table, hold down Shift and drag the line between Columns A and B to the right until the last three columns are 1 inch wide (refer to the number on the right side of the QuickTip box). Release the mouse button, and you now have evenly spaced columns at the right side of the table.

Adjusting column width in this manner is not very precise, but if you already have text in the columns and can see that the columns are wide enough, or if the measurements don't really matter, this method is adequate.

Sometimes you simply want to be sure that the columns are wide enough to display each cell's information on one line (for example, a list). To adjust a column's width to fit the text in its cells, position the cursor in the column you wish to adjust, and from the QuickMenu choose Size Column to Fit. Columns adjusted in this manner expand to the right, thus reducing the width of columns to the right.

If you want exact column measurements, position the cursor in any cell of the column you want to adjust and choose T<u>a</u>ble, <u>F</u>ormat from the Property Bar. WordPerfect displays the Properties for Table Format dialog box (from here on, we'll call this simply the Table Format dialog box). Click the Column tab (see Figure 10.21).

Tip #125 from
Laura and Read

You can also choose the Table Format dialog box from the QuickMenu.

Figure 10.21
The Table Format dialog box is used for formatting table columns, as well as tables, table rows, and table cells.

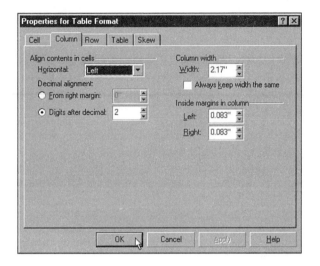

PART

III

CH

10

In the upper-right corner of the dialog box, type the measurement you want in the <u>W</u>idth box. Also, choose Always <u>K</u>eep Width the Same to prevent proportional sizing of columns from affecting this particular column.

Specifying Measurements
You can specify the column width measurement in decimals (the default unit of measurement) or in fractions of an inch, such as 1 5/16. Other units of measurement include centimeters (2.55c = 1 inch), points (72p = 1 inch), or WordPerfect units (1200w = 1 inch). WordPerfect automatically converts these measurements into the default measurement type you are using. This works anywhere that requires a measurement.

CHANGING TABLE SIZE

After you create a table, you often discover that it has too many or too few columns or rows. You learned earlier how to add rows at the end of a table by pressing Tab while in the last cell of the table. You can also insert or delete rows or columns at any location in the table.

To add rows to your table, position the cursor where you want the new row or rows and choose T<u>a</u>ble, <u>I</u>nsert from the Property Bar; or choose <u>I</u>nsert from the QuickMenu. WordPerfect displays the Insert Columns/Rows dialog box (see Figure 10.22).

Figure 10.22
The Insert Columns/Rows dialog box enables you to add rows or columns to your table.

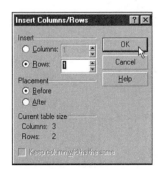

By default, WordPerfect assumes that you want to insert a single row preceding the current cursor position.

Tip #126 from
Laura and Read

The easiest and quickest way to insert a single row before the current cursor position is to press Alt+Insert. You can also click the Insert Row icon on the Property Bar.

Choosing <u>B</u>efore inserts the specified number of rows or columns at the location of the cursor, pushing the rows down or columns to the right to make room for the new rows or columns. Choosing <u>A</u>fter adds another row or column following the location of the cursor. This option is particularly useful when adding columns at the right of the table.

Note

Keep in mind that columns or rows you add or insert assume the special formatting attributes—such as lines and text formats—of the column or row that is selected when you choose <u>I</u>nsert.

To decrease the size of a table, you can delete rows or columns. Position the cursor in the first row or column you want to delete, and from the Property Bar T<u>a</u>ble menu (or from the Quick-Menu) choose <u>D</u>elete. Specify the number of columns or rows you want to delete and click OK. The Delete dialog box also enables you to delete the contents of only specified rows or columns.

Tip #127 from
Laura and Read

The easiest and quickest way to delete a single row at the current cursor position is simply to press Alt+Delete.

JOINING AND SPLITTING CELLS

If you use a table for complex purposes, such as a form, you often need cells of varying sizes. You can join and split cells to create such cells.

To join two or more contiguous cells (for example, all the cells along the top row of a table), simply select the cells you want to join and from the Property Bar T<u>a</u>ble menu, choose <u>J</u>oin, <u>C</u>ell; or from the QuickMenu, choose <u>J</u>oin Cells. WordPerfect joins the cells, which now appear as one large cell. Figure 10.23 shows an invoice title added after joining the cells.

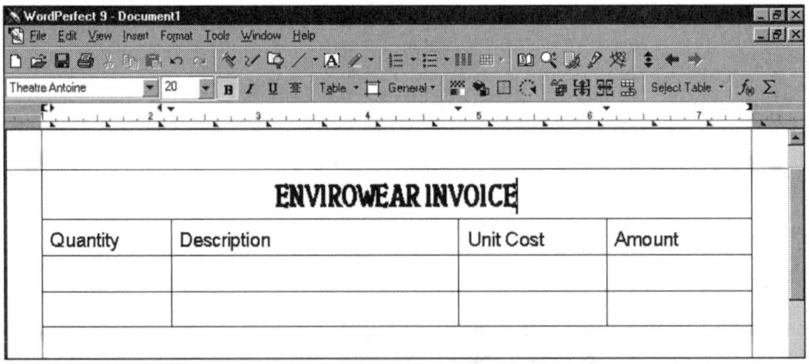

Figure 10.23
You can join several table cells—for example, all the cells in the first row—making them one large cell across the top.

You can use this method to join any number of cells in rows, columns, or blocks. Joined cells become one cell, occupying the space formerly occupied by the individual cells.

WordPerfect also enables you to split a cell into two or more cells. To split a cell, follow these steps:

1. Position the cursor in cell you want to split.

2. From the Property Bar Table menu choose Split, Cell; or from the QuickMenu menu choose Split Cell. WordPerfect displays the Split Cell dialog box (see Figure 10.24).

Figure 10.24
The Split Cell dialog box enables you to split a cell into two or more rows or columns.

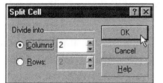

Indicate the number of columns or rows you want to divide the cell into, and click OK. You can further divide split cells as much as you need to. However, splitting a cell into additional rows also expands the other cells in the same row to accommodate the size of the split cell.

You can split and join cells even more quickly by using the QuickSplit feature, which enables you to use the mouse to visually split and join cells. To use QuickSplit to split or join cell columns, follow these steps:

1. From the Property Bar Table menu, choose Split, QuickSplit Column. WordPerfect changes the mouse pointer as shown in Figure 10.25, and also displays a dashed line and QuickTip measurements that indicate where the split will occur.

Figure 10.25
You can use QuickSplit to quickly split cells into columns or rows.

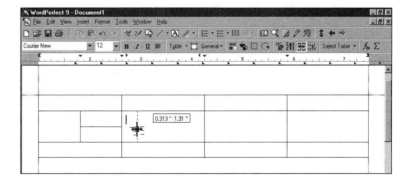

2. Position the mouse where you want the split to occur and click the mouse.

3. Split the same cell or other cells as needed.

4. If you need to join cells (for example, you accidentally split a cell, or need to join several cells so you can split them differently), hold down the Shift key and drag across the cells to be joined.

5. Turn off QuickSplit by choosing Table, Split, QuickSplit Column once again.

You can also use QuickSplit to split or join cells by rows. Choose Table, Split, QuickSplit Row and follow the same procedures just described.

CHANGING ROW STRUCTURE

WordPerfect automatically determines the amount of vertical space in a row based on the amount of text in its cells. The cell requiring the most vertical space sets the height for the entire row.

You can easily and quickly change a row's height by dragging the bottom line of the row up or down. WordPerfect displays a QuickTip showing the size the row will become when you release the mouse button.

Sometimes you need to set a specific row height, either to limit the amount of text you can enter into the row's cells or to make sure that a row contains a minimum amount of space, regardless of whether the cells contain data. A good example of the latter situation is a calendar in which you may want a fixed row height, regardless of the number of events on any given day. To fix row height, follow these steps:

1. Access the Table Format dialog box (by choosing Format from the QuickMenu or from the Property Bar Table menu.)

2. Click the Row tab. WordPerfect displays options for formatting a row (see Figure 10.26).

Figure 10.26
To format an entire row of cells, click the Row tab in the Table Format dialog box.

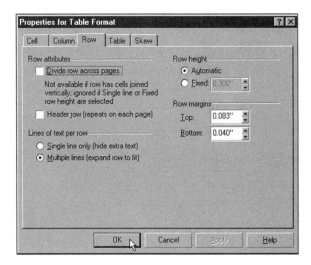

3. In this dialog box you set the row height and the number of lines of text per row. Although the options don't appear related in the dialog box, you can combine row height and lines of text per row in these ways:

   • Automatic and Multiple Lines—This combination, the default, automatically adjusts the row height to accommodate as many lines as necessary.

- **F**ixed and **M**ultiple Lines—This combination uses a fixed height and enables you to enter multiple lines, but only up to the specified height. You use this combination when you create a calendar, for example.

Make sure that any fixed height you select is high enough to accommodate at least one line of text. Otherwise, text that may appear onscreen will not print.

- A**u**tomatic and **S**ingle Line Only—This combination automatically adjusts the row height to accommodate a single line of text, regardless of the text's height (font size). If you choose these options and press Enter while entering text in your table, the cursor automatically advances to the next cell.
- **F**ixed and **S**ingle Line Only—This combination maintains a fixed height but enables you to enter only one line of text. The font size for that line of text must be small enough to fit into the specified row height.

PART

III

CH

10

4. Type the amount of space you want (for example, 1-inch fixed height for a calendar row), and click OK.

By default WordPerfect does not allow rows that contain multiple lines to span printed page breaks. This can create problems if you have rows with an unusually large number of lines, since you end up with large blank spaces at the bottom of the page. Some tables even contain so much text that a row exceeds the height of the entire page! To avoid these problems, simply choose **D**ivide Row Across Pages.

CREATING HEADER ROWS

Because a table can consist of up to 32,767 rows, it may span several pages. If you create a long table, you may want certain information (such as column headings) to repeat at the top of each page. Such rows are called *header rows*. To create a header row, follow these steps:

1. Position the cursor in the row you want to designate as a header row.
2. Access the Table Format dialog box.
3. Click the Row tab.
4. Choose Header **R**ow (Repeats on Each Page)
5. Click OK.

WordPerfect displays an asterisk (*) next to the cell reference in the general status area of the application bar (for example, `Cell A1*`) to indicate that the row is a header row.

Header rows don't have to begin with the first row, but if you want more than one header row, the rows you specify must follow one another.

CREATING SKEWED ROWS AND COLUMNS

Tables often require header rows where text doesn't quite fit horizontally. Although you can rotate text (see the section "Formatting Cells," later in this chapter), you can enhance the readability of your table by using *skewed*, or angled, cells and text.

The table shown in Figure 10.27 includes both a skewed row and a skewed column. To skew table rows or columns, follow these steps:

1. Access the Table Format dialog box and click the Skew tab (see Figure 10.28).

Figure 10.27
You can skew the cells in the top row, or in the left or right columns, along with the text they contain. You can also join skewed corners for a cleaner look.

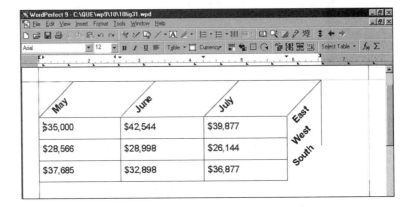

Figure 10.28
You can use the Skew tab of the Table Format dialog box to skew rows or columns.

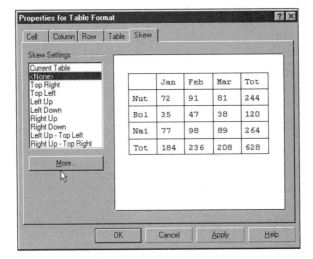

2. Click any of the available Skew settings. The preview box displays the effect of the skew style.

3. To customize the skew settings, click More. WordPerfect displays the Edit Skew dialog box (see Figure 10.29)

Figure 10.29
To customize how rows or columns are skewed, use the Edit Skew dialog box.

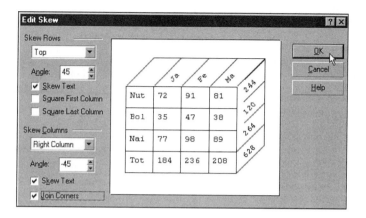

4. Choose from among these options (use the preview box to see what each option will do):

- Skew Rows—You can choose to skew the top row or none at all. You cannot skew a bottom row or a row in the middle of the table.

- Angle—By default, WordPerfect skews at a -45 degree angle, but you can increase or decrease the angle from -70 degrees (leaning far to the left), to +70 degrees (leaning far to the right).

- Skew Text—Choose this option to make the text align with the skewed cell.

- Square First Column—If the skewed row leans to the right, you may want to square the first column. If it leans to the left, this option could clip some of the cell's contents.

- Square Last Column—Square the last column if the skewed row leans to the left.

- Skew Columns—You can choose to skew the left or right columns, or none at all. You cannot skew both right and left columns in the same table.

- Join Corners—If you skew both a top row and a column, and if they lean toward each other, you can choose to have them join corners. This means that the total of their angles does not exceed 90 degrees, and the outermost corners of their row and column join in a square (refer to Figure 10.27).

FORMATTING TABLE TEXT

The preceding section focuses primarily on features that help you create the layout, or structure, of a table. It is also important that you make sure that the text itself contributes to the effectiveness of your presentation. Therefore, you need to understand how text attributes and text alignment apply to table cells.

UNDERSTANDING FORMATTING PRECEDENCE

Each time you choose a text formatting option, you have to consider whether that attribute should apply to the entire table, to a column, or to a cell or group of cells. Whether a change you make affects a cell depends on the priority that change has. Changes you make to a specific cell or group of cells have precedence, or priority, over changes you make to columns. Changes made to cells or to columns have precedence over changes made to the entire table.

Suppose, for example, that you specify that the data in a single cell should be centered (the heading of a column, for example) and then specify that the data for the entire column should be decimal-aligned. The change made to the column has no effect on the center-alignment change you make to the individual cell.

Keep this in mind, especially as you format columns. Any changes to a cell you may have made (and forgotten about) are not changed when you specify something different with column or table formatting.

FORMATTING TEXT IN COLUMNS

To modify the text formatting of all the cells in a column, position the cursor in the column you want to format, access the Table Format dialog box, and click the Column tab. WordPerfect displays the dialog box controls for formatting columns (see Figure 10.30).

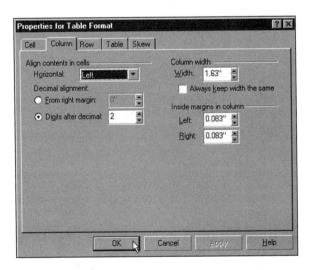

Figure 10.30
To format columns, use the Column tab in the Table Format dialog box.

Tip #128 from
Laura and Read

To format several adjoining columns simultaneously, select cells on the same row from all the columns you want to include. Then access the Table Format dialog box and click the Column tab.

Perhaps one of the most commonly needed column formats is the horizontal alignment of text, which you change in the Align Contents in Cells area of the Table Format dialog box.

Choose from the following options:

- Horizontal—Use the drop-down menu to choose Left, Right, Center, Full, or All alignment.

→ For a complete description of text alignment types, **see** Chapter 3, "Basic Formatting," **p. 57**

- From Right Margin—Enables you to align numbers at the decimal point, and the decimal point aligns at the distance you specify from the right margin of the cell.

- Digits After Decimal—Enables you to align numbers at the decimal point, and the decimal point aligns with enough space to accommodate n number of digits. The actual distance varies depending on the font size.

Tip #129 from *Laura and Read*	If you want to decimal-align a column of numbers, but want them to appear farther from the right edge of the table column, choose From Right Margin in the Column tab of the Table Format dialog box.

PART
III
CH
10

In addition to column width, explained earlier in this chapter in the section "Changing Column Widths," you can also specify the left and right text margins for your columns. The default is 0.083 inch (1/12 inch).

FORMATTING CELLS

Within cells, you format text as you normally do in a document. Simply select the text and add whatever attributes you want. However, you can also format a cell so that any text you add to the cell automatically acquires the cell's attributes.

For example, if you want all the text in a cell to be bold, first select the cell (move the mouse pointer to the edge of the cell, and click when the pointer turns to an arrow), and then click the Bold button on the toolbar or press Ctrl+B.

After you format a column of cells, as described in the preceding section, you may find that you also need to change the justification or attributes of a single cell or group of cells within that column.

To change the format of a single cell, other than for text attributes, position the cursor in the cell you want to change, access the Table Format dialog box, and click the Cell tab. WordPerfect displays the controls for formatting cells (see Figure 10.31).

To change the format of a group of cells, select the cells you want to change and access the Table Format dialog box. The changes you choose from the Cell tab then apply to each of the selected cells.

Note	Although it might seem logical to click the Row tab to format all the cells in a row, you must select all the cells first and then click the Cell tab from the Table Format dialog box to format the row of cells.

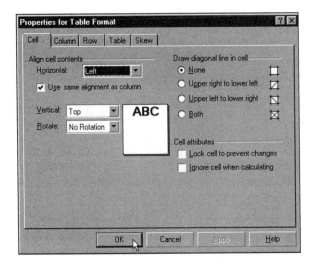

Figure 10.31
To format cells in a table, use the Cell tab in the Table Format dialog box.

Many of the options for formatting cells are identical to those used for formatting columns, such as the alignment options. Other options used only for formatting cells include

- Use Same Alignment as Column—By default, each cell assumes the attributes that are in effect for the column in which it resides. Thus, when you first choose the Table Format dialog box Cell tab, the Use Same Alignment as Column check box is selected. If you select a justification that differs from the column type, WordPerfect deselects this box. To reassign the column defaults, click Use Column Justification. WordPerfect automatically turns off any cell attributes that conflict with the default column formats.

- Vertical—By default, WordPerfect vertically aligns all text in a cell at the top of the cell. Choose Bottom or Center to change the vertical alignment of the text in a cell. In addition, you can rotate the text within a cell by choosing 90 Degrees, 180 Degrees, or 270 Degrees.

Note

When WordPerfect rotates text, it actually takes text you type and places it in graphics text boxes. To edit the information in rotated cells, you must click the text in the cell, make your changes in the Text edit screen, and click Close.

→ For more information on working with text graphics boxes, **see** Chapter 12, "Adding Graphics to Documents," **p. 317**

- Lock Cell to Prevent Changes—This option protects a cell from being altered. For example, if you want to prevent a user from entering data in certain cells in a form, you can lock them.

- Ignore Cell When Calculating—If the cell contains numbers that you don't want calculated during a math operation, you can specify that WordPerfect ignore the numbers.

→ For information on using formulas and calculations in WordPerfect tables, **see** Chapter 15, "Importing Data and Working with Other Programs," **p. 403**

■ Draw Diagonal Line in Cell—You can add diagonal lines to cells by choosing one of the options: <u>N</u>one, <u>U</u>pper Right to Lower Left, <u>U</u>pper Left to Lower Right, or <u>B</u>oth.

FORMATTING AN ENTIRE TABLE

Most of the changes you make to tables are to columns and cells. Sometimes, however, you might want to use a certain format as a default for an entire table. When you click the Table tab in the Table Format dialog box, WordPerfect presents the same controls used for columns and cells (see Figure 10.32).

Figure 10.32
For changes that affect the entire table, use the Table tab in the Table Format dialog box.

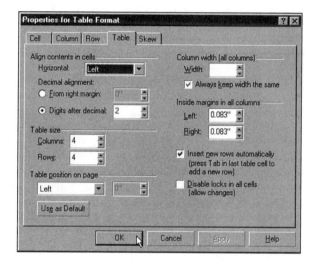

The options you select apply to the entire table, except to columns or cells you already modified.

Three options apply only to tables:

■ Table <u>P</u>osition on Page—By default, tables are full-justified in your document. This option lets you change the justification of the table itself, not the text in the cells of the table.

■ Insert <u>N</u>ew Rows Automatically—Deselect this check box to prevent WordPerfect from adding a new row to the table when you press Tab in the last cell of the table.

■ <u>D</u>isable Locks in All Cells—This option lets you quickly disable any cell locks you may have set. After you finish modifying the locked cells, select this box again to reset the locks.

CHANGING TABLE LINES, BORDERS, AND FILLS

One part of a table's effectiveness is lines, which help the reader better understand the information. For tables in which a user needs to fill in information, lines also help the user know where to enter appropriate data. By default, WordPerfect surrounds each cell with a single line, giving the appearance that the table also is surrounded by a single line. In fact, there is no border at all around a WordPerfect table. In addition to lines, you can fill the entire table or individual cells with varying patterns, colors of shading, or even images.

UNDERSTANDING DEFAULT LINE STYLES

The default style for table lines is a single line. Although it may appear that a single line appears on all four sides of a cell, only two sides typically make up a cell: the left and the top. If you were to "explode" a typical table of three rows and three columns, the cells would resemble the cells shown in Figure 10.33. (Notice that lines appear on the right and bottom sides of cells on the right and bottom of the table.)

Figure 10.33
An exploded WordPerfect table illustrates default line segments.

A1	B1	C1
A2	B2	C2
A3	B3	C3

When you specify a line style other than the default, you force WordPerfect to display that style at the location you specify. But you must be careful: If you specify a single line for the right side of a cell, even though its adjoining single cell line does not print, the line does not align with the other single lines in that column. In Figure 10.34, for example, notice that the single line between cells A2 and B2 does not align with the other lines between columns A and B. To avoid this situation, make changes only to the top and left sides of cells whenever possible.

Figure 10.34
If you change lines other than the default left and top lines, your table lines may not align properly.

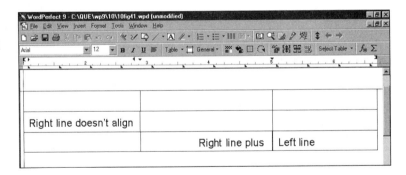

If you change both adjoining cell sides, you can create interesting effects because both lines print (refer to Figure 10.34, where two adjoining single lines appear to create a single thick line).

CHANGING CELL LINES

Changing the default single line between cells is simple. You can change to another line style or decide to use no line at all. To change a table cell line style, follow these steps:

1. Position your cursor in the cell.

2. From the Property Bar, choose Table, Borders/Fill. Alternatively, you can press Shift+F12, or you can choose Borders/Fill from the QuickMenu. WordPerfect displays the Properties for Table Borders/Fill dialog box (see Figure 10.35).

   This dialog box defaults to controls for the outside of the current selection and lists the current style for each of the line segments included in the selected cells. Unless you change them, each line uses the default (single line).

Figure 10.35
The Table Borders/Fill dialog box is used to change line styles for cells, groups of cells, the entire table, or the table border.

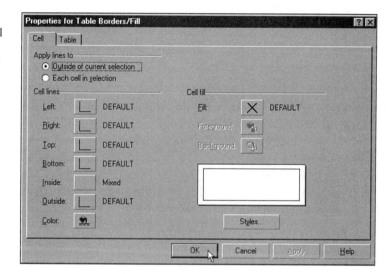

PART

III

CH

10

3. Click the palette button of the cell's line segment you want to change (for example, Bottom). WordPerfect displays a palette of line style choices (see Figure 10.36).

Figure 10.36
You can choose a table line style from a palette of choices.

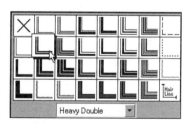

4. Move the mouse pointer to the style you want to use. The name of the style appears in a drop-down list at the bottom of the palette. If you want to see more styles, click the drop-down list.

5. From the palette or the drop-down list, select the style you want. The preview box shows the result of the selection.

6. After choosing each line style you want, click OK or press Enter. WordPerfect makes the change to your table.

Note

Depending on the resolution of your computer's monitor or the scale of your document display, single lines may not appear at all, or double lines may appear as a thicker single line. To be sure you have the correct line, you can increase the zoom percentage of your document.

If you select more than one cell, the Borders/Fill dialog box changes, and the default choice considers the group of cells as one large cell, with additional inside lines. Options you choose include

- Left, Right, Top, or Bottom—Changes in these line styles affect only one side of the group of cells. For example, if you choose Left, only the left line of the left column of cells changes.

- Inside—Only those lines that separate cells change with this option.

- Outside—All the lines on the outer edges of the groups of cells change. Changing this option automatically changes the styles of the left, right, top, and bottom styles. If you then change an individual side, the word *Mixed* appears beside this button.

Tip #130 from
Laura and Read

If you want to change most of the lines to a certain style, change the Outside line style first, and then make changes to individual sides.

TURNING OFF CELL LINES

To turn off the line between two cells, position the cursor in one of the cells, choose Borders/Fill from the QuickMenu, and change the appropriate line segment to <None> (click the × on the palette).

To turn off all the cells in a table, select all the cells, select Borders/Fill from the QuickMenu, and change all the Inside and Outside lines to <None>.

Whenever you choose <None> as the line style, WordPerfect displays instead a light gray gridline. The gridline does not print, but it does help you know where the cell lines are located. Figure 10.37 shows table gridlines for a table that contains no cell lines.

Figure 10.37
If you select <None> as your line style, WordPerfect still displays a grid to help you see where your cells are located.

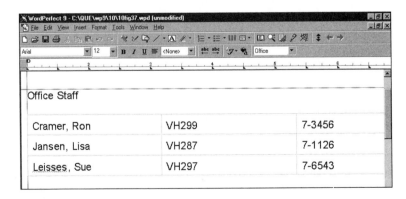

Note

You may be able to use SpeedFormat to turn off lines. Choose SpeedFormat from the QuickMenu, select the No Lines No Border style, and click Apply. If you previously made changes to any cell line, SpeedFormat will not affect that change.

You can also change the default line style to none by choosing Borders/Fill from the QuickMenu, and then clicking the Table tab. Then in the Default Cell Lines area, click the Line button and choose <None>. Note, however, that any changes you made to individual line segments still print.

Tip #131 from
Laura and Read

If you are used to using *parallel columns (page 215)* to format your text, consider using tables without lines instead. The effect is the same, but working with tables is much easier than working with parallel columns.

CREATING CUSTOM LINES

In addition to using predefined line styles, you can create your own custom line styles and effects. Furthermore, you can save your custom lines in style templates or in SpeedFormat table styles and use them over and over.

To create a custom line (for example, a colored single and dashed line), follow these steps:

1. Position the cursor in the cell, or select the group of cells, where you intend to use the new style. (This is not terribly important, however, because you can create the style first and then use it later.)

2. From the QuickMenu, choose Borders/Fill, and from the Borders/Fill dialog box, choose Styles. WordPerfect displays the Graphics Styles dialog box (see Figure 10.38).

Figure 10.38
You can use the Graphics Styles dialog box to create a new graphics line style.

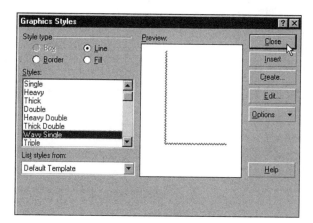

> **Note**
>
> Note that in the Graphics Styles dialog box you can create or edit box, line, border, or fill styles. The procedures for each type are similar.

3. Click Create. WordPerfect presents the Create Line Style dialog box (see Figure 10.39).

Figure 10.39
The Create Line Style dialog box, as it appears after following the steps to create a custom line, is used to customize your line styles.

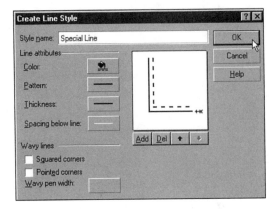

4. In the Style Name text box, type a unique name (for example, Special Line).

5. Change the color, pattern, and thickness of the first line by using the corresponding palette buttons.

6. Click Add to add another line to the style. Note that the arrow in the preview box points at the currently selected line. You can use the up and down arrows beneath the preview box to select lines in the style.

7. Change the Color, Pattern, and Thickness of the second, or any other, line, using the corresponding palette buttons.

8. If you want spacing between the lines, select a spacing width from the Spacing Below Line palette.

9. Click OK to return to the Graphics Styles dialog box. The name of the newly created style appears on the list of available styles.

10. Click Close to return to the Borders/Fill dialog box.

If you want to keep your new line style only in the current document, simply use the line style wherever you want and save the document. However, if you think you want to use this line style in other documents, you can save it in a template.

→ For details on working with customized styles, **see** Chapter 9, "Formatting with Styles," **p. 225**

CHANGING BORDERS

The border around a WordPerfect table is separate from the lines that surround each of the cells in the table. By default, a WordPerfect table border has no border style. To change a border style, follow these steps:

1. From the Table menu or from the QuickMenu, choose Borders/Fill.

2. From the resulting Table Borders/Fill dialog box, click the Table tab to display table-related lines and fill options (see Figure 10.40, shown with several options chosen).

Figure 10.40
You can use the Table tab of the Table Borders/Fill dialog box to change your table border.

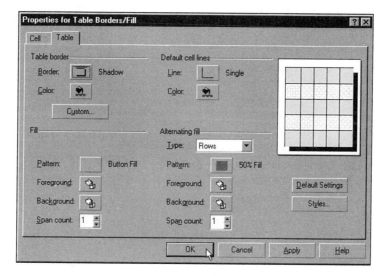

3. In the Table Border area, choose a border style from the Border palette. Note the resulting effect in the preview box.

4. Click Apply to apply the change but to remain in the dialog box, or click OK to apply the changes and return to your table.

> **Note**
>
> If you choose specific styles for both the border and the outside table cell lines, both styles print.

In addition to the standard list of border styles, you can customize your border to include special combinations of lines, shading, and even drop shadow border effects.

To customize a table border, follow these steps:

1. Access the Table Borders/Fill dialog box and click the Table tab (refer to Figure 10.40).

2. Select any border style that approximates what you want. (Unless a border style is selected, you can't customize the border!)

3. Click Custom to display the Customize Border dialog box (see Figure 10.41).

4. Change the Line Style for any of the sides selected. If All is checked, then all sides are changed at the same time.

5. Click Color to choose a line style color (see Figure 10.42). If you click Use Line Style Color, the customize screen reverts to the color of the line style you originally selected.

Figure 10.41
You can use the Customize Border dialog box to change the border style—for example, by adding a drop shadow to the table.

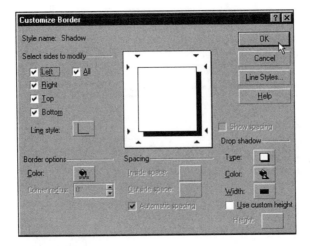

Figure 10.42
You can choose a new line color from the palette or choose Use Line Style Color to force your line to use the default color of the selected line style.

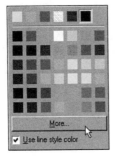

6. To add a drop shadow, choose the Type, Color, and the Width you want.

7. When you are satisfied with your changes as shown in the preview box, click OK.

8. Click OK again to apply the custom border to your table.

As with line styles, you can also save custom border styles.

→ For more information on how to save styles for future use, **see** Chapter 9, "Formatting with Styles," **p. 225**

CHANGING FILLS

WordPerfect enables you to fill individual cells, groups of cells, or the entire table with black, colors, or shades of black or color. Unless you have a color printer, however, the most practical use for this feature is to shade cells you want to set apart from the rest of the table. Suppose, for example, that you want to set off the column headings from the rest of a table. To shade a cell or group of cells, follow these steps:

1. Position your cursor in the cell (or select the group of cells) you want to change.

2. From the Table menu or the QuickMenu, choose Borders/Fill. WordPerfect displays the Table Borders/Fill dialog box.

3. From the Cell Fill area, click the Fill Palette button. WordPerfect displays a palette of fill patterns (see Figure 10.43).

Figure 10.43
The fill cell palette offers an array of fill patterns, including gradient fills.

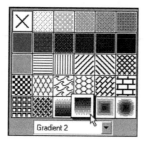

4. Click the fill pattern you want.

 5. Change the foreground color or the background color, as desired. Usually the foreground color is the pattern.

6. If what you see in the preview box is what you want, click OK to apply the fill style and to return to the table.

Tip #132 from *Laura and Read*	If you plan to print text in a cell, even when using a non-color printer, use a light color such as yellow, or if you are filling with a dark color, choose 20% fill or less. Higher percentages of shading with darker colors usually make reading text contained in that cell difficult.

You can select different shading or fill styles for any number of cells in your table. You can even create your own custom fills, including gradient shading and special patterns.

Tip #133 from *Laura and Read*	You can create white text on black background cells by using the reverse.wcm macro that comes with WordPerfect. Simply select the cells you want to change, and then choose Tools, Macro, Play, and play the reverse.wcm macro. The macro lets you choose the background color, the text color, and whether the cells should be a table header.

→ For more information on how to use WordPerfect macros, **see** Chapter 24, "Experts and Macros," **p. 685**

TROUBLESHOOTING

MOUSE PRACTICE MAKES PERFECT

I'm not too steady with the mouse. When I try to use the table grid to create a table, I sometimes get the wrong number of rows or columns.

As you practice, you'll get better at choosing just the right size. If you make a mistake, just click the Undo button on the toolbar (or choose Edit, Undo). The table goes away, and you can try again.

BUT I DIDN'T WANT THAT THERE!

Sometimes when I try to select cells in a table, the content of those cells ends up in some other part of the table.

You're probably inadvertently using WordPerfect's drag-and-drop feature. After selecting part of the cells you want, you're letting the mouse button go, and then clicking the already selected cells again and dragging to what should have been the last cell in your selection. When you release the mouse button, the first selection of cells is moved (dropped) into the new location. If this happens, just click the Undo button on the toolbar (or choose Edit, Undo) and try again.

TABLE COLUMN ALIGNMENT

I changed the format of my table column to decimal-aligned, but the text still appears left-aligned.

This is an easy mistake to make. When you used the Table Format dialog box, you probably forgot to click the Column tab, so all you formatted was a single cell.

To correct the problem, position the cursor in that column again, and then choose Format from the QuickMenu. This time, click the Column tab and make the desired changes.

EDITING ROTATED TEXT

I rotated text in some table cells, but I now need to change the text, and I can't figure out how to edit it.

When WordPerfect rotates text, it actually takes text you type and places it in graphics text boxes. To edit the information in the rotated cells, you click the text in the cell, make your changes in the Text edit screen, and click Close.

→ For more information on working with text graphics boxes, **see** Chapter 12, "Adding Graphics to Documents," **p. 317**

JUSTIFICATION CHANGES AREN'T ACCEPTED

After making a justification change to a column, one of the cells doesn't seem to accept the new change.

This is usually because you formatted a single cell at some point. To make the cell match the rest of the column, position the cursor in that cell, choose Format from the QuickMenu, and with the Cell tab selected, make sure the Use Column Justification check box is selected.

PLACING GRAPHIC IMAGES

I can't seem to position my graphic image properly in a table cell.

Graphic images require enough room to display properly. You may have to reduce the size of the graphic image or increase the width or height of the table cell. There is no exact rule for accomplishing this task, so keep trying (and using Undo) until you get it the way you want it.

PROJECT

So many potential uses for tables exist that an entire book could be written describing samples and exploring tables options. Here's just one possible use.

Suppose you need to create a telephone message form for your business. Follow these steps:

1. Create a table, with four columns and seven rows. Figure 10.44 shows the simple table that you will transform into a complex form.

Figure 10.44
To create a complex form, begin with the basic table structure.

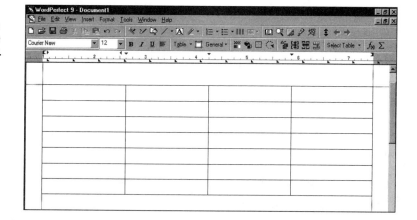

2. Select cells B1 through D1 and use the QuickMenu to join the cells.
3. Use Borders/Fill to change the left line of cell B1 to None.
4. Join cells A2 and B2, and join cells C2 and D2.
5. Join cells A3 and B3, and join cells C3 and D3.
6. Select cells A4 through B6 and choose Borders/Fill to change the inside lines to none.
7. Join cells C4 and D4.
8. Join cells C5 through D6.
9. Join cells A7 through D7, and drag the bottom line of row 7 to allow for about two inches of message space.
10. Select cells A8 through C8, and use Borders/Fill to turn off the inside and top lines.

The structure of the message form is shown in Figure 10.45.

Now add the text content of the message form, using Figure 10.46 as a reference. Insert your company graphic in cell A1, and type your company name and address in cell B1 (if necessary, adjust the height of the row by dragging the bottom line). Instead of using bullets for the "please call" options, simply choose a character from Insert, Symbol (or Ctrl+W), followed by a space.

Figure 10.45
After you modify the table structure to fit your needs, you can add text and graphic data.

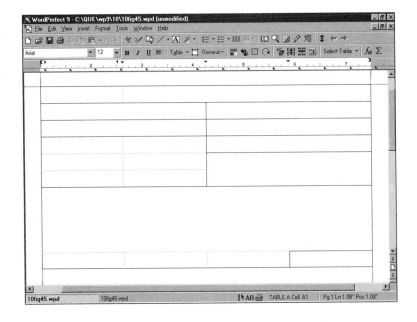

Figure 10.46
A complete phone message form, created from a WordPerfect table.

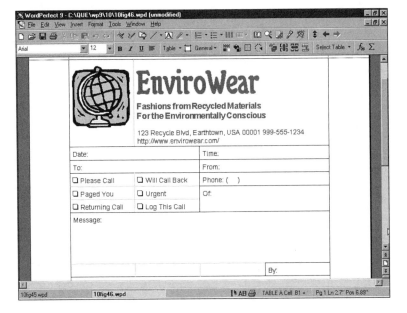

CHAPTER 11

ORGANIZING INFORMATION WITH LISTS AND OUTLINES

In this chapter

UNDERSTANDING OUTLINES

Not all text is narrative prose. Sometimes you use WordPerfect to create structured lists, such as the following, that summarize and organize information:

- Agendas
- Notes for a speech
- A summary of points covered in a class or workshop
- Overhead transparency lists
- To-do lists
- Structured reports with executive summaries

Any time you need to organize information in lists, WordPerfect can help with numbered, bulleted, and text lists and *outlines (page 296)*. Figure 11.1 shows examples of four types of WordPerfect lists.

Figure 11.1
WordPerfect enables you to create numbered and bulleted lists, as well as outlines to help you organize information.

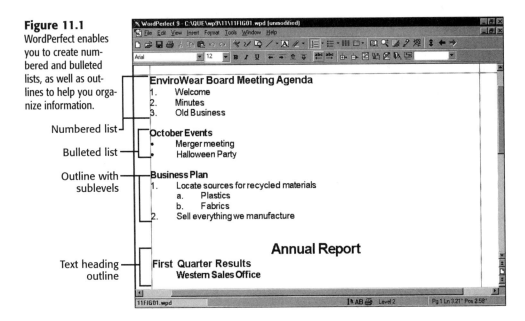

WORKING WITH BULLETED AND NUMBERED LISTS

In Chapter 1, "Getting Comfortable with WordPerfect," you learned to use QuickBullets. When you type an asterisk (*) and then press the Tab key, WordPerfect automatically inserts a bullet, followed by an indented paragraph. If you look behind the scenes in WordPerfect's Reveal Codes, you see that WordPerfect applies a paragraph style to each bulleted item (see Chapter 9, "Formatting with Styles," for more information on the Styles feature.)

Creating bullets to help accentuate items in a list is quick and easy using QuickBullets, but you also can control exactly which bullet you want to use. You can even decide later, if you want, to use numbers instead of bullets.

CREATING BULLETED LISTS

To create a bulleted list, follow these easy steps:

1. Choose Insert, Outline/Bullets & Numbering (a daunting menu entry). WordPerfect displays the Bullets and Numbering dialog box.

2. Click the Bullets tab to display a list of predefined bullet list styles (see Figure 11.2).

Figure 11.2
You can use the Bullets tab of the Bullets and Numbering dialog box to choose a bullet style for your list.

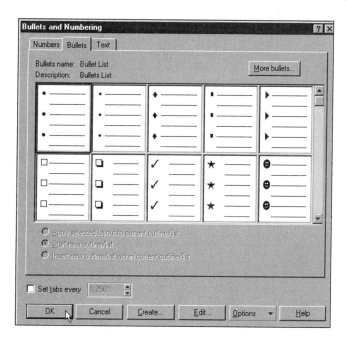

PART

III

CH

11

3. Click the style you want to use and click OK. WordPerfect inserts the chosen bullet style, which includes the bullet character and an indented paragraph.

4. Type the text of the first bullet.

5. Press Enter, and WordPerfect inserts the next bullet (see Figure 11.3).

6. Repeat steps 4 and 5 until you finish the list, and then press Enter one last time.

7. Press Backspace to erase the last bullet and to turn off the bullet paragraph style.

Note

You can also create a bulleted list by clicking the Bullet button on the toolbar, which places the currently selected bullet style in your document. To turn off the bullet style, simply click the Bullet button again.

Figure 11.3
When you use a bullet style, pressing Enter automatically adds a new, bulleted line.

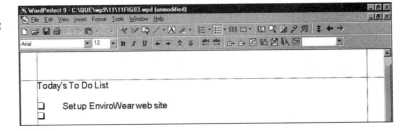

CREATING NUMBERED LISTS

Most people forget that computers are very good at keeping track of and calculating numbers. This includes numbered lists, and WordPerfect is excellent at making sure your numbered list is correct.

You create numbered lists very much the same way you create bulleted lists:

1. Choose Insert, Outline/Bullets & Numbering.

2. Click the Numbers tab and choose a number style (see Figure 11.4).

Figure 11.4
WordPerfect provides several predefined numbered list styles.

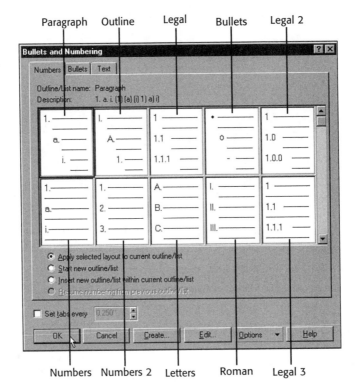

3. Click OK, and WordPerfect places a number style in your document that includes a number, followed by a period and an indent code.

Tip #134 from
Laura and Read

You can start a numbered list quickly by clicking the Numbering button on the toolbar.

---

4. Type some text, and when you press Enter, WordPerfect automatically increments the number for you.

5. Press Backspace or click the Numbering button on the toolbar to turn off the numbered list.

EDITING LISTS

Before long you'll want to know how to vary or edit the list. For example, you might want an extra blank line between each outline item, or you might need to add a new numbered line. The following are some of the ways to modify a bulleted or numbered list:

- Add an extra line while creating the list—If you are creating a list for the first time, after you press Enter, simply press Enter again to move the bullet or number down one line.

- Add an extra blank line after creating the list—Position the cursor on the line you want to move. Press Home to move the insertion point to the left end of the text, and press Enter to move the line down.

- Insert a new line—Position the cursor at the end of the line preceding the location where you want to insert a new line and press Enter. WordPerfect inserts a new number or bullet. Type the text of the new bulleted paragraph.

Automatic Renumbering
Note that when you add or remove a numbered line, WordPerfect automatically assigns the correct number in sequence, and also increases or decreases the numbers of each line following the change. This powerful feature can save you lots of time because you don't have to retype the numbers each time you make a change.

Tip #135 from
Laura and Read

Because numbered lists are so easy to create and to edit, you should get in the habit of using them even for short lists. Simply click the Numbering button on the toolbar, or press Ctrl+H to begin a numbered list.

 If pressing Ctrl+H turned off outline numbering in your paragraph, see "How Did I Turn Off Outline Numbering?" in the Troubleshooting section at the end of this chapter.

- Remove a line—Delete the text and bullet or number, as you do any text you want to remove. If you're using numbers, WordPerfect automatically renumbers your list.

- Change a normal text paragraph to a bullet or number—If you have already typed the text of the bullet (for example, a paragraph you want to highlight with a bullet), click the Bullet button or the Numbering button on the toolbar. WordPerfect adds the bullet or number style to the paragraph.

- Change a bulleted or numbered paragraph to normal text—If you decide you don't want a bullet paragraph, position the cursor anywhere on the paragraph and click the Bullet button on the toolbar. To convert a numbered paragraph to normal text, click the Numbering button on the toolbar.

Tip #136 from
Laura and Read

To toggle between bulleted or numbered paragraphs and normal text, you can click the Bullet button on the toolbar, or you can simply press Ctrl+H.

CHANGING THE BULLET OR NUMBERING STYLE

Changing the numbering or bullet style can be as easy as selecting a different predefined style or as complex as creating an entirely new bullet or numbering style.

Suppose, for example, you want to change a numbered list to one that uses capital letters. Follow these steps:

1. Access the Bullets and Numbering dialog box by choosing Insert, Outline/Bullets & Numbering.

Tip #137 from
Laura and Read

You can bypass the menus to access the Bullets and Numbering box by clicking the drop-down menu on the Numbering button or the Bullet button on the toolbar, and then choosing More from the palette of choices.

2. Click the Numbers or Bullets tab, depending on the style you want to change to.

Note

You can change any list from one style type to another. For example, you can change a numbered list to a bulleted list, and vice versa.

3. Click the style you want, for example, the Letters style (refer to Figure 11.4).

4. Choose one of the listed options:

- Apply Selected Layout to Current Outline/List—This option appears when the insertion point is located within a WordPerfect list of any kind. Selecting the option applies the selected style to the entire list (see Figure 11.5).

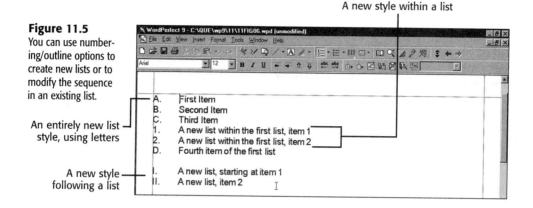

Figure 11.5
You can use numbering/outline options to create new lists or to modify the sequence in an existing list.

An entirely new list style, using letters

A new style following a list

A new style within a list

- $\underline{S}$tart New Outline/List—This option starts a new style at the insertion point. If you are in the middle of a list, the new style does not affect items before the insertion point—only those after it. If you are at the end of a list, it simply starts a new list, beginning at number 1 if you are using numbers.

- $\underline{I}$nsert New Outline/List Within Current Outline/List—If the insertion point is resting on a list paragraph, that paragraph becomes the first item in a new list. Items added after it are also part of the same list style. Items in the original list, however, are not changed (refer to Figure 11.5).

- $\underline{R}$esume Numbering from Previous Outline/List—If you turned off the list style, and inserted other normal text (including hard returns), you have the option of picking up where you left off, both in style and numbering sequence. If you choose another style, this option is not available (it is grayed out) and you must start a new list.

5. You also can choose a different tab setting for your numbered lists. For example, if the default 1/2 inch is too wide, click Set $\underline{T}$abs Every and enter the amount in the counter box (for example, 1/3).

Tip #138 from
Laura and Read

Reducing the amount of tab space between the bullet or number and the text can give your list a tighter, cleaner look. However, don't make the amount too small because wider, two- or three-digit numbers in numbered lists may cause the text to look uneven.

6. Click OK to apply the new style and options to your list.

PART
III

CH
11

WORKING WITH OUTLINES

WordPerfect was one of the first programs to offer fully functional outlining capabilities. Unfortunately, the feature was somewhat difficult to master, and as a result it is still one of WordPerfect's best-kept secrets. WordPerfect 9 changes all that with its easy-to-use, yet powerful, outlining feature.

Outlines work very much like lists, but add another dimension. For example, a typical list includes items that all have the same relative importance. Outlines items, on the other hand, are arranged hierarchically to show their relative importance. Consider the two lists shown in Figure 11.6.

Figure 11.6
Outlines are like lists, but add sublevels for greater depth in organizing information.

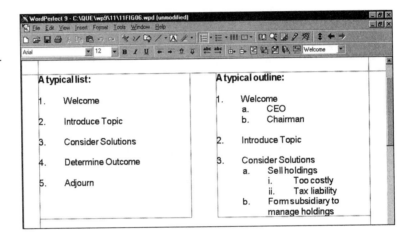

In Figure 11.6, the list presents only one level of relatively equal information, numbered 1, 2, 3, and so on. The outline, however, presents multiple levels. Each level is identified by its indentation and by its numbering style. For example, the first proposed solution, item a under point 3, contains two sublevels that explain the reason for the proposal.

Note
You can use up to nine outline levels. WordPerfect does not allow you to tab past the ninth level.

The advantages of working with outlines become evident after you begin working with them. They are easy to create, they are even easier to edit, and they make the task of organizing information a snap. You'll soon wonder how you ever got along without this feature.

CREATING AN OUTLINE

WordPerfect offers several outline styles, and the numbered paragraphs style is the default. To create a simple numbered paragraph outline, position the insertion point at the left margin, and then follow these steps:

Note

> Although WordPerfect offers myriad options, we'll first step you through the basics to show you just how easy it is to create a multilevel outline. We'll return to the details after that.

1. Choose Insert, Outlines/Bullets & Numbering. WordPerfect displays the Bullets and Numbering dialog box, with the Numbers tab and Paragraph style selected (refer to Figure 11.4).

Note

> If you've recently used another number of bullet outline system, you may have to click the Numbers tab and select the Paragraph outline style.

2. Click OK, and WordPerfect places a number, followed by a period and an indent in your document (for example, 1.).

Tip #139 from
Laura and Read

> You can also begin a numbered paragraph outline by clicking the Numbering button on the toolbar, or by pressing Ctrl+H.

Caution

> Make sure the insertion point is positioned horizontally where you want the outline to begin (usually at the left margin of the document), and also on a blank line. If the insertion point is located inside an existing paragraph, WordPerfect converts the paragraph to a numbered outline paragraph when you turn on outlining.

3. Type the content of the first paragraph—for example, Welcome (refer to the outline in Figure 11.6 for sample text you can type).

4. To insert the next number, press Enter.

5. To move the number down another line before you type, press Enter.

6. To create the next level, press Tab. WordPerfect moves to the next tab stop and changes the number to a letter (for example, a).

7. Type the content of the first subtopic.

8. Press Enter, and WordPerfect inserts the next number at the same level as the preceding paragraph (for example, b).

9. Type the second subtopic, and press Enter.

10. Before typing, press Shift+Tab to move the letter to the left and change it to a number (for example, 2).

11. Continue typing and inserting numbers until you finish the outline. Remember to press Enter to add a new numbered line, and to use Tab to move to the next level, or Shift+Tab to return to a previous level.

12. Press Enter one last time and then press Backspace to delete the unneeded outline number and to turn off outlining.

Tip #140 from
Laura and Read

You can also end a numbered paragraph outline by clicking the Numbering button on the toolbar, or by pressing Ctrl+H.

UNDERSTANDING OUTLINES

Now that you understand how easy it is to create an outline, you can explore other options and features.

OUTLINE TERMINOLOGY

If you understand outline terminology, it's easier to understand the feature. The following are some of the terms used to describe WordPerfect's outline features:

- Outline item—A paragraph of an outline, identified by a single number or bullet.

- Body text—Any non-outline text. Such paragraphs might appear between outline items in an outline, and also include blank lines (for example, a hard return code).

- Level—*Outline level* refers to the horizontal position of the outline item, relative to other outline items. For example, items at the left margin are at the first level. Outline items that appear at the first tab stop are at the second level, and so on.

- Family—A group of outline items that belong together. For example, in Figure 11.6, items 1.a and 1.b are all part of the item 1 family of outline items, and items 3.a.i and 3.a.ii are part of the 3.a family.

- Promote—To give an outline item more importance, by moving the paragraph to the left. The item is also said to have been moved up a level.

- Demote—To give an outline item less importance, by moving it to the right. The item is also said to have been moved down a level.

USING THE OUTLINE PROPERTY BAR

When the insertion point is located within an outline, WordPerfect displays several Outline tools on the Property Bar (see Figure 11.7).

Figure 11.7
You can use Outline buttons on the Property Bar to work with your outlines.

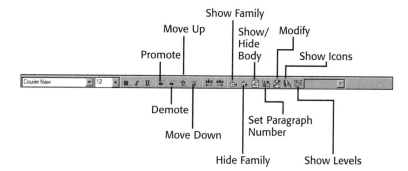

The options represented by these buttons include the following:

- Promote—Changes the current outline level to the previous, higher level. The cursor can appear anywhere in the text of the current outline level. This action has the same effect as pressing Shift+Tab when the insertion tab immediately follows the outline number.

- Demote—Changes the current outline level to the next, lower level. This is the same as pressing Tab when the insertion point immediately follows the outline number.

- Move Up—Moves an outline item, or selected family, up one line, while preserving the outline level. You can click several times to keep moving the item up in the outline.

- Move Down—Moves an outline item, or selected family, down one line, while preserving the outline level.

- Show Family—If you have hidden the sublevels of the current outline item, this option enables you to show all the sublevels again.

- Hide Family—Hides all the sublevels of the currently selected outline item. If the item has no sublevels, this option has no effect.

- Show/Hide Body—This option hides all non-outline text, such as titles, narrative paragraphs, and even blank lines (hard returns). Click the button again to show the body text along with the outline. This is particularly useful when you're using text outline headings, and you want to collapse the narrative into an outline format (see the section "Creating Text Outline Headings," later in this chapter.)

- Set Paragraph Number—Click this button to display the Set Paragraph Number dialog box (see Figure 11.8). Although you can select only numbers, the value of the current outline item changes accordingly, for example, a. changes to c. if you change the value from 1 to 3. This is particularly useful if you want to begin a new outline within the same document.

- Modify—Use this option to modify the current paragraph style (see the section "Creating and Editing Outline Styles," later in this chapter).

PART

III

CH

11

Figure 11.8
You can use the Set
Paragraph Number
dialog box to set the
current number of an
outline item.

- Show Icons—This option displays outline icons to the left of the outline itself (see
  Figure 11.9). T represents body text, and 1, 2, and so on indicate the levels of the outline items. You can click a number to select the item and its family.

Figure 11.9
The Show Icons option
displays outline level
indicators in the left
margin.

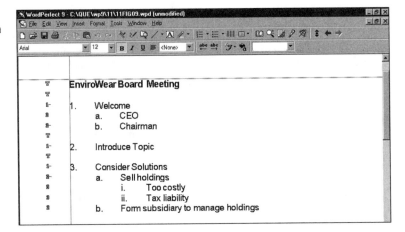

- Show Levels—Use this option to collapse or expand an outline. For example, if you
  want to display only first-level outline items, click this option and select One. All other
  levels remain hidden until you select Nine to show all levels again.

EDITING OUTLINE TEXT

Editing the text in an outline is as easy as editing any other text. However, you may also
find that you accidentally add or remove outline numbers as you edit your text.

If you accidentally add a paragraph number (for example, you press Enter and add the number), press Backspace to remove the number, and press Backspace again to remove the blank
line.

If you accidentally remove a paragraph number (for example, you press Backspace when you
didn't intend to), click the Numbering button on the toolbar, or press Ctrl+H. Alternatively,
you can press Backspace again to position the cursor at the end of the previous line, and
press Enter to add the paragraph number.

HIDING AND SHOWING OUTLINE FAMILIES

If your outline is fairly extensive, with lots of text and sublevels, you can hide some of the text by hiding families or showing only certain levels.

To hide all the sublevels of a specific outline family, follow these steps:

1. Position the cursor anywhere on the first line of the top level of the family you want to hide.

> **Note**
>
> You cannot hide an outline family if the cursor is to the left of the outline number because the outline features disappear from the Property Bar.

 2. Click the Hide Family button on the Property Bar. WordPerfect collapses the outline for that family, showing only the top outline level and hiding all the others (see Figure 11.10).

Figure 11.10
You can collapse the sublevels in an outline family by using the Hide Family button.

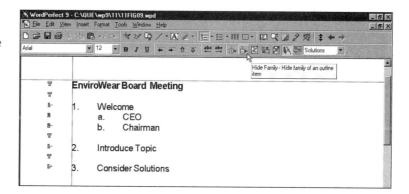

> **Note**
>
> When you hide a family of outline text, a design flaw in WordPerfect also hides body text that follows a sublevel (refer to Figure 11.10). If you intend to print your outline with family text hidden, you may need to insert another blank line (hard return) following the hidden family. If you then unhide the family, you will have to remove the extra blank line.

Tip #141 from
Laura and Read

If you select Show Icons, and the outline level numbers appear in the left margin, you can double-click an outline level number to hide (or show) its family.

 To show all outline levels in a family, click the Show Family button on the Property Bar.

You can also display only the top levels of an outline, hiding all the rest. This is sometimes referred to as *collapsing* an outline. For example, you could have an agenda that displays two levels for all the participants, but hides the third level, where you list details that you don't want them to see.

 To collapse an outline, showing only the top levels, click the Show Levels button on the Property Bar, and choose the number of levels you want to display (for example, Two). To expand an outline to show all levels, click the Show Levels button, and choose Nine.

Caution

If you choose <None> from the Show Levels menu, you hide the entire outline, and the Show Levels button disappears from the Property Bar. The only way you can redisplay your outline is to choose View, Toolbars, and select the Outline toolbar. You can then click the Show Levels button on the toolbar and select the number of levels you want to display.

Note

When you collapse an outline, a bug in WordPerfect also hides body text that follows hidden sublevels. If you intend to print your collapsed outline, you may need to insert blank lines (hard returns) to restore the spacing you want. If you then expand the outline, you will have to remove the extra blank lines.

MOVING AND COPYING IN AN OUTLINE

Selecting outline items or families and moving or copying them is a bit trickier than simply cutting and pasting, as you are used to doing.

To select an outline family—for example, just a single outline item—you can use any of the following methods:

- Using the mouse, select the line beginning at the *left* of the outline number, and continuing to the end of the text for the outline item, and *including* the hard return.

Caution

To fully select an outline item, you must also include the hard return at the end of the line. Positioning the cursor exactly to the left of an outline number is difficult. Therefore, you should use one of the other methods for selecting an outline item or family.

- Using the mouse, position the pointer in the left margin, opposite the outline item you want to select. When the pointer turns to an arrow, double-click to select the outline item. This selects the outline number, the text of the outline item, and also the hard return at the end of the line.
- Using the keyboard, position the cursor on the first line of the outline item, and press Home twice. Then press and hold down Shift while moving the cursor to the next line of the outline. Continue holding the Shift key, and press Home twice to move to the left of the next item's outline number.

These methods also work when selecting an outline item along with its sublevels (the entire family). In addition, consider these procedures:

- To select an entire family, first click the Show Icons button on the Property Bar to display outline level numbers in the left margin. Then click the level number that corresponds to the family you want to select, and WordPerfect selects the entire family (the outline item and its sublevels), along with the hard return at the end of the last item.

- You can also hide all the sublevels of the family, and then simply select what appears to be a single outline item. WordPerfect selects the sublevels along with the family's "parent" outline item.

After you select the portion of the outline you want to cut, copy, or delete, choose the appropriate action from the Edit menu, from the toolbar, or by using the keyboard.

To paste an outline item or family, position the cursor at the left margin (to the left of the outline number), and choose Paste from the Edit menu, from the toolbar, or by using the keyboard.

Tip #142 from
Laura and Read

Although the Windows graphical interface begs you to use the mouse, when working with outlines, the keyboard can be much quicker and more precise. You can press the Home key twice to move to the left of an outline number, and use the Shift key along with cursor movement to select text.

Tip #143 from
Laura and Read

Instead of cutting and pasting an outline family, you can hide the family, and then use the Move Up or Move Down buttons to move the parent along with the family to a new location. Then unhide the family.

ADJUSTING OUTLINE LEVELS

The real power of a WordPerfect outline is the capability to add or remove outline entries and to adjust the levels of those entries. As you do, WordPerfect automatically renumbers your entries.

To add an outline item, position the cursor following the preceding item and press Enter. WordPerfect inserts a new outline number at the same level as the preceding outline item. Before typing, press Tab to demote the item, or press Shift+Tab to promote the item.

Adjusting outline levels after you type the entries is just as easy. Position the cursor on the first line of the outline item you want to adjust, press Home to move the cursor to the beginning of the line (but following the outline number), and press Tab to demote the item, or press Shift+Tab to promote the item.

RENUMBERING AN OUTLINE

Normally you do not have to worry about outline numbering because WordPerfect takes care of it automatically for you. When you add or remove lines, or adjust the level of an outline item, WordPerfect also adjusts the numbering so you don't have to.

However, if you want to set the numbering differently than what WordPerfect displays, you can do that, too. For example, if you begin a second outline in your document, WordPerfect tries to continue with the numbering sequence from the first outline. To instead have the numbering start over for the second outline, follow these steps:

1. Position the cursor where you want to change the outline number. Normally you do this before beginning the new outline, but you can also place the cursor on an existing outline item.

2. Click the Set Paragraph Number button on the Property Bar. WordPerfect displays the Set Paragraph Number dialog box (see Figure 11.11).

Figure 11.11
You can set a new outline number value with the Set Paragraph Number dialog box.

3. Set the number you want to use and click OK.

Note

Although you can select only numbers, the value of the current outline item changes accordingly. For example, a. changes to c. if you change the value from 1 to 3.

WordPerfect changes the outline number to the one you selected. Figure 11.12 shows the new numbering, along with a heading for the new outline section. If you change the number in an existing outline, WordPerfect also automatically adjusts the numbers at the same level within the same family.

Figure 11.12
Changing the value of an outline number causes WordPerfect to renumber the numbers that follow it.

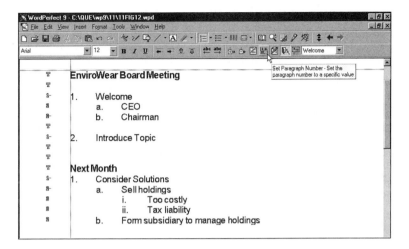

CREATING TEXT OUTLINE HEADINGS

WordPerfect also helps you create structured documents by using outline headings. Consider the document shown in Figure 11.13. Each section heading is a text outline style, and the corresponding level number appears in the left margin. In fact, you work with text heading outlines much more like you work with styles than you do with outlines.

PART
III

CH
11

Figure 11.13
You can create structured text documents using the text headings outline format.

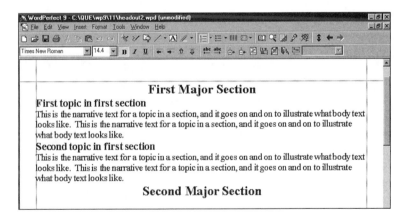

One method for creating text outline headings is to create a regular numbered outline first. Make all major section headings outline level one, secondary section headings outline level two, and so on. However, do not apply outline headings to the narrative paragraphs included in the sections. These should be body text. When you complete the outline (see Figure 11.14), then follow these steps:

Figure 11.14
One method for creating text outline headings is to create a regular numbered outline first.

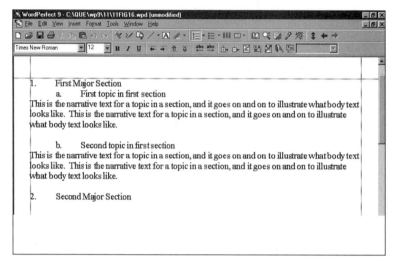

1. Choose Insert, Outline/Bullets & Numbering. When WordPerfect displays the Bullets and Numbering dialog box, click the Text tab (see Figure 11.15).

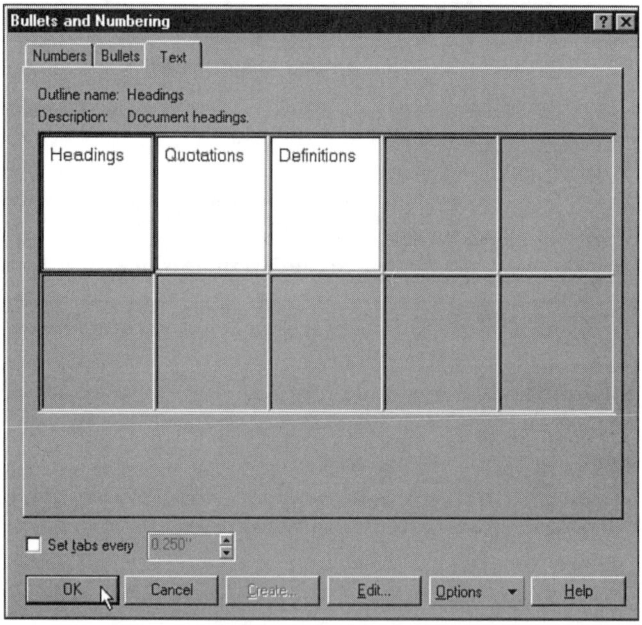

Figure 11.15
You can choose a text heading outline style from the Text tab of the Bullets and Numbering dialog box.

2. Click the text style you want to use, typically the headings style, and click OK.

WordPerfect now changes the numbered outline to a heading outline (refer to Figure 11.13).

Caution

After you convert a numbered outline to a text heading outline, you cannot change it back to a numbered outline without a great deal of effort. If you think you might want to use the numbered outline again, you should save the numbered outline before converting it to a text heading outline.

A second method for creating a text heading outline is to add heading styles to section and topic headings. You can also use this method to convert regular text to a structured text heading outline.

To add heading styles to new or existing text, follow these steps:

1. Position the cursor on the line you want to make a heading (either a new line or existing text).

2. Choose Format, Styles. WordPerfect displays the Styles dialog box (see Figure 11.16).

Figure 11.16
The Styles dialog box includes default text heading outline styles.

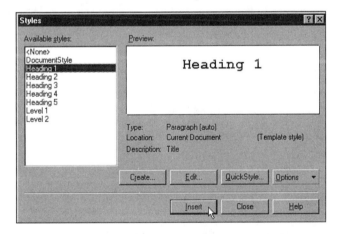

3. Select the heading style you want. The heading number (for example, Heading 1) should correspond to the outline level you want. WordPerfect also displays the effect of that style in the preview box.

4. Click Insert to apply the heading style to the current paragraph.

5. Repeat steps 1–4 for all other headings in the document.

After you create the text heading outline, you can use most of the tools on the Property Bar to work with the document. For example, you can use the following:

- Show Icons—If you click this button, WordPerfect displays outline level numbers and text body icons in the left margin (refer to Figure 11.9). You can double-click outline level numbers in the margin to show or hide outline families.

- Show Levels—Use this to display only certain levels, such as major section headings. All sublevels and their associated body text are hidden.

- Promote/Demote—You can adjust the text heading outline levels by clicking the Promote or Demote buttons. For example, if you want to make a topic level heading a section heading, you could simply promote the topic.

- Move Up/Down—Use these buttons to rearrange headings.

- Hide Body—This works only on a single family at a time.

Note
The Set Paragraph Number option does not work in text heading outlines.

→ To learn how text heading outline styles can be useful when you create and edit Web page documents, **see** Chapter 21, "Publishing Documents on the World Wide Web," **p. 569**

Creating and Editing Outline Styles

WordPerfect offers a very good selection of number and bullet styles. However, if the style you really need isn't available, you can create your own. Sometimes that may involve simply editing an existing style to make it more like what you want.

To create a new outline style, follow these steps:

1. Choose Insert, Outline/Bullets & Numbering to access the Bullets and Numbering dialog box.

2. If you can, find a style that's already close to what you want, and select it.

Tip #144 from
Laura and Read
You can save time and effort by creating an outline style based on an existing outline style.

3. Click Create. WordPerfect displays the Create Format dialog box (see Figure 11.17).

4. Type a name for your new style in the Outline/List Name box, and add the option Description.

5. Choose the type of outline you want: Single Level List, or Multilevel List.

6. You can choose a Number Set (see Figure 11.18), although this isn't entirely necessary.

Figure 11.17
You can use the Create Format dialog box to create or edit an outline style.

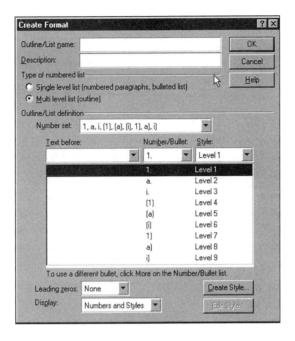

Figure 11.18
You can use predefined numbers sets or create your own in a custom outline style.

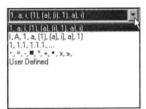

7. The dialog box lists all the levels used in this outline style, and at the top of the list are the following controls:

   • Text Before—If you want text to appear before each outline number (for example, "Section"), type that text in this box.

   • Number/Bullet—You can click the drop-down list and choose a number or bullet, or scroll down the drop-down list and click More (see Figure 11.19), which takes you to the Symbols dialog box, where you can choose from dozens of bullet icons (see Figure 11.20). After you choose the number or bullet you want, you can also add punctuation, such as a period, a colon, or parentheses.

   • Style—This applies predefined styles to the text and number or bullet you select. For example, the Level 1 style adds an indent code. You can further create and use formatting styles by choosing Create Style, creating the style, then selecting it from the Style drop-down list. See Chapter 9 for more information on creating and editing styles.

PART

III

CH

11

Figure 11.19
A drop-down menu offers several bullet and number styles, or you can choose More.

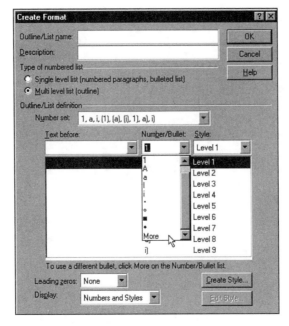

Figure 11.20
The Symbols dialog box offers dozens of possible bullet icons that you can use in a custom outline style.

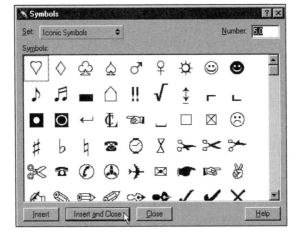

8. After you create or edit the style to your satisfaction, click OK to return to the Bullets and Numbering dialog box. Your new style now appears among the other styles (see Figure 11.21).

9. To use the style, click OK.

If you save your document, you also save the outline style with the document. However, if you want to save your style for use with other documents, you must access the Bullets and Numbering dialog box, and choose Options. Then save the style as described in Chapter 9.

Figure 11.21
Custom outline styles appear in the palette of styles available in the Bullets and Numbering dialog box.

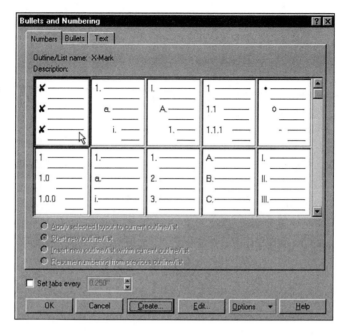

TROUBLESHOOTING

HOW DID I TURN OFF OUTLINE NUMBERING?

I pressed Ctrl+H as you suggested, but it turned off the outline number of my paragraph.

Indeed, Ctrl+H (or clicking the Numbering button on the toolbar) turns off outline numbering for the *current* paragraph. You must first press Enter and *then* turn off outline numbering for the blank numbered line you just created. If you accidentally turn off numbering for a paragraph, simply position the cursor anywhere in the paragraph and click the Numbering button on the toolbar, or press Ctrl+H.

SKIPPING CURSOR

I can't seem to move the cursor to the left of my paragraph number. Instead, when I press the left-arrow key, it skips up a line.

Press Home once to move to the left of the numbered line. Then press Home again to move to the left of the paragraph number.

PROJECT

One of the easiest, yet most functional, uses for the outline feature is to create an agenda. When you use the default paragraph numbering style, not only can you create a numbered list, but you can also use other outline features to customize the agenda.

The following steps help you prepare an agenda that you can customize, using one version for yourself, and one for those attending your meeting:

1. Turn on the default paragraph numbering by clicking the Numbering button on the toolbar, or press Ctrl+H.

2. Create a fully defined agenda, using Tab to create sublevel information. As shown in Figure 11.22, make sure to add notes to yourself in the outline's sublevels, since the audience will see only everything you place in level one.

Figure 11.22
You can create a detailed agenda for yourself using the default paragraph numbering style.

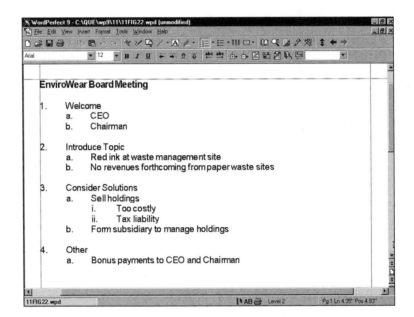

3. Print a copy for yourself.

4. Click the Show Levels button on the Property Bar, and choose One to hide all levels except level one (see Figure 11.23).

5. Sometimes hiding levels also removes extra blank lines between outline items. If necessary, add hard returns to add the needed blank lines.

6. Print a copy for those attending the meeting.

7. If you need to revise the agenda, show all levels again (click the Show Levels button on the Property Bar and choose Nine). Then repeat steps 2–6.

Figure 11.23
You can use the Show Levels option to show only the levels of the agenda you want everyone to see.

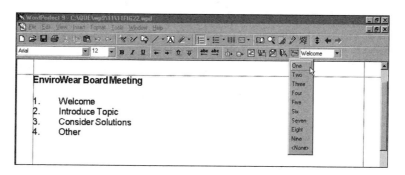

WORKING WITH GRAPHICS

CHAPTER 12

ADDING GRAPHICS TO DOCUMENTS

In this chapter

INSERTING GRAPHIC IMAGES

Although WordPerfect can do wonders with your text alone, it also provides a dazzling array of graphic elements that can jazz up nearly any document. Graphic images are one of the many graphic elements; you can also use horizontal and vertical lines, text borders, graphic shapes such as arrows, and background graphics called watermarks.

> **Caution**
>
> Working with graphics is *fun*! You can spend lots of time fiddling with graphics elements and have a great time following your creative instincts. However, remember that the basic content of the document should be your first concern. Then you can apply a judicious amount of graphics to enhance or illustrate what you say in the document.

INSERTING CLIP ART

When you think graphics, you think pictures. Indeed, graphic images not only are easy to use, but what you learn about working with images applies also to nearly every type of graphic element used in WordPerfect. The easiest of all graphic images to use is *clip art*, which is predesigned artwork that comes with WordPerfect. To insert a clip art image in your document, follow these easy steps:

1. Position the cursor at the location where you want to insert the graphic image.

2. Choose <u>I</u>nsert, <u>G</u>raphics, <u>C</u>lipart, or click the Clipart button on the toolbar. WordPerfect displays the Scrapbook dialog box (see Figure 12.1), which includes clip art, along with photos, video, and audio clips.

Figure 12.1
The WordPerfect Scrapbook provides more than 10,000 clip art images (on CD-ROM), as well as photos and audio and video clips.

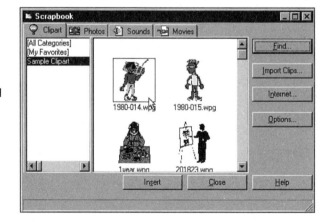

3. Scroll through the list of images and click the one you want.

4. Click In<u>s</u>ert to place the image in your document.

Tip #145 from
Laura and Read

You can also place a clip art image in your document by dragging it from the Scrapbook dialog box and dropping it in your document at the precise location where you want it.

Note that the image pushes aside the text that surrounds it, in the shape of a rectangle (see Figure 12.2). Note also in the figure that a special Graphics Property Bar appears to help you manipulate and modify the image.

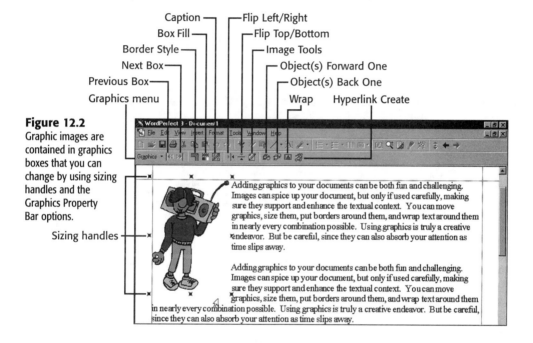

Figure 12.2
Graphic images are contained in graphics boxes that you can change by using sizing handles and the Graphics Property Bar options.

The rectangle that surrounds the image is called a *graphics box*, and when selected is surrounded by eight black boxes called *sizing handles* (refer to Figure 12.2). If you click elsewhere in the document, these handles disappear. If you click the image, you select the object, and the sizing handles appear again.

Image or Box?
Images, and nearly all graphic or other inserted objects, are placed inside graphics boxes. As you work with graphics, you need to remember whether you're working with the graphics box (the container), or with the image (the content) itself. For example, you can change the border style or the size and shape of the box. Independent of any changes you make to the graphics box, you also can change the size and attributes such as brightness or contrast of the image within the box.

 If you are unable to delete an image you've inserted, see "Making It Go Away" in the Troubleshooting section at the end of this chapter.

 If you are unable to make changes to a graphics box, see "Editing a Graphics Box "in the Troubleshooting section at the end of this chapter.

If you can't seem to select a graphics box, see "Difficulties Selecting a Graphics Box" in the Troubleshooting section at the end of this chapter.

RESIZING AND MOVING GRAPHICS

Now the fun begins. Unless you are very, very lucky, the graphic image probably isn't the right size or in exactly the right location. Fortunately, moving and sizing a graphics box is extremely easy.

To move a box, first select the box by clicking *once* on the image. Note that the mouse pointer changes to a four-way arrow (see Figure 12.3), which indicates that you are about to move the object. Drag the image to the precise location you want and release the mouse button to drop the image. You can do this over and over, until you place the image exactly at the right spot.

Figure 12.3
You can use the mouse to drag images and drop them where you want them.

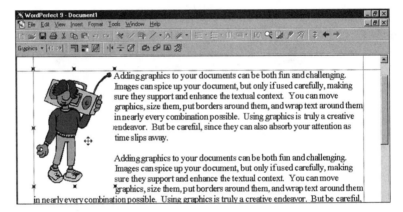

> **Caution**
>
> Be careful not to *double*-click an image. Double-clicking any graphics box enables you to edit the contents of the box. If you double-click an image, you open WordPerfect's graphics editor. If this happens by mistake, simply click outside the graphics image area (for example, in the text) and start over.

To modify the size of the graphics box, use the sizing handles. Point at any of the corner sizing handles, and the mouse pointer turns into a two-way diagonal arrow (see Figure 12.4). Click and drag the sizing handle toward the center of the image to make it smaller, or away from the image to make it larger. Using the corner sizing handles also forces the image to grow or shrink proportionally.

To change the size of the graphics box, and also distort the image it contains, point at any of the four side handles so that the mouse pointer turns into a vertical or horizontal two-way arrow (see Figure 12.5). Click and drag the handle to change the shape of the box. You can create some very interesting effects by using the side handles, such as short, fat giraffes, or long, skinny pigs!

Figure 12.4
Corner sizing handles enable you to enlarge or reduce the size of an image proportionally.

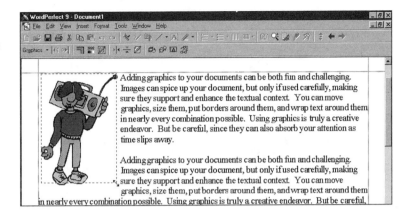

Figure 12.5
Dragging side handles distorts the image, sometimes in interesting ways!

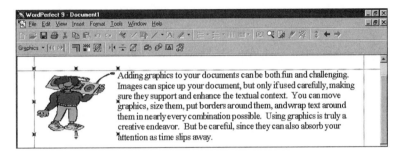

SETTING BORDER, WRAP, AND FILL OPTIONS

PART
IV
CH
12

Although the graphics box takes up rectangular space in your document, you might want to add a border to set it off more clearly from your text. To add a border to your graphics box, follow these steps:

1. Select the image by single-clicking it. The sizing handles indicate the box you select.

 2. Click the Border Style button on the Property Bar to display a palette of border styles (see Figure 12.6).

Figure 12.6
You can add a variety of border styles to graphics boxes.

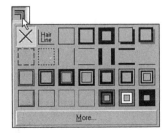

3. Click the border you want to use. WordPerfect adds the border to the graphics box (see Figure 12.7).

Figure 12.7
A border around your image helps set it off from the text.

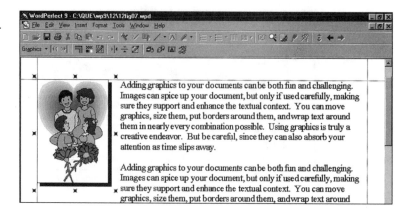

Tip #146 from
Laura and Read

Don't forget that simply pointing at the style on the palette for a moment enables you to preview the style in the document before you actually select it.

 In addition to borders, you can create a background for the box, which fills the box behind the image. WordPerfect calls this a *fill pattern*. With the graphics box selected, click the Box Fill button on the Property Bar and choose a fill pattern from the palette (see Figure 12.8).

Figure 12.8
You can fill in the background behind an image with a variety of fill patterns, including gradient shading.

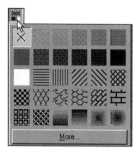

Using predefined borders and fills is a good place to start. But as you become more experienced with what looks good, you can customize your graphics boxes to make them more distinctive.

Notice the More button in Figure 12.6 and Figure 12.8. This is just one way to access the Box Border/Fill dialog box (see Figure 12.9, which shows a border already selected). You can also access this dialog box by clicking the Graphics button on the Property Bar and choosing Border/Fill; or you can simply right-click the image and choose Border/Fill from the QuickMenu.

Figure 12.9
The Box Border/Fill dialog box gives you greater control over the properties of your graphics box.

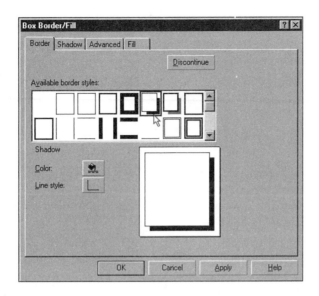

On the Border tab of the Box Border/Fill dialog box, you find the same palette of styles you find behind the Border Style button on the Property Bar. The default style is to include a bit of spacing between the image and the text, without any line. Here you can choose a different line style, and click Color to select a line color from a palette. Clicking the Discontinue button has the same effect as clicking the <None> style in the upper-left corner of the list.

The Fill tab offers the same palette of choices you find on the Property Bar, with the following additions (see Figure 12.10):

- If you choose a solid pattern, you can choose a color from the Foreground palette. Changing the Background color has no effect on solid colors.

Figure 12.10
The Fill tab of the Box Border/Fill dialog box enables you to add patterns, gradient shading, and even image backgrounds.

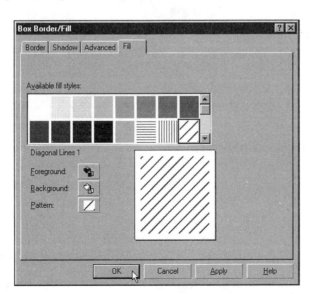

PART

IV

CH

12

- If you choose a pattern, you can also specify the foreground and the background colors. Pattern lines use the foreground color.

- If you choose a gradient shading pattern, you choose a start color and an end color. WordPerfect blends the background from one color to the other.

The Advanced tab enables you to further customize your borders and fills (see Figure 12.11). Custom options include the following:

- You can change the amount of space between the border and the image by changing the inside spacing. Select a predefined spacing amount, or specify an exact measurement, as shown in Figure 12.11.

- You can choose rounded corners for the box, and you can even specify how round the corner radius should be.

- You can modify the style and angle of your gradient shading. For example, if you want to create a linear reflective effect, you can adjust a light starting color to 50% vertical offset against the darker ending color. You can also change the rotation angle (for example, 45%), and then adjust the horizontal offset as needed.

Figure 12.11
You can adjust spacing between the text, the graphic image, and the surrounding box in the Advanced tab of the Box Border/Fill dialog box.

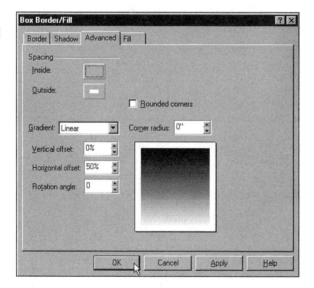

The Shadow tab enables you to add an offset shadow to the graphics box in any direction (see Figure 12.12). Begin by choosing the general direction of shadow you want, then use the scrollbars or the counter boxes to specify the exact shadow height and shadow width. You can also change the shadow color.

By default, text wraps around both sides of a graphics box. If you want to change the way it wraps, click the Wrap button on the Property Bar (see Figure 12.13). Point at each menu option and observe the effect on the text surrounding the graphics box. Click an option to apply it to a graphics box.

→ To learn what all the options mean and how to use them, **see** "Making WordPerfect Text Work with Graphic Objects," **p. 348**

→ To see how to use graphic objects, **see** Chapter 13, "Customizing Graphic Shapes and Images," **p. 347**

Figure 12.12
The Shadow tab of the Box Border/Fill dialog box enables you to create attractive drop shadows.

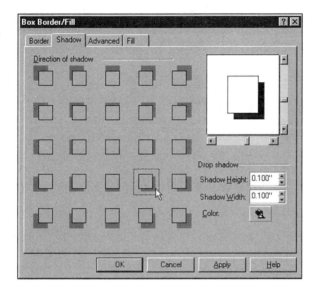

Figure 12.13
WordPerfect enables you to wrap text around your graphics nearly any way you want.

PART
IV

CH
12

USING THE SCRAPBOOK

WordPerfect's Scrapbook is a power tool for organizing and finding just the right graphic image for your document. You access the Scrapbook by choosing Insert, Graphics, Clipart, or by clicking the Clipart button on the toolbar. WordPerfect displays the Scrapbook (see Figure 12.14).

Note

The Scrapbook itself does not contain graphic images, but instead is a catalog of images available for you to use.

Figure 12.14
The Scrapbook is
WordPerfect's system
for helping you man-
age and use graphic
and other multimedia
images.

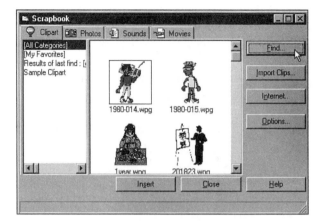

By default, WordPerfect displays the basic collection of installed clip art images. The other tabs in the dialog box display installed photographs, sound files, and video clips.

Although you can scroll through the collection to find the image you want, you can also use the Find feature to search for images based on filenames or keywords. To find a Scrapbook item, click Find. WordPerfect displays the Find Scrapbook Item dialog box (see Figure 12.15).

Figure 12.15
The Find Scrapbook
Item dialog box helps
you search for images
using keywords, file-
names, and file types.

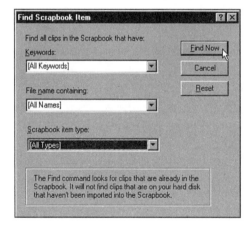

SEARCHING FOR SCRAPBOOK IMAGES

You can search for clip art images using one or more of the following options:

- Keywords—All images in the basic clip art collection have keywords assigned to them. Type a keyword to see which images might fit.

- File Name—If you know the name of the file, or even if you know only part of the file-name, you can type the name in the File Name Containing edit box.

- Scrapbook Item Type—There are many graphic image types, and each is identified by the filename extension. For example, WordPerfect's standard format typically ends in

.WPG. Internet graphic images usually end in .JPG or .GIF. If you have imported different graphic images to your Scrapbook, you can search for the images based on their image type.

Suppose you want to find all of the images that have to do with money. To find an image using a keyword, follow these steps:

1. Click Find to open the Find Scrapbook Item dialog box (refer to Figure 12.15).
2. Type the keyword in the Keywords edit box (for example, *cash*).
3. Click Find Now.

WordPerfect searches for all images that have matching keywords and displays the results, as shown in Figure 12.16. Note the new category on the left side of the dialog box: Results of Find. You can return to the complete list of images by clicking [All Categories]. You can then also return to the found images by clicking the Results of Find category.

Figure 12.16
WordPerfect creates a separate Scrapbook category to display the results of a search for graphic images.

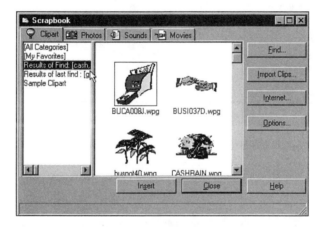

PART

IV

CH

12

Tip #147 from
Laura and Read

Keywords in the initial release of the WordPerfect 9 Scrapbook are separated by commas, which can prevent WordPerfect from finding them. To work around this problem, type the keyword once followed by a comma and once again without a comma (for example: cash, cash).

Note

If you close the Scrapbook, all Results of Find categories are lost, except the most recent one. When you open the Scrapbook again, the result of your last search is listed as Results of Last Find.

ADDING KEYWORDS TO SCRAPBOOK IMAGES

You can add your own keywords to images in the Scrapbook. Simply select the image, click Options, and choose Item Properties. WordPerfect displays the Scrapbook Item Properties dialog box (see Figure 12.17). Add any new keywords in the Keywords edit box, separating each keyword with a space (do *not* use commas to separate keywords). Click OK to return to the Scrapbook.

Figure 12.17
Use the Scrapbook Item Properties box to add keywords or to assign an image to one or more categories.

USING SCRAPBOOK CATEGORIES

If you have an extensive collection of clip art, you can organize it into specialized categories. To create and use categories, follow these steps:

1. Choose Options, Create Category, and when prompted, type a category name and choose OK. WordPerfect then displays the category in the list at the left of the Scrapbook.

2. Select an image you want to include in the new category.

3. Choose Options, Item Properties to access the Scrapbook Item Properties dialog box (refer to Figure 12.17).

Note

Note that you can also add new categories from the Scrapbook Item Properties dialog box.

4. Click the category you want to add the image to.

5. Click OK.

After you create a category, you can also use the Options button to rename or remove it.

Note Removing a category, or even a single scrapbook image, does not delete it from your hard disk. It simply removes it from the Scrapbook.

IMPORTING IMAGES TO THE SCRAPBOOK

You can import individual graphics images to your Scrapbook, as well as clip art collections from earlier versions of WordPerfect.

To import individual graphic images, follow these steps:

1. From the Scrapbook, select the category to which you want to import the image.

Tip #148 from *Laura and Read* When importing graphics, do so to a category you have created, not to [All Categories]. Finding and deleting graphics from [All Categories] is difficult, whereas deleting graphics from your own category is easy because you can simply delete the entire category.

2. Click Import Clips and then use the Insert File dialog box to browse to the graphic image you want to import.

3. Click Open to import the image.

4. WordPerfect displays the Scrapbook Item Properties dialog box (refer to Figure 12.17). Add keywords if you like, assign the image to one or more categories, or add a new category for the image. Click OK to add the image to your Scrapbook.

Note If you select several images to import at one time, WordPerfect asks if you want to set properties for each item. Unless you are importing relatively few images, answer no, and set image properties later. Otherwise, you are stuck either setting the properties or having to click Cancel for each and every imported image.

PART

IV

CH

12

WordPerfect 7 and 8 also shipped with useful graphics that you can import into your WordPerfect Scrapbook. In addition, other collections of clip art are available at the Corel Web site. Such collections typically come in a single file that ends with the .SCB filename extension.

To import such collections, follow these steps:

1. In the Scrapbook, create a new category to which you will import these graphic images.

2. Click Import Clips.

3. Browse to find the .SCB file (for example, compact.scb, which is the name of the sample clip art used in WordPerfect 8). Click Open.

4. Although WordPerfect warns that this may take a few minutes, it usually takes only a few seconds to import the collection. When asked if you want to delete the original file, answer No.

That's it!

USING CD CLIP ART

When you install WordPerfect, by default, only a handful of images are actually copied to your computer (or to your network). The rest of WordPerfect's extensive collection, including over 12,000 clip art images, remain on your CD-ROM.

> **Note**
>
> If you're using a network version of WordPerfect, you should ask your system administrator to copy the clip art folders to a network drive that is accessible by everyone. But if you're an individual WordPerfect user, unless you have a lot of hard disk space, you probably won't want to copy the entire collection to your hard drive.

To use the CD clip art, follow these easy steps:

1. Insert the CD-ROM that contains the graphic images (this varies depending on which version of the Office 2000 suite you have).
2. If the CD automatically displays an installation screen, close it.
3. Open the Scrapbook. WordPerfect automatically finds the graphics on the CD and adds several new categories to your scrapbook.
4. Click a category, and then select and insert a graphic image as you usually do.

You should be aware of the following when using CD clip art:

- When the CD is in the CD-ROM drive, all CD images are available. If the CD is removed, the categories remain visible in the Scrapbook but the images do not.
- You cannot change the item properties for CD images. However, you can copy a CD image to one of your own categories where you can then change the properties.
- You can remove the CD categories (there are many), but you first must remove the CD, and then you must delete each category separately.

USING LINES AND BORDERS

Although images are the most obvious graphic elements one adds to a document, other elements such as lines and borders also add visual impact and help organize the text in the mind of the reader. Horizontal lines can help identify divisions or sections of text—for example, a horizontal line that separates the heading information of a memo (TO:, FROM:, and so on) from the message of the memo. Vertical lines help the reader follow the flow of text—for example, in the columns of a newsletter.

INSERTING HORIZONTAL AND VERTICAL LINES

To insert a horizontal line that extends from one margin to the other, simply place the cursor where you want the line, and choose Insert, Line, Horizontal Line, or press Ctrl+F11. WordPerfect places a thin, single, black line in your document (see Figure 12.18). Because the line is a graphical line, not based on text characters, it fits perfectly between the margins even if you later change the margins or the font of the document.

Figure 12.14
Easy to add, horizontal lines help separate sections of text.

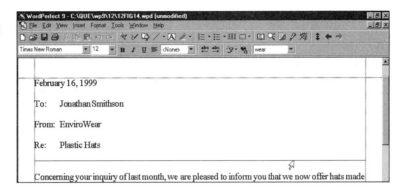

Inserting vertical lines works the same way. Simply position the cursor where you want the vertical line (for example, at the left margin), and choose Insert, Line, Vertical Line, or press Ctrl+Shift+F11. WordPerfect inserts a thin, single, black vertical line in your document that extends from the top to the bottom margin. Note, however, that because the vertical line sits nearly on top of the text, this default location is not terribly useful.

Fortunately, you can easily create custom lines that are any length, size, or color, and that you can place anywhere in the document. Because lines are graphic objects, you can also move and edit default horizontal or vertical lines.

To move a line (for example, to move the vertical line just to the left of the left margin), follow these steps:

1. Move the mouse pointer toward the line until it changes to an arrow.
2. Click the line to select it. WordPerfect treats the line just like it does any graphics box. Sizing handles appear, and the mouse pointer changes to a four-way arrow (see Figure 12.19).

PART

IV

CH

12

Figure 12.19
If you select a graphics line, you can move and size it the same way you do any graphic image.

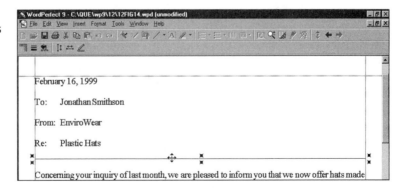

3. Drag the line to the new location (for example, about 1/10 inch to the left).
4. Click anywhere in the text to deselect the line.

Indeed, you treat graphic lines as you do any other graphic object. Here are some examples:

- To delete a line, simply select it and press Delete or Backspace.

- To change the size or shape of a line, drag the sizing handles. For example, to make a thicker line, drag any of the sizing handles from the center of the line until you see the size you want. By default, WordPerfect creates a solid black line.

- To edit a line, right-click it and choose Edit Horizontal (or Vertical) Line from the QuickMenu, or simply double-click the line. Alternatively, you can select the line, and choose Edit, Edit Graphic Line from the menus.

Whether you choose to edit an existing line or to create a custom line, the dialog box and the options are the same. Choose Insert, Line, Custom Line, and WordPerfect displays the Create Graphics Line dialog box (see Figure 12.20), which is identical to the Edit Graphics Line dialog box you get if you choose to edit an existing graphics line.

Figure 12.20
You can create a custom line length, thickness, or color by using the Create Graphics Line dialog box.

In the Create Graphics Line dialog box you can create a vertical or horizontal line, and preview the results before inserting the line into your document. Options for creating or editing a *horizontal* graphics line include the following:

Tip #149 from
Laura and Read

If you edit a horizontal line and select Vertical Line, you remove the horizontal line and replace it with a vertical line.

- Line Style—By default, WordPerfect inserts single, black lines. You can click the palette button to choose from other predefined line styles (see Figure 12.21). The drop-down list at the bottom of the palette gives you the same choices as clicking the Line Styles button at the bottom of the dialog box.

Figure 12.21
WordPerfect offers many predefined line styles to choose from when creating a custom line.

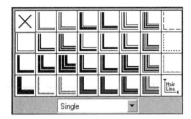

- Line Color—You can choose a different color from the palette. If you want to reset the color, choose Use Line Style Color from the palette.

- Line Thickness—You can choose a new line thickness from the palette, or specify an exact thickness in the counter box on the palette.

- Space Above Line/Space Below Line—These options appear only when creating or editing horizontal lines. To put distance between the line and its surrounding text, choose more space from the palette buttons.

- Length—The default length for horizontal lines is the distance between the left and right margins. If you want a longer or shorter line, specify the length here.

- Horizontal—This option refers to the location where the line begins or how it is aligned horizontally. The left, right, center, and full options are obvious. Set enables you then to specify a measurement in the At box that indicates the exact location where the lines begin, relative to the left edge of the paper. By default, when you choose Set, WordPerfect gives you the location of your cursor, and adjusts the line length to extend from that point to the right margin.

- Vertical—By default, WordPerfect places a horizontal line at the baseline (bottom of the characters) on the line of text your cursor is on. If you choose Set, you then specify the distance from the top edge of the paper to where the line begins.

When editing or creating a vertical line, the dialog box changes slightly, and some of the options work differently. The following are some examples:

- Border Offset—This appears only when you're creating or editing vertical lines and is used to specify the amount of space between the vertical line and the text to its right.

- Length—The default length for vertical lines is the distance between top and bottom margins. If you want a longer or shorter line, specify the length here.

- Horizontal—You can align a vertical line at the left, right, or center of the text, or set the exact horizontal location of a vertical line on the page. If you choose Column Aligned, the At box changes to After Col, and you indicate which column the line should follow.

- Vertical—Here you can align a vertical line at the top, bottom, or center, or from the top to bottom margin of the text (full). If you choose Set, you then specify the distance from the top edge of the paper to where the line begins.

PART
IV

CH
12

→ To learn more about creating newspaper style columns, **see** "Setting Up Columns," **p. 215**

Tip #150 from
Laura and Read

If you want to create different lines between each of the columns (for example, one thick line and one thin line) or otherwise customize the lines between columns, use this Custom Line feature. However, if all you want is single thin black lines between your columns that extend from the top to the bottom margins, choose Format, Columns, Border/Fill to access the Columns Border/Fill dialog box. Then choose the Column Between style. No fuss, no muss.

ADDING BORDERS TO PARAGRAPHS AND PAGES

You can apply line styles to surround text paragraphs and document pages. These text borders are very similar to borders used for graphics boxes. Unlike lines you insert, borders are styles you apply to various WordPerfect elements such as text paragraphs and columns. The information on customizing borders in the section "Setting Border, Wrap, and Fill Options," earlier in this chapter, applies also to text and page borders.

→ For more information on adding line borders to paragraphs and pages, **see** Chapter 7, "Formatting Lines and Paragraphs," **p. 171**

→ For more information on adding line borders to paragraphs and pages, **see** Chapter 8, "Formatting the Page," **p. 193**

INSERTING SHAPES

If you think adding clip art and lines is fun, wait until you start adding shapes. Beginning with version 8, WordPerfect added the capability to draw graphic shapes directly on a document, a feature that has been dramatically enhanced in WordPerfect 9.

WordPerfect's *graphic shapes* fall into three basic categories. Although each has similar characteristics, you create, edit, and manipulate each slightly differently:

- Lines—Each of the line types has a beginning and end, and you can even add arrow heads or tails to them.
- Closed shapes—These include boxes, circles, action buttons, and specialty shapes.
- Callout shapes—These are similar to closed shapes, but they also enable you to add text in them to make it easier to create callouts.

You can access shapes in one of the following ways:

- From the menus—Choose Insert, Shapes to display the Draw Object Shapes dialog box (see Figure 12.22).
- From the Graphics toolbar—Choose View, Toolbars, and then select the Graphics toolbar and click OK; or simply right-click the WordPerfect toolbar and choose Graphics. WordPerfect displays the Graphics toolbar, from which you can choose various shapes (see Figure 12.23).

Figure 12.22
The Draw Object Shapes dialog box offers a complete array of graphic shapes, but it is a bit more clumsy to use than the toolbar buttons.

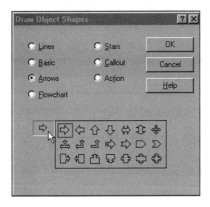

Figure 12.23
The Graphics toolbar makes it quick and easy to add a graphic shape to your document.

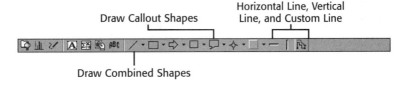

 ■ From the Draw Combined Shapes button on the WordPerfect 9 toolbar—This button combines several of the most useful shapes into one easily accessible button.

The following sections concentrate on the Draw Combined Shapes button. You'll probably want to use the menus and Graphics toolbar as well to explore the full range of graphic shapes.

PART
IV

CH
12

ADDING LINE SHAPES

 To examine the choices available on the Draw Combined Shapes button, click the drop-down arrow on the right side of the button. WordPerfect then displays a palette of choices (see Figure 12.24). These include several line styles, closed objects, and callout styles.

Figure 12.24
The most commonly used graphic shape types are included on the Draw Combined Shapes button on the toolbar.

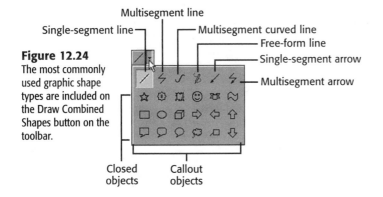

To draw a line shape on your document, follow these steps:

1. Click the line style you want to use from the Draw Combined Shapes palette (refer to Figure 12.24). WordPerfect displays the icon for that style on the button, and the button appears to be selected.

2. Move the mouse pointer to the text area and note that it is a crosshairs shape.

3. Position the pointer where you want the line to begin.

Tip #151 from
Laura and Read

These procedures are used for creating both lines and arrows. You can save time by always starting lines at the tail of the imaginary arrow, and ending them at the arrow head.

4. Click and drag to the opposite end of the line.

Tip #152 from
Laura and Read

You can draw a line from a center point by holding down the Ctrl key while you drag your line. As you drag away from the center point, the line extends an equal distance in the opposite direction.

5. If you're creating a single-segment line or arrow, release the mouse button to add the line on top of your text.

For other line types, the procedures vary slightly:

- If you're creating a multisegment line, click to change directions. Drag to the next juncture and click. Continue until you reach the end, then double-click the mouse to complete the line.

- If you're creating a multisegment curved line, click each time you want to start a new curve. As you drag the mouse in a new direction, note that WordPerfect rounds the line on both sides of the point that you click. To complete a curved line, double-click.

- Free-form drawing works just like drawing with a pencil. Click and drag in any direction, and WordPerfect draws a line to match. Release the mouse button to complete the line.

Tip #153 from
Laura and Read

You can draw free-form segments of multisegment lines or arrows by holding down the mouse button instead of releasing it before you change directions. When you want to resume straight lines again, release the mouse button.

After you complete your line shape, note that WordPerfect places the shape in a graphics box, complete with sizing handles (see Figure 12.25). The shape also covers any text or other objects that lie beneath it. You can adjust the size of the box or move the box as needed.

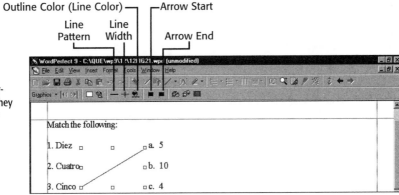

Figure 12.25
Graphic shapes are easy to use, and layered on your text, they add pizzazz to your document.

Caution

If you add several shapes or objects in the same area, it can become difficult to accurately select and move or modify some of the objects. If this happens, simply right-click where you think the object is, choose Select Other from the QuickMenu, and select the object you want.

With the shape selected, WordPerfect displays the graphics line editing tools on the Property Bar (refer to Figure 12.25).

The following are some of the changes you can make to a shape:

- Shadow—From the palette of choices, you can create a drop shadow in any of four directions.

- Shadow Color—The shadow color is a solid color and not a lighter version of the shape's color. For example, if you want a gray shadow for a black object, you must choose gray as the shadow color.

- Line Pattern—Choose from solid and dashed or dotted lines. If you click the large ×, you get no line.

Caution

If you choose no line for a line shape, you lose arrowhead options on the Property Bar. Simply double-click the line (guess where it is!) to display the Object Properties dialog box, where you can make all the changes you need.

- Line Width—Choose the width of your line.

- Outline Color (Line Color)—Choose the color you want the line to appear.

- Arrow Start—Change the look at the beginning of the line by using one of the arrow heads or tails from the palette (see Figure 12.26).

- Arrow End—You can change the look at the end of the line. Note that you can actually have two arrowheads, two tails, or any other combination you like.

Figure 12.26
You can create attractive and functional arrows by adding arrow tails and heads to graphic lines.

- Object(s) Forward One or Object(s) Back One—If you create more than one shape in the same area, you can layer the objects in the order you want.

- Wrap—By default, text does not wrap around the shapes, but instead the shapes appear in front of the text. You can change the way text wraps just as you do for any graphics box.

ADDING CLOSED OBJECT SHAPES

The lines of *closed object shapes* come together, such as in a circle, and thus their inside area is closed. By default, such objects are drawn with thin single lines and are filled with an aquamarine-like green color (your results may vary).

You draw closed shapes differently from the way you draw open shapes. Let's use a five-point star to illustrate the procedure:

1. Click the drop-down palette on the Draw Combined Shapes button to display the list of available shapes (refer to Figure 12.24).

2. Click a closed object, such as the five-point star. WordPerfect displays the star on the button, and the pointer turns into crosshairs.

3. Position the pointer at one corner of the area you intend to fill with the shape (for example, the upper-left corner).

4. Click and drag the pointer to the opposite corner (for example, the lower-right corner).

5. Continue holding the mouse button while you move the pointer, until you have exactly the right size and proportions.

Tip #154 from
Laura and Read

If you hold the Shift key down while dragging the mouse, WordPerfect constrains the object to be symmetrical–for example, a circle instead of an oval or a square instead of a rectangle.

6. Release the mouse button to place the object on the document (see Figure 12.27).

Figure 12.27
Closed object and call-out shapes are filled with color. Note the glyph, which is used to change the style of a graphic shape.

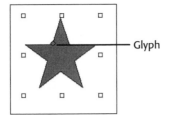

— Glyph

If the object has one or more *glyphs*, which are small pink-colored diamond handles, you can manipulate the shape or the perspective of the shape. For example, on the five-point star, you can drag the glyph toward the center of the object to create a skinny starfish look. You can drag it away from the center to create a fat sheriff's star look.

You can, of course, use the sizing handles to further change the shape or size of the object, and you can move the object to the exact location where you want it.

In addition, with the shape selected, WordPerfect also displays the graphics shape editing tools on the Property Bar (refer to Figure 12.25). The buttons are the same as those used for lines, except that the Arrow Start and End buttons are replaced by the Fill Style palette and buttons to change the foreground and background fill colors.

Tip #155 from
Laura and Read

If you want to create a contoured area around which text wraps—for example, to reserve space for something you must paste into the printed copy—you can create a closed object shape. Then change the wrap option to contoured, both sides; change the line style to none, and change the fill color to white.

Note

Although you can make many changes to the properties of closed objects from the Property Bar, you have more precise control and more options by double-clicking the object and using the Object Properties dialog box.

ADDING CALLOUT SHAPES

Callout shapes are similar to closed object shapes, and are created by following the same procedures. The difference is that after you create a callout, WordPerfect also creates a text box inside it, where you can type text to go along with the callout (see Figure 12.28).

You can create a callout in several ways:

- Type text to fill in the callout text box—By default, such text is centered both horizontally and vertically, but you can change the text just as you do other text in your document. For example, you can change the alignment or change the font or color.

Text box handles

Figure 12.28
A callout is a closed
object shape with
a text box.

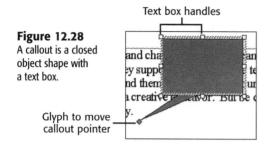

Glyph to move
callout pointer

■ Use the sizing handles to change the size of the callout area—If what you type exceeds the space of the callout area, WordPerfect does not automatically expand the box, so you need to use the sizing handles to resize the area.

■ Reorient the callout pointer—Drag the glyph at the end of the callout pointer to any side of the callout, and stretch the pointer until it's directed at the callout source (see Figure 12.29).

Figure 12.29
You can move the
callout pointer to any
side of the callout by
dragging the glyph.

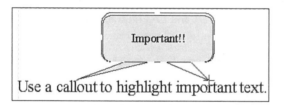

■ Use other options on the Property Bar to modify the callout object—For example, you can change the fill pattern or color, position the callout behind text by changing the wrap option, and so on.

■ Right-click the object and use the QuickMenu for other tools, such as wrap, position, or size.

Tip #156 from
Laura and Read

Instead of using new text in a callout text box, you can position the callout so that it encloses text already in the document. If you simply want to see through the callout to the text behind, turn off the fill pattern. If you want to keep the fill pattern and still see the document text, change the callout's wrap option so that it appears behind text.

USING WATERMARKS

In expensive bond paper, a *watermark* in the paper itself lends a distinctive look. Hold a piece up to the light, and you see an image—perhaps along with words—that helps identify the paper brand or content. WordPerfect watermarks also add a distinctive look by adding a lightly shaded graphic image behind the text of your document.

Watermarks are extremely easy to create:

1. Position the cursor at the beginning of the document.

Repeating Watermarks

Watermarks function like headers in that they appear on every page, beginning at the page where you insert the watermark code, continuing until you turn off the watermark.

---

2. Choose Insert, Watermark. WordPerfect displays the Watermark dialog box (see Figure 12.30).

Figure 12.30
You can use the Watermark dialog box to create or edit background watermark graphics.

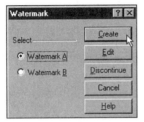

3. If this is a new watermark, and the first one you've created in this document, choose Watermark A, and click Create. WordPerfect next displays a blank, full page where you create or edit the watermark graphic. Figure 12.31 shows what the Watermark screen looks like after you have added a watermark.

Figure 12.31
A watermark image is text or a graphic image, displayed at 25% brightness.

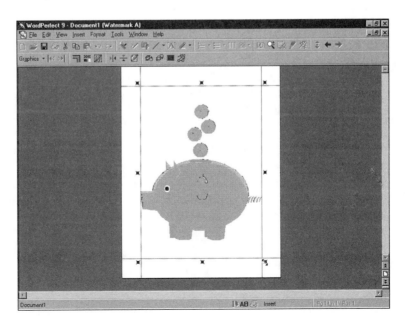

4. You can use graphics from any source that you would use in the document itself. For example, you can click the Clipart button to display the Scrapbook.

5. Scroll through the Scrapbook list until you find the graphic image you want.

6. Select the graphic and click Insert to place it on the Watermark screen (refer to Figure 12.31).

Note that the graphics box, complete with sizing handles, fills the entire page. The image itself is shaded lightly so as not to interfere with the text that will appear on top of it. You can size and position the graphic image just as you do any other graphic image, using the mouse and the sizing handles.

Click outside the graphics box area (in the margins, for example), and WordPerfect displays on the Property Bar the following options for modifying the watermark (see Figure 12.32):

You can add other images, and size and position them by clicking the Clipart, Image, or Insert File buttons.

You can choose whether to place the watermark on odd pages, even pages, or both, by clicking the Watermark Placement button.

You can change the shading of the watermark by clicking the Shading button. By default, both text and graphics watermarks are shaded only 25% of their full color (or darkness).

Figure 12.32
The Watermark
Property Bar helps
you modify a water-
mark graphic.

Caution

Rarely do you need or want to make a watermark darker. Doing so usually conflicts with document text in front of the watermark. More often, you may need to lighten the watermark to make it less conspicuous.

When you're satisfied with the look of the watermark, click the Close button on the Property Bar. If the watermark graphic is selected (that is, if you can see the sizing handles), you can close the Watermark editing screen by choosing File, Close. WordPerfect then returns you to the document editing screen and displays the watermark in the background (see Figure 12.33).

Figure 12.33
Watermarks can add attractive, as well as useful, backgrounds to a text page.

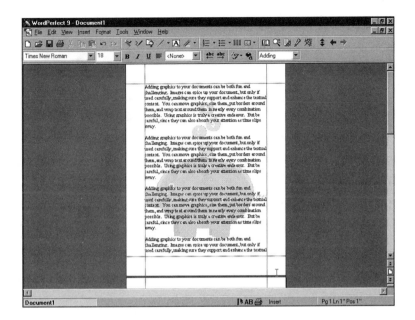

TROUBLESHOOTING

MAKING IT GO AWAY

I inserted the wrong image, but I can't seem to use Delete or Backspace to get rid of it.

WordPerfect does not delete the box code when you backspace or delete unless Reveal Codes is on. You can, of course, turn on Reveal Codes to delete the graphics box code, but an easier way is to click the object to select it. Now, pressing Backspace or Delete does indeed remove the image.

EDITING A GRAPHICS BOX

I want to edit my graphics box, but can't find the tools I need.

Don't forget that you must first select a graphic image, so that the sizing handles appear, before the Graphics menu and other graphics buttons appear on the Property Bar. You must deselect it to get back your normal text editing tools.

DIFFICULTIES SELECTING A GRAPHICS BOX

You tell me to select a graphics box, but for some reason I can't do so.

If you add several shapes or objects in the same area, it can become difficult to accurately select and move or modify some of the objects. If this happens, simply right-click where you think the object is, choose Select Other from the QuickMenu, and select the object you want.

WHERE DID ALL THIS COME FROM?

I tried to select a graphic image, but now there's a funny-looking hashed line around the edge of the graphic and a toolbar down the left side.

If you double-click a graphic image, WordPerfect opens the image in the draw program editor (actually, it opens the image in Corel Presentations). Click outside the graphics box (for example, in the text), and WordPerfect closes the editor. In the future, to select an image, just single-click it.

PROJECT

Using WordPerfect's graphics features, your creative genius can kick into high gear. But adding attractive graphics doesn't have to be time-consuming or difficult. In this example, we'll add a talking child to an article describing earth-friendly environmental policies.

Begin by creating your text. This is an extremely important first step because you don't want to add graphics until you've settled on how much text you have and where it should be located (see Figure 12.34).

Figure 12.34
Before adding graphics, you should create, edit, and format your text.

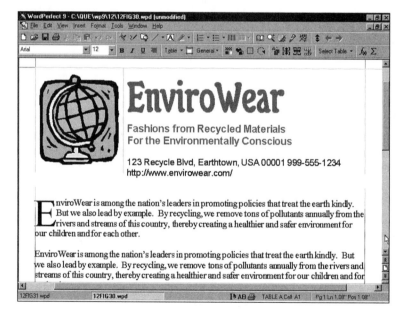

To add the child, follow these steps:

1. Position the cursor where you want the child to appear—for example, at the right side of the document.

 2. Click the Clipart button on the toolbar.

3. Scroll through the Scrapbook until you find the child, and click Insert.

4. Position and size the image exactly where you want it.

5. Right-click the image, choose Wrap, and change the wrap to contour on the left side of the image.

6. Click the Draw Combined Shapes button and choose a callout shape style.

7. Draw the callout shape to the upper left of the child.

8. Type the text of the callout in the text box; for example, `Show me how to take care of my planet!`.

9. Click outside the text box to deselect the callout, and then click the callout.

10. Drag the glyph to reposition the callout pointer, so that it points at the child's mouth.

11. Use the QuickMenu or the Property Bar to change the callout's color (for example, to light yellow) and the callout's wrap (for example, contour on the left side).

The end result, as shown in Figure 12.35, looks great, and as you can see, it wasn't at all difficult to create.

Figure 12.35
You can insert graphics and callouts to add emphasis and pizzazz to your documents.

CHAPTER **13**

CUSTOMIZING GRAPHIC SHAPES AND IMAGES

In this chapter

MAKING WORDPERFECT TEXT WORK WITH GRAPHIC OBJECTS

Graphic elements such as clip art, lines, or watermarks can do wonders to spice up an otherwise mundane document. However, the core of the document is still the text. Getting text and graphics to coexist in your document requires some skill and a lot of patience. In addition to what you learn here, trial-and-error also will be your teacher.

Caution

Using graphics, especially on computers that have limited memory (that is, RAM), increases the chances of program crashes. Save your work frequently while working with graphics to avoid losing painstaking work.

WRAP OPTIONS

When you insert a graphic image in your document, you insert a rectangular graphics box that contains the image. How the body of your text interacts with the graphics box, or with the image it contains, depends on the *wrap (page 384)* method you choose.

By default, WordPerfect wraps text on both sides of a graphics box rectangle. To see other wrap options, right-click the graphics box and choose W$\underline{r}$ap from the QuickMenu (see Figure 13.1).

Figure 13.1
You can choose wrap options from the Wrap Text dialog box.

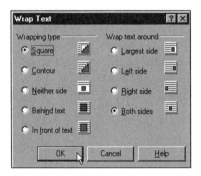

WordPerfect offers five basic options for wrapping text around an image (see Figure 13.2 for examples of each):

- $\underline{S}$quare—This option leaves a small margin of white space between the outside of the graphics box rectangle and the text that surrounds it. The side the text appears on depends on the other options you choose. For example, you can choose to wrap text on both sides, on the left or the right sides, or only on the largest side (the side with the most text).

- $\underline{C}$ontour—Using the $\underline{C}$ontour option, you can wrap the text so that it contours to the image contained in the box, instead of to the box itself (refer to Figure 13.2). This can result in a very professional-looking document. You can also specify which sides the text appears on. Note, however, that if you add a border of any kind to a contoured graphics box, the wrap option reverts to $\underline{S}$quare.

Figure 13.2
Wrapping text means making room around a graphics box for the text that surrounds it. You can also wrap text in front of or behind text.

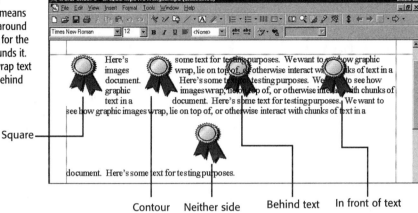

Square

Contour   Neither side
(no wrap)   Behind text   In front of text

If you use the Contour wrap option, you should check the wrapped text to make sure the image has not split words and that the way the words wrap makes sense. Consider not only the visual result, but also the text flow; because wrapped images interrupt the text flow, you need to verify that the reader will be able to follow along.

- Neither Side—This option means you do not wrap text around the box, but instead, leave blank spaces on each side of the graphic image. In effect, the text wraps only on the top and bottom of the graphic image. For example, equation graphics boxes, by default, do not wrap on either side.

- Behind Text—When you place an image behind the text, or in front of the text, you effectively turn off wrapping altogether. This option is used whenever you need to position an image without disturbing the text around it, such as in a poster (see Figure 13.3).

Figure 13.3
By turning off the wrap option, placing a larger image in front of the text and a smaller image behind the text, you create a sense of three-dimensional depth in a sign or poster.

PART

IV

CH

13

■ In <u>F</u>ront of Text—When you place an image in front of the text, you also effectively turn off wrapping altogether. You often use this option in documents such as posters where covering part of the image with text doesn't interfere with what's being presented (refer to Figure 13.3).

Tip #157 from
Laura and Read

An even easier way to select a wrap style is to click the Wrap button from the Property Bar. As you pause the mouse pointer over each option, WordPerfect previews the effect in the document itself. You can click an option to apply it to the selected graphics box.

WORKING WITH GRAPHIC LAYERS

If you add more than one graphic element at the same location, you create *layers* of graphics. The bottom layer is the image you inserted first, and the top layer is the graphic you inserted most recently. If you select an object and also move it, that object moves to the top layer. To specify the order of the graphic layers, you can right-click the objects.

By changing the size and order of the objects in the layers, you can combine graphics into rather interesting and effective images. For example, in Figure 13.4, three images have been added. If you want the stack of coins in front of the piggy bank, and the dollar bill floating behind the coins, you must change the order of the layers.

 If you're having trouble selecting the graphics box you want, see "Selecting the Correct Graphics Box" in the Troubleshooting section at the end of this chapter.

 If you accidentally double-click an image, see "Exiting the Graphics Editing Screen" in the Troubleshooting section at the end of this chapter.

Figure 13.4
Three graphic images inserted in a document at the same location are layered one on top of the other.

To change the order of graphic object layers, follow these steps:

1. Click the object you want to change (for example, the piggy bank object).

Tip #158 from
Laura and Read

If you select an image, but the sizing handles don't seem to match the graphics box for that image, click again until you select the correct box. This works even if the box you want to select is hidden behind another image.

2. Click the Graphics menu on the Property Bar (see Figure 13.5), or right-click the object and choose O<u>r</u>der from the QuickMenu.

Figure 13.5
You can access Graphics menu commands from the Property Bar or from the QuickMenu.

3. From the menu choose one of the following options:

- To F<u>r</u>ont—This moves the object all the way forward, to the top layer.
- To <u>B</u>ack—This moves the object all the way backward, to the bottom layer.
- For<u>w</u>ard One—This moves the object forward only one layer. Other objects may still remain on top of or in front of it.
- Bac<u>k</u> One—This moves the object back only one layer, so other objects may remain beneath or behind it.

4. Repeat steps 1–3 until all the objects are in the proper order.

Now, after you adjust the size (by dragging the sizing handles of the graphics box) and position (by dragging the graphics box) of the graphic objects, you create the effect of a composite graphic image, as shown in Figure 13.6.

Figure 13.6
You can size, position, and change the layer order of multiple graphics to create the effect of one image.

Text, Images, and Layers

Setting some images to wrap in front of the text and others to wrap behind the text creates two separate groups of graphic layers, each separated by the text itself. If you try to make a graphic that's behind the text move to the front, it only moves to the top layer of all the images that reside behind the text. Likewise, moving an image that's in front of the text all the way to the back causes it to move only to the bottom layer of all the images that reside in front of the text.

CHANGING SIZE AND CONTENT OPTIONS

Moving and sizing objects with the mouse is quick and easy, but not always perfectly accurate. If you're creating a complicated layout of text and graphics, you might find it easier to use dialog boxes to specify exact locations, sizes, and content of the graphics boxes.

To specify an exact size for a graphics box, follow these steps:

1. Select the graphics box.

2. Click the Graphics menu button on the Property Bar.

3. Choose Size from the menu. WordPerfect displays the Box Size dialog box (see Figure 13.7).

Figure 13.7
You can use the Box Size dialog box to specify an exact height or width of an image.

4. Set the width and height and click OK.

The options for width and height include the following:

- Full—This means that the graphic will extend from margin to margin.

- Set—Use this option to specify the exact measurement of the graphics box. This is particularly useful when you want several images to be exactly the same size, such as in a photo gallery.

- Maintain Proportions—Unless you intend to distort the image, you should set the exact size of one side, and then choose this option for the other.

ANCHORING IMAGES

By default, WordPerfect images are *anchored* to a page. That is, if you move the text, the images remain at the same location on the page. You can also anchor images to paragraphs or to characters. In these cases, the images move as the text moves. To set the exact position of a graphic image, follow these steps:

1. Select the image.

2. Click the Graphics menu on the Property Bar and select Position.

3. Choose one of the following methods from the Attach Box To drop-down list for anchoring the graphic, and specify the image's precise location:

   - Page—This is the default anchor when you insert a graphic image. The position options change in the Box Position dialog box (see Figure 13.8) if you select a different anchor. You can adjust the horizontal position relative to the left edge of the paper, the margins, or text columns. You set the vertical position relative to the top edge of the page, or to the top or bottom margins. Typically, the image moves with the text of the page it is anchored to, but if you check Box Stays on Page, the image remains on the current page (for example, page 1).

Figure 13.8
Options for anchoring an image to a page are found in the Box Position dialog box.

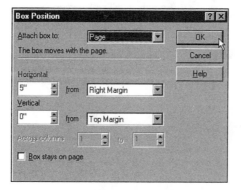

   - Paragraph—If you choose to attach the box to a paragraph (see Figure 13.9), then the box moves with the paragraph. You can specify the horizontal position relative to the left edge of the paper, to the margins, or the center of the paragraph. You set the vertical position relative to the top of the paragraph. With the box anchored to the paragraph, when you drag the box with the mouse, a pushpin appears to show you which paragraph the box is anchored to (see Figure 13.10).

   - Character—The image moves as the character it is anchored to moves. Note in Figure 13.11 the many options for positioning the image relative to the character. The preview box shows the effect of each option. Character anchoring is a more precise way to attach an image to your text, but it also can cause problems with the text that surrounds it because the line height of the text changes to accommodate the graphic image (see Figure 13.12).

PART

IV

CH

13

Figure 13.9
You can choose
Paragraph in the Box
Position dialog box to
display these options.

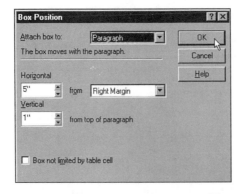

Figure 13.10
When an image is
anchored to a para-
graph, a pushpin
appears as you move
the graphic to show
you where it is
anchored.

A pushpin indi-
cates the location
of the paragraph
anchor.

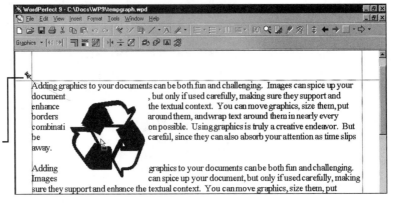

Figure 13.11
You can choose the
Character anchor type
to display these
options, which enable
you to preview the
results.

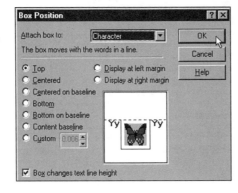

Figure 13.12
If you anchor an image to a character, you cause the text line height also to change to the height of the graphics box.

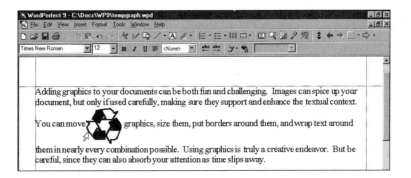

4. Click OK to apply the specified positioning to the image.

⚠️ *If you're having trouble with graphics not moving when you edit your text, see "Anchoring Images Correctly" in the Troubleshooting section at the end of this chapter.*

ADDING CAPTIONS

Image captions are useful for identification. Not only can you add text description, but you also can add figure numbers that automatically sequence throughout the document.

To add a caption, follow these easy steps:

1. Select the graphic.

2. Click the Graphics menu on the Property Bar and choose Caption. WordPerfect displays the Box Caption dialog box (see Figure 13.13).

Figure 13.13
The Box Caption dialog box enables you to create, edit, and position captions for a graphics box.

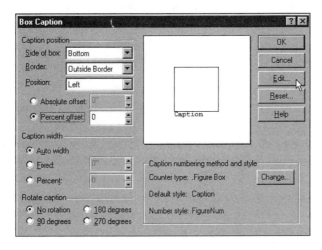

Note

You cannot add captions to graphic shapes such as lines or arrows, but you can add them to clip art and other images you place in a graphics box.

3. Click Edit to create the text of the caption. WordPerfect automatically places the figure numbering style along with the text *Figure n* (where *n* is the number of the box to which you're adding a caption). If you don't want that information, press Backspace once to delete it.

4. Type the caption information. Use the Property Bar to modify the font, size, and other attributes of the text.

Caution

The font of the caption is based on the document default font. If you change the font in the text, but don't change the default font, the caption font may not match your text.

5. Click the Close button on the Property Bar to return to your text, or just click in the text area. WordPerfect adds the caption to your graphics box, as shown in Figure 13.14.

Figure 13.14
Captions add information and are numbered sequentially to help you refer the reader to the images in your document.

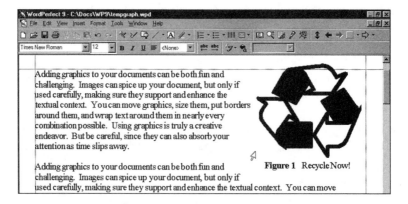

Note

When you add a caption outside the graphics box border, the graphics box extends to include the caption, but the border surrounds only the image. Document text wraps around both the image and the caption.

By default, WordPerfect creates captions that appear at the bottom left, outside the graphics box border. Using the Box Caption dialog box (refer to Figure 13.13), you can modify the caption to fit your needs. The options include the following:

- Side of Box—You can place the caption on the top, bottom, right, or left of the graphics box.

- Border—You can place the caption inside or outside the box border.

- Position—You can position the caption at the left or right, top or bottom, or center of the side you select. Or you can be even more precise by specifying an exact offset, by measurement or by a percentage of the available width.

- Caption Width—You can let WordPerfect do that calculating for you, or you can specify an exact measurement or percentage of available space for the width of your caption.

- Rotate Caption—If you place the caption on either side of the graphics box, you might want to rotate the caption 90 degrees (left side) or 270 degrees (right side). Rotating top or bottom captions doesn't make much sense, but you can do it.

- Caption Numbering Method and Style—By default, WordPerfect counts boxes according to the types of boxes they are. For example, each figure box is numbered sequentially, as are text boxes, equation boxes, and so on. You can change the box type, which also changes the box number. However, unless you are working with a long document where box numbers are important, you do not need to change the box type.

- Reset—Use this option if you want to delete a caption. This also sets options back to their original defaults.

ADDING TEXT BOXES AS GRAPHIC OBJECTS

Text boxes are similar to graphics boxes except that their content is text instead of graphic images. Text boxes are useful for adding labels to your document—for example, on top of a graphic image.

CREATING TEXT BOXES

To create a text box, follow these steps:

1. Position the cursor where you want to place the text box.

2. Click the Text Box button on the toolbar, or choose Insert, Text Box from the menu. WordPerfect places in your document a text box with a single-line border, aligned at the right margin (see Figure 13.15). The hash marks around the text box and the blinking cursor indicate that WordPerfect is waiting for you to add or edit text.

Figure 13.15
A text box is distinctive in that it is surrounded by hash marks, and the blinking cursor indicates where to type or edit text.

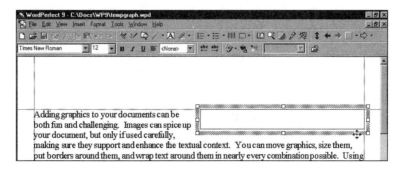

3. Type, edit, and format the text of the text box. If the text wraps, or if you press Enter, the box expands vertically.

4. Drag the right center sizing handle far enough the left that you don't have a lot of extra white space in the right side of the box.

5. Move the box itself by positioning the mouse pointer at the edge of the box (the pointer becomes a four-way arrow), and drag the box to the desired location.

6. Click outside the box to deselect it.

Selecting Text Boxes

To edit a text box, click the text area of the box. To move a box, however, you must move the mouse pointer to the edge of the box until you see the four-way arrow. To select a box to delete it, you must first click the edge of the box. Otherwise, you only delete text within the box.

You can apply all box formatting options to text boxes, the same way you do to graphics boxes. For example, you can change the way text wraps around the text box, the border, the background, and so on.

Tip #159 from
Laura and Read

If you want to add a text label to a graphic image, create a text box and wrap it in front of the text. You may have to change the order of the graphic image and the text box so that the text box appears in front of the image.

ROTATING TEXT

Often you need labels that aren't horizontal. Fortunately, you can easily rotate the text within a text box. To rotate text in a text box, follow these steps:

1. Select the box. Remember that you must click at the edge of the box, not in the text area, so that the Graphics Property Bar appears.

2. Click the Graphics menu on the Property Bar and choose Content. WordPerfect displays the Box Content dialog box (see Figure 13.16).

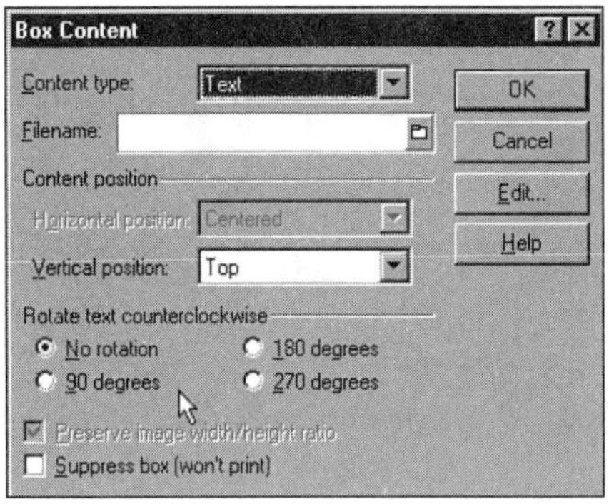

Figure 13.16
You can use the Box Content dialog box to rotate text in a text box.

3. From the Rotate Text Counterclockwise section, choose <u>9</u>0, <u>1</u>80, or <u>2</u>70 degrees.

> **Note**
>
> You can rotate the contents of a text box only in 90-degree increments. If you need to rotate text at some other angle, you must create the text as a graphic drawing object.

➔ For more information on adding custom text images, **see** Chapter 14, "Adding Drawings and TextArt," **p. 373**

4. Click OK to rotate the text in the text box.

If you rotate text, the editing process for that text changes. When you click the text box that contains rotated text, WordPerfect opens a Text Box Editor screen (see Figure 13.17). Although it appears that you have the whole screen to work with, WordPerfect limits the editing area to match the width of the text box itself. Make any changes you want and click the Close button on the Property Bar to return to the document.

Figure 13.17
When editing rotated text, you use the Text Box Editor screen. Note that text wraps at the text box margins, not at the margins of the editing screen.

> **Note**
>
> Selecting a text box that contains rotated text is a bit difficult because no matter where you click on the box, you enter the Text Box Editor screen. To select such a text box, right-click the box, and from the QuickMenu choose Select Bo<u>x</u>.

Tip #160 from
Laura and Read

If you intend to add a lot of text to a rotated text box, select the box first and drag the side sizing handles to give yourself more room. Then click the center of the box to enter the Text Box Editor screen.

PART
IV

CH
13

STICKY NOTE BOXES

One particularly useful text box style is the sticky note text box. This box is similar to other text boxes, but it contains a yellow background and it wraps in front of your document text, just like a sticky note! Unfortunately, this custom text box is a bit hard to find unless someone shows you where it is.

To add a sticky note to your document, follow these steps:

1. Position the cursor on the line where you want the sticky note.

2. Choose Insert, Graphics, Custom Box. WordPerfect displays the Custom Box dialog box (see Figure 13.18).

Figure 13.18
Among styles available in the Custom Box dialog box is the Sticky Note Text style.

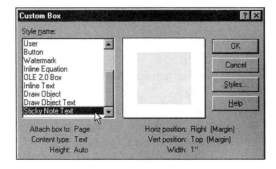

3. Scroll through the Style Name list box, and select Sticky Note Text.

4. Click OK to add a sticky note text box to your document.

You edit and manipulate the sticky note text box the same way you do any text box. Because the box covers text, you might want to remove it before printing.

→ For information on WordPerfect's document collaboration features such as Comments, Document Compare, Document Review, and Corel Versions, **see** Chapter 17, "Collaborating on Documents," **p. 475**

WATERMARK TEXT BOXES

Watermarks need not be only graphic images. You can also create your own text watermarks.

To create a text-based watermark, follow these steps:

1. Choose Insert, Watermark from the menu.

2. If you're creating a new Watermark A, click Create.

3. In the Watermark A editing screen, add text and format it. For example, you can change the font, the font size (72 points equals 1 inch high), center the text horizontally, or center the page vertically (by choosing Format, Page, Center).

4. Note in Figure 13.19 that WordPerfect automatically changes solid black text to 25% gray. However, you can also lighten or darken that shading by choosing Format, Font, and by changing the font's shading percentage.

5. If you want, you can also add graphic images along with your text.

6. Click the Close button to add the watermark to your document.

Figure 13.19
Text used as a water-mark appears at 25% black. You can use text along with images in a watermark.

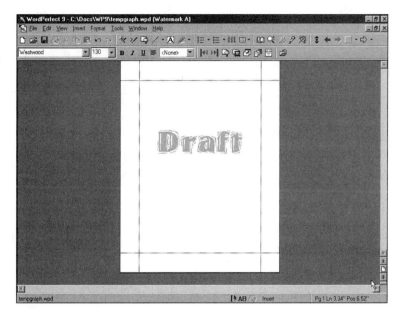

→ For information on using WordPerfect's watermark feature, **see** Chapter 12, "Adding Graphics to Documents," **p. 317**

CUSTOMIZING GRAPHIC IMAGES

In Chapter 12, "Adding Graphics to Documents," and so far in this chapter, we have focused on modifying and manipulating the graphics box, or the container of the graphic image. Borders, sizing, backgrounds, and wrapping are all elements that apply largely to the box border. But graphics boxes are like windows through which you view the contents—you can also modify or customize what you see inside the graphics box.

CHANGING BOX CONTENTS

You can change the contents of a graphics box, or the way the image is displayed, without affecting the size, border, or other changes you have made to the graphics box itself.

→ For details on graphics boxes, **see** Chapter 12, "Adding Graphics to Documents," **p. 317**

To change the contents of a box, first select the box, and then from the Graphics menu on the Property Bar, choose Content. WordPerfect displays the Box Content dialog box (see Figure 13.20), where you have the following options:

PART

IV

CH

13

Figure 13.20
You can use the Box Content dialog box to change the image or to change the type of content used in a box.

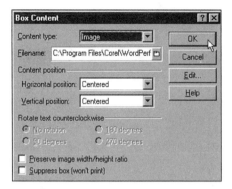

- Content Type—Typically, content is an image. However, you can also choose Empty (a box with nothing in it), Text, or Equation. A final choice, Image on Disk, is useful if you want to display and print the image with the document, but don't want to store a copy of the image in the document itself. For example, if you specify that the graphics used for a letterhead logo remain on disk, then you don't store a separate copy of the image with each letter you produce.

Caution

If you choose to use the Image on Disk option, the image does not print if someone else who does not have access to that image tries to print the document. In a network environment, be sure that images you want everyone to be able to use are accessible by everyone before using this option.

Note

If you edit the image (for example, you double-click the image and open it in the Draw program), the content type changes to OLE object and the filename changes to `Corel Presentations 9 Drawing`.

→ For more information on using the Draw program, **see** Chapter 14, "Adding Drawings and TextArt," **p. 373**

- Filename—You can use the Browse button to find and insert a graphic file into the current box, replacing the one that's already there.

- Content Position—These settings affect where the content appears within the box. By default, images are centered both vertically and horizontally. However, if you change the box size, you might want to position the image at the left or right, or at the top or bottom of the box. If the content of the box is text, you can also rotate the text in 90-degree increments.

- Preserve Image Width/Height Ratio—If you drag the side sizing handles when reshaping a box, the graphic image also becomes distorted. Check this option to prevent image distortion.

- Suppress Box (Won't Print)—This option means that WordPerfect prints the document with space reserved for the image, but does not print the image nor the box border or caption, if any.

USING IMAGE TOOLS

WordPerfect's image tools enable you to customize a graphic image itself. You can move the image, rotate it, flip it, size it, or change its brightness and contrast.

To access the image tools, first select the graphics box of the image you want to edit and then click the Image Tools button on the Property Bar or right-click the graphics box and choose Image Tools from the QuickMenu. WordPerfect displays the Image Tools dialog box (see Figure 13.21).

Figure 13.21
The Image Tools dialog box enables you to modify the image inside a graphics box.

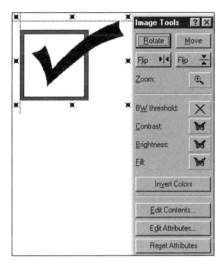

Typically you choose an option and use the mouse, or select from palettes of options to make changes to the image. The following are some of the options:

- Rotate—Click this option, and WordPerfect displays four diagonal sizing handles at the corners of the image, but inside the graphics box. Drag a handle to the right or left to rotate the image inside the box.

Tip #161 from	When you rotate an image, often the edges of the image don't fit within the box without being trimmed. To avoid this, first scale the image to a smaller size, and then rotate it.
Laura and Read	

- Move—After clicking this option, drag the image in any direction. Remember that the graphics box is like a window through which you view the graphic image. If you move part of an image beyond the border of the graphics box, you place it out of sight, and that part of the image does not display.

Tip #162 from	You can move an image beyond the edge of a graphics box border if you want to crop or trim part of the image. For example, if the very bottom of an image isn't pertinent to your document, you can move the image down far enough that the edge of the box crops the bottom of the image.
Laura and Read	

- Flip—You can flip the image horizontally, flip the image vertically, or both.

- Zoom—Clicking this option gives you a palette of three choices (see Figure 13.22). The magnifying glass enables you to click and drag an area of the image. WordPerfect then zooms to that area. Clicking the up/down arrow displays a scrollbar that enables you to decrease (up) or increase (down) the size of the graphic image. The 1:1 option restores the image to its full, original size.

Figure 13.22
The three image zoom tools enable you to crop an image, scale it, or restore it to its original size.

> **Caution**
>
> If you size the image by cropping it, WordPerfect resizes the graphics box to match the cropped image. If you restore the image, it goes back to being the complete image, but it's small enough to fit inside the newly defined box. You have to drag the box sizing handles to restore the graphics box shape and size.

- BW Threshold—If you want to print the image in black and white (without shades of gray), choose one of the options on the BW Threshold palette. To turn color back on, click the large × button on the palette.

- Contrast—This palette, which is similar to the Brightness palette shown in Figure 13.23, enables you to adjust the dark/light contrasts in an image.

Figure 13.23
The Brightness palette enables you to choose a preset brightness. The Contrast palette looks similar and works the same way.

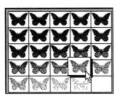

- Brightness—This palette (refer to Figure 13.23) helps you choose a shading for the colors of the image. Watermark images, for example, use buttons from the bottom row of the palette.

- Fill—These options generally aren't terribly useful. The blue butterfly is the default (as shown in the Brightness and Contrast palettes) when you're using all of the image's colors. The others display only those parts of the image that are black and white.

- Invert Colors—This option creates a negative of the image.

- Edit Contents—This option opens the image in the drawing editor.

→ For more information on the drawing editor, **see** Chapter 14, "Adding Drawings and TextArt," **p. 373**

- Edit Attributes—If you need to make precise settings to a variety of attributes, you can choose this option to display the Image Settings dialog box (see Figure 13.24), where you select the attributes you want to change, specify exact settings, preview the results in the preview box, and click OK to apply them to the image.

- Reset Attributes—If you want to restore all the original image settings, choose this option.

Figure 13.24
The Image Settings dialog box enables you to specify by exact numbers the changes you want and to preview them.

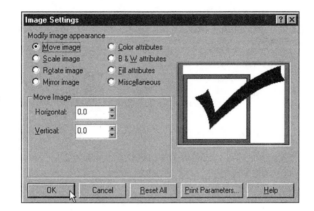

To close the Image Tools dialog box, click anywhere in the document, or click the Close button on the dialog box.

EDITING IMAGES IN PRESENTATIONS

The preceding sections deal with modifying an entire image—for example, its brightness or rotation. However, if you install Corel Presentations as part of the Office 2000 suite (which is highly recommended), that program also serves as the drawing editor in WordPerfect. With it you have a full range of options for editing WordPerfect clip art and other graphic images. For example, you can remove or add parts of images and change coloring.

→ To learn more about using the drawing editor (Corel Presentations) to edit images, **see** Chapter 14, "Adding Drawings and TextArt," **p. 373**

IMPORTING GRAPHICS

One of WordPerfect's strengths is its capability to import graphic images from a variety of sources. WordPerfect clip art is in the .wpg (WordPerfect Graphics) format, but there are many different graphic formats in use today. You can insert most types of graphic formats from other programs, as well as from photographs.

PART

IV

CH

13

INSERTING OTHER GRAPHIC TYPES

To insert a graphic image other than WordPerfect's clip art images, choose Insert, Graphic, From File. WordPerfect opens the Insert File dialog box, which is identical to the Open File dialog box. You can use this dialog box to browse to various graphic files.

> **Note**
>
> The preview box may not be able to display all the file types that you can import. If you're not sure whether you can import a certain image type, just try it and see what happens.

When you identify the file you want, select it and click Insert. WordPerfect automatically converts and imports the following graphic file types (the graphic format is followed by the typical filename extension used by that format):

Graphic File Type	Filename Extension
Bitmap	`.bmp, .dib`
CALS compressed bitmap	`.cal`
CompuServe GIF	`.gif`
Computer Graphics Metafile	`.cgm`
Corel PhotoPaint 6	`.cpt`
Encapsulated PostScript	`.eps`
Enhanced Windows Metafile	`.emf`
FAX/TIFF	`.tif`
JPEG bitmap	`.jpg, .jpe`
MicroGrafix Picture Publisher 4	`.pp4`
OS/2 bitmap	`.bmp`
PC Paintbrush graphic	`.pcx`
Portable network graphic (PNG)	`.png, .gif`
TIFF graphics	`.tif`
Windows cursor	`.cur`
Windows icon	`.ico`
Windows metafile	`.wmf`
WordPerfect Graphics 5	`.wpg`
WordPerfect Graphics 6/7/8/9	`.wpg`

Even if you don't use the WordPerfect graphics editor (Corel Presentations), it's likely that the graphics program you use can save its files in one of these formats.

Vector Versus Bitmap Images

WordPerfect graphics are *vector* graphics because they are created by drawing lines between reference points, or vectors. If you move the vectors, the line changes, but it also remains smooth because it's being drawn from one point to another. Other programs, notably paintbrush-type programs, create *bitmap* graphics by filling in areas with dots, or *bits*. If you change the size of a bitmap image (for example, to make it larger), you often see jagged edges because WordPerfect can't fill in the missing dots.

Whenever possible, save and use graphics in a vector format because these give you the greatest flexibility as you size them for your document.

INSERTING GRAPHICS FROM A SCANNER

One great way to obtain images for documents is to use a scanner. For example, you can scan family photos to put together a book of memories.

You can set up WordPerfect to interact directly with your scanner. Suppose, for example, that you have a Hewlett-Packard ScanJet. Follow these steps, which are typical for most scanners:

1. Choose Insert, Graphics, Select Image Source. WordPerfect displays the list of scanners in the Select Source dialog box, shown in Figure 13.25).

Figure 13.25
WordPerfect Office 2000 supports several types of scanners so that you can use WordPerfect 9 to scan images directly into your documents.

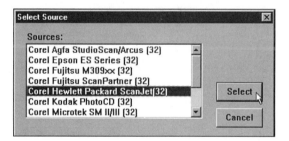

2. Choose the device that matches your scanner (for example, Corel Hewlett Packard ScanJet), and click Select.

3. Make sure your scanner is connected to your computer and is turned on.

4. Place the item to be scanned on the scanner.

5. Choose Insert, Graphics, Acquire Image. WordPerfect starts your scanning software.

6. Scan a preview image, make adjustments as necessary, and then make a final scan.

PART
IV

CH
13

Note

The software for each scanner varies, and so do the specific procedures. Most, however, are relatively simple to understand and use.

7. WordPerfect deposits the scanned image directly in your WordPerfect document (see Figure 13.26 for an example of a scanned image). You can move or size the image, add borders, or modify the image by using image tools.

Figure 13.26
Scanned images, such as photos, fit nicely in WordPerfect documents.

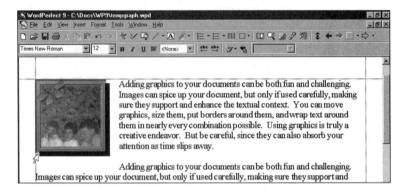

Tip #163 from
Laura and Read

The Contrast and Brightness controls in the Image Tools dialog box are particularly useful for lightening or darkening scanned photographs.

 If you're having trouble making scanned images look good in WordPerfect, see "Choosing the Right Size for Scanned Images" in the Troubleshooting section at the end of this chapter.

INSERTING GRAPHICS FROM THE INTERNET

Another great source for graphic images is the Internet. Web sites contain graphic images that may be just what you need. Some sites offer collections of free buttons, lines, and other kinds of clip art.

Caution

Just because images can be downloaded from the Internet does not mean they are free. Copyright laws and restrictions apply to Internet graphics as they do to print graphics. If you aren't sure whether you can use a graphic image, you should ask the owner of the Web site that contains the image.

To use an image from an Internet Web site, follow these steps:

1. In your Internet browser, right-click the image you want to download.
2. From the pop-up menu, choose Save Image As, in Netscape, or Save Picture As, in Internet Explorer.
3. Provide a name and local destination (for example, `c:\myfiles\webimage.jpg`). Use the same filename extension as used on the Web site—for example, `.gif` or `.jpg`.
4. Click OK to save the image.
5. Switch to WordPerfect and choose Insert, Graphics, From File.
6. Browse to the location where you saved the image, select the image, and choose Insert.

WordPerfect converts the image from the Internet format (`.gif` or `.jpg`) and places it in the document (see Figure 13.27 for an example of an Internet image, at both normal and enlarged sizes). You then can move or size the image, add borders, or modify the image by using image tools.

Figure 13.27
Graphics captured from the Web also import nicely into WordPerfect. Note, however, that small Web graphics, when enlarged too much, begin to display jagged edges.

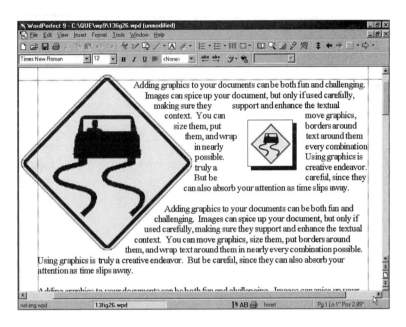

> **Note**
>
> Try to capture and use images that are close to the size you want. Small images, when enlarged in WordPerfect, tend to look jagged. Larger images, when made small, sometimes lose critical parts. This is the nature of bitmapped graphics, and beyond choosing the right size to begin with, there really is nothing you can do to improve the quality of the image.

→ For more information on editing bitmap images, such as scanned images or images from the Internet, in WordPerfect's Presentations program, **see** Chapter 14, "Adding Drawings and TextArt," **p. 373**

TROUBLESHOOTING

SELECTING THE CORRECT GRAPHICS BOX

I have several graphics boxes, some sitting on top of others. How can I select just the one I want?

Normally, to select a box you click it once. If there are several boxes, just click again (wait a moment between clicks), and note that the sizing handles change each time you do. When the sizing handles match the image you want, it's selected. You can also right-click on the stack of images, choose Select Other, and then select the image you want from the list of images displayed.

EXITING THE GRAPHICS EDITING SCREEN

I clicked a graphic, but my screen seemed to go all haywire, with a funny-looking line around the image and a toolbar on the left side of the screen. What happened?

You probably double-clicked the image. Single-clicking selects the image, but double-clicking edits the image. In the case of a graphics box, WordPerfect takes you to the drawing editor, hence the different toolbars. To close the image editor, click in your text, outside the graphics box. Or you can click the Close button on the toolbar.

CHOOSING THE RIGHT SIZE FOR SCANNED IMAGES

I scanned a picture of my family, but it doesn't look very sharp in my WordPerfect document.

Scanned graphics are bitmapped graphics and aren't designed to be enlarged. When you enlarge them, they turn out the way you describe. To get the best picture quality possible, right-click the graphic, choose Size, and set both the Width and Height to maintain proportions. This might reduce the size of the image, but it will make the image look much better. If you need a larger image, you should rescan the image, setting the saved size to match the size you need.

ANCHORING IMAGES CORRECTLY

I just used the Make It Fit feature, but now my graphics are all over the place and they don't fit with the text anymore.

This is one peril of using the Make It Fit feature. If your graphic images are anchored to the page, they remain in place even when the text moves (for example, when you use Make It Fit). You can reduce this problem by anchoring graphic images to paragraphs or characters, so that the images move as the text moves. In any case, you need to check your document and perhaps make adjustments to the position of your graphics boxes.

PROJECT

A common, and very practical, use for text boxes is to use them as labels in combination with graphic images or shapes. Suppose you want to make a flyer for the Humane Society Walkathon that's taking place next Saturday. You just happen to have a nifty graphic, and want to make the flyer look like a posted memo note.

Follow these steps to make the sign:

1. Open a new, blank document.
2. Choose Insert, Graphics, Clipart, or click the Clipart button on the toolbar.
3. From the Scrapbook, choose the memo note and click Insert.
4. With the image selected, click Graphics on the Property Bar, and choose Size.

5. In the Box Size dialog box, choose F<u>u</u>ll for the width, and F<u>u</u>ll for the height.

6. Click the Zoom button on the toolbar and choose Full Page so you can see the entire page (see Figure 13.28).

Figure 13.28
Set the horizontal and vertical size of the image to Full to fill the page.

7. Click the Wrap button on the Property Bar and select Behind Text. This enables the text box to coexist on the same page as the text.

8. Deselect the image. The easiest way is to click in the margin, but you can also right-click the image and choose <u>U</u>nselect Box from the QuickMenu.

9. Click the Text Box button on the toolbar, or choose <u>I</u>nsert, Te<u>x</u>t Box from the menu. WordPerfect displays a one-line, relatively small text box.

10. Using the Property Bar, change the font size (for example to 50 points) and the font style if you wish.

11. Type the text.

12. Drag the sides of the text box to move it, size it, and arrange the text so it fits properly within the memo note area.

13. Right-click the edge of the text box and choose <u>B</u>order/Fill from the QuickMenu.

14. Click <u>D</u>iscontinue to turn off all borders.

15. Make any final minor adjustments and save the image, which should look somewhat like the example in Figure 13.29.

Figure 13.29
You can combine a text box with a graphic image to create an attention-getting flyer that communicates your message.

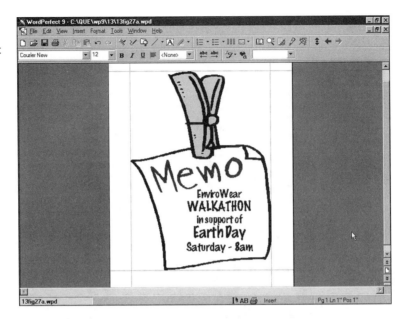

These steps are the basic procedure for adding a text box to an image. However, you will find that some experimentation is required to get just the right font, font size, and location. Fortunately, WordPerfect makes it quick and easy. Besides, isn't this more fun that typing that boring report?

CHAPTER **14**

Adding Drawings and TextArt

In this chapter

ADDING DRAWINGS BY USING PRESENTATIONS

WordPerfect's Draw feature is so powerful that it deserves special attention. Adding someone else's graphics and drawing cool shapes are fun and useful, but with the Draw program you can add your own custom graphics and even modify graphics from other sources.

 When you choose Insert, Graphics, Draw Picture, or click the Draw Picture button on the toolbar, WordPerfect opens an editing window in which you can create and edit graphics using the tools found in the Corel Presentations drawing program (see Figure 14.1). In addition to the window, you also see somewhat different toolbars, and at the left side of the screen a tool palette that looks a lot like some of the tools you use when working with graphic shapes and boxes. Further, if you click some of the menu items, you'll note that certain features you're used to seeing are gone, replaced by other features you've never heard of before.

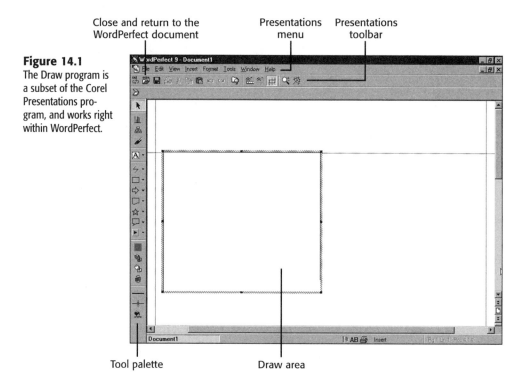

Figure 14.1
The Draw program is a subset of the Corel Presentations program, and works right within WordPerfect.

Close and return to the WordPerfect document

Presentations menu

Presentations toolbar

Tool palette

Draw area

Using Corel Presentations

The Presentations program is a full-featured drawing and slide show presentation program. If you start Presentations by itself, typically it expects you to create a slide show. However, you can also use it as a drawing program. This chapter focuses only on the drawing features that are most useful to you as you work with Presentations inside WordPerfect.

For complete information on Presentations, see Que's *Special Edition Using WordPerfect Office 2000*.

WORKING WITH DRAW

When you create a new Draw figure, WordPerfect limits you to a predetermined portion of the WordPerfect screen. You can stretch or shrink that editing window to fit your needs.

> **Note**
>
> For the sake of brevity, we refer to the Draw Picture program simply as Draw (for example, "Use Draw to create a text line").

If you want to edit a Draw image, double-click it to open an editing window the same size as the image's graphics box.

However, if you want to open a larger editing window, hold down the Alt key and double-click the image. WordPerfect opens a separate Corel Presentations drawing window (see Figure 14.2). This window can be sized as large you'd like it to be. You can even maximize the window to a full screen. Using this separate window can make it easier to see and work with your drawing. When you close the window and return to your document, WordPerfect scales the drawing to fit the original image window in your document.

Figure 14.2
If you use the Alt key while double-clicking an image, you open a larger Presentations editing screen.

Tip #164 from
Laura and Read

When editing a graphic image in WordPerfect, hold down the Alt key and double-click to open a full Corel Presentations editing screen.

⚠ If you're frustrated by the results you get as you experiment with the Draw program, see "Using Undo" in the Troubleshooting section at the end of this chapter.

USING SHAPES IN A DRAWING

The processes for creating shapes in WordPerfect and in Draw are almost identical. In fact, shapes may even be easier to use directly in WordPerfect because you don't have to enter and exit Draw. Nevertheless, what you know about WordPerfect shapes applies to creating and working with your own artwork in Draw.

There are, however, a few differences that may make using Draw worth your time:

- Draw has a greater number of shape drawing tools. These include the closed multisided curved and straight line objects, and lines drawn with Beziér curves.

- By default, when you create a shape in WordPerfect, the shape wraps in front of the text. When you create a shape in Draw, it becomes part of a WordPerfect graphics box, and text wraps around that box in a square.

- Because Draw shapes are in graphics boxes, you can also use captions and borders with them.

- You can blend shapes from one color to another, and even (partially) from one shape to another.

- You can add 3-D effects to any shape.

- You can warp shapes into other predefined shapes.

→ For information on how to create and manipulate various shapes, such as lines, closed objects, and call-outs, **see** "Inserting Shapes," **p. 330**

→ For information on how to add 3-D and warp effects, **see** "Adding Special Effects to Text," **p. 383**

ADDING TEXT TO A DRAWING

Although WordPerfect is the premiere program for creating, editing, and formatting text, when it comes to graphical presentation of text, Draw offers several advantages, including the following:

- Text rotated at any angle

- Gradient shaded text

- Text shaped to curved objects

- Three-dimensional text

- Text warped to fit predefined shapes

In WordPerfect, you can rotate text in text boxes only in 90-degree increments. However, if you want to angle text at 45 degrees, for example, you need to create the text in Draw and add the graphics box containing the text to your document.

To create text in Draw, follow these steps:

1. Choose Insert, Graphics, Draw Picture, or click the Draw Picture button on the toolbar. WordPerfect opens the Draw editing window (refer to Figure 14.1).

2. Click the drop-down menu or the Text Objects button on the Draw tool palette to display text options (see Figure 14.3), which include the following:

- Create a text box when you want to create more than one line of text.
- Create a text line when you want to limit the text to just one line.
- Create a bulleted list.
- Create text with special effects, such as that created by TextArt or QuickWarp.

Figure 14.3
Draw offers a variety of ways to create text objects.

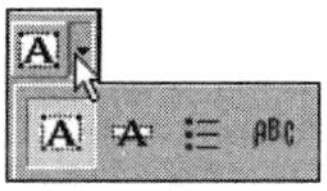

Tip #165 from
Laura and Read

Often working with text lines, rather than text boxes, is more efficient in the long run because you can rotate and rearrange text more easily.

---

3. Click the tool you want (for example, text line) and move the mouse pointer to the area of the screen where you want to start the text line. Note that the mouse pointer becomes crosshairs.

4. Click to begin the text line.

5. Type the text.

6. Select the text where you want to change or add the formatting, such as font, size, and bold.

Note

If you select the font, size, and color *before* creating text, what you select applies to all the text objects you create during the editing session. When you exit the Draw session, however, Draw reverts to the standard black, 36-point, Times New Roman font.

7. To close a text box, click anywhere else on the Draw screen. To close a single line of text, you can also just press Enter.

Although you already selected a font size, you may want to make some adjustments. You can drag the sizing handles of a text box in Draw to make the text larger or smaller. To size a text object, follow these steps:

1. Single-click the text box you want to size. Note that Draw displays only four sizing handles (see Figure 14.4).

2. Drag any of the sizing handles to enlarge or reduce the text proportionally.

3. Hold down the Shift key while dragging a sizing handle to stretch the text horizontally or vertically.

PART

IV

CH

14

Figure 14.4
Text objects in Draw have only four sizing handles. Pressing Shift while dragging a handle enables you to distort the text.

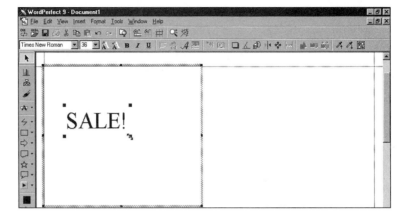

To rotate a text object, follow these steps:

1. Single-click the text box you want to rotate to select it.

 2. Click the Rotation Options button on the toolbar, and choose <u>S</u>elect Rotation, or right-click the object and choose <u>R</u>otate from the QuickMenu. WordPerfect places rotation and skewing handles around the outside of the text box, and an axis in the center of the box (see Figure 14.5).

Figure 14.5
You can rotate text at unlimited angles in Draw.

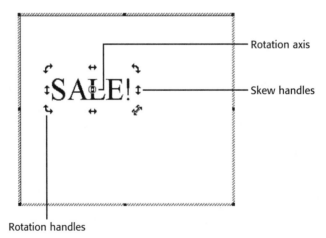

3. Drag a corner handle to rotate the text on its axis (see Figure 14.6).

4. Drag a side handle to skew the text (see Figure 14.7).

Finally, before returning to your document, you should make the Draw screen approximately the same size as the text box. The borders of the Draw screen become the borders of the graphics box that contains the special text, and you don't want too much empty space between the text and borders of the box. Simply move the text object to the upper left of the Draw screen, and then drag the sizing handles of the Draw screen to fit the text box (see Figure 14.8). Click in your document to close the Draw screen.

Figure 14.6
When you drag a rotation handle, Draw displays an outline showing where the image will be when you release the mouse button.

Figure 14.7
You can drag a side handle to skew the text, and Draw previews the location of the skewed object.

If you tried to use the menus to return to your document and can't figure out how to make Draw work, see "How to Get Out of the Draw Screen" in the Troubleshooting section at the end of this chapter.

Tip #166 from
Laura and Read

You can add as many graphic elements as you want to a single draw screen, including clip art, shapes, and text.

MODIFYING TEXT APPEARANCE

In WordPerfect you can change a font's style and color. In Draw you can make many other changes as well. To modify a text object in Draw, select the text object and choose Format, Font. Alternatively, you can press F9 or right-click the object and choose Font. WordPerfect displays the Font Properties dialog box, which offers a wide range of font options.

PART
IV

CH
14

Figure 14.8
You should try to make the size of the WordPerfect graphics box match the size of the objects it contains.

The Font tab (see Figure 14.9) enables you to choose font type (Face), size, color, and other basic attributes, and to preview the results.

→ For information on using fonts, **see** Chapter 3, "Basic Formatting," **p. 57**

Figure 14.9
You can use the Font tab of the Font Properties dialog box to modify text objects in Draw.

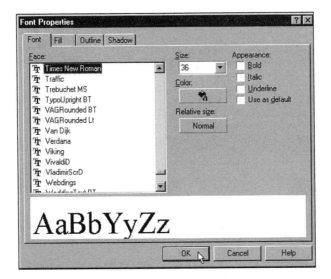

The Fill tab (see Figure 14.10) offers three options:

- Click the Fill Style - None button (the button with the large ×) to display only the outline of the text.
- Click the Fill Style - Pattern button (the default, refer to Figure 14.10) to choose from a palette of pattern choices. Foreground color is the pattern color, and Background color is what shows through the pattern. You can reverse the colors for a negative effect.

Figure 14.10
With the Fill tab, you can use solid colors, patterns, or gradient shading.

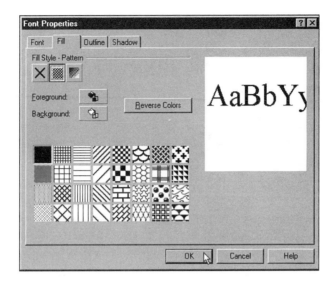

- Click the Fill Style - Gradient button to choose from a palette of *gradient* shaded fills (see Figure 14.11). You can also use <u>R</u>everse Colors to switch the order of the gradient colors. To customize gradient settings, click Gradient <u>S</u>ettings to display the Gradient Settings dialog box (see Figure 14.12), where you can change the angle (for example, 45 degrees to match rotated text), or the horizontal offset or vertical offset (where the foreground color is the stronger color). You can even specify the exact number of steps in the shading, although the default is the smoothest.

Figure 14.11
You can quickly select from among several preset gradient styles from the fill style gradient palette.

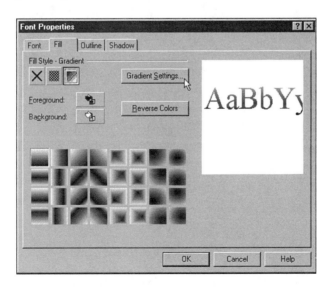

Figure 14.12
You can customize
gradient shading in
text in the Gradient
Settings dialog box.

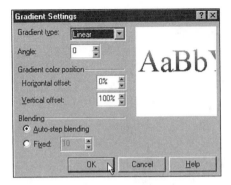

The Outline tab (see Figure 14.13, which shows the style palette selected), enables you to change the color, style (for example, solid or dashed), or thickness of the line that surrounds the text. You can also choose None (the large ×) from the style palette to remove the font border line altogether.

Figure 14.13
You can choose ×
(None) or one of the
line styles from the
line style palette.

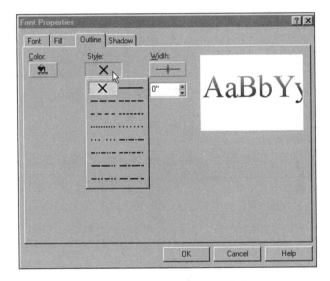

The Shadow tab (see Figure 14.14) enables you to create a shadow for the text in any of the directions you select. You then can further define the shadow side-to-side offset or up-and-down offset by dragging the scrollbars or by specifying a measurement in the counter boxes. Finally, you can change the shadow color and make it transparent (objects from behind the shadow can be seen) or not transparent (the shadow is a solid color).

Note

Shadow transparency works only with other objects in the Draw screen, not with text or other objects in your document.

Figure 14.14
It's easy to add or customize shadows on the Shadow tab of the Font Properties dialog box.

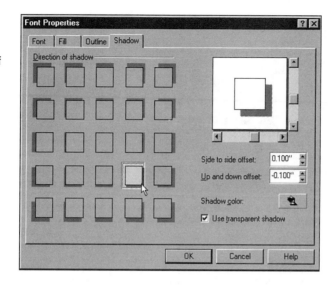

When you finish your text modifications, click OK to return to the Draw screen. An example of text changes you can make in Draw is shown in Figure 14.15, where the text has gradient shading, no border line, and a transparent gray shadow.

Figure 14.15
It's easy to customize text, as in this text that displays a different font, gradient shading, no border line, and a transparent gray shadow.

ADDING SPECIAL EFFECTS TO TEXT

Draw includes two special-effects options that apply to text as well as to other graphics objects. Quick 3-D adds dimension and shading to text, and QuickWarp fits text into a predefined shape.

To access the Quick 3-D dialog box, select the text object and choose Tools, Quick 3-D (see Figure 14.16). The options you use depend on the look you're trying to achieve. Options include the following:

- Rotation—You can click a predefined rotation angle, or make your own adjustments to the X, Y, or Z axes of the letters.

- Color Adjustment—The percentage of color applies to the face of the letters. The 3-D shadow is automatically made proportionally darker.

- Perspective—On the Perspective tab (see Figure 14.17), you can choose Linear, Parallel, or Inverse, as shown by the samples.

- Depth—You can specify how deep the 3-D effect should be.

PART
IV

CH
14

Figure 14.16
You can add 3-D effects to text from preset or customized styles in the Quick 3-D dialog box.

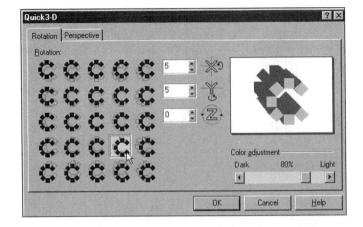

Figure 14.17
You can change the 3-D perspective on the Perspective tab of the Quick 3-D dialog box.

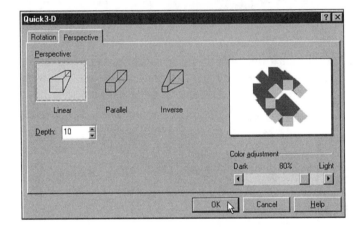

The QuickWarp feature is similar to TextArt (see the section "Creating TextArt" later in this chapter), but with only limited options. When you *warp* text, you make it change its shape to fit another predefined shape. Choose Tools, QuickWarp to display the QuickWarp dialog box (see Figure 14.18, which shows a shape selected). You can click a shape, preview it, and click OK to add the effect to your text.

Tip #167 from
Laura and Read

You can add both the QuickWarp and the Quick 3-D effects to a text or graphic object. For added effect, you can also apply either effect more than once to the same object.

Figure 14.18
You can warp text to fit a predefined shape in the QuickWarp dialog box.

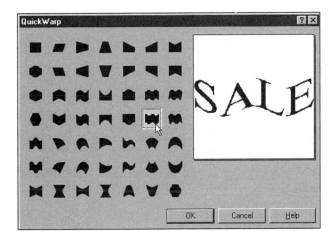

CONTOURING TEXT TO SHAPES

You can contour text to other shapes, such as circles, half-circles, of even flat-sided objects. To contour text to the outside of a circle, for example, follow these steps:

1. Create the text line you want to contour.

2. Create the shape you want the text to contour to—for example, a circle, created from the Basic Shapes button on the tool palette.

3. Select both the text and the shape. If they are the only two objects on the Draw screen, you can choose Edit, Select All. If there are other objects on the screen, click the shape object, and then hold down the Ctrl or the Shift key and click the text object.

4. Choose Tools, Contour Text. WordPerfect displays the Contour Text dialog box (see Figure 14.19).

Figure 14.19
You can use the Contour Text dialog box to contour text to another Draw shape.

5. Choose the text position from the Position Text drop-down menu. Choices include Top Left, Top Center, Top Right, Bottom Left, Bottom Center, and Bottom Right.

6. If you want to display the contoured text without the graphic object, leave the Display Text Only box checked.

7. Click OK to contour the text (see Figure 14.20).

PART

IV

CH

14

Figure 14.20
You can hide or leave visible the object that text is contoured to.

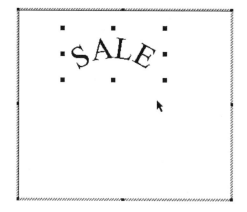

EDITING WORDPERFECT GRAPHICS IN PRESENTATIONS

WordPerfect ships with a collection of some 12,000 clip art images. Not enough, you say? Using the Draw program (Presentations), you can pull apart, modify, combine, or customize many of those clip art images to create just the image you need.

→ For information on using WordPerfect's clip art images, **see** Chapter 12, "Adding Graphics to Documents," **p. 317**

All this is possible in part because WordPerfect graphics are *vector* graphics. This means that clip art images are actually a combination of many images, each of which can be separated from the original clip art and modified.

Vector Versus Bitmap Graphics

WordPerfect graphics are *vector* graphics because they are created by drawing lines between reference points, or vectors. If you move the vectors, the entire line changes. Other programs, notably paintbrush-type programs, create *bitmap* graphics by filling in areas with dots, or bits.

Modifying clip art images is an artistic endeavor, determined by your needs and by what you think looks good. Nevertheless, the basic procedures are the same no matter what you want to modify. For example, suppose you want to make a flyer with an easel background for the announcement. You look through the clip art list and don't find an easel, but you do notice that one clip art image has a man standing at an easel that just might do the trick.

To modify a WordPerfect clip art image in Draw, follow these steps (but don't be afraid to experiment along the way!):

1. Insert the clip art image in your document (for example, the man standing at the easel, from the Scrapbook, 201823.wpg).

2. Double-click the image to open it in Draw.

Tip #168 from
Laura and Read

Don't forget that you can open an image in a larger Presentations editing screen by holding down the Alt key and double-clicking the image.

3. Click a part of the image you want to get rid of. If the sizing handles seem to indicate a larger selection than you anticipated, double-click the image again to begin separating the parts of the image. Eventually, you see sizing handles around that part of the image you want to work with—for example, the parts of the man's figure or the illustration on the easel (see Figure 14.21).

Figure 14.21
You know which part of an image you are deleting by the location of the sizing handles.

Sizing handles ⏌

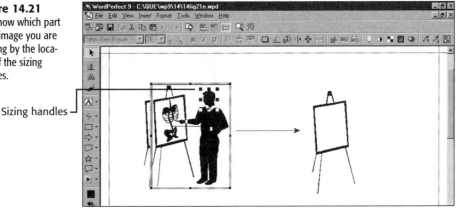

4. You can make changes to any object in the group of objects. Some changes you might make include the following:

- Delete an object—For example, if you want to remove the image of the man, select it and press Delete.

- Change colors—For example, you could change the easel border to brown.

- Change a shape—You can drag the sizing handles to skew or change the size of the object.

- Add other objects—For example, you could add a text line to the easel. You can even add other clip art images to the image.

5. When you finish modifying the clip art image (refer to Figure 14.21, which shows the modified clip art image), click outside the Draw window to return to your document, or click the Close Drawing button on the toolbar.

As you work with clip art images using Draw, you begin to understand how clip art designers do their work, which makes it easier for you to create your own images. You also discover certain limitations to editing existing clip art.

For example, clip art designers often use layers of solid colors as backgrounds to an entire image. When you remove the background from one part of an image, unfortunately you also remove it from other parts. Figure 14.22 shows how removing a solid black background can

PART
IV

CH

14

adversely affect an image. You want to keep the face, but not the neck on down, of the doctor clip art.

Figure 14.22
Clip art images are composed of layers. Removing a layer may remove more from an image than you expect. You can add a new background layer to the area you do keep.

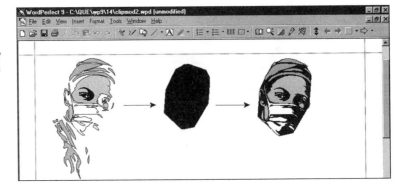

To remedy this sort of problem, you sometimes can add solid objects that cover just the part of the object you want to keep and then send that object to the back, or bottom layer. The black then shows through again as lines on the image (refer to Figure 14.22).

EDITING BITMAP GRAPHICS IN PRESENTATIONS

You've searched high and low, and the very best graphic image you can find is a bitmap image from the Internet. But you still need to make a couple minor changes. Fortunately, Presentations also includes a bitmap editor that you can use right from within WordPerfect.

> **Note**
>
> *Bitmap* images, created in paintbrush-type programs, are drawn by filling in areas with dots, or bits. Bitmaps are more difficult to modify because many bits must be changed. For example, just to change a line you must erase the bits of the old line, and draw all the bits of the new line.

To edit a bitmap image in WordPerfect, follow these steps:

1. Insert the image in your document. Typically, you choose <u>I</u>nsert, <u>G</u>raphics, <u>F</u>rom File. You then browse to find the file and click <u>I</u>nsert.

2. Double-click the image to open the image in Draw. To give yourself more room to work, hold down the Alt key while double-clicking to open a larger editing area.

3. Double-click the image again to open it in the bitmap editor (see Figure 14.23).

4. You have a whole new set of tools available, including the paintbrush, flood fill, and air brush. Some of the ways you can modify the image include the following:

   - Erase—Use the eraser to remove parts of the bitmap image you don't want.

   - Zoom—Choose <u>V</u>iew, <u>Z</u>oom to zoom in on the bits, thus making it easier to modify bit-by-bit (see Figure 14.24).
   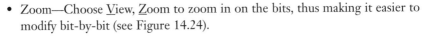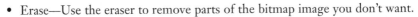
   - Paintbrush—The paintbrush enables you to draw, freehand, in different colors and with different brush widths. You can use smaller brush widths for more detailed changes.

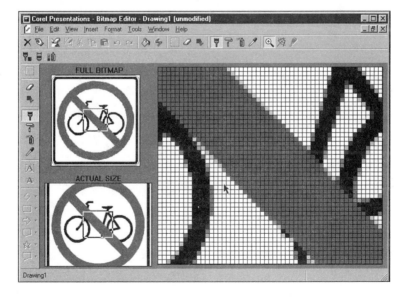

Figure 14.23
The bitmap editor is a paintbrush-type program within the Draw program.

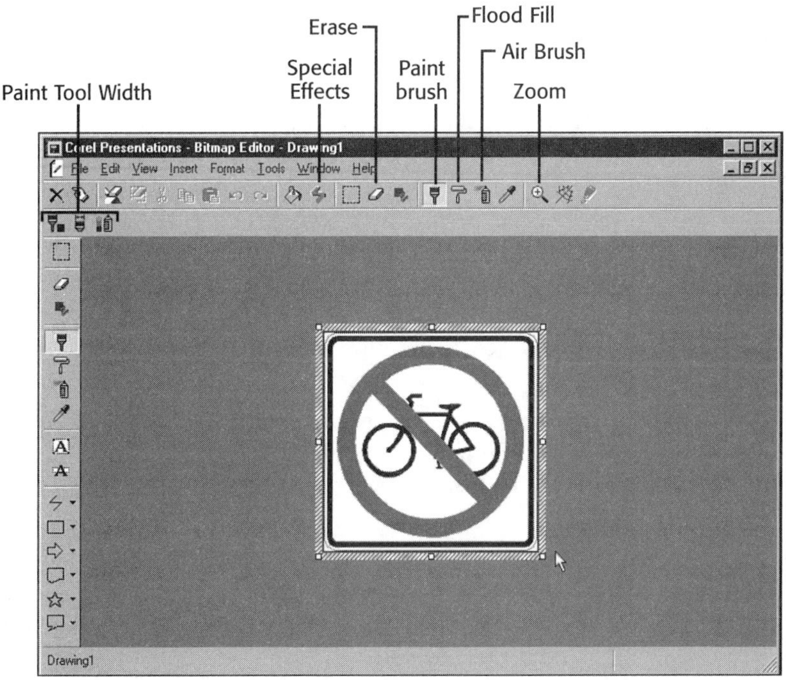

Figure 14.24
You can use Zoom in the bitmap editor to get in close to the individual picture bits.

- Flood Fill—Choose a color, and then click this tool in an area of color to replace that color with the new color. This requires a closed area to work; otherwise, the paint floods into other areas.

- Air Brush—Using this tool is like using a can of spray paint. Try it!

- Special Effects—Click this button to open the Special Effects dialog box that enables you to blur, soften, sharpen, emboss, or add other special effects to the bitmap image.

> **Note**
>
> You can, and very well may, spend hours editing bitmap images. You'll discover almost immediately how difficult it is to make precise changes to an image. Just remember that you really don't have a choice if you want to edit a bitmap image, but that you do have special effects tools at your disposal to do things you can't do with vector graphics. Also, don't forget to use the Undo button when you make mistakes.

Have you messed up the graphic image beyond hope? See "Aborting Bitmap Editing" in the Troubleshooting section at the end of this chapter.

5. When you're done, click the Close button on the toolbar. On the other hand, if you've made a terrible mess of things, and would prefer to start over, click the Close Bitmap Editor button on the toolbar. Then click <u>C</u>lose to close the bitmap editor without saving the changes you made.

> **Note**
>
> If you opened the Presentations window to edit your image, you can use the menu to close the editor. Choose <u>F</u>ile, <u>C</u>lose Bitmap Editor, or <u>F</u>ile, C<u>a</u>ncel Bitmap Editor. However, if you opened the regular Draw screen, choosing <u>F</u>ile, <u>C</u>lose causes WordPerfect to close the entire document.

6. Click outside the Draw window to return to your document, or if you opened the larger Presentations window, choose <u>F</u>ile, <u>C</u>lose and Return to update the image and return to your document (see Figure 14.25).

Figure 14.25
Even bitmap images can be modified with the bitmap editor to fit your needs.

CREATING TEXTART

TextArt is a text effects program that enables you to shape words and short phrases into pre-defined shapes and add shadows, textures, and dimensions to the text. In some ways it's like a super version of the Quick 3-D and QuickWarp features found in the Draw program (see the preceding section for information on Quick 3-D and QuickWarp).

TextArt is most often used for logos, banners, flyers, and the like. With a little effort, you can create stunning text effects.

CREATING TEXTART TEXT

To create TextArt in a WordPerfect document, choose Insert, Graphics, TextArt. WordPerfect opens a large graphics box, along with the TextArt dialog box (see Figure 14.26).

Figure 14.26
You can use the TextArt dialog box to create and modify a TextArt image in a WordPerfect graphics box.

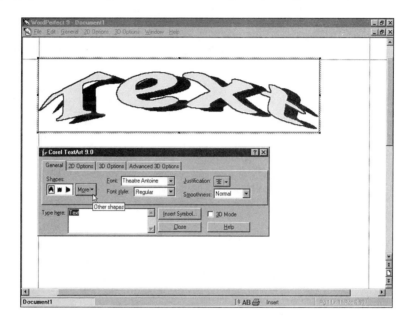

The Type Here box displays the word *Text* and the graphics box displays the TextArt effect on the word *Text*, using settings you selected the last time you used the TextArt feature. To add your own words, type them in the Type Here box. You can also add special characters by clicking the Insert Symbol button, or by pressing Ctrl+W. Note, however, that you can insert only a limited number of special characters, not the entire range of symbols normally available in the Insert Symbol dialog box.

Note

Although you can type a great deal of text in the Type Here box, generally your TextArt is more effective if you limit it to just a few short words.

You next apply several options to the text you typed, including the following:

- Shapes—WordPerfect displays only three shapes, but click the More button, and you have access to 57 different shapes (see Figure 14.27). Click the shape you want, and WordPerfect squeezes and warps the text into that shape (refer to Figure 14.26).

Note

Depending on the speed of your computer and the amount of memory you have, TextArt can take up to several seconds to update changes you make. Be patient, and be sure to save your work often!

PART

IV

CH

14

Figure 14.27
You can warp text to
57 predefined
TextArt shapes.

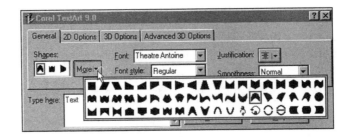

 If you seem to have lost the TextArt dialog box, see "Getting the TextArt Program Back" in the Troubleshooting section at the end of this chapter.

- Font—You can choose a font from a list of your installed Windows fonts.

> **Note**
>
> The amount of text, the font, and the shape you choose have, perhaps, more impact on what the TextArt shape will look like than any of the other options. Don't be afraid to try out several combinations until you find exactly what you're looking for.

- Justification—Normally this option has little effect on your TextArt because the text fills the entire graphics box. However, if you change the size of the graphics box after creating the text, WordPerfect aligns the text according to your selection.

- Smoothness—The resolution of the TextArt drawing can affect display and printing times. Normally you do not need to change this setting.

- 3D mode—This option adds another dimension to the object, but you might also want to make other changes on the 3D tabs.

ADDING 2-D TEXTART OPTIONS

After you create the text, font, and shape you want, you can adjust the pattern, color, shadows, and so on. Begin by clicking the 2D Options tab to find the following options:

- Pattern—You can choose None (you get a solid color), No Fill (you get only text outlines), or one of the patterns displayed on the palette (see Figure 14.28).

> **Note**
>
> If you click the 3D Mode check box, options on the 2D tab are grayed out. Likewise, if the box is not checked, options on the 3D tabs cannot be used.

- Shadow—You can click this button to display the shadow palette. You can select the direction and depth of the shadow, as well as the text color and the shadow color.

Choosing Colors
Choosing the right color combination for the text and shadow should be one of your first tasks. Look for colors that complement each other, but that make the text readable. Also, if you plan to print to a black-and-white printer, such as a laser printer, choose colors whose grays complement each other. For example, yellow prints as a very light gray, whereas blue and red print nearly black.

Figure 14.28
You can choose a solid color (None) or transparent text, or use a pattern with your TextArt text.

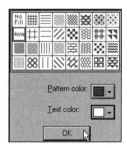

- Outline—From the outline palette (see Figure 14.29), you can choose the thickness and color of the line that outlines the text. Again, you can change the text color to complement the line color.

Figure 14.29
You can use the outline palette to choose a line style to go along with your TextArt text.

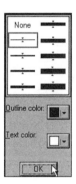

- Rotation—Unlike typical graphic objects that maintain their original shape while rotating, TextArt text skews as it rotates in order to stay within the graphics box and also to stay within the predefined TextArt shape you chose (see Figure 14.30). You can come up with some very interesting shapes using this option.

Figure 14.30
When you rotate TextArt text, it remains within the graphics box boundaries.

- Text Color—If you didn't already choose color when choosing shadow or outline, you can do so here.
- Preset—If you're not feeling particularly creative, or you're in a hurry, you can choose from a limited number of predefined 2-D effects.

PART
IV

CH
14

Caution

If you choose any preset setting, you also lose all your carefully customized settings. Try these presets first, before spending time coming up with your own custom settings.

ADDING 3-D TEXTART OPTIONS

You can click the 3D Options tab to display the options available if you choose to display your TextArt in three dimensions (see Figure 14.31). These options, and some of the things you can do with them, include the following:

■ Lighting—Lighting 1 and 2 function the same, but Lighting 1 is the text color and Lighting 2 is the shadow color. Click the color palette to change the color, and click the light source palette to choose a direction the light comes from (see Figure 14.32).

Figure 14.31
The 3D Options tab enables you to add another dimension to your TextArt text.

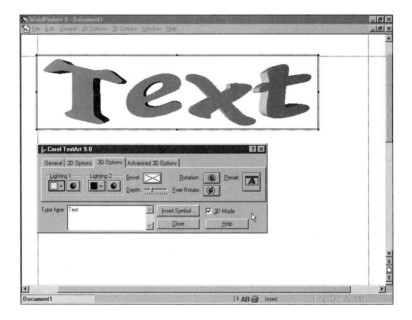

Figure 14.32
The light source palette helps you visualize the direction light comes from as it shines on your 3-D text.

- Bevel—This option enables you to shape the edge of the text, as if the letters were carved like wood molding. Choose a beveled shape from the palette (see Figure 14.33) to add this effect.

Figure 14.33
You can bevel the sides of 3-D text with interesting effects.

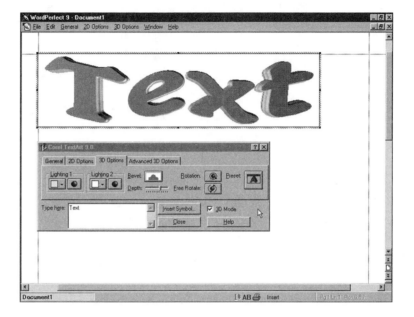

- Depth—You can use the slider to increase or decrease the depth of the beveled edge.
- Rotation—You can rotate the entire TextArt image left or right, up or down, by choosing from several preset rotations (see Figure 14.34).

Figure 14.34
Preset rotation angles make it easy to rotate 3-D TextArt text.

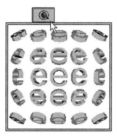

- Free Rotate—If you prefer to rotate the text yourself, click this option, and then use the mouse to drag the TextArt up, down, left, or right.
- Preset—Again, if you prefer to let TextArt do the work for you, you can choose from a palette of predefined 3-D settings.

PART

IV

CH

14

Caution

Don't forget that choosing a preset 3-D option cancels all other settings you may have painstakingly set up.

The Advanced 3D Options tab doesn't mean you have more complicated settings, but simply that you have more options (see Figure 14.35).

Figure 14.35
The Advanced 3D Options include textures.

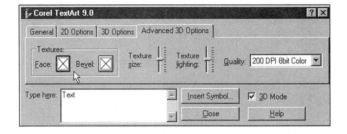

On this tab you can change the following settings, some of which are shown in Figure 14.36:

- Textures—WordPerfect provides a palette of interesting textures (nuts, tiles, fabrics, wood, and so on) that you can apply to the face of the text, to the bevel edge of the text, or both (see Figure 14.37).

- Texture Size—Use the slide control to increase (up) or decrease (down) the size of the texture pattern. If you want larger peanuts, for example, slide up. The size control applies to both the face and the bevel, if you use textures on both.

Figure 14.36
3-D TextArt text is shown here with advanced options.

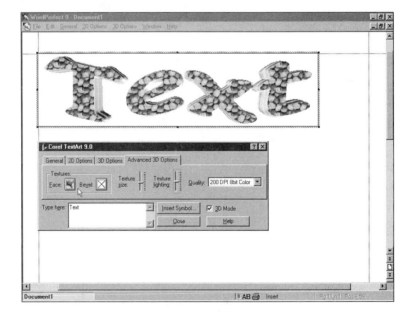

- Texture Lighting—This option controls the contrast between the Lighting 1 and Lighting 2 colors you selected on the 3D Options tab.

- Quality—Unfortunately, this option doesn't indicate how good your TextArt looks, but how well it will print on a color printer. *DPI* refers to the number of dots per inch that print, and *bits* refers to the richness of the colors you can use, especially for textures and gradient shadings.

Figure 14.37
These textures can be applied to the face or the side of 3-D TextArt text.

USING TEXTART IN DOCUMENTS

WordPerfect places TextArt images inside graphics boxes. As a result, they work like any other graphics box. You can add borders to the box, choose various wrap options, and size or move the box.

If you size the box using the side sizing handles, you also change the shape of the original TextArt.

If you choose to wrap the TextArt box in front of or behind your text, you can make it appear that the TextArt and text are designed to work together.

Figure 14.38 shows how a TextArt image combines with regular text to create a logo.

Figure 14.38
TextArt in a graphics box can interact with regular document text to create useful effects.

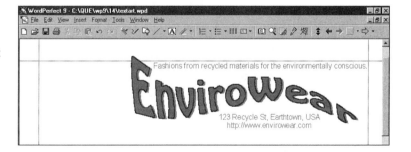

TROUBLESHOOTING

USING UNDO

It seems like nothing I do turns out right. Pretty soon my graphic is a complete mess. Is there anything I can do besides delete it?

Even artists have rags to wipe up their messes. Although it may seem absurdly elementary to mention this, you really must think Undo whenever you try something that you don't like. You should use Undo immediately, because if you wait, you may not be able to restore whatever you messed up.

HOW TO GET OUT OF THE DRAW SCREEN

When I edit an image and choose File, Close, WordPerfect closes my entire document. I want to close just the Draw editor.

If you click the Close button on the toolbar, WordPerfect closes just the editor. If you chose to use the larger Presentations screen (holding down Alt while double-clicking the image to be edited), the menu is different and you can indeed choose File, Close and return to the document.

ABORTING BITMAP EDITING

I've messed up my bitmap editing so badly, and it seems I can only undo one action. I don't want to save the whole mess by returning to the Draw screen. What can I do?

Fortunately, you can abort a bitmap editing session by clicking the Cancel Bitmap button on the Bitmap toolbar. This returns you to the Draw screen without keeping any changes you may have made. In the Draw screen, you have multiple levels of Undo, but you don't in the bitmap editor.

GETTING THE TEXTART PROGRAM BACK

When I'm working with TextArt, I seem to lose the TextArt dialog box.

The TextArt program is separate from WordPerfect. When you accidentally switch back to WordPerfect, you hide the TextArt program. Simply double-click the TextArt image to restore the TextArt program dialog box.

PROJECT

It's all the rage these days. Text with fuzzy shadow backgrounds that seem so real it appears the text is really floating off the page. Can you do that in WordPerfect? You bet. It's not a simple menu item, but it's easy to do using a combination of Draw text and bitmap editing. Figure 14.39 shows some text with the nifty shadow background.

Figure 14.39
Using both the Draw and bitmap editors, you can create this modern-looking shadow effect.

To create something like that, follow these steps:

1. Begin by choosing Insert, Graphics, Draw Picture; or click the Draw Picture button on the toolbar.

2. In the Draw screen, create the text. You can create shadows for anything, including shapes, but let's stick with the text shown in the example.

> **Note**
>
> It's important to make sure the basic object is complete before making a shadow copy. Otherwise, you'll just have to come back and do it all over again.

3. Select the text object (the sizing handles should be visible), and then hold down Ctrl while dragging a copy of the object to another part of the screen.

4. Click the font color palette and change the text copy to light gray.

5. Choose Tools, Convert to Bitmap to make the text copy a bitmap image. You'll get a warning about how irreversible this is. Laugh at the danger as you click Convert.

6. Double-click the new bitmap image to open the bitmap editor.

7. You're going to blur the image, so you need a little extra room at each side of the image. Move the pointer toward each side sizing handle, and when the pointer turns to a two-way arrow, click once. This creates the necessary room.

8. Choose Format, Set Transparent Color, check the No Transparent Color check box, and click OK. This makes the background white, which is the color that meshes with the blurred image.

9. Choose Tools, Special Effects, or click the Effect button on the toolbar. WordPerfect displays the Special Effects dialog box (see Figure 14.40).

Figure 14.40
The Special Effects dialog box enables you to blur bitmap images.

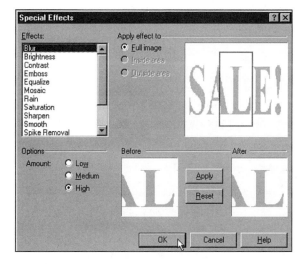

10. Click Blur, select High, and click OK. The blurred edge now mixes nicely with the white background.

11. Go back now, and choose Format, Set Transparent Color, and uncheck the No Transparent Color Box. Click OK. Note in Figure 14.41 how the white color blends with the edge of the blurred text, but otherwise, the rest of the background is transparent.

Figure 14.41
Blurred images mix the object's color with the background color.

12. Click the Close button on the toolbar to return the Draw editor with the blurred bitmap image.

13. Right-click the blurred image, and from the QuickMenu choose To Back.

14. Align the two text images so that the blurred image is a shadow to the regular text image.

15. Choose Edit, Select All, and then click the Group button on the toolbar; or right-click the objects and choose Group.

16. Size the graphics box to the size of the text object and click in your text to close the Draw editor.

That's it! Position the text wherever you want in your document. Although this might not be the quickest procedure you'll ever try, as you become more experienced at it, you'll find it takes only a minute or two, and that it's easy to add this effect to text or other graphics objects.

PART V

Integrating Information from Other Sources

CHAPTER **15**

IMPORTING DATA AND WORKING WITH OTHER PROGRAMS

In this chapter

MOVING INFORMATION IN WINDOWS

In today's office, information is created in a variety of programs. The smartest workers learn how to move and reuse that information, instead of creating it over and over again. Although some information comes in specific, proprietary formats, in many cases information can be moved easily from one place to another.

USING THE CLIPBOARD

The key to moving data in Windows is the Windows Clipboard. Despite the clever name, the Clipboard really is an area of your computer's memory that is reserved for temporarily holding information you place there. You can retrieve the information and use it wherever you want, as often as you want, until you replace the information with something else or until you turn off your computer.

Tip #169 from
Laura and Read

You can view the current contents of the Clipboard if you have installed the Windows 95/98 Clipboard viewer. Click the Start button, choose Programs, Accessories, System Tools, and then click Viewer. If you haven't installed the viewer, you can do so from the Control Panel, using the Windows tab of the Add/Remove Programs dialog box.

In WordPerfect, you can cut or copy information in a variety of ways, including by using the Edit menu, the toolbar, the QuickMenu, and keystrokes such as Ctrl+X or Shift+Del to cut, and Ctrl+V or Shift+Ins to paste.

→ If you need a review of the many ways you can cut and paste in WordPerfect, **see** Chapter 2, "Opening and Editing Documents," **p. 35**

Typically, each time you copy or cut information, Windows clears the Clipboard and adds what you've cut or copied. You can, however, add more than one selection to the Clipboard at a time. Choose Edit, Append to add more items to the Clipboard. Then when you paste, WordPerfect pastes all appended items at once.

Note

You can append only text selections to the Clipboard. You cannot append graphics.

When you move text in WordPerfect, you normally also move the formatting codes associated with that text. When you paste the text, you also paste its formatting codes. If the surrounding text happens to have the same formatting, the codes automatically disappear, but if it doesn't, WordPerfect inserts the formatting codes to preserve the original format of the source text, as shown in Figure 15.1.

You can, however, paste the text into your document in a variety of other ways. Choose Edit, Paste Special to access the Paste Special dialog box (see Figure 15.2). You then use this dialog box to paste using the following formats or options:

- WordPerfect 9 Data—This option is equivalent to the normal Paste option; it inserts text as native WordPerfect 9 information.

Figure 15.1
Text imported by cutting and pasting often brings formatting codes along with it.

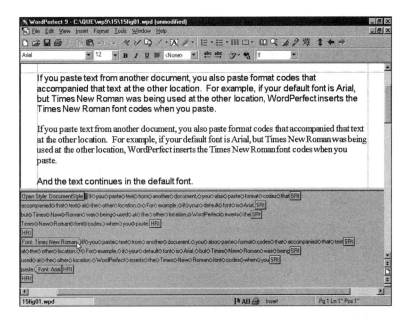

Figure 15.2
For greater control over how you import Clipboard data, use the Paste Special dialog box.

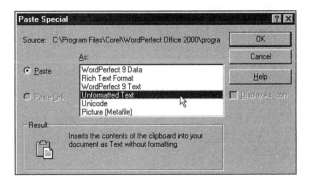

- Rich Text Format—Rich Text Format (RTF) is a quasi-standard method for translating some formatting between different programs. For example, although the Bold codes might be different for WordPerfect than they are for Word, RTF uses a Bold code that both can understand.

- WordPerfect 9 Text—This pastes only the text of the selection, not formatting or graphics.

- Unformatted Text—This option pastes only the most generic version of the selection in your document. All formatting, graphics, and so on are lost.

- Unicode—This is a relatively recent standard for text interchange; it tries to make sure that codes for foreign characters, among other things, are the same in all programs.

- Picture (Metafile)—This pastes the contents of the Clipboard into a graphics box. You can then size the box and position it as you do any graphics box (see Figure 15.3).

Figure 15.3
You can use the Picture option in the Paste Special dialog box to paste text into a graphics box, which you can then move and size. Note the graphic toolbar and the sizing handles around the text box.

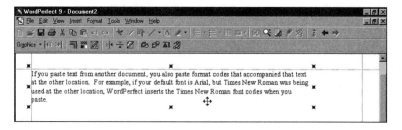

Note

The number and type of options in the Paste Special dialog box can change depending on the source of the information you copy.

Although you have many options to choose from, if all you really want to copy is the information itself, without formatting, simply choose the Unformatted Text option.

DRAG AND DROP

One handy yet often overlooked method for cutting and pasting is drag and drop. The procedure is so simple that we often forget to use it. Follow these steps:

1. With the mouse, select the text you want to move.
2. Point the mouse pointer at the selected text so that the pointer turns to an arrow.
3. Click and hold down the mouse button and drag the pointer to the location where you want to paste the text. The mouse pointer appears with an arrow, a piece of paper, and an insertion point to indicate exactly where you will paste the text.
4. Release the mouse button to drop the text in its new location.

The text remains highlighted so you can move it again if you missed your mark. Of course you can also use Undo.

→ For details on cutting, copying, and pasting text, **see** Chapter 2, "Opening and Editing Documents," **p. 35**

Drag and Drop or Cut and Paste?
Using drag and drop to move text is best suited for relatively short distances; dragging text from page 1 to page 8, for example, where lots of scrolling is required before you can drop the text, just isn't very practical. Sometimes regular cut and paste methods make more sense.

Tip #170 from
Laura and Read

One of the best uses for drag and drop is in tables, where you drag the contents of table cells along with cell formatting. You can even drag entire rows or columns within a table.

COPYING AND PASTING BETWEEN WORDPERFECT DOCUMENTS

As you undoubtedly know, WordPerfect enables you to work with up to nine open documents at a time. Not only can you switch among documents to refer to information in them, but you can easily move information from one WordPerfect document to another. The most obvious method is simply to cut or copy text in one document, switch to another, and paste the text there. Easy. Done.

A not so obvious method, but one that is easy to use, is drag and drop. Note in Figure 15.4 that two document tabs appear at the bottom of the WordPerfect screen. The current (active) document is highlighted (if you're not sure, simply check the title bar for the name of the current document).

Figure 15.4
Document tabs at the bottom of the WordPerfect screen enable you to switch between documents, and also to drag and drop text from one document to another.

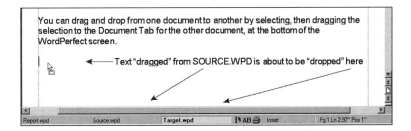

To drag and drop from one WordPerfect document to another, follow these steps:

1. First, go to the target document and position the cursor where you want to paste text. When you return here with text you've dragged from the other document, you don't want to have to scroll to find your target before you can drop the text.

2. Switch to the source document (by clicking the document tab at the bottom of the screen).

3. Select the text (or graphics, or table, and so on) that you want to copy.

4. Click the selection and quickly drag it toward the document tab of the target document.

Tip #171 from
Laura and Read

If you move too slowly toward the document tab, the document begins to scroll, and WordPerfect thinks you want to paste in the current document. If this happens, release the mouse button in the source document (which pastes the selection), choose Undo, and start over again.

5. Hold the pointer on the target document tab until WordPerfect switches to the target document.

6. Move the mouse pointer into the document area and release the mouse button to paste the document where you want it.

COPYING AND PASTING BETWEEN PROGRAMS

The same principles you use when moving information within a program apply when moving information between programs. The Windows Clipboard serves as the great information storage tank, and text, graphics, and even other information can be retrieved and converted so that it can be used in the target program.

Suppose, for example, that you have a paragraph in a Word document that you'd like to use in a WordPerfect document. To move information from one program to another, follow these steps:

1. Open the source program (for example, Word).

2. Select the information you want to move.

3. Cut or copy the selection.

4. Switch to the target program (for example, WordPerfect).

5. Paste the information.

Information you copy from one program to another often carries styles and other attributes from the source program. If you open the Reveal Codes window, as shown in Figure 15.5, you see that Word text also inserts style codes, font codes, and other codes to preserve the original formatting of the text from the source document.

Figure 15.5
Pasting text from Word may also import Word's default format codes.

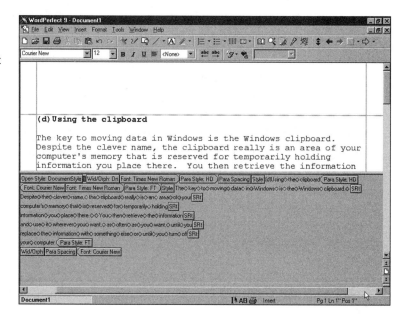

If you don't want all the formatting, but only the text, simply choose <u>E</u>dit, Paste <u>S</u>pecial, and then select Unformatted.

USING OLE LINKING AND EMBEDDING OPTIONS

OLE is object linking and embedding. When you paste information from another program, WordPerfect can embed the information, and Windows can remember where the information came from. When it comes time to edit the embedded information, simply double-click it. Windows opens an editing window within WordPerfect, and switches you to the source program so that you can edit in the original program, using that program's menus, keystrokes, and other procedures. When you finish, you return to WordPerfect with the updated information by clicking in the WordPerfect document.

Tip #172 from *Laura and Read*	If you use normal methods of copying and pasting information, WordPerfect inserts only the information you're copying and does not create an OLE link back to the original program. However, you can choose Edit, Paste Special and choose the format associated with the original program to paste the information and to establish the OLE link.

Tip #173 from *Laura and Read*	If you drag and drop the information from the other program to WordPerfect, WordPerfect automatically establishes an OLE link. The procedure is similar to dragging and dropping text between WordPerfect documents: Find the target in WordPerfect, and then go to the source program and drag the selected information to the WordPerfect button on the Windows taskbar. When WordPerfect appears, drop the information in the WordPerfect document.

You can also create new OLE objects within WordPerfect. For example, you can create a Word document or even a PowerPoint slide inside a WordPerfect document. To create an OLE object that you embed in a WordPerfect document, follow these steps:

1. Choose Insert, Object to display the Insert Object dialog box (see Figure 15.6).

Figure 15.6
You can use the Insert Object dialog box to insert OLE objects.

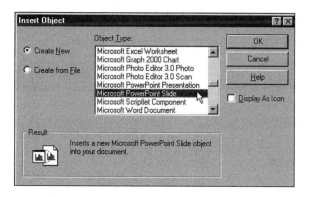

2. Select the object type from the list of options. Only the OLE-capable programs (called *OLE servers*) that are installed on your system appear on the list.

3. Click OK. The OLE server application starts and takes control of WordPerfect's menus and toolbars. It also opens an editing window in which you can use all the application's procedures to create the object (see Figure 15.7). This is called *in-place editing*.

Figure 15.7
You can edit, in place, OLE objects such as PowerPoint slides.

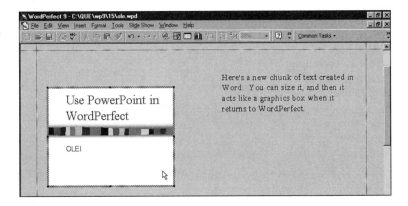

4. Close the OLE editing window by clicking in the document. WordPerfect takes control of menus and toolbars again.

Note

Some OLE server applications do not support in-place editing. Instead, they open a completely separate application window where you create or edit the object. You then exit the application to return to WordPerfect.

You can also embed or create a link to an existing OLE object created by another application. To create an OLE link, follow these steps:

1. Choose Insert, Object to open the Insert Object dialog box.

2. Click Create from File.

3. Browse to find the file you want to insert.

4. By default, WordPerfect inserts the file as an embedded object. However, if you choose Link, WordPerfect inserts the object and also creates a link to the original file so that changes made to that file are reflected in the WordPerfect document.

5. Click OK to insert the object in your document.

Tip #174 from
Laura and Read

Don't forget that many applications allow you to drag and drop objects from their programs into WordPerfect.

Extremely large WordPerfect documents are unwieldy and take up a lot of disk space. If you're having trouble with such documents, it may have to do with OLE. See "Keeping Files Small" in the Troubleshooting section at the end of this chapter.

WORKING WITH OTHER WORD PROCESSING DOCUMENTS

Let's face it. WordPerfect may be the best word processing program in town, but marketing muscle has helped Microsoft lay claim to a large portion of the Windows word processing turf. If you're lucky, your organization has standardized on WordPerfect alone. But more likely, you're faced with having to work on documents created initially in other word processing programs.

Fortunately, WordPerfect has kept pace with the need for interchangeability with other programs. In fact, Corel has placed a great deal of emphasis on providing up-to-date and accurate document conversions in WordPerfect 9. Whether your other word processing program is WordPerfect 5.1 for DOS or Word 2000, you'll find it easier than ever to use WordPerfect to work with these documents.

OPENING AND CONVERTING FILES FROM OTHER WORD PROCESSING PROGRAMS

The first step to working with a document from another word processing format is to open it in WordPerfect. Access the File Open dialog box, find the file, and click Open. WordPerfect briefly displays the conversion information box, and then opens the document in WordPerfect.

Automatic File Conversion
In earlier versions of WordPerfect, a conversion dialog box indicated the format of the document and ask you to confirm the format before opening it. In WordPerfect 9, perhaps because you may not even know the format of the document being converted, WordPerfect takes charge and converts and opens the document without your intervention.

By default, WordPerfect supports and converts a limited number of common modern formats, including the following:

> ANSI/ASCII (Windows and DOS; Text, Delimited, C/R L/F to SRt)
>
> HTML (Hypertext Markup Language)
>
> IA5
>
> Word 6.0/7.0 for Windows
>
> Word 97
>
> RTF
>
> RTF Japanese
>
> SGML

Unicode

Windows Write

WordPerfect 5.1/5.2 (Far East)

WordPerfect Compound File

XML (Extensible Markup Language; UTF-8, UTF-16 Big Endian and Little Endian)

If you try to open one of your old documents, and WordPerfect tells you the format of the document is not supported, don't despair. In addition to the limited default conversions included with your original WordPerfect installation, you can also install other conversion sets. The following are some of the conversions available (along with the latest version for each):

Ami Pro (3.0)

DisplayWrite (5.0)

IBM DCA

Kermit

Microsoft Word (many older versions for both DOS and Windows)

MultiMate (through MultiMate Advantage II)

OfficeWriter (6.2)

VolksWriter (4)

WordPerfect (4.2)

WordStar 2000 (3.0)

WordStar (7.0)

XyWrite III Plus (4.0)

Note

To install new conversion filters, start up the WordPerfect Office 2000 Setup program and choose Add New Components. Skip the Office 2000 components, and at the next screen select the conversion filters you need. Also skip the writing tools, and choose Install. The whole process takes only a few minutes.

USING DATA FROM UNSUPPORTED FORMATS

Despite WordPerfect's extensive support for automatic file conversions, you're bound to discover a document sometime that can't be opened in WordPerfect. When you try to open such a file, WordPerfect displays the Convert File Format dialog box (see Figure 15.8), and the Convert File Format From box shows Unsupported Format. There are a few methods for dealing with this problem:

- If you know the source of the document (for example, WordPerfect 4.2), make sure you have installed the necessary conversion filters. If you think you know what program created the file, but aren't sure what version, try various options to see if you can open the file.

- If you have the original program used to create the file, open the document in the other program and see if you can save it to an intermediate format, such as RTF, that WordPerfect understands. You might lose some formatting in the translation, but you'll retain the content of the document.

- When all else fails, you can usually open the file as an ASCII file. Try the CR/LF to SRt option first because it converts the hard returns at the end of ASCII lines to soft returns, thus preserving text paragraphs.

Figure 15.8
If WordPerfect can't convert a file, it displays the Convert Format dialog box, where you can choose an alternate conversion format.

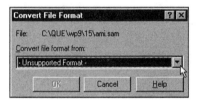

Caution

Always use the ASCII import as a last resort because you lose all document formatting with this option. ASCII imports also usually require extensive editing.

Editing a Converted Document

Although WordPerfect does a great job of converting a wide variety of document formats, inevitably you'll find that certain things don't convert cleanly.

The first reason is that WordPerfect tries to maintain the exact format of the original document. Because other word processing programs use different default layouts, this often causes WordPerfect to add margin, font, or style codes to the converted document that you wouldn't find in a typical WordPerfect document. For example, Figure 15.9 shows the Reveal Codes screen from a converted Word document, along with its opening styles in the Styles Editor dialog box.

The second reason is that WordPerfect doesn't always know how to handle certain formatting. When WordPerfect guesses, it sometimes guesses wrong.

The resulting converted WordPerfect document must be cleaned up to become a truly usable document. The following are some strategies you can use to complete the conversion process:

- Open Reveal Codes and see what kinds of codes you have to deal with. It may be that you can simply delete a few codes and be back to a standard WordPerfect layout.

Figure 15.9
You can use Reveal Codes to determine what codes, such as margins, tab sets, or styles, must be changed or deleted from an imported document.

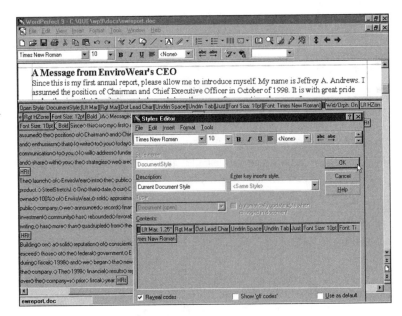

Tip #17517

Don't forget that you can delete codes by using the mouse to click and drag codes out of the Reveal Codes window.

- In Reveal Codes, double-click the initial Open Style: Document Style button to display the document default codes (refer to Figure 15.9). Only codes that differ from WordPerfect's default codes appear in this dialog box. Remove any codes that shouldn't be there.

- Use the Spell Checker, which often finds legitimate words combined with special characters.

- Use Find and Replace to match codes or characters and to replace them with the appropriate codes or with nothing. For example, you might replace the typical Word margin setting of 1.25 inches with nothing, which returns the document to the default 1-inch WordPerfect margin. Although using Find and Replace can be a bit tedious, once you're familiar with what you need to replace, this can save you a lot of time.

- Use macros if you have a lot of documents to clean up. You can use macros to set up, find, and replace various codes so you don't have to do these things manually.

SAVING AND EXPORTING TO OTHER WORD PROCESSING PROGRAMS

So, you're the only maverick in the office. They tell you you'll have to switch to Word someday, but you insist on keeping your trusted WordPerfect. Fortunately, you also exchange documents with your co-workers, even if they don't use WordPerfect. You already know how to open and edit their documents. To send your documents to them in a format they can use, you simply use Save As to save the document. To save a document in a different format, follow these steps:

1. Choose File, Save As. WordPerfect displays the Save As dialog box.

2. Type the name of the file you want to use, unless you intend to use the same name.

3. Click the File Type drop-down menu and select the file format you want to convert to (for example, MS Word 97 for Windows). In most cases WordPerfect adds the appropriate filename extension (for example, .doc).

4. Click Save. WordPerfect converts the document into the selected format.

If you continue to work on the document and save it again, WordPerfect prompts you with the Save Format dialog box (see Figure 15.10). Unless you want to change back to the WordPerfect format, click the conversion format (for example, MS Word 97 for Windows) and click OK.

Figure 15.10
When you save a document whose original format is other than the current version of WordPerfect, WordPerfect asks which format you want to save it to.

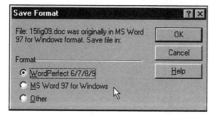

Note

When you convert and open a document from another format, you get the same Save Format dialog box the first time you save it. If you intend to keep the document in WordPerfect format, click OK, and WordPerfect does not prompt you again.

IMPORTING AND USING DATABASE DATA

Data conversion typically centers on word processing information. But you can also convert and use data from other sources, such as databases and spreadsheets.

CONVERTING TO WORDPERFECT FORMATS

WordPerfect's database format is the merge data file. Each record is separated by an end record code, and each field is separated by an end field code (see Figure 15.11). This structure is typical for any flat-file database—that is, individual records are divided into common fields.

Figure 15.11
Merge data files separate records and fields with merge codes.

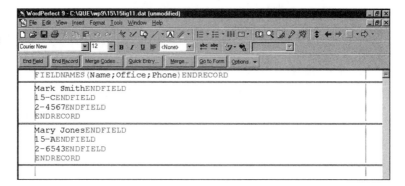

Any database that uses a similar structure can be converted into a WordPerfect data file.

Flat Versus Relational Databases

Relational databases do not convert well to a typical merge data file format because they are too complex. Records with one set of fields relate to other records with a different set of fields. Each set of records, typically, is its own database. Because only information that can be extracted in a flat format (one type of record and set of fields) can be imported into a WordPerfect merge data file, you must import separately each table of a relational database.

To import a database into a WordPerfect format, follow these steps:

1. Choose Insert, Spreadsheet/Database, Import. WordPerfect displays the Import Data dialog box (see Figure 15.12).

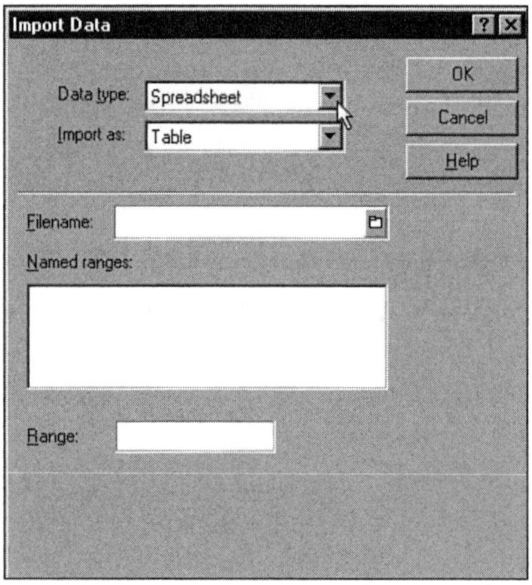

Figure 15.12
The Import Data dialog box enables you to import many database and spreadsheet formats.

2. From the Data Type drop-down menu, select the format of the database you want to import. Database formats supported by WordPerfect include the following:

- Clipper
- dBASE
- FoxPro
- Paradox
- ODBC (Microsoft's Open Database Connect standard—for example, Microsoft Access 97), and ODBC (SQL)
- ASCII and ANSI *delimited* text

Note

Nearly any database program can create database files of ASCII delimited text. ASCII is plain text, and delimiters separate the records and fields of such text. Typical delimiters include commas, spaces, and quotation marks.

Tip #176 from
Laura and Read

If you convert a lot of the same type of ASCII delimited files, you can select Tools, Settings and use the Convert tab of the Convert Settings dialog box to set the ASCII delimiters you use most often.

3. From the Import As drop-down menu, select the target format in WordPerfect. Options include the following:

- Table—Each row is a database record, and each column is a field in a record.
- Text—Each line is a database record, and each field in the line is separated by a tab.
- Merge Data File—Records and fields import with merge codes (refer to Figure 15.11). This can be particularly useful if you want to manage or reuse the data in merge letters, and so on.

→ For more information on using merge data files, **see** Chapter 23, "Assembling Documents with Merge," **p. 645**

4. Browse to find a database filename of the same type as the data you selected.

5. The bottom portion of the screen changes depending on the type of database you import (see Figure 15.13). The ASCII delimited type, for example, asks you to specify just what the delimiters are. The example shows that fields are separated by commas, and records are separated by a combination line feed and carriage return. Change the delimiters, if necessary, to match those used in the database. Other databases enable you to choose which fields to import for each record. This can be particularly useful if the number of database fields is large.

Figure 15.13
In the Import Data dialog box, you can specify the delimiters to be used when importing an ASCII delimited database.

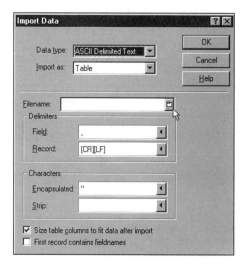

6. Click OK to import the database into your WordPerfect document.

Tip #177 from
Laura and Read

With many database types, you can open the database directly through the Open File dialog box. When you do, WordPerfect recognizes the database format and automatically displays the Import Data dialog box with all the appropriate information already filled in.

If you import a database from a program such as Paradox, you may also see one or more of the options in the Import Data dialog box, shown in Figure 15.14.

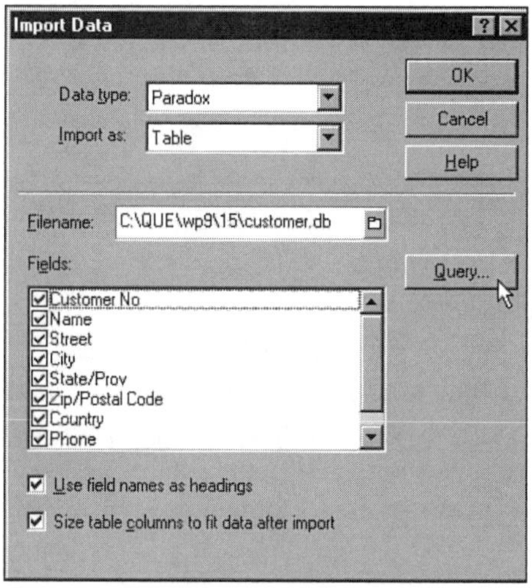

Figure 15.14
In the Import Data dialog box, import options are available when importing more complex data such as a database from Paradox.

The options include

■ Query—You can set criteria before importing data so that you get only the data you need (see Figure 15.15). For example, if you want only the records for customers from the United States, you could query the database and have it extract and import only those Country records that equal U.S.A..

Figure 15.15
When importing a database, you can use the Define Selection Conditions dialog box to extract and import records that meet criteria you set.

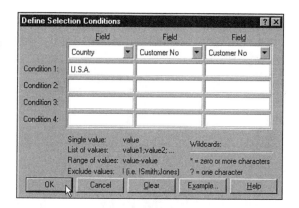

Tip #178 from
Laura and Read

If you're not sure how to use the query criteria, click Example for hints and examples.

■ Fields—If the database contains a large number of fields, you might want to limit the number of fields that you import into the WordPerfect document. Select the ones you want to import, and deselect the ones you want to exclude.

■ Table—(not shown in Figure 15.14) If the file has multiple record types, each must be imported separately. Choose the record set you want from the Table list.

LINKING DATABASE DATA

WordPerfect also enables you to link an imported database so that changes to the original database can be updated in WordPerfect. To link a database to a WordPerfect document, follow these steps:

1. Choose Insert, Spreadsheet/Database, Create Link. WordPerfect displays the Create Data Link dialog box (refer to Figure 15.14, which is identical to the Create Data Link dialog box).

2. Choose the data type, the target format (Link As), the name of the database, and other options.

3. Click OK to import the database, with links to the original database file.

You can also update the link and choose other link options from the Insert, Spreadsheet/Database menu:

- Edit Link—This option returns you to the Edit Data Link dialog box (refer to Figure 15.14, which, again, is the same as the Create Data Link dialog box), where you can change the name of the file, the target format, the fields to be imported, and so on.

- Update—This option displays the Update dialog box, which asks if you want to update all links. If you answer Yes, WordPerfect goes back to the original database and refreshes the data in the WordPerfect document.

- Options—This displays the Link Options dialog box (see Figure 15.16). You can choose to automatically update linked data when the document opens. By default, WordPerfect also displays link icons in the left margin of the document to let you know you have a linked database.

Figure 15.16
You can use the Link Options dialog box to specify how a linked database or spreadsheet should be updated. Note the link icon in the document margin.

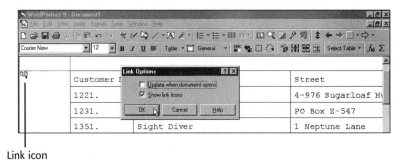

Link icon

SORTING DATABASE DATA IN TABLES

Sorting database information in WordPerfect tables is easy and practical. To sort table information, follow these steps:

1. Position the insertion point anywhere in the table.

2. Choose Tools, Sort, or press Alt+F9. WordPerfect displays the Sort dialog box (see Figure 15.17).

Figure 15.17
You can use the Sort feature to sort data in tables.

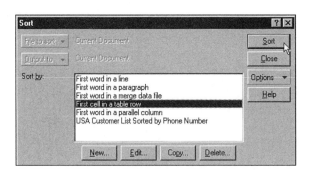

Note

WordPerfect enables you to sort information from a variety of formats, including tables, merge files, lines, and paragraphs. The procedures described here apply generally to other sorting as well.

3. Choose the type of sort you want. By default, the first time you sort a table, WordPerfect assumes that you want to sort by the first word in the first cell of each table row.

4. Click Sort to perform the sort.

Caution

Be sure to save your work before you perform any sort. By default, you cannot undo a sort, and you want to be able to return to a correct copy of the document if something goes wrong.

Note

Imported database tables already have header rows that do not get sorted with the rest of the data. In tables you create, you must use the Row tab of the Table Format dialog box to specify header rows *before* sorting. Otherwise, the header rows get sorted along with everything else.

If sorting by the first word of the first cell isn't what you had in mind, you can select a definition from the Sort By list and click Edit. You can also click New to create a new definition.

Note

It's usually best to leave original default sort definitions alone and to create new ones if you need different sort criteria. That way you always have at least one unchanged example if you need to refer to it.

To create a new sort definition, follow these steps:

1. Access the Sort dialog box (refer to Figure 15.17).

2. Click New. WordPerfect displays the New Sort dialog box (see Figure 15.18).

3. Edit the sort description (for example, USA Customer List Sorted by Phone Number).

4. Make sure Table Row is selected.

5. Edit the sorting rules, using these options:

   • Key—The first sorting rule is also the first key. You can choose Add Key at End of the rules, Insert Key Between other rules, or Delete Key if there are two or more in the list.

   • Type—You can choose Alpha or Numeric from the drop-down list. Alpha sorts in alphabetic order, and Numeric sorts by numeric value. In an Alpha sort, for example, 11 comes before 2.

- Sort Order—Choose Ascending (that is, A–Z) or Descending (that is, Z–A) from the drop-down list.

- Column—Specify the column of data to sort on.

- Line—Specify which line to sort on, if there is more than one line of text in the cells (for example, a multiline address).

- Word—Specify which word to sort on. 1 means the first word, 2 the second word, and so on. To count from the end of the line, specify -1 for the last word, -2 for the next-to-the-last word, and so on.

Figure 15.18
You can use the New Sort dialog box to set up a new sort definition.

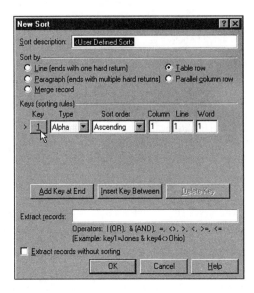

Tip #179 from
Laura and Read

When sorting by last name, specify -1. If you specify 2, you sort on the second name, even for people who have three names (for example, *Mary Anne Fitzpatrick*, sorts by *Anne*.)

- Extract Records—You can discard records that you don't want and sort the remaining records. Simply set up one key and specify what it should contain (for example, key1=U.S.A.).

6. Click OK to return to the Sort dialog box.

Setting up sort criteria takes some getting used to. Remember that the second key applies only *after* the first key has finished sorting. For example, you might make the first key sort by zip code to group everyone by zip code, and then make the second key sort by last name to alphabetize each zip code group. See Figure 15.19, which shows the setup for sorting a customer list by phone number and extracts only records that contain U.S.A. in the second column.

Figure 15.19
The Edit Sort dialog box shows criteria for sorting a U.S.A.-only customer phone list.

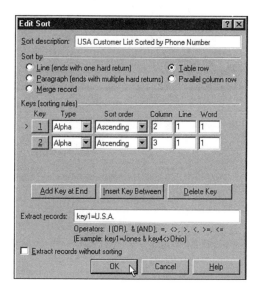

Before sorting, you should consider at least one more option. Click Options in the Sort dialog box and choose Allow Undo after sorting if you want to be able to undo your sort. This setting remains in effect until you change it.

Finally, click Sort and see what happens. You will likely have the opportunity to use Undo and try it again.

USING DATABASE DATA WITH MERGE

Importing database information to a WordPerfect merge data file is faster and easier than typing all the data over again, but wouldn't it be even nicer if you could merge directly from the database file itself so you don't have two separate databases?

You can! To merge directly from a database file, follow these steps:

1. Create a merge form file.

→ For information on creating merge documents, **see** Chapter 23, "Assembling Documents with Merge," **p. 645**

2. Access the Merge dialog box (by selecting Tools, Merge or pressing Shift+F9), and choose Perform Merge. WordPerfect displays the Perform Merge dialog box (see Figure 15.20).

3. Choose the type of database source file you'll use by clicking the Data Source drop-down menu, which includes the following options:

   - File on Disk, for Paradox and WordPerfect merge data files
   - Address Book, for Corel Central address book files
   - ODBC, for Access, dBASE, or FoxPro files

Figure 15.20
In the Perform Merge dialog box you can specify a database file in place of a standard merge data file.

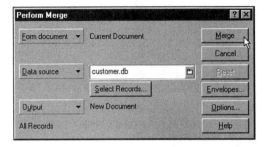

4. Choose the options you want, such as <u>S</u>elect Records to query the database, or <u>E</u>nvelopes if you want to merge address information to envelopes along with the merge document.

5. Click <u>M</u>erge to perform the merge. WordPerfect merges the data directly from your database file with the merge form document.

IMPORTING AND USING SPREADSHEET DATA

Another important type of data that you might need in a WordPerfect document comes from spreadsheets. Because spreadsheets are typically arranged in rows and columns, what better way to present spreadsheet data than in a WordPerfect table?

CONVERTING SPREADSHEET DATA

WordPerfect can convert data from nearly any modern spreadsheet program, including Quattro Pro, Excel, and others. To import a spreadsheet into WordPerfect, follow these steps:

1. Choose <u>I</u>nsert, Sp<u>r</u>eadsheet/Database, <u>I</u>mport.

Tip #180 from
Laura and Read

If you simply open a spreadsheet, WordPerfect opens the Import Data dialog box and fills in most of the spreadsheet information for you.

---

2. From the Data <u>T</u>ype drop-down menu, select Spreadsheet.

3. From the <u>I</u>mport As drop-down menu, select the target format in WordPerfect. Options are the same as for databases, WordPerfect tables, plain tab delimited text, and WordPerfect merge data files. Table is the default format.

4. Browse to find the filename of the spreadsheet you want to import.

5. Click in the <u>N</u>amed Ranges box, or press Tab. WordPerfect displays any named ranges it finds in the spreadsheet, and shows the upper-left and lower-right cells of the range (for example A1...F8).

Tip #181 from *Laura and Read*

> Because spreadsheets can be much larger than a typical word processing page, it helps to create named ranges in the spreadsheet program to make it easier to extract only portions of a spreadsheet in WordPerfect.

6. If there are no named ranges, or you want to specify a different range, in the Range box type the upper-left and lower-right cells of the area of the spreadsheet you want to import.
7. Click OK to insert the selected portion of the spreadsheet in a WordPerfect table (see Figure 15.21).

WordPerfect 9 - C:\QUE\wp9\15\15fig21.wpd (unmodified)
File Edit View Insert Format Tools Window Help
Arial
10
Table
General
Select Table
1st 2nd 3rd 4th Total
Madison 399 465 232 355 1451
Monona 56 59 61 65 241
Rio 5 3 7 6 21
Total 460 527 300 426 1713

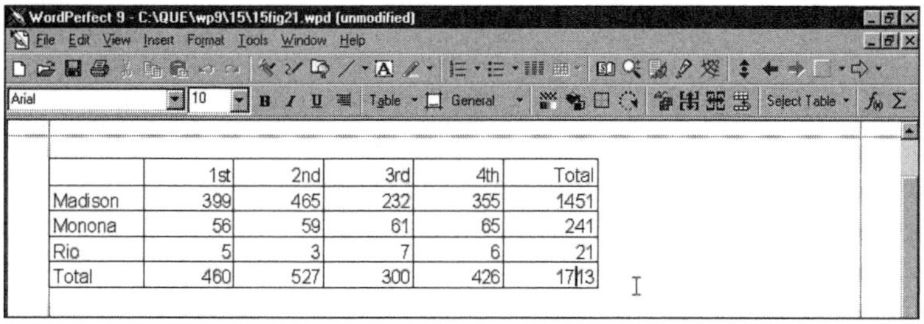

Figure 15.21
An imported spreadsheet looks like any other WordPerfect table, except that it can also include table formulas.

Linking Spreadsheet Data

You can also link spreadsheet data to a WordPerfect table the same way you link database data (see the section "Linking Database Data," earlier in this chapter.) The functions and options for each are identical.

Using Spreadsheet Formulas in Tables

One huge difference between typical tables and tables that contain imported spreadsheets is that the latter also include formulas, and such tables function just like spreadsheets. In fact, even WordPerfect tables you create can also be made to function like spreadsheets by using formulas.

To work with formulas in WordPerfect tables, use the following options:

- The Formula toolbar—Position the insertion point in the table and from the Property Bar choose Table, Formula Toolbar. Alternatively, you can right-click the table and choose Formula Toolbar from the QuickMenu. WordPerfect displays a formula bar and buttons to assist in working with table numeric data (see Figure 15.22, which also shows a formula in the Formula text box because the insertion point is in cell F5, which contains a formula).

Formula toolbar   Formula text box

Figure 15.22
A table can contain
formulas that function
like those in a spread-
sheet.

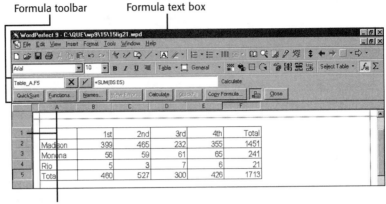

Row/column indicators

 ■ Row/column indicators—If the Formula toolbar is already displayed, click the Turn Row/Column Indicators On or Off button, or choose Table, Ro_w/Col Indicators from the Property Bar. WordPerfect displays spreadsheet-like row and column indicators (refer to Figure 15.22).

Working with formulas in WordPerfect tables is perhaps even easier than working with a spreadsheet program. Consider the price list table in Figure 15.23, which illustrates some of the following options you have in creating and working with table formulas:

■ The Formula text box—Here you can type formulas (for example, to show a 7% discount price, in cell D2 you enter C2-(C2*.07).

Figure 15.23
This price list uses
table formulas to cal-
culate discount prices.

Caution

Be sure your insertion point is in the cell where you want the formula *before* you click the Formula text box. Otherwise, you'll enter a formula where you didn't expect to.

- Accept Formula—Enters the formula into the table cell. You can also press Enter.

- Cancel Formula—Cancels the formula you may have been building. You can also press Esc.

- QuickSum—Click this button to quickly add all contiguous numeric cells above the cell that contains the insertion point. If the first cell above that point is blank, then QuickSum adds contiguous cells to the left.

> *If you're having trouble making a column of text add properly, see "Ignoring Values in Text Cells" in the Troubleshooting section at the end of this chapter.*

- Functions—You can choose from a complete array of spreadsheet functions from the Table Functions dialog box (see Figure 15.24). Click a function to display a brief description of what it does and how to use it.

Figure 15.24
WordPerfect enables you to use a complete set of spreadsheet formula functions, such as the one used to calculate a periodic payment.

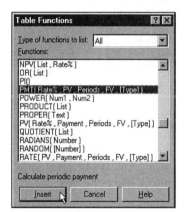

- Names—You can name cells and ranges of cells, and use those names in table formulas. You can even link the values of named cells in one table to formulas in other tables, or in floating cells.

- View Error—If you get an error message (if you build a formula incorrectly, for example), click this button to find out why you got the error and how to fix the problem.

- Calculate—You can force the table to recalculate. By default, tables do not automatically calculate when you make changes, as do most spreadsheets. To change the default, choose Table, Calculate, and choose Calculate Table in the Calculate dialog box (see Figure 15.25).

Figure 15.25
You can use the Calculate dialog box to set automatic calculation options.

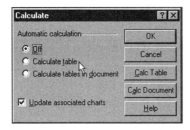

- QuickFill—This option enables you to begin a series of numbers in a row or column, and then select the entire column and fill in the rest of the cells automatically.
- Copy Formula—The Copy Formula dialog box (see Figure 15.26) enables you to copy a formula to a specific cell, or down or to the right *n* number of cells.

Figure 15.26
You can use the Copy Formula dialog box to copy formulas to other parts of a table, just as you do in a spreadsheet.

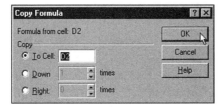

You can also use the row/column indicators to select entire rows or columns, by simply clicking the row or column indicator. You can use drag and drop to move the selected row or column.

You can also access the Table menu on the Property Bar and choose Format to change column alignments and other features. Choose Numeric Format from the same menu to apply formats such as currency and percentages (see Figure 15.27).

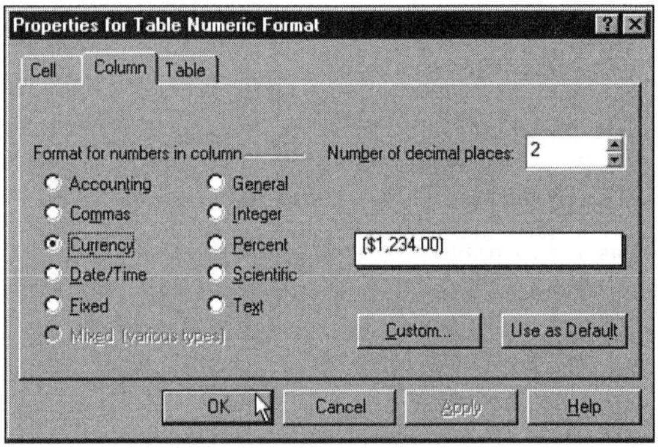

Figure 15.27
You can use the Properties for Table Numeric Format dialog box to set formatting for numbers, such as currency, percentage, and so on.

USING FLOATING CELLS

Floating cells are another way of working with spreadsheet data, but in a somewhat unusual way. Floating cells are invisible cells that display their content as if they are part of the text that surrounds them. In Figure 15.28, for example, the discount percentage displayed in the floating cell is also referenced in the formulas in Column D that show the discounted price. If you change the value in the floating cell, the discounted price amounts also change.

Figure 15.28
A floating cell looks like other text, but the data is contained between two floating cell codes, shown here in Reveal Codes.

To create a floating cell, its formula, and numeric format, follow these steps:

1. Position the insertion point where you want the floating cell.
2. Choose Insert, Table or press F12. WordPerfect displays the Create Table dialog box (see Figure 15.29).

Figure 15.29
You can use the Create Table dialog box to create a floating cell.

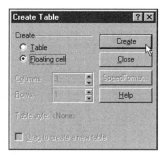

3. Choose Floating Cell and click Create. WordPerfect inserts a pair of floating cell codes in your document (refer to Figure 15.28).
4. Turn on the Formula toolbar if it's not already visible by choosing Table, Formula Toolbar from the Property Bar.

PART

V

CH

15

5. Click the Formula text box, and then create the formula for the floating cell. Click the Accept Formula button to place the formula in the floating cell.

Tip #182 from
Laura and Read

You can point to table cells or other floating cells to build formulas in the Formula text box.

---

6. Choose Table, Numeric Format from the Property Bar and select a numeric format for the floating cell (for example, Percent, to two decimal places).

That's it! Now as you make changes to the table or other floating cells, you can right-click any of these and choose Calculate from the QuickMenu.

Tip #183 from
Laura and Read

One particularly good use for floating cells is a mortgage loan letter. If you've ever seen a form letter from the bank telling you what your mortgage rate will be, you know they don't sit down and type each of the loan figures in by hand. Indeed, you can create similar documents by using floating cells that contain the principal, interest rate, and number of payment periods, and yet another to calculate the amount of each payment. When you change the principal or the interest percentage and calculate the document, all the other cells automatically update quickly and easily.

TROUBLESHOOTING

PASTING UNFORMATTED TEXT

Sometimes when I paste text, it's not the right font.

When you copy text from another source, you also copy formatting codes. To paste unformatted text, choose Edit, Paste Special, and choose Unformatted.

INSTALLING ADDITIONAL CONVERSION FILTERS

I've got some old WordPerfect files that WordPerfect 9 can't seem to open. I really need these files.

By default, WordPerfect installs only a limited number of relatively modern conversion filters. You can access the WordPerfect Office 2000 installation CD-ROM and choose Add New Components to install the remaining sets of conversion filters. You may be surprised at how many formats WordPerfect converts—many more than any other current word processing program.

KEEPING DATA UP-TO-DATE

I imported information from a company database, but now someone updated the database and my document doesn't match.

Instead of importing a database that might change, choose Insert, Spreadsheet/Database, Link. That way, if the database changes, you need only update the link, not the whole database.

ADDING A FORMULA TO A FLOATING CELL

I can't seem to add a formula to a floating cell.

Open Reveal Codes and make sure the insertion point is positioned between the floating cell codes. Then you can use the Formula toolbar to create a floating cell formula.

IGNORING VALUES IN TEXT CELLS

I created an invoice using a table, but when I calculate the total due, it's always wrong. I checked the formulas and they're all correct.

Check to see if your formula includes a text cell, and whether that text cell contains any numbers. WordPerfect ignores text and uses the numeric value of a cell that contains both text and numbers. For example, if you're adding an entire column, and the top cell contain an invoice number, the value of the invoice number is added to the total of the column.

To avoid this problem, right-click the cell, choose F*o*rmat, and in the Cell tab of the Table Format dialog box, choose *I*gnore Cell When Calculating. Then recalculate the table, and the formula should now yield the correct result.

KEEPING FILES SMALL

Some of my documents are getting huge and taking up a lot of disk space. All I've done is drag some data into them from Excel.

This is a common problem with documents that contain OLE objects. For example, a WordPerfect document with a simple clip art object might be only 25KB in size, but if you edit the graphic in the Draw program, it becomes an OLE object and the document increases in size to over 100KB. If you open the OLE link (for example, double-clicking a clip art graphic image), you can delete the object and insert the clip art image again to eliminate the OLE link. The only other way to avoid this is to avoid using OLE, since this is a problem associated with the OLE technology, not with WordPerfect itself. You have to determine whether you want small files, or the convenience of editing objects in place in WordPerfect.

PROJECT

WordPerfect's built-in spreadsheet capabilities, along with the ability to import database data, enable you to create wonderfully powerful documents. Suppose, for example, you want to build an invoice that links to a company price list. As the prices change in the database and are updated in the price list, so too do the numbers in the invoice. Consider, for example, the invoice/price list shown in Figure 15.30, which is the result of a carefully set up database table and table formulas.

Note

For details on how to perform some of the tasks in these procedures, refer to the appropriate sections of this chapter.

Figure 15.30
You can combine a linked database of prices with a table and table math to create an automatically updated invoice.

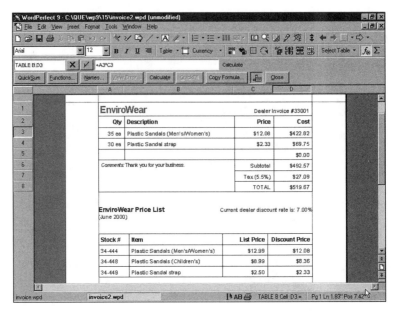

To create the invoice/price list document, begin by creating the price list:

1. Choose Insert, Spreadsheet/Database, Create Link. You want to link rather than import the data so that you can update the price list from the database as it changes.

2. In the Create Data Link dialog box, specify the database from which the information is drawn. Also, limit the fields you link to those you need for the price list (for example, Part Number, Description, and List Price). Click OK to create the linked database of prices.

3. Insert a fourth column to the right of the table and adjust the column widths as necessary. Use Format to right-align the last two columns, and use Numeric Format to have them display for currency.

4. Above the table, create a floating cell that indicates the dealer discount: Current dealer discount rate is:. Use Numeric Format to format the floating cell (7%) for percent.

Note

You must turn on the Formula toolbar to create the percentage as a formula in the floating cell and to create other formulas used in these procedures.

5. In the first Discount Price cell of the price list, create a formula that multiplies the floating cell (above the table) by the list price (to the left of the cell). Check to make sure the formula works correctly (for example, +FLOATING_CELL_A*C2).

6. Copy the formula all the way down the price list.

Now you're ready to create the table for the invoice (refer to Figure 15.30). Position the cursor at the very top of the document and insert a table with the structure and labels shown in Figure 15.31.

→ For information on creating and editing a table structure, **see** Chapter 10, "Organizing Information with Tables," **p. 251**

The table includes the following:

- Joined cells for the Invoice heading and for the comment box
- Right-aligned Columns A, C, and D.
- Numeric formatting for currency in Columns C and D.

Figure 15.31
You should create the structure, formatting, and labels of a table before adding the math formulas.

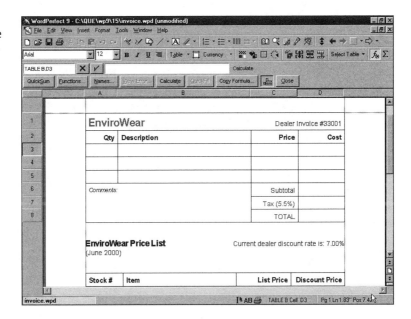

Next, create the table formulas that link the price list values to the invoice and calculate the charges, by following these steps:

1. Create a formula in the first blank cell in Column D (for example, D3) that multiplies the quantity times the Price (for example, A3*C3). WordPerfect displays the value $0.00 in D3.

2. With the insertion point in cell D3, copy the formula to match the number of rows that can contain an order item (for example, two times).

3. Click in the Subtotal cell of Column D and click QuickSum on the Formula toolbar. Again, WordPerfect displays $0.00.

4. Click the Tax cell of Column D and create a formula that multiples the subtotal times the tax in Column C (5.5%). Edit the formula to read D4*(-C5). Because WordPerfect interprets (5.5%) as *minus* 5.5%, you effectively change it to a positive value.

5. Finally, click the TOTAL cell of Column D, and create a formula to add the Subtotal and Tax cells from Column D.

Finally, you need to add information and prices from the price list. Follow these steps:

1. Copy product descriptions from the price list to the invoice (you can hold down Ctrl while dragging and dropping to copy, rather than move, the information).

2. Click in the cell in Column C, to the right of the description, and then click the Formula text box.

3. Click the cell in the price list that contains the discounted price. WordPerfect displays, for example, TABLE_A.D2 in the Formula text box.

4. Click the Accept button; or press Enter to place the formula/value in the invoice table.

Tip #184 from
Laura and Read

You could automate these steps by creating a macro that creates a new row in the Invoice table, copies the description to that row, and then creates a link from that row to the product list price. See Chapter 24, "Experts and Macros," for more information on recording and playing macros.

---

5. Repeat steps 1–4 for each product purchased.

6. Type the quantity ordered in Column A of the invoice (for example, 35 ea).

Note

WordPerfect ignores text in cells and uses the value of any numbers it finds.

---

7. Right-click the table and choose Calculate.

If all goes well, the correct values display in the appropriate cells (refer to Figure 15.30). If not, check your formulas to make sure they're created correctly.

Now, as you change the quantity ordered, the discount percentage, or the list price, and calculate again, the invoice updates automatically to give a correct total invoice.

Note

This chapter only begins to reveal the power of WordPerfect's table/spreadsheet capabilities. If you already know about spreadsheets, you'll quickly discover how to perform similar functions in WordPerfect. If you're new to spreadsheets, experiment with tables and formulas and you'll soon learn just what WordPerfect can do.

CHAPTER 16

INSERTING CHARTS

In this chapter

CREATING DATA CHARTS

WordPerfect communicates words effectively, and WordPerfect tables present numbers well. But numbers and words are often more effective when accompanied by charts that present information graphically.

WordPerfect's data chart feature can convert otherwise boring or unintelligible figures into bar charts, pie charts, and more. You can even link charts to tables of data right in WordPerfect.

To create a chart in WordPerfect, choose Insert, Chart. WordPerfect opens a chart editing window and a datasheet filled with sample data, along with the editing tools from the Presentations chart program (see Figure 16.1). A *datasheet* is a small spreadsheet.

Figure 16.1
When you create a chart, WordPerfect first displays a bar chart, complete with sample data.

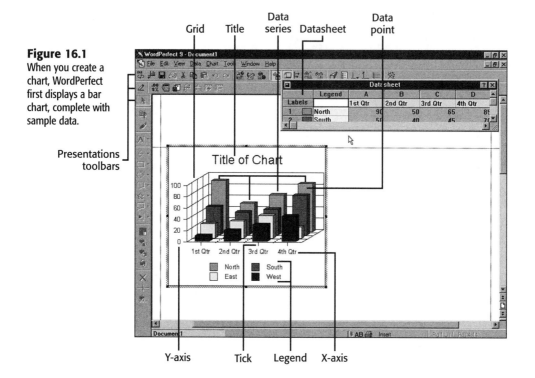

ENTERING DATA IN DATASHEETS

The foundation for any chart is a series of numbers, and labels to identify those numbers (refer to the datasheet in Figure 16.1). Often, you create such numbers in a spreadsheet, and you can then import that data into the WordPerfect chart. You can also create the numbers in a WordPerfect table, and create the chart based on the table data. Finally, you can enter the numbers directly in the chart's datasheet.

If you use the datasheet for chart numbers, consider the following (see Figure 16.2):

- You can drag and size the datasheet to display a larger spreadsheet-like area.
- The legend identifies rows, or *series* of data—for example, the figures for the North, South, East, or West regions.
- Each series (that is, row) is represented by a color, along with the legend name.
- The labels refer to columns of data—for example, 1st Quarter, 2nd Quarter, and so on.
- Labels appear horizontally along the *X-axis* of the chart.
- The values of labels (sometimes broken down by series) are matched with numbers that appear vertically along the *Y-axis* of the chart.

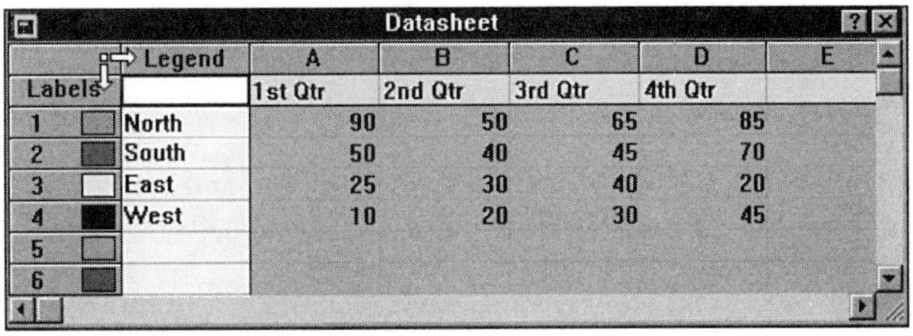

Figure 16.2
You can use the datasheet to prepare the underlying data for a chart.

	Legend	A	B	C	D	E
Labels		1st Qtr	2nd Qtr	3rd Qtr	4th Qtr	
1	North	90	50	65	85	
2	South	50	40	45	70	
3	East	25	30	40	20	
4	West	10	20	30	45	
5						
6						

You edit labels and data the same way you do in a Quattro Pro spreadsheet. For example, you can click a cell and type replacement data. You can also select entire rows or columns by clicking the row or column indicator, and you can drag, size, copy, or delete the selected data. As you enter each number, WordPerfect automatically updates the chart to reflect the new number.

If you want to start from scratch, choose Edit, Clear All, and then click Yes when asked if you want to clear all the data. You can also click the upper-left cell (refer to Figure 16.2, where the pointer displays both the row and column select arrows), then press Delete. When prompted, you can choose to clear Data (the default), Format, or Both. Click OK to clear the data.

The chart editor in Presentations also enables you to use several menu options, along with corresponding toolbar buttons to assist in editing the datasheet. Choose Data to access the following options:

- Format—You can change the numeric formatting of selected cells (for example, to display currency or percentage). These changes appear in the chart only if you use data labels.
- Column Width—You can change the width of columns in the datasheet.
- Formulas—You can create formulas in the datasheet, by using the Row/Column Formulas dialog box (see Figure 16.3), but you do not have nearly the power nor flexibility you have in a spreadsheet or even in a WordPerfect table. If you plan to use

complex formulas, you should create the data in a spreadsheet or table, and then import the data (see the section "Importing Data into Datasheets," later in this chapter).

Figure 16.3
The Rows/Columns Formula dialog box enables you to create simple formulas in the datasheet.

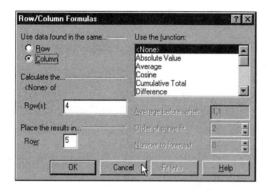

■ Recalculate—If you use formulas in the datasheet, and later change the data, you should recalculate the datasheet to make sure you have the correct results.

■ Sort—Select an area of data and sort it top to bottom, or left to right, in ascending or descending order.

Caution

You sort only that which you've selected. If you select only the legend text, for example, you sort only the text but not the data on the rows represented by the legend. You then have data that does not match the legends or labels.

To sort entire rows, including the legends and the data, click on the row indicators, and drag to select all the rows you want to sort. To sort entire columns, including data labels, click the column indicators and click and drag to select the columns you want.

If you sort your data incorrectly, but now can't get the original, correct data back, see "Saving It Anytime" in the Troubleshooting section at the end of this chapter.

■ Exclude Row/Column—If you don't want a certain row or column to appear in the chart, select the row or column and click this button. WordPerfect also partially hides the data in the datasheet (the numbers and text appear in light gray).

■ Include Row/Column—If you want use a row or column that you've excluded, select that row or column and click this option. The data also reappears in the datasheet.

■ Range Highlighter—This option, on the View menu, lets you change the background colors in the rows and columns of the datasheet. It does not change the colors used to represent data in the chart itself.

To return to your WordPerfect document, click the document. The datasheet and Presentations tools disappear, leaving the data chart in a graphics box. Click the document again to deselect the data chart graphics box.

To edit the data chart, double-click it to return to the chart editor.

 If the chart doesn't look as good as it did while you were editing it, see "Don't Worry, Just Print It" in the Troubleshooting section at the end of this chapter.

IMPORTING DATA INTO DATASHEETS

Often the data you need for a chart already exists in a spreadsheet. You can import that data or link it to the chart. To import data from a spreadsheet, follow these steps:

 1. Choose Data, Import, or click the Import button on the toolbar. WordPerfect displays the Import Data dialog box (see Figure 16.4).

Figure 16.4
You can use the Import Data dialog box to import chart information from a spreadsheet.

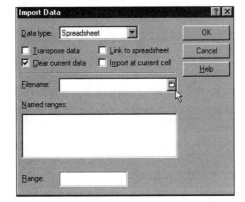

2. Choose the Data Type. Typically, you import data from a spreadsheet, but you can also import numbers from ASCII or ANSI delimited text.

3. Specify a Filename. If you browse for a file, by default WordPerfect searches for Quattro Pro spreadsheets. You can, however, import from Lotus, PlanPerfect, or Excel, or from spreadsheet programs that can save data in those formats.

4. Select a range from the Named Ranges box. You can also select a specific range in the Range box.

Tip #185 from
Laura and Read

If you prepare a spreadsheet that is to be used in a WordPerfect document, it helps to name *ranges*, or small sections of the spreadsheet, to facilitate importing it into a chart or table.

---

5. Choose from the following options:
   - Transpose Data—Typically, the heads of columns in a spreadsheet become the labels (the X-axis). To make the rows of a spreadsheet the X-axis, you transpose the data (that is, rows become columns, and columns become rows).

- **C**lear Current Data—You can merge spreadsheet data with what's already in the datasheet, but typically, you need to clear the data first.

- **L**ink to Spreadsheet—Choose this option to link the spreadsheet and the chart so that changes to the spreadsheet also appear in the chart.

- I**m**port at Current Cell—Unless you choose this option, WordPerfect imports the spreadsheet data to the upper-left cell of the datasheet.

Caution

Be sure to include the row and column headings in the range you import from the spreadsheet. Otherwise, spreadsheet numbers appear in the place of labels and legends. If you don't have text labels in the spreadsheet, you can avoid this problem by positioning the cursor in cell A1 of the datasheet and using the Import at Current Cell option. You then must add the legend and labels by hand.

Tip #186 from
Laura and Read

When you import data from a spreadsheet, it often includes rows or columns that you really don't want to include in the chart. In the datasheet, select those rows or columns and choose **D**ata, **E**xclude to hide them and to exclude them from the chart.

CREATING A CHART BASED ON A TABLE

You can create a data chart using information you create in a WordPerfect table. This way, not only do you present the graphic illustration of the data, but you also present the data itself in case the reader wants to examine it more closely (see Figure 16.5). An added benefit is that changes you make to the table update quickly and easily in the data chart.

Figure 16.5
If you base a chart on a WordPerfect table, the reader can refer to both in the document.

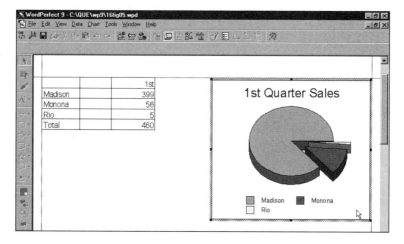

To create a data chart based on a WordPerfect table, follow these steps:

1. Create the table first. Make sure it includes the numeric information you want, and also text labels (column headings) and legend/series (row headings).

2. If you intend to include the entire table in the chart, go to the next step. Otherwise, select those cells you want to include.

3. Choose Insert, Chart.

WordPerfect opens the chart editing window and a chart that uses the table data (refer to Figure 16.5). No datasheet is necessary because the table serves that purpose.

To update a chart based on changes you make to its table, click the table, and choose Table, Calculate. WordPerfect recalculates any table formulas that need to be updated, and also updates the chart with the new data.

→ If you're not familiar with WordPerfect's table math capabilities and want to learn how to use this powerful feature, **see** Chapter 15, "Importing Data and Working with Other Programs," **p. 403**

CHOOSING CHART TYPES

The type of data you use and how you want to present it determine what kind of chart you use. By default, WordPerfect opens a three-dimensional bar chart. To see the wide variety of chart types available after opening a chart editing window, choose Chart, Gallery. WordPerfect displays the Data Chart Gallery (see Figure 16.6) dialog box, where you can choose from among 11 types of charts, and several styles for each:

■ Area—These are like line charts, but are filled in from the line down to the X-axis (see Figure 16.7).

Figure 16.6
The Data Chart Gallery dialog box displays several styles for 11 different chart types.

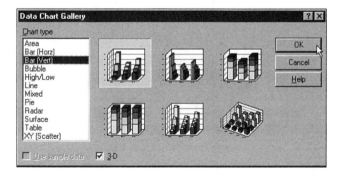

Note

If you click the Data Chart Gallery button on the toolbar, the palette presents only a limited number of gallery types.

Figure 16.7
An area chart is like a line chart, with everything filled in between the X-axis and the data line.

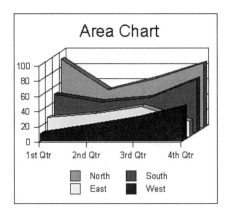

Charts by Example
If you insert a new chart and change the chart type before adding data, WordPerfect changes the datasheet to show you, by example, what kind of data you need for each type of chart. You can also click Help in the Data Chart Gallery dialog box to access WordPerfect's online help, which shows examples of each chart type and describes in more detail how and when you typically use each type.

- Bar (Horizontal/Vertical)—Each data point is represented by a bar in this commonly used type of chart. Vertical bar charts plot values against the Y-axis, and horizontal charts plot against the X-axis. Bar charts work best when they represent relatively small amounts of comparative data. Otherwise, they can be confusing to the reader.

- Bubble—This type chart is used to plot three different values on two axes (see Figure 16.8). For example, you can plot units sold, gross profit, and net profit.

Figure 16.8
A bubble chart can plot three different values on two axes.

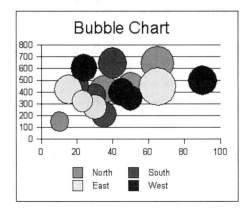

- High/Low—Often used to show stock market fluctuations, the high/low chart plots four values: the value at the beginning of a specified time period, the value at the end of the period, and the spread between the highest and lowest points at any time during the period (see Figure 16.9).

Figure 16.9
A high/low chart is often used to show stock market fluctuations.

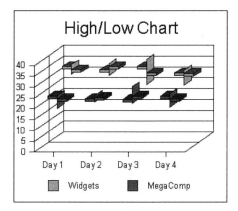

■ Line—This type of chart is excellent for showing trends, even with large numbers of data points (see Figure 16.10). For example, attendance over a one-month period, with 30 data points, is easier to visualize with a line chart than with a bar chart.

Figure 16.10
A line chart makes trends over a period of time easy to understand.

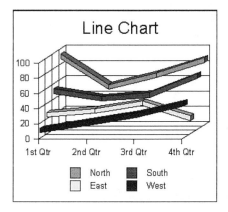

■ Pie—Pies, by definition, are whole (1, 100%, and so on). The pie slices represent fractions of the whole. You can use up to nine slices in a single chart (see Figure 16.11).

■ Radar—This type chart enables you to compare the relative strength of several data points. For example, you can plot team statistics in several categories (see Figure 16.12), and easily see how each team compares.

■ Surface—This type chart represents data values as a topography that bulges and dips like the contours of a landscape (see Figure 16.13). The color of the topography changes as the surface rises and falls. For example, you can use a surface chart to show business profits and losses as the peaks and valleys of a mountain range.

Figure 16.11
A pie chart represents parts of a whole (100%).

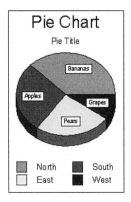

Figure 16.12
A radar chart compares the relative strength of several data points.

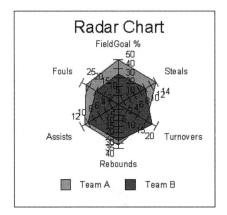

Figure 16.13
A surface chart shows peaks and valleys topographically.

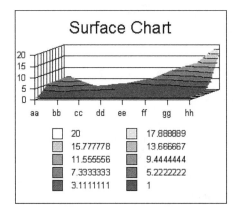

■ Table—Although this appears to be just a fancy table, cells of the table can also reflect the values they contain by their shading (see Figure 16.14).

Figure 16.14
A table chart shows table cells highlighted according to the values they contain.

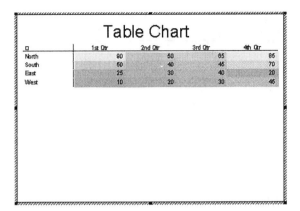

PART

V

CH

16

■ XY Scatter—This type of chart is unique in that the top row of the datasheet contains values, not text labels (see Figure 16.15). The data points in the chart represent the relationship between the data in the series and the data in the top row of the table that appears on the X-axis.

Figure 16.15
An XY scatter chart shows the relationship between the series data and the X-axis values.

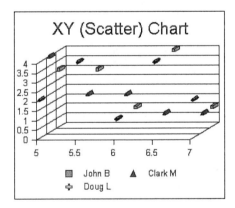

■ Mixed—Sometimes part of the data you want to show works best in a line chart, but another part is more understandable when represented by an area or bar chart (see Figure 16.16). You can use a mixed chart in this situation.

Figure 16.16
You can mix different chart types–such as bar, line, and area charts–within the same chart.

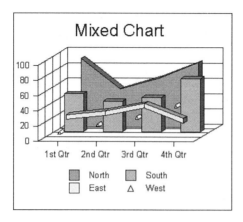

CHANGING CHART LAYOUT

You can further modify chart types by changing their layout. For example, you can choose to display the chart in a flat two-dimensional layout, or give it some depth by adding a three-dimensional layout.

 Each chart type can be modified, albeit some more than others. Consider, for example, the bar chart type, which is a typical example of available layout options. To modify a chart layout, choose Chart, Layout/Type, or click the Layout button on the toolbar. WordPerfect displays the Layout/Type Properties dialog box (see Figure 16.17).

Figure 16.17
Use the Layout/Type Properties dialog box to choose chart layout options.

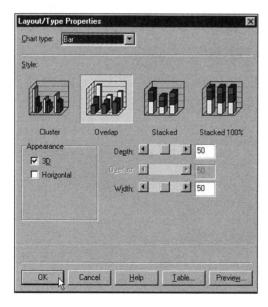

Among the layout choices for bar charts are the following:

- Cluster—Series bars are grouped beside each other.
- Overlap—Series bars are grouped, overlapping each other.
- Stacked—Series bars are stacked one on top of the other, with the height of the bar determined by the cumulative value of each bar.
- Stacked 100%—This option displays all the datapoints in a column as parts of the whole, just like a pie chart does. For example, 50 and 50 display at exactly the same height as do 33 and 33.

Other options include 3-D (including depth of the bar), no 3-D (including amount of overlap), width of the bars, and horizontal orientation.

PART

V

CH

16

Tip #187 from
Laura and Read

Although 3-D charts look nifty, a plain 2-D chart can sometimes be more effective in communicating the information in the chart. Sometimes less is more.

The layout options for pie charts, another commonly used chart type, are shown in Figure 16.18.

Figure 16.18
Options for changing pie charts are quite different from typical bar chart options.

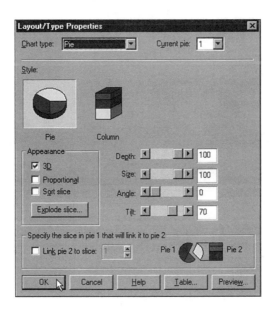

These include the following:

- Column—This is a stacked 100% bar chart.

- Proportional—If you have more than one pie chart (remember, you can have up to nine pie charts), this option enables each to be smaller or larger, depending on the total value of the parts of the pie.

- Sort Slice—Choosing this option arranges the slices of the pie in descending value, beginning at the 3 o'clock mark, and continuing counterclockwise around the pie.

- Explode Slice—If you want a slice to separate from the pie for emphasis, use this option. You can explode one or more slices from the pie (see Figure 16.19).

Tip #188 from
Laura and Read

The easiest way to explode a slice from a pie chart is simply to click the pie slice in the chart editor and drag it away from the pie.

- Link Pie 2 to Slice—This option, illustrated in Figure 16.19, enables you to show how a second pie represents a single slice in the first pie.

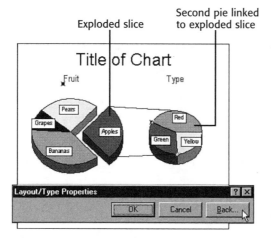

Figure 16.19
You can link a second pie to represent the details of a single slice in the first pie.

- Depth—This measures the thickness of the pie (like the thickness of a coin), with 100 the thickest and 0 the thinnest.

- Size—This number is the percentage of the size of the other pie (for example, you can set Pie 2 at 50% the size of Pie 1).

- Angle—This refers to the location, clockwise, of the beginning of the first slice in the pie. By default, the first slice starts at the 3 o'clock position.

- Tilt—In addition to 3-D depth, you can also modify the tilt of the pie. You can even tilt each pie differently.

Most of the other chart types include layout options similar to those described for bar and pie charts. If you're not sure what an option does, try it, and then click Preview to see the effect on the chart. WordPerfect then displays a minimized Layout/Type Properties dialog box (refer to Figure 16.19). Click OK to accept the changes, or Back to return to the full dialog box to make further changes.

ADDING TITLES

After you complete the data in the datasheet and select a chart type and layout, you're ready to begin modifying the various chart elements that enhance the reader's comprehension of what the chart represents.

You can probably focus better on the chart if you hide the datasheet. Choose View, Datasheet to toggle the datasheet off, or click the View Datasheet button on the toolbar.

To change the title of the chart, choose Chart, Title, or double-click the title. WordPerfect displays the Title Properties dialog box (see Figure 16.20).

Figure 16.20
You can create or edit the title in the Title Properties dialog box.

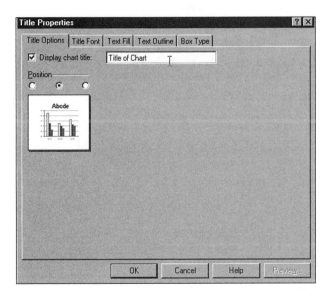

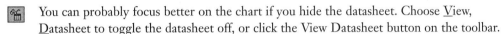

Tip #189 from
Laura and Read

The easiest way to access the dialog boxes and options for modifying chart elements is simply to double-click the element you want to change. When you get used to this, you'll rarely use menus or buttons to change chart elements.

The Title Options tab enables you to edit the title in the Display Chart Title text box. If you uncheck that option, the chart displays no title. Finally, you can also specify whether to display the title at the left, center, or right of the chart.

Tip #190 from
Laura and Read

You can drag the title box anywhere you want in the chart editing screen. However, if you want to return the title to its original position, right-click the title and choose <u>R</u>eset Text.

To change the look of the title, use the Title Font, Text Fill, and Text Outline tabs, each of which enable you to modify the text in attractive and interesting ways. For example, you can change the font, size, and color, modify the type of fill pattern used (including gradient shading), and add a line around the outside edge of each character (an outline line).

→ For more information on modifying text using Presentations, **see** Chapter 14, "Adding Drawings and TextArt," **p. 373**

Finally, you can add a box border around the title by choosing a style from the Box Type tab (see Figure 16.21). If you choose a box style, WordPerfect gives you one more tab on the Title Properties dialog box for modifying the fill used with the title box.

Figure 16.21
You can add a border to a title on the Box Type tab of the Title Properties dialog box.

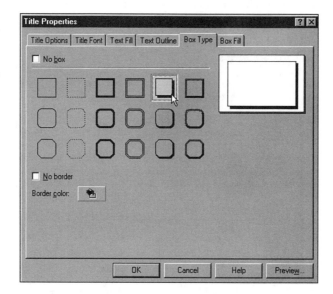

ADDING AND MODIFYING LEGENDS

 Legends help readers quickly identify what various elements on a chart represent. To add or modify a legend, choose <u>C</u>hart, Le<u>g</u>end, or click the Legend button on the toolbar. WordPerfect displays the Legend Properties dialog box (see Figure 16.22).

On the Type/Position tab of this dialog box you can use the following options:

- <u>L</u>egend Type—The elements of the legend can be arranged vertically or horizontally.

- <u>P</u>osition—Click one of the buttons around the edge of the preview box to select a position for the legend.

- Display Legend—If you don't want a legend—for example, if you need more room for the chart itself—uncheck this option.

- Place Legend Inside Chart—If you need more room for the chart, and there's an unused area inside the chart, use this option in combination with the Position option to place the legend inside the chart.

- Display Legend Title—Most people recognize a legend when they see one, but if you want to make sure, or if you want to call it something else, choose this option and change the legend title.

Figure 16.22
You can modify the chart legend by using the Legend Properties dialog box.

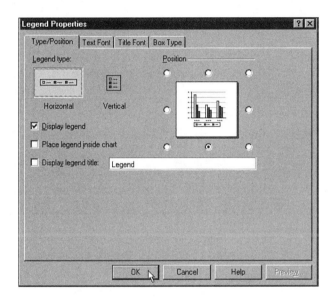

The other tabs in this dialog box enable you to change the font of the legend labels or the font of the legend title, or to add a box around the entire legend. Figure 16.23 shows a legend surrounded by a box, vertically arranged at the left of the data chart.

Figure 16.23
Legends, which you can place on any side of a chart, help readers identify the different series of data in a chart.

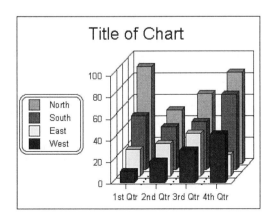

MODIFYING X- AND Y-AXIS LABELS AND PROPERTIES

The X- and Y-axis options vary depending on whether they represent column headings (labels) or values. To discover the options for an X-axis that represents column headings, choose <u>C</u>hart, <u>A</u>xis, <u>X</u>. WordPerfect displays the X-Axis Properties dialog box (see Figure 16.24).

Figure 16.24
You can modify X-axis options with the X-Axis Properties dialog box.

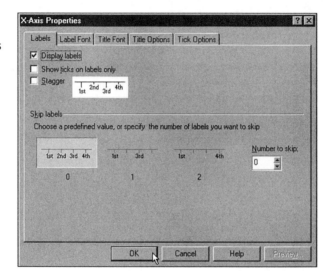

The Labels tab enables you to control how labels are displayed. Often labels contain more text than conveniently fits in the small amount of space available. The options on this tab include the following:

- Displa<u>y</u> Labels—You can, of course, choose not to display the labels at all. This isn't usually a real choice if you want your readers to know what the data relates to.

- Show <u>T</u>icks on Labels Only—If you skip labels, you then can specify whether you still want to show the tick marks.

- <u>S</u>tagger—You can stagger the labels so odd labels appear at one vertical position, and even labels appear at another.

- S<u>k</u>ip Labels—You can choose predefined values (for example, skip all even labels), or specify how many to skip (for example, skip 3 to display every fourth label).

You can use the Label Font tab to change the font of the labels (column headings) or the title of the X-axis.

The Title Options tab (see Figure 16.25) enables you to add a title to the Display <u>T</u>itle box, and to display it. You can also display the title horizontally or vertically. Displaying the title vertically requires a brief title (for example, one word), and even then, this option takes up so much space that it forces the data chart to shrink dramatically.

Figure 16.25
You can use the Title Options tab of the X-Axis Properties dialog box to add a title to the X-axis.

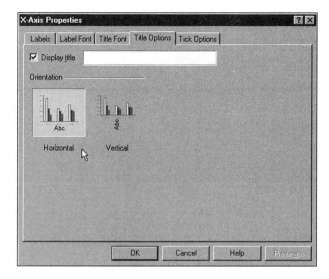

The Tick Options tab (see Figure 16.26) enables you to display major and minor tick marks, pointing away from the chart (out), or into the chart. Major tick marks correspond to the X-axis labels, and minor tick marks separate these major chart elements.

Figure 16.26
Tick marks help the reader associate labels or data values with the data in the chart.

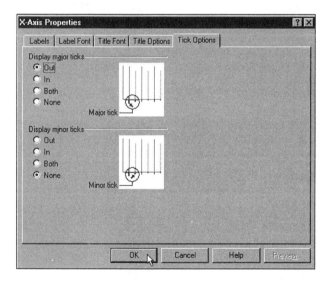

To discover the options for a Y-axis that represents numeric values, choose Chart, Axis, Primary Y. WordPerfect displays the Primary Y Axis Properties dialog box (see Figure 16.27). Font, title, and tick options are identical to those found on the X-Axis Properties dialog box.

Figure 16.27
You can use the Primary Y Axis Properties dialog box to establish how values display.

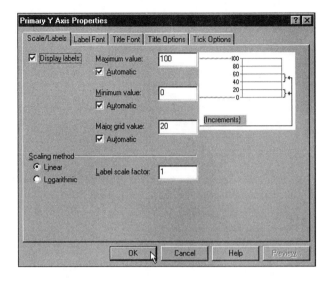

The Scale/Labels tab of this dialog box enables you to specify what values to display. Typically you use linear scaling, which enables you to set a maximum value, a minimum value, and the major grid value, which is the amount of increment between the numbers.

Tip #191 from
Laura and Read

If all the values are relatively high, you can distinguish the data points better by setting a higher minimum value. For example, showing the range from 80 to 100, instead of 0 to 100, makes it easier to tell the difference between a data point that represents 95 and one that represents 92.

Note

The options for X- and Y-axes are similar for all the data chart types except pie charts, which don't have a Y-axis, and table charts, which enable you to change the properties for table cells based on the values they contain.

EDITING SERIES ELEMENTS

A *series* represents all the data points in a row of the datasheet. Each series has its own color, shape, and style. To modify the properties of a series, choose Chart, Series or click the Series button on the toolbar. WordPerfect displays the Series Properties dialog box (see Figure 16.28). You can select the series you want to change by clicking the forward or back buttons at the left of the Series box.

If you're having trouble printing your chart so you can distinguish the different series, see "Printing Contrasting Series in Charts" in the Troubleshooting section at the end of this chapter.

Figure 16.28
You can modify how series of data are displayed in the Series Properties dialog box.

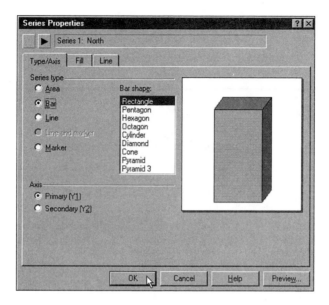

Series types, found on the Type/Axis tab of the Series Properties dialog box, include the following:

- Area—The data is represented as an area chart, the data points connected, and the area filled in, down to the X-axis.

- Bar—Several bar shapes are available, including cylinders, cones, pyramids, and so on. Even in 2-D layouts, many of these shapes use gradient shading to simulate dimension.

- Line—Only one option is available: a line that connects data points in a series. However, you can use the Line tab of this dialog box to change the thickness, style, and color of the line.

- Line and Marker—This option is not available if the chart is 3-D. You use markers to highlight the data points in a line chart.

- Marker—When used with lines, markers of different shapes and sizes can effectively distinguish between series. For example, for one series you might use a star, and for another, a triangle. You can also specify the size of the marker.

You can also choose to plot a series against a secondary Y-axis. In some charts, one series might be so different in value from the rest of the series that the differences in its data points are barely discernible. To remedy that, you can plot the series against a second Y-axis, scaled for the values in the series, which appears at the right of the chart. Select the series, and choose Secondary (Y2). The chart shown in Figure 16.29 shows the result of applying different series types, with one series (the markers) plotted against a secondary Y-axis.

Figure 16.29
You can use a secondary Y-axis to set off series of two markedly different values.

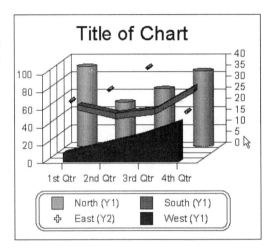

Finally, you can use the Fill and Line tabs of the Series Properties dialog box to modify the color, fill style, and lines of any of the series shapes.

Tip #192 from
Laura and Read

If you single-click a series on the chart or the legend, you can use the Presentations toolbar at the left of the screen to choose fill style, colors, and lines.

MODIFYING OTHER CHART ELEMENTS

If you haven't already found enough options for modifying your chart, here are a few more (see Figure 16.30, which shows several of the following options).

Figure 16.30
You can modify the frame and grid that surround a chart. Be careful that things don't get too cluttered!

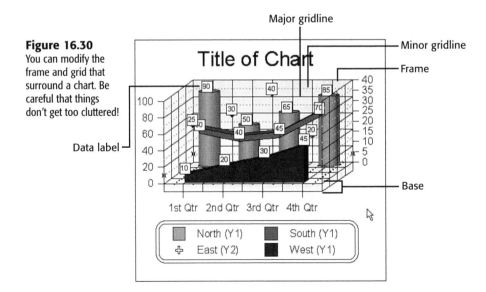

The following chart elements can easily be modified:

- Grids—Grids help the reader quickly associate values displayed on the Y-axis with data points in the chart. To modify a chart's grids, choose <u>C</u>hart, <u>G</u>rids, or click the Grids button on the toolbar to access the Grid Properties dialog box. You can choose whether you want to display horizontal or vertical grid lines, what style and color you want to use, and how many major and minor gridlines to use. Major gridlines usually have labels or values associated with them, and minor gridlines further subdivide the values of the major gridlines.

PART

V

CH

16

Tip #193 from	Don't forget that you can change the elements of a chart most quickly by double-clicking
Laura and Read	the element to display its properties dialog box.

- Frames—Gridlines are contained inside a chart frame, which is like a border to the chart. To modify the chart frame, choose <u>C</u>hart, <u>F</u>rame. You can choose which sides the grids should appear on (for example, left, back, front, bottom, and so on), what line style and color you want, and whether to include a base.

- Data labels—Typically you display labels only on the X- and Y-axes. However, you can also display the values of data points by using data labels. Choose <u>C</u>hart, Data La<u>b</u>els to display the Data Labels dialog box, where you can choose the position (outside or inside series element) and the font and box style used to display the labels.

Caution

If you click the Labels button on the toolbar, you display all labels, which usually adds only data labels to the chart because axis labels are typically already displayed. However, if you click the button again, you turn off all these labels, not just the data labels.

- Perspective—In 3-D charts only, you can change the horizontal and vertical angles of the chart to change the chart's perspective. This sometimes helps make data more visible. To change perspective, choose <u>C</u>hart, <u>P</u>erspective, and make changes in the Perspective dialog box.

- Base—The platform on which the 3-D chart sits is called the *base*. You can change its height in the Frame Properties dialog box.

CREATING ORGANIZATION CHARTS

Organization charts (usually called *org charts*) visually show relationships between various persons in an organization. The Draw program (based on Presentations) enables you to create and modify org charts, which then appear as graphics boxes within your WordPerfect document.

To create an org chart, choose <u>I</u>nsert, <u>G</u>raphics, <u>D</u>raw Picture. This opens up the Presentations/Draw editing screen, complete with Presentations toolbar.

Next choose Insert, Organization Chart. The mouse pointer turns to a hand. You can click and drag the area of the editor you want to use for the org chart, or simply single-click the editing screen to use the entire editing area.

WordPerfect next displays the Layout dialog box (see Figure 16.31), where you choose an initial organization structure. Click the structure you want (the default is Single, Top Down) and click OK. If you're not sure which layout to use, select the default, which you can change later.

Figure 16.31
You must choose a layout for your org chart before you can proceed.

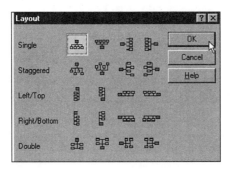

WordPerfect Draw places a basic org chart in the editing screen, and toolbar and Property Bar buttons appear to aid in modifying the chart (see Figure 16.32).

CHOOSING AN ORG CHART LAYOUT

Layout refers to the relationship and orientation of the boxes that represent persons in the organization. If you decide to change the layout you selected when you created the chart, follow these steps:

1. Choose Edit, Select All to select the entire org chart.

2. Choose Format, Branch Structure to access the Branch Layout dialog box (see Figure 16.33).

3. Make changes as follow:
   - The Structure tab offers options that refer to how boxes at the same organizational level are laid out. The more boxes you have at the same level, the smaller they become. Staggering the boxes, or arranging them vertically instead of horizontally, may allow them to take up less space, and thereby become larger.

- The Orientation tab of the Branch Layout dialog box enables you to make the org chart progress from left to right, right to left, top to bottom, or bottom to top.

Figure 16.32
You can use Presentations tools to create or modify an org chart.

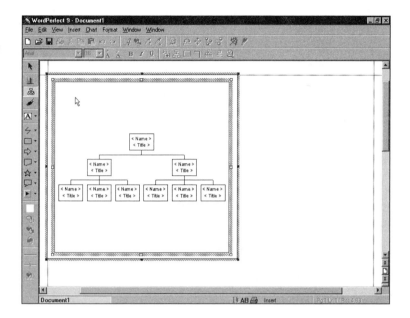

Figure 16.33
You can change the layout or structure of an org chart by using the Branch Layout dialog box.

If changes you make don't affect what you expect them to, see "Modifying an Entire Branch" in the Troubleshooting section at the end of this chapter.

ADDING AND REMOVING SUBORDINATES AND COWORKERS

The real work in developing the org chart comes in establishing relationships between various persons by adding, removing, and relocating boxes in the chart. Whether you organize the boxes first or fill in names and titles first doesn't really make much difference. Eventually you must do both.

To delete an individual, click the box and press Delete.

To add an individual, click a box near where you want to add the person. Then, depending of the type of box you want to add, choose one of these options:

- Manager—To insert a box above the currently selected box, choose Insert, Manager. WordPerfect inserts one box as the supervisor or manager.

- Coworker—To add a person at the same organizational level as the currently selected person, choose Insert, Coworkers. WordPerfect displays the Insert Coworkers dialog box (see Figure 16.34). You can choose how many coworkers to insert and whether they should go to the right or the left of the currently selected box.

Figure 16.34
You can use the Insert Coworkers dialog box to add persons at the same level.

- Subordinate—To add a subordinate to the currently selected person, choose Insert, Subordinates. The Subordinates dialog box enables you to specify how many boxes to add.

- Staff—A staff person is not part of the line authority of an organization. Thus the relationship is shown with a dotted line, and the staff person is shown off to the side and beneath his or her supervisor (see Figure 16.35). To add a staff person, click the supervisor's box, and then choose Insert, Staff. In the Insert Staff dialog box, indicate the number of staff members to insert and click OK.

You can also rearrange the boxes by clicking and dragging them to new locations, using these options:

- To move a person to a different manager, drag the box to the manager's box so that the box being dragged displays a downward-pointing arrow (see Figure 16.36). When you release the mouse button, the box is added at the end of the list of coworkers beneath that manager.

Figure 16.35
Staff boxes are connected with dotted lines, off to the side of the chart.

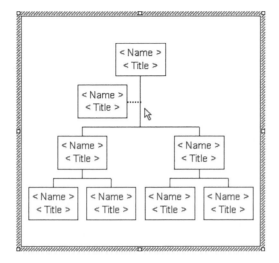

Figure 16.36
You can move a worker by dragging the person's box to a new manager's box.

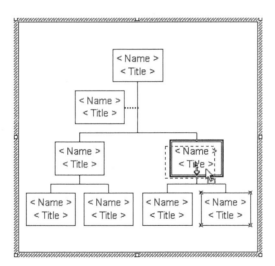

Caution

When you delete or move a box, you really are moving the position in the organization, not just the person. Thus, moving a box also moves the entire branch beneath the box. If you want to move just the person—for example, because he or she took a new job and his or her position will be filled by someone else—delete the person's name from the box and add it to another box at a new location.

- To change the position of a coworker, drag the box to another coworker's box until a right- or left-pointing arrow is displayed (see Figure 16.37). Release the mouse button to place the person at the left or the right of the coworker.

Figure 16.37
To rearrange the order of coworkers, drag a worker's box to another box until a horizontal arrow appears.

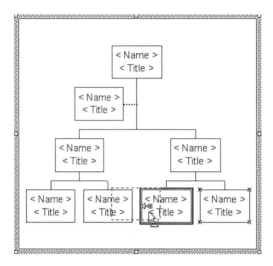

- You can copy a box by holding down the Ctrl key while clicking and dragging the box to a new location. This is a great way to add new employees to the chart.

ADDING AND MODIFYING ORG CHART BOX CONTENT

At some point you have to enter names or titles in the boxes. But you also have several options when it comes to adding org chart information.

Org charts tend to be hierarchical, very much like the organization of a WordPerfect outline. You can create a WordPerfect outline of your organization, and then import the outline to create the org chart.

→ For information on creating WordPerfect outlines, **see** Chapter 11, "Organizing Information with Lists and Outlines," **p. 289**

To import a WordPerfect outline as an org chart, follow these steps:

1. Create and save a WordPerfect outline, making the organization correspond to outline levels (see Figure 16.38).

2. Create an org chart in WordPerfect, choosing any standard layout that is likely to match up well with your outline. At this point you should be in the Draw/Presentations screen, with the default sample layout in the editing window.

3. Choose C̲hart, I̲mport Outline, and in the Insert Text dialog box, find the outline you created and saved in WordPerfect.

4. Click Insert, and WordPerfect imports the outline, replacing the sample org chart with one that matches your outline (see Figure 16.39).

Figure 16.38
You can create a WordPerfect outline of your organization, and then import the outline into an org chart.

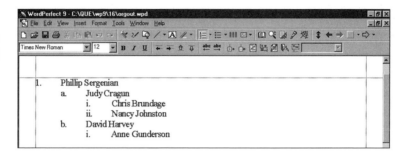

Figure 16.39
An imported outline quickly customizes an org chart.

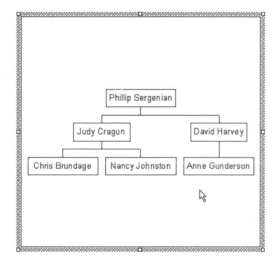

That's it! You now can edit the text in the boxes, or reorganize the boxes and relationships.

Tip #195 from
Laura and Read

After you edit an org chart, you can also export the data of the chart to a WordPerfect outline, by choosing Chart, Export.

You can, of course, add text directly to org chart boxes. To do so, double-click a box, and WordPerfect enlarges the box and displays a cursor inside it (see Figure 16.40). Type the person's name, and then press Tab to advance to the next field (Title) in the box. You can also click elsewhere in the org chart to close this box.

Figure 16.40
You can press Tab to move from field to field, and to add or edit org chart text.

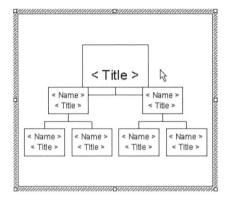

> **Note**
>
> If you don't replace the field code (for example, <Title>), the final org chart displays nothing for that field.

If you don't need the additional title field, or if you want to add other fields for each box, follow these steps:

1. Select the box or branch of boxes you want to change. To select a branch, click the top box in the branch, and then choose Edit, Select, Branch. To select all the boxes in the org chart, choose Edit, Select All.

2. Choose Format, Box Fields. WordPerfect displays the Box Fields dialog box (see Figure 16.41).

Figure 16.41
You can add or remove data entry fields for org chart boxes in the Box Fields dialog box.

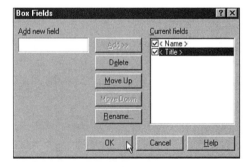

3. To remove a field for the selected boxes, uncheck the box next to it in the Current Fields box. If you don't need the field at all, you can Delete the field.

4. To add a different field, type a name for the field in the Add New Field box and click the Add>> button.

5. You can change a field by selecting it and clicking <u>R</u>ename, <u>M</u>ove Up or M<u>o</u>ve Down (for example, to display the title above the name).

6. Click OK to accept your choices and to display the new fields in your org chart boxes.

CHANGING ORG CHART STYLES

The structure and content of the org chart are your primary concern, just like the content of WordPerfect documents comes first. However, just as you do with a WordPerfect document, you can also make your org charts look good.

To modify an org chart box, follow these steps:

1. Select the box or boxes you want to modify.

2. Choose Fo<u>r</u>mat, Box <u>P</u>roperties, or right-click the box and choose Box <u>P</u>roperties from the QuickMenu. WordPerfect displays the Box Properties dialog box (see Figure 16.42).

PART

V

CH

16

Figure 16.42
You can modify the style of org chart boxes by using the Box Properties dialog box.

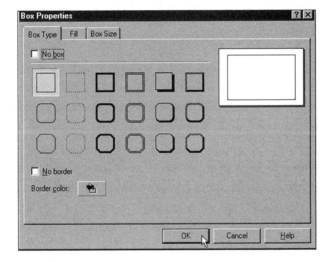

3. On the Box Type tab, click the style you want to use. You can also change the border color.

4. On the Fill tab, change the fill pattern (including gradient shading) and color.

5. The Box Size tab (see Figure 16.43) enables you to adjust the size of the org chart's boxes. By default, boxes automatically adjust so that they become smaller as more boxes and text are placed at the same level. You can specify that boxes adjust instead to the largest size in the branch or the entire org chart. You can also force text to adjust its size to fit the box. If you manually adjust the box size, you can make boxes that are larger than those sized automatically. Note that you can reset the size options and start over again without having to cancel all your Box Properties dialog box choices.

Figure 16.43
You can change the
org chart's box sizes
by using the Box Size
tab of the Box
Properties dialog box.

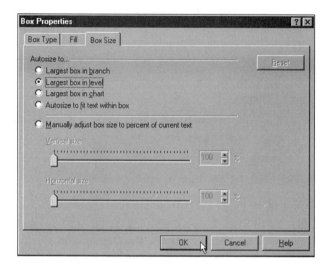

6. Click OK to apply the properties to the selected boxes.

One nifty formatting feature is the ability to pick up the attributes from one box and drop them onto another box.

To pick up box attributes, click the box to select it, and then choose Format, Get Attributes or click the Get Attributes button on the toolbar.

To drop box attributes on another box, select the box or boxes you want to modify and choose Format, Apply Attributes or click the Apply Attributes button on the toolbar.

You can also modify connectors between boxes in the org chart. Select the branches you want to change (or select the whole org chart, if you want to change all connectors). Then choose Format, Connectors. In the Connectors dialog box (see Figure 16.44), you can choose whether to show staff or subordinate connectors, whether to use right-angle or direct connectors, and the line style, color, or thickness of each type of line.

Figure 16.44
You can change the
type or style of box
connectors in the
Connectors dialog box.

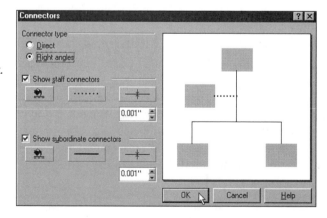

Tip #196 from
Laura and Read

If you don't like either of the connector choices, you can deselect the Show Connectors boxes and then use Draw/Presentations tools to add your own lines or arrows as objects on top of the org chart.

You can also adjust vertical and horizontal spacing between boxes. This can be particularly useful if you want to make the org chart more proportional (as tall as it is wide, for example). Select the boxes or branches you want to adjust, and choose For̲mat, Box S̲pacing. WordPerfect displays the Box Spacing dialog box (see Figure 16.45). Adjust vertical spacing by increasing or decreasing parent-to-child spacing. Change horizontal spacing by adjusting sibling-to-sibling spacing.

Figure 16.45
You can adjust the spacing between org chart boxes in the Box Spacing dialog box.

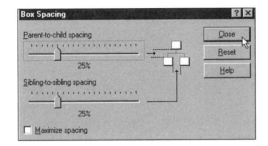

COLLAPSING AND ZOOMING ORG CHART BRANCHES

If you create a large org chart to map the structure of your entire company, you can selectively display parts of that structure without having to delete sections you don't want to display.

To collapse the subordinates of a selection, click a box, and then choose V̲iew, C̲ollapse Subordinates or click the Collapse/Expand button on the toolbar. WordPerfect hides the subordinates, but displays a small downward-pointing arrow in the box to indicate that there's more that you can't see (see Figure 16.46). When you return to your WordPerfect document, this indicator does not display. To expand the subordinates, click the arrow, or click the Collapse/Expand toolbar button again, or choose V̲iew, E̲xpand Subordinates.

To display only one section of the org chart—for example, a department or group—click the head of that part of the org chart and choose V̲iew, Zoom to B̲ranch, or click the Zoom Branch button on the toolbar. WordPerfect hides all other parts of the org chart, and also displays an upward-pointing arrow at the top box of the zoomed branch. To return to the entire chart, click that arrow, or click the Zoom button on the toolbar, or choose V̲iew, Z̲oom to Chart.

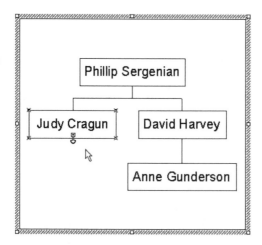

Figure 16.46
You can hide subordinates in the org chart, but an arrow indicates that they're still there.

TROUBLESHOOTING

DON'T WORRY, JUST PRINT IT

When I'm editing my chart data, the chart looks great. But when I return to my WordPerfect document, the chart looks lousy.

What you're seeing is only a display problem. Don't worry. When you print the chart, it'll look just fine.

SAVING IT ANYTIME

I sorted data in my datasheet, but I did it wrong and can't remember what it looked like. There doesn't seem to be any undo.

Unfortunately, Undo doesn't work while you're editing a chart. But you can save as often as you like. Simply click the Save button on the toolbar; or press Ctrl+S. That way, if you make a mistake, just exit the WordPerfect document, and open the last saved copy. You should always save your work before trying something new or complicated. Did you already lose your work? Sorry, but now you'll know for the next time.

PRINTING CONTRASTING SERIES IN CHARTS

In my document the data charts look fine, but when I print them, I can hardly distinguish between the different chart series.

This is common when you print to a black-and-white printer, such as a laser printer. You can try to change the series colors to use clearly different shades of gray, but if you have more than a few series, this may not be satisfactory. A more effective solution is to change the fill patterns of the series so they clearly contrast (for example, diagonal lines in different directions).

MODIFYING AN ENTIRE BRANCH

I changed the layout of my org chart, but only part of the chart changed.

You must select all the branches you want to change. To select the whole chart, choose <u>E</u>dit, Select <u>A</u>ll.

PROJECT

You're getting to the point where you can do some really fancy and also highly useful projects in WordPerfect. Let's suppose you've been keeping track of EnviroWear's annual sales in the major market, as well as in the smaller markets, and that you now need to present that information to the board of directors. Although they're highly intelligent people, they're also busy, so they want to know right now how you're doing. The other little twist is that the second-quarter report for the Monona store seems wrong, so you've put in a call to the Monona manager to check those figures.

On page 33 of the annual report, you want to insert the sales figures, and you'd also like to use an attractive chart to represent those figures. If the Monona numbers change, you want to reflect those changes as quickly as possible.

Begin by importing the data from the spreadsheet into a table. If you link, rather than import, the spreadsheet data, you can update the numbers when they arrive. Figure 16.47 shows the beginnings of the annual report with the table of data.

Figure 16.47
A linked spreadsheet, imported to a table, can be the beginnings of an impressive chart.

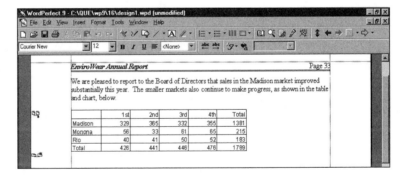

→ For details on how to link or import spreadsheet data to a WordPerfect table, **see** Chapter 15, "Importing Data and Working with Other Programs," **p. 403**

The chart you want to create doesn't need the totals row and column, but it's important to show those in the table. To create a bar chart based on just the data, select the first four rows and the first five columns, which include labels and data, but exclude the totals. Right-click the selection and choose <u>C</u>hart. WordPerfect opens the chart editor, as shown in Figure 16.48.

Figure 16.48
The chart editor uses
only the data you
select in the table.

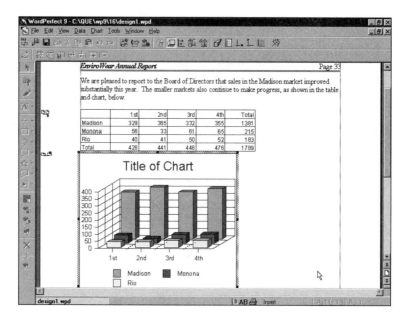

Certainly the chart shows that Madison is doing well, but it's hard to see any progress in the smaller markets. To remedy that problem, you need to plot the two smaller markets against a secondary Y-axis. Take the following steps, but be creative along the way and choose any other options you want:

1. Modify the title. Double-click the title, and in the Title Properties dialog box, use the Title Options tab to change the title (for example, EnviroWear Sales). Make other changes to the font or appearance of the text.

2. Change the smaller market series. Double-click a Monona data bar, and in the Series Properties dialog box, choose Secondary (Y2). Also change the series to a line type. Do the same for the Rio series. While you're there, you might also change the Madison series to something more interesting, such as a cylinder-shaped bar.

3. Add Y-axis titles. Charts aren't very useful if the reader doesn't know what the data points represent. Double-click a number on the primary Y-axis, and on the Title Options tab of the Primary Y-Axis Properties dialog box, add the title Large Market. Repeat this procedure for the secondary Y-axis, adding the title Smaller Markets.

4. Add a title to the labels. The reader doesn't have any idea what 1st, 2nd, 3rd, and 4th mean. Double-click a label, and on the Title Options tab of the X-Axis Properties dialog box, add 1999 Sales by Quarter.

5. Click in the WordPerfect document to close the chart editor. WordPerfect displays the chart, along with the table and text shown in Figure 16.49.

Figure 16.49
Using a secondary Y-axis, and changing the chart types for the two small market series, you can better illustrate their progress over the year.

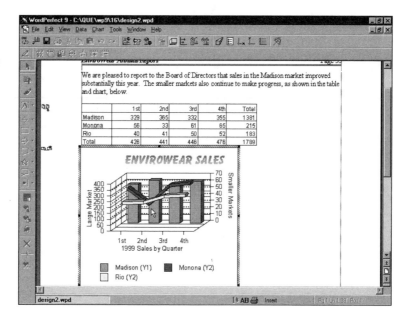

But wait…you were right. The Monona manager calls to tell you that the figures for the second quarter were indeed better than reported. Because it's only moments before the presentation to the board, you change the 33 in cell C3 to 53, right-click the table, and choose Calculate. WordPerfect updates the totals in the table, and also updates the chart, as shown in Figure 16.50. You print that page, insert it in the report, and hustle off to your meeting with the board.

Figure 16.50
You can calculate a table, and the chart based on that table updates automatically.

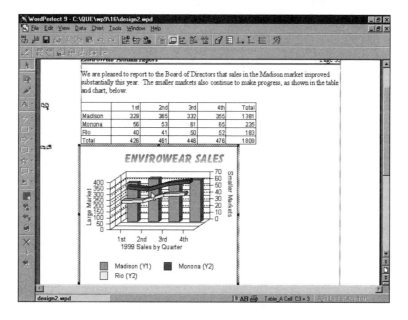

Publishing Documents

CHAPTER 17

COLLABORATING ON DOCUMENTS

In this chapter

INSERTING DOCUMENT COMMENTS

Those sticky notes have really taken off, haven't they? They take up an entire aisle at the office supply store—along with all the desk accessories to hold them. I've got one on my monitor right now that reminds me of my submission dates!

WordPerfect offers an electronic equivalent to sticky notes—it's called a *document comment*. Comments can be inserted into a document, and they remain invisible until you open them. They aren't printed and they don't affect the formatting of the document. Consider the following uses:

- Store an idea as a comment, and then return to the comment later to develop the idea.
- Create a comment to remind yourself (or someone else) to come back and check the accuracy of a statement.
- Place instructions inside comments throughout onscreen forms to eliminate the need for printed instructions on how to fill out the form.

Comments are a valuable collaboration tool. Every member of a team that works on a document can insert his or her own comments, which can easily be differentiated from other comments. These comments might include suggestions for improving the document, changes to facts and figures, corrections, feedback, follow-up instructions, and other types of editing queries.

Setting Up User Information

If you take a few seconds to fill in some information, your comments can be identified with your initials and a color. Choose Tools, Settings, Environment. Type your name and initials in the text boxes. Click the User Color button to choose a color from the palette. (The color is used for the comment balloon icons that appear when you insert a comment.)

CREATING COMMENTS

When you're ready to create a comment, click the text that you want to comment about. You don't have to be at the beginning of a line or at the top of a paragraph. You'll find that when you view the comment, an arrow points to the spot where you created the comment, so it's easy for the reviewer to see exactly what you are talking about.

To create a comment, choose Insert, Comment, Create. The insertion point moves into the comment editing window (see Figure 17.1). The Property Bar now has some helpful buttons for creating and editing comments.

Insert your initials. Insert your name. Insert the date. Insert the time.

Figure 17.1
Comments are cre-
ated in a separate
editing window. The
Property Bar in this
window has buttons
for creating com-
ments.

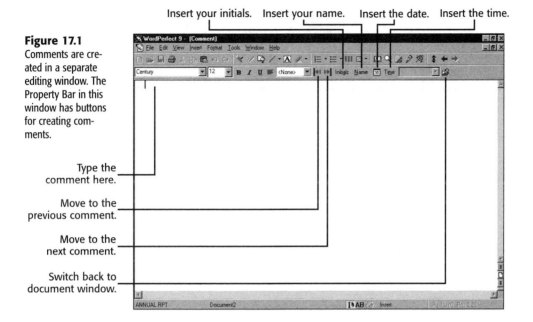

Type the
comment here.

Move to the
previous comment.

Move to the
next comment.

Switch back to
document window.

Tip #197 from
Laura and Read

If you've already typed the text that you want to put in a comment, select the text, and
then choose Insert, Comment, Create. The selected text is copied into the comment editing
window.

Type the text of the comment in the window. Using the buttons on the Property Bar, insert
your initials, your name, the date, or the time. Click the Close button on the Property Bar
when you're done.

In Page view, you can see the comment balloon icon (with the initials and the color you
chose in Environment Settings) inside the left margin. If you don't specify initials or a user
color in Environment Settings, the comment icon looks like a white bubble (see Figure
17.2). If you can't see these icons, click the Zoom button and choose Page Width, or click
the left horizontal scroll arrow until the left margin space comes into view.

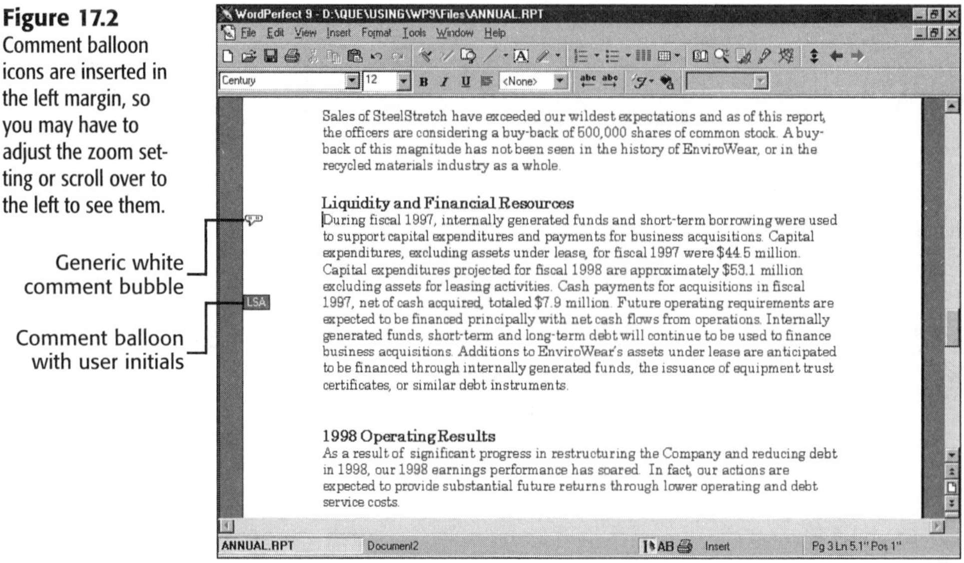

Figure 17.2
Comment balloon icons are inserted in the left margin, so you may have to adjust the zoom setting or scroll over to the left to see them.

Generic white comment bubble

Comment balloon with user initials

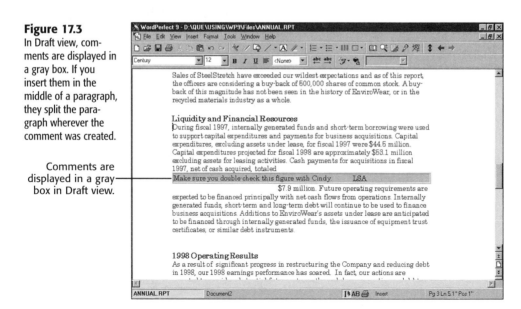

If you still can't see the margin icon after you've adjusted the zoom (or scrolled over to the left), see "Enabling Margin Icons" in the Troubleshooting section at the end of this chapter.

In Draft view, comments appear in the text inside a gray box. If you created the comment in the middle of the line, the beginning of the line appears above the comment box; the end of the line appears below (see Figure 17.3). Most people find the gray comment boxes too distracting, so they switch to Page view, where the comments stay hidden.

Figure 17.3
In Draft view, comments are displayed in a gray box. If you insert them in the middle of a paragraph, they split the paragraph wherever the comment was created.

Comments are displayed in a gray box in Draft view.

VIEWING AND WORKING WITH COMMENTS

Page view is the preferred mode for working with comments because the comments stay hidden until you are ready to look at them. To view the contents of a comment, click the balloon icon in the left margin. The comment text appears in a balloon, with the arrow pointing down to the text where you created the comment (see Figure 17.4).

Figure 17.4
The arrow at the bottom of the comment balloon points to the place in the text where you inserted the comment code.

Comment balloon —

Comment arrow —

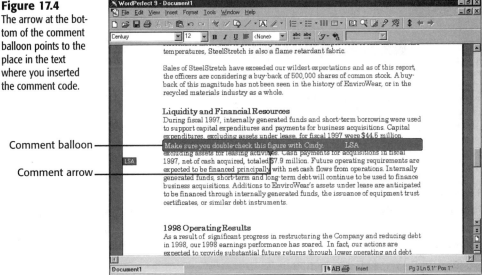

PART

VI

CH

17

You can do a few other things with comments:

- To edit a comment, right-click the comment icon or the comment text and choose <u>E</u>dit.

- While you're in the comment editing window, choose <u>F</u>ile, <u>P</u>rint to print the comment.

- To delete a comment, right-click the comment icon or comment text and choose <u>D</u>elete.

Tip #198 from
Laura and Read

> To strip out all the Comment codes in one fell swoop, use Find and Replace to search for comment codes and replace them with nothing. See "Searching for Codes" in Chapter 5, "Using the Writing Tools," for the steps to insert a code in the Find and Replace dialog box.

- To convert a comment to text, click after the comment. Choose <u>I</u>nsert, Co<u>m</u>ment, Convert to <u>T</u>ext. The text of the comment is inserted right where you created the comment—it replaces the comment code.

Tip #199 from
Laura and Read

Remember that you can delete a code by clicking and dragging it out of the Reveal Codes window.

- You can view information about when a comment was created, even if the date and timestamps weren't used. First, click the comment balloon icon to display the comment text. Right-click the comment text, and then choose Information. The Comment Information dialog box appears (see Figure 17.5).

Figure 17.5
The Comment Information dialog box lists the author, his or her initials, and the user color, with the date and time the comment was created.

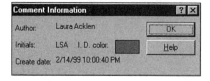

Using the Highlight Tool

Even the most stubborn opponents of automation can't deny the efficiency of working with information electronically. But hey, you go ahead—print the document and highlight the important passages with a highlighter pen. I'll stay right here and highlight the text onscreen with WordPerfect's Highlight tool and a few mouse clicks.

Just like a highlighter pen, the Highlight feature paints a bar of transparent color over the text. Just think about it—you can ask fellow collaborators to choose different colors, or you can use different colors to color code certain types of information.

There are two ways to highlight text:

- To highlight existing text, select it, and then click the Highlight button. The currently selected color is used to highlight the text (see Figure 17.6).

- You can turn on the Highlight feature so that you can select text and apply highlighting in one step. Click the Highlight button, and the mouse pointer changes to a pen highlighter. Click and drag through the text you want to highlight. When you release the mouse button, WordPerfect applies the highlighting. When you're finished highlighting text, click the Highlight button again to turn highlighting off. Again, the currently selected color is used.

Highlight button

Figure 17.6
Just as you can use a highlighter pen to emphasize important information on a printed document, you can use WordPerfect's Highlight feature to highlight text onscreen.

Highlighted text—

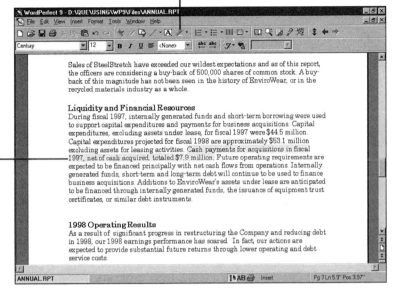

To remove highlighting from a section of text, click in the text, and then click the Highlight button. You can remove multiple instances of highlighting all at once by selecting the text that contains the highlighted sections and choosing Tools, Highlight, Remove.

The default highlight color is yellow, but you can choose any color you like from the palette. Click the arrow next to the Highlight button to open the color palette, where you can select another color. It's a good idea to choose a light color—the darker colors can make it difficult to read the highlighted text.

Note

When you select a different highlight color, the change is sticky, which means that the new color replaces the default color.

Highlighted text prints out in color on a color printer, and it prints as shaded text on a black-and-white printer. To print the document without the highlighting, you can temporarily hide the highlighting (but not the text on which the highlighting appears). Choose Tools, Highlight, Print/Show.

Note

If you're planning on sending this document to someone else to review onscreen, be nice—don't use so much highlight that the reader burns out his or her retinas trying to read the text.

REVIEWING DOCUMENTS

The Internet is the world's virtual post office—these days it seems as though *everyone* has an email address. Collaborating with people all over the world is as simple as attaching a file to an email message and distributing it. But when you have a handful of people working on the same document, keeping track of the revisions can be a nightmare.

WordPerfect's Document Review feature can be used by both reviewers and the document's author. First, a reviewer uses Document Review to insert revisions (in a unique color). Then, you (the author), use the Document Review feature to find every revision (no matter how small). Each reviewer has a unique color, so each revision can be traced back to the person who made it. You can accept or reject each change, because *you* have control over the document!

MAKING REVISIONS

If someone has sent a document to you, you are considered the *reviewer*. You'll have your own color, so your changes can easily be distinguished from those of other reviewers.

To add revisions with Document Review, open the document, and then follow these steps:

1. Choose File, Document, Review. The Review Document dialog box appears (see Figure 17.7).

Note

If a document has already been saved with revision marks, the Review Document dialog box appears automatically when you open that document. Click Cancel if you don't want to use Document Review.

Figure 17.7
You can use the Document Review feature as a reviewer or as the author.

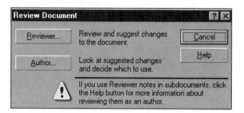

2. Click Reviewer. A Reviewer Property Bar appears at the top of the document. Your color is displayed in the Set Color button. Colors that have already been used are displayed, with the user name, in the Other User Colors list box (see Figure 17.8).

Other user colors

Figure 17.8
The Reviewer Property
Bar lists the other
reviewers next to their
user colors.

Click the Set Color
button to change
your user color.

Click here when
you're done.

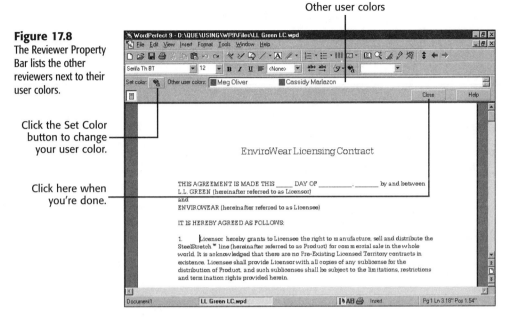

3. If you want to change your color, click the Set Color button, and then choose a color from the color palette.

4. Make your revisions to the document. If you add text, it appears in your user color. Deleted text appears in your user color, with a line running through it (to indicate strikeout text).

> **Note**
>
> You can edit revisions made by other reviewers, but you can't edit text that has been deleted by another reviewer. The only way to release that text is to review the document as the author and reject the deletion.

5. When you're finished, click the Close button on the Reviewer Property Bar.

> **Caution**
>
> You won't be able to see the revision marks in the document window, so don't panic when you don't see your changes. They are there—they just aren't displayed in the user color.

When you're revising a document, you can do just about anything to it—you can change the margins, change the font, add headers and footers, add graphics, and so on. However, your user color is only tied to textual changes—that is, whatever you type in. For example, if you create a header, the header text appears in your user color.

→ For the steps to create a header, **see** "Adding Headers and Footers," **p. 209**

Tip #200 from
Laura and Read

Each reviewer is identified by the user name in the User Information section of Environment Settings. If you share a computer, you have to remember to type your name and initials each time you start WordPerfect, or your revisions will be identified with someone else's name. A macro that does that for you would be very handy.

→ For more information on creating macros, **see** Chapter 24, "Experts and Macros," **p. 685**

REVIEWING A MARKED-UP DOCUMENT

As the document's author, you have control over which revisions are actually made and which are discarded. As you review the document, each revision is selected. You can accept or reject each change individually, or you can accept or reject all changes at once.

To review a document as an author, open the document, and then follow these steps:

1. Choose <u>A</u>uthor in the Document Review dialog box to display the Reviewer Property Bar at the top of the document (see Figure 17.9). This Reviewer Property Bar contains buttons for accepting and rejecting the revisions.

Click the Go to Next Annotation button
to start reviewing the document.

Click here to
reject a revision.

Figure 17.9
You can selectively accept or reject each revision individually, or you can choose to accept or reject all of them at once.

Click here to
accept a revision.

Revision marks

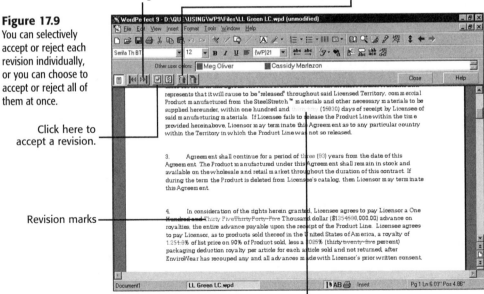

Red revision marks turn horrible
colors when selected.

2. Click the Go to Next Annotation button to start reviewing the changes. WordPerfect selects the first revision and waits for you to accept or reject it.

Beware! When a revision is selected, some user colors look positively hideous and others are impossible to read. My nice bright red revisions turned lime green on white when selected. Yuck! So I fooled around a little bit and tried to find the best colors to recommend for the reviewers. Dark red, dark blue, olive green, teal, green, magenta, orange, and bright blue are okay. Bright red, violet, dark green, dark gray, tan, and dark pink are horrendous.

3. Use the buttons on the Reviewer Property Bar to review the document:

- Click the Go to Previous Annotation button to move to the previous revision.
- Click the Go to Next Annotation button to move to the next revision.
- Click the Insert Current Annotation in the Document button to accept the revision.
- Click the Delete Current Annotation from the Document button to reject a revision.
- Click the Insert All Annotations in Document button to accept all the revisions at once.
- Click the Delete All Annotations from Document button to strip out all the revisions.

PART

VI

CH

17

Tip #201 from
Laura and Read

Change your mind about accepting or rejecting a revision? Click the Undo button to recover rejected revisions.

4. Click the Close button when you're finished, and then save the document.

⚠ *If your revisions show up as black text instead of appearing in the user color, see "My Review Color Is Broken" in the Troubleshooting section at the end of the chapter.*

COMPARING DOCUMENTS

Despite all the advantages electronic file transfers can bring, you might be reluctant to distribute your documents electronically because of the possibility of accidental (or intentional) changes being made to the text.

Only by comparing a reviewed document to the original can you be sure no unauthorized changes were made. The Document Compare feature compares two copies of a document and inserts revision marks for you. If text has been added, it's displayed in redline; if text has been deleted, it's copied back into the document as strikeout text. If so much as a space has been changed, you'll know about it.

Note

The Document Compare feature is designed to compare two documents in WordPerfect format. If you try to compare a document in a different format, you'll get unpredictable results.

Using the Compare Documents Feature

To compare two documents, open the reviewed copy of the document, and then follow these steps:

1. Choose File, Document, Compare to display the Compare Document dialog box (see Figure 17.10).

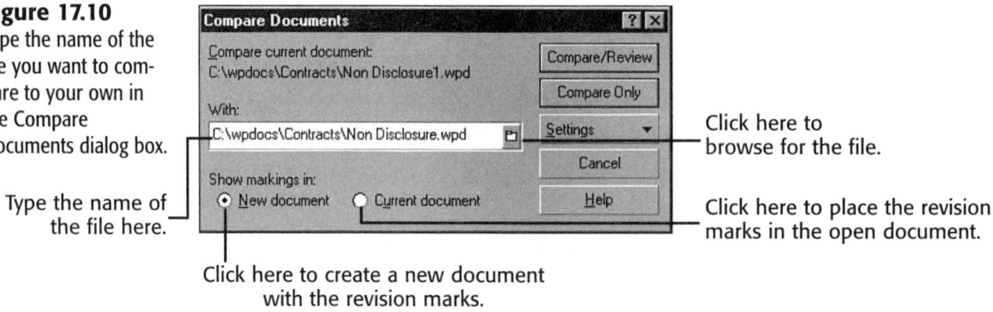

Figure 17.10
Type the name of the file you want to compare to your own in the Compare Documents dialog box.

Type the name of the file here.

Click here to browse for the file.

Click here to place the revision marks in the open document.

Click here to create a new document with the revision marks.

2. Type the filename for your copy of the document, or click the Files icon to browse for the file.

3. Choose one of the two options:

   • Click Compare Only to compare the two documents and insert revision marks.

   • Click Compare/Review if you want to compare the two documents, and then review the document as an author. (This is a new option in WordPerfect 9.)

When the comparison is complete, a Document Compare Summary page is created at the top of the document (see Figure 17.11). Scroll down past this page to review the document. Text that has been inserted appears in red, and text that has been deleted appears as strike-out text.

If you choose Compare/Review after the compare is complete, WordPerfect sets you up to review the document as an author, with the Document Review feature (discussed earlier in this chapter, in the section "Reviewing a Marked-Up Document").

Because WordPerfect inserted all those revision marks in your document, it only seems fair that WordPerfect should take them back out. Choose File, Document, Remove Markings to display the Remove Markings dialog box (see Figure 17.12). Choose one of the options to remove the redline/strikeout text.

Figure 17.11
The Document Compare Summary page is a useful report to save as confirmation that the two documents are identical.

Attributes for the deleted text

Attributes for the inserted text

Summary of changes

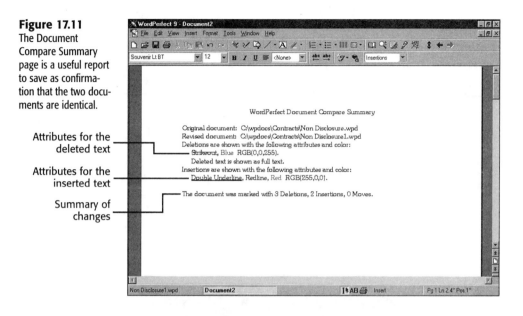

Figure 17.12
You can use the Remove Markings dialog box to strip out redline and strikeout text in any document, not just a compare document.

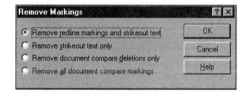

If you're not pleased with the way the redlined text looks and prints, you can change the way that text is formatted. Choose File, Document, Redline Method to open the Redline dialog box (see Figure 17.13). Choose a method for marking redlined text. If you choose one of the margin marking options, you can alter the redline character that appears inside the margin.

Figure 17.13
If you're not happy with the way your printer handles redline text, choose one of the margin marking options.

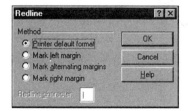

CUSTOMIZING THE DOCUMENT COMPARE FEATURE

The magnet that attracts so many loyal users is the incomparable capability to customize WordPerfect features. The Document Compare feature is no exception, and users of previous versions of WordPerfect will be pleased with the depth of the new Document Compare Settings options that were added to WordPerfect 9.

There are separate customization options for the Compare Only option and the Compare/Review option. Both can be accessed in the Compare Documents dialog box, so choose File, Document, Compare to open this dialog box.

To customize the Compare Only option, click the Settings button, then choose Compare Only to open the Document Compare Settings dialog box (see Figure 17.14). There are now five tabs in the dialog box, compared to two tabs in later releases (build 393 and beyond) of WordPerfect 8.

Click here to turn off
the summary report.

Figure 17.14
The Options tab of the Document Compare Settings dialog box controls how the compare is carried out.

Enter the enclosure character for text to skip.

Select which elements to include in the comparison here.

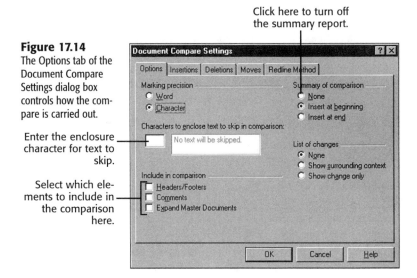

The Settings dialog box has four other tabs:

- Insertions—Click the Insertions tab to select an attribute for marking new text. The default is for redline, double-underline. You can also choose a different color and an enclosure character for the new text.

- Deletions—Click the Deletions tab to choose an attribute for deleted text (besides strikeout). You can choose a different color, and you can select an enclosure character. You can also choose how you want deleted text shown.

- Moves—Click the Moves tab to choose where moved text appears. You can choose a color for moved text.

- Redline Method—Click the Redline Method tab to select a different type of redline marking. The options are identical to those in the Redline Method dialog box you open by choosing File, Document, Redline Method.

To customize the Compare/Review option, click the Settings button, and then choose Compare Then Review to open the Compare-Then-Review Settings dialog box (see Figure 17.15).

Figure 17.15
You can customize the Compare/Review option in the Compare-Then-Review Settings dialog box.

Type an enclosure character for text to skip here.

Select the elements to include in the compare here.

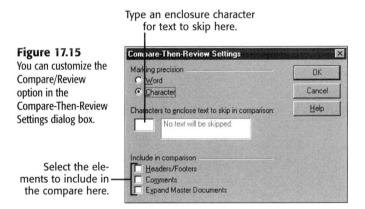

USING COREL VERSION CONTROL

First introduced in WordPerfect 8, Corel's Version Control may very well be the most powerful tool you have for collaborating on documents with other WordPerfect users. As each person revises a document, the real challenge is coming up with a system for naming all the different versions. Not only that, but you need to keep track of who made the revisions and when.

Stop wracking your brain, and let Corel's Version Control keep track of all the different versions of a document. Everything—the original document and the revisions—is saved together in one big file, so you eliminate the problem of having different versions of the same file scattered all over the place.

On a network, Corel Version Control manages revisions from multiple sources. Whenever a user saves a version of the file, his or her name, along with the date and time that version was saved, is shown in the document's history list. Using this history list, you can open any of the previous versions of the file in just a few seconds.

ARCHIVING FILES

Corel Version Control describes the process of saving a version as *archiving*, which means you are filing away a copy of the file. (Archiving also describes the process of moving inactive files off your hard drive and onto floppy disks.)

→ For more information on moving files around, **see** "Moving Files and Folders," **p. 82**

You can create a permanent archive or a temporary archive. Both can be retrieved later. The difference between the two is that you set a maximum number of temporary archives, and when that number is reached, older archives are removed to make room. Permanent versions are kept until you decide to remove them.

You can't create an archive on an unnamed document, so save and name the file first. Then choose File, Version Control, Save Current. If this is the first time a version has been saved for this document, you'll get the New Version dialog box (see Figure 17.16); otherwise, you'll see the dialog box in Figure 17.17.

Click here for a
permanent version.

Figure 17.16
When you enable Corel Version Control on a document, you can turn on compression and specify where you want the version files stored.

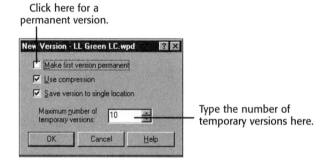

Type the number of temporary versions here.

Figure 17.17
You can type comments about your revisions in the Version Properties dialog box. These comments are visible in the properties sheet for the file.

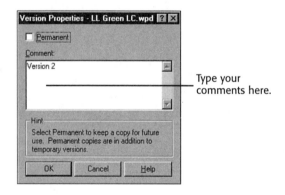

Type your comments here.

In the New Version dialog box, choose from the following options:

- Choose Make First Version Permanent to create a permanent archive.

- Deselect Use Compression if you don't want Corel to compress all the different versions to save space.

- Deselect Save Version to Single Location if you want to save the Corel Version Control files (.cv) in the same folder as the original file. Otherwise, the versions are saved in the \programfiles\corel\shared\versions folder.

- If necessary, adjust the maximum number of temporary versions for this document.

Tip #202 from
Laura and Read

By default, the maximum number of temporary versions is 10 and the versions are stored in the `\programfiles\corel\shared\versions` folder. You can change these, and other default settings, in the Control Panel. Open the Control Panel and double-click the Corel Version Control icon. Type the new number in the Default Number of Temporary Versions text box. Type another folder name for the version files in the Path text box.

The second time you save an archive, you get a different dialog box. The Version Properties dialog box (refer to Figure 17.17) gives you a comment window, where you can type remarks about this version. This is an excellent place to explain the reasoning behind the revisions. These comments can be viewed by others when they look at the file's history.

If you are having trouble creating archives on your network, see "I Can't Save a Revision with Corel Version Control" in the Troubleshooting section at the end of this chapter.

VIEWING A FILE'S HISTORY

A history of archive activity can be viewed from any file browser, such as Explorer or My Computer, or from any file management dialog box in WordPerfect.

Right-click the filename, and then choose Properties. If Corel Version Control has been enabled for this file, you'll see a Corel Versions(TM) tab. Click this tab to view the file history (see Figure 17.18). You can get to the same information if you right-click a file and choose Corel Versions, History.

PART
VI

CH

17

Click here to delete the version.

Click here to print the history.

Figure 17.18
If Corel Version Control has been enabled, there is a Corel Versions(TM) tab in the file's Properties dialog box.

Click here to save the version to a file.

This archive is permanent.

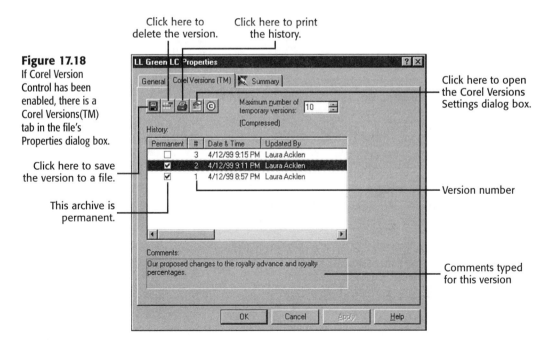

Click here to open the Corel Versions Settings dialog box.

Version number

Comments typed for this version

The history list shows all the archives that have been saved for this document. The number of the archive—along with the date, time, and name of the person who updated the document—is listed. If a check mark appears in the Permanent column, that version was saved as a permanent archive.

 If you ever need to extract one of the archives to send it to someone as a separate file, select the archive, and then click the Save As button. Corel Versions suggests a filename that incorporates (v#), where the # stands for the archive number in the history list, but you can type your own name in the Save Version As text box of the Save As dialog box (see Figure 17.19).

Figure 17.19
You can either accept the suggested name or type a new filename to copy an archive to a separate file.

Type a new filename here.

RETRIEVING AN ARCHIVED FILE

The beauty of tracking your revisions with Corel Version Control is the fact that you can retrieve any of the previous versions in just a few seconds. Compare that to spending several minutes (or hours) trying to figure out which file you need by the filename or date.

To retrieve an archive, choose File, Version Control. Choose Retrieve Current to open an archive for the file you currently have open or choose Retrieve Document to open an archive from another document on your system (or the network).

Caution
If the current file, or the file that you select in a file list, doesn't have versions attached to it, you'll get an error message that the file does not contain version information to retrieve.

In the Retrieve Version dialog box (see Figure 7.20), select the version, and then choose Retrieve. When the confirmation message box appears, choose Yes if you want to replace the current document with the selected archive. Choose No if you want to save the archive with a new name (WordPerfect displays another message, telling you the new name of the file).

Caution
Be careful about replacing the original file with the selected archive. You'll be replacing both the document onscreen (if the document is open) and the file on disk with that version of the document. The other archives are still saved with the document, however, so you'll be able to retrieve them whenever you want.

Figure 17.20
You can select the archive you want to work with in the Retrieve Version dialog box.

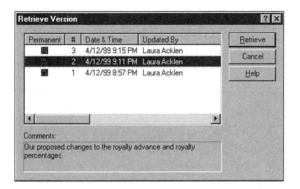

> ⚡ If you get an error message when you try to retrieve an archive from a file that you know has archives, see "The Version Information Is Missing" in the Troubleshooting section at the end of this chapter.

DELETING ARCHIVES

As you learned earlier in this chapter, when you save your revisions to a file, the archive can be created as a permanent archive or a temporary archive. When the maximum number of temporary archives is reached, the oldest temporary archive is deleted to make room for the newest temporary archive. Permanent archives are kept until you delete them. You can delete an archive, or the entire file with all the archives, from any file list.

 To delete an archive from a file, right-click the filename, choose Properties, and then click the Corel Versions(TM) tab. Select the archive you want to delete, and then click the Delete button. Read the confirmation message carefully, then choose Yes to delete the archive or choose No if you chicken out.

MOVING AND COPYING COREL VERSIONS FILES

It's your lucky day—one of your co-workers has offered to help you with an important contract negotiation. So that you can both work on the legal documents, you need to move the files to the company network. Some of these files have been heavily revised, so they contain multiple archives. In order to keep the archives attached to the right file, you have to use the Corel Versions commands to move and copy the file. You can move and copy an archive file from any file list.

To move or copy a file with archives, right-click the filename, and then choose Corel Versions, File, Move (or Copy). Select the folder where you want to move (or copy) the file. If necessary, type a new name in the File Name text box, and then choose Save.

Caution

If you don't use this procedure to move or copy a Corel Version Control file, the archives won't be available.

TROUBLESHOOTING

ENABLING MARGIN ICONS

I've just created a bunch of comments, and even though I changed the zoom setting to Page Width, I can't see the comment icons. What's up with that?

There is a setting in the Display Settings dialog box that enables and disables the display of margin icons. Choose Tools, Settings, Display. Place a check mark next to Margin Icons to enable them. You can use this option if you ever want to hide the comment balloon icons from view.

MY REVIEW COLOR IS BROKEN

I'm reviewing a document with the Reviewer Property Bar displayed and a nice bright blue user color all picked out. But my revisions aren't displaying in blue—they show up as black text like the rest of the document.

Revisions to a document should appear in the user color, whether you are reviewing the document as a reviewer or as an author. If the revisions are displayed in black text, there may be a conflict with the Windows system colors on your system. Choose Tools, Settings, Display. In the Document tab, deselect Windows System Colors.

I CAN'T SAVE A REVISION WITH COREL VERSION CONTROL

I'm working on a network, and whenever I try to save my revisions (using the Save Current command on the Version Control menu), I get an error message. The message says I don't have sufficient rights to save files in this folder.

Most network administrators set aside an area for shared files and folders on the network. They grant full rights to this area so people can share documents with each other. If you use Version Control and you want to share the document, keep your files in the shared area. Also make sure your system administrator gives you (and other collaborators) rights to the folder where the versions files are stored (\programfiles\corel\shared\versions).

THE VERSION INFORMATION IS MISSING

I've just opened a file from a shared folder on the network. When I choose File, Version Control, Retrieve Current, I get an error message that the file does not contain version information to be retrieved. I know this file has archives—why can't I get to them?

When you move and copy files that have archives, you have to use a certain procedure so the archives follow the file. If you don't use the commands on the Corel Versions menu, the file information isn't mapped correctly, and the archives aren't found.

Have the person who moved or copied the file into the shared folder try again. This time, tell the person to right-click the file and choose Corel Versions, File, Move (or Copy).

PROJECT

If you've ever had to read a hard copy with revision marks, you know it's difficult to read redlined text. Not only that, but some printers don't do such a great job printing redline. So, what can you do?

WordPerfect's Font Map feature gives you the flexibility of changing a font attribute (in this case, redline) to another font, font size, or font style. You can have the redline text appear in another font, so the redline text stands apart from the rest of the text. It's a good idea to pick a font that is stylistically different so it's easy to differentiate between the regular text and the redlined text. For example, if you use a serif font, such as Times New Roman, for the body text, choose a sans serif font, such as Arial, for the redlined text.

When you edit the font mapping, you are doing it for the current printer, not a specific document, so you don't need to open the document first.

Choose Format, Font, Settings, Edit Font Mapping. Select the font that you are using for the body text in the Printer font Face list box (such as Times New Roman). Scroll through the Automatic Font Change list box and choose Redline. Choose a font in the Redline font Face list box (such as Arial). If you place a check mark in the Map Individual Styles check box, you can choose a different font size and style. For example, you might want to use italics or bold to further emphasize the redlined text.

Figure 17.21 shows how the redline text in the Arial font looks with the Times New Roman text.

Figure 17.21
Changing the redline text to a different font makes it easier for someone to read a hard copy of a document with revision marks.

Redline text is in Arial.

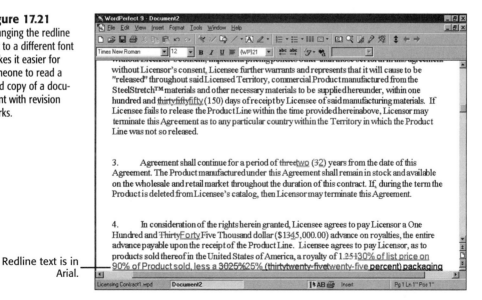

CHAPTER **18**

Working with Large and Multipart Documents

In this chapter

INSERTING BOOKMARKS

Just as you can place a bookmark in a book, you can insert bookmarks into a long document, and then jump from section to section with just a few mouse clicks. In their simplest form, bookmarks help you to navigate through a long document. Raise the bar a little, and you'll use bookmarks to create hypertext links within a document. Raise the bar a little higher, and you'll use bookmarks to position the insertion point, or to move to the next prompt, in a template. This chapter focuses on creating bookmarks to navigate through long documents.

➔ If you are ready to create a link to another part of a document, **see** "Creating Hypertext Links," **p. 546**

➔ For more information on creating templates, **see** "Creating Custom Templates," **p. 623**

INSERTING A BOOKMARK

A bookmark can be created to mark the beginning of a new chapter or section, a table or chart, the start of illustrative pages, or a section of text that is frequently revised—any position within a document. A bookmark can also be created to locate and select a portion of the text. The advantage of selecting text before you create the bookmark is that when you jump to that bookmark, the text is selected and you can then take action on the selection (such as moving or copying it).

Follow these steps to create a bookmark:

1. Click where you want to insert the bookmark, or select the text you want to use to create the bookmark.

> **Caution**
>
> If you've selected a chart or graphic object, the bookmark command won't be available. Click in the document window to deselect the object, and then select the text around the object if you want to include it in the selection.

2. Choose <u>T</u>ools, <u>B</u>ookmark to display the Bookmark dialog box (see Figure 18.1).

Figure 18.1
All the bookmarks for a document are listed in the Bookmark dialog box. Double-click a bookmark in the list to jump to that part of the document.

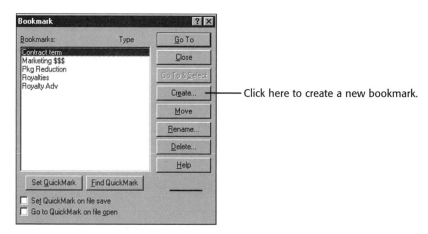

Click here to create a new bookmark.

Note

If you've upgraded from WordPerfect 7, note that the Bookmark command has been moved from the Insert menu to the Tools menu.

3. Click Create. The Create Bookmark dialog box appears (see Figure 18.2). If you've clicked in the document, the text following the insertion point appears in the Bookmark Name text box. If you selected text, the selected text appears in the Bookmark Name text box, and there is a check mark in the Selected Bookmark check box.

Figure 18.2
You type a name for the bookmark in the Create Bookmark dialog box.

4. If necessary, type another name for the bookmark in the Bookmark Name text box. Click OK to return to the Bookmark dialog box.

Now that you know how to create bookmarks, you're probably wondering how you're going to use them to move around. Bookmarks are integrated into the Go To feature, so you can use Go To when you want to jump to a bookmark. Or you can open the Bookmark dialog box and choose one there. Here's how you use Go To to select a bookmark:

- Press Ctrl+G, or double-click the position information on the status bar, to open the Go To dialog box (see Figure 18.3). Click Bookmark in the Go to What list box, and then choose a bookmark from the Select Bookmark drop-down list (see Figure 18.4).

Figure 18.3
You can use the Go To dialog box to move to any page, bookmark, line, edit position, top of current page, or bottom of current page. You can also have Go To reselect the last selection.

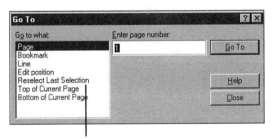

Click here to reselect the last selection.

- Choose Tools, Bookmark. Select a bookmark, and then choose Go To. If you created the bookmark with selected text, and you want that text selected when you move to the bookmark, click Go To & Select.

Bookmarks can be moved, renamed, and deleted in the Bookmark dialog box:

- To move a bookmark, click in the text where you want to place the bookmark. Choose Tools, Bookmark. Select the bookmark, and then choose Move.

- To rename a bookmark, choose <u>T</u>ools, <u>B</u>ookmark. Select the bookmark, and then click <u>R</u>ename. Type a new name for the bookmark in the Rename Bookmark dialog box, and then click OK.

- To delete a bookmark, choose <u>T</u>ools, <u>B</u>ookmark. Select the bookmark in the <u>B</u>ookmarks list box, and then click <u>D</u>elete. Click <u>Y</u>es to delete the bookmark, or click <u>N</u>o if you change your mind.

Caution

If you accidentally delete an important bookmark, you can click the Undo button to restore it. It's a good idea to click Undo immediately after you delete the bookmark, or you risk the possibility of undoing the wrong action.

Tip #203 from
Laura and Read

Although you can't print out a list of your bookmarks, you can create a screen shot with the Bookmark dialog box open. You can then paste the screen shot into a blank document and print it out for future reference. Choose Tools, Bookmark to open the Bookmark dialog box. Press Alt+PrintScreen to copy the screen to the Clipboard. In a document, press Ctrl+V or click the Paste button on the toolbar to paste in the screen shot. Finally, click the Print button to print the screen capture.

INSERTING QUICKMARKS

A *QuickMark* is a one-time-use bookmark that you can use to save your place in a document. You can have WordPerfect create a QuickMark at the insertion point whenever you save a document. The next time you open the document, you can jump to the QuickMark with one keystroke, or you can have WordPerfect take you there automatically.

To create a QuickMark, click in the text where you want to set the QuickMark, and then choose <u>T</u>ools, <u>B</u>ookmark, Set <u>Q</u>uickMark. Or you can press Ctrl+Shift+Q to create the QuickMark.

To find a QuickMark, press Ctrl+Q or choose <u>T</u>ools, <u>B</u>ookmark, <u>F</u>ind QuickMark. You can also open the Go To dialog box, and then choose QuickMark from the S<u>e</u>lect Bookmark drop-down list (see Figure 18.4).

Figure 18.4
After you create a QuickMark in a document, QuickMark appears on the S<u>e</u>lect Bookmark drop-down list.

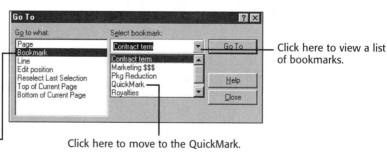

Click here to view a list of bookmarks.

Click here to move to a bookmark.

Click here to move to the QuickMark.

If you want WordPerfect to take care of setting the QuickMark whenever you save a document, choose Tools, Bookmark. Place a check mark in the Set QuickMark on File Save check box. Put a check mark in the Go to QuickMark on File Open check box if you want to jump to the QuickMark when you open the document again.

ADDING FOOTNOTES AND ENDNOTES

Footnotes and *endnotes* provide additional information about what is being said in the body of the text without interrupting the flow of that text. They may contain reference details, such as the name of the author, the title of the work, and the page number where the information can be found. They may also provide parenthetic or interpretive explanations of technical material.

Note Footnotes and endnotes should not contain essential information because their very location indicates that the author does not consider them required reading.

The process of creating and editing footnotes and endnotes is virtually identical. Because footnotes are more popular, this chapter focuses on them. The differences are mostly self-explanatory, so you shouldn't have problems using the information here to create endnotes.

PART
VI

CH
18

CREATING AND EDITING FOOTNOTES

A footnote has two parts: the footnote reference number and the footnote text. The footnote reference number is placed in the text when you create the footnote. The footnote text, along with a corresponding footnote number, is inserted at the bottom of the page. If the footnote is lengthy, WordPerfect splits the footnote and carries it over to the next page.

You can follow these steps to create a footnote:

1. Click in the text where you want the footnote reference number to appear.

2. Choose Insert, Footnote/Endnote to open the Footnote/Endnote dialog box (see Figure 18.5). WordPerfect suggests a footnote number, based on where you are in the document (before or after existing footnotes).

Figure 18.5
You can choose to create a footnote or an endnote in the Footnote/Endnote dialog box.

Click here to create an endnote.

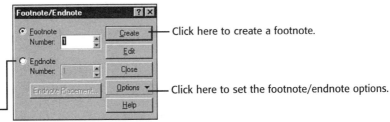

Click here to create a footnote.

Click here to set the footnote/endnote options.

Tip #204 from *Laura and Read*	If you want to create an endnote rather than a footnote, select E**n**dnote Number, and then click **C**reate.

Tip #205 from *Laura and Read*	If you're working in parallel columns, you are able to create only endnotes, not footnotes. Both footnotes and endnotes can be inserted in newspaper columns.

3. Choose **C**reate. What happens next depends on the view you're using. In Page view, the insertion point is placed at the bottom of the page in the footnote editing area (see Figure 18.6). In Draft view, the insertion point is moved into a footnote/endnote editing window. Either way, you have some new buttons on the Property Bar.

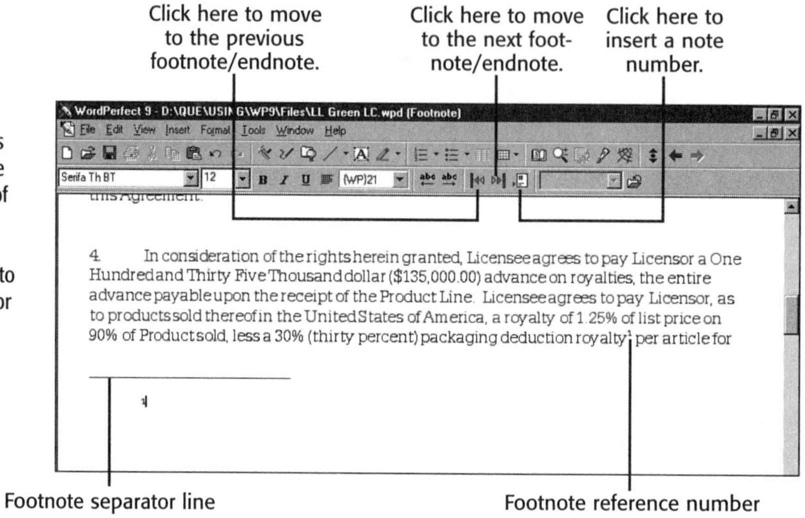

Click here to move to the previous footnote/endnote.

Click here to move to the next foot-note/endnote.

Click here to insert a note number.

Figure 18.6
The footnote area is at the bottom of the page, right on top of the bottom margin, so you can reduce the bottom margin to make more room for footnotes.

Footnote separator line

Footnote reference number

Tip #206 from *Laura and Read*	In Draft view, you can see the footnote numbers in the text, but you can't see the footnote text at the bottom of the page. Because they aren't displayed in the text, you have to create and edit footnotes in a separate footnote editing window. I strongly recommend switching to Page view when you're working with footnotes and endnotes because you don't have to keep switching back and forth from the footnote editing window to the document editing window.

4. Type the text of the footnote.

Tip #207 from *Laura and Read*	If you accidentally delete the note number in the footnote text, click the Note Number but-ton to reinsert the number. Don't type the number yourself, or WordPerfect won't be able to update the note numbers as you edit the document.

5. Click the Close button (or in Page view, click in the body text) to move the insertion point back into the text area. The footnote reference number appears in the text (see Figure 18.7).

 If your footnote numbers reset to 1 at the beginning of each page (and you don't want them to), see "My Footnote Numbers Keep Going Back to 1" in the Troubleshooting section at the end of this chapter.

Figure 18.7
The footnote reference number is tied to a footnote code so that the footnote numbers can be updated as you edit the document.

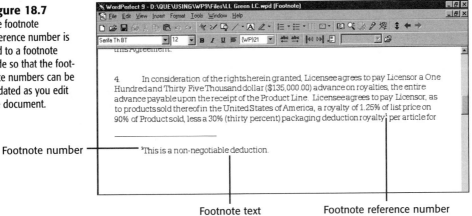

Footnote number

Footnote text   Footnote reference number

 Editing footnotes in Page View mode is simple—just click in the footnote area and make your changes. To edit a footnote in Draft view, choose Insert, Footnote/Endnote, type the number of the footnote you want to edit, and then choose Edit. When you're done, click the Close button on the Property Bar.

To delete a footnote, select the footnote reference number in the text, and then press Delete. Because this deletes the footnote code, both the footnote reference number and the footnote text are removed.

 If you are having trouble deleting a footnote, see "I Can't Get Rid of a Reference Number" in the Troubleshooting section at the end of this chapter.

You might decide after you've typed in the text of the footnote that the footnote should appear elsewhere in the paragraph. Or you might decide that you need to create a footnote that's almost identical to this one, so you want to copy the footnote, and then make the small changes. Moving and copying footnotes is easy—just cut or copy, and then paste the footnote reference number, just as you would any other piece of text. Because the footnote reference number represents the footnote code, you're actually copying and moving the code without having to turn on Reveal Codes.

→ *If you need a refresher on how to move and copy text,* **see** *"Moving and Copying Text,"* **p. 46**

By default, endnotes are grouped together at the end of the document, rather than printed at the bottom of a page. You can control where the endnotes are compiled with endnote placement codes. For example, a long document can be divided into smaller files, perhaps at major headings or sections, and then combined for final formatting. If you want the endnotes compiled at the end of each section, rather than at the end of the document, insert an endnote placement code at the bottom of each file.

→ For more information on breaking large documents into smaller pieces, **see** "Working with Master Documents and Subdocuments," **p. 512**

To insert an endnote placement code, choose Insert, Footnote/Endnote, Endnote Number, Endnote Placement. Choose Insert Endnotes at Insertion Point if you're compiling all the endnotes together, or choose Insert Endnotes at Insertion Point and Restart Numbering if you're compiling endnotes at the end of each section and you want to restart numbering at one in each section.

Caution

If the insertion point is inside the footnote area, the Footnote/Endnote option on the Insert menu isn't available. You have to click in the text and move the insertion point out of the footnote area to make the Footnote/Endnote option available.

FORMATTING FOOTNOTES

WordPerfect makes some assumptions for you so that you can create and edit footnotes without having to worry about creating a separator line or making sure there is enough room between the body text and the footnote text. The footnote number is a superscripted Arabic numeral, and the first line of the footnote is indented. You might have reasons for changing these settings, and it's easy enough to do.

Choose Insert, Footnote/Endnote, Options, Advanced to open the Advanced Footnote Options dialog box (see Figure 18.8), where you can tweak the footnote options.

Choose a numbering
method here.

Figure 18.8
You can make adjustments to footnote formatting in the Advanced Footnote Options dialog box.

Click here to edit the footnote text style.

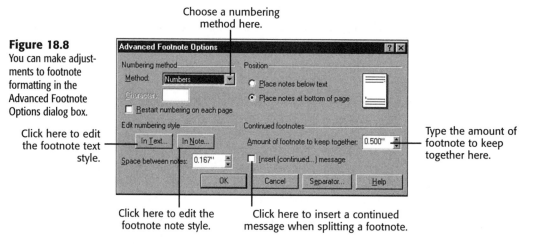

Type the amount of footnote to keep together here.

Click here to edit the footnote note style.

Click here to insert a continued message when splitting a footnote.

Here are some of the changes you can make in the Advanced Footnote Options dialog box:

■ Click the Method drop-down list arrow and choose a different numbering method (lowercase/uppercase letters, lowercase/uppercase Roman, or characters).

- Click In <u>T</u>ext to edit the style for the footnote reference number.
- Click In <u>N</u>ote to edit the style for the footnote text.

Tip #208 from *Laura and Read*	It's fairly common to have footnote text in the same font as the document text, but in a smaller size. Click In <u>N</u>ote to edit the footnote style, and then choose a smaller size from the Font Size drop-down list.

- Adjust the space between footnotes in the <u>S</u>pace Between Notes text box.
- In the <u>A</u>mount of Footnote to Keep Together, specify how much footnote text you want kept together if the footnote is split across two pages.
- Put a check mark next to <u>I</u>nsert (Continued…) Message if you want WordPerfect to insert a continued message next to the separator line when a footnote is split across two pages.

Tip #209 from *Laura and Read*	If a footnote is particularly long, you can force it to split between two pages. Press Ctrl+Enter to push the rest of the footnote text to the next page.

- Click Se<u>p</u>arator to open the Line Separator dialog box (see Figure 18.9). Make any necessary adjustments to the format of the separator line. You can also choose <u>O</u>ptions, Separator (in the Footnote/Endnote dialog box) to open the Line Separator dialog box.

Figure 18.9
You can set the spacing, positioning, length, and line style for the separator line in the Line Separator dialog box.

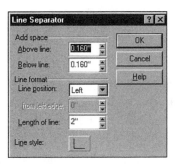

Endnotes are grouped together on a page, so there are fewer options to set for them than there are for footnotes. In the Footnote/Endnote dialog box, choose E<u>n</u>dnote Number, <u>O</u>ptions, <u>A</u>dvanced to display the Endnote Options dialog box (see Figure 18.10), which is an abbreviated version of the Advanced Footnote Options dialog box.

If you ever need to make manual adjustments to the footnote numbers, in the Footnote/Endnote dialog box, select <u>O</u>ptions, Set <u>N</u>umber to open the Footnote Number dialog box (see Figure 18.11). If you choose E<u>n</u>dnote Number first, you get the Endnote Number dialog box, which looks the same as the Footnote Number dialog box.

Figure 18.10
Because endnotes are grouped together on a page, there is no need to position them, include a separator line, or print a continued message.

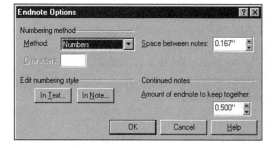

Figure 18.11
You can use the Footnote Number dialog box to adjust footnote numbering.

Making Global Changes to Footnotes or Endnotes

Footnotes and endnotes, like headers, footers, page numbers, and graphics box captions, are considered a part of the document's substructure. As such, they are formatted differently than the rest of the text. WordPerfect uses the settings in DocumentStyle to format these elements. So if you change the font at the top of the document, your footnotes/endnotes (and other elements) appear in the initial document font (or the font selected in the DocumentStyle).

To make global changes to the document and the substructure, place all the formatting codes in the initial document style. Choose File, Document, Current Document Style to edit the DocumentStyle.

CONVERTING FOOTNOTES AND ENDNOTES

If you're really lucky, you have a boss or a professor who never changes the formatting guidelines for your reports. In the real world, however, that's not likely. One day you need footnotes, the next day, endnotes. And vice versa.

WordPerfect ships with two macros that completely automate the process of converting footnotes to endnotes and endnotes to footnotes. They are called footend and endfoot (original, huh?).

→ For a complete list and the steps to run the shipping macros, **see** "Running the Shipping Macros," **p. 689**

There are two ways to run these macros:

- You can turn on a Shipping Macros toolbar for quick access to the macros that come with WordPerfect. Right-click the toolbar, choose <u>M</u>ore, and then place a check mark next to the Shipping Macros toolbar (see Figure 18.12). (You have to scroll down to see this one.) Now, click the Convert Foot to End button, or the Convert End to Foot button.

Figure 18.12
The More option on the toolbar QuickMenu takes you to a complete list of available toolbars.

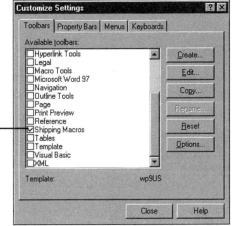

Place a check mark here.

- Choose <u>T</u>ools, <u>M</u>acro, <u>P</u>lay. In the Play Macro dialog box, scroll through the list of macros, and then double-click Footend or Endfoot. If you don't see these two macros, switch to the `\program files\corel\wordperfect office 2000\macros\wpwin` folder. Still no luck? You may have to copy the macros from the `\corel\macros\wpwin` folder on the WordPerfect Office 2000 CD-ROM.

Caution

You can't select a portion of the document, and then run the macro to convert only specific footnotes or endnotes. The footend macro converts every single footnote to an endnote and the endfoot macro converts every single endnote to a footnote.

SIMPLIFYING A COMPLEX DOCUMENT WITH CROSS-REFERENCES

Navigating a complex document can be made much easier with *cross-references*. References to other pages, figures, tables, and definitions show a reader how fragments of information are linked together. (You may have noticed that this book is liberally sprinkled with cross-references to guide you to other parts of the book that discuss related or complementary features.)

A cross-reference can point to a page, chapter, or volume number; a footnote or endnote number; a paragraph/outline number; a caption number; a counter; or any combination of these. It can be as simple as "see 'Contract Terms' on page 35," or as complex as "refer to footnote 5 on page 78 in chapter 13."

When you create a cross-reference, you mark the place in the text where you want to insert the reference information. Then you mark the *target*, or the item that you are referencing. The two marks share a common name—that's how they are matched up when you generate the cross-references.

MARKING REFERENCES

References and targets can be marked in any order—so you can mark the text as you type, or you can come back later and do it all at once. A reference in the text that refers to a non-existent target displays a ? where the reference information should be. After you mark the target and generate the document, the question marks are replaced with the reference information.

Follow these steps to create a reference:

1. Type the descriptive text that precedes a reference. For example, type "see 'Contract Terms' on page ".

2. Position the insertion point where you want the reference to appear. Make sure you leave a space between the descriptive text and the reference.

3. Choose Tools, Reference, Cross-Reference. The Cross-Reference bar appears below the Property Bar (see Figure 18.13). The default reference type is page (for a page number), so if you're inserting a page number reference, you're all set to go.

> **Note**
>
> In WordPerfect version 7, the Cross-Reference command is on the Generate menu.

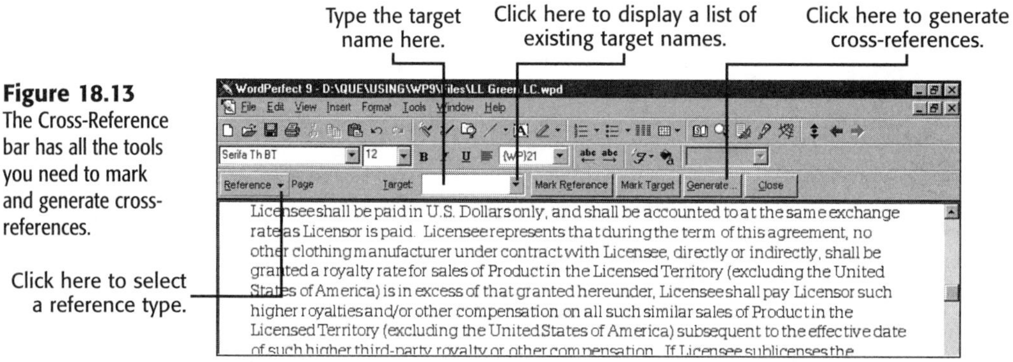

Type the target name here.   Click here to display a list of existing target names.   Click here to generate cross-references.

Figure 18.13
The Cross-Reference bar has all the tools you need to mark and generate cross-references.

Click here to select a reference type.

4. If necessary, click Reference to choose a reference type from the drop-down list (see Figure 18.14).

5. Click in the Target text box and type a target name for the reference (or if you've already marked the target, click the drop-down list arrow and choose the target name from the list).

Coming Up with Target Names
The target name that you use to mark the reference must exactly match the target name that you use to mark the target. Target names are not case sensitive. If you're unsure of the target name, try marking the target first. When you mark the references to that target, the target name will already be in the list. Highly complex documents can have similar target names, in which case you should mark targets (and their associated references) one at a time.

Figure 18.14
The default reference type is set to Page, which inserts a page number for the target.

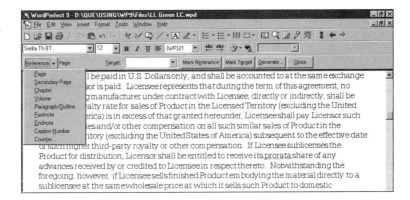

6. Click Mark Reference. WordPerfect inserts a reference code at the insertion point, and a question mark is used as a placeholder (see Figure 18.15).

Figure 18.15
If you haven't marked the target yet, a question mark serves as a placeholder.

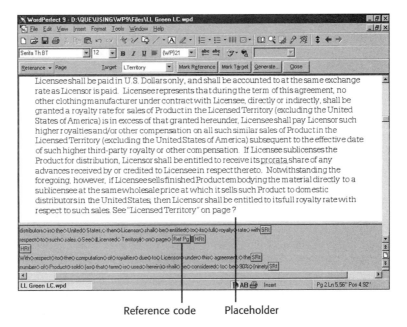

Reference code   Placeholder

PART

VI

CH

18

Creating Hypertext Links with Cross-References

Cross-references are a great way to point out related or complementary information in a long or multipart document. If the document is destined for a Web page or onscreen viewing, turn the reference text into a hypertext link that the reader can click to jump to the target. That way readers can jump back to their places and continue reading.

MARKING TARGETS

The trick to marking a target is to insert the code in the right place. Text references are easy—just click at the beginning of the phrase, paragraph, or section before you insert the code. To reference a footnote or endnote, you need to insert the code in the footnote or endnote text, not next to the footnote reference, as you might think. If you're referencing a graphics box, turn on Reveal Codes and position the red cursor right after the graphics box code. If you're marking a counter as a target, click before the counter.

Follow these steps to mark a target:

1. Position the insertion point either by clicking in the text or turning on Reveal Codes and positioning the red cursor.

2. If the Cross-Reference bar isn't displayed, choose Tools, Reference, Cross-Reference. The Cross-Reference bar appears below the Property Bar (refer to Figure 18.13).

3. Click in the Target text box and type the target name, or click the drop-down list arrow to choose a target from the list.

4. Click Mark Target. WordPerfect inserts a [Target (*target name*)] code at the insertion point.

 If you made a few mistakes when you marked targets and references, see "I Typed the Wrong Target Name" in the Troubleshooting section at the end of this chapter.

GENERATING AUTOMATIC CROSS-REFERENCES

When you generate the cross-references in a document, WordPerfect matches the target names in the reference and target codes and inserts the reference information in the text. Depending on the complexity of the document and the references you've created, generating can really tax your system's resources. For this reason, it's a good idea to save the document beforehand.

To generate a document, click the Generate button on the Cross-Reference bar, press Ctrl+F9, or choose Tools, Reference, Generate to display the Generate dialog box (see Figure 18.16). Click OK to generate the document.

 If the Generate button is grayed out, see "The Generate Button Isn't Available" in the Troubleshooting section at the end of this chapter.

→ *If you aren't sure whether you should select the Save Subdocuments option in the Generate dialog box, see "Generating Document References in Master Documents," p. 516*

Figure 18.16
The Generate option updates all the marked entries in a document at once.

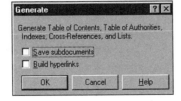

Tip #210 from
Laura and Read

If you're working on someone else's document, and the references are so messed up that you don't know *where* to start, you might consider stripping out all the target and reference codes and starting over. Use Find and Replace to search for both the target codes and the reference codes, replacing them with nothing.

→ To review the steps to use the Find and Replace feature to search for codes, **see** "Searching for Codes," **p. 130**

CREATING A CROSS-REFERENCE TO A GRAPHICS BOX COUNTER

Counters are used to number graphics boxes, usually within the caption. For example, I could use a counter to automatically number each figure in this chapter. Counters can be used to number all types of graphics boxes (figure, table, text, user, or equation). You can create a reference to any type of graphics box by referencing the counter.

Follow these steps to create a cross-reference to a graphics box counter:

1. Create a caption for each type of graphics box used in the document. This activates the counters for the graphics boxes.

→ For more information on creating graphics box captions, **see** "Adding Captions," **p. 355**

2. If the Cross-Reference bar isn't already displayed, choose Tools, Reference, Cross-Reference.

3. Type the descriptive text that precedes the reference. For example, type See Figure . Make sure you leave a space between the reference text and the reference.

4. Click Reference, and then choose Counter from the drop-down list to display the Counter dialog box (see Figure 18.17).

PART
VI

CH
18

Figure 18.17
You can select the type of graphics box that you want to reference in the Counter dialog box.

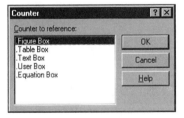

5. Click the graphics box counter type, and then click OK.

6. Type a target name in the Target text box or select the target name from the drop-down list.

7. Click Mark Reference.

8. Click the graphics box you are referencing.

9. Type the target name in the Target text box or select the target name from the drop-down list.

10. Click Mark Target.

11. Click outside the graphics box (to deselect the box).

12. Click Generate, OK.

 If you break a cross-reference when you move a graphics box, see "Discombobulated Graphics Box References" in the Troubleshooting section at the end of this chapter.

WORKING WITH MASTER DOCUMENTS AND SUBDOCUMENTS

The Master Document feature is ideally suited for any large project—an employee manual, a college dissertation, or a complex legal contract, for example. Writers often collaborate on a large project and then combine their work into one document. Without WordPerfect's Master Document feature, combining separate efforts is a time-consuming task that presents many challenges in numbering pages, creating a table of contents, setting up headers and footers, and generating cross-references.

Here's how it works: You create a document with links to other files. This is the *master document*. A *subdocument* is one of the linked files. When you expand the master document, each of the subdocuments is opened into the master document, which results in one huge document. Now you can work on all the text as a whole. You can search through the entire work, generate document references, make global formatting changes, and so forth. When you condense the master document, the subdocuments are saved and removed from the master document, leaving only the subdocument codes. For this reason, creating prefatory pages and introductory materials is easy because you don't have to scroll through all the text.

BREAKING UP AN EXISTING DOCUMENT INTO SUBDOCUMENTS

Breaking up an existing document into subdocuments is simple—just select a section and save it to a file. You can divide the document into as many logical or manageable sections as you want. If necessary, you can create subdocuments within subdocuments. Subdocuments can be expanded independently, so you have complete control over how much of a document you work with at a time.

 To create subdocuments from an existing document, select the section of text that you want to save in a subdocument. Keep in mind that you might someday use this subdocument in other master documents. With the text selected, click the Save button. In the Save dialog box (see Figure 18.18), choose Selected Text, and then click OK to display the Save File dialog box. Type a name for the new file, and then choose Save.

Figure 18.18
If you click the Save button with text selected, you can choose between saving the entire file and just the selected text.

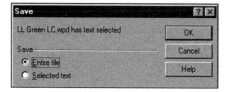

CREATING A MASTER DOCUMENT

A master document is just a regular WordPerfect document, with text and formatting codes. What turns a regular document into a master document is the links to other documents—the subdocuments. There isn't anything special about a subdocument—it's a regular WordPerfect document, too, with text and formatting codes.

You may already have a master document shell, especially if you just finished saving sections of text into files (as described previously) so they can be subdocuments. If you haven't done this, go ahead and type whatever headings or introductory material you need before the text of the first subdocument. Click where you want to insert the subdocument text, and then choose File, Document, Subdocument. The Include Subdocument dialog box appears (see Figure 18.19). Select the subdocument file, and then click Include.

Tip #211 from
Laura and Read

You can also right-click in the left margin space and choose Subdocument to display the Include Subdocument dialog box.

PART

VI

CH

18

Figure 18.19
The Include Subdocument is one of many different file management dialog boxes in WordPerfect.

Select a file in the list.

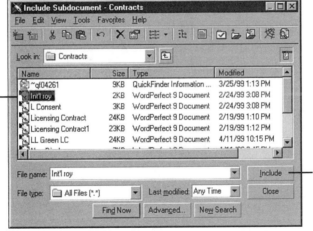

Click here to insert the subdocument code.

Tip #212 from
Laura and Read

The Reference toolbar includes buttons for working with master and subdocuments. Right-click the toolbar, and then choose Reference. There are three buttons: Subdocument, Expand Master, and Condense Master.

What happens next depends on your view mode. If you're in Page view, you have to scroll over to the left to see the subdocument icon in the margin (see Figure 18.20). If you're in Draft view, the name and path of the subdocument is displayed in a comment (see Figure 18.21).

Figure 18.20
In Page view, the position of subdocument codes is marked by icons in the left margin.

Subdocument icon ——

Subdocument code ——

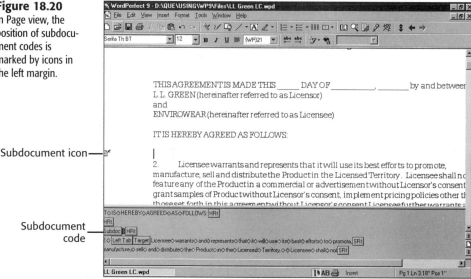

Figure 18.21
In Draft view, a subdocument is displayed as a comment.

Subdocument comment ——

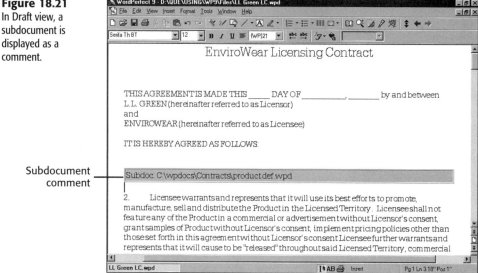

Rearranging Subdocuments

Subdocuments can easily be rearranged in a condensed master document. Turn on Reveal Codes and select the [Subdoc] code. Press Ctrl+X to cut the code. Click where you want to insert the subdocument code, and then press Ctrl+V to paste the code.

It's a little more complicated to rearrange expanded subdocuments, but it *can* be done. Turn on Reveal Codes and make sure you include the [Subdoc Begin] and the [Subdoc End] codes when you select the text of the subdocument. Press Ctrl+X, click where you want to insert the subdocument text, and then press Ctrl+V.

EXPANDING AND CONDENSING MASTER DOCUMENTS

When you expand a master document, each subdocument is inserted into that master document. You can then work with all the text at once. You can do a global search and replace, mark the text for an index or a table of contents, apply styles, and proof for whitespace and consistent formatting; you can perform any task that involves working with the entire document.

 To expand a master document, choose File, Document, Expand Master. The Expand Master Document dialog box opens, with a list of the subdocuments (see Figure 18.22).

Figure 18.22
You can select the subdocuments you want to expand in the Expand Master Document dialog box.

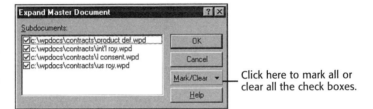

Click here to mark all or clear all the check boxes.

A subdocument that has a check mark in its check box will be opened and inserted in the master document. If you remove a check mark, that subdocument won't be opened. So you can expand only the subdocuments that you want to work with. Click OK to expand the subdocuments.

PART

VI

CH

18

Tip #213 from
Laura and Read

If you have a long list of subdocuments and you only want to expand one or two of them, it's quicker to deselect them all, and then select the one or two that you want. To deselect all the subdocuments at once, choose Mark/Clear, Clear All. When you're ready to expand all the subdocuments, you can reselect them. Choose Mark/Clear, Mark All to mark them all at once.

Caution

If one of the subdocuments has been moved or deleted, you get an error message. You can either type a new path and filename or browse for the file. If you're not sure where the file is, choose Skip. Network users should make sure they are mapped to the drive where the subdocuments are stored.

Note

  There are three different subdocument margin icons. The one with the up arrow is the [Subdoc Begin] code, the one with the down arrow is the [Subdoc End] code, and the one with the arrow tilting down to the left is a condensed subdocument [Subdoc *path/filename*] code.

When you condense a master document, you get to select which subdocuments are condensed and which are saved. By selectively condensing certain subdocuments, you can work on related sections of a document without "wading through" the rest of the text. Even a huge 500-page legal brief can be easily revised by breaking it up into subdocuments, and then expanding and condensing only those sections that you want to work with.

 To condense a master document, choose File, Document, Condense Master. The Condense/Save Subdocuments dialog box appears (see Figure 18.23).

This file will be condensed, but not saved.

Figure 18.23
In the Condense/Save Subdocuments dialog box, you can place a check mark next to a file to save or condense it.

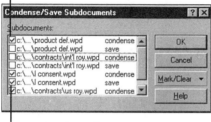

This file will be condensed and saved.

Once again, the Mark/Clear button opens a drop-down menu of options that you can use to condense all or clear all and to save all or clear all. Otherwise, you can place a check mark next to the files that you want to condense and save.

Tip #214 from
Laura and Read

You should *always* condense a master document before you save it. Otherwise, you save the same information twice and consume twice the disk space.

Caution

Think carefully before you choose to save your changes to a subdocument, especially if the subdocument belongs to a colleague. To save your changes without overwriting the original file, move or copy the original file before you condense and save the subdocument. There is no provision for saving a subdocument under a different name.

⚠ *If you have some stray subdocument text that won't disappear, or if the filename is missing in the Condense/Save Subdocuments dialog box, see "I Accidentally Deleted a Subdocument Code" in the Troubleshooting section at the end of this chapter.*

GENERATING DOCUMENT REFERENCES IN MASTER DOCUMENTS

When you generate document references for a master document, WordPerfect automatically expands the master document, generates the document references, and then condenses the master document again. If this procedure modifies any subdocuments, by default WordPerfect saves the modified subdocuments over the originals. If you don't want changes saved to the subdocuments, you can deselect the option to save subdocuments in the Generate dialog box (refer to Figure 18.16).

➔ For information on creating a table of contents, **see** "Creating a Table of Contents," **p. 522**

➔ For the steps to create an index, **see** "Creating Indexes," **p. 532**

➔ To learn how to create a table of authorities, **see** "Creating a Table of Authorities or a Bibliography," **p. 526**

→ To learn how to create a list in a long document, **see** "Assembling Lists," **p. 537**

FORMATTING TRICKS

The key to working with master documents and subdocuments is learning how to create subdocuments that can function independently of the master document. The formatting codes that are necessary in a subdocument can cause problems in the master document, and vice versa.

Automatic Code Placement, for the most part, is a great timesaver. It eliminates a lot of frustration from not positioning the insertion point correctly when formatting (those of us who worked in versions of WordPerfect before the advent of Automatic Code Placement thought it was magical).

However, in the case of subdocuments, the Auto Line Formatter component of the Automatic Code Placement feature can strip out redundant codes, resulting in a subdocument that can no longer stand on its own. For example, let's say you have a double-spaced master document. When you expand a subdocument with a double-spacing code in it, the Auto Line Formatter strips out that code, because it's redundant. When you save the subdocument, it is saved as a single-spaced document.

Now you're thinking "yeah yeah yeah, but what can I do about it?" You can place your formatting codes in an open style at the top of the subdocument…that's what. For this example, line spacing codes in an open style won't be deleted by the Auto Line Formatter.

Here are some other things to consider as you format master documents and subdocuments:

- If you want each subdocument to start on a new page, you can either insert a hard page between each subdocument code in the master document, or you can insert a hard page at the top of each subdocument.

- Formatting codes in a subdocument can cause conflicts with codes in the master document. For example, if the master document has Header A defined, that header remains in effect only until another Header A code is reached. If the first subdocument has a Header A defined, that header replaces the header you defined in the master document. This can work to your advantage, however, if you want new header text at the beginning of each chapter or section.

- Styles in a master document override subdocument styles with the same name, so the subdocuments are reformatted according to the codes in the master document's styles. These same-name styles are saved with the subdocument, although styles with unique names are added to the master document's list of styles. Consider creating a *template (page 614)* that contains the styles for your project, and then distributing the template among your colleagues so that they can use the styles when they create subdocuments.

- You can mark text for a table of contents, *table of authorities (page 526), list (page 537)*, index, or cross-reference in both the master document and subdocument. You might find it easier to mark document references in an expanded master document. If you're marking headings for a table, list, or index, you might want to define a style for your headings with all the formatting plus the mark text codes.

- To number an expanded master document sequentially, place a page numbering code to start numbering pages with 1 immediately after the introductory pages (such as the table of contents).

PART

VI

CH

18

- If you're working on a book, you probably want to increment the chapter numbers in each subdocument. Place a chapter number increment code at the beginning of each subdocument. At the beginning of the master document, insert a page number position code and a chapter number method code.

- If a document is to be printed on both sides of the paper, it's common practice to begin a new chapter or major section on the right side. You can accomplish this by placing a [Force: Odd] code in an open style at the top of each subdocument.

- Don't place footnote or endnote option codes in the subdocuments. These codes, which control spacing between footnotes, separator lines, and whether numbering should restart on each page, should only be placed in the master document.

- In most cases, footnotes should be numbered sequentially throughout a document. However, if you decide to restart the numbering in each subdocument, you need to place a footnote number set code in an open style at the top of each subdocument.

- You can opt to place all endnotes at the end of the document, or at the end of each subdocument. If you opt for the former, place an endnote placement code at the end of the master document and choose Insert Endnotes at Insertion Point in the Endnote Placement dialog box. For the latter, insert an endnote placement code at the end of the subdocument and choose Insert Endnotes at Insertion Point and Restart Numbering in the Endnote Placement dialog box.

- Marking text for cross-references in subdocuments is tricky because you have to remember the target names. Because expanding the master document compiles a list of all the marked targets, you might prefer to mark targets and references in an expanded master document.

TROUBLESHOOTING

MY FOOTNOTE NUMBERS KEEP GOING BACK TO 1

When I insert a footnote on a new page, the numbering starts over at 1.

The Restart Numbering on Each Page option is selected in the Advanced Footnote Options dialog box. To use continuously numbered footnotes for the entire document, choose Insert, Footnote/Endnote, Options, Advanced. In the Advanced Footnote Options dialog box, remove the check mark next to Restart Numbering on Each Page.

I CAN'T GET RID OF A REFERENCE NUMBER

I just deleted a footnote, but the footnote reference number is still in the paragraph.

The footnote number in the footnote itself and the footnote number in the document are two separate entities. Deleting the text of a footnote and the number in the footnote area doesn't automatically remove the footnote reference number (you have to do it manually). On the other hand, deleting the footnote reference number deletes everything at once.

I Typed the Wrong Target Name

I made a few mistakes when I marked my targets and references. In one case, I've typed the wrong target name. On the next page, I need to move the reference. Can I correct these mistakes without starting over?

If you make a mistake typing the target name, you need to delete the reference code and mark the reference again. If you just need to move the reference, select the explanatory text and the ? (or the reference information, if you've already generated the cross-references). You'll be selecting the text and the reference code, which can also be done in Reveal Codes if you prefer. Press Ctrl+X to cut the code, click where you want to insert the reference code, and then press Ctrl+V to paste the code.

The Generate Button Isn't Available

I've got the Cross-Reference bar displayed, but the Generate button is grayed out. The Generate option on the Reference menu is grayed out as well.

If the insertion point is inside one of the substructure elements (such as a graphics box caption, a footnote, an endnote, a header, or a footer), the Generate option isn't available. Click in the document text. When you move out of the substructure's area, the Generate button becomes available.

Discombobulated Graphics Box References

I just moved a graphics box and now the reference information is incorrect. I've tried generating the document, but the reference is still wrong.

When you click and drag a graphics box to move it somewhere else in the document, the target code doesn't go with it. The two become separated, so the reference information isn't accurate. There are a couple ways to avoid this.

First, you can turn on Reveal Codes and carefully select both the box code and the target code, and then use Cut and Paste to move the selection.

Or you can insert the target code in the graphics box caption. Right-click the graphics box, and then choose Caption. You can delete the default caption text, and then choose Tools, Reference, Cross-Reference. Select the target name from the list, and then choose Mark Target. Click in the document to get out of the caption, and then deselect the graphics box. No matter where you move this box, the target code stays with it.

I Accidentally Deleted a Subdocument Code

I'm finished revising a master document, so I opened the Condense/Save Subdocuments dialog box to condense the subdocuments. I condensed all the subdocuments, but there is still some text that belongs to a subdocument in my master document. When I look again at the Condense/Save Subdocuments dialog box, I see that the filename for that subdocument is missing. What's happened?

You've accidentally deleted one or both of the beginning or ending subdocument codes. When you do this, the subdocument text becomes a part of the master document. To rectify the situation, select the text and save it (using the original subdocument name). Then reinsert the subdocument code.

If you are making heavy revisions to a document, you might want to turn on the option to get a confirmation message before deleting codes. Choose Tools, Settings, Environment. Click the Prompts tab, and then select Confirm Deletion of Codes and Stop Insertion Point at Hidden Codes.

PROJECT

Cross-references make navigating through a long document much easier because they point out relationships between fragments of information. But even with the most detailed cross-reference, the reader must still go looking for the target information.

If the document is destined for a Web page or onscreen review, you can turn reference text into a *hyperlink (page 546)* that takes you directly to the target.

First, create a bookmark for the target:

1. Click near the target.
2. Choose Tools, Bookmark, Create.
3. Type a name for this bookmark, and then click OK. You can use the same name as the target.

Second, create a hyperlink to the bookmark:

1. Select the reference text.
2. Choose Tools, Hyperlink to open the Hyperlink Properties dialog box.
3. Click the Bookmark drop-down arrow to display a list of bookmarks for the document.
4. Choose the bookmark that you want to link to.
5. Click OK to create the hyperlink.

The hyperlink text appears in a different color. You can also choose Make Text Appear as a Button in the Hyperlink Properties dialog box for a different effect. To open the Hyperlink Properties dialog box so you can edit a hyperlink, right-click the hyperlink text, and then choose Edit Hyperlink.

→ This is just the beginning of things you can do with hyperlinks. **See** Chapter 20, "Interactive and Multimedia Documents," **p. 545**

CHAPTER 19

GENERATING TABLES, INDEXES, AND LISTS

In this chapter

CREATING A TABLE OF CONTENTS

Continuing in the fine tradition of providing powerful, yet easy-to-use long document tools, WordPerfect supports a five-level table of contents. Although any text that you mark in the document can be added to a table of contents, the most common entries are chapter names and section headings. You can automate the process of marking headings for a table of contents by using WordPerfect's heading styles, or by adding the mark text codes to your own heading styles. (I'll get back to that later in this section.)

Creating a table of contents entry is simple: You select the text that you want to appear (in most cases, a heading), and then choose the appropriate table of contents level. WordPerfect surrounds the selected text with Mark Text codes. When you generate the table, WordPerfect grabs the text between the Mark Text codes, positions it in the correct table of contents level, and inserts a current page number next to it.

MARKING TEXT

Selecting text for a table of contents can be a little tricky. You have to make sure that you don't include formatting codes, such as bold or italic, within the Mark Text codes. Otherwise, those codes affect the format of that entry and can potentially cause problems with other entries. If you do get some codes by accident, you'll know right away because, after you generate the table, you'll be able to see that certain entries are formatted differently.

To select text for a table of contents entry, follow these steps:

1. Choose Tools, Reference, Table of Contents to display the Table of Contents feature bar (see Figure 19.1).

Figure 19.1
The Table of Contents feature bar has buttons for each level in a table of contents, so marking a selection can be done with one click.

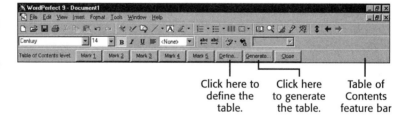

Click here to define the table.

Click here to generate the table.

Table of Contents feature bar

2. Turn on Reveal Codes (by pressing Alt+F3) and select the text that you want included in the table. Start selecting at the first letter of text and stop at the last letter so you don't accidentally include a formatting code.

3. Click one of the Mark buttons (refer to Figure 19.1) to mark this selection for a particular level in the table. For example, click Mark 1 to mark this entry for the first level in the table. Each table of contents level is indented by one more tab stop, so the second, third, fourth, and fifth levels are really sublevels of Level 1.

Tip #215 from
Laura and Read

If you want an automatic paragraph number to be included with a table of contents entry, make sure you include paragraph numbering codes when you select the text. If you don't want the paragraph numbers to appear in the table, start selecting right after the paragraph number (but don't include the tab or indent code that follows the paragraph number).

Note

If you're upgrading from version 7, note that the Table of Contents command is now under Tools, Reference, instead of Tools, Generate.

WordPerfect inserts a mark text code [Mrk Txt ToC] on either side of the selection. To expand the code so you can see the level for the entry, click the code in Reveal Codes. When you're finished marking text, you're ready to define where the table should be placed and how the entries should appear.

Tip #216 from
Laura and Read

You can edit the *outline styles (page 297)* so that headings created with the styles are automatically marked for a table of contents. Choose Insert, Outline/Bullets & Numbering. Select the outline style that you used in the document, and then choose Edit. Select the level that you want to edit in the list, and then click Edit Style. If necessary, place a check mark in the Show 'Off Codes' check box. Click right before the Codes to the Left Are ON-Codes to the Right Are OFF code. Hold down the Shift key, and then press the right arrow to move past the off code. Choose Tools, Reference, Table of Contents to display the Table of Contents feature bar at the bottom of the screen. Click a Mark button to mark the heading text for a particular level in the table. Click OK. A [Mrk Txt ToC] code is inserted in the on side and another on the off side. If necessary, repeat these steps for other outline levels.

PART

VI

CH

19

DEFINING TABLES

You can define a table of contents whenever you like—before or after you've marked the entries. Defining the table is a two-part process. First, you create a page for the table, which in most cases is at the top of the document. Second, you define how you want the table of contents to look. You choose the number of levels and the position and format of the page number that goes along with each entry. You can make global changes to the way table of contents entries are formatted by editing the five table of contents styles (one for each level).

Follow these steps to define a table of contents:

1. If necessary, create a new page and type a title for the table of contents.

2. Click on the line where you want the first entry to appear (usually 2–3 lines down from the title).

3. If the Table of Contents feature bar is displayed, click Define. Otherwise, choose Tools, Reference, Table of Contents to display the feature bar, and then click Define. The Define Table of Contents dialog box appears (see Figure 19.2).

Figure 19.2
In the Define Table of Contents dialog box, you can choose the number of levels for the table, and then select how you want the page numbers to appear.

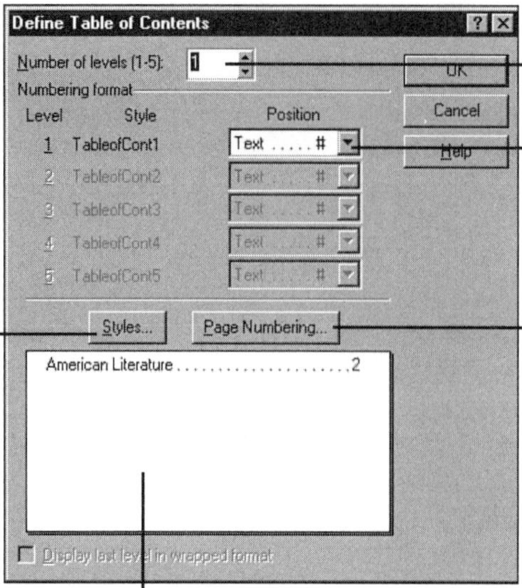

Click here to edit the table of contents styles.

Set the number of levels here.

Click here to choose a page number position.

Click here to choose a page number format.

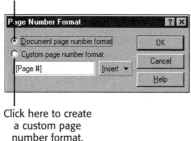

Preview the formatting for each entry on this sample document.

4. Type the number, or click the spinner arrows to set the Number of Levels (1–5).

5. Click the drop-down arrow for each available level and choose a page number position. (Depending on what you choose in step 4, some of the levels may not be available.)

6. Click Page Numbering to open the Page Number Format dialog box (see Figure 19.3). Select the document's page number format, or create a custom page number format, and then click OK.

→ For a complete discussion of creating customized page number formats, **see** "Switching to a Different Page Numbering Scheme," **p. 199**

Click here to use the page number format that you defined in the document.

Figure 19.3
In the Page Number Format dialog box, you can create a custom page number with page, chapter, and volume numbers.

Click here to create a custom page number format.

7. To edit the table of contents styles, click Styles. Select one of the TableofCont styles, and then click Edit. Click OK to return to the Define Table of Contents dialog box.

→ For more information on editing styles, **see** "Editing Styles," **p. 238**

8. Click OK. WordPerfect inserts the text <<Table of Contents will generate here>>.

Now, you've defined the table of contents so that when you generate the table, the table of contents entries have a place to go. You're almost done. Now you need to do two more things:

- So that the first page of text following the table of contents starts on a new page, insert a *hard page (page 195)* at the end of the table of contents.

- Reset page numbering to 1 if you don't want the table of contents pages included in the page count. If you've formatted the table of contents page numbers in Roman numerals, you might want to switch to Arabic numerals for the body text.

GENERATING TABLES

When you generate a document, WordPerfect compiles all the document references and creates tables, lists, and indexes. Generating a document takes a lot of processing power, so before you begin, save the document.

When you generate a document, all the document references (that is, the table of contents, the table of authorities, the index, lists, and cross-references) are generated at once. When you regenerate a document, the old tables, lists, and indexes are deleted from the document and rebuilt. This way, any entries that you've deleted are removed.

To generate a document, click the Generate button on the Table of Contents feature bar, or choose Tools, Reference, Generate. Or you can press Ctrl+F9. The Generate dialog box appears (see Figure 19.4).

Figure 19.4
When you generate a document, all the document references are updated at once.

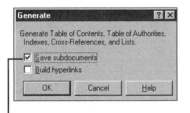

Click here to save subdocuments.

PART

VI

CH

19

Note

By default, the Generate feature updates the document references in *subdocuments (page 512)*. This can be extremely time-consuming because WordPerfect must open each subdocument, generate the references, and then save the subdocument. If you have links to subdocuments in this document, and you *don't* want to generate them, deselect Save Subdocuments in the Generate dialog box.

Click OK to generate the table of contents. Figure 19.5 shows a sample table of contents.

Figure 19.5
This table of contents has two levels, with no dot leaders for the second level.

The first level has dot leaders.

The second level doesn't have dot leaders.

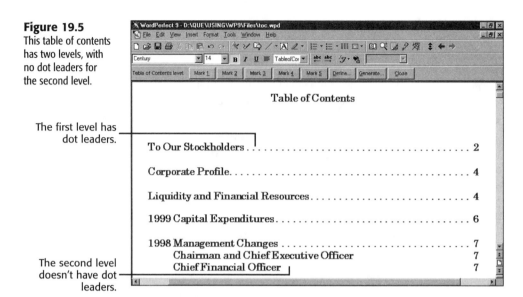

Tip #217 from

Laura and Read

You can edit table of contents entries after you've marked them. Simply revise the text between the two [Mrk Txt ToC] codes, and then regenerate the table.

⚠ *If some of your table of contents headings didn't make it into the table of contents, see "The Table of Contents Is Missing Entries" in the Troubleshooting section at the end of this chapter.*

⚠ *If some of the entries in the table of contents are bold or italic and others are not, see "Several Table of Contents Entries Are Bold" in the Troubleshooting section at the end of this chapter.*

CREATING A TABLE OF AUTHORITIES OR A BIBLIOGRAPHY

A *table of authorities* is sort of a table of contents for a legal document. It lists the authorities, which are the legal references to other cases, statutes, rules, citations, regulations, amendments, and so on, that appear in the brief. You can use the Table of Authorities feature to create a bibliography for any document that requires the identification of sources.

A table of authorities (or bibliography) can be divided into sections to separate the different sources. For example, a typical table of authorities might be divided into sections for cases, statutes, and regulations. A bibliography might have sections for newspaper articles, journal articles, and books.

Before you start marking text in a document, sketch out a rough draft of the table of authorities (or bibliography) so you have an idea of how many sections you need and what they will be called. Why? Because you'll need to specify a section when you mark an entry. (This is similar to marking a table of contents entry for a particular level.)

MARKING THE FIRST AUTHORITY

The first time you mark an entry for inclusion in a table of authorities, you define the actual text to be included in the table, so it's called *marking the full form*. As usual, when you're ready to mark the entries, you should turn on Reveal Codes (by pressing Alt+F3) so you can see exactly what you are selecting.

Follow these steps to mark an entry as a full form:

1. Choose Tools, Reference, Table of Authorities to display the Table of Authorities feature bar (see Figure 19.6).

Figure 19.6
The Table of Authorities feature bar has buttons that really speed up the tedious process of marking entries.

Table of Authorities feature bar

2. With Reveal Codes on, select the text that you want to appear in the table of authorities. Take note of nearby formatting codes—you may or may not want to include them in the selection.

> **Note**
> You can mark text for a table of authorities in the body text, as well as in footnotes, endnotes, and graphics box captions.

3. Click Create Full Form to display the Create Full Form dialog box (see Figure 19.7).

Figure 19.7
You can use the Create Full Form dialog box to specify the name of the section where you want the table of authorities entry inserted.

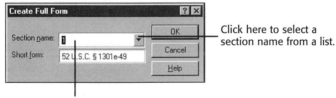

Click here to select a section name from a list.

Type a section name here.

PART
VI

CH
19

4. Type the name of the section in the Section Name text box, or click the drop-down list arrow and choose an existing name from the list.

5. Edit the portion of the selected text that appears in the Short Form text box or just type a one- or two-word abbreviation. The short form is the unique identifier that ties together the first authority and the following occurrences.

> **Note**
> The short form name must be unique, but it should also be descriptive enough so that you can easily associate the short form name with the full form.

6. Click OK. The Table of Authorities Full Form editing window appears, with the text that you selected at the top of the window (see Figure 19.8).

Figure 19.8
You can freely edit an entry so that it appears exactly as you want it to in the table.

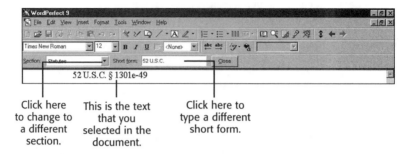

Click here to change to a different section.

This is the text that you selected in the document.

Click here to type a different short form.

Note

One of the advantages that the Table of Authorities feature has over the Table of Contents feature is the ability to edit the table entry separately from the text entry. In fact, the table entry can look completely different from the text entry because you can freely add *font attributes (page 66),* indentation, and blank lines—whatever you think is necessary to make the entry in the table of authorities easier to read.

7. Edit the text so that it looks exactly the way you want it to appear in the finished table. You can add or remove font attributes, indent text, add hard returns, and so on.

→ If you need a quick peek at the steps for indenting text, **see** "Indenting Text," **p. 176**

→ If you want to use font attributes, **see** "Emphasizing Important Text," **p. 64**

8. When you are finished, click <u>C</u>lose. WordPerfect inserts a [ToA: *section name; short form text;* Full Form] code. The Full Form part of the code identifies it as a full form code (as opposed to a short form code, which is explained in the next section).

If you later edit a table of authorities entry, the text in the full form won't be modified. You must edit the full form to update the entry for the table. To edit a full form, click the <u>E</u>dit Full Form button on the Table of Authorities feature bar. When the Edit Full Form dialog box appears (see Figure 19.9), select the full form in the list, and then click OK. This is a little confusing, so stick with me here—the full form is identified by its short form name in the Edit Full Form dialog box.

Figure 19.9
If you revise the text of a table of authorities entry in the document, you need to make those same revisions to the full form.

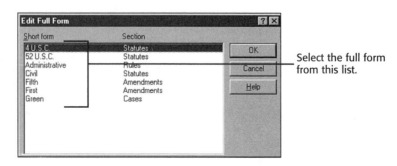

Select the full form from this list.

When you're in the table of authorities full form editing window (refer to Figure 19.8), you can revise the text, choose another section, or assign a different short form name.

MARKING SUBSEQUENT AUTHORITIES

After you've finished marking the full form, you can go through the document and mark subsequent occurrences with the short form. This step is the quickest because you don't have to select the text—you simply click in the text and choose the short form from a list.

Follow these steps to mark an authority by using the short form:

1. Click in the authority/text.
2. Click the Short form drop-down list arrow, and then select the short form in the list. If the short form is already displayed, you can skip this step.
3. Click Mark. WordPerfect inserts an abbreviated code in the document: [ToA:,*short form text*;].

Tip #218 from
Laura and Read

The last short form name you used is displayed in the Short form list box, so it's easy to continue marking subsequent occurrences of an authority. Simply click in the authority, and then click Mark. You might also consider using the Find feature in tandem with the Table of Authorities feature bar to quickly search for and mark all subsequent occurrences of each authority.

→ To get more information on searching for text, **see** "Searching for Text by Using Find and Replace," **p. 129**

 If the list of short forms is getting cluttered with short forms that you don't use anymore, see "Obsolete Short Forms" in the Troubleshooting section at the end of this chapter.

PART

VI

CH

19

DEFINING AND GENERATING TABLES

Just as you did for a table of contents, you have to create a page for the table of authorities (or bibliography) entries. You probably want the entries on a page by themselves, with headings for each section. You can create this page before or after you mark the authorities. When you have defined each section, you're ready to generate the table.

Follow these steps to define a table of authorities:

1. If necessary, press Ctrl+Enter to create a new page for the table.
2. If you want to set a page number format for the table of authorities pages, choose Format, Page, Numbering.

→ If you really want to get fancy with the page numbers, **see** "Adding Page Numbers," **p. 197**

3. Click where you want a section of the table to appear.
4. Type a heading for the section, and then press Enter a few times to insert some space between the heading and the entries.
5. Click the Define button on the Table of Authorities feature bar. (If the feature bar isn't displayed right now, choose Tools, Reference, Table of Authorities). The Define Table

of Authorities dialog box appears (see Figure 19.10). The section names that have been used in this document, along with the three default sections, are listed next to the default numbering scheme, which is *dot leaders (page 173)* trailing out to the page number at the right margin.

Figure 19.10
In the Define Table of Authorities dialog box, choose the section of authorities that you want to insert.

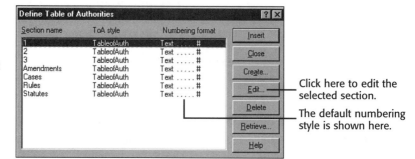

Click here to edit the selected section.

The default numbering style is shown here.

6. Click the section name, and then click Insert. WordPerfect inserts the following text at the insertion point: <<Table of Authorities will generate here>>.

7. Repeat steps 3–6 to define the location of each remaining section.

Tip #219 from
Laura and Read

Consistency across documents is important. When you have figured out how you want to do something, such as set up a table of authorities, for example, you can save time by retrieving that information from another document. To retrieve a table of authorities definition from another file, click the Retrieve button in the Define Table of Authorities dialog box to open the Retrieve ToA Definitions dialog box. Type the name of the file in the Filename text box, or click the Files icon to browse for it. When you've selected the file, the definitions for that document are displayed in the Name list box. Choose the definition, and then click OK to add them into the Define Table of Authorities dialog box.

Tip #220 from
Laura and Read

If the next page is the beginning of the body text, make sure you reset the page numbers back to 1 at the top of that page so that the table of authorities pages don't throw off the document page numbers.

By now you're hooked on the ability to customize virtually every aspect of the WordPerfect program, and you wouldn't even consider using another product that offered less flexibility. When you define a table of authorities, you have the ability to customize the format of each of its sections. You can even edit the table of authorities style and change the defaults for all future tables.

To customize the format of a particular section, select the section in the Define Table of Authorities dialog box (refer to Figure 19.10). Click Edit to open the Edit Table of Authorities dialog box (see Figure 19.11).

Click here to choose a page number position.

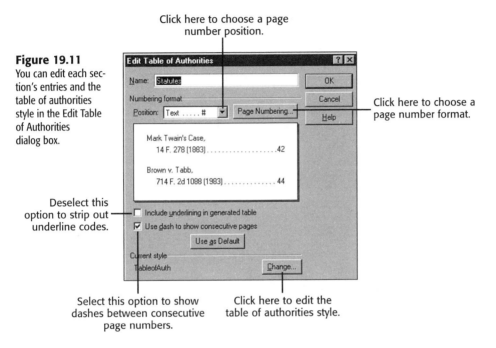

Figure 19.11
You can edit each section's entries and the table of authorities style in the Edit Table of Authorities dialog box.

Click here to choose a page number format.

Deselect this option to strip out underline codes.

Select this option to show dashes between consecutive page numbers.

Click here to edit the table of authorities style.

After you've marked all the entries, defined the location for each section's entries, and made the necessary adjustments in the Edit Table of Authorities dialog box, you're ready to generate the table. If the Table of Authorities feature bar is displayed, click the Generate button. Otherwise, choose Tools, Reference, Generate (or press Ctrl+F9). Choose to save changes to subdocuments or to build hyperlinks, and then click OK to build the table.

PART
VI
CH
19

Caution

If you've accidentally typed a short form name incorrectly, or if you have short forms that don't have corresponding full forms, you'll get an error message when you generate the table. The problem entry will be preceded by an asterisk in the first section of the table so you can see which entries need repair. If the incorrect short form name has been used, simply delete the short form code and reinsert it. If the full form is missing, find the first occurrence of the authority, delete the full form, and then create a new full form.

WordPerfect searches through the document for each entry and inserts the page number(s) where the entry is found (see Figure 19.12).

Figure 19.12
This is an example of a table of authorities in a legal brief.

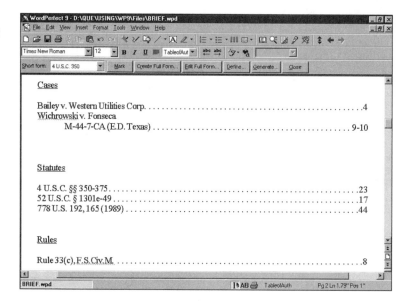

CREATING INDEXES

Take a look at the index at the back of this book and ask yourself, "Would I want to create one of these by hand?" Probably not, unless you're a wonderfully patient individual who can tolerate tedium well. I'm not, so I use WordPerfect's Index feature to help me create indexes for my lengthy documents.

Some say a good index can make or break a reference book. I hope the index for this book has already saved you some time (and frustration). The key to a good index is anticipating the needs of the reader. You need to try to think of all the ways a reader might try to look something up and then point them in the right direction.

There are two methods to create an index; the one you use depends on how much time you have, and how much control you want over the process. If you mark the entries by hand, you have maximum control, but you may need to spend a lot of time doing it. Or you can create a concordance file with a list of index information and let WordPerfect compile the index for you; this is fastest, but you have minimal control. For the best of both worlds, you can use a combination of both methods.

CREATING CONCORDANCE FILES

A *concordance file* is a list of words or phrases that you want included in the index. When you generate the index, WordPerfect compares the entries in the concordance file with the text and, if a match is found, inserts the index entry with a page number. The advantage of creating a concordance file is that it's much faster than selecting and marking every index entry manually. The disadvantage is that you lose some flexibility.

To create a concordance file, start with a blank document, and then type the index entries. Type only one entry per line, and make sure you press Enter at the end of the last line. Click the Save button, and then give the concordance file a name. You'll be prompted for the name and location later, when you generate the index.

Caution

Concordance file entries are not case sensitive, so if you type Recycling, the words *recycling* and *RECYCLING* are considered matches. However, when the index is created, WordPerfect uses the capitalization in the concordance file, not the capitalization in the document.

This important because when you create the concordance file, you need to make sure that you use the capitalization that you want to see in the index.

Tip #221 from
Laura and Read

You've got a pretty good memory if you can remember all the entries you want in the index! Even with gingko, my memory isn't that good, so I add entries to the concordance file while I'm working on a document. I keep both documents open and switch back and forth between the two.

WordPerfect automatically marks each entry in the concordance file as a heading—you don't have to do a thing. However, if you want an entry to be listed as a subheading in the index, you have to mark that entry manually. See the next section for the steps to mark an index entry.

Tip #222 from
Laura and Read

It is usually easiest to work with the concordance file if it's in alphabetical order. In just a few seconds, you can sort the entries alphabetically. At the top of the file, choose Tools, Sort. Select First Word in the Line, and then choose Sort. As you add entries, you can repeat this process to keep the list in alphabetic order.

MARKING INDEX ENTRIES BY HAND

Tedious? Yes. Precise? Absolutely. Marking every index entry in a document is a definite time investment. The hope is that your investment pays off by making all sorts of information easier for a reader to find.

Marking index entries is simple—you select the text, and then click one of the buttons on a handy Index feature bar to mark the text for the index. Indexes have two levels, so you can mark an entry as a heading or as a subheading (underneath a heading).

Every instance of an index entry has to be marked. Otherwise, the list of page numbers next to the entry won't be complete. After you mark the first occurrence, use the Find feature to locate the other occurrences in the document, and then move on to the next index entry.

To mark text for an index, follow these steps:

1. Choose Tools, Reference, Index. The Index feature bar appears over the text (see Figure 19.13).

Figure 19.13
The Index feature bar has buttons to speed up the process of marking the entries and creating the index.

Index feature bar

2. Select the text for the entry. (You can be a little sloppy selecting text here because if you accidentally grab an underline or bold code, WordPerfect won't apply the attribute codes to index text.)

3. Click in the Heading text box to mark this entry as a heading; click in the Subheading text box to mark this entry as a subheading. WordPerfect inserts the selected text in the text box.

4. If you are marking this entry as a subheading, type the heading that you want it to fall under in the Heading text box.

Tip #223 from
Laura and Read

The heading and subheading text don't *have* to match the text that you selected in the document. You can type exactly what you want to appear in the index heading (and subheading). This is helpful when the text in the document doesn't fit well in the index.

5. Click the Mark button to insert the index code.

The next time you have to mark this entry, you can either select the text, and then click in the Heading text box (to insert the selection), or you can select an entry off the Heading and Subheading lists.

Caution

When you revise a document, you're likely to make some changes to index entries. Because these changes aren't automatically reflected in the index codes, you need to delete the old code, and then insert a new one for the revised entry. In Reveal Codes, click and drag the old index code out of the Reveal Codes window to delete it. Select the entry, and then mark it as a heading or subheading. The next time you generate the index, the entries is updated.

DEFINING AND GENERATING INDEXES

Defining an index is similar to defining a table of contents or a table of authorities, except an index is assembled at the end of a document. To define an index, follow these steps:

1. Move to the end of the document and press Ctrl+Enter to create a new page.

2. At the top of the new page, type a heading for the index.

3. If necessary, choose Tools, Reference, Index to display the Index feature bar.

4. Click the Define button on the Index feature bar to display the Define Index dialog box (see Figure 19.14).

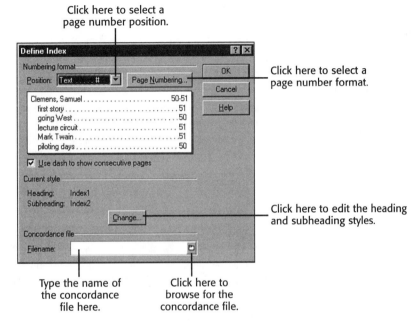

Click here to select a
page number position.

Figure 19.14
You can use the
Define Index dialog
box to select a page
number format and
position. You can also
edit the heading and
subheading styles and
specify a concordance
file.

Click here to select a
page number format.

Click here to edit the heading
and subheading styles.

Type the name of
the concordance
file here.

Click here to
browse for the
concordance file.

5. If you want to use the default settings, you can skip to step 6. Otherwise, make the necessary changes to the following:

- Click the Position drop-down list arrow and choose a position for the page numbers in the list.

- Click Page Numbering to use a custom page number format.

- Click Change if you want to edit the two index styles.

- Type a filename in the Filename text box or click the File icon to browse for the concordance file.

6. Click OK. The following text is inserted at the insertion point: <<Index will generate here>>. An Index definition code is also inserted.

7. Click Generate. Choose to save changes to subdocuments or to build hyperlinks, and then click OK to build the index. Figure 19.15 shows a sample index.

Figure 19.15
This is a sample of an index that might appear in the back of a WordPerfect reference book.

It's stylish to start each index section with a capital letter.

You can easily insert a short graphics line under the capital letter.

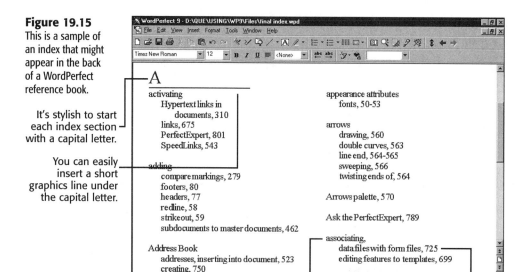

Heading   Subheading

Tip #224 from
Laura and Read

Flip back to the index in this book. Notice that the index is formatted into three columns? Have you *ever* seen an index not formatted in columns? To format your index in newspaper columns, see "Defining Newspaper Columns," in Chapter 8, "Formatting the Page."

 When you generated the index, if you got an error message that said one of the concordance file entries was too long, see "A Concordance Entry Is Too Long" in the Troubleshooting section at the end of this chapter.

An index has a lot more entries than a table of contents or table of authorities. The number of errors generally rises in proportion to the number of entries, so indexes tend to be more problematic than tables. After you generate the index, you may have some things to fix:

- Misspelled entries—Make a note of the page number for the misspelled entry, move to that page, and then turn on Reveal Codes (by pressing Alt+F3). When you locate the Index code for that entry, click on it or move to the left of it so the code expands and shows you the heading (and subheading) text. If the text is misspelled in the document, go ahead and correct it, but what you really need to focus on is the text in the heading or subheading because that's what shows up in the index. When you find the index code with the misspelled heading or subheading text, click and drag it out of the Reveal Codes window, and then re-create it.

- Entries with similar spellings—If you've got multiple entries with similar spellings, you need to consolidate them into one entry. For example, if you have an entry for Recycling Initiative and another for Recycling Initiative*s*, you need to decide which entry you want to keep, and then delete and re-create the index codes for the other entry. Rather than use the Find feature to look for every index code, make a note of the page numbers so you can zero in on a page at a time.

- Remove outdated entries—Turn on Reveal Codes (by pressing Alt+F3), locate the index code, and then click and drag it out of the Reveal Codes window.

- Solitary headings—If you see a heading that needs a subheading, you can go back and add another index code for a subheading, or you can delete and re-create the original code with heading and subheading text.

- Scattered subheadings—If you see subheadings that would make more sense if they were combined into one subheading, you need to re-create the index codes for those subheadings. Make a note of the page numbers, move to the first page, and turn on Reveal Codes (by pressing Alt+F3). Delete the code, and then re-create it with the new subheading. Repeat for the other index entries with inadequate subheadings.

- Too many subheadings—A good rule of thumb is to have no more than a dozen sub-headings under a heading. Of course, there are exceptions—witness the monster index at the end of this book! You can create a new heading and divide the subheadings between the original heading and the new heading. Of course, this means you have to delete and re-create codes. Decide which subheadings you want grouped under a new heading, and then delete the index codes for that subheading. When you re-create the index codes for those entries, use the new heading.

- Unexplained entries—If you've got entries in the index that don't appear in your con-cordance file, there must be some index codes in the document. You can strip them out with the Find and Replace feature. Choose Edit, Find and Replace. In the Find and Replace dialog box, click in the Find text box, and then choose Match, Codes. Type i to jump to the Index code, and then choose Insert & Close. Leave the Replace With text box blank or with <Nothing> in it. Choose Replace All.

- Misplaced entries—When you generate an index, subheadings are automatically alpha-betized under the heading. If you have subheadings that are out of order, there may be an extra space in front of the heading or subheading text. This can happen when you select text in the document, and then insert it into the Heading or Subheading text box. You know the drill by now—make a note of the page numbers, turn on Reveal Codes (by pressing Alt+F3), delete the code, and then re-create it.

ASSEMBLING LISTS

A *list* is just what it sounds like—it's a list of items in a document. You might want to gener-ate a list of all the figures or illustrations, with the numbers of the pages where they can be found in the document. If you have graphic boxes, you can have WordPerfect automatically place the caption text from each type of *graphics box (page 319)* into a separate list. You can create multiple lists to handle all the different elements in your document (such as figures, tables, charts, and equations).

MARKING ENTRIES

Assembling a list is just like creating a table or an index—you mark the entries, define the list, and then generate the list. To create a list, you have to mark the text that you want included in it. For example, to mark a table, select the table title or heading for the list (for example, Table 1.3. Continuing Education Classes), not the actual table definition code.

Caution

If you mark a graphics box that doesn't include a caption, an entry is inserted in the list with a page number, but the entry is blank. In other words, you have a dot leader and a page number, but no text. Either create a caption for the figure or mark a title or heading instead.

Follow these steps to mark an entry for a list:

1. Choose Tools, Reference, List to display the List feature bar (see Figure 19.16).

Figure 19.16
Use the buttons on the List feature bar to speed up the process of marking entries, defining lists, and generating lists.

Type the name of the list here.

List feature bar

2. Turn on Reveal Codes (by pressing Alt+F3) and select the text that you want to appear in the list.

Caution

You can't be sloppy when you're selecting text for a list—any formatting codes that fall between the mark text codes will affect that entry in the list (and possibly all the following entries).

3. If the name of the list is already displayed in the List text box, you can skip to step 4. If this is the first entry you've marked for a list, type the name of the list in the List text box. Otherwise, click the List drop-down list arrow and select the name of the list.

4. Click the Mark button. WordPerfect inserts [Mrk Txt List] codes on either side of the selection.

Note

You can see which list an entry is assigned to if you expand the [Mrk Txt List] code. In Reveal Codes, move the red cursor before a code to expand it.

To revise a list entry, edit the text between the two [Mrk Txt List] codes. You can remove an entry completely by clicking and dragging one of the codes out of the Reveal Codes window (the mate is deleted automatically).

DEFINING AND GENERATING LISTS

Long and multipart documents tend to have more elements than the average document, and keeping track of them can be very time-consuming, both for the creator and for the reader. Creating a separate list for figures, tables, equations, and other elements can help you keep things organized.

Tip #225 from *Laura and Read*	Generating a list of figure captions is a great way to check for consistency in figure numbering and to make sure the caption text is adequately descriptive.

You can define multiple lists in a document, each on its own page, or embedded in the body text. You can define lists before or after you mark up the document. Follow these steps to define a list:

1. Click in the document where you want a list to appear.

2. If you want the list on a page by itself, press Ctrl+Enter to insert a hard page.

3. Type a title for the list, and then press Enter a few times to create space between the title and the list entries.

4. If the List feature bar is displayed, click the Define button. Otherwise, choose Tools, Reference, List to display the feature bar, and then click Define. The Define List dialog box appears (see Figure 19.17). The names of lists that you've already used when marking entries appears.

Figure 19.17
In the Define List dialog box, you can choose the list that you want to insert.

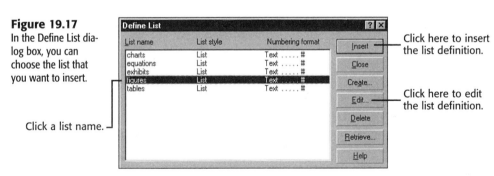

Click a list name.

Click here to insert the list definition.

Click here to edit the list definition.

5. Select a list name in the list box. By default, the entry has dot leaders out to the page number, which is positioned at the right margin. The page number format being used in the document is used on the list page numbers.

Note	If you're defining lists before marking entries in the text, you might not see any list names in the List Name list box. To create a new list, click Create, type a name for the list, and then click OK. Go ahead and create the list with the default settings; you can modify them from the Define List dialog box.

Tip #226 from
Laura and Read

Consistency across documents is important. When you've figured out how you want to do something, like build a list, for example, you can save time by retrieving that information from another document. To retrieve a list name from another file, click the Retrieve button in the Define List dialog box to open the Retrieve List Definitions dialog box. Type the name of the file in the Filename text box, or click the Files icon to browse for it. When you've selected the file, the list definitions for that document are displayed in the Name list box. Choose one or more list names, and then click OK to add them into the Define List dialog box.

6. To accept the default settings and insert a list definition code in the document, click Insert. WordPerfect inserts the following text in the document: <<List will generate here>>.

7. Repeat steps 1–6 to insert definition codes for all the list names. Click Close when you're done.

Tip #227 from
Laura and Read

If the next page is the beginning of the body text, make sure you reset the page numbers back to 1 at the top of that page so that the List pages don't throw off the page numbers of the document.

If you want to modify the defaults, select a list name in the Define List dialog box, and then click Edit to display the Edit List dialog box (see Figure 19.18), where you have the following options:

■ Click the Position drop-down list arrow and choose a position for the page numbers in the list.

■ Click Page Numbering to use a custom page number format.

■ Click Change if you want to edit the list style.

■ If you want WordPerfect to insert the caption text in the list, click the List Box Captions Automatically drop-down list arrow and choose the type of box this list is intended for. For example, if this is a Figures list, choose Figure Box.

When you're ready to generate the lists, click the Generate button. Choose to save changes to subdocuments, or to build hyperlinks, and then click OK to assemble the lists. Figure 19.19 shows a sample list.

 If the captions are missing from a list of figures, see "Blank Entries in a Figure List" in the Troubleshooting section at the end of this chapter.

Figure 19.18
You can use the options in the Edit List dialog box to edit the default page number position and page number format. You can also select to have WordPerfect automatically insert caption text in the list.

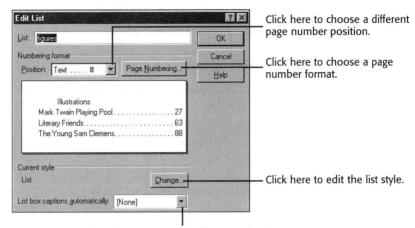

Click here to choose a different page number position.

Click here to choose a page number format.

Click here to edit the list style.

Click here to choose the box type for the captions to be inserted in the list.

Figure 19.19
Lists make it easier for the creator and the reader to keep track of where supportive elements are located.

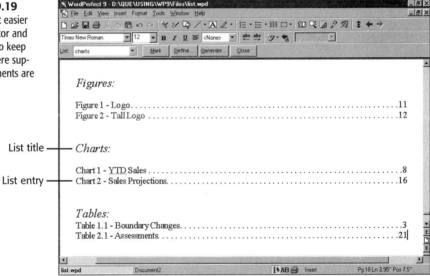

List title

List entry

TROUBLESHOOTING

THE TABLE OF CONTENTS IS MISSING ENTRIES

I've just generated a table of contents, but not all the headings are showing up: I marked three levels of headings for the table, but only two appear.

You have probably defined the table for only two levels, but marked for three. Turn on Reveal Codes (by pressing Alt+F3) and find the [Def Mark] code at the top of the table of contents page. Double-click the code to edit it. In the Define Table of Contents dialog box, click the up spinner arrow to increase the number of levels to three, and then click OK.

Because you've edited the original code, there is no duplicate code to delete. Regenerate the table—the third-level headings should show up now.

SEVERAL TABLE OF CONTENTS ENTRIES ARE BOLD

After making some revisions and marking new entries for the table of contents, I regenerated the table. All the new entries are bold, but the rest of the table is not.

When you select text to mark for a table of contents, you have to make sure that you don't include any formatting codes in the selection. If you do, those formatting codes are copied into the table of contents along with the selected text. You can turn on Reveal Codes (by pressing Alt+F3) and delete the [Bold] codes, but the next time you generate the table, they'll be back. A permanent solution is to go back to each new entry and delete the first [Mrk Txt ToC] code (which automatically deletes its mate). Then, position the insertion point on the first character and select only the text of the heading (plus any styles that are in place), but not the [Bold] codes. If necessary, choose Tools, Reference, Table of Contents to display the Table of Contents feature bar. Click a Mark button to reinsert the [Mrk Txt ToC] codes. Repeat for the other headings, and then regenerate the table.

OBSOLETE SHORT FORMS

While making heavy revisions, I removed some of the authorities that had been marked with a full form. Even though the full forms are gone, the short forms still show up in the list. Is there any way to strip out these obsolete short forms?

Short form information is stored in the document prefix. If you haven't had any contact with it until now, it's invisible, you can't edit it, and it is the root of all document evil. Rebuilding the document prefix fixes all manner of problems. First, make sure the file isn't already open. Then open a blank document, type an x, and then press Enter. Click Insert, File. Select the file, and then click Insert. Delete the *x* and the blank line, and then resave the file. Save this document under the original filename so you don't have duplicate files lying around. When the document prefix is rebuilt, only the short forms that are used in the document appear in the list.

A CONCORDANCE ENTRY IS TOO LONG

I've just generated an index, and I get an error message that says "Unable to generate: concordance entry is too large," followed by the offending entry. What is the length limit on concordance file entries?

A concordance file entry must not be longer than 63 characters. I tested this a bit and got flaky results between 55 and 60 characters, so your best bet is to keep the entries down to 50 characters or so.

BLANK ENTRIES IN A FIGURE LIST

I've just generated a list of figure captions, and some of the entries only have page numbers—there isn't any caption text, just dot leaders and page numbers. What did I do wrong?

There is a setting in the Edit List dialog box where you can choose to have WordPerfect automatically copy the caption text into the list. If you haven't selected a box type, the captions won't be copied into the list.

Choose Tools, Reference, List. Click the Define button on the List feature bar. Select the list name for the figures, and then click Edit. Click the List Box Captions Automatically drop-down list arrow, and then choose the type of box you have used.

PROJECT

When you import (and convert) a Microsoft Word 97 document with a table of contents, Word's table of contents styles are imported as well. The conversion process does its best to interpret Word's formatting, but the results are not always perfect. You can edit these styles to change the appearance of the table entries.

Follow these steps to edit the Word 97 table of contents styles:

1. Click at the top of the table of contents page.
2. Choose Tools, Reference, Table of Contents to display the Table of Contents feature bar.
3. Click Define to open the Define Table of Contents dialog box.
4. Click Styles to open the Table of Contents Styles dialog box (see Figure 19.20).

Figure 19.20
You can select a style in the Table of Contents Styles dialog box and edit it in the Styles Editor.

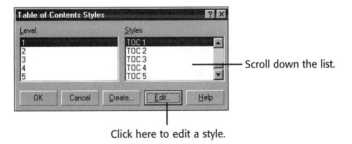

Scroll down the list.

Click here to edit a style.

5. Scroll down through the Styles list box until you see the TOC 1 through TOC 9 styles. The numbers correspond to levels, so start with the TOC 1 style.
6. Click the TOC 1 style, and then click Edit. The Styles Editor opens (see Figure 19.21). (Don't ask me where the Small Caps code comes from—in Word 97, the table of contents didn't have any small caps text in it!)
7. If you don't have Reveal Codes selected, select it now. Now you can see the codes in the TOC 1 style. To expand a code, click it or move the red cursor to the left of the code. To delete a style, click and drag it out of the Reveal Codes window. To edit a code, double-click it.
8. Make the changes by using the menu in the Styles Editor rather than the WordPerfect 9 menu.

Figure 19.21
You can use the menus in the Styles Editor to insert formatting codes in the style.

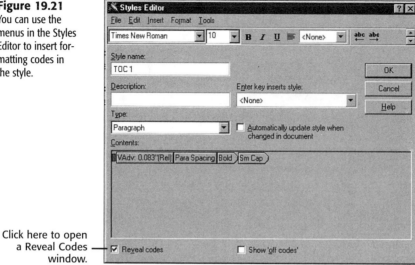

Click here to open a Reveal Codes window.

9. Click OK when you're done.

10. Select the TOC 2 style, and then click Edit. Make your changes, and then click OK.

11. Continue selecting the TOC styles until you've edited the styles that are in use for this document. In other words, if there are four levels in the table of contents, you should edit TOC 1 through TOC 4.

CHAPTER 20

INTERACTIVE AND MULTIMEDIA DOCUMENTS

In this chapter

RETHINKING THE CONCEPT OF DOCUMENTS

Technological advances over the years have gradually increased the power of the written document to communicate more effectively. The typewriter made it easier to read the written word. Early word processors helped writers to organize—by offering the capability of cutting and pasting—and to proofread documents. Not too long ago, elements of desktop publishing—including complex layout and graphics—crept into the word processing arena.

Today we're on the verge of another leap forward, as technology enables us to get at information differently. No longer must we read a document on a printed page. Instead we can read it on a computer screen. No longer must we follow a document from beginning to end, but we can jump from one place to another, or even from one document to another. Further, because we're not tied to paper and print, we can add multimedia elements, including sound or video.

CREATING HYPERTEXT LINKS

The first step in creating a nonlinear document is to link sections together so that the reader can jump from one place to another. You do this by creating *bookmarks*, which are like targets where you want to land, and then by creating *hyperlinks*, which enable you to jump from where you are to a bookmark.

Tip #228 from
Laura and Read

Before setting bookmarks in your document, you might want to visually sketch out how you view the organization of your document, including places readers will most likely want to go (bookmarks), and places from which you expect them to link. This makes it easier to systematically go through the document and add bookmarks and hyperlinks.

CREATING LINKS WITHIN DOCUMENTS

To create a bookmark in a document, follow these steps:

1. Go to the spot in the document you want to bookmark.
2. Choose Tools, Bookmark. WordPerfect displays the Bookmark dialog box (see Figure 20.1, which shows a bookmark already displayed).
3. Click Create to display the Create Bookmark dialog box (see Figure 20.2).

Note

The Create Bookmark dialog box attempts to guess at the bookmark name, based on the text following the insertion point. Often these names are long, and not always descriptive. You should change them to shorter, recognizable, and descriptive bookmark names.

4. Type the name of the bookmark, and click OK to set the bookmark and to return to the document.

Figure 20.1
You can use the
Bookmark dialog box
to create and manage
your document's
bookmarks.

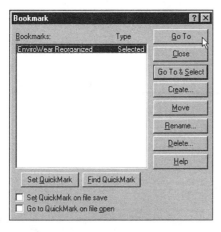

Figure 20.2
The Create Bookmark
dialog box suggests
using adjacent docu-
ment text, which you
can edit or replace
with something
shorter or more
descriptive.

If you select text before setting the bookmark, WordPerfect uses the selected text for the bookmark name. WordPerfect also identifies the bookmark type as Selected (refer to Figure 20.1), which means that both the location and the selected text are part of the bookmark.

Bookmarks can be used any time—for example, to quickly go to a bookmark while editing. You can also set a QuickMark, which does not require a name, by choosing Set QuickMark (refer to Figure 20.1). You can access the QuickMark or other bookmarks by choosing Tools, Bookmark. You then click the bookmark you want to go to and click Go To.

You can also access your bookmarks by choosing Edit, Go To or pressing Ctrl+G. In the Go To dialog box, click Bookmarks and select a bookmark from the drop-down list (see Figure 20.3). Click Go To to jump to the selected bookmark.

PART

VI

CH

20

Figure 20.3
The Go To dialog box
is an easy way to
jump to your docu-
ment bookmarks.

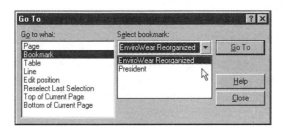

If you choose Set QuickMark on File Save, and also Go to QuickMark on File Open, the QuickMark is automatically set at the point of the insertion point each time you save the document, and when you open it again, WordPerfect jumps directly to that bookmarked location. If the bookmark type is selected, you can also click Go To & Select, which causes WordPerfect to jump to the bookmark and select the bookmarked text.

After you have created bookmarks, you can create hyperlinks to those bookmarks. To create a hyperlink, follow these steps:

1. Create or find the text you want to link from. You should choose text that suggests to the readers that they can get more information by following the link.

Tip #229 from
Laura and Read

For very long documents, you can create a table of contents or menu at the beginning of the document, and then use those entries to link to sections of the document.

2. Select the text or object to be linked.

Note

You cannot link from nothing. However, you *can* link from graphic objects as well as text. Whatever you link, you must select it first.

3. Choose Tools, Hyperlink. WordPerfect displays the Hyperlink Properties dialog box (see Figure 20.4).

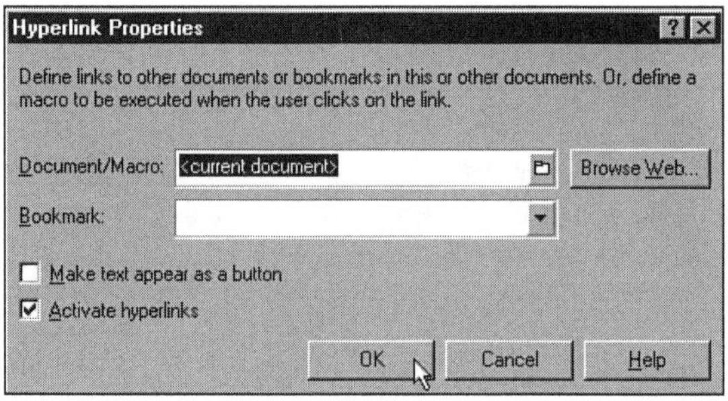

Figure 20.4
The Hyperlink Properties dialog box enables you to create links to bookmarks, to other documents, and even to Web or email addresses.

4. Click the Bookmark drop-down list, and select the bookmark you want to jump to.

5. Choose one or both of these options, if needed:
   - Create button link—Normally linked text appears in a different color from the regular text, typically blue, and underlined (see Figure 20.5). This is a visual cue to the reader that clicking the text links to another location. If you really want to get the reader's attention, select the Make Text Appear as a Button option, which creates a button from the text you selected, as shown also in Figure 20.5.

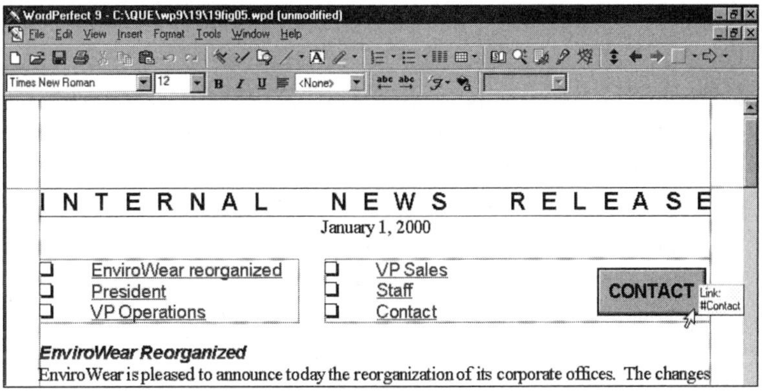

Figure 20.5
Hyperlink text usually appears underlined and in blue, but you can also display linked text as buttons.

- Activate links—By default, hyperlinks you create are *active*, which means that if you click them, you jump to the targeted bookmark. If you deselect Activate Hyperlinks, the text continues to appear linked (underlined and blue), but if you click the link, nothing happens.

Tip #230 from
Laura and Read

If you want to edit many linked text locations by using the mouse, choose Tools, Hyperlink, and deselect Activate Hyperlinks. You can then edit links without the fear of accidentally jumping to a bookmark. When you're through editing, choose Tools, Hyperlink again to activate all links.

6. Click OK to return to your document. WordPerfect displays the hyperlink using the options you selected (refer to Figure 20.5).

After you create a link, assuming that hyperlinks are active (the mouse pointer appears as a hand), click the link to jump to the target bookmark.

Caution

Because hyperlinked documents are not linear, it can become easy for a reader to get lost while following hyperlinks. You can help the reader by inserting links that jump back to the top of the document, or that return to a table of contents or menu.

Tip #231 from
Laura and Read

WordPerfect enables you to draw action shapes, such as forward, back, return, or home buttons, like those found in Web browsers (choose Insert, Shapes, Action). You can link those shapes to bookmarks, thus helping the reader navigate your document.

PART

VI

CH

20

If you change your mind and need to edit or delete a bookmark or hyperlink, consider these options:

- If you know where the code is located, move the insertion point to that location and open Reveal Codes (by choosing View, Reveal Codes or pressing Alt+F3). Then delete the bookmark or hyperlink code.

- To remove a bookmark, which might be difficult to find in a document, choose Tools, Bookmark. In the Bookmark dialog box, select the bookmark you want to remove and choose Delete.

- To rename a bookmark, access the Bookmark dialog box and choose Rename. This has the same effect as editing a bookmark, because there is nothing else to change.

- To edit a hyperlink, right-click the link, and choose Edit Hyperlink. WordPerfect displays the Hyperlink Properties dialog box (refer to Figure 20.4). Change the link and click OK. Note that you can also use the menus (by choosing Tools, Hyperlink), but the insertion point must already be on the hyperlinked text, which is a bit tricky if the link is active.

- To edit the text of a hyperlink button, right-click the button and choose Select. Double-click the button graphics box to edit the text (for example, to change the text font). You can also right-click the button and choose other graphics box options such as Border/Fill to change the look from a button to some other type of box.

LINKING TO DOCUMENTS

You can also create hyperlinks from one document to another, and even to specific bookmarks within the target document. To create a hyperlink to another document, follow these steps:

1. Create the target document. If you intend to link to specific locations in the document, create bookmarks to identify those locations.

2. In the document from which you want to link, select the text or object you want to link and choose Tools, Hyperlink. WordPerfect displays the Hyperlink Properties dialog box (refer to Figure 20.4).

3. Type the filename of the document you want to link to, or click the browse button at the right of the text box to browse for the file.

Caution

When linking to another document, be sure to include the full drive and path, along with the filename. Otherwise, WordPerfect might not be able to find the file when you try to link to it.

Tip #232 from
Laura and Read

If you're linking documents on a network drive for use by others, use UNC (universal naming convention) instead of drive letters. Others on the network may not have mapped their drives the same way you have. For example, instead of `drive:\path\filename`, you should use `\\server\volume:\path\filename`.

4. If you're linking to a bookmark in the target document, type the name of the bookmark in the <u>B</u>ookmark edit box or select a bookmark from the <u>B</u>ookmark drop-down list.

Tip #233 from	If you browse to choose the filename of the target document, WordPerfect also reads
Laura and Read	ahead and returns a list of valid bookmark names in the <u>B</u>ookmark drop-down list.

Caution	You should link to bookmarks by using the same upper- and lowercase characters found in
	the bookmark. Although WordPerfect ignores case, Web pages don't, and you might find
	that links don't work simply because the case in the bookmark and the link don't match.

5. Click OK to return to your WordPerfect document.

When you click a link to another document, WordPerfect opens that document. If you also specified a target bookmark, WordPerfect then jumps to that location.

Tip #234 from	If you intend for the reader to return to the original, or *home*, document, you should also
Laura and Read	place a link in the target document that jumps back to the home document. Remember that
	you can link text or graphic objects, such as action buttons.

LINKING TO MACROS

You can also create a link to a macro, so that when you click the link, WordPerfect executes the macro. Macros could perform an action (such as sorting a table), or could launch another program (such as the Windows Calculator).

To link to a macro, follow these steps:

1. Create the macro you want to execute.

→ For information on creating and using macros, **see** Chapter 24, "Experts and Macros," **p. 685**

2. In the document to which you want to link the macro, select the text or object from which you want to link.

3. Choose <u>T</u>ools, Hyperlink. WordPerfect displays the Hyperlink Properties dialog box (refer to Figure 20.4).

4. In the <u>D</u>ocument/Macro edit box, type (or browse for) the name of the macro you want to execute.

5. Click OK to save the link and return to your document.

Now you can simply click the link to execute the macro.

PART

VI

CH

20

CREATING LINKS TO THE INTERNET

The Internet has revolutionized the way we share information. The World Wide Web is a rich source of information. And many companies also use an intranet to store and share information via Web pages. Either way, using external (Internet) or internal (intranet) Web sites, you can create links so that with just a click of a button, the reader can jump from your WordPerfect documents to Web documents.

Note

WordPerfect does not distinguish between Internet and intranet documents. Web documents are the same, and you access them the same, whether they're available to the whole world or just to your company site.

USING AUTOMATIC HYPERLINKS

By default, WordPerfect automatically creates links to Web site addresses and even to email addresses. Type a Uniform Resource Locator (URL), followed by a space or hard return, and WordPerfect underlines the address, highlights it in blue, and creates a hyperlink to that address (see Figure 20.6).

Figure 20.6
If you type a space following a Web or email address, WordPerfect automatically creates a hyperlink.

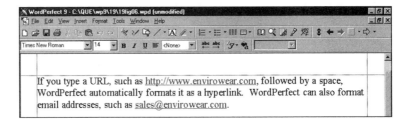

What's a URL?

A URL (Uniform Resource Locater) is the standard method for describing a World Wide Web address. For example, in the following address you find three distinct components:

`http://www.mycompany.com/sales/june/report.html`

The first is the protocol being used to "serve" you the information (`http://`). The second is the name of the Internet computer, or Web server, which consists of at least the domain name (`mycompany.com`) along with any other names that distinguish more than one server in that domain. The final component is the path to the specific document you want, ending in the actual filename (`/sales/june/report.html`).

Caution

Do not add a period or other end-of-sentence punctuation following a URL or email address before typing the space or pressing Enter. Doing so adds that punctuation to the address, and as a result the link will not work.

WordPerfect also distinguishes between URLs and email addresses, and creates an email link when it finds an address that contains the @ symbol.

When you click an Internet link in a WordPerfect document, WordPerfect launches your default browser (for example, Netscape Navigator), and goes to the designated Web site. If you click an email address, WordPerfect launches your default mail program so you can create a mail message.

Note

What you believe to be your default mail program may not be what Windows thinks it is. If you click a mail link, and it opens a mail program that's not what you usually use (for example, Outlook), you have to change your system settings to recognize your mail program. Go to the Windows Control Panel, double-click the Internet Settings icon, click the Programs tab, and from the Mail drop-down list, select your default email program.

Some do not like this automatic hyperlink feature, especially for printed documents, because links appear underlined and serve no useful linking purpose. To turn off the feature, follow these steps:

1. Choose Tools, QuickCorrect.
2. Click the SpeedLinks tab (see Figure 20.7).

Figure 20.7
You can turn off automatic hyperlink formatting in the SpeedLinks tab of the QuickCorrect dialog box.

3. Deselect Format Words as Hyperlinks When You Type Them.
4. Click OK to return to your document.

This setting remains until you change it again. Now by hand you must create hyperlinks to Web and email addresses. Note, however, that changing this setting does not remove links you have already created.

USING SPEEDLINKS

SpeedLinks are like QuickCorrect words in that you type one word (for example, @EnviroWear), and WordPerfect automatically changes it to another (for example, EnviroWear without the @ symbol) and also adds a hyperlink to the corrected text (for example, http://www.envirowear.com).

To create a SpeedLink, follow these steps:

1. Choose Tools, QuickCorrect.
2. Click the SpeedLinks tab (refer to Figure 20.7).
3. In the Link Word box, type the word you want to appear in your document.
4. In the Location to Link To box, type the URL you want to link to.

> **Note**
>
> You can use SpeedLinks to link to an Internet URL or email address, or to another document. Use the browse button to find another document to link to.

5. Click Add Entry to add the SpeedLink to the list. WordPerfect adds the @ symbol to the beginning of the word.
6. Click OK to return to your document.

To use the SpeedLink, type the @ symbol followed by the SpeedLink word (for example, @EnviroWear). WordPerfect inserts the SpeedLink word as a hyperlink.

> **Caution**
>
> Do not use fully capitalized words or acronyms as SpeedLinks. When you do, WordPerfect also capitalizes the hyperlink, which then may not link properly because many Web site addresses are case sensitive.

CREATING, EDITING, AND DELETING INTERNET LINKS

To create an Internet link without using the automatic hyperlink feature, follow these steps:

1. Select the text or object to which you want to attach a hyperlink.
2. Choose Tools, Hyperlink to access the Hyperlink Properties dialog box (see Figure 20.8, shown here with a URL).
3. In the Document/Macro box, type the complete URL (for example, http://www.envirowear.com). If you want to create a link to an email address, type mailto: followed by the email address (for example, mailto:sales@envirowear.com).

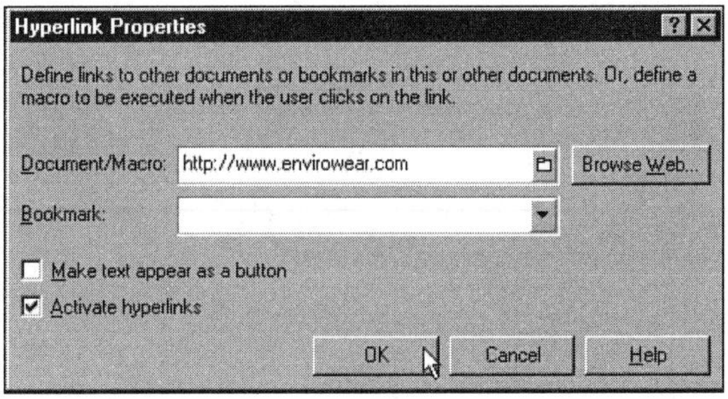

Figure 20.8
You can use the Hyperlink Properties dialog box to create links to Web site URLs and email addresses.

Hyperlink Properties	? ☒

Define links to other documents or bookmarks in this or other documents. Or, define a macro to be executed when the user clicks on the link.

Document/Macro: `http://www.envirowear.com` ☐ Browse Web...

Bookmark: ▼

☐ Make text appear as a button
☑ Activate hyperlinks

OK   Cancel   Help

4. If you are linking to a bookmark within a Web page, type the name of the bookmark in the Bookmark box.

5. Click OK to add the hyperlink to the selected text or object.

To edit a hyperlink, right-click the link and choose Edit Hyperlink from the QuickMenu. Then, in the Hyperlink Properties dialog box, make any needed changes.

Caution

When entering a URL by hand, be sure to carefully type the URL, including all special characters, such as the tilde (~). Generally, you should use lowercase characters. Some Web servers distinguish between upper- and lowercase characters, and using an uppercase character in the URL might not work.

To remove a hyperlink, open the Reveal Codes window (by choosing View, Reveal Codes or pressing Alt+F3) and delete the hyperlink codes. There is no way to remove a hyperlink code using the menus or dialog boxes.

 If you are having trouble making your Internet links work, see "Checking Links" in the Troubleshooting section at the end of this chapter.

EMBEDDING SOUNDS IN DOCUMENTS

You know documents have changed when they can talk back to you! Indeed, you can include recorded sound clips in your documents.

Note

Before you can use sound in a WordPerfect document, you must have a sound-capable computer (with a working sound card and speakers). If you intend to record your own sounds, you also need a microphone that's compatible with your sound card.

INSERTING SOUNDS

Assuming that your computer is wired for sound (that is, that your computer has a sound card, a microphone, speakers, and the appropriate sound software), follow these steps to add sound to a WordPerfect document:

1. Choose Insert, Sound. WordPerfect displays the Sound Clips dialog box (see Figure 20.9).

 If you're not getting any sound from your system, see "Getting Wired" in the Troubleshooting section at the end of this chapter.

Figure 20.9
The Sound Clips dialog box lists clips already in the document, and also enables you to add or record clips.

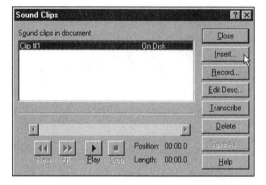

2. Click Insert to select and insert a sound clip into the document. WordPerfect displays the Insert Sound Clip into Document dialog box (see Figure 20.10).

Figure 20.10
In the Insert Sound Clip into Document dialog box, you can specify the name of the sound file to insert.

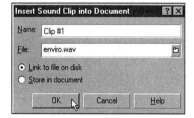

3. Browse to find the sound file you want. In this dialog box, you also have the following options:

- Name—You can change the name of the clip to something that describes it better than Clip #1, Clip #2, and so on.
- Link to File on Disk—This leaves the sound file on disk, either on your local hard drive or on a network drive. This also means the document will have a smaller file size, and that others might not have access to the sound file if they use the document.

Note

Typically, sounds used in Windows, especially voice recordings, are stored in .wav file format. However, you can also insert other types of sound files, such as music MIDI (.mid) files. The only requirement is that the proper sound drivers are installed in Windows to play these other sounds.

If you're having trouble playing MIDI files, see "Installing Sound and Video Drivers" in the Troubleshooting section at the end of this chapter.

- Store in Document—Selecting this option makes for a large file size, but it also means that regardless of where the document goes, the sound file travels with it.

4. Click OK to close both the Insert Sound Clip into Document and Sound Clips dialog boxes and return to your document. WordPerfect displays a sound (speaker) icon in the left margin (see Figure 20.11, which also shows other sound linking options).

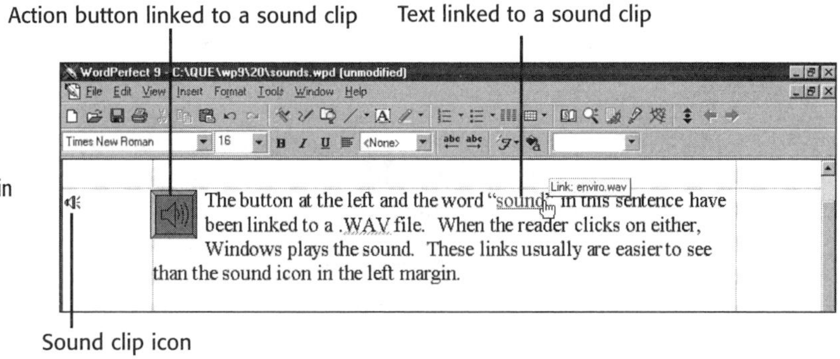

Action button linked to a sound clip   Text linked to a sound clip

Figure 20.11
The speaker icon in the left margin indicates that there is a sound clip inserted in the document. You can click the icon to play the sound.

Sound clip icon

To play an inserted sound clip, click the speaker icon in the left margin.

Note

Depending on your view of the document, you may not see what's in the margins. You can decrease the zoom percentage, or scroll horizontally to the left to see the sound icon.

RECORDING SOUNDS

You can also record your own sound file by using your computer's microphone. To do so, follow these steps before inserting the sound, as described previously:

1. Choose Insert, Sound to access the Sound Clips dialog box (refer to Figure 20.9).

2. Click Record. WordPerfect launches the Windows Sound Recorder program (see Figure 20.12).

If your microphone doesn't seem to work, see "Is the Right Switch On?" in the Troubleshooting section at the end of this chapter.

PART
VI

CH
20

Figure 20.12
With a microphone and the Windows Sound Recorder, you can record sounds to insert in your documents.

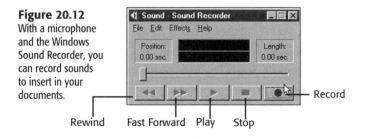

Rewind   Fast Forward   Play   Stop   Record

3. Get your microphone and text ready, and click the Record button.

4. When you finish recording, click the Stop button.

5. Click the Play button to review the sound, and use other Sound Recorder tools to edit the selection (for example, clip it, amplify it, or even add an echo).

6. Choose File, Save (or Save As), and save the sound file; remember its name and location for future reference.

Now you need to follow the procedures for inserting a sound, using the file you just recorded.

TRANSCRIBING RECORDINGS

One use for embedding a sound recording in a document is to later transcribe that recording (for example, a dictated memo). WordPerfect enables you to listen, and repeat as often as necessary, while typing the transcription. To transcribe a sound, follow these steps:

1. Choose Insert, Sound to access the Sound Clip dialog box (refer to Figure 20.9).

2. Select the sound clip you want to transcribe and click Transcribe. WordPerfect displays the Transcription feature bar (see Figure 20.13).

Note

The transcription feature is a throwback to the days when one person would dictate a document into a tape recorder and another would write down the spoken word. However, recording long documents as computer sound files is not very practical, primarily because they take up a lot of computer disk space.

Tip #235 from
Laura and Read

One alternative to recording and transcribing text is to use the Dragon Dictation feature in the WordPerfect Office 2000 suite. This feature enables you to convert your speech into commands and words on-the-fly, thus avoiding the creation of large sound files. For information on Dragon Dictation, see Que's *Special Edition Using WordPerfect Office 2000*.

Figure 20.13
The Transcription feature bar helps you play segments of sound clips as you transcribe a recording.

Tip #236 from
Laura and Read

You can activate the Transcription feature bar quickly by right-clicking the sound icon in the left margin of the document and choosing Transcribe.

3. Click the Play button to begin the sound.

4. Click the Pause button (which replaced the Play button when you began to play the sound.)

5. Type the text you heard.

6. Click the Replay button to repeat just the most recent segment you listened to. You can repeat as often as you like.

7. Click Play again to continue. When you click Pause and Replay, WordPerfect repeats only the segment from which you stopped last to your current location.

8. Repeat steps 3–6 until you finish transcribing the document.

9. Click Close to close the Transcription feature bar.

LINKING SOUNDS

The biggest problem with inserting a sound as described in the preceding section is that the sound icon often is hidden from view in the left margin. The reader might have no idea that there's a sound included with the document.

You can create a more visible sound link by using the procedures described earlier in this chapter for linking a document to text or to a graphics object (for example, an action button). When asked to supply the name of the document (refer to Figure 20.4), instead give the name and location of the sound file. A more visible document link can help ensure that the reader knows to listen to a sound clip (refer to Figure 20.11).

EMBEDDING VIDEO IN DOCUMENTS

You can also insert motion video clips in your WordPerfect documents. However, this type of media is inserted and played as an *OLE object (page 409)*, which means it is embedded in the WordPerfect document, but linked to another program, which plays it.

→ For more information on OLE, **see** Chapter 15, "Importing Data and Working with Other Programs," **p. 403**

> **Note**
>
> Typically, Windows video files use the `.avi` filename extension. Other types of video clips, such as QuickTime (`.mov`) files also can be embedded in WordPerfect documents.

To insert a Windows `.avi` video clip, follow these steps:

1. Choose Insert, Object. WordPerfect displays the Insert Object dialog box.

2. Click Create from File (see Figure 20.14).

3. Browse or type the name of the video file you want to insert.

4. You can choose among these options:

   - Link—If you don't want the video clip to become part of your document, you can link to a copy on your computer or on the network by choosing this option.

Figure 20.14
You can insert OLE objects, such as video clips, using the Insert Object dialog box.

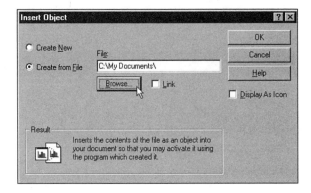

- Display As Icon—You can display a still image (the first video frame) in your document, or you can choose this option to display an icon that lets the reader know a video image is available for viewing.

- Change Icon—If you select Display As Icon, this button appears; otherwise, you do not see it. Click the button to display the Change Icon dialog box (see Figure 20.15). Here you can select a new icon to represent the clip, and also provide your own custom label to identify the clip. Click OK to return to the Insert Object dialog box.

Figure 20.15
If you display the OLE clip as an icon, you can select a different icon than the one suggested by WordPerfect.

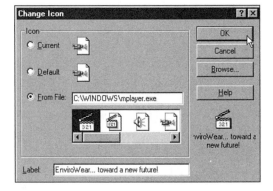

5. Click OK to insert the video clip.

Figure 20.16 shows two video clips—one of which is displayed as the first frame of the video clip, and the other of which is represented as an icon. Both are in graphics boxes, which you can move and resize as needed. Note, however, that if you increase the size of the video frame, you decrease the quality of the image.

To play the clip, choose one of these options:

- If you inserted the video frame without the link or icon options, you can double-click the frame, and then double-click it again to begin playing the clip in place in the document. You can also play the clip by clicking the Play button on the Windows Media

Player controls, which appear in place of the WordPerfect menus and toolbars (see Figure 20.17).

Figure 20.16
Video clips can be displayed using the first frame of the clip, or can be represented by an icon.

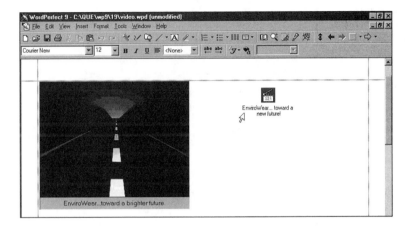

Figure 20.17
The Windows Media Player replaces WordPerfect menus and toolbars so you can start, stop, or rewind a video clip.

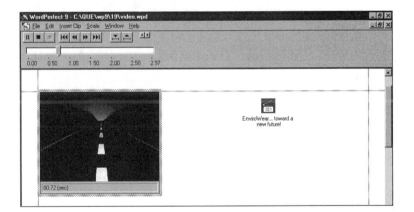

Playing Media Clips
The Windows Media Player is just one of many programs that can play video clips. If you have installed another player as your default media player, such as the RealPlayer G2, that program will launch it in place of the Windows Media Player.

- If you linked the video clip, or if you used an icon to represent the video clip, you can double-click the object to launch the Media Player, which appears as a separate control program and viewing window (see Figure 20.18). You can use the player's controls to start, stop, rewind, and so on.

The Windows Media Player, like other media players, offers a variety of options, including whether to include a caption, how to display lapsed time (time, frames, tracks), and so on. You can experiment with the player that appears on your system to discover some of the options available for presenting a video clip.

Figure 20.18
The Media Player operates as a detached, separate program when associated with a linked or icon-represented video clip.

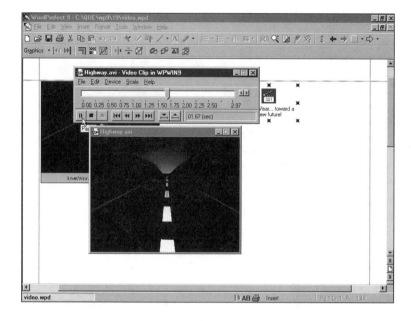

PUBLISHING INTERACTIVE AND MULTIMEDIA DOCUMENTS

Printing traditional documents requires a printer. It's quite simple, really. But publishing interactive and multimedia documents sometimes isn't quite so straightforward.

REQUIREMENT FOR VIEWING DOCUMENTS

For readers to be able to read your documents, they must have computers that can do one or more of the following:

- Use WordPerfect—Although you can convert documents to Word, that doesn't necessarily mean that all links, sounds, video clips, and so on convert correctly. If the people who must read your documents don't use WordPerfect, they may not get the full picture.

- Connect to the Internet—If you have links that connect to Web pages, you must be connected to the Internet via a local or dial-up connection if you want to view linked Web sites. If some of your readers don't have Internet access, you need to make sure the document is still effective without its Internet links.

- Play sound files—Nearly every computer these days comes equipped with sound cards and speakers. But that's not universally true, and it's also not a given that needed sound drivers are installed. One person may be able to play .wav files, for example, but not MIDI files.

- Play video clips—Not every computer is set up to play even standard Windows .avi files. If you use other video formats, for example QuickTime files, the user might first have to install the QuickTime player.

As a publisher of electronic documents, you must make decisions about what's important, who your target audience is, and what percentage of your audience is likely to be able to read your document. Sometimes you can take steps to ensure that they can, such as convincing your computer support department that everyone needs sound cards and speakers, or that everyone should have QuickTime video players installed.

Finally, you also can, and should, design your documents so that they're still effective, communicating essential information, even without Internet links, sounds, or video clips.

PUBLISHING TO PDF

One exciting new addition to WordPerfect 9 is the capability to publish documents to Adobe's PDF format (Portable Document Format). This process creates documents that match the originals in terms of layout, fonts, and special effects, but that can be viewed with the Acrobat reader instead of requiring that users have WordPerfect installed on their system.

> **Note**
>
> Adobe Acrobat is a free reader that understands PDF-formatted documents. Many Web sites routinely publish documents in PDF format, and many users already have installed Acrobat. They may see it only as an automatic plug-in to their Web browser, but they can also start the program from the Start, Programs menu. Also, just double-clicking a PDF document in the Windows Explorer automatically starts Acrobat and views the PDF document.

To publish a WordPerfect document to PDF format, follow these steps:

1. Save the document one last time in WordPerfect format. You may need to come back to the original version later.

2. Choose File, Publish to PDF. WordPerfect displays the Publish to PDF dialog box (see Figure 20.19).

Figure 20.19
Use the Publish to PDF dialog box to create documents that anyone can read using the Adobe Acrobat reader.

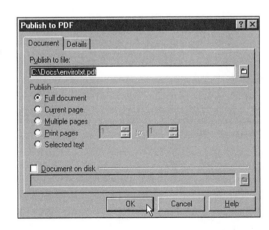

3. Specify the name of the PDF file in the Publish to File edit box. Typically, this is the name of the WordPerfect file, with a `.pdf` filename extension.

4. Choose what you want to publish (full document, current page only, and so on). If you want to publish a document other than the current document, you can choose Document on Disk and specify the name of the file in the edit box.

5. If you click the Details tab (see Figure 20.20), you can choose from among these options:

- Compression—By default, the PDF publisher uses LZW compression to make the size of the PDF file smaller. You can also use the JPG format from the drop-down menu, specifying a quality factor that affects the size of the PDF file. You can also choose no compression at all.

- Output—The PDF published normally creates files that also include color (RGB). From the Output All Objects As drop-down menu, you can also choose Gray for a black-and-white PDF file, or CMYK if you are preparing the document for professional press printing.

- Text and Fonts—You can choose whether to include fonts in the document, whether to include graphics, and so on. Unless you know that you need these options, it's usually best to accept the default settings.

Figure 20.20
You can choose several output methods to reduce the size of the PDF file or to adjust the quality of the final result.

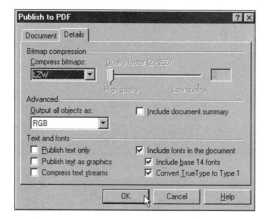

6. Click OK to publish the document to the PDF format.

WordPerfect publishes PDF documents so quickly that it's easy to think nothing has happened. You can verify the PDF format by starting Adobe Acrobat and opening the PDF file you just created (see Figure 20.21).

Caution

Although Adobe is very good at converting your WordPerfect documents to PDF format, not everything converts perfectly. For example, WordPerfect's special characters, including Smart Quotes, don't translate at all. In addition, some spacing between characters isn't perfect. Before you distribute the PDF version of your documents, you should check it to make sure you can live with these minor problems.

Figure 20.21
The Adobe Acrobat reader enables anyone, even non-WordPerfect users, to see your documents exactly as you intend them to appear. They can easily zoom in or out, print, or even use hyperlinks if you include them.

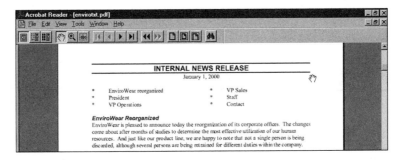

TROUBLESHOOTING

CHECKING LINKS

I clicked a hyperlink to a Web site and Netscape Navigator starts, but it won't display the Web site.

This could be one of several problems. Can you go to any site at all in Netscape Navigator? If so, then check the URL in the WordPerfect hyperlink to make sure it's typed correctly, including upper- and lowercase. If you can't reach other sites in Netscape Navigator, make sure you're connected to the Internet (for example, that you've established a dial-up connection if you're not connected directly to the Internet).

Some companies set up firewalls to prevent others from accessing company networks. These firewalls also sometimes prevent employees from accessing anything beyond the company networks. If this seems to be the case, consult with your computer support department about possible solutions.

INSTALLING SOUND AND VIDEO DRIVERS

I've got a video file linked properly, but it won't play.

Not everyone installs the necessary video players and drivers when they set up their Windows system. Further, some video formats require special players (for example, .mov files require the QuickTime player for Windows from Apple). Make sure all necessary drivers and players are installed.

GETTING WIRED

How come I can't hear any sound files on my computer?

Although it is quite unusual these days, some computers do not have the necessary hardware installed to enable you to record sound files. You must have a sound card, a microphone, and speakers, in addition to the necessary software to make them work.

If you do have the necessary hardware and software, have you ever heard sounds, but now you can't? Some speaker systems use power from the computer, or from batteries. If you turn on the power without batteries installed, the speakers actually turn off the sound. Try turning off the power.

IS THE RIGHT SWITCH ON?

I have all the right hardware, but I still can't record sound files.

Some microphones have switches you can use to turn them on and off. Some also have switches that adapt the microphone to different types of sound cards. Make sure your switch settings are correct for the type of microphone and sound card you are using.

PROJECT

Well-designed documents are easy for the reader to navigate. For example, in Chapter 18, "Working with Large and Multipart Documents," you learned how to create a table of contents to help the reader quickly find sections of a document. You can combine those tools with WordPerfect's linking ability to make it even easier for the reader.

For example, consider the EnviroWear Annual Report shown in Figure 20.22. You have no idea how long the document is, whether you must start at the beginning, or whether you might skip to more important sections later in the document.

Figure 20.22
Reading an entire annual report can be a daunting prospect. You can make the job easier by adding navigation aids.

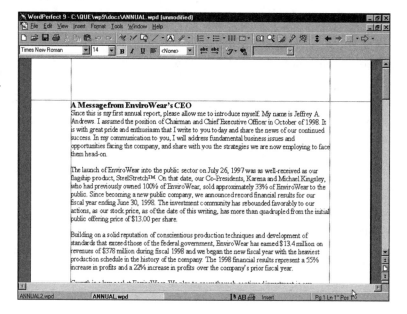

To begin, you can generate a table of contents that shows the location of various sections of the annual report. Further, you can link table of contents entries to their related section headings.

To create automatic table of contents hyperlinks, follow these steps:

1. Mark table of contents entries, and insert the table of contents definition at the beginning of the document.

→ For information on how to mark, define, and generate a table of contents, **see** "Creating a Table of Contents," **p. 522**

2. Generate the table of contents. When WordPerfect displays the Generate dialo g box (see Figure 20.23), choose Build Hyperlinks before clicking OK.

Figure 20.23
WordPerfect can automatically generate hyperlinks along with a table of contents.

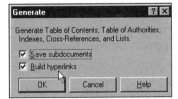

Tip #237 from

Laura and Read

If you define the table of contents to display without page numbers, WordPerfect creates hyperlinks using the table of contents entries. Otherwise, hyperlinks appear only on the page numbers.

WordPerfect automatically generates a table of contents, complete with hyperlinked section entries (see Figure 20.24).

Figure 20.24
A hyperlinked table of contents makes it easy for readers to jump directly to different sections of the document.

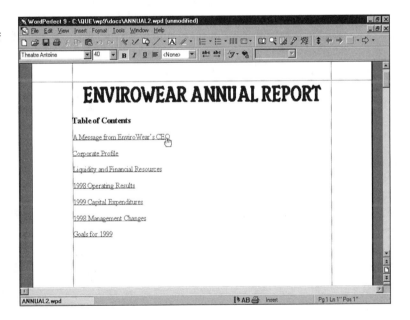

Now you want to make it easy for a reader to return to the table of contents in case he or she doesn't want to read the entire report sequentially.

To create a linked action button that returns to the table of contents, follow these steps:

1. Go to the top of the document (or to the beginning of the table of contents), and choose Tools, Bookmark, Create. Provide the name of the bookmark (for example, Top of Report) and click OK.

2. Go to the end of the first section of the report (for example, the end of the CEO's message).

3. Choose Insert, Shapes, and click Action to display action button options (see Figure 20.25).

Figure 20.25
WordPerfect provides several action buttons that you can draw as shapes and hyperlink to other locations in the document.

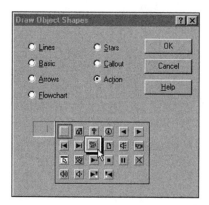

4. Choose the one you want (for example, the Return icon) and click OK.

5. In the document, click and drag to create the action button. WordPerfect draws the button, and the sizing handles indicate that the button is selected. Move and size the button as needed, and also change button properties, such as color, from the Graphics Property Bar.

6. Choose Tools, Hyperlink to display the Hyperlink Properties dialog box.

7. Click the Bookmark drop-down list and choose the bookmark that takes you back to the top (for example, Top of Report).

8. Make sure Activate Hyperlinks is selected before choosing OK.

WordPerfect displays a hyperlinked action button (see Figure 20.26). If you click the button, you jump immediately to the bookmark at the top of the report.

Figure 20.26
You can add hyper-linked text or other instructions along with a hyperlinked graphic image to help readers who might not know to click the link.

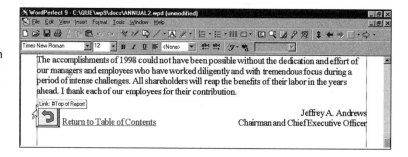

Tip #238 from
Laura and Read

Some readers may not know to click the button to return to the table of contents. You might also need to add instructions, such as "Click button to return to top." Or you might add hyper-linked text that duplicates the action of the button (for example, "Return to top of report").

CHAPTER **21**

PUBLISHING DOCUMENTS ON THE WORLD WIDE WEB

In this chapter

UNDERSTANDING HTML

One of the most interesting phenomena in the past few years has been the development of the World Wide Web, usually referred to simply as the Web. Made possible by the development of the *Internet* over the past 20–30 years, the Web enables anyone—from large corporations to individuals—to create and publish information that is easily and readily available to anyone anywhere in the world. Today such phrases as "check out my Web site" to "dot com" are part of our everyday vocabulary.

Part of the success of the Web lies in the basic nature of Web documents. Unlike proprietary word processing formats that require specific word processors to be read, edited, or printed, Web document are standard *ASCII* (pronounced "ask-key") text documents that you can create with any common text editor.

At the heart of the Web page is HTML (Hypertext Markup Language), which consists of tags that describe document formatting. This concept should be familiar to WordPerfect users, who are used to seeing formatting codes in the Reveal Codes window. Most HTML tags are used in pairs: one to turn on a formatting feature and another to turn it off. For example, the markup tags used to add boldface to a word look like this:

```
<strong>text in bold</strong>
```

A Web document is placed on a *Web server*, a computer that does nothing more than honor requests to "serve up," or send, documents to those who want to see them.

Finally, you use a Web *browser* to view Web pages. When you specify a uniform resource locator, or URL (which is a Web page address), your browser contacts the designated Web server over the Internet and requests a document. The server sends the HTML document to your computer, and then your browser translates it into the attractively functional Web page you see on your screen (see Figure 21.1).

Figure 21.1
Web servers send HTML text documents over the Internet to computers that use Web browser software to view them.

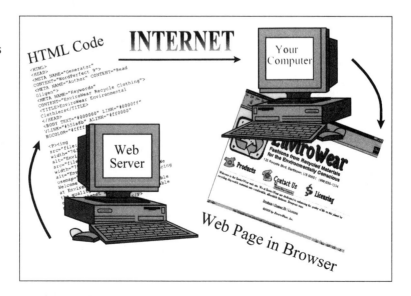

Table 21.1 lists many of the terms you need to know as you work with Web pages in WordPerfect.

TABLE 21.1   WEB TERMS USED IN WORDPERFECT

Term	Description
Home page	The initial screen people see when they visit a Web site.
Browser	Software used to view Web pages, such as Netscape Navigator and Internet Explorer.
HTML	The coding used to create documents that can be viewed on the Web.
URL	The addressing protocol used to identify Web pages.
Tag	Codes used to mark up text in HTML; usually used in pairs, such as `<strong>` (bold on) and `</strong>` (bold off).
Link	A place on a Web page that a user can click to jump to another URL. Linked text usually appears underlined. When the mouse pointer passes over a link, the pointer changes to a hand.

USING CODE VERSUS WYSIWYG EDITING

You'd probably never consider editing a WordPerfect document entirely in Reveal Codes. Instead, you simply apply formatting and gauge the results by the WYSIWYG (what-you-see-is-what-you-get) document you see onscreen. You know something is bold because it looks bold, not because you see the bold codes that surround it.

Web page publishing programs also help insulate you from having to see, and in most cases even know about, HTML tags. You create the document in a WYSIWYG environment, and the program then converts it into the required HTML format so that Web servers and browsers can understand it.

WordPerfect includes an Internet Publisher feature to enable you to develop Web documents in a WYSIWYG/WordPerfect environment. Many of the formatting features and procedures you use in a WordPerfect document can also be used as you create a Web page.

HOW WORDPERFECT CHANGES TO WORK WITH WEB DOCUMENTS

Perhaps the most difficult task you have is to learn just what you *can't* use in WordPerfect as you create your Web pages. Fortunately, WordPerfect helps you by changing its menus and toolbars to allow you to use only the features that follow HMTL standards.

Consider the Format menu, for example. Figure 21.2 shows the Format menu as you're used to seeing it, and Figure 21.3 shows the WordPerfect Format menu you get when using Internet Publisher.

Figure 21.2
The regular
WordPerfect Format
menu offers many
formatting choices.

Figure 21.3
WordPerfect's Internet
Publisher offers far
fewer formatting
choices.

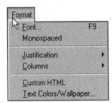

In addition to the standard toolbar, WordPerfect also adds a second toolbar just for Internet Publisher features (see Figure 21.4).

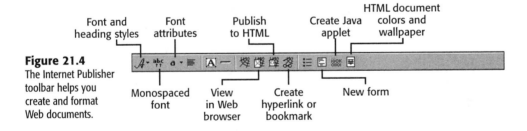

Figure 21.4
The Internet Publisher
toolbar helps you
create and format
Web documents.

 If you still get the regular WordPerfect menus and toolbars after changing to a Web document view, see "Using the Internet Publisher Menus" in the Troubleshooting section at the end of this chapter.

CREATING NEW WEB DOCUMENTS

You can use a couple different methods to create a Web page in WordPerfect. One is to use a PerfectExpert project to help guide you through the process. Another is to create the Web page without that help. Finally, you can convert existing documents into Web pages.

USING THE WEB PAGE EXPERT

If you've never created a Web page before, using the WordPerfect Web Page Expert can help you make sure you don't miss anything. To begin working on a new Web page project, follow these steps:

1. Choose File, New from Project, or press Ctrl+Shift+N. WordPerfect displays the PerfectExpert dialog box (see Figure 21.5, which shows the Web Document project already selected).

Figure 21.5
Among WordPerfect PerfectExpert projects is one for creating a Web page.

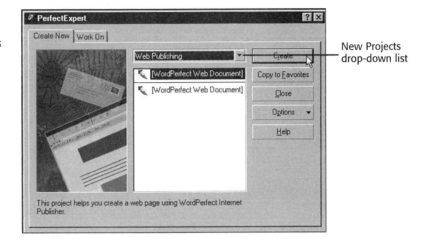

New Projects drop-down list

2. Click the Create New tab if it's not already selected.

3. Click the Projects drop-down list and select Web Publishing. WordPerfect lists Internet Publisher projects, such as WordPerfect Web Document (refer to Figure 21.5).

4. Select the project and click Create. WordPerfect opens a new blank Web document and displays the PerfectExpert at the left of the screen (see Figure 21.6).

You're now ready to begin a new Web page. See the next section, "Converting Existing Documents to HTML Format," for a detailed description of how to use various HTML features, and for a description of some of the things you want to look for as you create a Web page.

Figure 21.6
The PerfectExpert, on the left, helps you create a Web document, on the right.

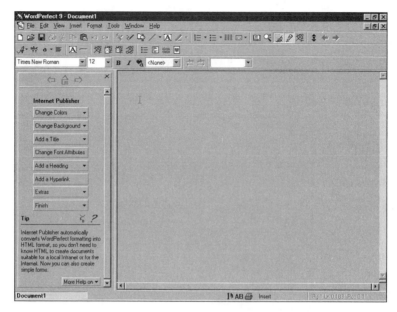

CONVERTING EXISTING DOCUMENTS TO HTML FORMAT

You can also convert existing documents to HTML documents. Keep in mind that you might lose some WordPerfect formatting options when you change to HTML.

> **Note**
>
> The procedures described in this section pertain also to Web documents created by using the PerfectExpert. Although you may arrive at the features a bit differently, the features themselves and the results are identical.

OPENING, VIEWING, AND SAVING AS

Converting a WordPerfect document is as simple as opening it, changing the way it's viewed, and saving it again. To convert a WordPerfect document to an HTML document, follow these steps:

1. Open the WordPerfect document as you normally do.

2. Choose View, Web Page. Alternatively, you can choose File, Internet Publisher, and then choose Format as Web Document. WordPerfect displays a warning (see Figure 21.7).

Figure 21.7
When you convert an existing WordPerfect document to a Web document, you lose certain formatting.

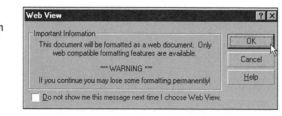

3. Click OK to convert the document to HTML format, and to view it *almost* as you will in a browser.

> **Caution**
>
> If you change to the Web Page view and save your document, you replace the original document. Generally you use the Save As option to save the document with a different name in HTML format.

4. To complete the conversion, you must save the document in HTML format. Choose File, Save As or press F3 to display the Save As dialog box.

> **Caution**
>
> Even if you begin a Web document by using the PerfectExpert, you must follow these steps to save your document as an HTML document. Otherwise, you save it as a WordPerfect document that won't display on a Web browser.

5. Click the File Type drop-down list and select HTML. WordPerfect adds the .htm extension to the original filename.

> **Tip #239 from**
> *Laura and Read*
>
> All Web servers require the filename extension .html, and some also permit the .htm extension. Ask your Webmaster if .htm is supported. Otherwise, use .html to be safe.

> **Caution**
>
> Web servers are very particular about upper- and lowercase letters used in Web page names. For example, if you save the file as MyPage.htm, a link to Mypage.htm will not find the document because the *p* is lowercased. Generally it's a good idea always to use lowercase.

6. Change the filename if you want, and click Save to save the converted file.

The converted, saved file is now a standard ASCII text file with HTML markup tags. It can be opened by a Web browser or by any word processor or text editor.

Subsequently, each time you save your Web page, WordPerfect asks if you want to save it in WordPerfect format or in HTML format. Choose HTML and click OK to preserve the HTML format of the saved file.

 If your Web server refuses to display your WordPerfect-created Web page, see "Saving As HTML" in the Troubleshooting section at the end of this chapter.

PREVIEWING WEB PAGES

Although WordPerfect appears to format your Web page in WYSIWYG fashion, in reality, it's *almost* WYSIWYG. Certain formatting just isn't going to look the same in WordPerfect as it does in your browser.

As you create a page, you should probably check your work in progress. To view a document in your Web browser, follow these steps:

1. Save your document. This isn't required, but it's always a good precaution before switching to your browser. Don't forget to save it in HTML format.

 2. Choose View, View in Web Browser. Alternatively, you can click the View in Web Browser button on the Internet Publisher toolbar. WordPerfect launches your default browser (for example, Netscape Navigator) and displays your Web page in the browser.

3. To switch back to WordPerfect, you can close your browser, although this isn't necessary. You can also click the WordPerfect tab on the Windows taskbar or press Alt+Tab until you switch to WordPerfect.

DOCUMENT PROPERTIES

HTML document properties are a bit different from typical WordPerfect document properties, but in some ways they are more important. For example, each HTML document has a title that isn't part of the Web page itself, but displays on the browser's title bar when someone visits your page. To access the HTML Document Properties dialog box shown in Figure 21.8, choose File, Properties.

Figure 21.8
You can set up the Web page title and other properties in the HTML Document Properties dialog box.

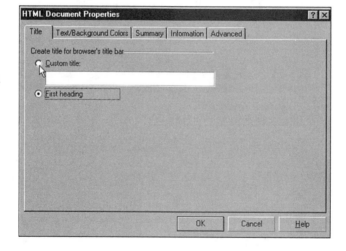

The Title tab enables you to provide a custom title or to use the text from the first heading in the document. There are three reasons to provide an accurate, meaningful title:

- When someone visits your Web site, the Web page title appears on the title bar of that person's browser (refer to Figure 21.14).

- If the person chooses to add your Web site to a list of bookmarks, or favorites, the title you provide also appears on the bookmarks or favorites list.

- Many search engines such as Lycos, AltaVista, and Yahoo! consider the words found in a Web page title as primary keywords to help find or identify the page.

Tip #240 from
Laura and Read

To help people find your page using Internet search engines, avoid using generic titles such as My Home Page. Instead, use unique and descriptive titles such as EnviroWear Environmental Clothiers.

→ To find out how to use the Text/Background Colors tab to choose color schemes for your Web page, **see** "Adding Color and Backgrounds," **p. 592**

The Summary tab looks much like the regular WordPerfect document summary, but a bit simpler (see Figure 21.9). The important information here is the keywords (separate each with a space) and the abstract. This information is inserted in the HTML document head as meta-information, which means that it's important information but doesn't appear as part of the document itself. Internet search engines key on this meta-information to help people find what they're looking for.

Note

If you're working with a new Web document, WordPerfect forces you to save the document before you can add document summary information.

Figure 21.9
You can use the Summary tab of the HTML Document Properties dialog box to provide information used by Internet search engines to tell people how to find your Web page.

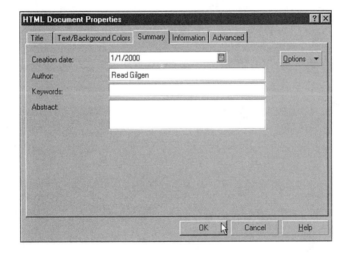

On the Advanced tab (see Figure 21.10) you can specify the base URL, and any other meta-information you'd like to add to the HTML document head. The base URL specifies the location of the HTML document that the current Web page relates to. That way, if you move the document, it doesn't lose track of graphics and other elements that remain at the base URL location.

ADDING TITLES AND HEADINGS

Even the title of this section is a bit misleading. In an HTML document, *title* does not refer to text on the Web page itself, but to the title you added in the HMTL Document

PART

VI

CH

21

Properties dialog box. *Title*, as we're used to using it, refers to the main heading in a document. In HTML terms, that's Heading 1.

Figure 21.10
You can add more meta-information and a base URL on the Advanced tab of the HTML Document Properties dialog box.

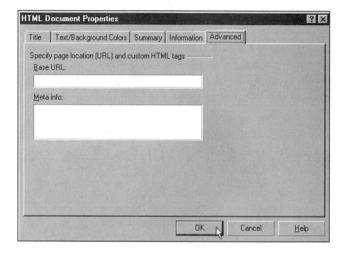

Web documents use headings to organize sections of a document, much like an outline style. Browsers interpret headings by applying a consistent font style and size to each heading type (see Figure 21.11). Heading 1 is the main heading, reserved for the title at the top of the document. Heading 2 is for major sections, Heading 3 for subsections, and so on.

Figure 21.11
Internet browsers such as Netscape Navigator give a consistent look to Web page headings.

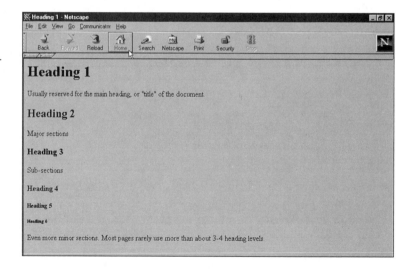

Caution

You might be tempted to use heading styles to make text appear large, bold, and so on. Don't. Heading styles should be used only for structural organization of the document because browsers interpret them differently, and because there is more to the heading style than just font and size. You should use attribute formatting (bold, font, size) for normal text formatting.

To apply a heading style to a paragraph (usually a short line), follow these steps:

1. Position the insertion point anywhere on the paragraph.

2. Choose Format, Font or press F9. WordPerfect displays the Font Properties dialog box, with the Paragraph tab selected (see Figure 21.12).

Figure 21.12
The Font Properties dialog box is one way to select heading styles.

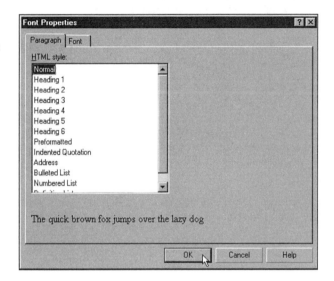

3. Click the heading style you want and click OK.

 You can also quickly access heading styles by clicking the Font/Size button on the Internet Publisher toolbar (refer to Figure 21.4). When you become familiar with heading styles, you'll probably use this button exclusively.

ADDING BODY TEXT

The HTML standard calls for automatic double-spacing between paragraphs. Each time you press Enter, WordPerfect automatically inserts the equivalent of a paragraph tag.

 Note

When you convert a regular WordPerfect document to HTML, WordPerfect converts double-spacing to quadruple spacing. You must remove these extra spaces (hard returns) by hand.

If you want to force a line break, without inserting the extra space, choose Insert, Line Break or press Ctrl+Shift+L. Note, however, that the two sections separated by the line break are part of the same paragraph, and paragraph formatting (such as a heading) applies to both.

PART
VI

CH
21

APPLYING TEXT FORMATTING

HTML allows relatively few other font or character formatting options. In the Font Properties dialog box (refer to Figure 21.12), note the styles listed, which include the following:

- Normal—This is the default paragraph style. Although typically it's a Times Roman type of font, users can change that default in their browser to make it larger, smaller, or a different font style. Most users leave this setting alone, however.

- Preformatted—Default HTML fonts are proportionally spaced. If you need a fixed-pitch, or monospaced, font to align characters horizontally, use this style, which typically is Courier.

Tip #241 from *Laura and Read*	Although WordPerfect allows you to insert spaces to align text, browsers generally ignore the spaces. Using the Preformatted style, however, you can insert spaces that browsers recognize, although the rest of the paragraph text also appears in the preformatted font.

- Indented Quotation—This is the HTML equivalent to WordPerfect's left/right indent. However, it indents only once, both on the left and right sides of the paragraph.

- Address—This italicizes the entire paragraph. In the early days of HTML this was a conventional method for designating a contact person's address.

ADDING BULLETS AND LISTS

In addition to basic paragraph font and size styles, you can also add special numbered or bulleted lists to help organize information on your Web page. There are three types of lists:

- Bulleted lists
- Numbered lists
- Definition lists

Bulleted lists are the most common, and arguably the most useful of these list types. To create a bulleted list, follow these steps:

1. Position the insertion point at the left margin.
2. Choose Insert, Outline/Bullets & Numbering. WordPerfect displays the Bullets and Numbering dialog box, shown in Figure 21.13. Alternatively, you can choose Format, Font, and click the Paragraph tab (refer to Figure 21.12).
3. Select Bulleted and click OK.
4. WordPerfect inserts a bullet at the left margin. Type the text of the bulleted item.
5. Press Enter to add another bullet at the same level (left margin).
6. To indent the bullet to the next level (to the right), press Tab. WordPerfect moves the insertion point to the next tab stop and also changes the bullet style.

Figure 21.13
The Bullets and Numbering dialog box enables you to use simple bulleted, numbered, or definition lists.

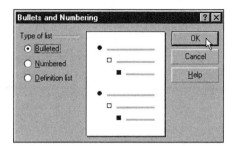

Note

Although you can press Tab several times, indenting a bullet many times, browsers only recognize and provide different bullets for three levels.

7. If you indent a line in a bulleted list, and then press Enter, the next line is indented at the same level as the previous line. To move back a level (to the left), simply press Shift+Tab.

8. If you need to change the level of a bullet, place the insertion point after the bullet, but preceding the text, and press Tab or Shift+Tab as required.

Note

WordPerfect's bullets probably won't match the bullets displayed in your browser, and they probably won't indent correctly. You must preview your Web page in your browser to see the bullets correctly displayed.

9. To end a bulleted list, press Enter and then press Backspace.

Caution

If you click the Bullet button on the regular WordPerfect toolbar, you might change the bullet style to one that doesn't allow bullet levels. If after you click the Bullet button, your bullets all suddenly become first-level bullets, click Undo to restore the HTML bullet style.

You can also add bullets to existing lines of text. Select the entire list and click the Insert Bullet button on the Internet Publisher toolbar. WordPerfect applies first-level bullets to all the selected lines. To indent a line, position the insertion point following the bullet, but before the text, and press Tab.

Numbered lists are similar to bulleted lists, but don't expect them to look like regular numbered outlines. HTML standards do not provide for true outline numbering. To create a numbered list, follow these steps:

1. Position the insertion point at the left margin.

2. Choose Insert, Outline/Bullets & Numbering. WordPerfect displays the Bullets and Numbering dialog box (refer to Figure 21.13). Alternatively, you can choose Format, Font, and click the Paragraph tab (refer to Figure 21.12).

3. Select <u>N</u>umbered and click OK. WordPerfect inserts an Arabic numeral 1 and a period.

4. Follow the same procedures as for adding a bulleted list, pressing Enter to add numbers, and using Tab and Shift+Tab to change the indent level.

Tip #242 from
Laura and Read

Because HTML does not allow for true outline numbering, some Web page authors like to apply the numbering style to first-level list items (1, 2, 3, and so on), but apply the bullet style to sublevel list items.

A definition list is different from the other two lists in that it allows only two levels: a term level and a definition level. To create a definition list like the one shown in Figure 21.14, follow these steps:

1. Position the insertion point at the left margin.

2. Choose <u>I</u>nsert, Outline/Bullets & <u>N</u>umbering. WordPerfect displays the Bullets and Numbering dialog box.

3. Select <u>D</u>efinition List and click OK.

4. Nothing appears to happen. Type the term and press Enter.

5. Press Tab to move to the Definition level. Type the definition and press Enter.

6. Press Shift+Tab to move back to the Term level.

7. Repeat steps 4–6 until you finish the list.

8. To close the list, press Enter twice and then press Backspace.

Figure 21.14
A definition list has only two levels: the term and the definition.

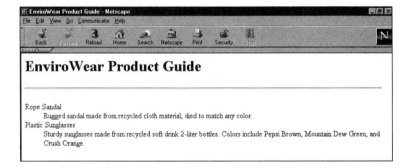

CREATING LINKS

The real power of the World Wide Web lies in the reader's ability to follow hyperlinks (usually referred to simply as *links*) to quickly jump from one location to another. Whether people who visit your site jump to another spot within the same Web document, to another document at the same Web site, or to an entirely different Web site anywhere else in the world is all the same.

→ For complete information on creating hyperlinks, **see** Chapter 20, "Interactive and Multimedia Documents," **p. 545**

The method for creating links in a Web document using Internet Publisher are identical to those described in Chapter 20, "Interactive and Multimedia Documents." Consider the following:

- You can create links from text or graphics objects. The user jumps by clicking on the text or object.

- Internal links enable a reader to jump to another location in the same document. You first create bookmarks, and then create links to those bookmarks.

- External links enable a reader to jump to another Web document, either one of yours or anywhere else on the Web.

  Typical links include

  - Links to a URL using the `http://` protocol (for example, `http://www.envirowear.com`)

  - Links to an email address using `mailto:` (for example, `mailto:sales@envirowear.com`)

  - Links to an FTP site to download a file (for example, `ftp://supportfiles.envirowear.com`)

Tip #243 from
Laura and Read

Don't forget that WordPerfect's QuickLink feature enables you to create a link simply by typing a URL, an email address, or an FTP site, followed by a space.

Adding Tables

As you develop your first Web page, you'll quickly discover how difficult it is to visually organize your text information. For example, you cannot use tabs or spaces to align text horizontally.

Caution

WordPerfect allows you to add spaces within WordPerfect, but Web browsers ignore these spaces, thus rendering useless all efforts to align text with spaces.

Fortunately, HTML does allow for the use of tables, and WordPerfect makes it easy to create and modify tables for use in a Web page. Many table features in HTML documents work the same as they do in regular WordPerfect documents, but others work differently or not at all.

→ For information on creating WordPerfect tables, **see** Chapter 10, "Organizing Information with Tables," **p. 251**

Part
VI

Ch
21

To create a table in a Web page, follow these steps:

1. Choose Insert, Table or press F12. WordPerfect displays the HTML Table Format dialog box (see Figure 21.15).

Figure 21.15
You can create and format a table using the HTML Table Format dialog box.

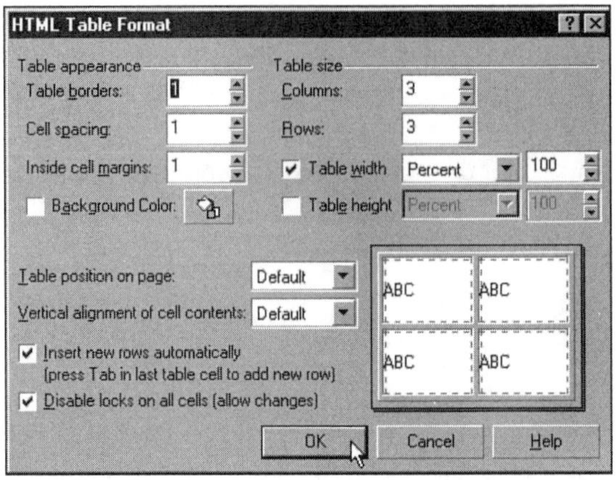

2. Specify the number of columns and rows you want.

3. Make changes in the basic format of the table.

4. Click OK to insert the table in your Web document (see Figure 21.16).

Figure 21.16
A table in an HTML document looks similar to a regular WordPerfect table.

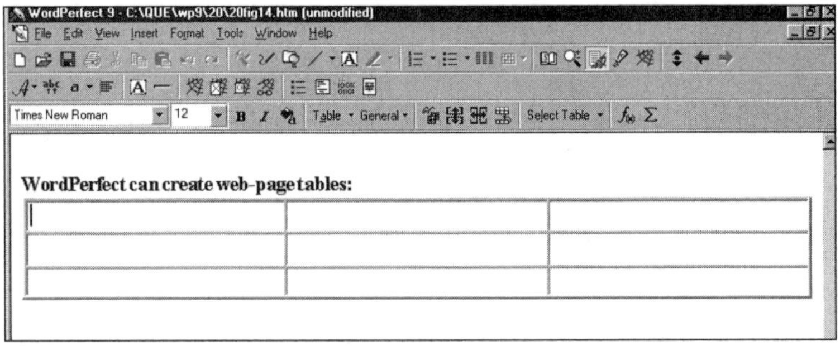

You now can use the following table features:

■ Add text or numbers, including formulas (although formulas are converted to numbers when published to HTML).

■ Apply numeric format to cells, columns, or the entire table.

■ Drag column lines to size columns. You can also use Size Column to Fit, but dragging row lines has no effect on the table when it's viewed in a Web browser.

■ Join or split cells.

- Add or delete rows or columns.
- Use row/column indicators and the formula bar.

Options for formatting Web page tables, however, are considerably different from what you're used to in normal WordPerfect tables, due to HTML requirements. To format a table, or its cells, rows, or columns, follow these steps:

1. Position the insertion point inside the table. WordPerfect displays the Table Property Bar.

2. Click the table menu button on the Property Bar and choose Format, or press Ctrl+F12. WordPerfect displays the Table tab of the HTML Table Properties dialog box, which is identical to the HTML Table Format dialog box (refer to Figure 21.15).

3. Click the tab of the table element you want to format (for example, Table, Row, Column, or Cell), and make your changes.

4. Click Apply to make changes to the table and continue with other formatting changes, or click OK to apply the changes and also close the dialog box.

Format options for each table element are limited by what is permitted in an HTML document. Some are similar to options available in WordPerfect tables, but others require some explanation.

On the Table tab of the HTML Table Properties dialog box (refer to Figure 21.15), be aware of the following:

- Table Appearance—Table borders are the thickness, measured in *pixels* of the lines around table. Cell spacing is the thickness of the lines between the cells. However, if you set Table Borders to zero, no table lines appear when displayed in a browser. Inside cell margins indicate the distance between the edge of a cell and the text it contains.

Measuring in Pixels

Most formatting measurements are based either on pixels or on a percentage of the screen because other units of measurement such as inches are relatively meaningless in a Web browser environment. A *pixel* is a single dot on your computer's monitor, but the number of pixels on a screen also depends on your computer's resolution settings. For example, a standard VGA setting measures 640 pixels horizontally, and 480 vertically, whereas super VGA (SVGA) resolution measures 800 pixels by 600 pixels.

If you specify a table width of 700 pixels, for example, but the visitor to your Web site can only view 640 pixels, he or she will not be able to see the entire table without using the horizontal scrollbar.

For this reason, many Web page designers prefer to use percentages so that the table adjusts to a percentage of the available screen width. For example, if you want the table to occupy 75% of the width of the screen, the table will take up 600 pixels on an SVGA monitor, but only 480 pixels on a standard VGA monitor.

Caution

What you see on your screen may not match what others see when they view your Web page. To the extent possible, design your Web page, including the width of tables and graphics, so that everyone, including those using low-resolution monitors, can view the whole page without having to scroll horizontally.

- Table Size—By default, the width of a table is 100% of the width of the screen, regardless of the resolution used by the person viewing the Web page. If you adjust the width of the table by dragging table lines, the value in the Table <u>W</u>idth box changes to indicate how many pixels wide it is.

- B<u>a</u>ckground Color—The color you choose fills all the table cells and hides whatever color or background wallpaper you use in the rest of your Web document.

The other tabs enable you to format entire rows, columns, or individual cells. The HTML standard also limits your options. Consider, for example, the Column tab, shown in Figure 21.17. You can set column widths by percentage or by pixel, change the background color, and specify how text should be aligned, both horizontally and vertically, within column cells.

Figure 21.17
You can format table columns with the Column tab of the HTML Table Properties dialog box.

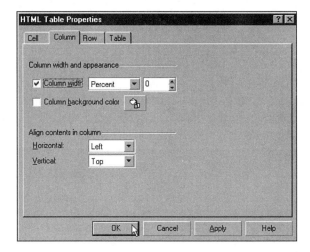

The Row tab enables you to set only the background color and text alignment of cells in a row.

The Cell tab enables you to set background color and text alignment. You can also lock cells, or prevent text wrap, but these have no effect on the Web page and are lost when you publish to HTML.

Although tables created with the Internet Publisher aren't as feature rich as regular WordPerfect tables, they are extremely useful for formatting data on a Web page.

Tip #244 from
Laura and Read

> You can use a table to simulate text columns on a Web page. For example, to create a two-column format, you create a table with only one row and two columns. You place all the text for the first column in cell A1, and the text for the second column in B1. You then format the table so that it does not display table borders.

Tip #245 from
Laura and Read

> Very old browsers often did not support viewing of tables, but most browsers today do. However, certain screen readers for the visually impaired read tables horizontally, row by row. If you use tables, consider whether the flow of information in them will make sense to *all* visitors to your Web page.

ADDING GRAPHICS

A great reason for the success of the World Wide Web has been the visual attractiveness of its sites. Indeed, graphics may be one of the most important elements of your Web page.

Caution

> Too many graphics on a page or graphics whose file size is too large can make for a long download by those using modems, or even by those using older, slower computers on a network. Make sure the graphics you use add real value to your Web page, and also look for ways to reduce their file size.

 If you're worried about the size of graphics files, see "Right-Sizing Graphics" in the Troubleshooting section at the end of this chapter.

What kind of graphic images can you use? Web browsers understand only a limited number of graphic formats. The two most common of these are GIF (Graphics Interchange Format), and JPG (or JPEG, Joint Photographic Experts Group). You also find variations on these formats such as animated GIF or interlaced GIF, as well as the newer PNG (Portable Network Graphic) format.

Fortunately, you need not worry too much about the type of graphic you use because WordPerfect converts your non-Web graphic images to the appropriate GIF format when you publish your page to HTML.

Tip #246 from
Laura and Read

> Besides using images with smaller dimensions, you can often make graphic image files smaller by using the JPG instead of the GIF format.

You add graphics to a Web page the same way you add them to any WordPerfect document, although where you can place them on a page is limited by HTML standards. To insert a graphic image, follow these steps:

1. Position the insertion point where you want to place the graphic. Don't worry about being too precise because you'll probably have to adjust the location later anyway.

PART
VI

CH
21

2. Choose Insert, Graphics, and then choose Clipart if you want to use WordPerfect's clip art collection, or From File if you have an image of your own.

→ For information on using and manipulating graphic images in a WordPerfect document, **see** Chapter 12, "Adding Graphics to Documents," **p. 317**, and Chapter 13, "Customizing Graphic Shapes and Images," **p. 347**

Many WordPerfect graphic options also apply to graphics you use in your Web page. For example, you can size or flip images, place borders around them, and so on. When you publish your Web page to HTML, WordPerfect converts images to the GIF format so that Web browsers can view them.

Tip #247 from
Laura and Read

Standard HTML does not provide for captions. However, if you create a caption for your graphic box in WordPerfect, when you publish your Web page to HTML, WordPerfect converts both the graphic image and its caption to a GIF format that can be displayed as a single image in your Web browser.

Before going much further, you should take time to establish the HTML properties of the graphic image. To do this, follow these steps:

1. Right-click the image and choose HTML Properties from the QuickMenu, or select the image and click the HTML Box Properties button on the Property Bar. WordPerfect displays the HTML Properties dialog box (see Figure 21.18).

Figure 21.18
Certain HTML properties, such as Alternate text, should always be set for graphic images.

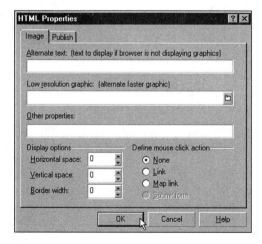

2. In the Alternate Text box, add a short description of the image. If users turn off graphics because they have slow modems, or if visually impaired people are using special readers, this alternate text will let them know what the image represents.

3. By default, nothing happens if a user clicks a graphic image. However, you can add a hyperlink to the image by choosing Link. You can then click the Link tab that appears and provide the URL, bookmark, or target frame, if any.

4. You can specify how much space there is to be between the text and the graphics box (horizontal and vertical, in pixels). You can also specify a border width, also in pixels. WordPerfect does not display the results, so you have to view the results in your Web browser.

5. Click OK to add the properties to your graphic image.

Note

We'll talk about the Map link and Submit form options in this dialog box later on, in the "Creating Forms" and "Using Image Mapping" sections in this chapter.

Perhaps the most difficult limitation to get used to is where you can place your graphics on the screen. In a typical WordPerfect document, you can position a graphic image precisely where you want it, and specify exactly how you want text to wrap around it. HTML provides only for a much cruder placement of graphics, typically at the left, center, or right of the screen.

To adjust the position of a graphic image in your Web page, select the graphic, and then select Graphics, Position from the Graphics Property Bar menu. WordPerfect displays the Box Position dialog box (see Figure 21.19), which offers the following choices:

■ Attach Box To Character—By default, the graphic image is attached to the character preceding the graphics box. As the character moves, so does the box. However, only one line of text is allowed on either side of the graphic image. You can align the image vertically at the top or the bottom of the line of text, or to points in between. Although this option offers some interesting possibilities, accurate graphic placement is quite tricky and requires a great deal of experimenting.

Figure 21.19
You can position graphics on a Web page using the Box Position dialog box.

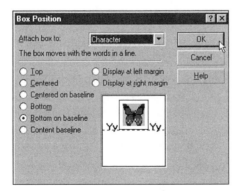

Note

Although WordPerfect offers the choice of placing a character-anchored graphic at the right or left, with text wrapping around it, this option does not work. In your browser, the graphic displays with only one line of text wrapping around it. To get true text wrapping, you need to use the Attach Box To Paragraph option.

■ Attach Box To Paragraph—Click the Attach Box To drop-down menu and choose Paragraph to view these options (see Figure 21.20), which more closely approximate typical HTML graphics placement. Although you're limited to left, right, and center positioning of the graphics box, this option allows text to wrap on one side or the other of the graphic image if you choose right or left alignment. Center alignment does not permit text wrapping at all.

Figure 21.20
You have better text wrapping options when you anchor an image to a paragraph.

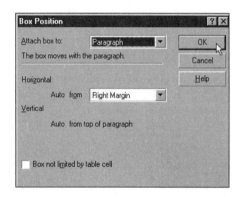

If you're like most people, creating just the right graphic image for Web pages really isn't an option because you just don't have the necessary artistic skills. Fortunately, there are plenty of resources for good graphic images, including the following:

■ WordPerfect's clip art—WordPerfect ships with approximately 12,000 clip art images. See Chapter 12, "Adding Graphics to Documents," for information on finding and adding these images to your Web page.

■ Images you modify using Corel Presentations—Although you might not find exactly the image you want as a clip art image, you should look at each clip art image as a collection of images. For example, you want a pair of blue jeans. None of the images is of just blue jeans, but one of the images shows a teenager wearing blue jeans. You can use Presentations to edit the image, removing everything except what you want. You then save just the image as its own WPG graphics file.

→ For information on manipulating and customizing clip art images by using the Draw program, **see** Chapter 14, "Adding Drawings and TextArt," **p. 373**

■ Images you create using Corel Presentations—If you have a specific layout of graphics and text that you can't seem to replicate in a WordPerfect Web page, you can create the layout in Presentations, and then group the objects in the layout and save them as an image that you then can insert into your Web page.

Note

You can save Presentations graphics in the standard WordPerfect (WPG) format, or use Save As to save them as GIF or JPG images. The key is to select the image first, and then save just the image, not the entire Presentations drawing screen.

■ Images from other Web sites—Often, while browsing the Web, you find just the image you'd like to use on your Web page. Capturing and using graphic images from other Web sites is quick and easy. Simply right-click the image in your browser, and from the QuickMenu, choose the option that enables you to save the image. Note where you save the image and its name, and then insert the image in your WordPerfect document.

Caution

Just because you can capture an image from the Web doesn't mean that it's legal to do so. Copyright laws apply to published materials on the Web, just as they do to printed materials. If you have questions about whether you can use an image, you should contact the owner of the Web page and ask permission.

Tip #248 from
Laura and Read

Many Web sites provide collections of free clip art, including graphic lines, buttons, bullets, and even animated GIF files. Two places to look are at the Netscape and Microsoft Web sites. You can also use any search engine, such as Lycos or Yahoo!, to find clip art sites.

Sizing Web page graphics can affect the quality of the graphic when it's displayed in a Web browser. In particular, bitmap graphics, such as GIF and JPG graphics, distort badly unless they appear in their original size. WPG graphics can be sized any way you like because they don't convert to bitmap graphics until you publish the Web page to HTML.

To ensure that a bitmap graphic remains at its proper size, follow these steps:

1. Select the graphic image.

2. Right-click the image and choose Size from the QuickMenu. WordPerfect displays the Box Size dialog box (see Figure 21.21).

Figure 21.21
You can use the Box Size dialog box to allow graphic images to display proportionally.

3. Choose Maintain Proportions for both the width and height, and click OK.

If you then find that the image is too large or too small, you really have no other option but to risk distortion by changing its size or re-creating the bitmap image in the proper size.

Tip #249 from *Laura and Read*	If you save a Corel Presentations graphic image as a GIF or JPG file, try to specify the exact dimensions you will need so you won't have to distort the image after inserting it into your WordPerfect Web page document.

ADDING COLOR AND BACKGROUNDS

By default, most browsers display Web pages with a gray background, which makes a page readable but not very exciting. Also by default, normal text is typically black, links are blue, and visited links are purple. Although users can change these settings in their browsers, you can, and should, control exactly what colors your Web pages display.

To change text colors, or color and wallpaper backgrounds, follow these steps:

1. Choose File, Properties, and click the Text/Background Colors tab of the HTML Document Properties dialog box (see Figure 21.22, which shows changed colors and background).

Figure 21.22
The Text/Background Colors tab of the HTML Document Properties dialog box enables you to change text colors and Web page background color, and to add a wallpaper background.

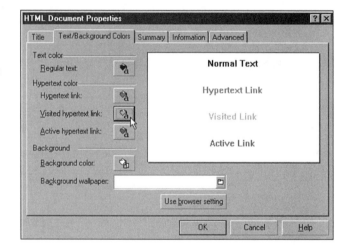

2. Using the color palette buttons, change the colors of each of the text components.

3. Using the color palette buttons, choose a background color that complements the text colors you have chosen.

Caution	Although unusual combinations of text and background colors can add pizzazz to your Web page, such combinations aren't a good idea if you expect people to read a lot of text. Dark text with contrasting light backgrounds are the easiest to read, and dark backgrounds with light text are better for introductory or menu pages where little reading is required.

4. You can choose a background wallpaper by clicking the browse button at the right of the Background Wallpaper text box. *Wallpaper* graphics are small images that Web

browsers download once and replicate as a background. WordPerfect ships with several wallpaper images, grouped by pattern types such as wood, paper, oil, stone, organic, designs, fabric, and nature.

Note

If you change the background color or add a wallpaper background, a display bug in the initial release of WordPerfect 9 may prevent you from seeing table lines, although tables display perfectly in a Web browser. You may need to turn off the background in WordPerfect while you edit tables and lines.

Tip #250 from
Laura and Read

You can capture wallpaper designs from other Web sites by right-clicking the Web page and choosing the appropriate Netscape Navigator or Internet Explorer menu option to save the background.

Note

A more logical location for changing backgrounds and text colors probably would be on the Format menu. Indeed, if you choose Format, Text Colors/Wallpaper, WordPerfect displays a different HTML Properties dialog box that, by the looks of it, should make selecting backgrounds easier. However, in the initial release of WordPerfect 9, this dialog box is clumsy and doesn't work nearly as well as the method described above. Nevertheless, this feature may well be improved in a subsequent service pack (update) for the program.

ADDING CUSTOM HTML CODE

If you already know HTML code and need to add coding that WordPerfect can't, you can insert it directly into a WordPerfect Web page. To insert custom HTML code, follow these steps:

1. Position the insertion point exactly where you want the HTML codes.

2. Choose Format, Custom HTML. Although you don't see it happen, WordPerfect inserts a pair of custom HTML style codes in your Web page document. You can see the codes by opening Reveal Codes (by choosing View, Reveal Codes or pressing Alt+F3).

3. Type the HTML codes, following standard HTML markup language conventions (for example, <OL> and </OL> to format a numbered list). WordPerfect displays what you type as red, double-underlined text (see Figure 21.23).

4. Move the insertion point and repeat steps 2–3 as required to complete the coding.

PART
VI
CH
21

Tip #251 from
Laura and Read

WordPerfect does not provide a means of indenting paragraphs. However, using the HTML tags for beginning and ending lists, you can create the same effect. Use custom HTML to insert <OL> at the beginning of a paragraph and </OL> at the end of the paragraph. Each pair of codes you add to the same paragraph indents the paragraph another five spaces.

Figure 21.23
If WordPerfect doesn't already offer an HTML formatting feature, you can add the HTML code, which when inserted appears red and double-underlined.

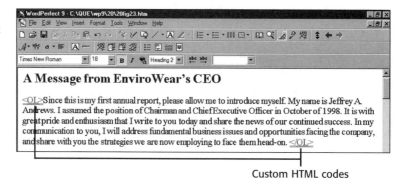

Custom HTML codes

CREATING INTERACTIVE WEB PAGES

Although the majority of user interaction with your Web page is likely to be clicking of links, you can also provide other ways for users to navigate your site or to communicate information back to you.

ADDING MAILTO LINKS

Perhaps the easiest and most common method of getting feedback is to include a mailto link. This type of link is a command to the user's browser to start up a mail program where the user can then create a message that is sent to the email address identified in the mailto link.

To create a mailto link, select the text or object you want to link, and choose Tools, Hyperlink, and in the Document text box of the Hyperlink Properties dialog box, type `mailto:` followed by the email address you want the mail to go to (for example, `mailto:sales@envirowear.com`). Note that there is no space between `mailto:` and the email address.

For your email links to work, the user has to have set up his or her browser to know what mail program to use. Although most people set up mail for their browsers, this is not universally the case. If you think your target audience may have problems with this, you might include a disclaimer on your Web page saying something like "This link requires a mail-enabled browser."

With a correct mailto link, and a correctly set up browser, clicking on the link opens the designated mail program, with the email address already placed in the To: line.

CREATING FORMS

Another, more structured, method for getting input is the use of forms. For example, a common use of forms is to collect required information from the user, and then to send that information via email to you or to someone you designate.

However, forms require two separate processes: one to collect and submit information, and another to process the information. The second process generally involves some sort of programming (often referred to as *CGI*, or Common Gateway Interface), placed on your Web page's server. If you plan to use forms on your Web page, you should contact the Webmaster (or Web server administrator) to find out what is required.

Note
Because of potential security problems, some Webmasters don't permit CGI or other programs on their servers.

 Assuming that you have access to a Web server with a program that can process your form, you can proceed to design the form. WordPerfect enables you to create forms that include check boxes, radio buttons, text boxes, lists, and so on. To create a form in a WordPerfect Web document, choose Insert, Form Items, and then choose from among the following menu options:

- Create Form—This places two form tags in your document to show where the form is located (see Figure 21.24, which shows a form with several options inserted).

Figure 21.24
WordPerfect enables you to build a form using text boxes, lists, check boxes, and more.

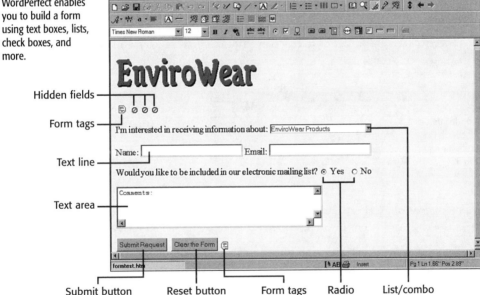

- Form Properties—After you create the form, you need to edit the form properties in the Form Properties dialog box (see Figure 21.25) to specify the URL where the processing program is located, as well as any MIME script, if required.

Note
Choosing Insert, Form Items, Properties, gives you the dialog box to change the properties for the form item immediately preceding the insertion point. For example, to change the properties for the form itself, position the insertion point following the opening form tag before choosing Properties.

Figure 21.25
You can use the Form Properties dialog box to specify what program will be used to process the data collected by the form.

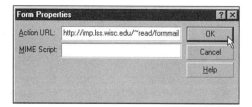

Tip #252 from
Laura and Read

You can double-click any form element to access its editing dialog box.

■ Hidden Field—In some cases, you want the form to submit information regardless of the information provided by the user. For example, you could include the email address to which the form's content is sent. The Hidden Field Properties dialog box enables you to provide a name and a value (see Figure 21.26, which shows values filled in). The form processor typically looks for certain named values (for example, Email) and then processes the value assigned to that name (for example, sends the information to sales@envirowear.com).

Figure 21.26
You can use hidden fields to provide information to the form processor without it being seen by the user.

Several options on the Form Items menu are designed to help you solicit information. You can create text instructions or prompts (refer to Figure 21.24), and then add these input fields:

■ Radio Button—When you want to offer several options, but allow the user to choose only one, you use radio buttons (refer to Figure 21.24). Use the Radio Button Properties dialog box (see Figure 21.27) to set the field values. Each button in the group must have the *same* name (for example, Mailing). One of the buttons, usually the most likely choice, can also be initially selected. You set a different value for each button (for example, Yes, No, Maybe) so that the form processor knows which button has been selected.

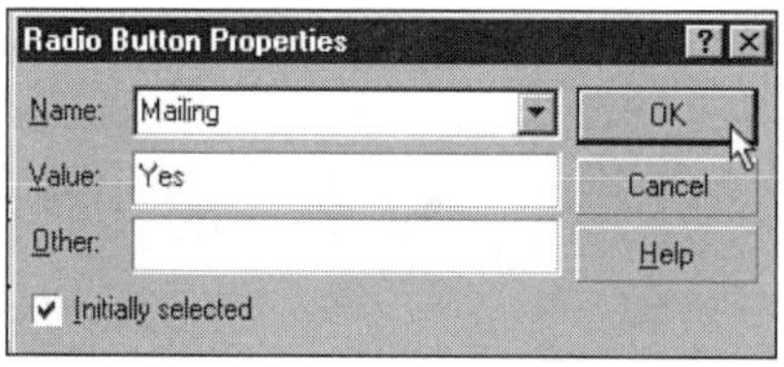

Figure 21.27
You can set the name and field values for radio buttons in the Radio Button Properties dialog box.

■ Check Box—If you want the user to be able to select as many or as few options as wanted, use a check box. You can also display boxes as initially selected.

■ Text Line—If you want to limit what a user types to just one line, use this option. In the Text/Password Properties dialog box (see Figure 21.28), you can also specify how wide the box should be, and the maximum number of allowable characters that can be typed. If you choose Password, the user sees an asterisk (*) for each character typed. The value of the box is processed the same for both text and passwords.

Figure 21.28
In the Text/Password Properties dialog box, you can specify the width of a text box, the number of permitted characters, and whether the entry is a password.

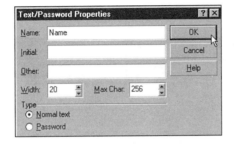

■ Text Area—This option enables the user to type larger amounts of information. You can specify the width of the area, the number of rows, how much text can be entered, and whether text wraps at the box margin.

■ Password—See Text Line, above.

■ Selection List—The Listbox/Combobox Properties dialog box (see Figure 21.29) enables you to create a list of items from which the user selects. Each item selected is processed by the name of the list, and you can allow more than one selection. When you choose Add, the Add Option dialog box enables you to assign a label in the Option text box (what the user sees in the list), and a Value (which is the information used by the form processor).

■ Combobox List—See Selection List, above.

Figure 21.29
Lists force users to choose from predefined options.

Finally, somewhere on the page you must include a means by which the users can submit their information. It's also a good idea to offer an option to clear all the information, in case a user wants to start over.

You can assign a label to the Submit or Reset button that appears on the button itself, and a name that the form's processor uses.

If you want something fancier than a standard Submit button, you can insert a graphic image by using the Submit Image option. The image works just like a regular Submit button.

Figure 21.30 shows a typical form displayed in a Web browser, and Figure 21.31 shows an example of the results of a form that has been processed by a CGI program.

Figure 21.30
In the Web browser, a user responds to the form's request for information.

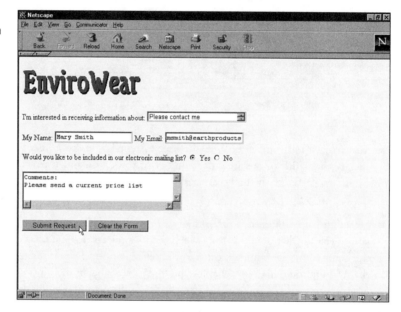

Figure 21.31
It's a good idea to create a feedback page to let the user know that the information was received.

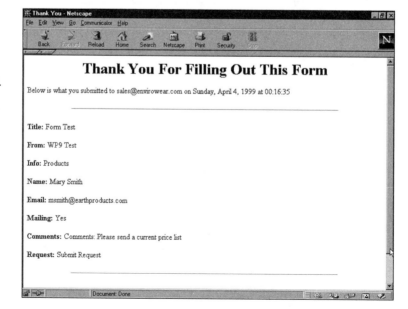

USING IMAGE MAPPING

Admit it. You think those underlined text menus look old-fashioned. What you really want is to be able to click on fancy-looking graphic images and have them link to other pages at your Web site.

Image mapping, the capability to tell the Web page what to do when a person clicks on a specific area of a page, in the past required that a program reside on the Web server to process the mapping information and requests. This was called *server-side* image mapping.

Recent changes in the HTML standard allow you to create *client-side* image mapping, which means that by using information you provide in your own Web page, you can tell the Web page what to do when a person clicks on a particular area of a page (see Figure 21.32 for an example of a mapped image used for a menu).

Figure 21.32
Mapped images can serve also as menus, linking users to other Web pages depending on where on the page they click.

To use a mapped image in your Web page, you first must enable the image to be mapped. Follow these steps:

1. Right-click the image and choose HTML Properties from the QuickMenu, or click the Box HTML Properties button on the Property Bar. WordPerfect displays the HTML Properties dialog box (refer to Figure 21.18).

2. Click the Map Link option. WordPerfect adds a Map Link tab to the dialog box.

3. Click the Map Link tab to access the image mapping options (see Figure 21.33).

Figure 21.33
You can use the Map Link tab of the HTML Properties dialog box to specify the name and location of image mapping codes.

4. If you're using a server-side image mapping program, provide its name and URL location in the CGI Script text box. However, you'll probably leave this box blank.

5. Because you're using client-side mapping, and because you want to include the HTML code for that mapping within the current document, leave the File box as is. However, you must give the map a name, for example, EnviroMenu.

6. Click OK to add the image mapping properties to the graphic image.

The second part of the mapping process requires you to insert HTML code that specifies the exact coordinates of the area of the graphic to be linked, and the links to follow when that area is clicked. This is code that must be inserted as custom HTML code. Choose Format, Custom HTML and insert the mapping code, as shown in Figure 21.34.

Figure 21.34
Image mapping codes appear as custom HTML code in WordPerfect, but are hidden when viewed in a Web browser.

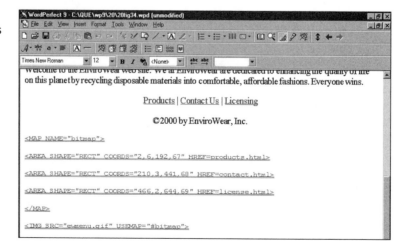

If you're a real gearhead, you might enjoy coding this yourself, including the mapping coordinates, but if you're like the rest of us, you'll need some help.

Fortunately, WordPerfect Office 2000 provides a Corel Presentations 9 macro to help in creating the image map coding. To use the macro, follow these steps:

1. Open Corel Presentations 9. It makes no difference whether you start with a drawing screen or a slide show.

2. Choose Tools, Macro, Play, and in the Macro Play dialog box, choose imgemap.wcm.

Note

By default, the WordPerfect Office 2000 installation program does not install the Presentations macros. If you did not install them, you must do so before you can use the image mapping macro.

3. The macro displays the Create HTML Image Map Code dialog box (see Figure 21.35). Specify the name of the image to be mapped (a GIF or JPG file), and the folder where you want to save the resulting bitmap.htm file that will contain the HTML image mapping code. If you also want to view a sample of how your image is mapped, choose Create a Sample Page. Click OK.

Figure 21.35
The Presentations imgemap.wcm macro first asks you to specify the name of the image to be mapped and where the resulting code will be stored.

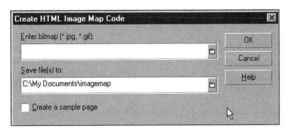

4. A dialog box appears, instructing you how to use the macro. Click OK to begin.

5. Your bitmap image appears on the Presentations screen, along with the Image Map dialog box.

6. Drag the first area you want to map, and then click Set Map in the Image Map dialog box (see Figure 21.36).

7. The Link to URL dialog box appears, where you type the URL location. If the URL is another document on your own Web site, and is in the same folder as the current page, simply type the name of the HTML document without a path. Otherwise, type the complete URL (http://...).

8. Repeat steps 6–7 until you map all the areas of the image you want.

9. Click Done in the Image Map dialog box.

PART

VI

CH

21

Figure 21.36
You can drag an area to be mapped and specify the URL it's linked to.

The macro creates HTML image mapping code and saves it in the bitmap.htm file in the location you specified. If you selected Create a Sample Page, the macro launches your browser and displays the image and its mapping for you to review.

Finally, to insert the image mapping code in your document, follow these steps:

1. Open the HTML document that contains the image you mapped.

2. Choose Format, Custom HTML. Although nothing appears to happen, continue with the next step.

3. Choose Insert, File, and then find and select the bitmap.htm file you created that contains the image mapping code. WordPerfect asks if this is ASCII text. Choose OK. WordPerfect inserts the image mapping code, in red and double-underlined (refer to Figure 21.34). Alternatively, you can open the bitmap.htm file, copy the code, and paste it as custom HTML code in your Web document.

4. Make sure the name of the image map matches the one you specified when you set the HTML properties of your image (for example, EnviroMenu). Be sure to match the case exactly.

5. Delete the line that identifies the image source (for example, <A HREF SRC=...>) because this is a duplicate reference to the image you already placed in your document.

Tip #253 from
Laura and Read

You can insert the image mapping code anywhere in your document because the browser finds the code based on the name of the mapping (for example, EnviroMenu). Thus you can place this code at the end of your document to keep it out of the way of the rest of your document.

6. Save your document (as HTML), and preview the document. As you pass the mouse over the mapped areas of the image (refer to Figure 21.32), note that the pointer changes to a hand and the URL appears on the status bar of your browser.

If you plan to do a lot of image mapping, you might want to invest in a third-party software program to help you generate the image mapping codes. One such program is MapEdit, by Boutell.COM (`http://www.boutell.com/mapedit`). With this program or one like it, you specify the name of the Web document, and it finds and opens for you the graphic image you want to map, helps you map it, and then generates the appropriate HTML code and automatically inserts it in your Web document. Also, although the Presentations macro allows you to map only rectangles, this map editing software enables you to map circles and irregular shapes.

PUBLISHING WEB PAGES

The moment of truth has arrived. You've worked long and hard to get your Web page ready, and now it's time to put it on a Web server for the whole world to see.

Consider the following as you prepare to publish your page:

- Do a final preview in your own Web browser. Check for content (spelling, for example), and layout (are things where they're supposed to be?).

- Check your links in your browser. Do they jump where they're supposed to?

- Determine the name of the server and the location where you will move your files. You should contact your Webmaster and work out these details, or you might not be able to move your files. For example, do you need a password? Do you have sufficient rights to create files on the server?

- Determine how you want to organize your files on the server. The safest way is to keep all your files in the same folder. For example, your graphics files might reside in the same location as your Web page (HTML) documents.

> **Caution**
> One of the most common problems in publishing a Web page is not placing all the required files in the proper location. Browsers don't tell you why you can't view a file, but it's painfully obvious when you get the broken image icon when you view your Web page.

- Make sure you have a network or Internet connection to the Web server.

⚠ *If your Web page has missing graphic images, see "Where, Oh Where, Is That Graphics File?" in the Troubleshooting section at the end of this chapter.*

USING THE BUILT-IN FTP PUBLISHER

The process whereby you move your Web files from your computer to a Web server is most often accomplished by using an File Transfer Protocol (FTP) program. You could, of course, make sure all your files are in one place on your local computer, connect to the server using an FTP program, and transfer the files to the proper location on the server.

However, WordPerfect makes it even easier than that with its built-in Publish to HTML option. To publish a Web page to a Web server, follow these steps:

 1. Choose File, Internet Publisher, and in the Internet Publisher dialog box click Publish to HTML. WordPerfect displays the Publish to HTML dialog box (see Figure 21.37).

Figure 21.37
You can use the Publish to HTML dialog box to transfer your Web page and its associated graphics files to a Web server.

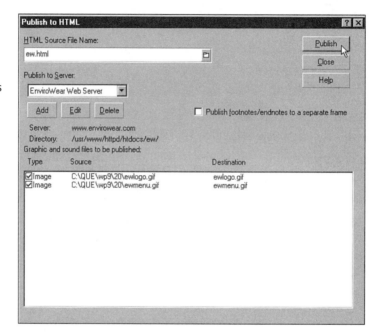

2. If the Web page was open already in WordPerfect, the name of the file appears in the HTML Source File Name text box. Otherwise, type the name of the file.

3. Click Add to set up a server to which you publish the file. WordPerfect displays the Server Information dialog box (see Figure 21.38).

4. Provide a description label in the Label text box.

5. Type the URL of the server. This should be only the name of the server, without directories (for example, www.envirowear.com).

6. If the name of the machine requires a port number, type it in the Port text box.

7. Provide your user ID, whether you want to be prompted for a password, and the password itself.

8. Specify the full path where the Web page is to go—for example, /usr/www/httpd/htdocs/ew/.

9. Click OK to add the server definition to the drop-down list of Web servers in the Publish to Server box (refer to Figure 21.37).

10. Click Publish to send the HTML file and all listed graphics to the server you selected.

Figure 21.38
You can set up server information you get from your Webmaster so you don't have to enter that information more than once.

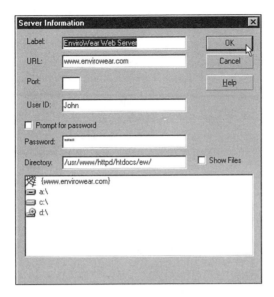

Caution

If you're using a dial-up connection to your Web server, make sure you're connected before attempting to publish your Web page.

Tip #254 from
Laura and Read

If you've already published your page before and are updating it, you can uncheck any unchanged graphic image files so you don't have to upload them again.

If you're lucky, you may be able to publish your Web pages directly to a local or network drive. Many corporate intranets, for example, permit you to save documents directly on network drives that are accessible with a browser.

To publish your Web pages to a network (or local) drive, set up a server in the Publish to HTML dialog box that includes just a server label, and a directory that includes the network drive along with the path to the location where the files are to be published. If you need a user ID and password, you can supply those, too, although often these are not required when you're connected to your network server.

⚡ *If your pages don't look good in some browsers, see "All Browsers Are Not Created Equal" in the Troubleshooting section at the end of this chapter.*

OTHER PUBLISHING OPTIONS

HTML-based Web pages are still the most common method of publishing and viewing Web documents. However, other options exist for getting your Web pages out to the rest of the world. WordPerfect now includes three such methods: publishing to PDF, publishing to Trellix, and using Extensible Markup Language (XML) and Standard Graphics Markup Language (SGML).

PART

VI

CH

21

PUBLISHING TO PDF

A serious drawback to HTML pages is the limitation of the HTML standard itself. Wouldn't it be better if you could publish pages that look *exactly* as pages do when formatted in WordPerfect?

Adobe Corporation has developed a specialized format that it calls the Portable Document Format, or PDF. It requires the Adobe Publisher to create the published files, and it requires that users install a PDF reader as a plug-in to their Web browsers. The PDF reader is free, but the publisher is not. Fortunately, WordPerfect now includes the PDF publisher as a built-in feature.

Note
You cannot publish Web-formatted pages to PDF. Only normal WordPerfect documents can be published to this format.

Using PDF documents with your Web page involves two steps:

1. Create the PDF document.

→ For information on how to create a PDF document from an existing WordPerfect document, **see** "Publishing to PDF," **p. 563**

2. In your Web document, simply create a link to the PDF file. For example, in the Hyperlink Properties dialog box, specify the name of the PDF file in the Document edit box.

Caution
If you use PDF documents along with your Web pages, be sure to transfer the PDF documents to your Web server. Also, it's usually best to place the PDF and Web documents in the same folder on the Web server. Do *not* include a local pathname in the link (for example, c:\myfiles\mydoc.pdf) or the Web server won't be able to find it.

Tip #255 from
Laura and Read
If you use PDF files, it's usually a good idea to add a note to your Web page letting users know they must have the free Adobe Acrobat reader installed. You might even include a link to the Adobe Web site (http://www.adobe.com) to make it easy for them to do so.

PUBLISHING TO TRELLIX

A dilemma that faces many of us who want to publish existing documents to the Web is that long documents are unwieldy in the HTML format, which lends itself better to being broken down into several shorter pages. Better yet, these pages should be linked in such a way that the reader can easily navigate the entire longer document.

WordPerfect 9 includes Trellix, an integrated program that helps you take existing longer documents and publish them as an organized and linked collection of smaller pages.

Note
A discussion of Trellix is beyond the scope of this book. For more information on this useful program, see Que's *Special Edition Using WordPerfect Office 2000*.

USING XML AND SGML

HTML is intended to give Web documents a uniform look, regardless of the computer and the software used to create the document. Unfortunately, as noted previously, HTML has several limitations, especially in document formatting.

Another, more advanced, standard for formatting Web documents is SGML (Standard Graphics Markup Language). SGML provides a method for defining each element in the content of a document. This allows advanced formatting to be applied to the SGML document so that the same content can be published multiple ways without changing or converting the content. For example, you can print a book in a large-page format and also in a smaller format, such as paperback that uses a smaller page size and font, as well as different margins, without changing the content file. Similarly, the same content can be published to the Internet or manipulated by a computer application. Support for SGML editing was initially available as a WordPerfect 8 feature.

The capability to edit XML (Extensible Markup Language) documents is new to WordPerfect 9. XML is a simplified version of SGML, and provides the power of SGML without the complexity.

Although a discussion of SGML and XML is beyond the scope of this book, you should be aware that you can edit these types of documents in WordPerfect, using the familiar WordPerfect interface.

TROUBLESHOOTING

USING THE INTERNET PUBLISHER MENUS

I started a Web page, but I still get the regular WordPerfect menu, not the Internet Publisher menu.

This happens from time to time, but you can fix it easily by right-clicking the menu bar and choosing Internet Publisher Menu. Likewise, if you close a Web page and still see the Internet Publisher menu, right-click the menu bar and choose WordPerfect 9 Menu.

RIGHT-SIZING GRAPHICS

I'm using a graphic I created in Corel Presentations, but although it looks fine on my screen in WordPerfect, it looks lousy in my Web browser.

Bitmap graphics, such as GIF and JPG graphics, cannot be enlarged without creating display problems. When you save a Corel Presentations image as a GIF or JPG file, specify also the exact size you need on your Web page so you don't have to change the size of the graphic in WordPerfect.

SAVING AS HTML

When I view my Web page in a browser, I see lots of strange characters on the screen—they begin with WPC—but I don't understand anything after that.

If you save your Web page, but forget to save it to the HTML format, that's what it will look like when viewed in a browser. Just open the file and save it again, this time as HTML.

WHERE, OH WHERE, IS THAT GRAPHICS FILE?

Everything looks good when I'm previewing my Web page, but after I publish it, some of the graphics are missing.

Several issues can affect your published Web page. First, you must be sure that all elements of the page, including graphics, are published to the target location. If you manually copy or FTP files, you may miss a file. Second, if you don't publish the page, the Web page may still refer to graphic images by their local designation—for example, `c:\graphics\image.gif`. Use WordPerfect's publishing option to avoid this. Finally, make sure the case of the file-names and locations is correct. Most UNIX-based Web servers distinguish between upper- and lowercase, whereas Windows does not. If your Web page says to use `Image.gif`, and the name of the file on the server is `image.gif`, the server won't know what file to use.

ALL BROWSERS ARE NOT CREATED EQUAL

My Web page looks good when I view it in my browser, but my friend says parts of it are messed up when she looks at it on the Web.

Not all browsers view the same HTML code in the same way. For example, even different versions of Netscape Navigator can view a page differently. If users are viewing your page on a Macintosh, or if they're using Internet Explorer and you're using Netscape Navigator, they may get different results. As a Web page creator, you should take the time to view your page in different browsers (usually Netscape Navigator and Internet Explorer) and on different platforms (PC and Mac), and then make adjustments to your page if possible so it looks good on all of them. If what you want to accomplish on your page just won't work in other browsers, you should note that on your page by including a link to the viewer download site that says something like "This page is best viewed using SuprBrowz. Click here to download the free viewer."

PROJECT

As noted several times in this chapter, one of your biggest challenges in creating Web pages is to recognize the limitations of HTML in formatting things to look like what you're used to seeing in WordPerfect. Even features that *seem* to be available in the WordPerfect Internet Publisher may not work in all situations.

One example is the aligment of text in columns. If you create a Web document and then choose Format, Columns, Format, WordPerfect displays the Web Columns dialog box shown in Figure 21.39. What WordPerfect doesn't tell you, however, is that the HTML codes it generates to create columns is recognized by recent versions of Netscape Navigator, but *not* of Internet Explorer.

Nevertheless, you still can create the *effect* of columns that both Netscape Navigator and Internet Explorer can display. You do this by creating a table with a single row, and as many columns as you want. Although this effect is most useful with columns of data, such as two columns of bulleted items, you can use it to simulate newspaper-style columns as well.

Figure 21.39
Although WordPerfect enables you to create columns in a Web page, some browsers do not recognize this formatting.

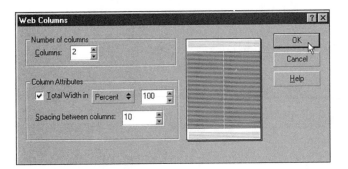

> **Caution**
>
> Although it's rare to find anyone using a browser that can't display tables, it's possible. Tables were not part of the earliest HTML standards, and very early versions of Netscape Navigator, for example, do not recognize tables.

Consider the list shown in Figure 21.40. Because it's a long list, the user has to scroll the Web page to see it in its entirety. If you place this list inside a table, it spreads out horizontally for easier access.

Figure 21.40
A long list is difficult to use because the user has to scroll to see it all.

To create columns by using a table, simply create the table as described in this chapter (see the section "Adding Tables"). Create just one row and the number of columns you need (for example, three). Consider the following:

- Use the HTML Table dialog box to set table borders to zero width so that the user doesn't see the table lines.

- In the Table tab of the HTML Table dialog box, set Vertical Alignment of Cell Content to Top. Otherwise, browsers vertically center text that doesn't fill as much of the cell as does text in other cells in the row.

- If you're creating a list and don't want double-spacing between lines (for example, in the lines of an address), insert a line break instead of a hard return (by choosing Insert, Line Break or pressing Ctrl+Shift+L).

- If you're placing text inside a table, you can cut and paste it into the cells. For newspaper-style columns, you have to determine how much text goes in each column because, unlike regular WordPerfect columns, WordPerfect can't calculate this for you.

- If you don't specify exact column measurements, Internet Explorer and sometimes Netscape Navigator try to format the column widths themselves. To avoid this, drag the column lines of the table right, and then left, back to the original spot. This is enough to set column widths that both browsers can use.

Using these tips, you can create a Web page that looks like the ones shown in Figure 21.41 (Netscape Navigator) and Figure 21.42 (Internet Explorer).

Figure 21.41
Tables can create the effect of columns in Netscape Navigator.

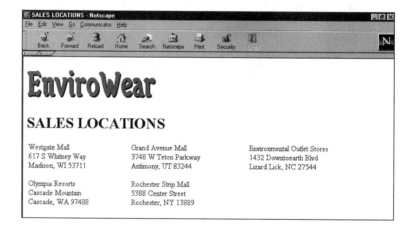

Figure 21.42
The same tables can create the effect of columns in Internet Explorer.

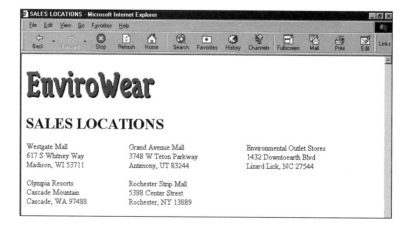

VII

AUTOMATING EVERYDAY TASKS

CHAPTER 22

BUILDING DOCUMENTS WITH TEMPLATES

In this chapter

USING WORDPERFECT'S TEMPLATES

Whether you realize it or not, you use a *template* every time you create a new document. The wp9us.wpt template (for the U.S. version of WordPerfect) is the default template in WordPerfect, and it contains all the default settings for new documents. Although the default template is blank except for the initial settings, a typical template is like a fill-in-the-blanks document. It contains the formatting, layout, and standard blocks of text—all you have to do is provide the content. Voilà! A document is created, ready to print, fax, or email. It takes about 90 seconds to create a fax cover sheet, not 3 to 4 minutes to edit another cover sheet, and certainly not 10 minutes to type it from scratch. Multiply that by the number of times you use a fax cover sheet, or invoice, or legal time sheet, and you've saved enough time to actually go *out* for lunch.

There are a wealth of templates included with WordPerfect—so many that you may not have to create your own for quite a while, if ever. When you do venture out and create your own template, you'll be able to use any of the existing templates as a model, so all you have to do is make minor adjustments. In just a few minutes, you can even turn your own documents into templates.

CHOOSING A PROJECT TEMPLATE

Beginning in WordPerfect 8, templates are called *project templates* because PerfectExpert projects act as the "front end" for the templates. Rather than open a template just as you would any other document, you select the project that you want to work on. The template is opened in the document window, and the *PerfectExpert panel* opens on the left side of the screen. You simply click the project buttons and choose from a list of options to alter the style, add other elements, and fill in the important text.

Tip #256 from
Laura and Read

The PerfectExpert is a powerful ally. When your users don't want to learn the ins and outs of WordPerfect just to create standard documents, it's your best friend. The easiest way to include the PerfectExpert in custom templates is to base your custom template on an existing WordPerfect template.

To create a new document based on a WordPerfect template, choose File, New from Project (or press Ctrl+Shift+N). The Corel PerfectExpert dialog box appears (see Figure 22.1). If necessary, click the Create New tab. Scroll through the list of projects, and then double-click the one you want to run.

Figure 22.1
In the Corel PerfectExpert dialog box, you can choose the PerfectExpert project you want to use to create a document from a template.

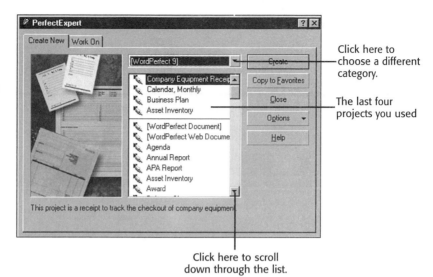

Click here to choose a different category.

The last four projects you used

Click here to scroll down through the list.

⚠ *If you get an "Error Creating Project" message when you try to open a project template, see "Missing or Damaged Template Files" in the Troubleshooting section at the end of this chapter.*

If you don't see the project you want, click the category drop-down list arrow at the top of the project template list and choose another category. Select WordPerfect 9 for a list of all the templates that ship with Corel WordPerfect Office 2000.

Tip #257 from
Laura and Read

If you have an Internet browser installed and running, you can go online and download more projects and templates from Corel's WordPerfect 9 Web site. Choose the Projects and Template Online category, and then double-click WordPerfect.

Caution

Many of WordPerfect's templates require personal information. If you haven't filled that in yet, you'll be prompted for it the first time you open a project template that uses the personal information. Skip down to the section "Filling in Personal Information," later in this chapter, and take care of that before you move on.

When you open a template, the PerfectExpert panel opens next to the template (see Figure 22.2). The buttons in the PerfectExpert panel give you options for customizing the template by choosing from the available variations.

PerfectExpert panel

Figure 22.2
PerfectExpert projects incorporate templates and PerfectExpert ask-and-you-shall-receive formatting to auto-mate many aspects of document production.

Click here to fill in the To and From information.

Click here to check spelling, print, fax, or save.

Now you can start building the document by clicking the buttons in the PerfectExpert panel. For example, in the Fax Cover Sheet project, click the Fill in Heading Info button to open the Fax Cover Sheet Heading dialog box, where you can type all the To and From information (see Figure 22.3). Remove the check mark next to any item that you don't want on the fax cover sheet. Click the drop-down list arrows to choose items that you've already used in these fields. Otherwise, type the information in the text boxes.

Figure 22.3
After you type the information in the Fax Cover Sheet Heading dialog box, WordPerfect inserts it in the appropriate places in the template.

Remove the check mark if you don't want to use the element.

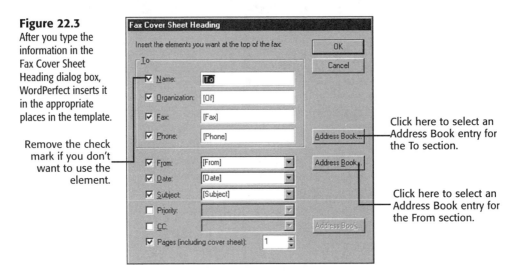

Click here to select an Address Book entry for the To section.

Click here to select an Address Book entry for the From section.

Click the top <u>A</u>ddress Book button to fill in information from an Address Book entry in the recipient's section. Click the bottom Address <u>B</u>ook button to fill in information in the sender's section. Click OK when you're done. The information is inserted into the template, and you're ready to continue creating the document.

FILLING IN PERSONAL INFORMATION

A good number of project templates require personal information (such as a name, company, address, and fax number), which you can type in once and have WordPerfect insert for you whenever it's necessary. If this information hasn't been created yet, you are prompted for it when you open a template that uses it (see Figure 22.4).

Figure 22.4
If you haven't filled in the personal information, you are prompted for it the first time you open a project template that uses it.

When you click OK, the CorelCENTRAL Address Book dialog box opens, with a list of available Address Books (see Figure 22.5). You need to select an Address Book entry that contains the personal information. Click the book with your personal information, select the entry in the list, and then click Insert. That's it—you're in.

Click here to add your
own information.

Figure 22.5
The list of Address Books in the CorelCENTRAL Address Book dialog box varies depending on how your system is set up.

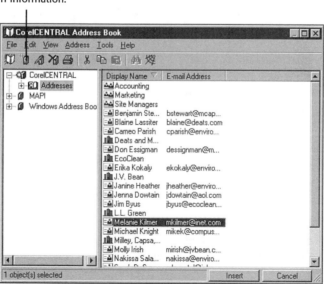

If you haven't created your own entry, click the Create a New Address Entry button on the toolbar. In the New Entry dialog box, select the kind of entry you want to create, and then click OK. The Properties dialog box for that kind of entry appears. Figure 22.6 shows the Person Properties dialog box.

Note

Users of WordPerfect 8 should notice that a new entry type has been added in WordPerfect 9–the Group entry.

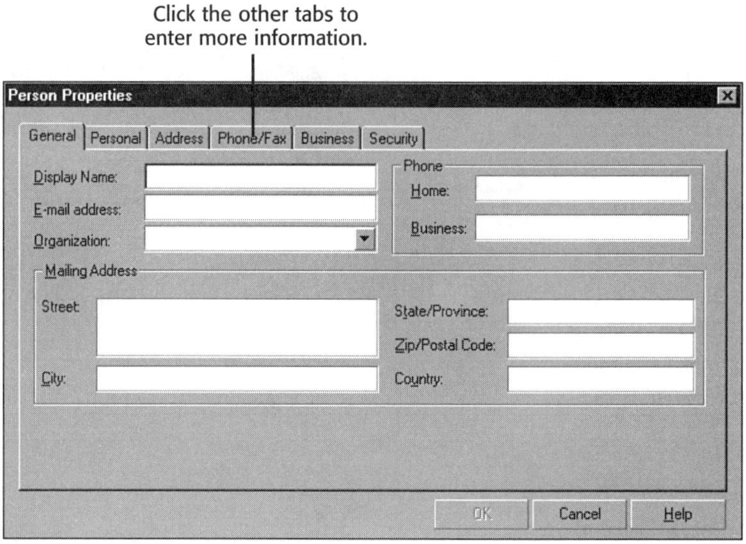

Click the other tabs to enter more information.

Figure 22.6
The Person Properties dialog box is the most comprehensive of the Properties dialog boxes, with six different tabs.

When you finish, choose OK to get back to the template. Now you can start building the document. If you like, skip back to the text below Figure 22.2 for a quick review of how to use the fax cover sheet project template.

EDITING PERSONAL INFORMATION

When you select a personal information entry in an Address Book, the entry becomes the default for all the templates. In many offices, computers are shared, so users need to select their own personal information entry in the Address Book.

To select a different personal information entry, open the PerfectExpert Projects dialog box by clicking File, New from Project (or by pressing Ctrl+Shift+N), and then choose Options, Personal Information. A message box appears and identifies the current personal information entry (see Figure 22.7). Click OK to open the CorelCENTRAL Address Book dialog box, where you can select another personal information entry.

Figure 22.7
The personal information can be changed each time a different user uses the computer.

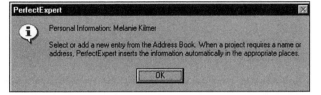

CUSTOMIZING WORDPERFECT'S TEMPLATES

Every new document you create is based on the *default template*, which contains all the default settings. Some of these settings are listed in Table 1.1 in Chapter 1, "Getting Comfortable with WordPerfect." This template can be customized to suit specific requirements. For example, if you want 1.5-inch margins, specific tab settings, and *widow/orphan protection (page 180)* always on, you can make these changes to the default template so that they are in place for all new documents.

WordPerfect's project templates are designed so that you can use them right away. They are generic enough to work in most situations, especially when time is more important than personalization. However, when you're ready to customize the templates, you can revise a template as easily as you revise any other document. It is especially important that you back up the original template before you start revising. If something goes wrong, you can always revert back to the original.

EDITING THE DEFAULT TEMPLATE

If you routinely use settings other than the defaults, you can place these settings in the default template. The next time you create a new document, the new default settings will be in place. Editing the default template is a little tricky. Rather than click on the [WordPerfect Document] entry in the list of projects and choose Options, Edit WP Template, you have to select the template file from the list of custom templates. I like to think that WordPerfect is designed this way to avoid accidental modifications—not just to confuse me.

Follow these steps to edit the default template:

1. Choose File, New from Project. If necessary, click the Create New tab.
2. Click the category drop-down list arrow and choose the Custom WP Templates category. By default, there are two templates in this folder: the default template and the QuickWords template (see Figure 22.8).

Figure 22.8
The Custom WP Templates category contains the default template, the QuickWords template, and any custom templates you create.

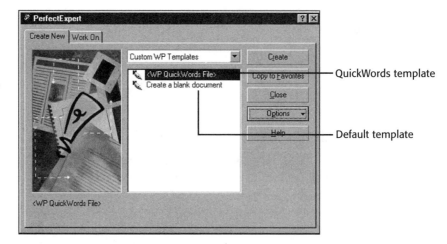

QuickWords template

Default template

You use the <WP QuickWords File> template when copying abbreviations or QuickWords from older templates so you can use them in WordPerfect 9. See the section "Copying Objects from Other Templates" later in this chapter for more information.

3. Select Create a Blank Document from the list.

4. Choose Options, Edit WP Template. The template opens in a document window, and the Template toolbar is displayed on top of the Property Bar (see Figure 22.9).

Figure 22.9
When you edit a template, the Template toolbar is added to the top of your screen.

Click here to insert a file.

Click here to close the template editor.

5. Revise the template as you would any other document. Bear in mind that your changes will be applied to every new document from here on out, so be careful about the type of formatting codes and text you include.

Tip #258 from
Laura and Read

Is the Edit WP Template option grayed out? If you select the [WordPerfect Document] entry in the list, and then click Options, the Edit WP Template option is grayed out because you can't edit the default template this way. Click the category drop-down list arrow and select Custom WP Templates. Select Create a Blank Document, and then choose Options, Edit WP Template.

It's better to *add* functionality to templates than to take it out. Your changes aren't written in stone, so if you decide to take some things back out of the template, it will only takes a minute. If you've removed functionality, it may take hours to re-create (and that's assuming that you have the expertise to do it).

Tip #259 from
Laura and Read

By default, any new styles you create are stored with the particular document. If you want to be able to use those styles with other documents, you need to save the new styles to the default template, which is available to all new documents. See the section "Saving a Style" in Chapter 9, "Formatting with Styles," for more information.

Note

The default template folder (specified in File Settings) is where the default template is stored. Any custom templates that you create are also saved to this folder. If the default template folder is set to a network drive, that drive must be accessible when WordPerfect is started. If the drive isn't available, the default template folder is set to `\windows\template` on the local drive. Templates that you create while the default template folder is set to your local drive are created in the `\windows\template` folder.

Backing Up Templates Before Making Revisions

Always make backup copies of your templates before you edit them. If something goes wrong, you can revert back to the original copy and start over.

In the Corel PerfectExpert dialog box, right-click the template that you want to revise. Choose Project Properties to display the Modify a Project dialog box (see Figure 22.10). The Command Line list box has the name of the folder and the name of the template file. Click in the text box, and then press End to move to the end of the entry. Scribble down the name of the file.

In the Open File dialog box, move to the `\program files\corel\wordperfect office 2000\template` folder. There are two types of files here. Template files are shown as WordPerfect 9 Documents; project files are shown as AST files. Right-click the template file, choose Rename, and then type `filename.old` as the new filename.

Tip #260 from
Laura and Read

Okay, here's your safety net. If you're on the stubborn side and you don't *want* to back up your templates, you can get fresh copies from the WordPerfect Office 2000 CD-ROM. The templates are stored in the `\corel\template` folder.

Figure 22.10
The Modify a Project dialog box has the name of the template file and the name of the project file for a selected project template.

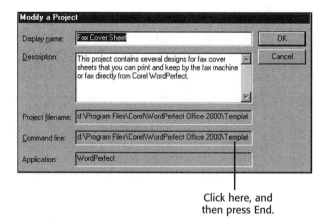

Click here, and
then press End.

REVISING WORDPERFECT TEMPLATES

Call me lazy, but adding my company logo was the full extent of my template customizing. If you're more ambitious, you might want to change the headings, select a different font, remove elements that you won't use, or modify the formulas used to calculate figures in tables.

Follow these steps to revise one of WordPerfect's templates:

1. Choose File, New from Project.
2. Select the template you want to revise.
3. Choose Options, Edit WP Template. The template is opened into the document window, and the Template toolbar is turned on (see Figure 22.11).

Template toolbar

Figure 22.11
You can edit a template as easily as you edit a regular document.

Click here to change the description text.

Click here when you're done.

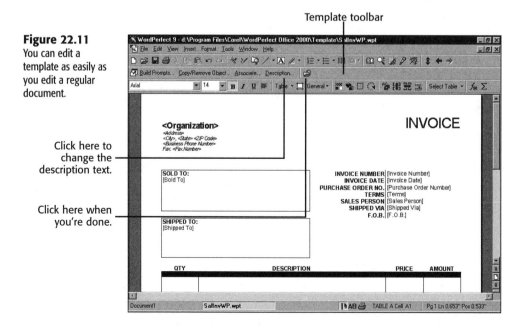

4. Using the same techniques that you use on a regular WordPerfect document, revise the template.

→ For more information on adding template prompts to help you remember what you're supposed to be typing, **see** "Using Prompt Builder," **p. 629**

Tip #261 from
Laura and Read

You can change the name that appears in the list of project templates. While editing a template, click the Description button on the Template toolbar, and then type a new name in the Template Description dialog box. Keep it short, so that the name doesn't extend too far over in the list.

5. Click the Close Template Editor button when you are through. When you are prompted to save your changes, click <u>Y</u>es.

Note

The modifications that you make in a template only affect new documents you create with the template; the documents that you've already created won't be affected at all.

CREATING NEW TEMPLATES

Creating a template from scratch is definitely a last resort. Two other options are much faster. First, you can save an existing document as a template. You're bound to have a least a couple "form" documents that you use over and over. Fax cover sheets come to mind, but so do supply requests, time sheets, network maintenance bulletins, expense reports, newsletters, equipment check-out sheets, and so on.

Second, you can revise an existing template, and then save your changes as a new template. You can use as your starting point one of your own templates or one of the templates that came with WordPerfect, and then just make the necessary adjustments. After all, a lot of effort goes into the development of a template—it would be a shame to let that go to waste.

BASING A TEMPLATE ON AN EXISTING DOCUMENT

For basic templates, basing a template on an existing document is the best option for building a library of templates that you can start using right away. Think of documents that you use often in which some of the information stays the same (such as memo headings and the sender's name) and some of the information changes (such as the recipient, date, subject, and content of the memo). Strip out the information that changes, leave the information that doesn't, and voilà—you've got yourself a template.

Note

This might seem like a complicated way to achieve the same result that you get by revising an existing document and saving it under a new name. But hang on for a second, there's more to it than that! Filling in a blank template is just the tip of the iceberg. You can build on the template later, adding automation features such as the ability to select information from the Address Book. Furthermore, system administrators can deploy templates with standardized styles, macros, toolbars, menus, and keyboards (you'll learn more on this later).

Follow these steps to create a template from an existing document:

1. In a blank document, choose File, New from Project.

2. Choose Options, Create WP Template. A blank template opens in the document window, and the Template toolbar is displayed at the top of the screen.

 3. Click the Insert File button (or choose Insert, File) to display the Insert File dialog box.

4. Select the filename for the existing document, and then choose Insert.

5. Strip out the variable text, and then make any other necessary revisions.

Tip #262 from
Laura and Read

By using a *QuickMark (page 500)*, you can position the insertion point in a specific place when creating a new document based on a template. For example, you might want to place the insertion point on the fax number line in a fax cover sheet template so that the user can type the fax number as soon as the document opens. Before you save the template, click where you want the insertion point to be, and then press Ctrl+Shift+Q to set a QuickMark. To find the QuickMark later (as you edit the template), press Ctrl+Q.

 6. Click the Close button when you're finished.

7. Click Yes when you're asked if you want to save the template. The Save Template dialog box appears (see Figure 22.12).

Figure 22.12
In the Save Template dialog box, you can type a description for the template and a name for the file, and then choose a category to store the template in.

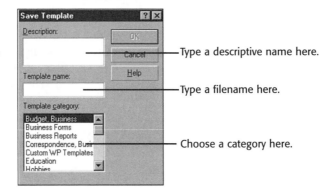

Type a descriptive name here.

Type a filename here.

Choose a category here.

8. In the <u>D</u>escription text box, type a descriptive name to appear in the template list.

9. Type a filename in the Template <u>N</u>ame text box. Don't type an extension—WordPerfect assigns the .wpt extension to templates so that they can be recognized as templates and not as documents.

10. Choose the category where you want the template stored in the Template <u>C</u>ategory list box.

11. Click OK to save and close the template.

Tip #263 from
Laura and Read

Templates cannot be password protected. If you want to password protect a template, you're better off saving it as a regular document and choosing <u>P</u>assword Protect in the Save As dialog box.

 If you can't find a template that you've just created in the list, see "My New Template Isn't Showing Up" in the Troubleshooting section at the end of this chapter.

After you've converted some of your documents to templates, you might want to consider how you can delegate some document production by distributing the template. For example, attorneys aren't crazy about learning the ins and outs of WordPerfect just to create and revise their own documents. If a savvy legal secretary were to create a library of templates, and then copy them to an attorney's computer, that attorney could create some fairly sophisticated documents without ever taking a class or reading a book. As you'll see in later sections of the book, you can actually create an environment that shields the user from the intricacies of the software by providing customized styles, menus, keyboards, and toolbars.

BASING A TEMPLATE ON ANOTHER TEMPLATE

One of the most basic concepts of document production is saving time by sharing work products. You revise an existing document (yours or someone else's), and then save it as a new file. Everyone benefits from the time and energy that goes into creating documents. This same concept carries over to templates. If the design you are looking for is similar to an existing template, by all means, edit the template, make the changes, and then save it as a new template.

To create a new template based on an existing template, follow these steps:

1. Choose <u>F</u>ile, Ne<u>w</u> from Project.

2. Select the template you want to revise.

3. Choose Options, Ed<u>i</u>t WP Template. The template is opened into the document window, and the Template toolbar is turned on.

4. Choose <u>F</u>ile, Save <u>A</u>s to open the Save Template dialog box (refer to Figure 22.12).

Tip #264 from
Laura and Read

I know you haven't made your changes yet, but I strongly recommend that you immediately save the template to a new name. If something terrible happens while you're editing the template, the original is unharmed, so you have the option of starting over.

5. In the <u>D</u>escription text box of the Save Template dialog box, type a descriptive name to appear in the template list.

6. Type a filename in the Template <u>N</u>ame text box. Don't type an extension—WordPerfect assigns the .wpt extension to templates so they can be recognized as templates and not as documents.

7. In the Template <u>C</u>ategory list box, choose the category where you want the template stored.

8. Click OK to save the template. Now you are free to make changes to the template without fear of harming the original file.

If you object to having two similar templates in the list, you can replace the original template with your customized template. After you're finished revising (and testing) the template, delete the original, and then rename this template file with the original template's filename.

WORKING WITH PROJECTS AND CATEGORIES

The same way files are organized into folders, templates are organized into categories. WordPerfect's projects are organized into 25 predefined categories. You can create your own categories, and then move and copy templates into them. You might want to set up a category for a new or intimidated user's templates, and then point to that category so only a few templates show up in the list.

You have the following options for managing projects and categories:

- Add projects to a category—You can select the category in the drop-down list. Choose Op<u>t</u>ions, A<u>d</u>d Project, and then answer the questions.

- Copy a project to another category—You can select the project, and then choose Op<u>t</u>ions, <u>C</u>opy Project. Choose the new category from the pop-up list.

- Move a project to another category—You can select the project, and then choose Op<u>t</u>ions, Mo<u>v</u>e Project. Choose a category from the pop-up list.

- Delete projects you no longer use—You can select a project, and then choose Options, Re<u>m</u>ove Project. Take a minute to review the Project Properties dialog box, and then click OK to confirm the removal (or bail out by clicking Cancel).

Note

> The Remove Project command doesn't delete the template from the hard drive; it just removes the reference to that project from the `projects.usr` file. If you want to remove the project entirely, you have to delete the file manually.

■ Create new categories—You can create your own categories for projects and templates. Choose Options, Create Category, and then type the name of the category in the Display Name text box. Click OK.

Tip #265 from
Laura and Read

> If you have temporary helpers come in when things get busy, group together the templates that you want them to use and put them in their own category. Select that category in the drop-down list so only the templates that you want the temps to use are displayed in the list.

■ Rename categories—You can rename a category. Select the category in the drop-down list, and then choose Options, Rename Category. Type the new name in the Display Name text box, and then click OK.

■ Delete categories that you no longer use—You can select the category in the drop-down list, and then choose Remove Category. Take a close look at the category name in the Display Name text box, and then confirm the deletion by clicking OK (or bail out by clicking Cancel).

⚠ *If you accidentally delete the wrong category and need to rebuild the* `projects.usr` *index file, see "My New Template Isn't Showing Up" in the Troubleshooting section at the end of this chapter.*

COPYING OBJECTS FROM OTHER TEMPLATES

Template objects are features that can be embedded into a template. They include Property Bars, toolbars, menus, styles, keyboards, macros, XML components, and QuickWords. When you customize WordPerfect by adding buttons to the toolbar or creating styles and macros, you are creating objects that are stored in the default template.

Think about the WordPerfect wizard at your firm. She has created custom toolbars for the company newsletter. She has added all the employees' names, clients' names, and company information to the QuickWords list. She has created standard styles for formatting company correspondence. She has customized the menus to remove unused features and to add features that are used often. She has customized WordPerfect in ways you can only dream of.

Count yourself lucky if you have someone like this in your company, because you can take advantage of all her hard work by simply copying the objects into your template(s).

Follow these steps to copy objects from another template:

1. Make a copy of the other template and give it a different name (such as `amelia` or `prodn`).

2. Copy the template to the `\program files\corel\wordperfect office 2000\ templates\custom wp templates` folder.

3. Choose File, New from Project.

4. Click the category drop-down list arrow and choose Custom WP Templates.

5. Select the default template (create a blank document) in the list, and then choose Options, Edit WP Template.

6. Click the Copy/Remove Object button on the Template toolbar to display the Copy/Remove Template Objects dialog box (see Figure 22.13).

Figure 22.13
In the Copy/Remove Template Objects dialog box, you can copy an object from one template to another.

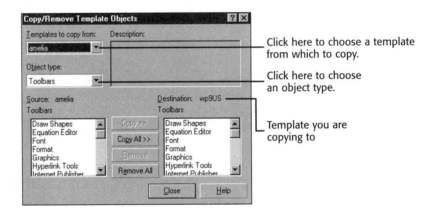

Click here to choose a template from which to copy.

Click here to choose an object type.

Template you are copying to

7. Click the Templates to Copy From drop-down list arrow and select the template that has the objects that you want to copy (for example, `amelia` or `prodn`). (This is the template from your office's WordPerfect genius.)

8. Click the Object Type drop-down list arrow and choose the object you want to copy. Depending on which object you choose to copy, the Source list displays a list of those objects. For example, if you choose Menu Bars in the Object Type drop-down list, a list of available menu bars appears in the Source list box (see Figure 22.14).

9. Select the item you want to copy in the Source list box and click Copy>>. Or you can click Copy All>> to copy all the items at once.

10. If the object names are identical, you get a message asking you to confirm the replacement. Click Yes.

11. Repeat steps 4 and 5 until you've copied all the objects that you want.

12. Click Close.

Figure 22.14
When you choose an object type, a list of items appears in the Source list box, where you can select and copy them to the other template.

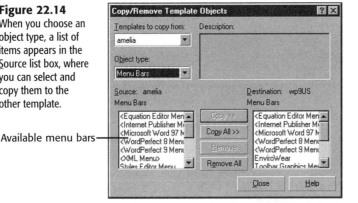

Available menu bars

Tip #266 from
Laura and Read

You can remove objects from a template as easily as you can add them. Follow the steps above, except in step 5, click Remove to delete the selected item or click Remove All to strip out all the items at once. Objects associated with the main document window can't be removed.

Tip #267 from
Laura and Read

Toolbars, menus, and custom keyboards can all be copied from one template to another in the Customize Settings dialog box (which you get by choosing Tools, Settings, Customize). Click Toolbars, Menus or Keyboards tab, and then click Copy. Click the Template to Copy From drop-down list arrow and choose the template you want to copy from. Choose the item that you want to copy from the list box. Click the Template to Copy To drop-down list arrow and choose the template you want to copy to. Click Copy.

Additional Objects Templates

Template objects can be stored in the default template or the additional objects template. The additional objects template is a secondary default template. The name and location of the additional objects template is found in the Template tab of the File Settings dialog box. You can use the objects in this template along with or in place of the objects in the default template.

In a networked environment, a system administrator can implement company standards by customizing an additional objects template and keeping it on a network drive. Each user has his or her own default template on the local drive, so each is free to customize WordPerfect. The additional objects template can be set up as read-only to prevent accidental modification.

USING PROMPT BUILDER

Let's say *you're* the WordPerfect wizard in the company and it's your job to develop templates for distribution to the rest of the staff. The experience level of your coworkers varies wildly—some employees understand how to fill in the blanks, and others don't.

The solution? Use Prompt Builder to create messages that ask users for information, and then plug that information into the template. It's as close as you can get to sitting right next to the users, explaining what they are supposed to do.

Follow these steps to insert prompts in a template:

1. In the Corel PerfectExpert dialog box, select the template you are developing, and then choose Options, Edit WP Template.

2. Click where you want to place the information that the user types.

3. Click the Build Prompts button on the Template toolbar to display the Prompt Builder dialog box (see Figure 22.15).

Figure 22.15
In the Prompt Builder dialog box, you can create messages that prompt the user for information.

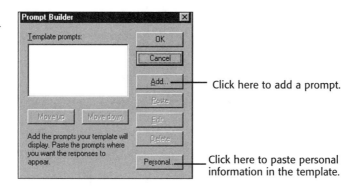

Click here to add a prompt.

Click here to paste personal information in the template.

4. Click Add to display the Add Template Prompt dialog box (see Figure 22.16).

Figure 22.16
In the Add Template Prompt dialog box, you can type the prompt text and select an Address Book field to link the prompt to.

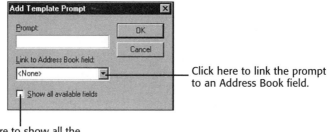

Click here to link the prompt to an Address Book field.

Click here to show all the available Address Book fields.

5. Type the message in the Prompt text box. You can type up to 60 characters, but you should try to keep it short (20 to 30 characters).

6. Click OK to add the prompt to the list in the Prompt Builder dialog box. Now that you've added the prompt to the list, you can paste it into the template.

7. Select the prompt in the Template Prompts list box, and then click Paste to insert it in the template. The prompt appears at the insertion point, with brackets around it (see Figure 22.17).

Figure 22.17
Using Prompt Builder, you can generate prompts that remind the user what to type.

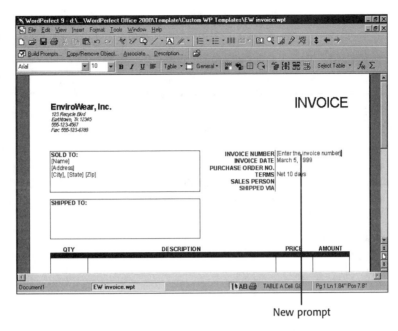

New prompt

When you open a template with prompts, the Template Information dialog box appears, with a list of the prompts in the template (see Figure 22.18).

Figure 22.18
The Template Information dialog box contains text boxes for each of the prompts in a template.

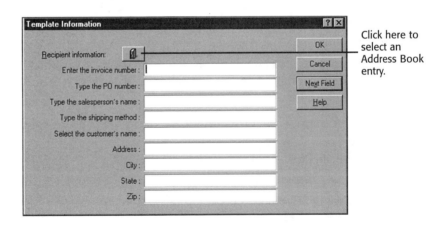

Click here to select an Address Book entry.

WORKING WITH TEMPLATE PROMPTS

As you revise a template with prompts, you might have to move a few of them around. You might even decide to delete a section of the template, rendering some of the prompts obsolete. The key is to keep the template prompts and Prompt Builder prompts in sync. You can remove prompt text from a template, but you'll see that prompt displayed the next time you use the template if you don't remove the prompts from the Prompt Builder list.

Here are a few things to keep in mind as you work with the template prompts:

- Moving prompts—Make sure you select the brackets ([ ]) on either side of the prompt text, and then cut and paste the prompt.

- Rearranging prompts in Prompt Builder—When you run a template, you are prompted to fill in the information in the order in which the prompts appear in the Prompt Builder list. So if you don't mind typing the zip code before the name, leave them alone. Otherwise, arrange the prompts in the order that's easiest for you to fill them in. Select the prompt that you want to move, and then click Move Up or Move Down.

- Deleting prompts—After you've deleted the prompt text in the template, you have to delete the prompt in the Prompt Builder dialog box; otherwise, you'll still be prompted to type in the information, even though it isn't inserted anywhere. In the Prompt Builder dialog box, select the prompt, and then click Delete, Yes.

- Editing prompts—You can delete the old prompt text in the template. Select the prompt in Prompt Builder, and then choose Edit. Revise the prompt text and/or change the Link to Address Book field (you'll learn more about this in the next section). Reinsert the new prompt.

LINKING PROMPTS TO ADDRESS BOOK FIELDS

Your company can have 5 employees or 5,000 employees—in either case the client information is the most valuable asset. Maintaining a centralized list of names, addresses, and phone numbers is essential, and with the CorelCENTRAL Address Books, it's easy to do. Using one of the Address Books on your system, you can insert client information directly into a template.

You still have to create a prompt for the information, but WordPerfect fills it in for you when you select an entry from an Address Book. Follow these steps to link a prompt to an Address Book field:

1. Edit the template, and then click where you want the Address Book information to appear.

2. Click Build Prompts. In Prompt Builder, click Add.

3. Type the prompt text in the Prompt text box.

4. Click the Link to Address Book Field drop-down list, and then select a field from the list (see Figure 22.19).

Caution

If you don't see the field you want, click the drop-down list arrow again (to close the list). Place a check mark next to Show All Available Fields, and then click the Link to Address Book Field drop-down list arrow again.

5. Click OK, and then paste the prompt into the template.

Figure 22.19
In the Add Template Prompt dialog box, you can link the prompt to an Address Book field.

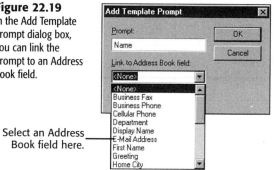

Select an Address Book field here.

When you run the template, the prompts appear in the Template Information dialog box (refer to Figure 22.18). Click the Address Book button to display the CorelCENTRAL Address Book dialog box, with a list of the Address Books on your system (refer to Figure 22.5).

When you select an Address Book entry and choose Insert, WordPerfect displays a Format Address dialog box (see Figure 22.20).

Figure 22.20
You can choose from one of the predefined address formats in the Format Address dialog box.

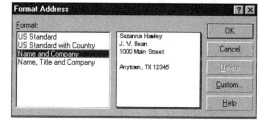

Select the address format that you want to use, and then click OK twice to plug the information in to the prompts that you linked to Address Book fields (see Figure 22.21).

INSERTING PERSONAL INFORMATION IN A TEMPLATE

Remember when you first used the Template feature and you had to create a personal information entry in the CorelCENTRAL Address Book? Guess what? You can insert information from that entry into a template, too. For example, if you want a user's name to appear in a Salesperson or an Author prompt, insert a personal field for the person's name in the template.

To insert data from the personal information entry in the CorelCENTRAL Address Book, click in the template where you want the information to appear. Open the Prompt Builder dialog box, and then click Personal. The Personal Fields dialog box appears (see Figure 22.22). Select a field, and then choose Paste.

Figure 22.21
After you select an entry from the Address Book, WordPerfect plugs that information in to the template, replacing the prompts.

Information from the Address Book

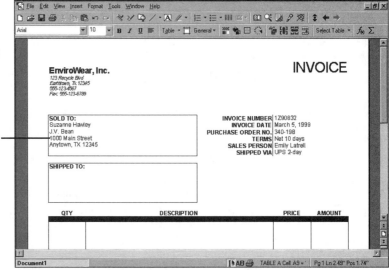

Figure 22.22
By using the Personal Fields dialog box, you can paste one of the personal information fields into the template.

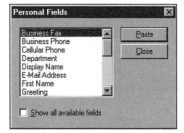

The personal information prompt appears in square brackets ([ ]), so it looks different from the other prompts, which appear in angle brackets (< >). When you run the template, the information is inserted from the Address Book (see Figure 22.23).

Note

You can't see the prompts you create for personal information in the Template Prompts list box (in the Prompt Builder dialog box).

Figure 22.23
Personal information prompts are surrounded with angle brackets, and regular prompts are surrounded by square brackets.

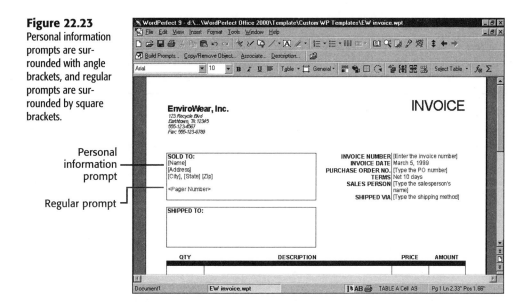

Personal information prompt ──

Regular prompt ──┘

CUSTOMIZING THE WORKING ENVIRONMENT

The toughest part of supporting computer users is catering to different levels of expertise. A manufacturing company, for example, might have a technician on the plant floor who needs to fill out production logs. Upstairs in the administrative offices, there is a temporary who has never worked with your company's documents before. Down the hall is the management team, which generates reams of reports, but doesn't seem too interested in learning the program.

If this is a typical day in your office, you've just found the perfect reason to implement templates. By using the Template feature and the PerfectExpert panel as your front-end to WordPerfect, users can crank out documents without ever learning how to use a menu.

ASSOCIATING MENUS AND KEYBOARDS

As you saw in an earlier section, you can attach objects to templates so that they are available only when you are using that template. Rather than create a monster list of menus or keyboards, you can embed them in templates. The same goes for macros—you can create macros and attach them to a template. From that point forward, they are template macros, so they don't even show up in the macros folder.

→ If you are intrigued by the idea of embedding macros in templates to reduce macro clutter, **see** "Creating Template Macros," **p. 697**

Now let's take this one step further. You can create an *association* to menus and keyboards so that they show up only in certain editing modes. As you change modes, the menu or keyboard layout changes dynamically and automatically.

The different editing modes in WordPerfect are

> Main Editing Window (normal document editing)
>
> Comments
>
> Endnotes
>
> Equation Editor
>
> Footers
>
> Footnote
>
> Graphics
>
> Headers
>
> Main
>
> Outline
>
> Tables
>
> Watermark

Follow these steps to create an associate to a feature:

1. Edit the template to open it in the editing window and display the Template feature bar.

2. Click Associate on the Template feature bar to display the Associate dialog box (see Figure 22.24).

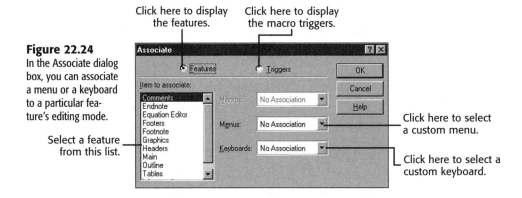

Figure 22.24
In the Associate dialog box, you can associate a menu or a keyboard to a particular feature's editing mode.

3. If necessary, choose Features.

4. Choose the editing mode you want to associate (Headers, Tables, Graphics, and so on).

5. Click the Menus or Keyboards drop-down list arrow and choose the menu (or keyboard) that you want to associate with this editing mode.

Caution

If the menu or keyboard that you want to use doesn't appear in the list, you haven't attached it to this template yet. Cancel out of the Associate dialog box, and then either create the menu or keyboard or copy it from another template. See the section "Copying Objects from Other Templates," earlier in this chapter, for more information.

Tip #268 from	To remove a menu or keyboard association, select the editing mode in the list, and then
Laura and Read	choose No Association from the Menus or Keyboards drop-down list.

6. Repeat steps 4 and 5 to define other associations.

7. Click OK when you're finished.

ASSOCIATING MACROS TO TRIGGERS

Macros work a little differently. You don't associate them with an editing mode, but with an event, or *trigger*. Table 22.1 lists the macro triggers and what they do.

For example, say you have set up a shared workstation for paralegals to use. These systems have templates to generate standard legal documents. In each template, you associate a macro with printing, so when the user sends a document to the printer, this macro runs and prompts for the client number. After this information is typed in (and plugged in to a resource usage log so you can bill the printing costs back to the client), the document is printed.

You could also associate a macro with opening a template. This macro would prompt for the paralegal's name and the client number, so the paralegal's time spent creating and printing the document could be billed back to the client.

TABLE 22.1   MACRO TRIGGERS

Macro Trigger	What Does It Do
Post Close	Runs in the active window after you close a window.
Post New	Runs after you open a new document by using File, New.
Post Open	Runs after you open a document by using File, Open.
Post Print	Runs after you send a job to the printer.
Post Startup	Runs when you start WordPerfect. This macro must be associated with the default template to work properly.
Post Switch Doc	Runs in the active window after you switch from another window.
Post Tables	Runs after you create a table definition, but before you type anything.
Pre Close	Runs before you close the window by choosing File, Close.
Pre New	Runs before you open a new document by using File, New.
Pre Open	Runs before you open another document by using File, Open.
Pre Print	Runs after you choose File, Print, but before the document is sent to the printer.
Pre Switch Doc	Runs in the active window before you switch to another window.
Pre Tables	Runs after you create a table (by using Insert, Table), but before the table definition is created in the document.

Follow these steps to associate a macro with one of these triggers:

1. Edit the template to open it in the editing window and display the Template feature bar.
2. Click <u>A</u>ssociate on the Template feature bar to display the Associate dialog box (refer to Figure 22.24).
3. Click the <u>T</u>riggers option.
4. In the <u>I</u>tem to Associate list box, select the trigger you want to use (see Figure 22.25).

Figure 22.25
In the Associate dialog box, you can assign a template macro to an event or a trigger.

Choose a trigger from this list.

Choose a template macro from this drop-down list.

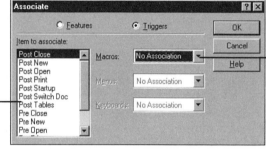

5. Click the <u>M</u>acros drop-down list arrow and choose the macro you want to associate with this trigger.

Caution

The macro you want to associate to a trigger must already be a part of the template, or it won't appear in the <u>M</u>acros list. If you don't see the macro you want, cancel out of the Associate dialog box, and then create the macro or copy it into the template. See the section "Copying Objects from Other Templates" earlier in this chapter for more information.

Tip #269 from
Laura and Read

To remove a trigger association, select the trigger, and then choose No Association in the <u>M</u>acros drop-down list.

6. Repeat steps 4 and 5 to define the other trigger associations.
7. Click OK when you're done.

Tip #270 from
Laura and Read

Template macros increase the size of the file, so try to avoid embedding large macros in your templates. The larger the template, the slower it runs.

Filling in Template Prompts
If you've created a template from scratch and you've added prompts to it, you're probably wondering how to display the Template Information dialog box, where users can fill in the prompts and have WordPerfect insert the information into the template. (You might want to refer to Figure 22.18 to refresh your memory.)

The answer is the `TemplateFill()` macro command, which starts the DoFiller feature. You can create a simple macro with just this command, and then associate it with the Post New trigger. If you already have a template macro associated with the Post New trigger, you can edit that macro and add the command to the macro. Choose <u>T</u>ools, Tem<u>p</u>late Macro, <u>E</u>dit to edit the template macro.

USING TEMPLATES FROM EARLIER VERSIONS OF WORDPERFECT

Heavy-duty template users don't want to hear that they can't use their existing templates in the newest release of WordPerfect. And they don't have to. The templates that you created in versions 6.1, 7, and 8 can be used in WordPerfect 9. Some may have to be converted, and those using Address Book fields may need some fine-tuning, but for the most part, your hard work won't go down the drain.

First, you have to copy the templates to the `\program files\corel\wordperfect office 2000\template\custom WP templates` folder. You can create subfolders in the `Custom WP Template` folder to organize the templates. These folder names appear as categories in the drop-down list (see Figure 22.26). This naming system helps keep the older templates separate from the templates that shipped with WordPerfect 9.

Figure 22.26
Subfolders of the Custom WP Templates folder appear as categories in the list.

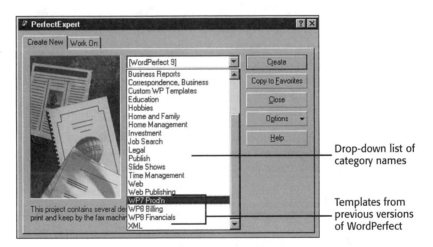

Drop-down list of category names

Templates from previous versions of WordPerfect

Former WordPerfect 6.1 users will have to convert their templates before they can use them in WordPerfect 9. You can convert a template by editing it and then saving your changes. Even if you haven't made any changes, this triggers the `tconvert.wcm` macro that converts the template. In the Corel PerfectExpert dialog box, click the category drop-down list arrow and choose Custom WP Templates (or choose the category that matches the subfolder you created in the Custom WP Templates folder). Select the template, and then choose O<u>p</u>tions, Ed<u>i</u>t WP Template. Click <u>Y</u>es to convert the template. Click <u>Y</u>es to overwrite the original template.

You can also run the `tconvert.wcm` macro manually by choosing <u>T</u>ools, <u>M</u>acro, <u>P</u>lay. Scroll down, and then double-click `tconvert`. When the Convert Template dialog box appears, type the name of the template or click the Files icon to browse for the file. Click OK to convert the template, and then save the template.

→ To learn more about macros, **see** Chapter 24, "Experts and Macros," **p. 685**

 If you try to convert an old template and get the error message "tconvert.wcm not found," see "`tconvert.wcm` *Not Found" in the Troubleshooting section at the end of this chapter.*

Tip #271 from *Lauɾa and Read*	You might run into problems using templates with links to Address Book fields that no longer exist. If the older version of WordPerfect is still available, edit the template in that version and remove all the links to Address Book fields. Next, edit the template in WordPerfect 9 and reselect the Address Book fields. Otherwise, edit the template in WordPerfect 9, delete the prompts, and then re-create them.

TROUBLESHOOTING

MISSING OR DAMAGED TEMPLATE FILES

When I choose <u>F</u>ile, Ne<u>w</u> from Project and double-click a project, the following error message appears: "Filename.wpt cannot be opened or retrieved: the file cannot be found."

The template file associated with this project is missing or damaged. You can get a fresh copy of this template file from the WordPerfect Office 2000 CD-ROM. If you're having problems with more than one project, you might want to do a custom installation of the PerfectExpert Projects so all the template and project files are refreshed. Keep in mind that if you reinstall the PerfectExpert Projects, any changes that you made to the WordPerfect templates will be lost (unless, of course, you saved your changes to a new template name).

To restore an individual template file, insert the WordPerfect Office 2000 CD-ROM in the drive, and then open the Open File dialog box and switch to the CD-ROM drive. Move to the `\corel\templates` folder. Select the template file(s). Right-click the selection and choose <u>C</u>opy. Move back to the `\program files\corel\wordperfect suite 2000\template` folder. Right-click in the file list, and then choose <u>P</u>aste.

To restore all the template and project files, run the Setup program. Click WordPerfect Office 2000 Setup. Choose Cus<u>t</u>om Setup. In the list of components, clear the check marks next to everything except WordPerfect 9, CorelCENTRAL 9, and Install As You Go Shared. Click the plus sign next to WordPerfect 9. Remove the check mark next to everything except PerfectExpert Project Files. Continue with the rest of the installation.

After you've restored the template(s), use the Refresh command to update the project list. In the Corel PerfectExpert dialog box, choose O<u>p</u>tions, Re<u>f</u>resh Projects, and then click OK.

Note

If a project file is missing or damaged, you'll still get the PerfectExpert panel when you open the template, but the buttons in the panel are for creating a generic document. They are not the buttons that control the template. You have the same two options that are described previously: You can copy an individual project file (with the same name as the template with an AST extension), or you can restore all the template and project files at once.

MY NEW TEMPLATE ISN'T SHOWING UP

I just created and saved a new template, but now I can't find it in the list. Where did the template get saved?

When you save a template, you type a description that appears in the project list and a template filename. The last step is to select a category where the template is saved. Because you don't have to type anything (you select a category from a drop-down list), it's easy to overlook that last step.

If you don't choose a category, WordPerfect stores the new template in the first category in the list: the Budget, Business category. In the Corel PerfectExpert dialog box, click the category drop-down list arrow and choose Budget, Business. Select the new template from this list, choose Options, Move Project, and then select the proper category from the pop-up list.

If the new template doesn't appear in the Budget, Business category (or in the other categories), you can rebuild the project index, which contains a list of all the templates and categories. Click Start, Find, Files or Folders. Type `projects.usr` in the Named text box, choose a drive to search in the Look In list box, and then click Find Now. When the file appears in the list, right-click it, and then choose Rename. Type `projects.old`, and then press Enter. Choose File, New from Project. WordPerfect should hesitate for a moment while the index is rebuilt, and then the list of projects should appear. Look in the Budget, Business category first.

tconvert.wcm NOT FOUND

I'm trying to convert an old WordPerfect 6.1 template, and I've tried editing the template and running the tconvert *macro. Either way, I'm getting the error message "tconvert.wcm Not Found." Where is this file?*

Either the macro wasn't installed or it's been moved. You can copy it directly from the Corel WordPerfect Office 2000 CD-ROM. Open the `\corel\macros\wpwin` folder on the CD-ROM. Right-click the `tconvert` file, and then choose Copy. Move to the `\program files\corel\wordperfect office 2000\macros\wpwin` folder. Right-click in the file list and choose Paste. Try converting the macro again.

If the file *still* can't be found, make sure the correct folder name is in File Settings. Choose Tools, Settings, Files. Click the Merge/Macro tab. The Default Macro Folder text box should have `\program files\corel\wordperfect office 2000\macros\wpwin` in it. If it doesn't, revise it.

PROJECT

You probably have users who are fighting the upgrade to WordPerfect 9 because they are afraid they'll lose all their hard work in customizing the program. Not so. You can transfer almost everything—addresses, macros, QuickWords, toolbars, keyboards, menus, templates, custom dictionaries, styles, labels, and of course, documents. WordPerfect uses the same file format as version 6.1, 7, and 8, so you won't have any problems opening and editing documents created in previous versions.

Tip #272 from
Laura and Read

Traditionally, Corel has developed a transition guide for people upgrading to the latest version of WordPerfect. These guides are stored in Corel's Knowledge Base at `http://kb.corel.com`. You can find them by searching the WordPerfect 9 documents for *transition* or *upgrading*.

A good bit of the customization that you do in WordPerfect is saved to the default template as objects. All you have to do is copy these objects from the default template for the previous version to the default template for WordPerfect 9.

Here are the steps for transferring over the custom templates, toolbars, styles, menus, keyboards, template macros, and QuickWords. These steps assume installation on a local hard drive:

1. Copy the templates that you created in the previous version to the `WP Custom Templates` folder for WordPerfect 9. The `WP Custom Templates` folder is in the `\program files\corel\wordperfect office 2000\templates` folder. If you have created subfolders for your templates, copy everything into the `WP Custom Templates` folder. (The subfolders will appear as categories in the list.)

2. Edit each of the templates (you don't have to do them all them right now), and then save them (even if you didn't make any changes). Editing a template triggers a conversion if one is necessary to make the template usable in WordPerfect 9.

3. The next step is to copy the objects from the old default template into the default template for WordPerfect 9. If you didn't copy the default template for the previous version of WordPerfect in steps 1 and 2, you need to do that now. The default template for the previous version needs to be copied into the `Custom WP Templates` folder for WordPerfect 9 (`\program files\corel\wordperfect office 2000\templates\custom wp templates`):

   - For version 8, copy the `wp8us.wpt` file from the `\corel\suite8\template\custom wp templates` folder.
   - For version 7, copy the `wp7us.wpt` file from the `\corel\office7\template` folder.
   - For version 6.1, copy the `standard.wpt` file from the `\office\wpwin\template` folder.

4. Edit the WordPerfect 9 default template. Choose File, New from Project. Click the category drop-down list arrow and choose WP Custom Templates.

5. Select Create a Blank Document from the list, and then choose Options, Edit WP Template. This step is a little tricky because now you have two Create a Blank Document entries. In my experience, the first one is the WordPerfect 9 default template and the second one is the default template for the previous version. Just to be on the safe side, right-click the first one and choose Project Properties. In the Project Template Properties dialog box, click in the Project Filename text box. Press End to move to the end of the line so you can see the filename—now you know which default template it is!

6. Click the Copy/Remove Objects button on the Template toolbar.

7. Click the Templates to Copy From drop-down list arrow, and then select the previous version's default template.

8. Click the Object Type drop-down list arrow and choose the type of object you want to copy. For example, choose QuickWords to copy the QuickWords (or abbreviations).

9. Select the items you want to copy, and then click Copy>>.

10. Click Close when you're done.

11. Save the changes to the template. You should make a backup copy of the template because you've just made some changes.

Styles won't show up in the template unless you specifically save them to the default template. If you still have the previous version of WordPerfect, copy the styles to the default template, and then copy the new template back over to the WordPerfect 9 Custom WP Templates folder, and try again. If you don't have the previous version, open a document that contains those styles in WordPerfect 9. Select the styles that you want, and then save them to the WordPerfect 9 default template.

→ For more information on copying styles to the default template, **see** "Saving Styles," **p. 240**

CHAPTER 23

ASSEMBLING DOCUMENTS WITH MERGE

In this chapter

GETTING FAMILIAR WITH MERGE TERMINOLOGY

Everyone calls it a *mail merge*, but you can really pull together any type of information—not just mail—to produce any type of document. The Merge feature is used most often to produce personalized letters, but it's also a very powerful tool for organizing key pieces of information.

As the term suggests, a *merge* is a combination of information from two different sources. Typically, you have a *form file*, which is the document, and one *data file*, which contains the information you want to insert. The form file is just a regular document with merge codes in it. The *merge codes* act as markers for the information from the data file.

A data file is organized into *records*, which contain *fields* for every piece of information. Using the mail merge example, the data file is a list of names and addresses and the form file is the letter. Each person has his or her own record, which is divided into fields, such as name, company, address, and phone. Think of a data file as an electronic Rolodex—only you can put a lot more than just names and phone numbers in it.

WORKING WITH DATA FILES

It's easiest to create a data file first, so you can use the *field names* in the form document. Field names are used to identify the merge field codes that you create to organize the data file. For example, a typical data file might contain these fields: Name, Company, Address, City, State, Zip, Phone, Fax, and Email. Field names are optional, though—you can use Field1, Field2, Field3, and so on if you prefer.

The main thing to keep in mind when you're creating the data file is that more fields mean more flexibility. For example, if you have three separate fields for the city, state, and zip code, you can sort the list by zip code. The same goes for the name—if you use one field for first name and one field for last name, you can sort by the last name and you can use the first name in a salutation. Each field can be acted upon individually. This is how the Publisher's Clearinghouse folks make those letters seem so personal. The last letter I received had my city and county broken out and used in the letter, as well as my name, address, and state. And these letters are extremely effective!

CREATING DATA FILES

It's easy to create a data file from scratch, but before you do, make sure you don't already have the information stored somewhere else. There are several ways to convert information from other sources into a merge data file. You might have a little cleanup to do, but at least you aren't entering the information all over again. The next several sections contain information on converting *tables (page 252)* and importing data into merge data files.

Follow these steps to create a data file from scratch:

1. Choose Tools, Merge or press Shift+F9 to display the Merge dialog box (see Figure 23.1).

Click here to
create the
data file.

Click here to work
with the Address Book.

Figure 23.1
In the Merge dialog
box, you can create a
data file and a form
document, and you
can merge these two
together.

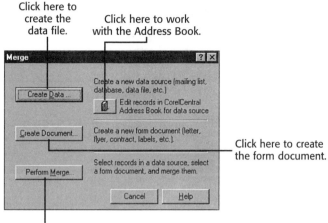

Click here to create
the form document.

Click here to merge the data file
and form document together.

→ For more information on pulling records directly from the Address Book during a merge, **see** "Merging with the Address Book," **p. 661**

2. Click Create Data to open the Create Data File dialog box (see Figure 23.2). This is where you create the field names.

Type the name of a field here.

Figure 23.2
In the Create Data
File dialog box, you
can create and edit
the field names for
the data file.

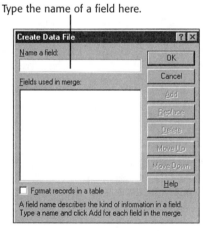

3. Type the name of the first field name in the Name a Field text box.

4. Press Enter or choose Add to insert the field name in the Fields Used in Merge list box.

5. Repeat steps 3 and 4 until you've entered all the field names. If you misspell a field name, or change your mind, select the field, and then choose Delete. Figure 23.3 shows a typical list of field names.

Figure 23.3
Here is a list of field
names that you might
use for a merge
data file.

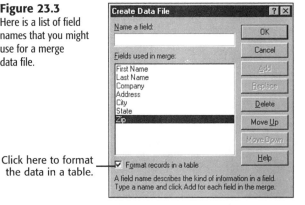

Click here to format
the data in a table.

Tip #273 from
Laura and Read

The order of the field names is important because this is the order in which you'll type the information. If you need to rearrange the field names, select a name, and then choose Move Up or Move Down.

---

6. If you want the records formatted into a table, place a check mark in the Format Records in a Table check box.

Tip #274 from
Laura and Read

Formatting a data file in a table has many advantages. In a table, each field has its own column, and each row is one record. Data files that aren't formatted as a table have merge codes that separate fields and records. You have to be especially careful when editing this type of data file so you don't accidentally delete one of the merge codes.

---

7. Click OK when you're finished. The Quick Data Entry dialog box appears (see Figure 23.4). You can use this dialog box to enter and edit records in the data file.

Note

If the Field Names button is grayed out in the Quick Data Entry dialog box, then field names weren't created in this data file. See the section "Adding Field Names to a Data File," later in this chapter, for the steps to add the field names.

---

8. Type the data for the first field, and then press Enter or Tab (or choose Next Field) to move down to the next field. Press Shift+Tab or choose Previous Field to move back up a field.

9. Continue entering the information in each field. When you press Enter in the last field, a new record is created. You can also choose New Record from any field to create a blank record.

Tip #275 from
Laura and Read

Don't include extra spaces or punctuation marks when you enter the data. For example, don't type a comma after the city. All formatting and punctuation marks should be in the form document.

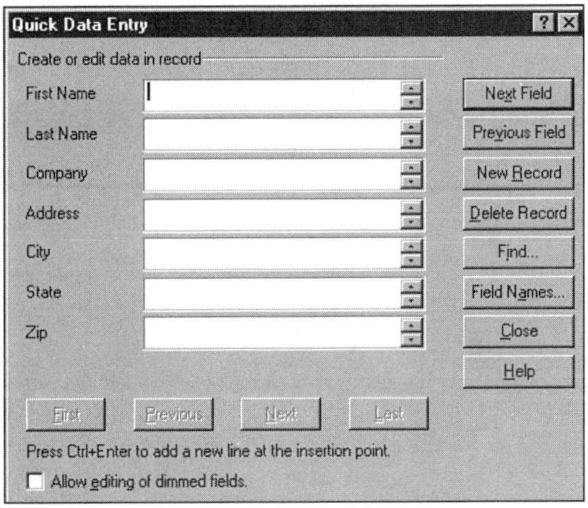

Figure 23.4
Most people prefer using the Quick Data Entry dialog box for creating and editing records in the data file.

PART

VII

CH

23

Tip #276 from
Laura and Read

You can move back and forth between records by clicking the Previous and Next buttons at the bottom of the Quick Data Entry dialog box. Click the First button to move to the first record; click the Last button to move to the last record.

10. Choose Close when you're finished.

11. Choose Yes to save the data file to disk. The Save File dialog box appears (see Figure 23.5).

12. Type a name for the data file in the File Name text box, and then click Save.

Note

WordPerfect suggests a .dat extension for data files. If you follow this suggestion, you can choose WP Merge Data (*.dat) from the File Type drop-down list and display only merge data files in the file list.

When the Save File dialog box closes, you can see the data that you've entered so far. Figure 23.6 shows the data in table format. Notice that the Merge feature bar has been added to the top of the screen. The generic Property Bar has also morphed into the Tables Property Bar with lots of buttons for working with tables.

After you've finished entering the information, you can always go back and edit it later. You can add and edit records directly (in the table), or you can click the Quick Entry button on the Merge feature bar to open the Quick Data Entry dialog box.

EDITING FIELD NAMES

If you need to edit the field names, you have to do so from the Quick Data Entry dialog box (refer to Figure 23.4). Click the Field Names button to open the Edit Field Names dialog box, where you can add, rename, and delete field names (see Figure 23.7).

Figure 23.5
You can type a name for the data file in the Save File dialog box.

WordPerfect suggests the extension .dat.

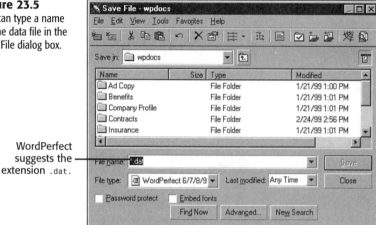

Each field name is a column.

Merge feature bar

Tables Property Bar

Figure 23.6
Formatting the records in a table has many advantages. Not only is it easier to read the information in table format, but you can easily manipulate the data by using the buttons on the Table Property Bar.

Each record is a row.

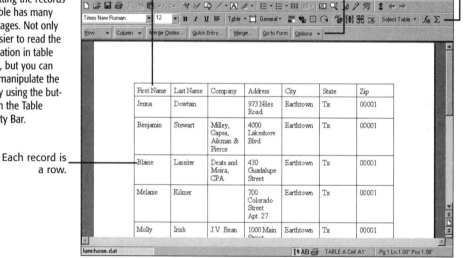

Caution

Beware! Renaming and deleting field names deletes the contents of that field in *every* record. When you use Delete, at least you get a warning message, so you have a chance to bail out; you don't get a warning when you rename a field name. Err on the side of caution and save the data file before you edit the field names.

Figure 23.7
From the Edit Field Names dialog box, you can add new fields, rename fields, and remove fields from the data file.

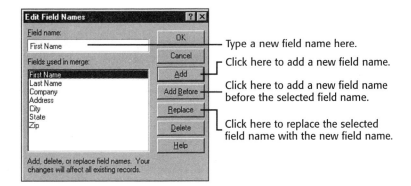

Type a new field name here.

Click here to add a new field name.

Click here to add a new field name before the selected field name.

Click here to replace the selected field name with the new field name.

Tip #277 from
Laura and Read

In large data files, you can use the Find feature to quickly locate records. In the Quick Data Entry dialog box, click the Find button to open the Find Text dialog box. Otherwise, choose Edit, Find and Replace (or press Ctrl+F) to open the Find and Replace dialog box. In either dialog box, type the text you want to search for in the Find text box, and then choose Find Next.

CONVERTING TEXT DATA FILES TO TABLES AND VICE VERSA

When you create a data file, you have a choice. You can create the data file as a table or as a text file. You can see what the table looks like in Figure 23.6. Figure 23.8 shows what a data text file looks like. If you've inherited a text data file from someone else, and you prefer to work with tables, you can convert the text data file into a data file table.

Click here to insert an end field code.

Click here to insert an end record code.

Figure 23.8
A data text file stores the field names in the first record.

Field names record at the top of the document.

Merge codes

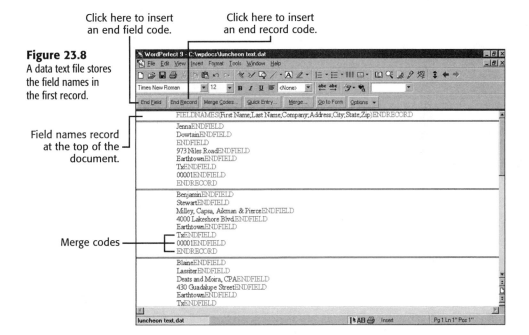

The following are the steps to convert a text data file into a table:

1. Press Ctrl+A to select the entire file.

2. Choose Insert, Table (or press F12). The Convert Table dialog box appears (see Figure 23.9).

Figure 23.9
In the Convert Table dialog box, you can choose the type of text you want to convert to a table.

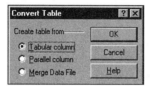

3. Choose Merge Data File and click OK. WordPerfect reads the field name record at the top of the data file and creates a column for each field and a row for each record.

You can also go the other way and convert a data file table to a text data file. Interestingly, you can even create a text data file from an ordinary table (without the field names). The following are the steps to convert a table into a text data file:

1. Move to the top of the document and turn on Reveal Codes (by pressing Alt+F3).

2. Move the red cursor to the left of the [Tbl Def] code (the table definition code).

3. Press Delete. The Delete Table dialog box appears (see Figure 23.10).

Figure 23.10
Depending on the type of table, you can choose to create the text data file with or without field names in the Delete Table dialog box.

Click here if you don't have field names.

Click here if you have field names.

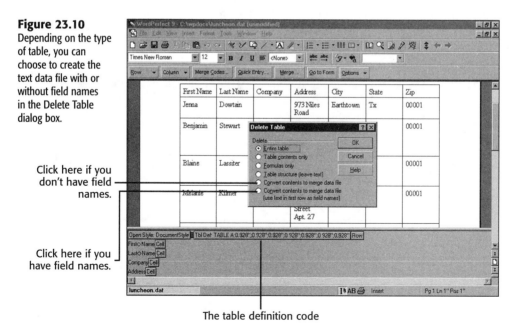

The table definition code

4. Choose Co̲nvert Contents to Merge Data File or Co̲nvert Contents to Merge Data File (Use Text In First Row as Field Names).

WordPerfect creates the text data file. If you started out with a table that didn't have field names, you can add those now (the steps are in the next section).

Tip #278 from
Laura and Read

In a lengthy text data file, it's easy to lose your place. If you turn on line numbering, you have a number next to each field, which not only helps you keep your place, but also makes it easier to spot records with missing fields. Line numbers restart numbering at the top of every page, so every record has the same line numbers. At the top of the data file, choose Format, Li̲ne, N̲umbering. Place a check mark next to Turn Line Numbering O̲n, and then click OK.

ADDING FIELD NAMES TO A DATA FILE

Often you inherit files from other users, who may or may not understand how to use the program. Such is the case with merge data files. Not everyone takes the time to create field names. Granted, you don't have to do it. As long as you don't mind referring to the fields by number, it's fine to leave the file that way. However, in files with lots of fields, field names are a necessity.

The first record of a text data file is the field names record. If you don't have an End Record code at the top of the data file, the data in the first record is assumed to be the field name data (this is bad).

In most cases, you see an End Record code at the top of the file. When a data file has been created without field names, the fields are numbered (for example, 1, 2, 3, 4, 5).

Follow these steps to add field names to a text data file:

1. Press Ctrl+Home to move to the top of the document. You'll see the End Record code that separated the field names record from the rest of the records. The insertion point should be at the beginning of the End Record code.

Tip #279 from
Laura and Read

If you don't see the End Record code, you need to insert it. Click the End R̲ecord button on the Merge feature bar, or press Alt+Shift+R.

---

2. Type a field name for the first field in the records.
3. Click the End F̲ield button to insert an End Field code.
4. Continue typing in the field names and inserting the End Field codes until you have one for every field in the record.
5. On a line underneath the last field, notice the End Record code, followed by a hard page (see Figure 23.11). Each record in a text data file is separated by a hard page. This ensures that when you merge the data file with a form document, the resulting documents are on separate pages.

Caution

If there is not an End Record code at the top of the file, click the End Record button, and then press Ctrl+Enter to insert the hard page.

Tip #280 from
Laura and Read

When I'm doing heavy-duty data entry, I really dislike taking my hand off the keyboard to click a button. Instead of clicking the buttons on the Merge feature bar, you can press Alt+Shift+F to insert an End Field code and press Alt+Shift+R to insert an End Record code.

Tip #281 from
Laura and Read

You can add field names to a data file table that doesn't have field names. Just add a row to the top of the table and place a field name in each column. You don't need to use the End Field and End Record codes because WordPerfect knows that each row is a record and each column is a field.

IMPORTING DATA INTO MERGE DATA FILES

You can use files from other applications as data files, and in some cases, you need not convert them prior to the merge. In addition to files from other word processing programs, WordPerfect supports the import of data files created in spreadsheet and database programs. If field names were used in the source application, they are recognized and used by WordPerfect.

Tip #282 from
Laura and Read

If you're upgrading to WordPerfect 9 from a previous version of WordPerfect, you can use the secondary merge files as data files.

Files from popular spreadsheet programs can be imported into WordPerfect and then used as merge data files. However, because spreadsheets are converted into tables, they are restricted by the same limitations as tables. For example, there is a 64-column limit on tables, so if the spreadsheet has more than 64 columns, the data in the remaining columns won't be imported. One workaround is to import smaller sections of the spreadsheet—this is where the convenience of named ranges becomes apparent. Another workaround is to save the spreadsheet as a database, and import it into WordPerfect. For example, you can save a Quattro Pro spreadsheet as a Paradox database file, and then import the Paradox database into WordPerfect.

→ If you want to convert a spreadsheet file into a data file table, **see** "Converting Spreadsheet Data," **p. 424**

→ If you want to create a link to a spreadsheet file, **see** "Linking Spreadsheet Data," **p. 425**

Figure 23.11
This text data file has a field name record so the fields can be identified by name instead of by number.

Field name record ——

Records are separated by a — hard page.

Each record ends with an end — record code.

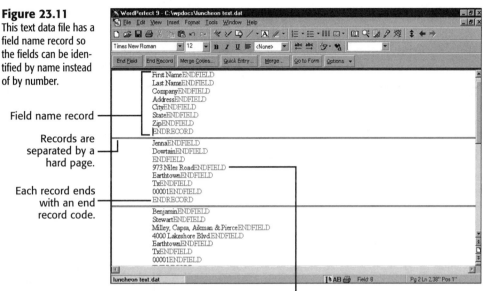

Each field ends with an end field code.

The database format in WordPerfect is the merge data file, so you can either convert the database file to a merge data file, or you can use it as is. You can also create links to a database file so that when you update the database, the data file information is updated as well.

→ If you want to convert the database file to a merge data file, **see** "Converting to WordPerfect Formats," **p. 415**

→ If you want to use the database file without first converting it to a data file, **see** "Using Database Data with Merge," **p. 423**

→ If you want to create a link to a database file, **see** "Linking Database Data," **p. 419**

CREATING FORM FILES

Relax—this is the easy part, and if you've already typed the document, you're almost done! An existing document can be turned into a form file in just seconds. You just insert the merge codes and save the document. Voilà! It's ready for a merge.

If you're creating the form file from scratch, make sure that you insert all the formatting codes you want in the finished documents. You definitely don't want to put formatting codes (or anything besides text) in the data file; otherwise, it is duplicated over and over again.

Note

If you're upgrading from a previous version of WordPerfect, you're accustomed to seeing the terms *form file* and *primary merge file* to describe the form document.

If you want to use an existing document, open it now. In a new document, type any text that you need to precede the information that you want to insert. Then follow these steps:

1. Choose Tools, Merge (or press Shift+F9) to open the Merge dialog box (refer to Figure 23.1).

2. Choose Create Document to open the Create Merge File dialog box (see Figure 23.12).

Figure 23.12
In the Create Merge File dialog box, you can convert the current document into a form document or you can create a form document from scratch.

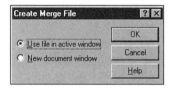

3. Choose Use File in Active Window, and then click OK. Choose New Document Window if you want to create a new merge file from scratch in another document window. The Associate Form and Data dialog box appears (see Figure 23.13).

Figure 23.13
In the Associate Form and Data dialog box, you can identify a data file or other data source for use with this form document.

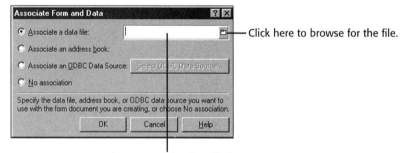

Click here to browse for the file.

Type the name of the data file here.

4. Type the name of the data file in the Associate a Data File text box or click the Files icon to search for the file. If you haven't created the data file yet, or you don't know where it is, choose No Association.

→ For more information on associating an Address Book with a form document, **see** "Merging with the Address Book," **p. 661**

5. Click OK. WordPerfect adds the Merge feature bar at the top of the document (see Figure 23.14). This document is now marked as a form document.

Note

If you associated a data file in step 4, that file is now tied to this one. Whenever you need to edit the data, just click the Go to Data button on the Merge feature bar. WordPerfect opens the data file in another window and switches you to that window. To go back to the form document, click the Go to Form button in the data file window.

Click here to insert
field codes.

Click here to switch to the data file.

Merge feature bar

Figure 23.14
The Merge feature bar
is included in every
form document and
data file that you
create.

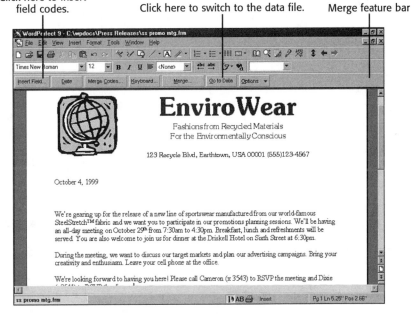

PART

VII

CH

23

6. Position the insertion point where you want to insert the first piece of information. For example, in a typical mail merge, you insert the name and address information at the top of the letter.

7. Click the Insert Field button on the Merge feature bar. The Insert Field Name or Number dialog box appears (see Figure 23.15). The field names (or numbers) in the associated data file appear in the Field Names list box.

Figure 23.15
In the Insert Field
Name or Number
dialog box, you can
select a field name
to insert in the form
document.

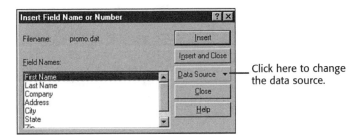

Click here to change
the data source.

Caution

If you haven't associated a data file yet, the Insert Field dialog box doesn't have a list box full of field names. Instead, you can type in a field name or number and insert it in the data file.

Tip #283 from
Laura and Read

When you associate a data file with a form document, it isn't written in stone. You can click the Data Source button in the Insert Field Name or Number dialog box and choose a different source. When you do, the field names from that source appear in the list.

8. Double-click a field name to insert it in the document. WordPerfect inserts the field name (or number) in parentheses, preceded by FIELD (see Figure 23.16).

Figure 23.16
Merge codes are displayed in a different color so you can pick them out from the rest of the text.

First Name merge code

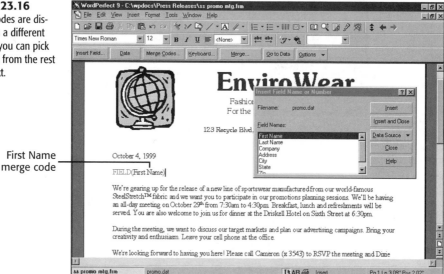

9. Continue inserting field names as necessary to complete the form document. Click Close to close the Insert Field Name or Number dialog box. Figure 23.17 shows a sample letter with the mailing address and salutation field codes.

Note

Make sure you include any necessary spaces, commas, or other punctuation between the field names.

Figure 23.17
A mailing address block and salutation have been constructed using field names from the data file.

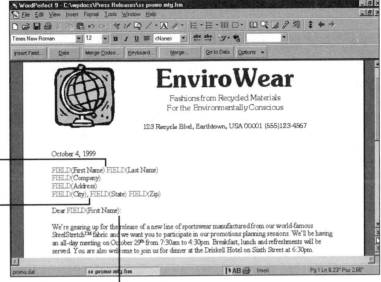

Space between the first and last names

Comma and space after the city

Colon after the first name

Tip #284 from
Laura and Read

Instead of typing in the date, you can insert a merge code that inserts the date for you when you run the merge. Click the Merge **C**odes button to open the Insert Merge Codes dialog box. Select Date in the **M**erge Codes list box, and then click **I**nsert.

The most readily understood use of the Merge feature is in a mail merge, where you are merging a letter with a list of addresses. It's important to point out that Merge can be used for much more. A form document might be an invoice or billing statement with a database file as the data source. Or how about a loan document, where the same information is plugged into a million different places? (You could import spreadsheet data into a loan application form document.) Or some day you might need to create 250 "Hello...My Name Is" labels for an awards dinner, in which case the form document would be a labels form. These are just a few examples—the possibilities are endless.

Converting a Merge File Back into a Normal Document
You can always turn a merge file (data file or form document) back into a normal document. In a form document, strip out all the merge codes by selecting and deleting them. Click the **O**ptions button on the Merge feature bar. Choose **R**emove Merge Bar. In a form document, you see a confirmation message that warns you that your data file association will be lost. In a data file, the message tells you that the file will not be recognized as a merge file. Click OK to continue or Cancel to bail out.

MERGING A FORM DOCUMENT WITH A DATA FILE

Now you've got a form document and a data file, so you're ready to go. If you've got the form document or data file open, you can click the Merge button on the Merge feature bar. Otherwise, choose Tools, Merge, Perform Merge to open the Perform Merge dialog box (see Figure 23.18).

Figure 23.18
You can identify the form document, the data file, and the output location in the Perform Merge dialog box.

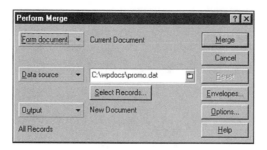

What you see in this dialog box varies depending on what files you have open (or if you have any files open at all). If you click the Merge button from the form document, Form Document is set to Current Document. If you've associated the form document with a data file, the name of that file appears next to Data Source.

If you've clicked the Merge button from the data file, the name of the file appears next to Data Source. If this data file is associated with a form document, the name of that document appears next to Form Document. Otherwise, you'll need to type the filename next to Form Document or click the Files icon to search for the file.

Finally, if you aren't running the merge from either document, you see a blank text box next to Form Document and None next to Data Source.

In any case, you need to fill in the blanks by typing the names of the files or clicking the Files icon to search for them. By default, Output is set to New Document. You can also merge to the current document. Click the Output drop-down list arrow to see the other three options:

- Printer—Sends the output directly to the printer.
- File on Disk—Creates a file and places the output in the file.
- Email—Sends the output via electronic mail. See the section "Merging to Email," later in this chapter, for more information.

When you have everything filled in, click Merge. WordPerfect matches up the field names (or numbers) in the form file and the field names (or numbers) in the data file and inserts the information into the form. The results are displayed in the current document or a new document, unless you chose to merge directly to the printer, a file, or email. Figure 23.19 shows the results of a mail merge.

Figure 23.19
WordPerfect combines the information from the data file with the text in the form document and creates a new document.

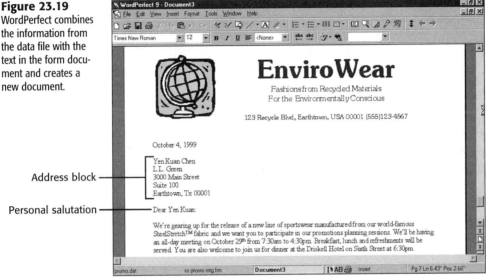

PART

VII

CH

23

Address block

Personal salutation

⚡ *If you got unexpected results when you merged the two files, see "This Isn't What I Expected" in the Troubleshooting section at the end of this chapter.*

Tip #285 from
Laura and Read

If you start a merge and then suddenly realize that you've done something wrong, press Esc to stop the merge.

Don't Save the Results
Unless you're merging to a file on disk so you can work with the results later, you don't need to save the results of a merge. If you do, you're duplicating the information that you have in the form document and data file. In most cases, you print the documents and then close the file without saving. Remember, it only takes a few seconds to run the merge again.

MERGING WITH THE ADDRESS BOOK

Corel's Address Book is integrated into all the suite applications, and it's well-suited for tracking all sorts of contact information. If you maintain a comprehensive Address Book, you might never create a data file again. During a merge, you can select records directly from the Address Book.

When you create a form document, you can associate the form with an Address Book instead of a data file (refer to Figure 23.13). If you need to switch to another Address Book, or if you created the form document with a different association, you can edit the association. There are several ways to do this, but the most direct is to click the Insert Field button on the Merge feature bar, and then click the Data Source drop-down arrow. Choose one of the Address Books from the list. I like using this method because I can see an updated list of field names right away.

After you insert the field codes from the Address Book, click the Merge button to open the Perform Merge dialog box, and then click Merge.

→ For the scoop on the Address Book, **see** "Working with the Address Book," **p. 673**

CREATING ENVELOPES DURING A MERGE

If you are producing letters, you probably need envelopes or labels for them. You can create an envelope form when you merge so it's all done together. If you need labels, you need to create a labels form document and insert the field codes, and then merge that form with the data file. See the section "Merging to Labels," later in this chapter, for more information.

Follow these steps to generate envelopes during the merge:

1. In the Perform Merge dialog box, click the Envelopes button. WordPerfect opens an envelope form document. If necessary, type the return address (or leave it out if your envelopes are preprinted).

2. Press Ctrl+End to move down to the mailing address block.

3. Click the Insert Field button to open the Insert Field Name or Number dialog box.

4. Double-click a field name (or number) to insert the field code. Include all the necessary spacing and punctuation between the fields (see Figure 23.20).

Figure 23.20
Creating the envelope during a merge has an advantage: Word-Perfect creates the envelope form document and integrates it into the merge process.

Click here to go back to the Perform Merge dialog box.

The return address might already be inserted for you.

Insert the field codes here.

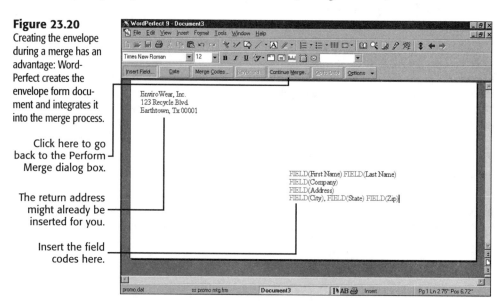

5. Click Continue Merge when you're finished. The Perform Merge dialog box appears (refer to Figure 23.18).

6. If necessary, specify a form document, a data file, and an output location.

7. Click Merge.

When a merge is complete, the insertion point is always on the last line of the last page, so don't panic if you don't see the letters right away. The envelopes are created at the end of the document, and you can either page up through the envelopes and proof them for accuracy, or you can press Ctrl+Home to move to the top of the document.

MERGING TO LABELS

Creating labels isn't integrated in the merge process, but it takes only a minute to create a labels form, associate it with the data file, and merge.

Follow these steps to merge to labels:

1. If you've already defined the labels, you can skip down to step 4. Otherwise, in a blank document, choose Format, Labels to open the Labels dialog box (see Figure 23.21).

2. Choose Laser Printed or Tractor-Fed to narrow down the list, and then select the label definition that matches your labels.

Just because your label isn't listed in the Labels box doesn't mean the definition doesn't exist. Check the layout (such as 3 columns by 10 rows) or the dimensions, and compare them to the definitions in the list. You'll probably find an exact match (or at least a close approximation).

Figure 23.21
You can choose label definitions for both laser-printed and tractor-fed printers in the Labels dialog box.

Select a label definition here.

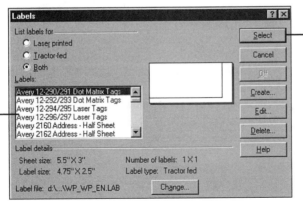

Click here to insert the definition in the current document.

3. Choose Select to insert the definition in the document.

4. Choose Tools, Merge, Create Document, Use File in Active Window to display the Associate Form and Data dialog box (refer to Figure 23.13).

5. Specify a data source, and then click OK. The Merge feature bar appears in the label document.

6. Click the Insert Field button to open the Insert Field Name or Number dialog box (refer to Figure 23.16).

7. Double-click a field name to insert it in the label. Make sure you include all the spacing and punctuation.

8. When you're finished inserting field codes, click Close to close the Insert Field Name or Number dialog box. Figure 23.22 shows a completed label form.

9. Click the Merge button on the feature bar. Verify the data source and output location, and then choose Merge to create the labels.

Tip #286 from
Laura and Read

You can take a shortcut when creating labels with the Address Book. Insert the label definition in a blank document, and then choose Tools, Address Book. Select the records, and then click Insert. Select a format in the Format Address dialog box, and then choose OK. WordPerfect creates a label for each record.

Figure 23.22
This form document is actually a sheet of labels, which will be filled in during the merge.

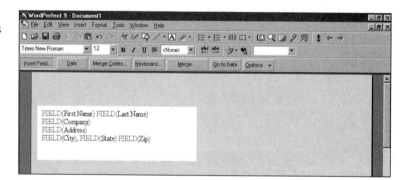

You can create a sheet of identical labels with the Merge feature. Create the label form and type the text of the label. Choose Tools, Merge, Perform Merge. In the Perform Merge dialog box, make sure Form Document is set to Current Document and Data Source is set to None. Click Options to open the Perform Merge Options dialog box (see Figure 23.23). Type the number of labels on the page in the Number of Copies for Each Record text box. Choose Merge.

Figure 23.23
You can enter the number of copies (labels) in the Perform Merge Options dialog box.

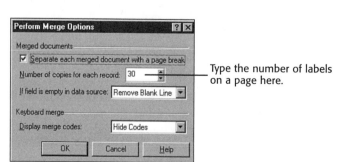

Type the number of labels on a page here.

> **Note**
>
> The maximum number of copies per record is 255, so that's the maximum number of identical labels you can create.

Figure 23.24 shows a page of identical labels. Here's an exception to the "don't save merge results" rule—you might want to save this label page for future printing.

> **Tip #287 from**
> *Laura and Read*
>
> If every other label is blank, you need to remove the page break at the end of the original label. Close this document without saving and switch back to the label form document. Position the insertion point at the end of the address and press Delete until only one label is displayed. Try the merge again.

Figure 23.24
Using the Merge feature, you can create a sheet of identical labels.

> **Caution**
>
> You might be tempted to send a partially used sheet of labels through your laser printer once again to print on the unused labels. However, the heat process from printing the sheet the first time can loosen unused labels, causing them to come off in the printer the second time around. Cleaning stuck labels from inside a laser printer is both time-consuming and costly.

MERGING TO EMAIL

Here's another intriguing possibility—you can create personalized messages and send them out via electronic mail. Think about it—you could send out meeting notices, press releases, billing statements, order confirmations, shareholder information, invoices, class schedules, responses to requests for information from your company's Web site—the list goes on and on.

Follow these steps to merge to email addresses:

1. From either the data file or form document, click the Merge button on the Merge feature bar. Otherwise, choose Tools, Merge, Perform Merge.

2. Set the form document and the data source.

3. Click the Output drop-down arrow and choose E-mail. The Merge to E-mail dialog box appears (see Figure 23.25).

Figure 23.25
You can select the field that contains the email address and type a subject for the messages in the Merge to E-mail dialog box.

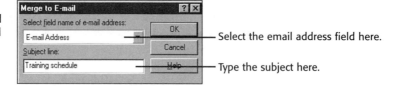

Select the email address field here.

Type the subject here.

> **Note**
>
> Changes to the Output settings in the Perform Merge dialog box are sticky, which means they stay in effect until you change the dialog box settings again.

4. Click the Select Field Name of E-mail Address drop-down list arrow and choose the field that contains the email address.

5. Type a subject in the Subject Line text box, and then click OK to return to the Perform Merge dialog box.

6. Choose Merge. The Choose Profile dialog box appears (see Figure 23.26).

Figure 23.26
You can select the Profile Name for your email system in the Choose Profile dialog box.

7. Select a profile from the Profile Name drop-down list, and then click OK to start the merge.

MERGING TO TABLES

Tables make popular form documents because they are incredibly flexible and easy to work with. You can merge a data file into a table form document, where each record has its own row, with the insertion of the Repeat Row merge code.

Follow these steps to create a table form document:

1. Create a table with one row and as many columns as you need for the fields.

→ For the steps to create a table, **see** "Creating Tables," **p. 254**

2. Click in the first cell (upper-left corner).

3. Choose <u>T</u>ools, <u>M</u>erge, <u>C</u>reate Document, <u>U</u>se File in Active Window. The Associate Form and Data dialog box is displayed (refer to Figure 23.13).

4. Select a data file, an Address Book, or an ODBC data source to associate with this form document, and then click OK.

5. Click the <u>I</u>nsert Field button to open the Insert Field Name or Number dialog box.

6. Double-click a field name to insert it in the table. Make sure you include all the necessary spacing and punctuation between the field codes. Press Tab to move to the next cell or just click in the cell.

7. When you're finished inserting field codes, click <u>C</u>lose to close the Insert Field Name or Number dialog box.

8. Click in the last cell of the last row, after any field codes or text.

9. Click the Merge <u>C</u>odes button on the Merge feature bar to open the Insert Merge Codes dialog box (see Figure 23.27).

Figure 23.27
The Insert Merge Codes dialog box includes a list of merge commands.

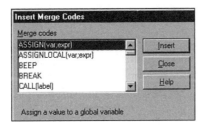

Note

The Repeat Row command is but one command in a long list of merge commands. The Merge feature has its own programming language for creating "intelligent" merge documents. Unfortunately, covering the merge commands is beyond the scope of this book. Don't despair—you've still got the help topics. On the Index tab of the Help Topics dialog box, type `Merge programming commands`, and then double-click the matching help topic in the list box. Finally, click the More Detailed Information button to display a list of commands.

10. Scroll down through the list, and then select the Repeat Row command.

11. Choose <u>I</u>nsert, and then choose <u>C</u>lose to close the Insert Merge Codes dialog box. The Repeat Row command is inserted in the last cell (see Figure 23.28). This command automatically creates a new row for each record in the data file.

12. Choose <u>M</u>erge to open the Perform Merge dialog box.

13. Specify a data source and verify the output location.

14. Choose <u>M</u>erge.

Figure 23.28
You need the Repeat Row command in the last cell of the table, after the field name, if you want the merge to create a new row for every record.

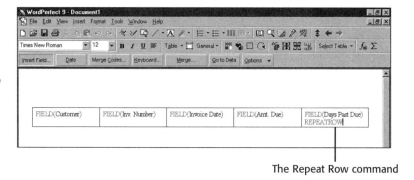

The Repeat Row command

Caution

If you have empty rows in the table, those fields were empty in the data source. If that's the case, print this table so you can see which gaps you need to fill, and then close the table without saving. Open the data source and enter the missing data. Save your changes, and try the merge again.

SORTING AND SELECTING RECORDS

Managing the data in your data source, whatever it might be, is an important part of your office automation system. You'll save hours if you can keep the information in that single source current. If you've been creating small data files for every project, stop right now. The more data files you have, the less likely you are to keep up with them.

It's easier to create larger data files where you can update everything at once. You can sort the records and then select only the records that you want to work with. For example, if you want to send a notice only to people living in a certain city, you can sort the records by the City field and then select the records that contain that city.

SORTING DATA FILES

By using the Sort feature, you can group together common records, making it easier to select them for a merge or to update the information in the records. Bulk mail, for example, must be sent out in zip code order. By using the Sort feature, you arrange the data file in zip code order before you merge.

The default sort is to arrange the records by the first column of the table or the first word in a merge data file. You can create your own sort if you want to sort by something else. The trick is to remember that when you specify the column number or the field number, this is really the field name. Right now, you can't choose from a list of field names in the Sort dialog box, so you have to remember to count the columns or count the fields so that you know the number of the field.

→ The steps for sorting a text data file are almost identical to those for sorting a data file table, so for more information, **see** "Sorting Database Data in Tables," **p. 420**

SELECTING RECORDS

Nine times out of ten, you work with a larger set of data than you need for the merge. I mean, how often do you send a letter or email to *everyone* in your Address Book? If the records have something in common, you can select them by specifying certain conditions. Or you can simply choose which records you want from the list.

Follow these steps to select records from a data file:

1. In the Perform Merge dialog box, make sure the data source is properly identified.

2. Click <u>S</u>elect Records to open the Select Records dialog box (see Figure 23.29).

Click here if you want to mark records manually.

Type the beginning record number here.

Figure 23.29
In the Select Records dialog box, you can define the selection criteria to select records in a data file.

Click here to specify a range of records.

Click a drop-down list arrow to choose a field.

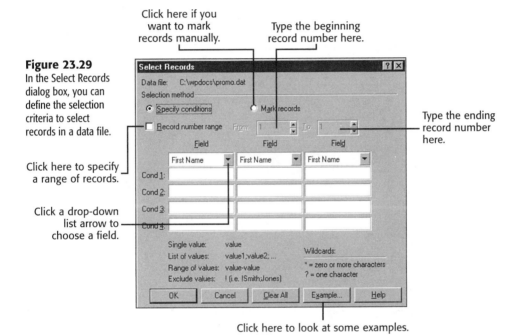

Type the ending record number here.

Click here to look at some examples.

3. If you want to specify a range of records, put a check mark next to <u>R</u>ecord Number Range, and then type the beginning number in the Fr<u>o</u>m text box and the ending number in the <u>T</u>o text box.

4. In the first column, click the <u>F</u>ield drop-down list and select a field from the list.

5. Type the condition that you want to set in the Cond <u>1</u> text box.

> **Note**
>
> Each condition line defines a set of records that are to be selected (or excluded) from the merge. Each column defines the field for which you want to set the condition(s). You can define more than one condition for a single row, so more than one field can be involved. Only records that meet all the conditions in the row are selected. Specifying more than one row of conditions selects records that meet *any* row of conditions.

6. If necessary, select a field from the Fi̲eld drop-down list and type the condition in the second column.

7. If necessary, select a field from the Field drop-down list and type the condition in the third column.

8. Repeat these steps to set any other conditions you want to use.

Tip #288 from
Laura and Read

If you've made a mess of things and you just want to start over, click C̲lear All to reset the fields and clear all the conditions.

9. Click OK when you're done to return to the Perform Merge dialog box.

 If you're missing records that match your conditions, see "Not All the Records Are Being Selected" in the Troubleshooting section at the end of this chapter.

When you aren't sure how to set a condition, WordPerfect gives you some excellent examples. Click the E̲xample button at the bottom of the dialog box to display the Examples of Selecting Records dialog box (see Figure 23.30). There is even a second page that you can look at—choose M̲ore to display the second page.

Figure 23.30
The Examples of Selected Records dialog box has a series of examples to help you understand how to set conditions.

	Field	Field	Field
	Last Name ▾	State ▾	First Name ▾
Cond 1:	-Ling	Iowa	
Cond 2:	Allens-Cohen	Arizona;New York	
Cond 3:	n"-p"		
Cond 4:	Gonzales	!California;Texas	

In this example, records that meet any of the following conditions will be merged:
1- Everyone up to and including the Lings who live in Iowa.
2- All of the Allens to the Cohens who live in Arizona and New York.
3- All people whose last name starts with "n", "o", or "p".
4- Everyone named Gonzales who does not live in California or Texas.

[Close] [More...] [Help]

Click here to view the second page of examples.

In some cases, it's easier to mark the records manually, especially in cases where there is no common ground. In this situation, choose M̲ark Records. The dialog box options change to those for selecting records directly from the data file (see Figure 23.31).

You can change which field appears first in the list. For example, you might need to see the cities, not the first and last names. Click the F̲irst Field to Display drop-down list arrow and choose a field from the list. Choose U̲pdate Record List to update the list with the new first field.

To select records, click the check box next to the record. If the records are one right after the other, click the first record, and then hold down the Shift key and click the last record.

Otherwise, click the first record, and then hold down the Ctrl key while you click the other records. Click OK when you're done to return to the Perform Merge dialog box.

Figure 23.31
Selecting Mark Records allows you to manually select records from the data file.

Type the beginning record number here.

Type the ending record number here.

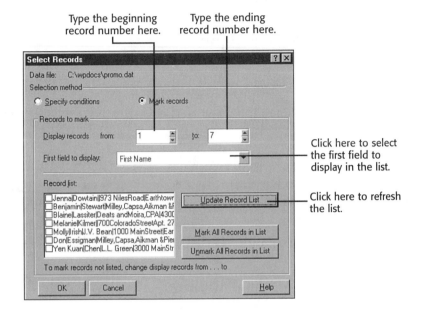

Click here to select the first field to display in the list.

Click here to refresh the list.

CREATING FILL-IN-THE-BLANKS FORMS

You may have a project that seems ideal for a merge, except that some of the information is variable, so it isn't well suited for a data file. Well, guess what—you don't have to have a data file to perform a merge. You can merge with the keyboard—in a manner of speaking.

A form document can be created with Keyboard codes that stop and wait for the user to type in the information, rather than pulling it from a data file. You can create a detailed message that explains what the user should be typing at this point. After the information has been entered, the merge moves on to the next Keyboard code.

Follow these steps to create a fill-in-the-blanks form:

1. If you've already created the document, open it now.

2. Choose Tools, Merge, Create Document, Use File in Active Window.

3. In the Associate Form and Data dialog box, choose No Association.

4. Click in the document where you want to insert the Keyboard code.

5. Click the Keyboard button on the Merge feature bar to open the Insert Merge Code dialog box (see Figure 23.32).

6. Type the prompt text that you want to appear, and then click OK to insert the Keyboard code in the form.

Figure 23.32
Type the message that you want to appear in the Insert Merge Code dialog box.

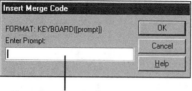

Type the message here.

7. Repeat steps 4–6 to insert any other prompts for this form document. Figure 23.33 shows a form document with four Keyboard codes that prompt for the heading information.

Keyboard code   Message text

Figure 23.33
The keyboard code includes the message text in parentheses.

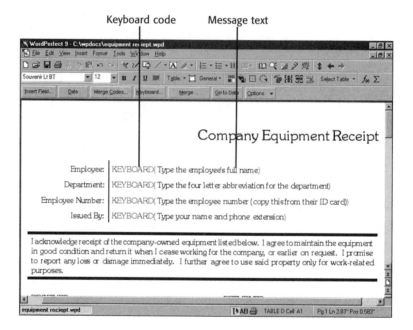

8. When you're ready to fill in the form, choose Tools, Merge, Perform Merge or click the Merge button on the Merge feature bar. Verify the location of the data file (if there is one), the form document, and the output, and then choose Merge. When a keyboard command is encountered, the merge pauses and displays the prompt message (see Figure 23.34).

9. Type the requested information, and then press Alt+Enter or Alt+Shift+C (or click the Continue button on the Merge feature bar) to continue the merge.

Tip #289 from
Laura and Read

You can get the best of both worlds by combining a typical merge of a data file and form document with the flexibility of a fill-in-the-blanks form. Just include keyboard codes in the form document where you want the user to type the information. The rest of the fields can be filled in from the data file.

Click here to halt the merge.

Figure 23.34
The prompt message that you type is displayed in a window at the bottom of the screen.

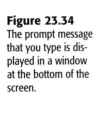

Click here to continue the merge.

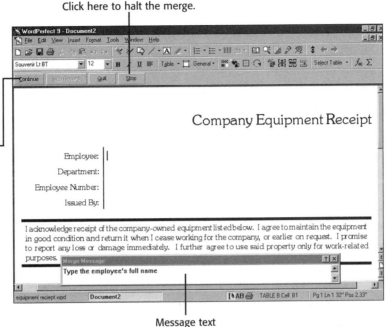

Message text

WORKING WITH THE ADDRESS BOOK

The CorelCENTRAL Address Book is accessible throughout the Corel WordPerfect Office 2000 suite of applications, so it's the perfect place to keep your contact information. You can keep track of all sorts of information: phone and fax numbers, addresses, email addresses, birthdays, personal greetings, job titles, assistant and manager names, and so on.

If you have other address books on your system, they are also available to you in the Corel applications, so you can maintain a centralized database of contact information and also use the other address books on your system.

Tip #290 from
Laura and Read

If you use the Address Book often, you can add a button to your toolbar that opens the Address Book. Right-click the toolbar to which you want to add the button, and then choose Edit. Choose Tools from the Feature Categories drop-down list, and then select Address Book. Choose Add Button, and click OK.

CREATING AND EDITING ADDRESS BOOK ENTRIES

The Address Book has been redesigned to store more information and to give you equal access to other address books on your system. If you're upgrading from WordPerfect 8, the installation program copies the records from the Address Book into the WordPerfect 9 Address Book. Records from the WordPerfect 7 and 6.1 Address Book can also be converted. See the section "Importing and Exporting Tips," later in this chapter, for more information.

To open the Address Book and add some entries, follow these steps:

1. Choose <u>T</u>ools, <u>A</u>ddress Book. The CorelCENTRAL Address Book dialog box opens. By default, the WordPerfect 9 Address Book is open. You can open another one by clicking the plus sign next to the category, and then clicking the name of the address book.

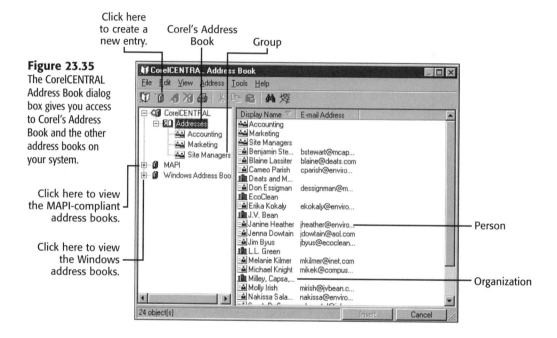

Figure 23.35
The CorelCENTRAL Address Book dialog box gives you access to Corel's Address Book and the other address books on your system.

Click here to create a new entry.
Corel's Address Book
Group

Click here to view the MAPI-compliant address books.

Click here to view the Windows address books.

Person

Organization

Changes to the Address Book Dialog Box

If you've upgraded from WordPerfect 7 or 8, you'll notice right away that the Address Book dialog box has been redesigned for WordPerfect 9. The left pane of the CorelCENTRAL Address Book dialog box has a list of all the address books on your system; the right side displays a list of records in the selected address book. There is a new toolbar with buttons for common tasks. The My Addresses and Frequent Contacts address books are rolled into one address book called Addresses. If you used the automatic dialer, brace yourself—it's gone. They may bring it back in a service pack, but the shipping release doesn't include it. Otherwise, the buttons you're used to seeing along the bottom of the dialog box have been moved to the menus and the toolbar.

---

2. Click the Create a New Address Entry button on the toolbar in the CorelCENTRAL Address book dialog box. The New Entry dialog box appears (see Figure 23.36).

Tip #291 from
Laura and Read

If you are creating records for members of the same organization, create the organizations first. As you create the records for the members, you can choose the organization from a drop-down list, which fills in the address information for you, so you don't have to type it in each time.

Figure 23.36
You can choose the type of address book entry you're creating in the New Entry dialog box.

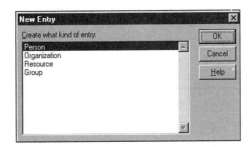

3. Choose one of the following options:

- Person—This is the most comprehensive entry you can create. There are six tabs where you can organize the information: General, Personal, Address, Phone/Fax, Business, and Security.

- Organization—This is a subset of the Person record, with three tabs: Address, Phone/Fax, and Security.

- Resource—You can maintain records about your company resources by identifying the name and type of the resource, the owner, the main phone number, and comments.

- Group—You can create a group of Address Book records to make it easier to broadcast messages and general correspondence.

Depending on the type of entry you choose, you get a blank record to fill in. Figure 23.37 shows an entry for a person. Type the information into the fields, pressing Tab to move to the next field and Shift+Tab to move back a field. Click the other tabs to enter data in additional fields.

 If you're getting the wrong information from the Address Book plugged into your templates (via prompts), see "Scrambled Information from the Address Book" in the Troubleshooting section at the end of this chapter.

Figure 23.37
The Person Properties dialog box has six tabs to help you organize data for an individual.

Click here to select an organization.

After you enter some records, you can do the following:

- Edit an entry—You can double-click the person, organization, or resource entries in the list. You can also select the entry and then click the Edit an Address Entry button. To edit a group, right-click the group, and then choose Edit to open the Properties dialog box for that group. Make your changes, and then click OK to save the changes or Cancel to discard the changes.

- Delete an entry—You can select one or more entries, and then press Delete. You can also click the Delete an Address Entry button.

Caution

You're working without a safety net when you delete records in the Address Book because there is no way to restore an entry that you've deleted in error.

- Move entries to another address book—You can select the entries in the list, and then click and drag them over to another address book (in the list in the left pane).

- Copy entries to another address book—You can select the entries, and then choose Edit, Copy. Open the other address book, and then choose Edit, Paste.

- Print entries—You can print the current record, selected records, or all the records. Select one or more records, and then click the Print button on the toolbar or press Ctrl+P to open the Print dialog box.

- Find text—You can click the Search for Specified Text button to open the Find dialog box (see Figure 23.38). Type the text you want to search for, and then click OK. If records are found that contain the search text, the dialog box expands and the records are listed below the Find text box.

Figure 23.38
In the Find dialog box, you can type the text you want to search for in the address book records.

- Sort the records—You can click the column heading for the field that you want to sort by. Click the column heading again to reverse the sort (ascending to descending and vice versa). You can then select the sorted records for printing, email, or merging. For example, you can print labels in zip code order if you sort the records by zip code before selecting them.

Caution

If you sort the Address Book records, and then exit the Address Book and try to use the sorted records in a merge, the sort doesn't stick. If you want to use sorted records in a merge, you have to convert the Address Book to a merge data file and then sort it. See the section "Importing and Exporting Tips" later in this chapter for more information.

■ Display different fields—To change the fields that are displayed, right-click a column heading. The Columns dialog box appears, with a list of all the fields (see Figure 23.39). Place a check mark next to each of the fields that you want to see listed.

Figure 23.39
You can mark the fields that you want displayed in the Address Book list in the Columns dialog box.

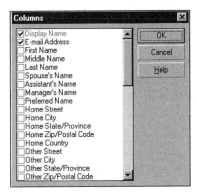

PART
VII
CH
23

■ Set a filter—You can expand or narrow down the list of records by specifying criteria that must be met for the record to be displayed. For example, you can display all the records for a given company name. Choose <u>V</u>iew, <u>F</u>ilter to display the Filter dialog box (see Figure 23.40). Click the first drop-down list arrow and choose a field. Click the operator button between the list box and the text box. Select an operator from the list. Type the text or value in the text box, and then click OK. To remove a filter, choose <u>V</u>iew, <u>R</u>emove Filter.

Figure 23.40
In the Filter dialog box, you can specify the criteria that must be met for the record to be displayed in the list.

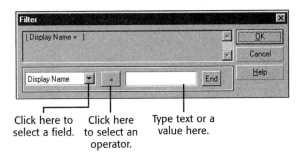

Click here to select a field. Click here to select an operator. Type text or a value here.

 ■ Create a new address book—You can create multiple address books to further separate the different types of records that you are maintaining. Click the Create a New Address Book button (or press Ctrl+N) to create a new address book. Select the type of address book in the New Address Book dialog box (see Figure 23.41). Depending on the type of address book you want to create, you'll get another dialog box where you can specify a name and other properties for the new address book.

Note

Your list of address book types might vary depending on the applications installed on your system.

Figure 23.41
You can select the type of address book you want to create in the New Address Book dialog box.

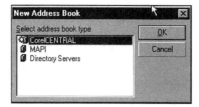

- Send email—You can select an address book entry, and then choose <u>T</u>ools, <u>S</u>end Mail to start composing a mail message. If there is an email address in the selected record, it's automatically inserted into the message. You can finish creating the message, and then send it as you normally would.

IMPORTING AND EXPORTING TIPS

Now that you know you can create a centralized repository for all your contact information, the question becomes "How can I get everything into the Corel Address Book?" or "How can I get the Corel Address Book records into another address book or another application?"

The answers are as varied as the different programs that you can use to create and maintain contact information. You've got a lot of options, so you're sure to find a way to import the information in or to export the information out.

Unfortunately, space considerations don't permit detailed steps for every type of import or export operation. The following list of general concepts for importing and exporting should get you moving in the right direction:

- Importing spreadsheet and database files—Use the steps in the "Converting to Word-Perfect Formats" section of Chapter 15, "Importing Data and Working with Other Programs," to import a spreadsheet or database file as a merge data file. After you have a merge data file, you can import that directly into the Address Book. During this process, you'll be able to "map," or match up, the field names from the merge text file with the Address Book field names, so you can be sure that the information from the merge data file is inserted in the right places.

If you get the error message "Invalid Field Name" when trying to import a merge data file into the Address Book, see "Invalid Field Name Error Message" in the Troubleshooting section at the end of this chapter.

- Importing other address books—In most cases, you'll be able to export your addresses from another address book (such as Outlook Express) into an ASCII (or comma-delimited) text file, which can be imported directly into the Corel Address Book. The field names that were used in the other address book will be listed next to the fields in the Corel Address Book. After you've matched up the field names, you can import the addresses.

- Exporting to a merge data file—The adrs2mrg macro that ships with WordPerfect converts the Address Book into a merge data file. You can either use the data file directly, or you can save the merge data file as an ASCII (DOS) delimited text file (see the following item).

→ To find out where the `adrs2mrg` macro is and how to run it, **see** Chapter 24, "Experts and Macros," **p. 685**

- Exporting to an ASCII delimited file—You can export the Corel Address Book to an ASCII delimited file (with field names intact) by converting the file to a merge data file and then saving the data file as an ASCII delimited file. Here's how: After you've converted the Address Book to a merge data file, delete the FIELDNAMES code, and then replace the semicolon after each field name with a colon, an ENDFIELD code, and a hard return. You can do this with Find and Replace if you like. In the Save As dialog box, choose ASCII (DOS) Delimited Text from the File Type drop-down list, and then save the file. If you don't want the field names, delete the entire FIELDNAMES record before you save the file to ASCII.

→ For the steps to insert a code in the Find and Replace dialog box, **see** "Searching for Codes," **p. 130**

- Converting/importing WordPerfect 7/8 Address Books—When you install WordPerfect 9, Setup looks for previous versions of the program. If a previous version is found, Setup copies the information found in the older Address Books into the WordPerfect 9 Address Book. If, for some strange reason this doesn't take place, you have a couple of options. You can cut and paste the records from the older Address Books to the WordPerfect 9 Address Book. Or, you can manually transfer the information over by exporting the addresses in WordPerfect 7 and 8 to an ABX file and then importing the ABX file into WordPerfect 9. Either way, there is a help topic on this in the Address Book help (choose <u>H</u>elp, <u>H</u>elp Topics, double-click Using CorelCENTRAL Address Book, and then double-click Moving from Corel Address Book 8). Make sure you follow the instructions to the letter.

- Converting/importing WordPerfect 6.1 addresses—You need to run the `adrs2mrg` macro to convert the addresses to a merge data file. Take a few minutes and add field names to the data file so that it's easier to import. You may have to make some adjustments because the WordPerfect 6.1 Address Book didn't use separate fields for city, state, and zip. After you save the file as a merge data file, you can import it into the WordPerfect 9 Address Book. This is where the field names you added come in handy. During the import process, you'll see a dialog box where you can map, or match up, the field names from the two Address Books. This way, you're sure the information is plugged into the right fields.

TROUBLESHOOTING

THIS ISN'T WHAT I EXPECTED

I just did a merge, but I'm not getting the results I need. There are blank spaces where there should be data. I've also got blank lines in the middle of a few addresses.

First, take a good look at the results. Can you detect a pattern? Is the state where the city should be? Are all the last names missing, or just one or two? When you're ready to proceed, close the merge results document without saving.

If you're having the same problem over and over, start with the form document. Make sure you have the right field codes in the right places. If you need to change a field code, select and delete the code, and then reinsert it. Save your changes and try the merge again.

If the problem occurs just in one or two entries, go straight to the data file and take a look at the records that are giving you trouble. Make sure the right information is in the right field. You might have actually typed the state in the city field by accident. Save your changes and try the merge again.

If the source file is a spreadsheet or database, you have to do your proofing in the originating program. If this is inconvenient, consider converting the file to a merge data file so you can edit it in WordPerfect.

NOT ALL THE RECORDS ARE BEING SELECTED

I've set up conditions to select a group of files, but not all the records that contain this information are selected. What's going on?

When you set conditions, you have to make sure that you aren't pairing contradictory conditions that in effect cancel each other out. For example, if you search for records that contain a certain city AND a company name, you won't find any of the records that contain that company name but are in a different city. Because every situation is different, it's a good idea to take a look at the examples. In the Select Records dialog box, click Examples. You can get to a second page of examples by clicking More in the Examples of Selecting Records dialog box.

INVALID FIELD NAME ERROR MESSAGE

I'm trying to import a merge data file in the Address Book, but I get an error message that says there is an invalid field name. What does this mean?

You probably have some punctuation in one of the field names. Open the data file and remove any punctuation marks from the field names. For example, if one of your field names is "City, State Zip", the Address Book sees the comma as a field separator so the City field is assumed to be one field and the State Zip field to be another. Resave the data file and try the import again.

SOME OF THE ADDRESS BOOKS ARE MISSING

Not all the address books are listed in the CorelCENTRAL Address Book dialog box. Where did they go?

The Windows logon information is used to determine the creator of each address book, so the address books are visible only to the person who created them. When you are logged on to the network, only the address books that you've created will show up in the CorelCENTRAL Address Book dialog box. In addition, new address books can be marked as Hidden (or Read-Only) as a security measure to protect against unauthorized access. If an address book is marked as Hidden, it won't appear to users who log on to that machine. If it's marked Read-Only, users won't be able to modify the records.

SCRAMBLED INFORMATION FROM THE ADDRESS BOOK

You want to use your customized WordPerfect 8 templates in WordPerfect 9. Most of them work just fine, but when a prompt is linked to an Address Book field, the wrong information is being inserted into the template.

The field names were changed in WordPerfect 9, so you probably need to rebuild your prompts and link them to the proper fields. In WordPerfect 9, open the template for editing. Delete the prompts that are linked to Address Book fields, and then reinsert them. Click Build Prompts, and then choose Add. In the Add Template Prompt dialog box, select Show All Available Fields. Type the prompt, and then choose the correct field from the list. Make sure that you save these changes.

PROJECT

Someone just handed you a disk with a long list of names and addresses. She wants it used in a mass mailing that has to go out by this afternoon's mail run. You open the file and discover to your dismay that it's a list of names and addresses without any merge codes. Short of retyping the list, you're wondering "how in the world can I turn this into a merge data file in just an hour?"

The answer? Stand back and let the Find and Replace feature work its magic. If you can figure out how the fields and records are divided, you can replace these elements with End Field and End Record codes. Here's how:

1. Open the file, and then immediately save it with a new name. This way, if your efforts backfire, you can always get back to the original list.

2. Turn on Reveal Codes so you can figure out what divides the fields and records. If there is a blank line between each record, then the separator is two hard returns. If the list is in a label format, there is probably a hard page between each record. See the note at the bottom of the steps for more information on different kinds of separators.

3. From the top of the document, press Ctrl+F to open the Find and Replace dialog box. Choose Match, Codes to open the Codes dialog box (see Figure 23.42).

4. Scroll down the list and select the code that separates the records. For example, if there is a blank line between the records, select HRt and click Insert twice to insert two hard return codes. If there isn't a blank line between the records, insert one hard return code. You should now see [HRt][HRt] (or [HRt]) in the Find text box.

5. Click in the Replace With text box, and then select the HRt code and click Insert.

6. Click the check box next to Display Merge Codes Only so that the list of codes now shows only the merge codes. Select the end record code, and then click Insert.

7. Remove the check mark next to Display Merge Codes Only to reveal the other codes. Select the HPg code, and then click Insert. The Find and Replace dialog box should now look like the one shown in Figure 23.43.

Figure 23.42
The same Codes dialog box is used to select codes that you want to search for and codes that you want to insert in place of the search codes.

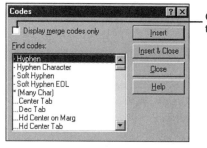

Click here to display the merge codes.

Figure 23.43
The Find and Replace feature is set to look for two hard returns that separate the records and replace them with the codes that separate records in a merge data file.

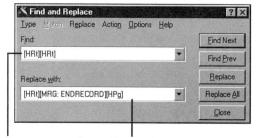

Search for two
hard returns.

Replace with a hard return, the
end record code, and a hard page.

8. Choose Replace All. Now it's time to insert the end field codes after each field in the record. You've figured out that each field is on a line by itself, so the separator is a hard return.

9. Click in the Find text box and delete the contents. Choose Match, Codes to open the Codes dialog box again. Select HRt, and then click Insert.

10. Click in the Replace With text box and delete the contents. In the Codes dialog box, click the check box next to Display Merge Codes Only. Select the End Field code, and then click Insert. Remove the check mark next to Display Merge Codes Only. Select HRt, and then click Insert and Close. The Find and Replace dialog box should now look like the one shown in Figure 23.44.

Figure 23.44
The Find and Replace feature is set to look for the hard return that separates the fields and replace it with the codes that separate fields in a merge data file.

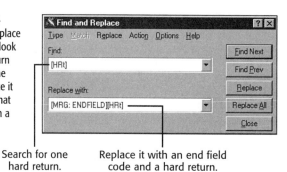

Search for one
hard return.

Replace it with an end field
code and a hard return.

11. Choose Replace <u>A</u>ll, and then close the Find and Replace dialog box. The next step is to identify the file as a merge data file and to name the fields.

12. Choose <u>T</u>ools, M<u>e</u>rge, Create <u>D</u>ata, <u>U</u>se File in Active Window, and then click OK. In the Create Data File dialog box, type a field name for every field in the file (even if you aren't planning on using them all in the form document). Click OK when you're finished, and then save the file to disk.

13. Now that you have the Merge feature bar displayed, go through the file and make sure that there is an End Field code at the end of every field and an End Record code at the end of every record. (This includes the field name record at the top of the document.) Make sure that every field is on a line by itself and that there is a hard page between each record. If there are missing field codes, click the End <u>F</u>ield or End <u>R</u>ecord buttons on the Merge feature bar to insert them.

14. Save your changes, and then continue on with creating the form document and merging the two together.

If you're converting a labels form into a merge data file, use the following Find and Replace operations:

Find	Replace With
[HPg]	[HRt][MRG:ENDRECORD][HPg]
[HRt]	[MRG:ENDFIELD][HRt]

Also, make sure that you delete the Paper Size/Type and the Labels Form codes at the top of the document. If you decide to use more than one field for the city, state, and zip, you can use the following search operation to break up the city and the state:

Find	Replace With
,<space>	[MRG:ENDFIELD][HRt]

If you used two spaces between the state and zip, you can use the following search operation:

Find	Replace With
<space><space>	[MRG:ENDFIELD][HRt]

The last record can be problematic, so make sure you check it before you save the file and merge.

If you're converting a file where each record is on a line by itself and the fields have a comma between them, use the following Find and Replace operations:

Find	Replace With
[HRt]	[MRG:ENDRECORD][HPg]
,<space>	[MRG:ENDFIELD][HRt]
"	<nothing>

The last operation removes any quotation marks that might be around text in one of the fields.

CHAPTER 24

EXPERTS AND MACROS

In this chapter

USING THE PERFECTEXPERT

In Chapter 1, "Getting Comfortable with WordPerfect," you learned how you can use the PerfectExpert to ask questions in your own words to identify potentially useful help topics. In Chapter 22, "Building Documents with Templates," you learned how to use the PerfectExpert *project templates (page 614)* to build specific types of documents. In this chapter, you'll learn how to use the "generic" PerfectExpert, which can guide you through the creation of all sorts of different documents. You can create documents with tables, columns, bulleted and numbered lists, graphics, shapes, borders, charts, outlines, headers, footers, page numbers, and so on. All the common formatting options, such as changing the margins, choosing fonts, setting tabs, using Make It Fit, adjusting line spacing, inserting symbols, and marking text, are available at the click of a button. You can even get to the document collaboration and proofing tools. In short, "it's in there."

To start the PerfectExpert, click the PerfectExpert button or choose <u>H</u>elp, Perfect<u>E</u>xpert. The PerfectExpert panel appears on the left side of the screen (see Figure 24.1). You may recall from Chapter 22 that you click the panel buttons to choose additional options. The buttons with a down-facing arrow display pop-up menus.

Figure 24.1
The PerfectExpert panel has buttons that open pop-up menus and other pages with additional options.

Down-facing arrow

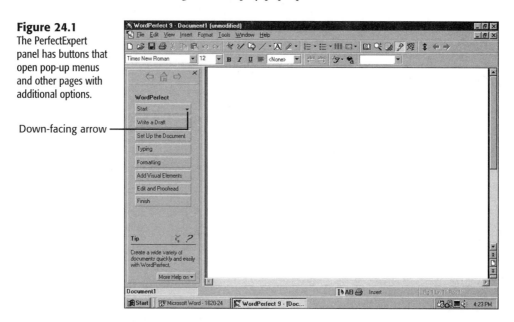

Clicking a panel button opens another page with more options (see Figure 24.2). If you want to move back to the previous page, click the Go Back button. As you continue to work in the PerfectExpert panel, the Go Forward button will become available.

Clicking the Web button next to the question mark launches your Internet browser (if available) and takes you to Corel's Learning Center on the Web.

Go Forward button

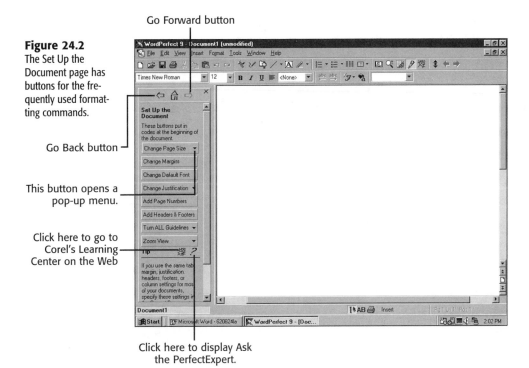

Figure 24.2
The Set Up the Document page has buttons for the frequently used formatting commands.

Go Back button

This button opens a pop-up menu.

Click here to go to Corel's Learning Center on the Web

Click here to display Ask the PerfectExpert.

Clicking the question mark displays the Ask the PerfectExpert tab of the Help Topics dialog box, where you can type a question in your own words and get a list of help topics to choose from.

→ To learn more about PerfectExpert, see "Asking for Help in Your Own Words," **p. 30**

By default, you are set to create the new document in a blank document window. You can, however, use the PerfectExpert to edit an existing document or project template. To do so, click the Start button in the PerfectExpert panel and choose New Project/Existing Document. In the PerfectExpert dialog box (see Figure 24.3), you can choose from the list of project templates or you can click the Work On tab and choose from a list of previously edited documents (work in progress).

→ To learn more about project templates, **see** Chapter 22, "Building Documents with Templates," **p. 613**

I've kind of saved the best for last, but you *have* to see what happens when you open the PerfectExpert panel in an existing document. Let me give you a quick example. With the PerfectExpert panel displayed, I opened a newsletter. When I click in various parts of the newsletter, the PerfectExpert panel pages change to display options that are relevant for the feature used for that section of the newsletter. When I click on a table, I get the Table page; when I click on a title, I get the Title Look page; when I click in the newsletter text, I get the Newsletter page.

PART

VII

CH

24

Figure 24.3
You can open a project template, or a recently edited document, in the PerfectExpert dialog box.

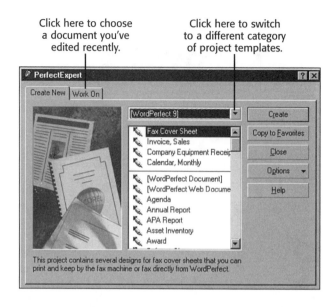

Click here to choose a document you've edited recently.

Click here to switch to a different category of project templates.

Note

This feature is perfect for the new (or timid) users because it is literally point-and-click document generation. All users have to do is click the PerfectExpert button to open the PerfectExpert panel where they can click buttons to get menus and dialog boxes that they may not have been able to find on their own.

USING MACROS TO AUTOMATE REPETITIVE TASKS

Think about your day-to-day activities and ask yourself how much of what you do is repetitive. You may be spending valuable time repeating the same steps over and over, not realizing that you can speed things up *considerably* with a macro.

What is a *macro*? Let me use a popular analogy to try and explain. A tape recorder records sounds on a cassette tape. You can turn the recorder on, record the sounds, and then turn the recorder off. The sound you recorded is there for you to access when you play the cassette tape back. The same is true for creating a macro, except instead of recording sounds, you record actions taken in a document window. You turn on the Macro Recorder, record your actions, and then turn off the Macro Recorder. Whatever you do between turning the Macro Recorder on and turning it back off is recorded in a macro. The next time you need to perform that series of steps, you play the macro back and it does the work, at lightening speed.

Now, before you skip this section because you think that macros are only for the technically proficient...think again. They can be simple, such as typing out your standard letter closing, setting up a landscape page with 10-point Arial, or inserting a page number. Or they can be very complex, such as asking a series of questions and generating a customized document with standard sections of text (such as legal documents, loan forms, and insurance policies).

Shortcut Keys Are Still in Place
Previous users of WordPerfect will be pleased to find that the same keystrokes that have been in use since the early DOS WordPerfect days still work in WordPerfect 9. You can still press Alt+F10 to play a macro and Ctrl+F10 to record a macro.

If you're lucky, your firm has distributed a standard set of macros for everyone's use. If this is the case, all you need to know is how to run them, so let's start there. Later on, I'll explain how to create your own macros.

PLAYING MACROS

The trick to playing macros that someone else has provided for you is knowing where they are stored. If you need to look around a bit, you can browse for them. Choose Tools, Macro, Play (or press Alt+F10) to open the Play Macro dialog box (see Figure 24.4). The shipping macros are displayed in the wpwin subfolder of the macros folder. From here, you can click the Look In drop-down list arrow and go looking for the macros folder. When you find it, double-click the macro that you want to play.

Click here to look around
for the macro folder.

Figure 24.4
By default, the Play Macro dialog box displays the contents of the wpwin folder.

Double-click a macro file to play the macro.

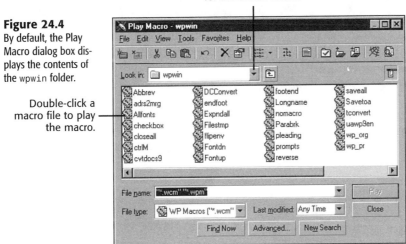

Tip #292 from
Laura and Read

The last nine macros that you played are listed at the bottom of the Macro menu. Choose Tools, Macro, and then select one from the list to play it.

RUNNING THE SHIPPING MACROS

WordPerfect ships with a collection of macros that are both helpful to use and to examine if you want to become familiar with the PerfectScript macro language. Many of these macros were available in previous versions of WordPerfect, so you're likely to see that your old favorites are still around.

- **Abbrev.wcm**—Opens an Abbreviations dialog box where you can select a *QuickWord (page 138)* and expand it in a document. The dialog box stays open so you can expand multiple QuickWords without opening the QuickCorrect dialog box each time.

- **adrs2mrg.wcm**—Opens an Address Book to Merge dialog box, where you can choose an *Address Book (page 673)* and then create a merge data file from the entire Address Book or just from selected records. This macro creates a text data file with a field name record at the top of the file.

- **Allfonts.wcm**—This macro searches for all the fonts that are installed for the current printer and generates a list of the fonts along with a short sample of text (see Figure 24.5). Depending on the number of fonts you have installed, it might take a few minutes to generate the list. Also, your printer might not have enough memory to be able to print the list.

⚠️ *If you don't see all these files in the macro list, see "Where Are the Rest of the Shipping Macros?" in the Troubleshooting section at the end of this chapter.*

Figure 24.5
The **Allfonts** macro compiles a list of the fonts that are installed for the current printer.

Total number of fonts

Sample text

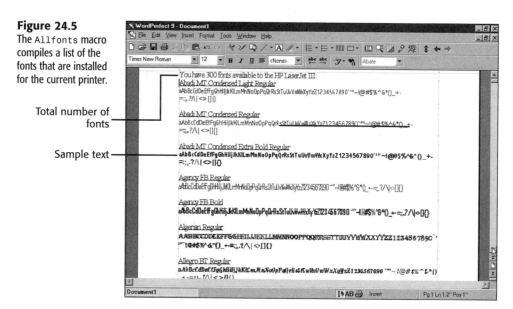

- **checkbox.wcm**—This macro creates a check box that you can click to insert an "x" in the box and click again to remove the "x". The check box is created as *hypertext (page 546),* so it will show up underlined and blue.

⚠️ *If you don't like blue, underlined check boxes, see "Changing the Hypertext Style" in the Troubleshooting section at the end of this chapter.*

■ `closeall.wcm`—This macro displays a Close All Documents dialog box, where you can selectively save open documents before they are closed (see Figure 24.6). If documents are unnamed, you can specify a name for the documents in the dialog box. A Save check box lets you decide which documents should be saved before they are closed.

Figure 24.6
In the Close All Documents dialog box, you can select which documents you want to save before you close them.

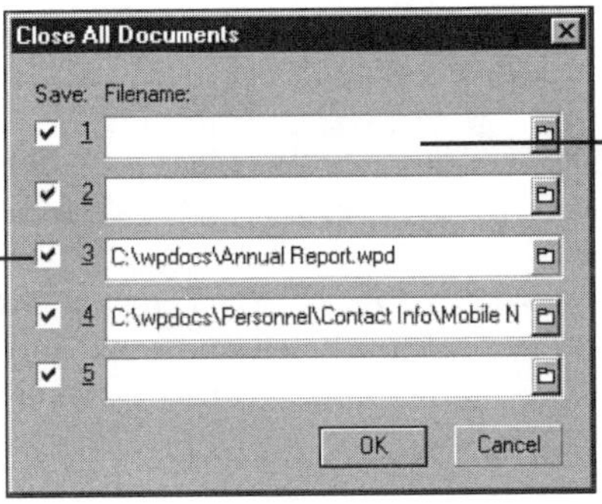

Remove the check mark if you don't want to save the document.

Type a filename here.

■ `ctrlm.wcm`—This macro displays the PerfectScript Command dialog box, where you can select, edit, and insert macro commands in a macro. You don't have to choose this macro from the Play Macro dialog box—you can just press Ctrl+M in the document window.

■ `cvtdocs9.wcm`—This macro opens the WordPerfect Conversion Expert dialog box, where you can choose to convert a single file, a directory (folder), or a directory (folder) and its subdirectories (subfolders) to several different WordPerfect formats. You can choose from WordPerfect 9, 8, 7, 6, and 5.1.

■ `DCConvert.wcm`—This macro converts WordPerfect *drop cap characters (page 187)* (that is, the first whole word is a drop cap) to a drop cap character that is Microsoft Word compatible (that is, a number of characters drop cap).

■ `endfoot.wcm`—This macro converts all the endnotes in the entire document to footnotes. You must be outside the footnote/endnote area to run this macro.

■ `Expndall.wcm`—This macro expands all the *QuickWords (page 138)* in the document, from the insertion point forward. In a lengthy document with complex QuickWords, you might decide to turn off Expand QuickWords as you type them and then expand them all at once with this macro.

■ `Filestmp.wcm`—This macro opens the File Stamp Options dialog box (see Figure 24.7), where you can choose to insert the filename or the filename and path into a header or footer. If the document has not been named when you run this macro, a filename code is placed in the header or footer. When you save and name the file, the filename (and the path) show up in the header or footer. If you select Change Font, a Font Properties dialog box appears so that you can select the font (or font size) that you want to use for the file stamp.

Figure 24.7
You can select the type of file stamp and a location for it in the File Stamp Options dialog box.

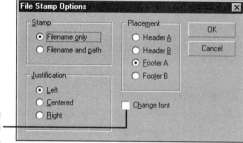

Click here if you want to use a different font.

- `flipenv.wcm`—This macro displays an Envelope Addresses dialog box, where you can type in the return address (unless you've already selected a personal information entry in the Address Book) and a mailing address. You can also select a mailing address from the Address Book. After you fill in the address information, you can choose an envelope size. The macro creates the envelope, only it flips it 180 degrees so that it is upside-down. This macro was created because some printers have trouble printing text within 1/4 inch of the top-left corner of an envelope, but they don't have a problem printing it within 1/4 inch of the lower right corner. If you have one of these printers, this macro allows you to print the return address closer to the edge of the envelope.

- `Fontdn.wcm`—This macro reduces the font size by 2 points. If you select text before running the macro, only the selected text is affected. Otherwise, the change takes place at the insertion point and remains in effect until you change the size again.

- `Fontup.wcm`—This macro increases the font size by 2 points. If you select text before running the macro, only the selected text is affected. Otherwise, the change takes place at the insertion point and remains in effect until you change the size again.

- `footend.wcm`—This macro converts all the footnotes in the entire document to endnotes. You must be outside the footnote/endnote area to run this macro.

- `Longname.wcm`—This macro is for everyone who got around the Windows 3.x/DOS eight-character filename, three-letter extension filenames by creating descriptive names in *document summaries (page 93)*. This macro converts those descriptive filenames into Windows 95/98 long filenames. When you run this macro, a Convert to Long Filenames dialog box appears (see Figure 24.8). You can either type the name of the drive and folder where the files are stored, or you can click the Files icon to open the Select Folder dialog box. Select the file(s) that you want to convert in the Select Files to Rename list, and then click OK. When the macro is finished, a record of the changes is created in a blank document (see Figure 24.9).

Figure 24.8
You can select the file(s) that you want to convert in the Convert to Long Filenames dialog box.

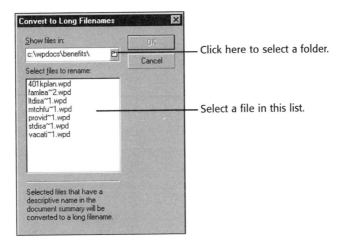

Click here to select a folder.

Select a file in this list.

Figure 24.9
When all the file-names have been converted, a record of the changes is generated.

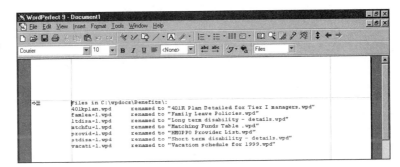

- `nomacro.wcm`—This macro selects hypertext that is linked to a missing macro.
- `Parabrk.wcm`—This macro displays a Paragraph Break dialog box, where you can choose a symbol or graphic to display at every paragraph break. The symbol or graphic is centered on the blank line between paragraphs.
- `pleading.wcm`—This macro displays the Pleading Paper dialog box (see Figure 24.10), where you can choose from a variety of options to generate a legal pleading paper.

Figure 24.10
Using the Pleading Paper dialog box, you can set up line numbers, vertical lines, margins, fonts, page numbers, line spacing, and justification for a legal pleading paper.

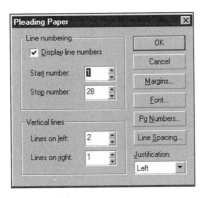

■ prompts.wcm—This macro opens Prompt Builder, which helps you create prompts for your templates. You can create messages that help guide the user along in using the template.

→ If the capability to create prompts in your templates sounds appealing to you, **see** "Using Prompt Builder," **p. 629**

■ reverse.wcm—This macro displays the Reverse Text Options dialog box (see Figure 24.11), where you can choose a color for the text and a color for the fill (or background). If you've selected text, you can place the reverse text in a text box. If you've selected table cells, the dialog box is a little different. You choose from three table-oriented options: C̲enter Text, L̲ock Cell, and H̲eader Row.

Caution

You must select the text or table cells that you want to modify before you run this macro. If you forget, you get a warning message and the macro doesn't run.

Figure 24.11
You can create white text on a black background, or many other combinations, in the Reverse Text Options dialog box.

Click here to select a text color.

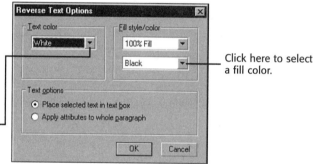

Click here to select a fill color.

■ saveall.wcm—This macro displays the Save Open Documents dialog box, which is similar to the Close All Documents dialog box shown in Figure 24.6. It works the same way: If you want to save a document, place a check mark next to the filename. If necessary, you can change the filename and path before saving the file.

■ Savetoa.wcm—This macro saves the current document, and then copies the file to a disk in drive a:. If you haven't named the document yet, you get the opportunity to do so.

■ tconvert.wcm—This macro displays the Convert Template dialog box, where you can type in the name of a template that you want to convert for use in WordPerfect 9. If you can't remember the name (or the location) of the template file, click the Files icon to search for it.

■ uawp9en.wcm—According to the documentation, this macro is used by the PerfectExpert. You must not delete this file from the macros folder, so don't even think about getting rid of it!

■ wp_org.wcm—This macro creates a basic *organization chart (page 457)* that you can start filling in immediately. You get the same results that you would if you chose I̲nsert, G̲raphics, D̲raw Picture to open the Presentations/Draw editing screen and then chose

Insert, Organization Chart, and selected the first Single option in the Layout dialog box.

- wp_pr.wcm—This macro opens an outline from a WordPerfect document in Presentations as a slide show. You can run the macro whether you have an outline in the document or not, but Presentations has a hard time figuring out what to put on the slides with a regular document. The document is saved as proutln.wpd. If there is already a file by that name, you are prompted to replace it.

Tip #293 from
Laura and Read

WordPerfect designed a toolbar with buttons for the most frequently used shipping macros. Right-click the toolbar, choose More, and then scroll down and place a check mark next to Shipping Macros.

 If you click one of the buttons on the Shipping Macros toolbar and you get an error message that the file can't be found, see "Where Are the Rest of the Shipping Macros?" in the Troubleshooting section at the end of this chapter.

CREATING MACROS

Now that you've played around with a couple of the shipping macros and you've got the general idea, you're ready to create a few of your own. Keep in mind that the first several attempts don't have to be perfect; you can keep recording the macro over and over again until you get it right.

Tip #294 from
Laura and Read

For all but the simplest macros, it's a good idea to jot down the sequence of events, so you do everything in the right order and you don't forget anything.

Follow these steps to record your own macro:

1. You can record a macro in a blank document or in an existing document. In fact, it's most practical to create the macro the next time you need to perform a certain series of steps: You'll be creating the macro and accomplishing your task at the same time.

2. Choose Tools, Macro, Record or press Ctrl+F10.

3. Type a name for the macro in the File Name text box.

Note A macro is automatically saved with the .wcm extension, which identifies it as a macro file.

4. If necessary, choose a location for your macro from the Save In drop-down list. By default, new macros are created in the shipping macros folder (\program files\corel\wordperfect office 2000\macros\wpwin).

Storing Macro Files

The names of the default macro folder and the supplemental macro folder are specified in Settings. Choose Tools, Settings or press Alt+F12. Click Files, and then click the Merge/Macro tab. If you need to change the location, click the Files icon at the end of the text box to browse for the folder. It's common practice to use the supplemental macro folder as a way to gain access to macros stored on a network.

5. Click Record. The Macro Edit feature bar is displayed underneath the Property Bar (see Figure 24.12). The recorder is now on, so you're ready to start recording your actions.

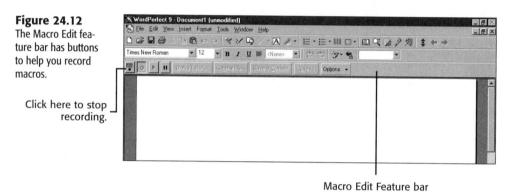

Figure 24.12
The Macro Edit feature bar has buttons to help you record macros.

Click here to stop recording.

Macro Edit Feature bar

6. Type the text, work with the features, and do whatever you want to record for future use.

⚡ *If you turn on the Macro Recorder and your fingers rebel against you and you make simple mistakes, see "I Made a Mistake While Recording a Macro" in the Troubleshooting section at the end of this chapter.*

Caution
The macro records all your actions, whether you use the keyboard or the mouse. One caveat—you have to use the keyboard to position the insertion point in the document window.

7. When you're finished, click the Stop Macro Play or Record button (or press Ctrl+F10) to stop recording. The Macro toolbar disappears, and you are returned to a normal document window. The actions that you took while you created the macro have been performed on the document, so you've essentially killed two birds with one stone.

⚡ *If you sometimes get an error message when you run a macro, see "I Get an Intermittent Error Message When I Run My Macro" in the Troubleshooting section at the end of this chapter.*

Now that you've created the macro, all sorts of possibilities open up. Macros that you use often can be placed at your fingertips by assigning them to keystrokes, toolbar buttons, menu commands, and Property Bars. I'll cover assigning macros later in the chapter, in the "Assigning Macros to Keystrokes, Toolbars, and Menus" section. The next section explains how you assign and create macros in templates so that they are available only in a specific template.

CREATING TEMPLATE MACROS

You can create macros specifically for use with a particular template. Because these macros are saved with a template, they do not appear in the list with the other macros. Therefore, they must be created in a template.

You can do a lot of the same things with template macros that you do with regular macros. You can assign a template macro to a keystroke, toolbar, menu, or Property Bar. See the section "Assigning Macros to Keystrokes, Toolbars, and Menus," later in this chapter, for the steps to assign a macro.

There are several ways to add a macro to a template:

- You can copy the macro from another template.
- You can copy the macro from a macro file.
- You can record the macro from scratch.

Follow these steps to copy a macro over from another template:

1. Edit the template that you want to add the macro to.
2. Click the Copy/Remove Object button on the template toolbar to open the Copy/Remove Template Objects dialog box.

→ If you need a refresher on the steps to edit a project template, **see** "Revising WordPerfect Templates," **p. 622**

→ For more detailed information on copying objects between templates, **see** "Copying Objects from Other Templates," **p. 627**

3. Click the Templates to Copy From drop-down list arrow and select the template that has the macros you want to copy.
4. Click the Object Type drop-down list arrow and choose Macros. A list of available macros appears in the Macros list box (see Figure 24.13).

PART **VII**

CH **24**

Figure 24.13
A list of macros in the selected template appears in the Macros list box, where you can select them for copying into the current template.

Macros in the selected template

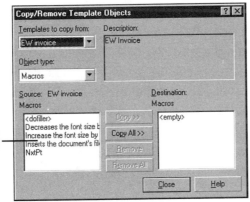

5. Select the macro you want to copy in the Macros list box and click C̲opy>>. Or you can click Cop̲y All>> to copy all the macros at once.

6. Click C̲lose, and then save your changes to the template.

If someone has already created a macro that you want to include with a template, you can copy it directly from the file. Follow these steps to copy a macro from a file:

1. Edit the template to which you want to add the macro.

2. Click the Copy/Remove Object button on the Template toolbar to open the Copy/Remove Template Objects dialog box.

3. Click the O̲bject Type drop-down list arrow and choose Macros on Disk.

4. In the S̲ource text box, either type the path for the macro that you want to copy or click the File icon to search for the macro file. When you locate the macro file, select it, and then click Select.

5. The path and name of the macro file are inserted in the S̲ource text box.

6. Click the C̲opy>> button.

7. Repeat steps 4–6 to copy other macro files to the template.

8. Click C̲lose when you're done.

The last method is to create the macro from scratch. The steps are slightly different from the ones you used earlier in the chapter. First, edit the template to which you want to add macros, and then follow these steps to create a template macro from scratch:

1. Choose T̲ools, Template Macro, R̲ecord. The Record Template Macro dialog box appears (see Figure 24.14).

The name of the current template

Figure 24.14
You can verify the name of the template, then type the name of the macro in the Record Template Macro dialog box.

Type the name of the macro here.

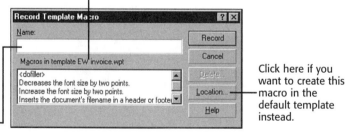

Click here if you want to create this macro in the default template instead.

2. Type a name for the macro in the N̲ame text box, and then click Record.

 If nothing happens after you enter the macro name and click Record, see "I'm Stuck in the Record Template Macro Dialog Box" in the Troubleshooting section at the end of this chapter.

3. Get busy recording whatever it is that you want to do in this macro.

4. Click the Stop Macro Play or Record button (or choose Tools, Template Macro, Record) to stop recording. The Macro toolbar disappears, and you are returned to a normal document window.

> **Note**
>
> In order for a macro to be associated with a *trigger (page 637)*, it must have been created as a template macro. For example, you could set up a pre-print trigger to run a macro that accepts client identification information so the printer resources can be billed back to the client.

→ To get the scoop on macro triggers, **see** "Associating Macros to Triggers," **p. 637**

CREATING QUICKMACROS

Ever have one of those days when you are forced into typing a long and complex phrase over and over again? You don't want to create a macro because it's not likely that you'll have to type that same information again. Wouldn't it be nice if you could create a temporary macro just for today? You can—it's called a *QuickMacro*.

QuickMacros are created as template macros—the only difference is that you don't name a QuickMacro. The QuickMacro is assigned to a temporary file for this session, and when you exit WordPerfect, the file is erased. You can have only one QuickMacro at a time. To replace a QuickMacro, simply create a new one. Follow these steps to create a QuickMacro:

1. Choose Tools, Template Macro, Record to display the Record Template Macro dialog box (refer to Figure 24.14).

2. Don't type a name—just press Enter or click the Record Button.

3. When you see the Macro toolbar, you can start recording the macro.

4. Click the Stop Macro Play or Record button (or choose Tools, Template Macro, Record) to stop recording. The Macro toolbar disappears, and you are returned to a normal document window.

When you're ready to play the QuickMacro, choose Tools, Template Macro, Play. In the Play Template Macro dialog box (see Figure 24.15), select Wp}00001, and then click Play.

Figure 24.15
A QuickMacro is given a temporary filename, which shows up in the Play Template Macro dialog box.

Click here to select the QuickMacro.

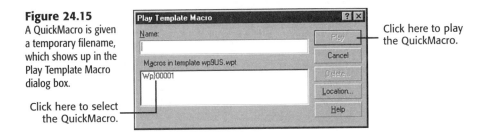

Click here to play the QuickMacro.

ASSIGNING MACROS TO KEYSTROKES, TOOLBARS, AND MENUS

There are a variety of different ways to put the macros you use the most right at your fingertips. You can assign a macro or a template macro to a keystroke (such as Alt+8), to a toolbar button, or to a menu. Macros (not template macros) can be also be assigned to the Property Bar. Let's start with the steps to assign a macro to a keystroke first, and then move on to the others.

ASSIGNING MACROS TO KEYSTROKES

Because you spend most of your time with your hands on the keyboard, macros that are activated by a keystroke are immensely popular. The only problem is that many other features are already assigned to shortcut keys. You can either choose one that isn't currently assigned or you can replace the current assignment.

→ For the steps to edit a project template, **see** "Basing a Template on Another Template," **p. 625**

The steps to assign a macro and a template macro to a keystroke are similar, so rather than repeat steps, I'll point out the differences as we go along. In every case, when you want to assign a template macro, you need to edit the template that contains the macro first. Then follow these steps to assign a macro to a keystroke:

1. Choose Tools, Settings (or press Alt+F12), and then click Customize. This opens the Customize Settings dialog box.

2. Click the Keyboards tab to display the available keyboards (see Figure 24.16).

Figure 24.16
You can select the keyboard that you want to edit in the Keyboards tab of the Customize Settings dialog box.

The default keyboard

Select a keyboard here.

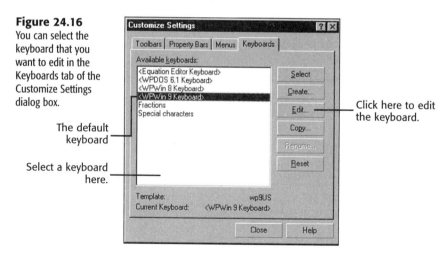

Click here to edit the keyboard.

3. If you want to edit the default keyboard, leave <WPWin 9 Keyboard> selected. Otherwise, select another keyboard.

4. Choose Edit to display the Keyboard Shortcuts dialog box. This is where you choose the keystroke and select a macro.

5. Select the shortcut key that you want to use from the <u>C</u>hoose a Shortcut Key list box.

6. Click the Macros tab to display the macro options (see Figure 24.17).

Figure 24.17
You can assign a macro to any key-stroke that you see in the list, even if the keystroke already has something assigned to it.

Select a shortcut key in the list.

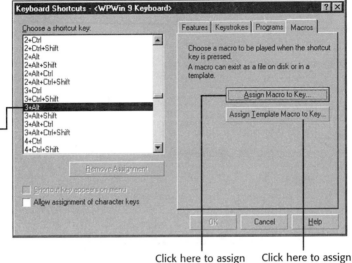

Click here to assign a regular macro.

Click here to assign a template macro.

7. Click <u>A</u>ssign Macro to Key to assign a regular macro to a keystroke; click Assign <u>T</u>emplate Macro to Key to assign a template macro to a keystroke.

8. Depending on which button you clicked in step 7, you see the Select Macro dialog box or the Select Template Macro dialog box. Either way, select the macro that you want to assign and then choose Select.

9. If you're assigning a template macro, skip this step. In the message box, choose <u>Y</u>es if you want the entire path to show up in the shortcut keys list; choose <u>N</u>o if you want only the name of the macro displayed in the list.

> **Caution**
>
> If the macro is not stored in the default macro folder or the supplemental macro folder specified in File Settings, make sure that you save the macro with the full path.

10. Repeat steps 5–9 to assign other macros to shortcut keys.

ASSIGNING MACROS TO TOOLBARS

Now that you understand the general concept, assigning macros to toolbar buttons is a snap. Again, the steps to assigning a regular macro and a template macro are similar, so I'll point out the differences we go along. Remember that if you want to assign a template macro to a toolbar button, edit the template first. Then follow these steps to assign a macro to a toolbar button:

1. Choose Tools, Settings (or press Alt+F12), and then click Customize. A list of available toolbars is displayed in the Customize Settings dialog box (see Figure 24.18).

→ For the steps to edit a project template, **see** "Basing a Template on Another Template," **p. 625**

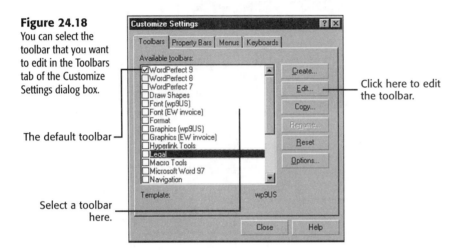

Figure 24.18
You can select the toolbar that you want to edit in the Toolbars tab of the Customize Settings dialog box.

The default toolbar

Select a toolbar here.

Click here to edit the toolbar.

2. Select a toolbar, and then choose Edit to open the Toolbar Editor dialog box. This is where you choose a macro to assign to a toolbar button.

3. Click the Macros tab to display the buttons to add a regular macro or a template macro (see Figure 24.19).

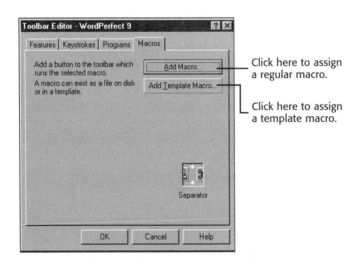

Figure 24.19
You can add a macro or template macro to a toolbar button in the Macros tab of the Toolbar Editor dialog box.

Click here to assign a regular macro.

Click here to assign a template macro.

4. Click Add Macro to add a macro to a toolbar button, or click Add Template Macro to add a template macro to a toolbar button.

5. Depending on your choice, you see the Select Macro dialog box or the Select Template Macro dialog box. In either case, select the macro, and then choose Select. If you've assigned a macro, you are prompted to save the macro with a full path name (Yes or No).

Caution

If the macro is not stored in the default macro folder or the supplemental macro folder specified in File Settings, make sure that you save the macro with the full path.

6. Repeat steps 3–5 to assign other macros to toolbar buttons.

A new button has been added to the selected toolbar. All macros have the same button picture—of a cassette tape (see Figure 24.20). Click and drag the new button to position it on the toolbar.

Figure 24.20
Macro buttons all use the same picture, that of a cassette tape. To identify each button, point to it and pause. This displays a Quick-Tip that tells you the name of the macro.

New macro button

Because the buttons are all the same, you need help differentiating the macro buttons. While you're editing a toolbar, you can modify the properties for a macro button. Double-click the button to display the Customize Button dialog box (see Figure 24.21), where you can type text to appear on the button and the message for the QuickTip.

Type the button text here.

Figure 24.21
You can type button text and the message that you want to appear in the Quick-Tip in the Customize Button dialog box.

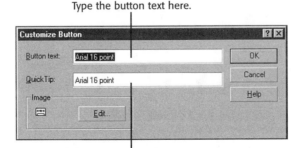

Type the QuickTip text here.

> **Note**
>
> Button text doesn't appear by default, so you have to change the button option settings to show text in a button. In the Toolbar Editor dialog box (refer to Figure 24.19), choose Options to open the Toolbar Options dialog box. Choose Text to display only the text, or Picture and Text to display both the picture and the text message.

Assigning Macros to a Property Bar

The steps to add a macro to a Property Bar are very similar to the steps to add a macro to a toolbar. The only difference is that you click the Property Bars tab, and then select the Property Bar that you want to edit. The Text Property Bar is the default, or the one that you see in a blank document. From here, you can repeat the preceding steps, starting at step 4.

ASSIGNING MACROS TO MENUS

If you aren't concerned about the clutter, you can put your macros right on the menu bar. The name of the macro (or whatever else you want to appear) shows up on the menu bar right next to the other menu items. To play the macro, you just click the name on the menu bar.

As usual, if you want to assign a template macro, you need to edit the template first. Then follow these steps to assign macros to the menu bar:

1. Choose Tools, Settings, and then click Customize.
2. Click the Menus tab to display a list of available menus (see Figure 24.22).

Figure 24.22
You can create customized menus or edit the existing menus in the Menus tab of the Customize Settings dialog box.

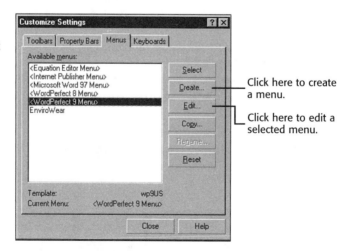

Click here to create a menu.

Click here to edit a selected menu.

3. Select a menu, and then choose Edit to open the Menu Editor dialog box. This dialog box is almost identical to the Toolbar Editor dialog box shown in Figure 24.19.
4. Click the Macros tab.

5. Click <u>A</u>dd Macro to assign a macro, or click Add <u>T</u>emplate Macro to assign a template macro. Depending on your choice, you see the Select Macro dialog box or the Select Template Macro dialog box.

6. In either dialog box, select the macro, and then click Select.

7. Choose <u>Y</u>es if you want to save the macro with the entire path, or choose <u>N</u>o if you don't want to. The name of the macro is added to the menu bar (see Figure 24.23).

> **Caution**
>
> If the macro is not stored in the default macro folder or the supplemental macro folder specified in File Settings, make sure that you save the macro with the full path.

8. Repeat steps 5–7 to assign other macros to shortcut keys.

Macro name on the keyboard

Figure 24.23
After you've added a macro to the menu bar, you can give it a friendlier name.

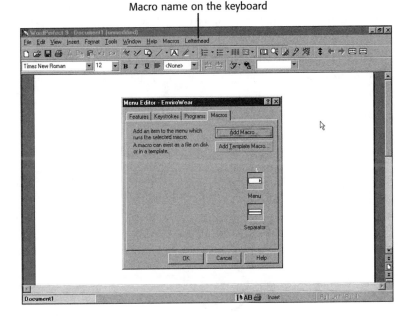

> **Tip #295 from**
> *Laura and Read*
>
> If you save the macro with the path, so you don't have to put it in the default macro folder, you'll see that the macro path takes up a lot of space on the menu bar. You can give the macro a friendlier name and a description that appears in the QuickTip. Double-click the macro name on the menu bar to open the Edit Menu Text dialog box, which looks similar to the Customize Button dialog box shown in Figure 24.21. Type a friendlier name for the macro in the <u>M</u>enu Item text box, then type a description in the QuickTip text box.

EDITING MACROS

Say someone in your company is in charge of developing and distributing macros for every-one else's use. If so, count yourself lucky and make sure you say thank you once in a while because if you ever want some changes made, that's who you'll have to go to.

However, if all you want to do is change a name, address, or other minor detail, you can save yourself some groveling by making the minor changes yourself. Furthermore, you may have an occasion to edit the macros that you created with the Macro Recorder.

When you open a macro, you'll see that rather than record your exact keystrokes (as earlier versions of the macro language did), the Macro Recorder actually records the *results* of your actions. For example, if you use the menus to change the margins, you can't see the actual menu commands that you selected. Instead, you see the margin change itself.

You can edit macros and template macros with essentially the same steps. However, if you want to edit a template macro, you have to edit the template first. Then follow these steps to edit a macro:

1. Choose Tools, Macro (or Template Macro), Edit. Depending on which type of macro you chose, you'll see the Edit Macro dialog box or the Edit Template Macro dialog box.

2. In either case, select the macro you want to edit, and then choose Edit. The macro appears in the document window (see Figure 24.24).

Figure 24.24
This macro sets up a letterhead page with margin settings, a font change, today's date, a salutation, and a closing.

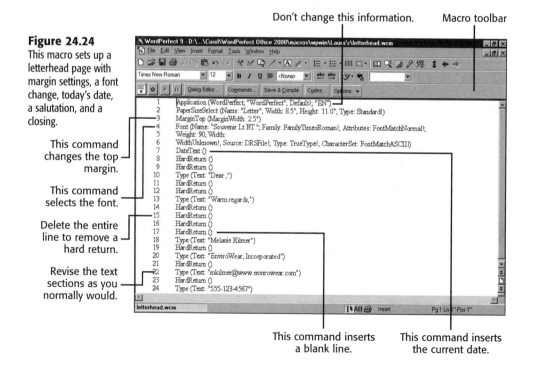

Don't change this information.   Macro toolbar

This command changes the top margin.

This command selects the font.

Delete the entire line to remove a hard return.

Revise the text sections as you normally would.

This command inserts a blank line.   This command inserts the current date.

Caution

Here's where things get a little tricky—you must use extreme care so that you don't accidentally delete (or modify) the macro commands. If you do, make sure you don't save your changes when you close the macro, and then start over.

3. Make the necessary corrections to the text portions of the macro. Unless you're comfortable with macro commands, it's a very good idea to leave them alone.

4. When you're finished, click the Close button on the menu bar to close the document window.

5. Choose <u>Y</u>es to save your changes to the macro.

If you're editing a macro that someone else has written, it's likely to be more complicated than the macro shown in Figure 24.24. You'll see lots of programming commands and you may be wondering where they come from.

WordPerfect's macro language is called Corel *PerfectScript*. It is a command-based language that can be used to write macros in all the WordPerfect Office 2000 applications. You can do a lot more with PerfectScript than just play back recorded commands. Macros can stop and prompt for input, and then, based on that input, go to a different section of the macro and execute the commands there. Macros can be structured to display messages and customized dialog boxes. Information from other WordPerfect Office 2000 applications can be combined. In fact, you can actually build complete document-building applications (or wizards) for those users with limited WordPerfect experience.

Note

The Software Developer's Kit (SDK) contains reference materials, OLE automation samples, and PerfectScript tools, as well as code generation wizards, tools, and utilities for third-party add-ons to WordPerfect. The SDK is located on the CD-ROM in the SDK folder.

Unfortunately, covering the PerfectScript macro language is beyond the scope of this book. Here are some places where you can go for help:

■ Consult the help topics. Specifically, open the help topic titled "Writing and editing macros using PerfectScript" under the heading "Recordings, Macros, and Automation Features" in the Contents tab of the Help Topics dialog box.

Note

If you can't find the macro help files, they may not have been installed yet. The fastest way to get the file is to copy it over directly from the CD-ROM. You can do this from within WordPerfect. Insert the CD-ROM in the drive, and then choose <u>F</u>ile, <u>O</u>pen. Go to the `\corel\shared\help` folder on the CD-ROM. Right-click the `wpmh9en.hlp` file, and then choose <u>C</u>opy. Go to the `\program files\corel\wordperfect office 2000\shared\help` folder on your hard drive. Right-click the file list and choose <u>P</u>aste.

■ If you're inserting commands in the PerfectScript Commands dialog box, you can select a command in the list to view a brief description.

- You can view the Reference Center information on PerfectScript & Macros. Click Start, and then choose Programs, WordPerfect Office 2000, Setup and Notes, Corel Reference Center. Double-click the PerfectScript & Macros book cover. You must have Adobe's Acrobat Reader installed to view the Reference Center materials, so if you don't already have it installed, you'll be asked if you want to install it now. Choose Yes to have Setup install the files for you.

- Buy a book that specifically covers macro programming with PerfectScript. Ask your local bookstore to do a search for you or go up to one of the online bookstores and search for *wordperfect macros*.

Gordon Is "the Man" Where WordPerfect Macros Are Concerned

You may recognize the name Gordon McComb, from other *Special Edition Using WordPerfect* books, or possibly from the "Macros" column that he wrote for *WordPerfect for Windows* magazine. Gordon is widely recognized as a leading authority on WordPerfect macros. Rumor has it that over the years, some of his applications have actually been incorporated into the program. Go to his site at www.gmccomb.com to look over his selection of macro books. (And no, I'm not getting paid to say this.)

USING MACROS FROM PREVIOUS VERSIONS OF WORDPERFECT

The basic structure of the programming language hasn't changed since WordPerfect 6. New commands have been added to take advantage of new features and to use existing features more efficiently. The majority of the old commands have been retained to ensure backward compatibility.

To convert macros from previous versions of WordPerfect, follow these steps:

1. Choose Tools, Macro (or Template Macro), Edit. Depending on which type of macro you choose, you'll see the Edit Macro dialog box or the Edit Template Macro dialog box.

2. In either case, select the macro you want to edit, and then choose Edit.

3. If you need to make some changes, do that now.

4. Click the Save & Compile button on the Macro toolbar. *Compiling* a macro is a dry run where the macro is checked for accuracy but isn't actually executed.

5. Correct any errors listed by the macro compiler, and then click the Save & Compile button again. When you don't get any more errors, close the macro and save your changes.

Note

You may notice that macros from previous versions run slower in WordPerfect 9. This is because those macros are optimized for the version they were created in. To optimize them for WordPerfect 9, you need to recompile them. When you open the macro for editing, make a dummy change, such as inserting a space and then backspacing over it. Click the Save & Compile button and then save the macro.

VISUAL BASIC—DO YOU NEED IT?

WordPerfect Office 2000 includes support for Microsoft Visual Basic for Applications (VBA) programming language, which can be used as an alternative to the PerfectScript programming language. WordPerfect gets a gold star for being the only mainstream word processor to offer two powerful programming languages that can be used separately or in combination.

So do you need it? It depends on whether you need to accomplish something that you can't do with PerfectScript. VBA is harder to learn and requires a much higher level of understanding of how WordPerfect operates. Prior experience with an object-oriented programming language is a definite plus.

> **Note**
> VBA support isn't installed by default, so if you want to use it, you have to install it with a Custom Setup. One caveat—make sure you disable your antivirus program when you install any part of WordPerfect Office 2000.

Unless you were living under a rock this spring, you heard about the Melissa virus and all the havoc it wreaked on companies such as Microsoft, Intel, and Dell. This virus, and many others like it, are easy to spread because of the way Microsoft Word handles macros in a document. You might have heard that by installing VBA support with WordPerfect 9, you are leaving yourself open to macro viruses. You're right to be concerned. If you've installed VBA support and you open a document that contains VBA macros (also called projects), the VBA macros are automatically triggered.

Thankfully, WordPerfect 9 is designed in such a way that the risk is minimal and easy to avoid with a good antivirus program. There are also extra security measures built in to the version of VBA that ships with WordPerfect. Just make sure that you impress upon anyone who will listen that they should never, ever, *ever*, disable their macro virus security just because it's a pain to bypass the warning messages every time they open a file with VBA macros embedded in it.

> **Tip #296 from**
> *Laura and Read*
>
> For more information on what VBA means to you, check out Gordon McComb's frequently asked questions (FAQ) document on VBA. Go to www.gmccomb.com/vbafaq.html.

After all the media hype surrounding viruses and how the email systems of many companies are brought down due to them, you would think that the employees would know better than to disable their virus protection. It just goes to show that no one is immune from computer viruses. Consider every file suspect until you've checked it out with an antivirus program that has the latest virus definitions installed, even if your best friend just gave it to you.

TROUBLESHOOTING

WHERE ARE THE REST OF THE SHIPPING MACROS?

I want to play the `allfonts` macro, but it doesn't appear in the list of macros. Where are the rest of the files?

During a typical installation, only a few of the shipping macros are installed. Why? Because some people won't use them and it's considered impolite to take up disk space unnecessarily, so Corel chose not to install the whole set as part of the typical installation. But you can copy the rest of them from the CD-ROM. Insert the CD-ROM in the drive, and then choose File, Open. Go to the `\corel\macros\wpwin` folder on the CD-ROM. Select the macros that you want to copy, and then choose File, Copy. Go to the `\program files\ corel\wordperfect office 2000\macros\wpwin` folder on your hard drive. Right-click in the file list, and then choose Paste.

I MADE A MISTAKE WHILE RECORDING A MACRO

In the middle of recording a macro, I realized that I'd made a mistake. What should I do?

Relax, it isn't the end of the world—the mistake is easily fixed. In fact, you might be surprised to learn that WordPerfect doesn't even record some of your mistakes in the macro.

You can stop recording the macro at this point and just start over, saving the completed macro over the incomplete macro. Or you can fix the mistake and go on. In most cases, the "fix" isn't recorded—only the final result of your actions.

I GET AN INTERMITTENT ERROR MESSAGE WHEN I RUN MY MACRO

I created a macro that changes the font and font size for selected text. When I run the macro, sometimes I get an error that says the macro is being cancelled due to an error on line 3. Other times, the macro runs just fine. I've reviewed the macro and I can't find anything wrong. What now?

Did you select text before you ran the macro? If not, the macro won't work. You've just run into a problem with *states*. If you record a macro that takes action on selected text, that macro expects a state of selected text when you run it. If it doesn't find that state, the macro can't run properly.

The same holds true for other conditions in WordPerfect. For example, if you write a macro that customizes graphics boxes, you better make sure there is a graphics box in the document before you run the macro.

I'M STUCK IN THE RECORD TEMPLATE MACRO DIALOG BOX

I'm trying to create a template macro from scratch. When I enter a name for the macro and click Record, nothing happens. I have to cancel out of the dialog box.

It sounds like the template file is damaged. If you're adding the template macro to the default template, you'll have to rename the default template and let WordPerfect create a new one when you start WordPerfect again. Unfortunately, this means you'll lose any customizations that have been made to the toolbars, keyboards, menus, styles, macros, and other objects that are stored in the default template.

Let me stop here and remind you how important it is to make a backup copy of your default template after you've done some customizing. It only takes a second, and it can save you hours. In fact, you might be able to recover by simply deleting the corrupted default template and renaming the backup copy. The name of the default template is `wp9us.wpt`, and you'll find it in the `\program files\corel\wordperfect office 2000\templates\Custom WP Templates` folder.

If you are adding a template macro to one of the project templates, try getting a fresh copy of the template from the CD-ROM. Look in the `\corel\template` folder on the CD-ROM. Right-click the template file, and then choose <u>C</u>opy. Switch to the `\program files\ corel\wordperfect office 2000\template` folder. Right-click in the file list and choose <u>P</u>aste.

CHANGING THE HYPERTEXT STYLE

I just created a check box in my document, and that blue underline stands out like a sore thumb. Is there any way to change the appearance of the check box?

Check boxes are created as hypertext, which by default appears underlined and in blue. Thankfully, you can modify the style used for hypertext. Keep in mind that if you alter the style, it will affect other hypertext codes in the document, so you might want the other hypertext codes to appear as buttons instead.

To modify the hypertext style, choose Fo<u>r</u>mat, <u>St</u>yles. In the Styles dialog box, choose <u>O</u>ptions, <u>S</u>ettings. If necessary, place a check mark in the <u>W</u>ordPerfect System Styles check box. Select WordPerfect heading styles and all other system styles, and then click OK. In the Available <u>S</u>tyles list box, select Hypertext, and then click <u>E</u>dit. In the Styles Editor dialog box, make sure there is a check mark in the Re<u>v</u>eal Codes check box. In the Reveal Codes window, delete the [Color: Blue] code, both [Und] codes, and the [Color: Black] code. Click OK, and then click Close. The check box should now appear black and not be underlined.

PROJECT

I know I said I couldn't cover any of the programming commands as much as I would like to. I just don't have the space here to do justice to the information. However, there is one very simple thing you can do that opens all sorts of possibilities in your macros. You can insert a pause, which causes the macro to stop and wait for input. When you press Enter, the macro continues. You can insert as many pauses in a macro as you like. And you can type as much text as you like during the pause.

A pause in a macro is similar to the Keyboard Merge command, where you can pause the process to type something and then continue the process. A fill-in-the-blanks form is a perfect candidate, but so is any document with standard blocks of text and a few places where you need to type in something different.

Follow along with these steps to insert a pause in a macro:

1. Choose Tools, Macro, Record (or press Ctrl+F10).

2. Start recording the macro. Do everything up to the point where you want to pause for input.

3. Click the Pause While Recording/Executing a Macro button on the Macro toolbar.

4. If necessary, type some text or perform other tasks.

5. Click the Pause While Recording/Executing a Macro button again to resume recording the macro.

6. Repeat steps 2–5 to continue recording the macro.

7. Click the Stop Macro Play or Record button when you're finished.

Figure 24.25 shows a macro that creates a memo form. There is a pause to type the recipient's name, the subject, and the date. The rest is filled in automatically.

Figure 24.25

This macro creates a memorandum form that allows you to type in the name of the recipient, the subject, and the date.

Pause to type in the recipient name.

Pause to type in the memo subject.

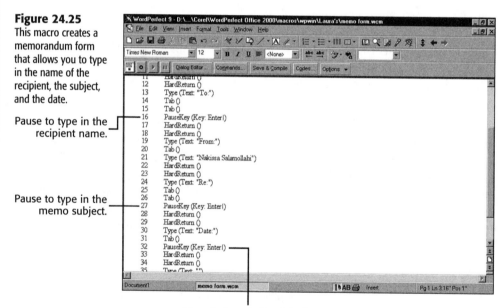

Pause to type in the date (or press Ctrl+D to insert the date).

INDEX

X-Z

Get **FREE** books and more...when you register this book online for our Personal Bookshelf Program

http://register.quecorp.com/

 Register online and you can sign up for our *FREE Personal Bookshelf Program...*unlimited access to the electronic version of more than 200 complete computer books—immediately! That means you'll have 100,000 pages of valuable information onscreen, at your fingertips!

 Plus, you can access product support, including complimentary downloads, technical support files, book-focused links, companion Web sites, author sites, and more!

 And you'll be automatically registered to receive a *FREE subscription to a weekly email newsletter* to help you stay current with news, announcements, sample book chapters, and special events, including sweepstakes, contests, and various product giveaways!

 We value your comments! Best of all, the entire registration process takes only a few minutes to complete, so go online and get the greatest value going—absolutely FREE!

Don't Miss Out On This Great Opportunity!

QUE® is a brand of Macmillan Computer Publishing USA.

For more information, please visit *www.mcp.com*